the Damron
eller®

| | |
|---|---|
| Publisher | Damron Company |
| President | Gina M. Gatta |
| Editor-in-Chief | Erika O'Connor |
| Cover Design | Kathleen Pratt |

*Board of Directors*
**Gina M. Gatta, Edward Gatta, Jr., Louise Mock**

*How to Contact Us*

| | |
|---|---|
| **Mail:** | 459 Fulton St #301, |
| | San Francisco, CA 94102 |
| **Email:** | info@damron.com |
| **Web:** | www.damron.com |
| **Fax:** | 415/703-9049 |
| **Phone:** | 415/255-0404 |

# Table of Contents

## United States

# Table of Contents

## International

## Tours

# Traveller Codes

Most of the codes used in this book are self-explanatory. Here are the few, however, that aren't.

➤—This symbol marks an advertiser. Please look for their display ad near this listing, and be sure to tell them you saw their ad in the *Damron Women's Traveller.*

**Popular**—So we've heard from the business and/or a reader.

**Mostly Women**—80-90% lesbian crowd.

**Mostly Gay Men**—Women welcome.

**Lesbians/Gay Men**—Roughly 50/50 mix of lesbians and gay men.

**LGBT**—Lesbian, Gay, Bisexual, and Transgendered.

**Gay/Straight**—A little bit of everything.

**Gay-Friendly**—LGBT folk are definitely welcome but are rarely the ones hosting the party.

**Neighborhood Bar**—Regulars and a local flavor, often has a pool table.

**Dancing/DJ**—Usually has a DJ at least Friday and Saturday nights.

**Transgender-Friendly**—Transsexuals, cross-dressers, and other transgendered people welcome.

**Live Shows**—From an open mic to live music.

**Multiracial**—A good mix of women of color and their friends.

**Beer/Wine**—Beer and/or wine. No hard liquor.

**Nonsmoking**—No smoking anywhere inside premises.

**Private Club**—Found mainly in the US South where it's the only way to keep a liquor license. Call the bar before you go out and tell them you're visiting. They will advise you of their policy regarding membership. Usually have set-ups so you can BYOB.

**Wheelchair Access**—Includes rest room.

**WiFi**—Wireless Internet access.

## ALABAMA

## Statewide

### PUBLICATIONS

**Ambush Mag** 504/522-8049 • LGBT newspaper for the Gulf South (TX through FL)

## Birmingham

### ACCOMMODATIONS

**Hampton Inn** 2021 Park Pl N (at 21st St N) **205/322-2100** • gay-friendly • also restaurant & lounge • WiFi • wheelchair access

### BARS

**The Garage Cafe** 2304 10th Terrace S (at 23rd St S) **205/322-3220** • 11am-close, from 3pm Sun-Mon • gay-friendly • great sandwiches • live music

**Our Place** 205/715-0077 • 4pm-midnight, till 2am Fri-Sat • mostly gay men • neighborhood bar • videos • gay-owned

**Wine Loft** 2200 1st Ave N **205/323-8228** • 5pm-close, clsd Sun-Mon • gay-friendly • wine bar • light food served

### NIGHTCLUBS

**Al's on 7th** 2627 7th Ave S (at 27th St) **205/321-2812** • lesbians/ gay men • neighborhood bar • dancing/DJ • drag shows • theme nights • 18+ • private club

**The Quest Club** 416 24th St S (at 5th Ave S) **205/251-4313** • 24hrs • mostly gay men • karaoke • dancing/DJ • 19+ Wed-Sun • drag shows • private club • patio • wheelchair access • cover charge

### CAFES

**Chez Lulu** 1909 Cahaba Rd **205/870-7011** • lunch & dinner Tue-Sun, Sun brunch, clsd Mon • plenty veggie • also bakery • live shows

### RESTAURANTS

**Bottega Cafe & Restaurant** 2240 Highland Ave S (btwn 22nd & 23rd) **205/939-1000** • 5:30pm-10pm, clsd Sun • some veggie • full bar • wheelchair access

**Highlands Bar & Grill** 2011 11th Ave S (at 20th St) **205/939-1400** • 5:30pm-10pm, clsd Sun-Mon • wheelchair access

**John's City Diner** 112 21st St N (btwn 1st & 2nd Ave N) **205/322-6014** • lunch weekdays & dinner Mon-Sat, clsd Sun • seafood & steak • full bar • wheelchair access

**Rojo** 2921 Highland Ave S (at 30th St) **205/328-4733** • 11am-10pm, clsd Mon, wknd brunch • Latin & American cuisine

**Silvertron Cafe** 3813 Clairmont Ave S (at 39th St S) **205/591-3707** • 11am-9pm, from 8am Sat • also full bar • more gay back

**Taj India** 2226 Highland Ave S **205/939-3805** • lunch & dinner • Indian • plenty veggie

### ENTERTAINMENT & RECREATION

**Terrific New Theatre** 2821 2nd Ave S (in Dr Pepper Design Complex) **205/328-0868**

**Tragic City Rollers** • Birmingham's female roller derby league • visit www.dixiederbygirls.com for events

### EROTICA

**Alabama Adult Books** 801 3rd Ave N (at 8th) **205/322-7323**

## Dothan

### NIGHTCLUBS

**Dothan Dance Club** 2563 Ross Clark Circle (at Hwy 52 West) **334/792-5166** • 11pm Fri, from 6pm Sat-Sun, clsd Mon-Th • gay/ straight • drag shows • cabaret • private club • gay-owned

## Huntsville

### ENTERTAINMENT & RECREATION

**Dixie Derby Girls** • Huntsville's female roller derby league • visit www.dixiederbygirls.com for events

## Mobile

### INFO LINES & SERVICES

**Pink Triangle AA Group** 251/479-9994 (AA#), 251/438-7080 (CHURCH) • 7pm Tue, Th & Sat • call for locations

### ACCOMMODATIONS

**Berney Fly B&B** 1118 Government St 251/405-0949 • gay-friendly • close to gay bars and restaurants • full brkfst • pool • jacuzzi • nonsmoking • WiFi

### BARS

**Flipside Bar & Patio** 54 S Conception St 251/431-8869 • open 4pm • lesbians/ gay men • neighborhood bar • non-smoking

**Gabriel's Downtown** 55 S Joachim St (off Government) 251/432-4900 • 7pm-close • lesbians/ gay men • videos • karaoke • patio • private club

**Midtown Pub** 153 S Florida St (at Emogene) 251/450-1555 • noon-2am • lesbians/ gay men • neighborhood bar • dancing/DJ • karaoke • food served

### NIGHTCLUBS

**B–Bob's Downtown** 213 Conti St (at Joachim) 251/433–2262 • 6pm-close, from 7pm Sat • mostly men • dancing/DJ • also gift shop • wheelchair access

## Montgomery

### ACCOMMODATIONS

**The Lattice Inn** 1414 S Hull St (at Clanton) 334/262–3388 • mixed gay/ straight • pool • nonsmoking • WiFi • wheelchair access

### NIGHTCLUBS

**Club 322** 322 N Lawrence St 334/263–4322 • 8pm-close, clsd Mon • lesbians/ gay men • dancing/DJ • drag shows

## Tuscaloosa

### NIGHTCLUBS

**Icon** 516 Greensboro Ave • 9pm-2am, clsd Sun-Mon • mostly gay men • dancing/DJ • drag shows

# ALASKA

## Statewide

### ENTERTAINMENT & RECREATION

**Out in Alaska** 1819 Dimond Dr, Fairbanks 99507 877/374–9958, 907/374–9958 • adventure travel throughout Alaska for LGBT travelers

## Anchorage

### INFO LINES & SERVICES

**AA Gay/ Lesbian** 336 E 5th Ave (at Community Center) 907/929–4528 • 6pm Mon

**Identity, Inc** 336 E 5th Ave 907/929–4528 • LGBT community center • newsletter

### ACCOMMODATIONS

**A Wildflower Inn B&B** 1239 I St (at 13th) 907/274–1239, 877/693–1239 • gay/ straight • close to hiking trails & scenic vistas • fun hosts • nonsmoking • WiFi • gay-owned

**Alaska Heavenly Lodge** 34950 Blakely Rd (at Mile 49 Sterling Hwy), Cooper Landing 907/595–2012, 866/595–2012 • gay-friendly • hot tub • cedar sauna • nonsmoking

**Anchorage Jewel Lake B&B** 8125 Jewel Lake Rd 907/245–7321, 877/245–7321 • gay/ straight • full brkfst • kids ok • WiFi • nonsmoking • gay-owned

**Arctic Fox Inn** 327 E 2nd Ct 907/272–4818, 877/693–1239 • gay/ straight • also apts • gay-owned

**City Garden B&B** 1352 W 10th Ave (at N St) 907/276–8686 • gay-straight • beautiful views of Mt McKinley • 10-minute walk to downtown area • nonsmoking • gay-owned

**Copper Whale Inn** 440 L St (at 5th Ave) 907/258–7999, 866/258–7999 • gay/ straight • located downtown • WiFi • nonsmoking • gay-owned • limited wheelchair access

**Gallery B&B** 1229 G St (at 12th) 907/274–2567 • gay/ straight • kids/ pets ok • wheelchair access • lesbian-owned

**Inlet Tower Hotel & Suites** 1200 L St (at 12th) 907/276–0110, 800/544–0786 • gay/ straight • kids/ pets ok • WiFi • wheelchair access • also bar & restaurant

**Renfro's Lakeside Retreat** 27177 Seward Hwy, Seward 907/288–5059, 877/288–5059 • gay-friendly • WiFi • furnished modern log cabins on Kenai Lake • seasonal • gay-owned

### BARS

**Bernie's Bungalow Lounge** 626 D St (at W 5th Ave) 907/276–8808 • gay-friendly • cocktail lounge • patio • food served

**Mad Myrna's** 530 E 5th Ave (at Fairbanks) 907/276–9762 • 4pm-2:30am, till 3am Fri-Sat • lesbians/ gay men • neighborhood bar • dancing/DJ • karaoke • food served • drag shows

**Raven** 708 E 4th Ave 907/276–9672 • 1pm-2:30am, till 3am wknds • lesbians/ gay men • neighborhood bar • wheelchair access

### RESTAURANTS

**Bear Tooth Theatre Pub & Grill** 1230 W 27th Ave 907/276–4200 • movie theater, pub & grill all in one

**China Lights** 12110 Business Blvd, Eagle River 907/694–8080 • 11:30am-10pm, till 10:30pm wknds

**Club Paris** 417 W 5th Ave 907/277–6332 • 11am-midnight, from 4pm Sun • perhaps the finest restaurant in town

**Garcia's** 11901 Business Blvd #104 (next to Safeway), Eagle River 907/694–8600 • 11am-midnight, from noon wknds • Mexican

**Ginger** 425 W 5th Ave (at D St) 907/929–3680 • lunch Mon-Fri, dinner nightly, bar from 3pm • Pacific Rim/ Asian

**Marx Brothers Cafe** 627 W 3rd Ave 907/278–2133 • 5:30pm-10pm, clsd Sun-Mon • great food & views

**Simon & Seafort's** 420 L St (btwn 4th & 5th) **907/274-3502** • lunch weekdays, dinner nightly • seafood & prime rib • full bar • great views

**Snow City Cafe** 1034 W 4th Ave (at L St) **907/272-2489** • 7am-3pm, till 4pm wknds

### ENTERTAINMENT & RECREATION

**Out North Contemporary Art House** 3800 DeBarr Rd **907/279-3800** • community-based & visiting-artist exhibits, screenings & performances

### BOOKSTORES

**Title Wave Books** 1360 W Northern Lights Blvd **907/278-9283, 888/598-9283** • 10am-8pm, till 9pm Fri-Sat, 11am-7pm Sun • largest independent bookstore in Alaska

### RETAIL SHOPS

**The Sports Shop** 570 E Benson Blvd **907/272-7755** • 10am-7pm, till 6pm Sat, noon-5pm Sun • women's outdoor clothing, adventure gear & equipment

### PUBLICATIONS

**Anchorage Press 907/561-7737** • alternative paper • arts & entertainment listings

### EROTICA

**Le Shop** 305 W Diamond Blvd (at C St) **907/522-1987** • 8am-1am

## Fairbanks

### ACCOMMODATIONS

**All Seasons B&B Inn** 763 7th Ave (at Barnette St) **907/451-6649, 888/451-6649** • gay-friendly • full brkfst • nonsmoking • WiFi • wheelchair access

**Billie's Backpackers Hostel** 2895 Mack Blvd **907/479-2034, 907/799-6120** • gay-friendly • kids ok • food served • women-owned

### CAFES

**Hot Licks Ice Cream** 3453 College Rd **907/479-7813** • seasonal

## Haines

### ACCOMMODATIONS

**The Guardhouse Boarding House** 15 Fort Seward Dr **907/766-2566, 866/290-7445** • lesbians/ gay men • in former jail of Fort William H. Seward • great views of Lynn Canal • bald eagle-watching • nonsmoking • WiFi • lesbian-owned

## Homer

### ACCOMMODATIONS

**Sadie Cove Wilderness Lodge** Kachemak Bay State Park **907/235-2350, 888/283-7234** • gay-friendly • 5 cabins • tree planted for every guest to offset carbon emissions • built from hand-milled driftwood • 3 full meals a day • nonsmoking

**Spit Sister B&B** Homer Spit Rd (at Harbor View Boardwalk #5, at Spit Sister Cafe) **907/235-4921 (SUMMER), 907/299-7748** • gay/ straight • full brkfst • kids/ 1 small pet ok • private deck • nonsmoking • WiFi • cafe downstairs • women-owned

### CAFES

**Spit Sister Cafe** Homer Spit Rd (at Harbor View Boardwalk #5) **907/235-4921 (SUMMER), 907/299-6868/ 6767 (WINTER)** • 5am-4pm • gay/ straight • WiFi • also B&B • women-owned

## Juneau

### ACCOMMODATIONS

**Pearson's Pond Luxury Suites & Adventure Spa** 4541 Sawa Circle **907/789-3772, 888/658-6328** • gay-friendly • B&B resort & spa • hot tub • nonsmoking

**The Silverbow Inn** 120 Second St **907/586-4146, 800/586-4146** • gay-friendly • full brkfst • also restaurant & bakery • alternative cinema • gallery • kids ok • nonsmoking • WiFi

### RESTAURANTS

**Hangar on the Wharf** 2 Marine Way Ste 106 **907/586-5018** • lunch & dinner • full bar • great fish & chips

## Ketchikan

### ACCOMMODATIONS

**Anchor Inn by the Sea** 4672 S Tongass Hwy **907/247-7117, 800/928-3308** • gay-friendly • nonsmoking • WiFi

### ENTERTAINMENT & RECREATION

**Southeast Sea Kayaks** 3 Salmon Landing **907/225-1258, 800/287-1607** • trip planning • tours • wilderness kayaking

## McCarthy

### ACCOMMODATIONS

**McCarthy Lodge & Ma Johnson's Hotel** **907/554-4402** • gay-friendly • full brkfst • also restaurant • kids ok • inside Wrangell St Elias nat'l park • nonsmoking

## Palmer

### ACCOMMODATIONS

**Alaska Garden Gate B&B** 950 S Trunk Rd **907/746–2333** • gay/ straight • full brkfst • hot tub • kids/ pets ok • WiFi • lesbian-owned

## Seward

### ENTERTAINMENT & RECREATION

**Puffin Fishing Charters** PO Box 606, 99664 **907/224–4653, 800/978–3346** • gay/ straight • day fishing trips

## Sitka

### ENTERTAINMENT & RECREATION

**Esther G Sea Taxi** 215 Shotgun Alley **907/738–6481, 907/747–6481** • marine wildlife tours • transportation service

# ARIZONA

## Bisbee

### ACCOMMODATIONS

**Casa de San Pedro B&B** 8933 S Yell Ln (at Hwy 92 & Palominas Rd), Hereford **520/366–1300, 888/257–2050** • gay-friendly • full brkfst • pool • hot tub • nonsmoking • WiFi • wheelchair access • gay-owned

**Copper Queen Hotel** 11 Howell Ave **520/432–2216** • gay-friendly • restored landmark hotel • kids ok • pool • nonsmoking • restaurant • wheelchair access

**David's Oasis Camping Resort** 5311 W Double Adobe Rd, McNeal **520/979–6650** • lesbians/ gay men • hot tub, rec room, cabins, RV & tent camping, also BYOB bar on wknds • pool • BYOB bar on wknds • WiFi • gay-owned

**Eldorado Suites** 55 OK St **520/432–6679** • gay-friendly • territorial architecture •WiFi • kitchens • nonsmoking

**Sleepy Dog Guest House** 212A Opera Dr **520/432–3057, 520/234–8166 (CELL)** • gay-friendly • reclaimed miner's cabin • patio • great views • very dog-friendly • lots of stairs • WiFi

### BARS

**St Elmo's** 36 Brewery Ave **520/432–5578** • 10am-2am • gay-friendly • live bands Fri-Sat

## Flagstaff

### ACCOMMODATIONS

**Abineau Lodge** 1080 Mountainaire Rd **928/525–6212, 888/715–6386** • gay/ straight • huskies on premises • cedar sauna • full brkfst • nonsmoking • WiFi • gay-owned

**The Historic Hotel Monte Vista** 100 N San Francisco St (at Aspen) **928/779–6971, 800/545–3068** • gay-friendly • live shows • full bar • nonsmoking

**Inn at 410** 410 N Leroux St **928/774–0088, 800/774–2008** • gay-friendly • full brkfst • WiFi • wheelchair access • gay-owned

**Motel in the Pines** 80 W Pinewood Blvd (exit 322), Pinewood **928/286–9699, 800/574–5080** • gay-friendly • 20 miles from Flagstaff • wheelchair access

**Starlight Pines B&B** 3380 E Lockett Rd (at Fanning) **928/527–1912, 800/752–1912** • gay/ straight • full gourmet brkfst • kids ok (call for details) • nonsmoking • WiFi • gay-owned

### BARS

**Charly's Pub & Grill** 23 N Leroux St (at Weatherford Hotel) **928/779–1919** • 8am-2am • gay-friendly • food served • some veggie • live shows nightly • patio • wheelchair access

**Monte Vista Lounge** 100 N San Francisco St (at Hotel Monte Vista) **928/774–2403** • noon-2am, from 11am Fri-Sun • gay-friendly • dancing/DJ • live bands • karaoke

### CAFES

**Macy's European Coffee House** 14 S Beaver St **928/774–2243** • 6am-8pm • food served • vegetarian/ vegan bakery

### RESTAURANTS

**Granny's Closet** 218 S Milton Rd **928/774–8331** • lunch & dinner • also sports bar

**Pasto** 19 E Aspen (at San Francisco) **928/779–1937** • lunch & dinner, clsd Sun • Italian • beer/ wine • wheelchair access

## Golden Valley

### EROTICA

**Pleasure Palace Adult Bookstore** 4150 US Hwy 68 (at Houck Rd) **928/565–5600**

## Grand Canyon

ACCOMMODATIONS

**Grand Canyon Lodge North** end of Hwy 67, North Rim 877/386-4383 • gay-friendly • at the North Rim of the Grand Canyon

**Grand Canyon Lodges** 928/638-2631 • gay-friendly • the only "in-park" lodging at the South Rim

## Jerome

ACCOMMODATIONS

**The Cottage Inn Jerome** 928/634-0701, 928/634-4148 • gay/ straight • full brkfst • kids/ pets ok • gay-owned

**Mile High Grill & Inn** 309 Main St 928/634-5094 • gay-friendly • cool hotel • also restaurant • lesbian-owned

## Lake Havasu City

INFO LINES & SERVICES

**Lake Havasu City AA** 877/652-9005

ACCOMMODATIONS

**Nautical Inn** 1000 McCulloch Blvd N 928/855-2141, 800/892-2141 • gay-friendly • beachfront hotel • full restaurant & bar • WiFi • pool

## Lake Powell

ACCOMMODATIONS

**Dreamkatchers Lake Powell B&B** 435/675-5828 • gay/ straight • spa on deck • full brkfst • WiFi • gay-owned

## Phoenix

**see also Scottsdale & Tempe**

INFO LINES & SERVICES

**Lambda Phoenix Center** 2622 N 16th St (at Virginia Ave) 602/635-2090 • space for many 12-step programs

**Phoenix Pride LGBT Center** 4442 North 7th Ave 602/712-0111 • 10am-9pm, till 10pm Fri-Sat, till 4pm Sun, clsd Mon

ACCOMMODATIONS

**Best Western Plus Scottsdale Thunderbird Suites** 7515 E Butherus Dr (at Scottsdale Rd), Scottsdale 480/951-4000, 800/951-1288 • gay-friendly • full brkfst • pool • nonsmoking • WiFi • kids/pets ok • also full bar • wheelchair access

**Clarendon Hotel & Suites** 401 W Clarendon Ave (at 3rd Ave) 602/252-7363 • gay/ straight • boutique hotel in midtown • pool • WiFi • wheelchair access • gay-owned

**FireSky Resort & Spa** 4925 N Scottsdale Rd, Scottsdale 480/945-7666, 800/528-7867 • gay-friendly • pool • garden courtyard spa • WiFi • wheelchair access

**Hotel San Carlos** 202 N Central Ave 602/253-4121, 866/253-4121 • gay-friendly • boutique hotel • rooftop pool • restaurant • WiFi

**Maricopa Manor B&B Inn** 15 W Pasadena Ave 602/274-6302, 800/292-6403 • gay/ straight • pool • hot tub • WiFi • wheelchair access • gay-owned

**Orange Blossom Hacienda** 3914 E Sunnydale Dr (btwn Recker & Hunt Hwy), Gilbert 480/755-4346, 877/589-8465 • gay-friendly • pool • gay-owned

**The Saguaro** 4000 N Drinkwater Blvd 480/308-1100 • gay-friendly • hip boutique hotel • pool • gym • nonsmoking • WiFi

**ZenYard** 830 E Maryland Ave 602/845-0830, 866/594-0242 • gay/ straight • private suites w/ kitchens • saltwater pool

BARS

**Bar 1** 3702 N 16th St (at E Clarendon) 602/266-9001 • 10am-2am • mostly gay men • neighborhood bar • karoke • WiFi

**BS West** 7125 E 5th Ave (in the Kiva Center), Scottsdale 480/945-9028 • 2pm-2am • lesbians/ gay men • dancing/DJ • shows • karaoke • wheelchair access

**Cash Inn Country** 2140 E McDowell Rd (at 22nd St) 602/244-9943 • 2pm-close, from noon wknds • mostly women • dancing/DJ • country/ western • karaoke • WiFi • wheelchair access

**Cruisin' 7th** 3702 N 7th St (near Indian School) 602/212-9888 • 6am-2am, from 10am Sun • mostly gay men • transgender-friendly • drag shows • karaoke • wheelchair access

**Kobalt** 3110 N Central Ave 602/264-5307 • 11am-2am • lesbians/ gay men • karaoke • live shows

**Oz** 1804 W Bethany Home Rd (at 19th) 602/242-5114 • 6am-2am • lesbians/ gay men • neighborhood bar • WiFi • wheelchair access

**Plazma** 1560 E Osborn Rd (at N 16th St) **602/266-0477** • 2pm-close, from noon wknds • lesbians/ gay men • neighborhood bar • karaoke • videos

**R Lounge** 4301 N 7th Ave (at Indian School Rd) **602/265-3233** • 5pm-2am, from 10am Th-Sun • mostly women • dancing/DJ • multiracial • karaoke • live /drag shows • wheelchair access • women-owned

**Rainbow Cactus** 15615 N Cave Creek Rd (btwn Greenway Pkwy & Greenway Rd) **602/971-1086** • 3pm-2am • lesbians/ gay men • neighborhood bar

**The Rock/ La Roca** 4129 N 7th Ave (at Indian School) **602/248-8559** • 2pm-2am, from 11am wknds • lesbians/ gay men • neighborhood bar • dancing/DJ • karaoke • live shows

**Roscoe's on 7th** 4531 N 7th St (at Minnezona) **602/285-0833** • 2pm-2am, from 10am wknds • lesbians/ gay men • sports bar • food served

**Stacy's @Melrose** 4343 N 7th Ave **602/264-1700** • 4pm-2am • lesbians/gay men • dancing/DJ

**The Twisted Peacock** 3108 E McDowell Rd (at 32nd St) **602/267-8707** • 2pm-2am, from noon wknds • mostly men • video bar

## NIGHTCLUBS

**Bar Smith** **602/229-1265** • 9pm-2am, till 3am Sat, clsd Sun • gay/ straight • full menu

**Karamba** 1724 E McDowell (at 16th St) **602/254-0231** • 9pm-close, clsd Mon-Wed • mostly gay men • dancing/DJ • drag shows • Latin wknds • wheelchair access

## CAFES

**Copper Star Coffee** 4220 N 7th Ave (at Indian School) **602/266-2136** • 6am-9pm, till 11pm Fri-Sat • coffee in a converted gas station • WiFi

## RESTAURANTS

**Alexi's** 3550 N Central Ave #120 (in Valley Bank Bldg) **602/279-0982** • lunch Mon-Fri, dinner nightly, clsd Sun • full bar • patio • wheelchair access

**AZ/88** 7553 E Scottsdale Mall, Scottsdale **480/994-5576** • 11:30am-1am (food till 12:30am)

**Barrio Cafe** 2814 N 16th St **602/636-0240** • lunch Tue-Fri, dinner Tue-Sun, Sun brunch, clsd Mon • Mexican • live music • lesbian-owned

**Coronado Cafe** 2201 N 7th St **602/258-5149** • lunch Mon-Sat, dinner Tue-Sat, clsd Sun

**DeFalco's Italian Deli** 2334 N Scottsdale Rd **480/990-8660** • best sandwiches in AZ

**Dottie's True Blue Cafe** 4151 N Marshall Way, Scottsdale **480/874-0303** • 7:30am-3pm, clsd Mon • plenty veggie • great brkfst • gay-owned

**Durant's** 2611 N Central Ave **602/264-5967** • lunch Mon-Fri, dinner nightly

**FEZ** 105 W Portland St (at Central) **602/287-8700** • 11am-midnight, from 8:30am wknds • Moroccan influence • full bar • patio

**Green** 2240 N Scottsdale Rd #8, Tempe **480/941-9003** • 11am-9pm, clsd Sun • new American vegetarian/ vegan

**Harley's Bistro** 4221 N 7th Ave (N of Indian School) **602/234-0333** • lunch Tue-Fri, dinner nightly, clsd Mon • lesbians/ gay men • Italian

**Los Dos Molinos** 8684 S Central Ave **602/243-9113** • lunch & dinner, clsd Sun-Mon • Mexican homecooking

**MacAlpines's Soda Fountain** 2303 N 7th St **602/262-5545** • 11am-7pm, till 8pm Fri-Sat, great milkshakes

**Malee's** 7131 E Main, Scottsdale **480/947-6042** • lunch & dinner • Thai • plenty veggie • full bar

**Mi Patio** 3347 N 7th Ave **602/277-4831** • 10am-10pm • Mexican

**Persian Garden Cafe** 1335 W Thomas Rd (at N 15th Ave) **602/263-1915** • lunch & dinner, dinner only Sat, clsd Sun-Mon • plenty vegan• WiFi

**Restaurant Mexico** 423 S Mill Ave, Tempe **480/967-3280** • 11am-9pm, till 10pm Fri-Sat, clsd Sun

**Rose & Crown** 628 E Adams St **602/256-0223** • 11am-2am • British pub

**Switch** 2603 N Central Ave **602/264-2295** • 11am-midnight, from 10am wknds • full bar • WiFi

**Ticoz** 5114 N 7th St (N of Camelback) **602/200-0160** • 11am-midnight • Latin cuisine • full bar • WiFi

**Vincent on Camelback** 3930 E Camelback Rd (at 40th St) **602/224-0225** • dinner Mon-Sat, clsd Sun • Southwestern • wheelchair access

## ENTERTAINMENT & RECREATION

**Arizona Roller Derby** • Arizona's female roller derby league • visit www.azrollerderby.com for events

**Lesbian Social Network** 480/946–5570 •
7:30pm-10pm Fri • popular informal social
evenings of games, videos & discussions •
smoke- & alcohol-free • call for location

**Soul Invictus** 1022 NW Grand Ave (near W
Van Buren St) 602/214–4344 • queer-friendly
art gallery & cabaret

**Stray Cat Theatre** 132 E 6th St (at
Performing Arts Ctr), Tempe 480/634–6435 •
provocative, off-the-beaten-path productions

### Bookstores

**Changing Hands** 6428 S McClintock Dr,
Tempe 480/730–0205 • 10am-9pm, from 9am
Sat, till 6pm Sun • new & used • LGBT section

### Retail Shops

**Off Chute Too** 4111 N 7th Ave (at Indian
School Rd) 602/274–1429 • 9am-9pm, till
10pm Fri-Sat, 10am-6pm Sun • LGBT gift shop
in Melrose District

### Publications

**Echo Magazine** 602/266–0550,
888/324–6624 • bi-weekly LGBT
newsmagazine

**Ion Arizona Magazine** 602/308–4662 •
entertainment guide for the AZ gay
community

**Women's Community Connection**
480/946–5570 • monthly newspaper w/ events
& lesbian resources

### Gyms & Health Clubs

**Pulse Fitness** 18221 N Pima Rd #H-130,
Scottsdale 480/907–5900

### Erotica

**Adult Shoppe** 111 S 24th St (at Jefferson)
602/306–1130 • 24hrs • several locations

**Castle Megastore** 300 E Camelback (at
Central) 602/266–3348 • 11am-11pm, tll 2am
Fri-Sat

**Fascinations** 10242 N 19th Ave #1-7
602/943–5859 • many locations

**Zorba's Adult Book Shop** 2924 N
Scottsdale Rd (N of Thomas), Scottsdale
480/941–9891 • 24hrs • video rentals &
arcade

## Prescott

### Accommodations

**The Motor Lodge** 503 S Montezuma St (at
Leroux) 928/717–0157 • gay-friendly •
nonsmoking • WiFi • gay-owned

## Sedona

### Accommodations

**Apple Orchard Inn** 656 Jordan Rd
928/282–5328, 800/663–6968 • gay-friendly •
full brkfst • hot tub • pool • hiking • scenic
views • nonsmoking • wheelchair access

**El Portal Sedona** 95 Portal Ln
928/203–9405, 800/313–0017 • gay-friendly •
suites in a 1910 adobe hacienda •
nonsmoking • food served • WiFi • wheelchair
acccess

**The Lodge at Sedona—A Luxury B&B
Inn** 125 Kallof Pl 928/204–1942,
800/619–4467 • gay/ straight • full gourmet
brkfst • pool • nonsmoking • WiFi •
wheelchair access

**Sedona Rouge Hotel & Spa** 2250 W Hwy
89-A 928/203–4111, 866/312–4111 • gay-
friendly • pool • nonsmoking • WiFi •
restaurant & bar • wheelchair access

**The Sedona Women's Institute** PO Box
127, 86339 928/254–1897 • women only •
"healing sanctuary" • retreats

**Southwest Inn at Sedona** 3250 W Hwy
89–A 928/282–3344, 800/483–7422 • gay-
friendly • pool • spa • workout room • WiFi •
nonsmoking

### Cafes

**Old Town Red Rooster Cafe** 901 N Main
St, Cottonwood 928/649–8100 • 8am-4pm

### Restaurants

**Judi's** 40 Soldiers Pass Rd 928/282–4449 •
lunch & dinner, clsd Sun • some veggie • full
bar

### Retail Shops

**Sedona Green Gallery & Gifts** 273 N Hwy
89A #K (btwn Jordan & Mesquite)
928/239–5353 • 10-15% discount to self-
identifying gay & lesbian customers

## Tucson

### Info Lines & Services

**AA Gay/ Lesbian** 3269 N Mountain Ave
520/624–4183 • many mtgs

**Wingspan, Southern Arizona's LGBT
Community Center** 430 E 7th St
520/624–1779, 800/553–9387 • 11am-2pm,
resources, youth support (3pm-8pm Mon-Fri)

### Accommodations

**Catalina Park Inn** 309 E 1st St (at 5th Ave)
520/792–4541, 800/792–4885 • gay/ straight •
full brkfst • nonsmoking • kids 10+ ok • WiFi •
gay-owned

**Desert Trails B&B** 12851 E Speedway Blvd **520/885–7295, 877/758–3284** • gay-friendly • unique adobe territorial on 3 acres bordering Saguaro Nat'l Park • far from the madding crowd • swimming • smoking outside only

**Hotel Congress** 311 E Congress St **520/622–8848, 800/722–8848** • gay/ straight • historic hotel • WiFi • also cafe, full bar & club

**La Casita Del Sol** 407 N Meyer Ave (btwn Church Ave & Franklin Ave) **520/623–8882** • gay/ straight • 1880s adobe guesthouse • nonsmoking • WiFi • gay-owned

**Royal Elizabeth B&B Inn** 204 S Scott Ave (at Broadway) **520/670–9022, 877/670–9022** • gay/ straight • full brkfst • pool • hot tub • kids ok • nonsmoking • WiFi • gay-owned

### BARS

**Club Congress/ The Tap Room** 311 E Congress (at Hotel Congress) **520/622–8848** • 11am-2am • gay-friendly • neighborhood bar • dance club from 9pm • karaoke • bands

**IBT's (It's About Time)** 616 N 4th Ave (at University) **520/882–3053** • noon-2am • lesbians/ gay men • dancing/DJ • live shows • karaoke • patio • wheelchair access

### CAFES

**Revolutionary Grounds** 606 N 4th Ave (at E 5th St) **520/620–1770** • 8am-8pm • plenty veggie/vegan/ gluten free • WiFi • also leftist bookstore

### RESTAURANTS

**Blue Willow** 2616 N Campbell Ave (at Grant) **520/327–7577** • 7am-9pm, from 8am wknds • brkfst served all day

**Cafe Poca Cosa** 110 E Pennington St **520/622–6400** • 11am-9pm, till 10pm Fri-Sat, clsd Sun-Mon • Mexican-influenced bistro • patio

### ENTERTAINMENT & RECREATION

**The Loft Cinema** 3233 E Speedway Blvd **520/795–0844, 520/322–5638** • Tucson's independent art house • pizza, beer & wine

**Tucson Roller Derby** **520/390–1454** • Tucson's female roller derby league • visit tucsonrollerderby.com for events

### BOOKSTORES

**Antigone Books** 411 N 4th Ave (at 7th St) **520/792–3715** • 10am-7pm, till 9pm Fri-Sat, 11am-5pm Sun • LGBT/ feminist • gifts • wheelchair access

### EROTICA

**Hydra** 145 E Congress (at 6th) **520/791–3711** • vinyl • leather • toys • shoes • lingerie

# ARKANSAS

## Crosses

### CAFES

**Crosses Grocery & Cafe** 4223 Hwy 16 (E of Elkins, outside Fayetteville) **479/643–3307** • 6am-8:30pm • on the Pig Trail • gay-owned

## Eureka Springs

### ACCOMMODATIONS

**The Grand TreeHouse Resort** 350 W Van Buren (at Pivot Rock Rd) **479/253–8733** • gay/ straight • outdoor showers up in trees • WiFi • gay-owned

**Heart of the Hills Inn** 5 Summit St (on Historic Loop) **479/253–7468, 800/253–7468** • gay/ straight • historic inn near downtown • full brkfst • private decks • nonsmoking • gay-owned

**Lookout Lodge** 3098 E Van Buren **479/253–9335, 877/253–9335** • gay-friendly • private entrances • kids/ pets ok • WiFi • nonsmoking

**Mount Victoria** 28 Fairmount St **479/253–7979, 888/408–7979** • gay-friendly • full brkfst & dinner • WiFi

**Out on Main** 269 N Main St (at Magnetic Rd) **479/253–8449** • gay/ straight • 3-room cottage • full kitchen • nonsmoking • WiFi • gay-owned

**Palace Hotel & Bath House** 135 Spring St **479/253–7474, 866/946–0572** • gay-friendly • historic bathhouse open to all • nonsmoking • WiFi

**Pond Mountain Lodge & Resort** **479/253–5877, 800/583–8043** • gay/ straight • mountaintop inn on 150 acres • cabins • pool • nonsmoking • jacuzzis • wheelchair access • lesbian-owned

**Red Bud Manor Inn** 7 Kingshighway **479/253–9649, 866/253–9649** • gay-friendly • full brkfst • WiFi • indoor hot tub • women-owned

**Roadrunner Inn** 3034 Mundell Rd **479/253–8166, 888/253–8166** • gay-friendly • lake views • reservations advised • guestrooms & log cabins • WiFi

**Texaco Bungalow** 77 Mountain St **888/253–8093** • gay/ straight • art deco service station rentals • gay-owned

**Tradewinds** 141 W Van Buren (at 23 N) **479/363-6189** • gay/straight • motel reminiscent of the motor inns of the '40s & '50s, mention Damron and receive 20% off BnB Suite rate • pool • pets ok • WiFi • gay-owned

**The Woods Teehouse Resort** 50 Wall St (off Hwy 62) **479/253-8281** • lesbians/gay men • cottages • some treehouse cottages • treehouse hot tub • kitchens • nonsmoking • gay-owned

### BARS

**Chelsea's Corner Cafe** 10 Mountain St (at Center St) **479/253-6723** • 11am-2am, till 10pm Sun • gay-friendly • dancing/DJ • patio • also restaurant • live shows • WiFi • women-owned

**Eureka Live** 35 N Main **479/253-7020** • 11am-1:30am, clsd Mon-Tue • gay/straight • dancing/DJ • food served • karaoke

**Henri's Just One More** 19 1/2 Spring St **479/253-5795** • noon-2am, clsd Tue • gay/straight • gay night Wed from 5pm • bar menu • live shows • WiFi

**Pied Piper Pub & Inn** 82 Armstrong (at Main St) **479/363-9976, 866/363-9976** • noon-midnight • gay-friendly • popular Reuben sandwich, fish & chips • also hotel

### CAFES

**Mud Street Cafe** 22G S Main St **479/253-6732** • 8am-3pm, clsd Tue-Wed

### RESTAURANTS

**Caribe Restaurant & Cantina** 309 W Van Buren **479/253-8102** • 4pm-9pm, clsd Tue, from noon wknds • also bar

**Ermilio's** 26 White St **479/253-8806** • 5pm-9pm • Italian • plenty veggie • full bar

**Gaskins Cabin Steak House** 2883 Hwy 23 N (Hwy 187) **479/253-5466** • 5pm-9pm, till 8pm Sun, clsd Mon-Tue • full bar • reservations suggested

## Fayetteville

### INFO LINES & SERVICES

**AA Gay/Lesbian** 568 W Sycamore **479/443-6366 (AA#)**

### ACCOMMODATIONS

**Hilton Garden Inn Bentonville** 2204 SE Walton Blvd (Exit 85, off I-540), Bentonville **479/464-7300, 877/782-9444** • gay-friendly • pool • kids ok • WiFi • wheelchair access

### CAFES

**The Common Grounds** 412 W Dickson St (at West) **479/442-3515** • 7am-midnight • full bar • also restaurant • lots of veggie

### RESTAURANTS

**Bordinos** 310 W Dickson St **479/527-6795** • dinner nightly, lunch Tue-Fri, clsd Sun • full bar

**Hugo's** 25 1/2 N Block Ave **479/521-7585** • 11am-10pm, clsd Sun

## Fort Smith

### BARS

**Kinkead's** 1004 1/2 Garrison Ave **479/226-3144** • 5pm-2am, from 7pm Fri-Sat, clsd Mon • gay/straight • neighborhood bar • dancing/DJ • draw shows • karaoke • WiFi • gay-owned

## Helena

### ACCOMMODATIONS

**The Edwardian Inn** 317 Biscoe **870/338-9155, 800/598-4749** • gay-friendly • 60 miles from Memphis • full brkfst • nonsmoking • WiFi

## Hot Springs

### ACCOMMODATIONS

**Park Hotel of Hot Springs** 211 Fountain St (at Central Ave) **501/624-5323, 800/895-7275** • gay/straight • WiFi

### BARS

**Another Rumor Bar & Grill** 1310 Central Ave **501/463-9221** • 6pm-2am, 4pm-midnight Sun, clsd Mon-Tue • lesbians/gay men • dancing/DJ • karaoke

## Little Rock

### ACCOMMODATIONS

**Legacy Hotel & Suites** 625 W Capitol Ave (at Gaines) **501/374-0100, 888/456-3669** • gay-friendly • nat'l historic property in downtown area • kids ok • WiFi • wheelchair access

## Bars

**Chaps** 2769 Pike Ave, North Little Rock **501/313-2836** • 7pm-2am • mostly gay men • neighborhood bar • older crowd • WiFi • wheelchair access

**Discovery** 1021 Jessie Rd (btwn Cantrell & Riverfront) **501/664-4784** • 9pm-5am Sat only • gay/straight • dancing/DJ • drag shows • male dancers • videos • 18+ • private club • wheelchair access

**Triniti Nightclub** 1021 Jessie Rd (btwn Cantrell & Riverfront) **501/664-2744** • 9pm-5am Fri only • lesbians/gay men • dancing/DJ • drag shows • male dancers • videos • 18+ • private club • wheelchair access

## Restaurants

**Bossa Nova** 2701 Kavanaugh Blvd (at Ash St) **501/614-6682** • lunch & dinner, Sun brunch, clsd Mon • Brazilian • plenty veggie

**Juanita's** 614 President Clinton (at River Market) **501/372-1228** • 11am-close, clsd Sun • Mexican • reservations recommended • live music

**La Hacienda** 3024 Cantrell Rd **501/661-0600** • lunch & dinner • Mexican

**Lilly's Dim Sum, Then Some/ B-Side** 11121 N Rodney Parham Rd **501/716-2700** • 11am-9pm, clsd Mon • contemporary Asian • plenty veggie • lesbian-owned

**Vino's Pizza** 923 W 7th St (at Chester) **501/375-8466** • 11am-close • beer/wine

## Entertainment & Recreation

**The Weekend Theater** 1001 W 7th St (at Chester) **501/374-3761** • plays & musicals on wknds • gay-owned

## Bookstores

**Wordsworth Books & Co** 5920 R St **501/663-9198** • 9am-7pm, till 6pm Fri-Sat, noon-5pm Sun • independent

## Retail Shops

**A Twisted Gift Shop** 1007 W 7th St (at Chester) **501/376-7723** • noon-midnight • gift shop

## Texarkana

### Bars

**The Chute** 714 Laurel St **870/772-6900** • 7pm-2am Th-Sat • lesbians/gay men • dancing/DJ • karaoke • drag shows

# CALIFORNIA

## Amador City

### Accommodations

**Imperial Hotel** 14202 Hwy 49 (at Water St) **209/267-9172** • gay-friendly • B&B • brick Victorian hotel • nonsmoking • full brkfst • restaurant & bar

## Anaheim

see Orange County

## Arcata

### Info Lines & Services

**Queer Humboldt** PO Box 45, 95518-0045 **707/834-4839** • "Humboldt County's online resource for the LGBT community" • includes links & events calendar • check out www.queerhumboldt.org

### Bars

**The Alibi** 744 9th St **707/822-3731** • lesbian/gay men • cocktail lounge w/ live music • neighborhood bar • also restaurant (8am-midnight) • young crowd

### Cafes

**Cafe Mokka** 495 J St (at 5th) **707/822-2228** • from noon • coffee & soups (bread bowls) • live music • also Finnish sauna & hot tubs

**North Coast Co-op** 811 I St **707/822-5947** • 6am-9pm • co-op store w/ bakery, deli & espresso cafe • WiFi

### Restaurants

**Wildflower Bakery & Cafe** 1604 G St **707/822-0360** • 9am-3pm & 5:30pm-9:30pm • popular • vegetarian • organic beer & wine

### Bookstores

**Northtown Books** 957 H St **707/822-2834** • 10am-7pm, till 9pm Fri-Sat, noon-5pm Sun • LGBT section • carries The L Word paper and other gay magazines

## Bakersfield

### Info Lines & Services

**Gay AA** 1001 34th St **661/322-4025 (AA#), 661/324-0371 (Alano Club #)** • 7:30pm Mon

### Accommodations

**The Padre Hotel** 702 18th St **661/427-4900** • gay/straight • sleek hotel with nightclubs, bar, cafe, and fine dining room

### Bars

**The Mint** 1207 19th St (at M) **661/325-4048**
• 6am-2am • gay/ straight • alternative • live music

### Nightclubs

**The Casablanca Club** 1825 N St (at 19th St)
**661/324-0661** • 9pm-2am, clsd Mon-Wed •
gay/ straight • neighborhood bar • dancing/DJ
• live entertainment • cabaret • drag shows •
videos • wheelchair access

## Berkeley

see East Bay

## Big Bear Lake

### Accommodations

**Grey Squirrel Resort** 39372 Big Bear Blvd
**909/866-4335, 800/381-5569** • gay/ straight •
20 cabins & 30 private rental homes • pool •
some nonsmoking • WiFi • lesbian-owned

## Big Sur

### Accommodations

**Lucia Lodge** 62400 Hwy"1 **831/688-4884,
866/424-4787** • gay-friendly • oceanview
cabins • also restaurant & lounge • WiFi

## Cambria

### Accommodations

**El Colobri** 5620 Moonstone Beach Dr
**805/924-3003** • gay-friendly • WiFi • pets ok

**FogCatcher Inn** 6400 Moonstone Beach Dr
**805/927-1400, 800/425-4121** • gay-friendly •
steps from Moonstone Beach • swimming •
WiFi • wheelchair access

**Sea Otter Inn** 6656 Moonstone Beach Dr
**805/927-5888, 800/966-6490** • gay-friendly •
heated pool • nonsmoking • WiFi • wheelchair
access

### Bars

**Mozzi's Saloon** 2262 Main St **805/927-4767**
• 1pm-11pm, Fri-Sat till 2am • gay-friendly
cowboy bar • live music

### Restaurants

**The Cambria Pub & Steakhouse** 4090
Burton Dr **805/927-0782** • 11am-9pm, till
10pm Fri-Sat, clsd Wed

## Carmel

see also Monterey

### Accommodations

**Best Western Carmel Mission Inn** 3665
Rio Rd **831/624-1841, 800/348-9090** • gay-
friendly • near Monterey Bay • pool • pets ok •
also restaurant & lounge • nonsmoking

**Cypress Inn** Lincoln & 7th **831/624-3871,
800/443-7443** • gay-friendly • pets very
welcome • owned by Doris Day • WiFi • also
restaurant & lounge

### Restaurants

**Flaherty's Seafood Grill & Oyster Bar** 6th
Ave (btwn Dolores and San Carlos)
**831/625-1500** • open daily 11am • wheelchair
access

**Rio Grill** 101 Crossroads Blvd **831/625-5436**
• lunch & dinner daily, Sun brunch • "Creative
American" • full bar

## Cayucos

### Accommodations

**Cayucos Beach Inn** 333 S Ocean Ave
**805/995-2828
, 800/482-0555** • gay-friendly • pets ok

**Seaside Motel** 42 S Ocean Ave **800/549-
0900**
• gay-friendly • conventional-looking `50s-
style motel with immaculate rooms • WiFi

### Bars

**Old Cayucos Tavern and Cardroom** 130 N
Ocean Ave **805/995-3209**
• 10am-2am • gay-friendly • live music •
liquor in the front, poker in the back

### Restaurants

**Schooners Wharf** 171 N Ocean Ave
**805/995-3883**
• lunch & dinner

## Chico

### Info Lines & Services

**Stonewall Alliance Center** 358 E 6th St (at
Flume) **530/893-3336** • HIV testing &
counseling • also recorded info • meetings •
events

## Chino

### Restaurants

**Riverside Grill** 5258 Riverside Dr (at Central)
**909/627-4144** • 8am-9pm

## Clearlake

**includes major towns of Lake County**

ACCOMMODATIONS

**Blue Fish Cove Resort** 10573 E Hwy 20, Clearlake Oaks **707/998–1769** • gay-friendly • lakeside resort cottages • kitchens • kids ok • pets ok by arrangement • boat launch facilities & rentals

**Edgewater Resort** 6420 Soda Bay Rd (at Hohape Rd), Kelseyville **707/279–0208, 800/396–6224** • "gay-owned, straight-friendly" • cabin • camping & RV hookups • lake access & pool • boat facilities • WiFi • kids/pets ok • lesbian-owned

**Featherbed Railroad B& B** 2870 Lakeshore Blvd, Nice **707/274–8378** • gay-friendly • pool • full brkfst • WiFi • pets ok

**Sea Breeze Resort** 9595 Harbor Dr, Glenhaven **707/998–3327** • gay/ straight • lakefront cottages • swimming • nonsmoking • WiFi • wheelchair access • gay-owned

## Cloverdale

**see also Healdsburg**

ACCOMMODATIONS

**Kelley & Young Wine Garden Inn** 302 N Main St (at 3rd) **707/894–4535** • gay-friendly • Queen Anne mansion • full brkfst • nonsmoking

RESTAURANTS

**Hamburger Ranch & Bar-B-Que** 31195 N Redwood Hwy **707/894–5616** • 7am-9pm • beer & wine • patio

## Concord

**see East Bay**

## Costa Mesa

**see Orange County**

## Davis

**see also Sacramento**

INFO LINES & SERVICES

**LGBTQIA Resource Center** Student Community Center, Ste 1400 **530/752–2452** • 10am-6pm, 9am-5pm Fri, clsd wknds • info • referrals • meetings • library • WiFi • wheelchair access

**LGBTQIA Resource Center** Student Community Center, Ste 1400 **530/752–2452** • 10am-6pm, 9am-5pm Fri, clsd wknds • info • referrals • meetings • library • WiFi • wheelchair access

CAFES

**Mishka's Cafe** 610 2nd St **530/759–0811** • 7:30am-11pm

BOOKSTORES

**The Avid Reader** 617 2nd St **530/758–4040** • 10am-10pm • general independent • readings

## East Bay

**includes major cities of Alameda and Contra Costa Counties: Alameda, Antioch, Berkeley, Concord, Danville, Fremont, Hayward, Lafayette, Newark, Oakland, Pleasant Hill, Richmond, San Leandro, Walnut Creek**

INFO LINES & SERVICES

**East Bay AA** 510/839–8900 • variety of LGBT-friendly mtgs

**Pacific Center for Human Growth** 2712 Telegraph Ave (at Derby), Berkeley **510/548–8283** • 10 am to 9 pm, till 4pm Sat, clsd Sun, offers sliding-scale psychotherapy, peer-facilitated support groups, HIV counseling • wheelchair access

**Rainbow Community Center of Contra Costa County** 2118 Willow Pass Rd #500, Concord **925/692–0090** • 10am-5pm Mon-Fri

ACCOMMODATIONS

**Hotel Durant** 2600 Durant Ave, Berkeley **510/845–8981, 800/238–7268** • gay/ straight • nonsmoking • WiFi • restaurant on premises

**Washington Inn** 495 10th St (at Broadway), Oakland **510/452–1776** • gay/ straight • historic boutique hotel • full brkfst • nonsmoking • also restaurant • wheelchair access

**Waterfront Hotel** 10 Washington St, Oakland **510/836-3800, 888/842–5333** • gay-friendly • pool • bar & restaurant • WiFi • wheelchair access

BARS

**The Alley** 3325 Grand Ave (btwn Lake Park & Elwood Aves), Oakland **510/444–8505** • 5pm-2am • gay/ straight • dive bar & restaurant • karaoke • trivia nights

**Cafe Van Kleef** 1621 Telegraph Ave (at Broadway), Oakland 510/763–7711 • 4pm-2am, clsd Sun • gay-friendly • eclectic crowd & live-music scene—from cabaret to blue grass to jazz • cover

**Club 21** 2111 Franklin St (at 21st St), Oakland 510/268–9425 • mostly gay men • dancing/DJ • mostly Latino/a • theme nights • videos

**Club BNB** 2120 Broadway, Oakland 510/444–2266 • 4pm-2am • popular • mostly gay men • dancing/DJ • drag shows • theme nights • wheelchair access

**The Port** 2021 Broadway (next to the Paramount Theater), Oakland

**White Horse** 6551 Telegraph Ave (at 66th), Oakland 510/652–3820 • 3pm-2am, from 1pm wknds (also Sun beer bust) • lesbians/gay men • dancing/DJ • karaoke • wheelchair access

**World Famous Turf Club** 22519 Main St (at A St), Hayward 510/881–9877 • 4pm-2am, from noon Sat-Sun • lesbians/gay men • dancing/DJ • drag shows • sports bar • huge patio • BBQs • live music • WiFi • near BART • wheelchair access

## NIGHTCLUBS

**Club 1220** 1220 Pine St (at Civic Dr), Walnut Creek 925/938–4550 • 4pm-2am • lesbians/gay men • dancing/DJ • theme nights • karaoke • WiFi • wheelchair access

## CAFES

**Actual Cafe** 6334 San Pablo Ave (at Alcatraz), Oakland 510/653–8386 • 7am-9pm, till 10pm wknds

**Au Coquelet Cafe** 2000 University Ave, Berkeley 510/845–0433 • 6am-2am • WiFi

**Bittersweet** 5427 College Ave (in Rockridge District), Oakland 510/654–7159 • 9am-7pm, till 9pm Fri-Sat

**Caffe Strada** 2300 College Ave (btwn Way & Durant), Berkeley 510/843–5282 • 6am-midnight • students • great patio • wheelchair access

**Cole Coffee** 6255 College Ave (btwn 62nd & 63rd Sts), Oakland 510/985–1958 • 7am-7pm • hip hideaway in lovely Rockridge

**Raw Energy** 2050 Addison St (btwn Shattuck & Milvia), Berkeley 510/665–9464 • 7:30am-7pm, 11am-4pm Sat, clsd Sun • organic juice cafe • gay-owned

**Victory Burger** 1099 Alcatraz Ave (at San Pablo), Oakland 510/653–8322 • 7am-9pm, till 10pm wknds • food served • events

## RESTAURANTS

**Arizmendi Bakery & Pizzeria** 4301 San Pablo Ave (at 43rd St), Emeryville 510/547–0550 • 7am-7pm, till 3pm Mon, clsd Sun • excellent pastries, breads & pizzas

**Banh Cuon Tay Ho** 344-B 12th St (at Webster), Oakland 510/836–6388 • 10am-9pm, till 8pm Sun, clsd Mon

**Cactus Taqueria** 5642 College Ave (at Shafter, in Rockridge), Oakland 510/658–6180 • 11am-10pm, till 9pm Sun

**César** 4039 Piedmont, Oakland 510/883–0222 • noon-11pm • Spanish tapas • full bar

**Connie's Cantina** 3340 Grand Ave (btwn Lake Park Ave & Mandana Blvd), Oakland 510/839–4986 • 10:30am-9pm, clsd Sun • popular • delicious homemade Mexican food • plenty veggie • patio • woman-owned

**Dopo** 4293 Piedmont Ave (btwn Glenwood & Echo), Oakland 510/652–3676 • lunch Mon-Fri, dinner nightly, clsd Sun • Italian • worth the wait

**Le Cheval** 1007 Clay St, Oakland 510/763–8495 • 11am-9pm, from 4pm Sun • popular • Vietnamese • wheelchair access

**Lois the Pie Queen** 851 60th St (off Martin Luther King Jr Hwy), Oakland 510/658–5616 • 8am-2pm, 7am-3pm wknds • popular • Southern homecooking & killer desserts

**Mama's Royal Cafe** 4012 Broadway (at 40th), Oakland 510/547–7600 • 7am-2:30pm, from 8am wknds • popular • come early for excellent wknd brunch • beer/wine • wheelchair access

**Rockridge Cafe** 5492 College Ave (at Forest), Oakland 510/653–1567 • 7:30am-3pm • popular • great brkfsts • plenty veggie

**Zachary's Chicago Pizza** 5801 College Ave, Oakland 510/655–6385 • 11am-10pm • popular • pizza that is worth the crowds & the long wait!

## BOOKSTORES

**Black Oak Books** 2618 San Pablo Ave, Berkeley 510/486–0698 • 11am-7pm • independent • new & used

**Diesel, A Bookstore** 5433 College Avenue, Oakland **510/653-9965** • 10am-9pm, till 10pm Fri-Sat, till 6pm Sun • independent

**Laurel Book Store** 1423 Broadway, Oakland **510/452-9232** • 10am-7pm, till 6pm Sat, 11am-5pm Sun • general • LGBT section • readings • wheelchair access • lesbian-owned

**Pegasus Books** 5560 College Ave (at Oceanview), Oakland **510/652-6259** • 9am-10pm, from 10am Sun • used books • magazines • great to browse while waiting for a table in Rockridge

## RETAIL SHOPS

**See Jane Run Sports** 5817 College Ave, Oakland **510/428-2681** • 11am-7pm, 10am-6pm Sat-Sun • women's athletic apparel

## EROTICA

**Good Vibrations** 2504 San Pablo Ave (at Dwight Wy), Berkeley **510/841-8987** • 10am-9pm, till 10pm Fri-Sat • clean, well-lighted sex toy store • workshops & events • wheelchair access

**Good Vibrations** 3219 Lakeshore Ave, Oakland **510/788-2389** • 10am-9pm, till10pm Fri-Sat • clean, well-lighted sex toy store • workshops & events • wheelchair access

# Elk

## RESTAURANTS

**Queenie's Roadhouse Cafe** 6061 S Hwy 1 **707/877-3285** • 8am-3pm, clsd Tue-Wed • fabulous all-day brkfsts • some veggie • lesbian-owned

# Eureka

## ACCOMMODATIONS

**Carter House Inns** 301 L St **707/444-8062, 800/404-1390** • gay-friendly • enclave of 4 unique inns • full brkfst • nonsmoking • kids ok • restaurant • wine shop • wheelchair access

**Trinidad Bay B&B** 560 Edwards St (at Trinity), Trinidad **707/677-0840** • gay-friendly • nonsmoking • WiFi • kids ok • full brkfst • gay- & straight-owned

## BARS

**Lost Coast Brewery** 617 4th St (btwn G & H Sts) **707/445-4480** • 11am-1am • gay-friendly • food served till midnight • beer/ wine • WiFi • wheelchair access • women-owned

**The Shanty** 213 3rd St (at C St) **707/444-2053** • noon-2am • gay/ straight • neighborhood bar • lesbian-owned

## NIGHTCLUBS

**Where's Queer Bill** 707/832-4785 • monthly queer events • check wheresqueerbill.com for info

## CAFES

**North Coast Co-op** 25 4th St (at B St) **707/443-6027** • 6am-9pm • co-op store w/ bakery, deli & espresso cafe

**Ramone's Cafe & Bakery** 209 E St (Old Town) **707/445-2923** • 7am-6pm

## RESTAURANTS

**Chalet House of Omelettes** 1935 5th St (at U St) **707/442-0333** • 6am-3pm, brkfst & lunch • wheelchair access

**Folie Douce** 1551 G St, Arcata **707/822-1042** • dinner only, clsd Sun-Mon • bistro • beer/ wine • reservations recommended • wheelchair access

## BOOKSTORES

**Booklegger** 402 2nd St (at E St) **707/445-1344** • 10am-5:30pm, 11am-4pm Sun • mostly used • wheelchair access • women-owned

## PUBLICATIONS

**The "L" Word** PO Box 272, Bayside 95524 • lesbian newsletter for Humboldt County • available at Eureka Natural Foods & Booklegger in Eureka • also at the co-op & North Town Books in Arcata

## EROTICA

**Good Relations** 223 2nd St **707/441-9570, 888/485-5063** • lingerie • toys • books • videos • wheelchair access • queer-owned/ run

# Fort Bragg

## ACCOMMODATIONS

**The Cleone Gardens Inn** 24600 N Hwy 1 (at Nameless Ln) **707/964-2788, 800/400-2189 (CA,NV & OR ONLY)** • gay-friendly • country garden retreat on 2.5 acres • hot tub • WiFi • nonsmoking • wheelchair access

**The Weller House Inn** 524 Stewart St (at Pine) **707/964-4415, 877/893-5537** • gay-friendly • 1886 Victorian • full brkfst • jacuzzi • nonsmoking • WiFi

## RESTAURANTS

**Cowlick's** 250B N Main St **707/962-9271** • delicious homemade ice cream, including mushroom ice cream (in-season)—it's actually quite good!

**Purple Rose** 24300 N Hwy 1 **707/964-6507**
• 5pm-9pm, clsd Sun-Mon • Mexican •
wheelchair access

ENTERTAINMENT & RECREATION

**Skunk Train California Western** foot of
Laurel St **707/964-6371, 866/457-5865** •
scenic train trips

## Fremont

see East Bay

## Fresno

INFO LINES & SERVICES

**Community Link** **559/266-5465** • info •
LGBT support, including LGBT youth group •
also publishes Newslink

**Fresno AA** **559/221-6907** • call or check
website (www.fresnoaa.org) for meetings

ACCOMMODATIONS

**The San Joaquin Hotel** 1309 W Shaw Ave
(at Fruit) **559/225-1309, 800/775-1309** • gay-
friendly • pool • WiFi • wheelchair access

BARS

**The Phoenix** 4538 E Belmont Ave (at Maple)
**559/252-2899** • 4pm-2am • mostly gay men •
country/western • bears • leather • multiracial
• videos • older crowd • popular beer busts •
patio • gay-owned

**Red Lantern** 4618 E Belmont Ave (at Maple)
**559/251-5898** • 2pm-2am • mostly gay men •
neighborhood bar • country/western • Latin
night Sat very popular • food Sun • patio •
WiFi • wheelchair access

NIGHTCLUBS

**Club Legends** 3075 N Maroa Ave
**559/222-2271** • 4pm-2am • gay/straight •
dancing/DJ • drag shows • pool & patio

RESTAURANTS

**Don Pepe's** 4582 N Blackstone Ave (at
Gettysburg) **559/224-1431** • 9am-9pm •
Mexican

**Irene's Cafe** 747 E Olive Ave (in Tower
District) **559/237-9919** • 8am-9pm • some
veggie • good hamburgers • beer/wine

**Sequoia Brewing Company** 777 E Olive
Ave (in Tower District) **559/264-5521** • 11am-
10pm, till midnight Fri-Sat, till 9pm Sun •
microbrewery w/ restaurant • live music

**Veni Vidi Vici** 1116 N Fulton (S of Olive Ave,
in Tower District) **559/266-5510** • California
fine dining • nightclub later

EROTICA

**Suzie's Adult Superstores** 1267 N
Blackstone Ave **559/497-9613** • 24hrs

## Garden Grove

see Orange County

## Grass Valley

see also Nevada City

## Gualala

ACCOMMODATIONS

**Breakers Inn** 39300 S Hwy 1 **707/884-3200**
• gay/straight • oceanfront • women-owned

**North Coast Country Inn** 34591 S Hwy 1
**707/884-4537** • gay-friendly • B&B
overlooking Mendocino coast • hot tub •
nonsmoking

BOOKSTORES

**The Four-Eyed Frog** 39138 Ocean Dr (in
Cypress Village) **707/884-1333** • 10am-6pm,
till 5pm Sun • independent

## Half Moon Bay

ACCOMMODATIONS

**Mill Rose Inn** 615 Mill St **650/726-8750,
800/900-7673** • gay-friendly • classic
European elegance by the sea • full brkfst •
hot tub • nonsmoking • WiFi • kids 10+ ok

RESTAURANTS

**Moss Beach Distillery** 140 Beach Wy (at
Ocean) **650/728-5595** • lunch & dinner, Sun
brunch • popular • steak & seafood • some
veggie • patio • even own ghost • wheelchair
access

**Pasta Moon** 315 Main St (at Mill)
**650/726-5125** • lunch & dinner • Italian • full
bar • live shows • wheelchair access

**Sam's Chowder House** 4210 N Cabrillo
Hwy (S of Pillar Point Harbor) **650/712-0245**
• lunch & dinner • great loster rolls and views

## Hayward

see East Bay

## Healdsburg

see also Russian River & Sonoma County

## Huntington Beach

see Orange County

## Idyllwild

### ACCOMMODATIONS

**The Rainbow Inn** 54420 S Circle Dr
**951/659-0111** • gay/ straight • full brkfst • kids
ok • nonsmoking • patio • fireplaces • WiFi •
also conference center • gay-owned

**Strawberry Creek Inn B&B** 26370 Hwy 243
(at S Cir Dr) **951/659-3202, 800/262-8969** •
gay-friendly • relaxing getaway w/ sundeck,
garden & hammocks • nonsmoking •
wheelchair access • gay-owned

### RESTAURANTS

**Cafe Aroma** 54750 North Circle
**951/659-5212** • 7am-10pm • great ambience
& food • live music most nights

## Irvine

**see Orange County**

## Joshua Tree

### ACCOMMODATIONS

**Kate's Lazy Desert** 58380 Botkin Rd,
Landers **845/688-7200** • gay-friendly • love
shack owned by Kate Pierson of the B-52s •
WiFi • nonsmoking

## Joshua Tree Nat'l Park

### ACCOMMODATIONS

**The Desert Lily** PO Box 139, 92252-0800
**760/366-4676, 877/887-7370** • gay-friendly •
artist-owned adobe-style B&B on 5 acres •
also cabins • clsd July-Aug • woman-owned

**Joshua Tree Highlands Houses**
**760/366-3636** • gay/ straight • private, fully
equipped rentals • near Joshua Tree Nat'l Park
• nonsmoking • kids/ pets ok • WiFi •
wheelchair access • gay-owned

**Sacred Sands** HCl Box 1071 A, 63155 Quail
Springs Rd (at Desert Shadows), Joshua Tree
**760/424-6407** • gay/ straight • private
outdoor living • spa • nonsmoking • WiFi •
gay-owned

**Spin & Margie's Desert Hideaway** 64491
29 Palms Hwy **760/366-9124** • gay-friendly •
hacienda-style B&B • suites w/ private patios

**Starland Retreat** Yucca Valley
**760/364-2069** • mostly gay men & radical
faeries, but women very welcome •
membership-only rustic rural camp • hot tub •
nudity permitted

### RESTAURANTS

**The Crossroads Cafe & Tavern** 61715 29
Palms Hwy **760/366-5414** • 7am-8pm, till
9pm Fri-Sat, clsd Wed

## Kernville

### ACCOMMODATIONS

**Riverview Lodge** 2 Sirretta St **760/376-6019**
• gay/ straight • riverfront resort • jacuzzi •
kids/ pets ok • nonsmoking • gay-owned

## La Mirada

### RESTAURANTS

**Mexico 1900** 11531 La Mirada blvd
**562/941-2016** • lunch & dinner • Mexican

## Laguna Beach

**see Orange County**

## Lake Tahoe

**see also Lake Tahoe, Nevada**

### ACCOMMODATIONS

**Alpine Inn & Spa** 920 Stateline Ave (Lake
Ave/ Hwy 50), South Lake Tahoe
**530/544-3340, 800/826-8885** • gay/ straight •
motel • just steps from casino • swimming •
lesbian & gay & straight-owned

**Black Bear Inn** **530/544-4451,**
**877/232-7466** • gay/ straight • full brkfst • hot
tub • fireplaces • nonsmoking • WiFi • gay-
owned

**The Cedar House Sport Hotel** 10918
Brockway Rd, Truckee **530/582-5655,**
**866/582-5655** • gay-friendly • full bar • WiFi •
kids/ pets ok

**Holly's Place** **800/745-7041, 530/544-7040**
• gay/ straight • cabins • fireplaces • kitchens •
hot tubs • nonsmoking • kids/ dogs ok • WiFi
• women-owned

**Spruce Grove Cabins** 3599-3605 Spruce
Ave, South Lake Tahoe **530/544-0549,**
**800/777-0914** • gay-friendly • full kitchens •
near Heavenly Ski Resort • hot tub • dog-
friendly • nonsmoking

**Tahoe Valley Lodge** 2241 Lake Tahoe Blvd
(at Tahoe Keys Blvd), South Lake Tahoe
**530/541-0353, 800/669-7544** • gay-friendly •
motel • pool • nonsmoking • WiFi

## RESTAURANTS

**Driftwood Cafe** 1001 Heavenly Vlg Way #1A 530/544-6545 • 7am-3pm • homecooking • some veggie • wheelchair access

**Passaretti's** 1181 Emerald Bay Rd/ Hwy 50, South Lake Tahoe 530/541-3433 • 11am-9pm • Italian • beer/ wine

## Lancaster

includes Palmdale

## Livermore

see East Bay

## Long Beach

### INFO LINES & SERVICES

**AA Gay/ Lesbian** 2017 E 4th St (at Cherry, at Gay & Lesbian Center) 562/434-4455 • 7pm Mon • lesbians/ gay men

**The Gay & Lesbian Center of Greater Long Beach** 2017 E 4th St (at Cherry) 562/434-4455 • 10am-9pm, till 4pm Sat, clsd Sun • activities & support groups • also newsletter

### ACCOMMODATIONS

**Beachrunners' Inn** 231 Kennebec Ave (at Junipero & Broadway) 562/856-0202, 866/221-0001 • gay/ straight • B&B • near beach • hot tub • nonsmoking

**Hotel Current** 5325 E Pacific Coast Hwy 562/597-1341, 800/990-9991 • gay/ straight • swimming • WiFi • wheelchair access

**Hotel Maya** 700 Queensway Dr 562/435-7676 • gay/ straight • luxury boutique resort hotel w/ waterfront Fuego restaurant • pets ok

**The Varden Hotel** 335 Pacific Ave (at 3rd St) 562/432-8950, 877/382-7336 • gay/ straight • urban boutique hotel • nonsmoking • WiFi • wheelchair access

### BARS

**The Brit** 1744 E Broadway (at Cherry) 562/432-9742 • 10am-2am • mostly gay men • neighborhood bar • patio • wheelchair access

**The Broadway** 1100 E Broadway (at Cerritos) 562/432-3646 • 10am-2am • lesbians/ gay men • neighborhood bar • karaoke Fri-Sat • wheelchair access

**The Crest** 5935 Cherry Ave (at South) 562/423-6650 • 2pm-2am, from noon wknds • mostly gay men

**The Falcon** 1435 E Broadway (at Falcon) 562/432-4146 • 8am-2am, from 7am wknds • mostly gay men but women very welcome • neighborhood bar • wheelchair access

**Flux** 17817 Lakewood Blvd (at Artesia), Bellflower 562/633-6394 • noon-2am • lesbians/ gay men • neighborhood bar • patio • theme nights

**Liquid Lounge** 3522 E Anaheim St 562/494-7564 • gay/ straight • neighborhood bar • food served • karaoke Fri-Sat • live music • patio • gay-owned

**Mineshaft** 1720 E Broadway (btwn Gaviota & Hermosa) 562/436-2433 • 11am-2am • popular • mostly gay men • bears

**Paradise Piano Bar & Restaurant** 1800 E Broadway Blvd (at Hermosa) 562/590-8773 • 3pm-1am, from 10am Sat-Sun • lesbians/ gay men • live entertainment

**Pistons** 2020 E Artesia (at Cherry) 562/422-1928 • 5pm-2am, from 2pm Sun • mostly gay men • bears • leather • patio

**Que Será** 1923 E 7th St (at Cherry) 562/599-6170 • 9pm-2am Tue, from 5pm Wed-Sat, from 3pm Sun, clsd Mon • gay/ straight • dancing/DJ • alternative • live music • cover after 9pm

**Silver Fox** 411 Redondo (at 4th) 562/439-6343 • 4pm-2am, from noon wknds • popular happy hour • mostly gay men • karaoke Wed & Sun • videos • wheelchair access

**Sweetwater Saloon** 1201 E Broadway (at Orange) 562/432-7044 • 10am-2am • popular days • mostly gay men • neighborhood bar • wheelchair access

### NIGHTCLUBS

**Club Ripples** 5101 E Ocean (at Granada) 562/433-0357 • noon-2am • popular • mostly gay men • more women Fri • dancing/DJ • theme nights • multiracial • food served • karaoke • videos • young crowd • patio

**Executive Suite** 3428 E Pacific Coast Hwy (at Redondo) 562/597-3884 • 5pm-2am, 2pm-11pm Sun • popular • lesbians/ gay men • dancing/DJ • Latin night Th • women's night Sat • wheelchair access

**Syren's Ladies Night** 5101 E Ocean Blvd (at Ripples Bar) **562/433-0357** • 7pm-2am Fri only • popular • mostly women • dancing/DJ • multiracial • food served • videos • live entertainment • karaoke • go-go girls • patio

### CAFES

**Birdcage Coffee House** 224 W 4th Street **562/628-9835** • 7am-7pm • wheelchair access • gay-owned

**Hot Java** 2101 E Broadway Ave **562/433-0688** • 6am-11pm, till midnight Fri-Sat • also soups, sandwiches, salads • WiFi

**The Library** 3418 E Broadway **562/433-2393** • 6am-midnight, till 1am Fri-Sat, from 7am wknds

### RESTAURANTS

**212 Degrees Bistro** 2708 E 4th St **562/439-8822** • 8am-2pm, clsd Mon • Mexican-inspired

**Cafe Sevilla** 140 Pine St **562/495-1111** • dinner only, Sun brunch • Spanish • also music & dancing

**Hamburger Mary's** 330 Pine Ave **562/436-7900** • 11am-2am • lesbians/gay men • full bar • dancing/DJ • Tue TG night

**Open Sesame** 5215 E 2nd St **562/621-1698** • lunch & dinner • Middle Eastern

**Original Park Pantry** 2104 E Broadway (at Junipero) **562/434-0451** • 6am-10pm, till 11pm Fri-Sat • int'l • some veggie • wheelchair access

**Two Umbrellas Cafe** 1538 E Broadway (btwn Gaviota & Falcon) **562/495-2323** • 8am-2pm, clsd Mon • gay-owned

**Utopia** 445 E 1st St **562/432-6888** • lunch Mon-Fri, dinner nightly, clsd Sun • seafood, California cuisine • plenty veggie

### RETAIL SHOPS

**Hot Stuff** 2121 E Broadway (at Junipero) **562/433-0692** • noon-8pm, 10am-6pm Sat-Sun • cards • gifts • adult novelties • serving community since 1980 • gay- & lesbian-owned

**So Cal Tattoo** 339 W 6th St, San Pedro **310/519-8282** • woman-owned tattoo & piercing shop • reservations recommended

### EROTICA

**The RubberTree** 5018 E 2nd St (at Granada) **562/434-0027** • 11am-9pm, till 10pm Fri-Sat, noon-7pm Sun • gifts for lovers • women-owned

# LOS ANGELES

Los Angeles is divided into 8 geographical areas:
LA—Overview
LA—West Hollywood
LA—Hollywood
LA—West LA & Santa Monica
LA—Silverlake
LA—Midtown
LA—Valley
LA—East LA & South Central

## LA—Overview

### INFO LINES & SERVICES

**Alcoholics Anonymous** 323/936-4343 & 735-2089 (EN ESPAÑOL), 800/923-8722 • call or check web (www.lacoaa.org) for meetings

**Crystal Meth Anonymous** 877/262-6691 • call or check website (www.crystalmeth.org) for meetings in LA County

**LA Gay & Lesbian Center** 1625 N Schrader Blvd (McDonald/Wright Building) **323/993-7400** • 9am-9pm, till 1pm Sat, clsd Sun • wide variety of services

**LA Gay & Lesbian Center's Village at Ed Gould Plaza** 1125 N McCadden Pl (at Santa Monica) **323/860-7302** • 9am-9pm, clsd Sun • cybercenter • cafe • theaters

### ENTERTAINMENT & RECREATION

**Bikes and Hikes LA** 8743 Santa Monica Blvd **323/796-8555, 888/836-3710** • bike/hike tour company

**The Celebration Theatre** 7051 Santa Monica Blvd (at La Brea) **323/957-1884** • LGBT theater • call for more info

**The Ellen DeGeneres Show** • you know you want to dance w/ Ellen! • check out ellen.warnerbros.com for tickets

**The Gay Mafia Comedy Group** • lesbians/gay men • improv/sketch comedy • gay-owned

**The Getty Center** 1200 Getty Center Dr, Brentwood **310/440-7300** • 10am-6pm, till 9pm Fri-Sat, clsd Mon • LA's shining city on a hill & world-class museum • of course, it's still in LA so you'll need to make reservations for parking (!)

**Griffith Observatory** enter on N Vermont St (in Griffith Park) **213/473-0800** • noon-10pm, from 10am wknds, clsd Mon

**Highways** 1651 18th St (at the 18th Street Arts Center), Santa Monica **310/315–1459** • "full-service performance center"

**LA Sparks** 310/426–6033, 877/447–7275 **(LA AREA ONLY)** • check out the Women's Nat'l Basketball Association while you're in Los Angeles

**Outfest** 213/480–7088 • LGBT media arts foundation that sponsors the annual LGBT film festival each July • see listing in Film Festival Calendar

**Women on a Roll** 310/578–8888 • "largest lesbian organization in California" • offering sporting, cultural & social events, as well as worldwide travel, for women

## PUBLICATIONS

**Adelante Magazine** 323/256–6639 • bilingual LGBT magazine

**Essential Gay & Lesbian Directory** 310/841–2800, 866/718–GAYS • business directory serving the LGBT community

**Lesbian News (LN)** 310/548–9888, 800/458–9888 • nat'l w/ strong coverage of Southern CA • see ad front color section

# LA—West Hollywood

## INFO LINES & SERVICES

**Visit West Hollywood** 8687 Melrose Ave, Ste M38 (at San Vicente) **800/368–6020, 310/289–2525** • Re-discover West Hollywood! When was the last time you visited? Website offers hotel packages and special events

## ACCOMMODATIONS

**Andaz West Hollywood** 8401 Sunset Blvd (at Kings Rd) 323/656–1234, 800/233–1234 • gay/ straight • on the Sunset Strip • rooftop pool • nonsmoking • WiFi • wheelchair access

**Chamberlain** 1000 Westmount Dr (near Holloway) 310/657–7400, 800/201–9652 • gay/ straight • boutique hotel • fitness center • rooftop pool • bistro restaurant & lounge

**The Elan Hotel Los Angeles** 8435 Beverly Blvd (at Croft) 323/658–6663, 866/203–2212 • gay/ straight • hip & trendy • kids ok • wheelchair access • gay-owned

**The Grafton on Sunset** 8462 W Sunset Blvd (at La Cienega) 323/654–4600, 800/821–3660 • gay/ straight • pool • sundeck • panoramic views • located in heart of Sunset Strip • wheelchair access

**Hotel Le Petit** 8822 Cynthia St (at Larrabee) 310/854–1114 • gay-friendly • all-suite hotel • hot tub • pool • kids ok • wheelchair access

**Le Parc Suite Hotel** 733 N West Knoll Dr (at Melrose) 310/855–8888, 800/578–4837 • gay-friendly • all-suite hotel • pool • tennis courts • kids/ pets ok • also restaurant • wheelchair access

**The London West Hollywood** 1020 N San Vicente Blvd 866/282–4560 • gay-friendly • luxury hotel • pool • WiFi • also Gordon Ramsay's restaurant

**Mondrian** 8440 Sunset Blvd 323/650–8999, 800/697–1791 • gay-friendly • home of trendy Skybar & Asia de Cuba restaurant

**Ramada Plaza Hotel—West Hollywood** 8585 Santa Monica Blvd (at La Cienega) 310/652–6400 • gay-friendly • modern art deco • pool & poolside WiFi • kids ok • wheelchair access

**San Vicente Bungalows** 845 N San Vicente Blvd (at Santa Monica) 310/854–6915 • gay/straight • newly restored and updated • gay-owned

**Sunset Marquis Hotel & Villas** 1200 Alta Loma Rd (1/2 block S of Sunset Blvd) 310/657–1333 • gay/ straight • full brkfst • sauna • hot tub • pool • WiFi • kids ok • wheelchair access

## BARS

**The Abbey** 692 N Robertson Blvd (at Santa Monica) 310/289–8410 • 11am-2am, from 9am wknds • lesbians/ gay men • popular • also restaurant • patio • wheelchair access

**Comedy Store** 8433 Sunset Blvd (at La Cienega) 323/650–6268 • 8pm-2am • gay-friendly • legendary stand-up club

**Fiesta Cantina** 8865 Santa Monica Blvd (at San Vicente) 310/652–8865 • noon-2am • lesbians/ gay men • raucous Mexican restaurant & bar

**Flaming Saddles** 8811 Santa Monica Blvd (at Larrabee St) 310/855–7501 • 3pm-2am, from noon wknds • mostly gay men • food served • karaoke

**Here Lounge** 696 N Robertson Blvd (at Santa Monica) 310/360–8455 • 4pm-2am • lesbians/ gay men • more women Fri for Truck Stop • swanky & stylish • DJ nightly

**Micky's** 8857 Santa Monica Blvd (at San Vicente) 310/657–1176 • noon-2am, after-hours wknds • mostly gay men • dancing/DJ • videos • younger crowd • food served • patio • gay-owned

**Revolver Video Bar** 8851 Santa Monica Blvd (at Larrabee St) 310/694–0430 • 4pm-2am, from noon wknds • popular • mostly gay men • a WeHo institution

## NIGHTCLUBS

**Girl Bar** 692 N Robertson (at The Abbey) • Wed night • popular • women only • dancing/DJ • visit girlbar.com for info

**Juicy Club LA** 8911 Santa Monica Blvd. (at Rage) **310/659-4551** • 9pm-3am 1st Sat • dancing/DJ

**Rage** 8911 Santa Monica Blvd (at San Vicente) **310/652-7055** • noon-2am, lunch Tue-Sun, dinner nightly • popular • mostly gay men • dancing/DJ • live shows • videos • 18+ wknds • wheelchair access

## CAFES

**Champagne French Bakery & Cafe** 8917-9 Santa Monica Blvd **310/657-4051** • 6:30am-9pm, till 11pm Fri-Sat • coffees & pastries as well as brkfst, lunch & dinner • some outdoor seating

**Grind House Cafe** 1051 N Havenhurst Dr **323/650-7717** • 6:30am-10pm • coffeehouse • WiFi • occasional live music

**Urth Caffe** 8565 Melrose Ave (btwn Robertson & La Cienega) **310/659-0628** • 6:30am-midnight • organic coffees, teas & treats • food served • plenty veggie & vegan • patio

## RESTAURANTS

**AOC** 8022 W Third St (at Crescent Heights Blvd) **323/653-6359** • dinner nightly • wine bar • eclectic • upscale

**Basix Cafe** 8333 Santa Monica Blvd (at Flores) **323/848-2460** • 7am-11pm • outdoor seating

**The Bayou** 8939 Santa Monica Blvd (at Robertson) **310/273-3303** • 6pm-2am • full bar • gay-owned

**Bossa Nova** 685 N Robertson Blvd (at Santa Monica) **310/657-5070** • 11am-midnight • Brazilian • beer/wine • patio • wheelchair access

**Cafe La Boheme** 8400 Santa Monica Blvd (btwn Benecia Ave & Fox Hills Dr) **323/848-2360** • 5pm-10pm Fri-Sat, till 11pm Sun-Th • American eclectic/California • full bar • patio w/ fireplace • wheelchair access

**Canter's Deli** 419 N Fairfax (btwn Melrose & Beverly) **323/651-2030** • 24hrs • hip after-hours • Jewish/American • some veggie • full bar • wheelchair access

**Cecconi's** 8764 Melrose Ave **310/432-2000** • 8am-midnight, classic Italian

**Falcon** 7213 Sunset Blvd (btwn Poinsettia & Formosa) **323/850-5350** • dinner Wed-Sat • gay/straight • California/cont'l fusion • full bar & lounge

**Hamburger Mary's Bar & Grill** 8288 Santa Monica Blvd **323/654-3800** • 11am-1am, till 2am Fri-Sat • lesbians/gay men • transgender-friendly • karaoke • drag shows

**Hedley's** 640 N Robertson Blvd **310/659-2009** • lunch & dinner, also wknd brunch, clsd Sun night & Mon

**The Hudson** 1114 N Crescent Heights Blvd **323/654-6686** • 4pm-2am, from 10am Sat-Sun

**Il Piccolino Trattoria** 350 N Robertson Blvd (btwn Melrose & Beverly) **310/659-2220** • lunch & dinner, clsd Sun • full bar • patio • wheelchair access

**Joey's Cafe** 8301 Santa Monica Blvd **323/822-0671** • 8am-10pm • a little bit coffeehouse, a little bit diner • popular at lunch

**Kokomo Cafe** 7385 Beverly Blvd (between La Brea Ave & Fairfax Ave) **323/933-0773** • 8am-4pm • diner • wheelchair access

**Lola's** 945 N Fairfax Ave (at Santa Monica) **323/654-5652** • 5:30pm-2am • great martinis

**Louise's Trattoria** 7505 Melrose Ave (at Gardner) **323/651-3880** • 11am-10pm • Italian • great foccacia bread • beer/wine • patio

**Lucques** 8474 Melrose Ave (at La Cienega) **323/655-6277** • lunch Tue Sat, dinner nightly • French • full bar • patio • wheelchair access

**Marix Tex Mex** 1108 N Flores (btwn La Cienega & Fairfax) **323/656-8800** • 11:30am-11pm, from 11am wknds • lesbians/gay men • some veggie • great margaritas • patio • wheelchair access

**Nyala** 1076 S Fairfax (at Whitworth Dr) **323/936-5918** • many Ethiopian, Nigerian & other African restaurants to choose from on this block

**St Felix** 8945 Santa Monica Blvd (at Hilldale) **310/275-4428** • 4pm-2am • small plates

**Tart** 115 S Fairfax Ave (at Farmer's Daughter Hotel) **323/937-3930, 800/334-1658** • 7am-midnight • Southern

**Taste** 8454 Melrose Ave (at La Cienega) **323/852-6888** • lunch & dinner, wknd brunch • upscale eclectic • full bar

**Versailles** 1415 S La Cienega (at W Pico) **310/289-0392** • lunch & dinner • Cuban

### Bookstores

**Book Soup** 8818 W Sunset Blvd (at Larrabee) 310/659-3110 • 9am-10pm, till 7pm Sun • LGBT section

### Retail Shops

**665 Leather** 8722 Santa Monica Blvd (at Huntley Dr) 310/854-7276 • noon-8pm, till 10pm Fri-Sat • custom leather & neoprene • also accessories & toys

**Marginalized Tattoo** 4228 Melrose Ave (at Vermont) 213/422-4801 • featuring Dave Davenport (aka "Dogspunk"), named best gay tattoo artist

### Gyms & Health Clubs

**24 Hour Fitness** 8612 Santa Monica Blvd, West Hollywood 310/652-7440 • recently renovated • tres gay

**The Easton Gym** 8053 Beverly Blvd (at Crescent Hts) 323/651-3636 • gay-friendly

**The Fitness Factory** 650 N La Peer Dr (at Santa Monica) 310/358-1838 • 6am-9pm, till 8pm Fri, 7am-4pm Sat, 8am-2pm Sun

### Erotica

**Circus of Books** 8230 Santa Monica Blvd (at La Jolla) 323/656-6533 • 7:30am-1am

**Hustler Hollywood** 8920 Sunset Blvd (at San Vicente) 310/860-9009 • 10am-2am • chic erotic department store • also cafe

**Pleasure Chest** 7733 Santa Monica Blvd (at Genesee), N Hollywood 323/650-1022 • 10am-midnight, till 1am Th-Sat

## LA—Hollywood

### Accommodations

**Hollywood Hotel – The Hotel of Hollywood** 1160 N Vermont Ave (at Santa Monica) 323/315-1800, 800/800-9733 • gay-friendly • full brkfst • pool • nonsmoking • WiFi • wheelchair access

**The Redbury** 1717 Vine St (at Hollywood) 323/962-1717, 877/962-1717 • gay/straight • WiFi • spacious flats • restaurant & bar

### Bars

**Boardner's** 1652 N Cherokee Ave 323/462-9621 • 4pm-2am • gay/straight • "a Hollywood legend & best-kept secret since 1942" • dancing/DJ • food served • theme nights

**Faultline** 4216 Melrose Ave (at Vermont) 323/660-0889 • 5pm-2am, from 2pm wknds, clsd Mon-Tue • popular • mostly gay men • cruisy • leather • bears • videos • patio

### Nightclubs

**Avalon** 1735 Vine St (at Hollywood Blvd) 323/462-8900 • gay/straight • one of LA's best dance music clubs • call for events

**Booby Trap** • check www.clubboobytrap.com for dates • mostly women • cute girls • dive bar

**TigerHeat** 1735 Vine (at Avalon) 323/467-4571 • 9:30pm-3am Th only • gay/straight • dancing/DJ • transgender-friendly • live shows • videos • 18+ • cover charge

### Restaurants

**101 Coffee Shop** 6145 Franklin Ave 323/467-1175 • 7am-3am • diner

**La Poubelle** 5907 Franklin Ave (at Bronson) 323/465-0807 • 5:30pm-midnight • French/Italian • some veggie • full bar • wheelchair access

**Musso & Frank Grill** 6667 Hollywood Blvd (near Las Palmas) 323/467-5123 • 11am-11pm, clsd Sun-Mon • the grand-dame diner/steak house of Hollywood • great pancakes, potpies & martinis!

**Off Vine** 6263 Leland Wy (at Vine) 323/962-1900 • lunch & dinner, wknd brunch • beer/wine

**Prado** 244 N Larchmont Blvd (at Beverly) 323/467-3871 • lunch & dinner, dinner only Sun • Caribbean • some veggie • wheelchair access

**Rockwell Table & Stage** 1714 N Vermont Ave (at Prospect, enter in alley) 323/669-1550 • 11am-midnight, brunch wknds

**Roscoe's House of Chicken & Waffles** 1514 N Gower (at Sunset) 323/466-7453 • 8:30am-midnight, till 4am Fri-Sat

### Bookstores

**Skylight Books** 1818 N Vermont Ave (at Melbourne Ave) 323/660-1175 • 10am-10pm • way cool independent in Los Feliz • great fiction & alt-lit sections

### Gyms & Health Clubs

**Gold's Gym** 1016 N Cole Ave (near Santa Monica & Vine) 323/462-7012 • 5am-midnight, 7am-9pm Sat-Sun • gay-friendly

## LA—West LA & Santa Monica

### Accommodations

**Casa Malibu** 22752 Pacific Coast Hwy, Malibu 310/456-2219 • gay-friendly • on the beach • WiFi

**The Georgian Hotel** 1415 Ocean Ave (btwn Santa Monica & Broadway), Santa Monica **310/395–9945, 800/538–8147** • gay-friendly • food served • wheelchair access

**Hotel Angeleno** 170 N Church Ln (at Hwy 405) **310/476–6411, 866/264–3536** • gay/straight • boutique hotel w/ landmark circular shape • pool • gym • nonsmoking • WiFi

**Hotel Erwin** 1697 Pacific Ave (at Venice Way), Venice Beach **310/452–1111, 800/786–7789** • gay/ straight • rooftop lounge & restaurant • gym • nonsmoking • WiFi

**Hotel Palomar** **310/475–8711, 800/472–8556** • gay/ straight • pool • wheelchair access

**The Inn at Venice Beach** 327 Washington Blvd (at Via Dolce), Marina Del Rey **310/821–2557, 800/828–0688** • gay-friendly • 43-room European-style inn • kids ok • WiFi • wheelchair access

**The Linnington** 2052 Linnington Ave **310/422–8825** • vacation rental • jacuzzi • kids ok • lesbian-owned

**The Malibu Beach Inn** 22878 Pacific Coast Hwy, Malibu **310/456–6444** • gay-friendly • balconies with views of the Pacific Ocean • onsite dining • WiFi

**Shutters on the Beach** 1 Pico Blvd, Santa Monica **310/458–0030, 800/334–9000** • gay-friendly • swimming • WiFi

**W Los Angeles** 930 Hilgard Ave (at Le Conte) **310/208–8765, 800/421–2317** • gay-friendly • suites • also restaurant • gym • day spa • pool

## BARS

**Artesia Bar** 1995 Artesia Blvd (at Green Ln), Redondo Beach **310/318–3339** • 7pm-2am, more women Mon • lesbians/ gay men • neighborhood bar • dancing/DJ Fri-Sat • karaoke • patio • wheelchair access

## CAFES

**The Novel Cafe** 2507 Main St, Santa Monica **310/396–7700** • 7am-1am, from 8am Sat, 8am-midnight Sun • coffeehouse • used bookstore

## RESTAURANTS

**Baja Cantina** 311 Washington Blvd (at Sanborn), Marina Del Rey **310/821–2252** • 10:30am-1am, also brunch wknds • full bar

**Border Grill** 1445 4th St (at Broadway), Santa Monica **310/451–1655** • lunch & dinner from famous "Two Hot Tamales" chefs • Mexican

**Cantalini's Salerno Beach Restaurant** 193 Culver Blvd (at Vista del Mar), Playa del Rey **310/821–0018** • lunch Mon-Fri, dinner nightly • Italian • homemade pastas • beer/ wine • live music Sun nights

**Cora's Coffee Shoppe** 1802 Ocean Ave (N of Pico Blvd), Santa Monica **310/451–9562** • 7am-3pm, from 7am wknds, clsd Mon • organic

**Gjelina** 1429 Abbot Kinney Blvd, Venice **310/450–1429** • pizzas & small plates • beer/ wine only

**Golden Bull** 170 W Channel Rd (at Pacific Coast Hwy), Santa Monica **310/230–0402** • 4:30pm-10pm, till 11pm wknds, Sun brunch • American • full bar

**Hamburger Habit** 11223 National Blvd (at Sepulveda) **310/478–5000** • popular • 10am-11pm, till midnight Fri-Sat

**Joe's** 1023 Abbot Kinney Blvd, Venice **310/399–5811** • lunch Tue-Fri, dinner nightly, wknd brunch, clsd Mon • French/ Californian

**Real Food Daily** 514 Santa Monica Blvd (btwn 5th & 6th), Santa Monica **310/451–7544** • 11:30am-10pm • organic vegan • beer/ wine • wheelchair access

**Seed Bistro** 11917 Wilshire Blvd **310/477–7070** • lunch Mon-Fri, dinner nightly, clsd Sun • vegan

**Wokcano** 1413 5th St, Santa Monica **310/458–3080** • 11am-12:30am, till 1:30am Fri-Sat • sushi bar & Chinese cafe

## ENTERTAINMENT & RECREATION

**Santa Monica Pier** Ocean Ave (at Colorado Ave), Santa Monica

**Will Rogers State Beach** Pacific Coast Hwy (at Temescal Canyon Rd) • gay beach

## EROTICA

**Pleasure Island** 18426 Hawthorne Blvd (btwn Artesia & 190th), Torrance **310/793–9477** • 11am-midnight, till 2am Fri-Sat

# LA—Silverlake

## BARS

**4100 Bar** 4100 Sunset Blvd (at Manzanita) **323/666–4460** • 8pm-2am • gay/ straight • neighborhood bar

**Cha Cha Lounge** 2375 Glendale Blvd (at Silverlake) **323/660–7595** • 5pm-2am • gay-friendly • hipster lounge • gay-owned

**Eagle LA** 4219 Santa Monica Blvd (at Hoover) **323/669–9472** • 4pm-2am, from 2pm wknds • popular • mostly gay men • leather • wheelchair access

**Good Luck Bar** 1514 Hillhurst Ave (nr Hollywood Blvd) **323/666–3524** • 7pm-2am, from 8pm wknds • gay-friendly • stylish dive bar

**Silverlake Lounge** 2906 Sunset Blvd (at Silver Lake Blvd) **323/663–9636** • 3pm-2am • gay/ straight • rock 'n' roll club • drag shows wknds

### NIGHTCLUBS

**A Club Called Rhonda** 213/482–2313 • gay/ straight • monthly party • "house, disco, & polysexual hard partying" • check www.rhondasays.net for info

**The Echo** 1822 W Sunset Blvd (at Glendale Blvd) **213/413–8200** • gay/ straight • dancing/DJ • live shows

**Full Frontal Disco** 4356 W Sunset Blvd (at Fountain) **213/626–2285** • last Sun only • gay/ straight • dancing/DJ • transgender-friendy

### RESTAURANTS

**Casita Del Campo** 1920 Hyperion Ave **323/662–4255** • 11am-midnight, till 2am Fri-Sat • popular • Mexican • patio

**Cha Cha Cha** 656 N Virgil Ave (at Melrose) **323/664–7723** • lunch & dinner • lesbians/ gay men • Caribbean • plenty veggie • wheelchair access

**Cliff's Edge** 3626 Sunset Blvd (at Griffith Park Blvd) **323/666–6116** • dinner only, wknd brunch • plenty veggie • romantic • outdoor seating

**Home** 1760 Hillhurst Ave, Los Feliz **323/669–0211** • 9am-10pm, patio

**The Kitchen** 4348 Fountain Ave (at Sunset Blvd) **323/664–3663** • 5pm-1am, from 11am Sat, till 10pm Sun • cozy diner • gay-owned

**Michelangelo Pizzeria Ristorante** 2742 Rowena **323/660–4843** • lunch & dinner

**Square One Dining** 4854 Fountain Ave (at Vermont Ave) **323/661–1109** • 8am-3pm • great brkfst

**Vermont Restaurant & Bar** 1714 N Vermont Ave **323/661–6163** • lunch Mon-Fri, dnner nightly, clsd Sun • gay-owned

### RETAIL SHOPS

**Syren** 2809 1/2 W Sunset Blvd **213/289–0334** • noon-10pm, clsd Mon • leather & latex

### EROTICA

**Romantix Adult Superstore** 3147 N San Fernando Rd **323/258–2867** • 24hrs

## LA—Midtown

### ACCOMMODATIONS

**Luxe City Center** 1020 S Figueroa St **213/748–1291** • gay/straight • urban oasis amidst skyscrapers and renowned landmarks ,

**O Hotel** 819 S Flower St **213/623–9904** • gay/ straight • restaurant • WiFi

**The Standard, Downtown LA** 550 S Flower St **213/892–8080** • gay/ straight • pool • restaurant • WiFi

### BARS

**Bar Mattachine** 221 W 7th St (at Broadway) **213/278–0471** • 5pm-2am • mostly gay men • craft cocktails

**Redline Bar** 131 E 6th St • 5pm-2am, clsd Mon • mostly gay men • dancing/DJ • food served

### NIGHTCLUBS

**Coco Bongo** 3311 S Main St **818/233–5322** • 9pm-2am, clsd Mon-Wed • mostly women • dancing/DJ • Latino/a • drag shows • go-go dancers • 18+

**Jewel's Catch One Disco** 4067 W Pico Blvd (at Norton) **323/734–8849 (HOTLINE), 323/737–1159** • call for hours, clsd Wed-Th • gay/ straight • dancing/DJ • theme nights • wheelchair access

**Mustache Mondays** 336 S Hill St (at W 4th St, at La Cita bar) **213/687–7111** • 9pm Mon only • lesbians/ gay men • dancing/DJ • transgender-friendly • queer fashionistas

### RESTAURANTS

**Bar & Kitchen LA** 819 S Flower St (at O Hotel) **213/784–3048** • traditional american cuisine with local Californian farm to table influences

**Border Grill Downtown** 445 S Figueroa St (at 5th St) **213/486–5171** • lunch & dinner, late-night cocktails • wheelchair access • owned by celebrity chefs Mary Sue Milliken & Susan Feniger

**Cassell's** 3266 W 6th St (at Vermont) **213/387–5502** • 8am-10pm, till midnight Fri-Sat • great burgers

**Doughboys Cafe** 8136 W 3rd St **323/852–1020** • 7am-10pm

## LA—Valley

**includes San Fernando & San Gabriel Valleys**

### BARS

**Cobra** 10937 Burbank Blvd (1 block E of Vineland), North Hollywood 818/760-9798 • 9pm-2am, till 3am fri-Sat, clsd Sun-Wed • popular • mostly gay men • dancing/DJ • wheelchair access

**The Other Door** 10437 Burbank Blvd (2 blocks E of Cahuenga), North Hollywood 818/508-7008 • 3pm-1:30am, from 1pm Fri-Sun • popular • gay/ straight • neighborhood bar • dancing/DJ • live bands • wheelchair access

**Oxwood Inn** 13713 Oxnard (at Woodman), Van Nuys 818/997-9666 (PAY PHONE) • 4pm-2am, 5pm-8pm Mon-Tue, clsd Sun • mostly women • neighborhood bar • dancing/DJ • karaoke • patio • one of the oldest lesbian bars in US • women-owned

### NIGHTCLUBS

**C Frenz** 7026 Reseda Blvd (at Sherman Way), Reseda 818/996-2976 • 3pm-2am, till 3am Sat • popular • lesbians/ gay men • neighborhood bar • dancing/DJ • multiracial • strippers • karaoke • patio • wheelchair access • gay-owned

**Rain** 12215 Ventura Blvd, Studio City 818/755-9596 • 9pm-2am Fri-Sat • gay/straight• dancing/DJ

### CAFES

**Aroma** 4360 Tujunga Ave, Studio City 818/508-0677 • 6am-11pm, from 7am Sun • coffeehouse w/ small bookstore

### RESTAURANTS

**Firefly Studio City** 11720 Ventura Blvd, Studio City 818/762-1833 • 5pm-2am, till midnight Sun, great beer braised mussels, full bar

### EROTICA

**Romantix Adult Superstore** 21625 Sherman Wy (at Nelson), Canoga Park 818/992-9801

## Manhattan Beach

see also LA—West LA & Santa Monica

### ACCOMMODATIONS

**Sea View Inn at the Beach** 3400 Highland Ave 310/545-1504 • gay-friendly • ocean views • pool • courtyard • nonsmoking • WiFi

### RESTAURANTS

**The Local Yolk** 3414 Highland Ave (at Rosecranz) 310/546-4407 • 6:30am-2pm • WiFi • wheelchair access

## Marin County

**includes Corte Madera, Mill Valley, San Anselmo, San Rafael, Sausalito, Tiburon**

### INFO LINES & SERVICES

**AA Gay/ Lesbian** 415/499-0400 • check www.aasf.org for meeting times

**Spectrum LGBT Center of the North Bay** 30 N San Pedro Rd # 160, San Rafael 415/472-1945 • drop-in hours: 11am-5pm Mon-Fri • wheelchair access

### ACCOMMODATIONS

**Acqua Hotel** 555 Redwood Hwy, Mill Valley 415/380-0400, 888/662-9555 • gay-friendly • nonsmoking • pets/ kids ok • WiFi • wheelchair access

**Casa Madrona Hotel & Spa** 801 Bridgeway, Sausalito 415/332-0502, 800/288-0502 • overlooks SF skyline

**The Lodge at Tiburon** 1651 Tiburon Blvd, Tiburon 415/435-3133, 800/762-7770 • gay-friendly • pool • nonsmoking • kids/ pets ok • WiFi • also restaurant & bar

**Waters Edge Hotel** 25 Main St, Tiburon 415/789-5999 • gay/ straight • boutique hotel • kids ok • nonsmoking • WiFi • wheelchair access

### RESTAURANTS

**Guaymas** 5 Main St (at ferry dock), Tiburon 415/435-6300 • gourmet Mexican • great views of the Bay

**Terrapin Crossroads** 100 Yacht Club Dr, San Rafael 415/524-2773 • 4pm-10pm, from 11am wknds, clsd Mon • a healthy down-home all-American eatery, taproom & lounge

### BOOKSTORES

**Book Passage** 51 Tamal Vista Blvd, Corte Madera 415/927-0960, 800/999-7909 • 9am-9pm • beloved independent which draws the biggest names to read • also cafe • WiFi

### RETAIL SHOPS

**Cowgirl Creamery** 80 4th St (at Tomales Bay Foods), Pt Reyes Station 415/663-9335 • 10am-6pm Wed-Sun • handmade cheeses • picnic lunches to go • women-owned

## Mendocino

ACCOMMODATIONS

**Agate Cove Inn** 11201 N Lansing St 707/937-0551, 800/527-3111 • gay-friendly • full brkfst • fireplaces • nonsmoking

**The Alegria Quartet & Oceanfront Inn Cottages** 44781 Main St 707/937-5150, 800/780-7905 • gay-friendly • located in the village • ocean views • nonsmoking • WiFi • kids ok

**Blair House & Cottage** 45110 Little Lake St (at Ford St) 707/937-1800, 800/699-9296 • gay-friendly • in former "home" of Jessica Fletcher of Murder, She Wrote • nonsmoking

**Brewery Gulch Inn** 9401 N Hwy 1 707/937-4752, 800/578-4454 • gay/ straight • oceanview B&B made of eco-salvaged redwood • full brkfst • jacuzzi • nonsmoking • WiFi

**Cottages at Little River Cove** 7533 N Hwy 1, Little River 707/937-5339 • gay/ straight • amazing ocean views • fireplaces • WiFi • kids/pets ok

**Dennen's Victorian Farmhouse** 7001 N Hwy 1 (at Hwy 128) 707/937-0697, 800/264-4723 • gay-friendly • nonsmoking • full brkfst • WiFi

**Glendeven Inn** 8205 N Hwy 1 (1.7 miles S of Mendocino), Little River 707/937-0083, 800/822-4536 • gay-friendly • charming farmhouse on the coast • full brkfst & wine bar • nonsmoking

**Hill House Inn** 10701 Palette Dr 707/937-0554, 800/422-0554 • gay/ straight • New England–style inn • also restaurant

**The Inn at Schoolhouse Creek** 7051 N Hwy 1, Little River 707/937-5525, 800/731-5525 • gay/ straight • B&B w/ cottages & suites • full brkfst • hot tub • fireplaces • WiFi • kids/pets ok • wheelchair access

**John Dougherty House** 571 Ukiah St (at Kasten St) 707/937-5266, 800/486-2104 • gay-friendly • jacuzzi • gay-owned

**Little River Inn Resort & Spa** 7901 N Hwy 1, Little River 707/937-5942, 888/466-5683 • gay-friendly • resort • ocean views, restaurant & bar • nonsmoking • WiFi

**MacCallum House Inn** 45020 Albion St (at Lansing) 707/937-0289, 800/609-0492 • gay/ straight • nonsmoking • WiFi • wheelchair access • kids ok • also popular restaurant & full bar w/ cafe

**Orr Hot Springs** 13201 Orr Springs Rd, Ukiah 707/462-6277 • gay-friendly • mineral hot springs, swimming, private rooms, yurts, cottages, and campsites, clothing-optional, guests must bring all own food • no pets • kids ok • mineral hot springs • pool • no food provided • reservations required

**Packard House** 45170 Little Lake St (at Kasten St) 707/937-2677, 888/453-2677 • gay-friendly • full brkfst • jacuzzi • nonsmoking • WiFi • gay-owned

**Sallie & Eileen's Place** 707/937-2028, 888/757-5223 • women only • cabin • hot tub • kitchens • fireplaces • kids/ pets ok • nonsmoking • lesbian-owned

**Sea Gull Inn** 44960 Albion St 707/937-5204, 888/937-5204 • gay-friendly • in the heart of historic Mendocino • nonsmoking • kids ok • WiFi • wheelchair access

**Stanford Inn by the Sea** 44850 Comptche-Ukiah Rd (at Coast Hwy 1 ) 707/937-5615, 800/331-8884 • gay-friendly • full brkfst • hot tub • pool • organic vegetarian restaurant • nonsmoking • WiFi • kids/ pets ok • wheelchair access

RESTAURANTS

**Cafe Beaujolais** 961 Ukiah St 707/937-5614 • lunch& dinner • reservations recommended • some veggie • wheelchair access

BOOKSTORES

**Gallery Bookshop** Main & Kasten St S 707/937-2665 • 9:30am-6pm, till 9pm Fri-Sat • independent • also children's bookstore

## Menlo Park

see Palo Alto

## Mill Valley

see Marin County

## Modesto

see also Stockton

BARS

**Brave Bull** 701 S 9th St 209/529-6712 • 7pm-2am, clsd Mon-Tue• lesbians/ gay men • dancing/DJ • karaoke Wed

**Tiki Lounge** 932 McHenry Ave (at Roseburg Ave) 209/577-9969 • 5pm-2am • lesbians/ gay men • neighborhood bar • multiracial • transgender-friendly • karaoke

## CAFES

**Deva Cafe** 1202 J St **209/572–3382** • 7am-3pm, 8am-noon Sun • live music • patio • wheelchair access

**Queen Bean** 1126 14th St **209/521–8000** • 7am-8pm, till 11pm wknds

## RESTAURANTS

**Minnie's Restaurant** 107 McHenry Ave **209/524–4621** • lunch Tue-Fri, dinner Tue-Sun, clsd Mon • full bar

## RETAIL SHOPS

**Mystical Body** 121 McHenry Ave **209/527–1163** • noon-8pm, clsd Sun-Mon • body piercing

## EROTICA

**Suzie's Adult Superstores** 115 McHenry Ave (at Needham) **209/529–5546** • 8am-midnight

# Monterey

## ACCOMMODATIONS

**Asilomar Conference Grounds** 800 Asilomar Blvd, Pacific Grove **831/372–8016, 888/635–5310** • gay-friendly • Arts & Crafts-style buildings designed by Julia Morgan • pool • WiFi

**Gosby House Inn** 643 Lighthouse Ave (at 18th), Pacific Grove **831/375–1287, 800/527–8828** • gay-friendly • B&B • full brkfst • some shared baths • nonsmoking • kids ok • wheelchair access

**The Monterey Hotel** 406 Alvarado St **831/375–3184, 800/966–6490** • gay-friendly • turn-of-the-century boutique hotel • WiFi

## NIGHTCLUBS

**Franco's Club** 10639 Merritt St, Castroville **831/633–2090** • 10pm-2am Sat only • lesbians/ gay men • dancing/DJ • Latino/a

## RESTAURANTS

**Old Fisherman's Grotto** 39 Fisherman's Wharf #1 **831/375–4604** • 11am-10pm

**Tarpy's Roadhouse** 2999 Monterey Salinas Hwy (at Canyon Dr) **831/647–1444** • lunch & dinner, Sun brunch • patios & gardens • full bar

## ENTERTAINMENT & RECREATION

**Ag Venture Tours** 831/761–8463 • customized wine-tasting, agriculture & sight-seeing tours of Monterey and Sata Cruz countries

# Morro Bay

see also San Luis Obispo

# Mountain View

## NIGHTCLUBS

**King of Clubs Nightclub** 893 Leong Dr (at Moffett Blvd) **650/968–6366** • 8pm-2am, clsd Mon-Tue • lesbians/ gay men • neighborhood bar • dancing/DJ • theme nights • karaoke • multiracial • transgender-friendly

# Napa Valley

## ACCOMMODATIONS

**Beazley House B&B Inn** 1910 First St, Napa **707/257–1649, 800/559–1649** • gay-friendly • historic inn • full brkfst • nonsmoking • very pet-friendly • WiFi • wheelchair access

**Brannan Cottage Inn** 109 Wapoo Ave (at Lincoln Ave), Calistoga **707/942–4200** • gay-friendly • B&B in Victorian cottage • full brkfst • 1 block from downtown • nonsmoking • WiFi

**The Chablis Inn** 3360 Solano Ave (Redwood Rd at Hwy 29), Napa **707/257–1944, 800/443–3490** • gay-friendly • stylish motel • pool • hot tub • kids/ pets ok • nonsmoking • wheelchair access

**The Chanric Inn** 1805 Foothill Blvd, Calistoga **707/942–4535, 877/281–3671** • gay/ straight • pool & spa • nonsmoking • WiFi • gay-owned

**Chateau de Vie** 3250 Hwy 128, Calistoga **707/942–6446, 877/558–2513** • gay/ straight • chateau w/ gardens • full brkfst • pool • pets ok • WiFi • gay-owned

**Hotel Yountville** 6462 Washington St, Yountville **707/944–5600** • gay-friendly • alongside Hopper Creek • spa • nonsmoking

**The Inn on First** 1938 1st St, Napa **707/253–1331, 866/253–1331** • gay/ straight • pets ok • WiFi • gay-owned

**Luxe Calistoga** 1139 Lincoln Ave (at Myrtle), Calistoga **707/942–9797** • gay-friendly • on historic main street • nonsmoking • wheelchair access

**Meadowlark Country House** 601 Petrified Forest Rd, Calistoga **707/942–5651, 800/942–5651** • gay-friendly • full brkfst • clothing-optional mineral pool, sauna & hot tub • nonsmoking • WiFi • gay-owned

**Napa River Inn** 500 Main St (at 5th), Napa 707/251-8500, 877/251-8500 • gay-friendly • luxury boutique hotel w/ spa • located in historic Napa Mill • WiFi

**North Block Hotel** 757 Washington Street, Yountville 707/944-8080 • gay/straight • modern boutique hotel with a restaurant & spa

RESTAURANTS

**Brannan's** 1374 Lincoln Ave (at Washington), Calistoga 707/942-2233 • lunch & dinner, brunch wknds • full bar • live jazz wknds • gay-owned

**Cindy's Backstreet Kitchen** 1327 Railroad Ave, St Helena 707/963-1200 • 11:30am-9:30pm

**Redd** 6480 Washington St, Yountville 707/944-2222 • lunch Mon-Sat, dinner nightly, Sun brunch • American • reservations required

**SolBar** 755 Silverado Trail (at the Solage Hotel), Calistoga 707/226-0850 • soul-food

**Tra Vigne** 1050 Charter Oak Ave (Hwy 29), St Helena 707/963-4444 • 11:30am-10pm • Northern Italian • also wine bar • reservations recommended

ENTERTAINMENT & RECREATION

**Absolutely Fabulous Tours** 707/320-8043 • specialize in offering wine tours of Sonoma, Napa, and surrounding areas to the LGBTQ community and their allies • lesbian-owned

**Cameo Cinema** 1340 Main St, St Helena 707/963-9779 • Cameo exists to entertain, inspire, educate and connect the community through the "art of storytelling"

BOOKSTORES

**Copperfield's Books** 1330 Lincoln Ave, Calistoga 707/942-1616 • 9am-7pm, till 9pm Fri-Sat, 10am-6pm Sun

## Nevada City

CAFES

**Java John's** 306 Broad St 530/265-3653 • 6:30am-4:30pm, from 7pm wknds

RESTAURANTS

**Friar Tuck's** 111 N Pine St (at Commercial) 530/265-9093 • dinner from 5pm • American/ fondue • live shows • full bar • wheelchair access

## Newport Beach

see Orange County

## Oakland

see East Bay

## Orange County

includes Anaheim, Costa Mesa, Garden Grove, Huntington Beach, Irvine, Laguna Beach, Newport Beach, Santa Ana

INFO LINES & SERVICES

**AA Gay/ Lesbian** Laguna Beach 714/556-4555 (AA#) • call or visit www.oc-aa.org for meeting times

**The Center Orange County** 1605 N Spurgeon St, Santa Ana 714/953-5428 • 9am-5pm Mon-Fri or by appt or event

ACCOMMODATIONS

**Best Western Plus Plus Laguna Brisas Spa Hotel** 1600 S Coast Hwy (at Bluebird), Laguna Beach 949/497-7272, 888/296-6834 • gay/ straight • resort hotel • free brkfst • pool • 99 steps to the beach • nonsmoking • WiFi • wheelchair access

**Best Western Raffles Inn & Suites** 2040 S Harbor Blvd, Anaheim 714/750-6100, 800/308-5278 • gay-friendly • pool • WiFi • walk to Disneyland

**Casa Laguna Inn & Spa** 2510 S Coast Hwy, Laguna Beach 949/494-2996, 800/233-0449 • gay-friendly • inn & cottages overlooking the Pacific • pool • kids/ pets ok • nonsmoking • WiFi • gay-owned

**Laguna Beach House** 475 N Coast Hwy, Laguna Beach 949/497-6645, 800/297-0007 • gay-friendly • hot tub • pool • kids ok • easy beach access • WiFi • wheelchair access

**The St Regis Monarch Beach** One Monarch Beach Resort, Dana Point 949/234-3426 • gay-friendly • restaurant • pool • nonsmoking • wheelchair access

**Surf & Sand Resort** 1555 S Coast Hwy, Laguna Beach 949/497-4477, 877/741-5908 • gay-friendly • restaurant & spa • WiFi • wheelchair access

BARS

**Club Cherry** 416 W 4th St (at Velvet), Santa Ana 714/232-8727 • Wed only • mostly women • dancing/DJ • also restaurant

**Frat House** 8112 Garden Grove Blvd (at Beach Blvd), Garden Grove **714/373–3728** • 4pm-2am • lesbians/ gay men • dancing/DJ • multiracial • drag shows & strippers • young crowd • wheelchair access

**Ibiza Bar & Nightclub** 18528 Beach Blvd **714/963–7744** • noon-2am, from 4pm Mon, from 2pm Sun • gay-friendly • neighborhood bar • dancing/DJ • wheelchair access • gay-owned

**Main Street Bar & Cabaret** 1460 S Coast Hwy, Laguna Beach **949/494–0056** • 4pm-2am • lesbians/ gay men • dancing/DJ Fri-Sat • karaoke • drag shows

**Tin Lizzie Saloon** 752 St Clair (at Bristol), Costa Mesa **714/966–2029** • 11:30am-2am • mostly gay men • neighborhood bar • wheelchair access

**Velvet Lounge** 416 W 4th St, Santa Ana **714/232–8727** • 11:30am-2am • lesbians/ gay men • dancing/DJ • girls night Wed • also restaurant

### NIGHTCLUBS

**Bravo** 1490 S Anaheim Blvd, Anaheim **714/533–2291** • more gay Th & Sat • gay/ straight • dancing/DJ • goth & electronica Sun • Latin music Wed & Fri-Sat

**Club Lucky Presents** 949/551–2998 • check www.clubluckypresents.com for weekly parties in OC

**El Calor** 2916 W Lincoln Ave (at E Beach Blvd), Anaheim **714/527–8873** • 8pm-2am • gay-friendly • dancing/DJ • mostly Latino/a • drag shows

### CAFES

**The Koffee Klatch** 1440 S Coast Hwy (btwn Mountain & Pacific Coast Hwy), Laguna Beach **949/376–6867** • 7am-11pm, till midnight Fri-Sat • brkfst & lunch • desserts • WiFi

**Zinc Cafe** 350 Ocean Ave (at Broadway), Laguna Beach **949/494–6302** • 7am-4pm, also market till 6pm • vegetarian • beer/ wine • patio • wheelchair access

### RESTAURANTS

**Cafe Zoolu** 860 Glenneyre St, Laguna Beach **949/494–6825** • 5pm-10pm, clsd Mon • beer/ wine • wheelchair access

**Dizz's As Is** 2794 S Coast Hwy (at Nyes Pl), Laguna Beach **949/494–5250** • open 5:30pm, clsd Mon • full bar • patio

**Madison Square & Garden Cafe** 320 N Coast Hwy, Laguna Beach **949/494–0137** • 8am-3pm, clsd Tue • dog-friendly

**Nirvana Grille** 303 Broadway St, Laguna Beach **949/497–0027** • dinner nightly • seasonal rooftop deck

**Three Seventy Common** 370 Glenneyre St, Laguna Beach **949/494–8686** • dinner only • upscale American bistro & martini bar

### ENTERTAINMENT & RECREATION

**San Onofre State Beach** on I-5, S of San Clemente (exit at Basilone Rd), Laguna Beach

**West St Beach** Laguna Beach • gay beach

### EROTICA

**Pink Kitty** 17955 Sky Park Cir, Ste A, Irvine **949/660–4990** • 10am-6pm • gay-owned

## Pacifica

### RESTAURANTS

**Nicks Seafood Restaurant** 100 Rockaway Beach Ave **650/359–3900** • 11am-10pm, from 8am wknds • live jazz wkds

## Palm Springs

### INFO LINES & SERVICES

**AA Gay/ Lesbian** **760/324–4880 (AA#)** • call for meeting schedule

**The LGBT Community Center of the Desert** 611 S Palm Canyon #201 **760/416–7790** • programs, education, recreation, social & counseling services

### ACCOMMODATIONS

**Ace Hotel Palm Springs** 701 E Palm Canyon Dr **760/325–9900** • gay/ straight • pool • restaurant • WiFi

**Caliente Tropics Resort** 411 E Palm Canyon Dr **760/327–1391, 888/277–0099** • gay/ straight • hot tub • pool • nonsmoking resort • kids ok • very pet-friendly • wheelchair access • gay-owned

**Calla Lily Inn** 350 S Belardo Rd (at Baristo) **760/323–3654, 888/888–5787** • gay-friendly • pool • "a tranquil oasis" • nonsmoking • WiFi

**Calmada Boutique Hotel** 3569 Calmada Rd, Pioneertown **760/228–3141** • gay/straight • pool • WiFi • resort 30 min from Palm Springs

**Casitas Laquita** 450 E Palm Canyon Dr (near Camino Real) **760/416–9999, 877/203–3410** • lesbian resort • pool • nonsmoking • small pets ok • WiFi • wheelchair access • lesbian-owned

**L' Horizon**  1050 E Palm Canyon Dr 760/323–1858 • gay-friendly • pool • restaurant on site • WiFi

**Rendezvous**  1420 N Indian Canyon Dr 760/320–1178, 800/485–2808 • gay-friendly • '50s chic • pool • WiFi

**Ruby Montana's Coral Sands Inn** 210 W Stevens Rd (at N Palm Canyon) 760/325–4900, 866/820–8302 • gay/ straight • resort • pool • kitschy 1950s chic • kids/ pets ok • WiFi • wheelchair access • lesbian-owned

**The Saguaro**  1800 East Palm Canyon Dr 760/323–1711 • gay-friendly • hip boutique hotel • food served • WiFi

**The Skylark** 1466 N Palm Canyon Dr (at Monte Vista) 760/322–2267, 800/793–0063 • gay/ straight • Pool • kitchens • pets ok • WiFi

## BARS

**DiGS** 36–737 Cathedral Canyon Dr (at 111), Cathedral City 760/321–0031 • 2pm-2am, from 10am Sun • lesbians/ gay men • neighborhood bar • karaoke • country/ western • patio

**Georgie's Alibi** 369 N Palm Canyon Dr 760/325–5533 • 11am-close, from 10am Sun • mostly gay men • neighborhood bar • food served • patio

**Hunter's Video Bar** 302 E Arenas Rd (at Calle Encilia) 760/323–0700 • 10am-2am • popular • mostly gay men • dancing/DJ • video bar • go-go boys Fri • theme nights

**Score** 301 E Arenas Rd 760/327–0753 • 6am-2am • mostly gay men • neighborhood bar • game bar

**Studio One 11** 67–555 E Palm Canyon Dr #A-103, Cathedral City 760/328–2900 • 3pm-2am • mostly gay men • dancing/DJ • karaoke • piano bar

**Toucan's Tiki Lounge** 2100 N Palm Canyon Dr (at Via Escuela) 760/416–7584 • noon-2am • lesbians/ gay men • dancing/DJ • live shows • drag shows • male & female go-go dancers wknds

## CAFES

**Oscar's Cafe & Bar** 125 E Tahquitz Way #108  760/325–1188 • 11am-9pm, till 10pm Fri-Sat, 5pm-8pm Sun for popular T-dance (summer only)

**Palm Springs Koffi** 515 N Palm Canyon (at Alejo) 760/416–2244 • 5:30am-8pm • WiFi

## RESTAURANTS

**Appetito Deli** 1700 S Camino Real 760/327–1929 • 11am-9pm, full bar, patio

**Billy Reed's** 1800 N Palm Canyon Dr (at Vista Chino) 760/325–1946 • 7am-9pm, till 10pm Fri-Sat • some veggie • full bar • also bakery • wheelchair access

**Blue Coyote Grill** 445 N Palm Canyon Dr 760/327–1196 • 11am-10pm, till 11pm Fri-Sat • Southwestern

**Bongo Johnny's** 214 E Arenas Rd 760/866–1905 • 8am-10pm, till 11pm Fri-Sat • burgers & sandwiches

**Cafe Palette** 315 E Arenas 760/322–9264 • 11am-10pm • live shows • also delivers

**The Chop House** 262 S Palm Canyon Dr 760/320–4500 • from 5pm • fine steaks and chops • reservations recommended

**Copley's** 621 N Palm Canyon Dr (btwn E Tamarisk Rd & E Granvia Valmonte) 760/327–9555 • 6pm-10pm • contemporary American • full bar

**The Crazy Coconut Bar & Grill** 166 N Palm Canyon Dr 760/327–8175 • 11am-10pm, till Th-Sat • burgers & fries • karaoke

**El Gallito** 68820 Grove St (at Palm Canyon), Cathedral City 760/328–7794 • 10am-9pm • homemade Mexican • beer/ wine

**Jake's** 664 N Palm Canyon Dr 760/327–4400 • lunch & dinner, wknd brunch, clsd Sun night & Mon • American bistro

**Las Casuelas** 368 N Palm Canyon Dr (btwn Arnado & Alejo) 760/325–3213 • 11am-10pm • Mexican

**Matchbox** 155 S Palm Canyon Dr (in Mercado Plaza, 2nd level) 760/778–6000 • 4pm-11pm, till 1am Fri-Sat • pizza

**Nature's Health Food & Cafe** 555 S Sunrise Way #301 760/323–9487 • 8am-7pm, 9am-5pm wknds • vegan/ vegetarian

**Peppers Thai Cuisine** 396 N Palm Canyon Dr 760/322–1259 • lunch & dinner

**Pinocchio in the Desert** 134 E Tahquitz Canyon Way 760/322–3776 • 7:30am-2pm • outdoor seating

**Pomme Frite** 256 S Palm Canyon Dr 760/778–3727 • dinner nightly, lunch wknds, clsd Tue • Belgian beer & French food

**Rio Azul** 350 S Indian Canyon Dr 760/992–5641 • dinner nightly, open for lunch wknds • Mexican

**Shame on the Moon** 69–950 Frank Sinatra Dr (at Hwy 111), Rancho Mirage **760/324–5515** • 5pm-9:30pm • cont'l • plenty veggie • full bar • patio • reservations recommended • wheelchair access

**Sherman's Deli & Bakery** 401 E Tahquitz Canyon Wy **760/325–1199** • 7am-9pm • kosher-style deli

**Spencer's Restaurant** 701 W Baristo Rd **760/327–3446** • 9am-2:30pm & 5pm-10pm • Sun brunch • upscale contemporary • reservations recommended

**Tootie's Texas Barbeque** 68-703 Perez Rd, Cathedral City **760/202–6963** • 11am-8pm, clsd Sun • the name says it all

**Towne Center Cafe** 44491 Town Center Wy, Palm Desert **760/346–2120** • 6am-8pm • Greek diner

**Trio** 707 N Palm Canyon Dr **760/864–8746** • dinner nightly • also lounge

**The Tropicale Restaurant & Lounge** 330 E Amado Rd **760/866–1952** • 4pm-11pm, from 11am wknds, till midnight Fri-Sat

**Wang's in the Desert** 424 S Indian Canyon Dr (at E Saturnino Rd) **760/325–9264** • from 5:30pm • Chinese • full bar

**Zin American Bistro** 198 S Palm Canyon (at Arenas) **760/322–6300** • lunch & dinner

### ENTERTAINMENT & RECREATION

**Desert Dyners** PO Box 5072, 92263-5072 **760/202–6645** • lesbian social club • membership required • hosts mixers, dances, dinners & golf • singles & couples welcome

### BOOKSTORES

**Q Trading Company** 606 E Sunny Dunes Rd (at Indian Canyon) **760/416–7150, 800/756–2290** • 10am-6pm • LGBT • also cards, gifts, videos, etc

### RETAIL SHOPS

**GayMartUSA** 305 E Arenas Rd (at Indian Canyon) **760/416–6436** • 10am-midnight

**Greetings** 301 N Palm Canyon Dr (at Amado ) **760/322–5049** • 9am-6pm, till 9pm Th-Sat

**Mischief** 210 E Arenas Rd (at Indian Canyon) **760/322–8555** • 11am-7pm, 10am-11pm Fri-Sat

**Off Ramp Leathers** 650 E Sunny Dunes Rd #3 **760/778–2798** • custom motorcycle leathers

### PUBLICATIONS

**Desert Daily Guide/ DDG Media Group** **760/320–3237** • LGBT weekly, travel, activity & lodging info for Palm Springs

### GYMS & HEALTH CLUBS

**WorkOUT Gym** 2100 N Palm Canyon Dr #C100 **760/325–4600** • 6am-9pm, 7am-8pm Sat, till 6pm Sun • gay-owned

**World Gym Palm Springs** 1751 N Sunrise Way (at Vista Chino) **760/327–7100** • 5am-10pm, 6am-8pm wknds • mostly gay men • day passes available • steam & sauna • club-quality sound system • wheelchair access • gay-owned

### EROTICA

**Gear Leather & Fetish** 650 E Sunny Dunes #1 (at S Calle Palo Fierro) **760/322–3363** • noon-7pm, till 9pm Fri-Sat

## Palmdale

**see Lancaster**

## Palo Alto

### ACCOMMODATIONS

**Creekside Inn** 3400 El Camino Real (at Page Mill Rd) **650/493–2411, 800/492–7335** • gay/straight • pool • kids ok • WiFi • nonsmoking • restaurant & lounge • wheelchair access

**The Epiphany Hotel** 180 Hamilton Ave • gay/straight • luxury boutique hotel that caters to the region's tech-savvy travelers • restaurant & bar • pets ok • WiFi

**Hotel Avante** 860 E El Camino Real, Mountain View **650/940–1000, 800/538–1600** • gay/ straight • in heart of Silicon Valley • pool • WiFi

### BOOKSTORES

**Books Inc** 855 El Camino Real **650/321–0600** • 9am-8pm, till 9pm Fri-Sa• LGBT section

### EROTICA

**Good Vibrations** 534 Ramona St **650/422–2790** • 10am-10pm, till 11pm Th-Sat • clean, well-lighted sex toy store • workshops & events

## Pasadena

### BARS

**The 35er** 626 /356–9315 • 3pm-1am, from 12:30pm Fri-Sun • gay/ straight • great neighborhood bar • food served

**The Boulevard Bar** 3199 E Foothill Blvd (at Sierra Madre Villa) **626/356–9304** • 4pm-2am, from 3pm Fri-Sun • mostly gay men • neighborhood bar • drag shows • karaoke • piano bar

### RESTAURANTS

**Kings Row** 20 E Colorado Blvd **626/793–3010** • 4pm-midnight, till 2am wknds • gastropub

**Lanna Thai** 400 S Arroyo Pkwy **626/577–6599** • 11am-10:30pm • Thai • full bar • wheelchair access

### ENTERTAINMENT & RECREATION

**The Huntington** 1151 Oxford Rd, San Marino **626/405–2100** • art collection • botanical gardens

## Paso Robles

### ACCOMMODATIONS

**Asuncion Ridge Vineyards & Inn** **805/461–0675** • gay-friendly • WiFi • gay-owned

**Hotel Cheval** 1021 Pine St **805/226–9995, 866/522–6999** • gay-friendly • WiFi

**The Oaks Hotel Paso Robles** 3000 Riverside Ave (at 24th St) **805/237–8700** • gay-friendly • perfect boutique-style hotel with many upscale amenitie • full brkfst • pool • WiFi • kids/pets ok • wheelchair access

### ENTERTAINMENT & RECREATION

**River Oaks Hot Springs Spa** 800 Clubhouse Dr **805/238–4600** • 9am-9pm, clsd Mon

## Petaluma

### RESTAURANTS

**Brixx** 16 Kentucky St (in Lanmart Bldg) **707/766–8162** • dinner from 4pm • popular • handmade pizzas & paninis • live bands Sat

### BOOKSTORES

**Copperfield's Books** 140 Kentucky St (btwn Western & Washington, downtown) **707/762–0563** • 9am-9pm, 10am-6pm Sun

## Placerville

### ACCOMMODATIONS

**Albert Shafsky House B&B** 2942 Coloma St (at Spring St/ Hwy 49) **530/642–2776, 877/262–4667** • gay-friendly • full brkfst • nonsmoking • WiFi • kids ok • lesbian-owned

**Rancho Cicada Retreat** 10001 Bell Rd, Plymouth **209/245–4841, 877/553–9481** • mostly gay men • secluded riverside retreat in the Sierra foothills w/ 2-person tents & cabin • swimming • nudity • gay-owned

## Pleasant Hill

see East Bay

## Pomona

### BARS

**Alibi East & Back Alley Bar** 225 S San Antonio Ave (at 2nd) **909/623–9422** • noon-2am, till 3am Fri • mostly gay men • dancing/DJ • karaoke • smoking patio

**The Hookup** 1047 E 2nd St (at Pico) **909/620–2844** • noon-2am • lesbians/ gay men • neighborhood bar • food served • karaoke • beer bust Sun • wheelchair access • gay-owned

### NIGHTCLUBS

**340** 340 S Thomas St **909/865–9340** • 7pm-2am , clsd Mon-Wed • lesbian/ gay men • also restaurant • dancing • drag shows

## Redding

### NIGHTCLUBS

**Club 501** 1244 California St (at Center & Division, enter rear) **530/243–7869** • 6pm-2am, from 3pm Th-Sun lesbians/ gay men • dancing/DJ • young crowd

## Redondo Beach

see also Los Angeles—West LA & Santa Monica

## Riverside

see also San Bernardino

### NIGHTCLUBS

**Menagerie** 3581 University Ave (at Orange) **951/788–8000** • 4pm-2am • lesbians/ gay men • dancing/DJ • karaoke • drag shows Th • wheelchair access

**VIP Nightclub & Restaurant** 3673 Merrill Ave (at Magnolia) **951/784–2370** • 5pm-2am • lesbians/ gay men • dancing/DJ • karaoke • drag shows • food served • 18+

## Russian River

includes Cazadero, Forestville, Guerneville, Monte Rio, Occidental & Sebastopol

### INFO LINES & SERVICES

**AA Meetings in Sonoma County** 707/544–1300 (AA#), 800/224–1300 • call for meeting times

**Russian River Chamber of Commerce & Visitors Center** 16209 First St (on the plaza), Guerneville **707/869–9000** • 10am-5pm, till 4pm Sun

**Sonoma County Tourism** 800/576–6662 • Sonoma County, located 30 miles from San Francisco, provides a genuine, independent, and adventurous wine country experience, featuring more than 425 wineries, 100-plus organic farms, and 55 miles of stunning Pacific coast
For a free visitors guide or information on hotels, wineries, events, spas, attractions, and dining in Sonoma County, visit www.sonomacounty.com or call 800-576-6662

### ACCOMMODATIONS

**Applewood Inn** 13555 Hwy 116 (at Mays Canyon), Guerneville **707/869–9093, 800/555–8509** • gay-friendly • full brkfst • pool • nonsmoking • WiFi • wheelchair access • also restaurant

**boon hotel & spa** 14711 Armstrong Woods Rd, Guerneville **707/869–2721** • gay/ straight • resort w/ full-service spa • kids/ pets ok • pool • nonsmoking • jacuzzi • WiFi • gay-owned

**Fern Grove Cottages** 16650 River Rd, Guerneville **888/243–2674** • gay-friendly • pool • kids/ pets ok • nonsmoking • WiFi

**Guerneville Lodge** 15905 River Rd (at Hwy 116), Guerneville **707/869–0102** • gay/ straight • WiFi • nonsmoking • gay-owned

**Highland Dell Resort** 21050 River Blvd (at Bohemian Hwy), Monte Rio **707/865–2300** • gay-friendly • WiFi • full bar & restaurant

➤**Highlands Resort** 14000 Woodland Dr, Guerneville **707/869–0333** • lesbians/ gay men • country retreat on 4 wooded acres • hot tub • swimming • clothing-optional pool

**Inn at Occidental** 3657 Church St, Occidental **707/874–1047, 800/522–6324** • gay-friendly • full brkfst • wheelchair access

**r3 Hotel** 16390 4th St (at Mill), Guerneville **707/869–8399** • lesbians/ gay men • pool • nudity ok • also restaurant • full bar • wheelchair access • gay-owned

**Rio Villa Beach Resort** 20292 Hwy 116 (at Bohemian Hwy), Monte Rio 707/865-1143, 877/746-8455 • gay-friendly • kids ok • nonsmoking • WiFi • gay-owned

**Village Inn & Restaurant** 20822 River Blvd, Monte Rio 707/865-2304 • gay/ straight • historic inn • nonsmoking • also restaurant & full bar • WiFi • wheelchair access • gay-owned

**West Sonoma Inn & Spa** 14100 Brookside Ln (at Main St), Guerneville 707/869-2470, 800/551-1881 • gay/ straight • 6-acre resort • pool • spa • some jacuzzis • nonsmoking • WiFi • wheelchair access

**The Woods Resort** 16484 4th St (at Mill St), Guerneville 707/869-0600, 877/887-9218 • mostly gay men • swimming • WiFi • wheelchair access • gay-owned

## BARS

**Mc T's Bullpen** 16246 First St (at Church), Guerneville 707/869-3377 • 10am-2am • gay/ straight • karaoke • bands • patio • WiFi • wheelchair access

**Rainbow Cattle Co** 16220 Main St (at Armstrong Woods Rd), Guerneville 707/869-0206 • 6am-2am • gay/ straight • neighborhood bar • DJ Bruce 3rd Sat

## CAFES

**Coffee Bazaar** 14045 Armstrong Woods Rd (at River Rd), Guerneville 707/869-9706 • 6am-8pm • cafe • soups • salads • sandwiches • WiFi

**Coffee Catz** 6761 Sebastopol Ave (at Hwy 116), Sebastopol 707/829-6600 • 7am-6pm, till 8pm Th, till 10pm Wed & Fri-Sat • live shows • WiFi • wheelchair access

**Roasters Espresso Bar** 6656 Front St (Hwy 116), Forestville 707/887-1632 • 6am-6pm, from 7am Sat-Sun • WiFi

## RESTAURANTS

**Aioli** 6536 Front St, Forestville 707/887-2476 • 9am-5pp, from 10am Sat • gourmet deli • beer/ wine • outdoor seating

**boon eat + drink** 16248 Main St (at Hwy 116), Guerneville 707/869-0780 • lunch & dinner • modern California bistro

**Cape Fear Cafe** 25191 Main St, Duncans Mills 707/865-9246 • 9am-2:30pm & 5pm-9pm (clsd Wed & Th off-season)

**Chef Patrick** 16337 Main St (at Hwy 116), Guerneville 707/869-9161 • dinner nightly

**Farmhouse Inn Restaurant** 7871 River Rd, Forestville 707/887-3300, 800/464-6642 • dinner, clsd Tue-Wed

**Garden Grill** 17132 Hwy 116, Guerneville 707/869-3922 • 8am-8pm • great burgers & sandwiches • some veggie • patio

**Main Street Station** 16280 Main St (at Church St), Guerneville 707/869-0501 • 11am-7pm • Italian restaurant & pizzeria • cabaret dinner shows nightly

**Mom's Apple Pie** 4550 Gravenstein Hwy N, Sebastopol 707/823-8330 • 10am-6pm • pie worth stopping for on your way to & from Russian River!

**River Inn Grill** 16141 Main St, Guerneville 707/869-0481 • 8am-3pm • local favorite • wheelchair access

**Seaside Metal Oyster Bar** 16222 Main St, Guerneville 707/604-7250 • 5pm-10pm, clsd Mon-Tue • a rustic seafood-based restaurant run by the duo behind SF's famous Bar Crudo

**Tahoe Chinese Restaurant** 6492 Mirabel Rd, Forestville 707/887-9772 • lunch & dinner Mon-Fri, dinner only Sat-Sun • some veggie

**Underwood Bar & Bistro** 9113 Graton Rd, Graton 707/823-7023 • lunch & dinner, clsd Mon

**Willow Wood Market Cafe** 9020 Graton Rd, Graton 707/823-0233 • 8am-9pm, from 9am Sat, brunch 9am-3pm Sun

## ENTERTAINMENT & RECREATION

**Pegasus Theater Co** 4444 Wood Rd (at Rio Nido Lodge, at Canyon Two Rd) 707/583-2343 • classic to contemporary plays

## RETAIL SHOPS

**Guerneville 5 &10** 16252 Main St, Guerneville 707/869-3404 • 10am-6pm • old-fashioned five & dime • lesbian-owned

**Sonoma Nesting Company** 16151 Main St, Guerneville 707/869-3434 • antiques & home decorating

## Sacramento

### INFO LINES & SERVICES

**Gay AA** 916/454-1100 • 24hr helpline

**Sacramento Gay & Lesbian Center** 1927 L St 916/442-0185 • noon-6pm Mon-Fri

### ACCOMMODATIONS

**Citizen Hotel** 926 J Street 916/447-2700 • gay-friendly • bar & restaurant • wheelchair access

**Governors Inn** 210 Richards Blvd (at I-5) 916/448-7224, 800/999-6689 • gay-friendly • pool • hot tub • nonsmoking • WiFi

**Inn & Spa at Parkside** 2116 6th St (at U St) 916/658–1818, 800/995–7275 • gay/ straight • full brkfst • jacuzzi • WiFi • also full-service spa • wheelchair access • gay-owned

### BARS

**The Depot** 2001 K St 916/441–6823 • 4pm-2am, from 2pm wknds • mostly gay men • neighborhood bar • transgender-friendly • live shows • videos • wheelchair access

**Dive Bar** 1016 K St 916 /737–5999 • 4pm-2am • gay/ straight • super cool water tank

**Hush** 2001 K St (at the Depot) 916/441–6823 • 1st Friday of the month women's dance party • videos • wheelchair access

### NIGHTCLUBS

**Badlands** 2003 K St 916/448–8790 • 6pm-2am • mostly gay men • dancing/DJ • wheelchair access

**Faces** 2000 K St (at 20th St) 916/448–7798 • 4pm-2am • popular • lesbians/ gay men • dancing/DJ • 3 bars w/ various theme nights • karaoke • videos • patio • wheelchair access • cover

### RESTAURANTS

**Chops** 1117 11th St (at L St, across from State Capitol Building) 916/447–8900 • lunch Mon-Fri, dinner nightly • steak & seafood • full bar

**Ernesto's** 1901 16th St 916/441–5850 • Mexican

**Ink Eats & Drinks** 2730 N St (at 28th) 916/456–2800 • lunch, dinner, late-night brkfst, wknd brunch • full bar • DJ wknds

**Jack's Urban Eats** 1230 20th St (at Capitol Ave) 916/444–0307 • 11am-8pm, from 5pm wknds

**Paesanos** 1806 Capitol Ave (at 18th) 916/447–8646 • 11:30am-9:30pm, from noon wknds • Italian • funky artwork • patio • full bar • also 8519 Bond Rd, 916/690–8646

**Pizza Rock** 1020 K St 916/737–5777 • 11am-10pm, till midnight Wed-Th, till 3am Fri-Sat

**Rick's Dessert Diner** 2401 J St 916/444–0969 • 10am-midnight, till 1am wknds, from noon Sun • coffee & dessert

**Thai Palace** 3262 J St (33rd St) 916/447–5353 • lunch & dinner

**Zócalo** 1801 Capitol Ave (at 18th St) 916/441–0303 • 11am-10pm • Mexican • full bar

### ENTERTAINMENT & RECREATION

**Lavender Library, Archives & Cultural Exchange of Sacramento** 1414 21st St 916/492–0558 • 4:30pm-8pm Th-Fri, noon-6pm wknds, clsd Mon-Wed

### RETAIL SHOPS

**Side Show Studios** 2111 28th St 916/391–6400 • 10am-10pm • tattoo studio • art gallery • reception w/ live music 2nd Sat • lesbian-owned

### PUBLICATIONS

**Outword Magazine** 916/329–9280 • statewide LGBT newspaper w/ Northern & Southern CA editions

### EROTICA

**G Spot** 2007 J St (at 20th) 916/441–3200 • gay-owned

**Kiss-N-Tell** 4201 Sunrise Blvd (at Fair Oaks) 916/966–5477 • clean, well-lighted erotica store • also 2401 Arden Wy, 916/920–5477

## San Bernardino

**see also Riverside**

### INFO LINES & SERVICES

**AA Gay/ Lesbian** 897 Via Lata, Colton 909/825–4700 • call or visit www.inlandempireaa.org for times

## San Clemente

**see Orange County**

## San Diego

### INFO LINES & SERVICES

**Live & Let Live Alano Club** 1730 Monroe Ave 619/298–8008 • 10:30am-10pm, from 8:30am wknds • various LGBT meetings (see www.lllac.org)

**San Diego LGBT Community Center** 3909 Centre St (at University) 619/692–2077 • 9am-10pm, till 7pm Sat, clsd Sun

**Women's Resource Center (WRC)** 3909 Centre St (at University, in SD LGBT Community Center) 619/692–2077 • variety of resources • health care referrals • social services • community activities

### ACCOMMODATIONS

**Andaz San Diego** 600 F St 619/849–1234 • gay/ straight • also restaurant& nighclub • rooftop pool • WiFi

**The Bristol Hotel** 1055 First Ave 619/232-6141, 800/662-4477 • gay/straight • hotel • kids ok • restaurant & bar • great collection of pop art • WiFi • wheelchair access

**Handlery Hotel & Resort** 950 Hotel Circle N 619/298-0511, 800/676-6567 • gay-friendly • pool • hot tub • nonsmoking • kids ok • WiFi • wheelchair access

**Inn at the Park** 525 Spruce St (btwn 5th & 6th) 619/291-0999, 877/499-7163 • gay-friendly • 1926 hotel • kids ok

**Keating House** 2331 2nd Ave (at Juniper) 619/239-8585, 800/995-8644 • gay-friendly • Victorian on Bankers Hill • full brkfst • nonsmoking • kids ok • WiFi

**Lafayette Hotel & Suites** 2223 El Cajon Blvd (btwn Louisiana & Mississippi) 619/296-2101, 800/468-3531 • gay-friendly • swimming • kids ok • also restaurant • internet access • nonsmoking • WiFi • wheelchair access

**Pier South Resort** 800 Seacoast Dr, Imperial Beach 619/621-5900 • gay/straight • steps from the ocean, restaurant on the beach

**Porto Vista Hotel** 1835 Columbia St 619/544-0164 • gay-friendly • unique European boutique hotel • food served • WiFi

**Scripps Inn** 555 Coast Blvd S (La Jolla ) 858/454-3391 • gay/straight • 14 room boutique B&B, short drive to Black's (gay)beach • pets OK

**The Sofia Hotel** 150 W Broadway 619/234-9200, 800/826-0009 • gay/ straight • kids/ pets ok • wheelchair access

**La Valencia Hotel** 132 Prospect St (La Jolla ) 858/454-0771 • gay/straight • in the heart of downtown La Jolla, ask for a beach view room • pool

## Bars

**The Brass Rail** 3796 5th Ave (at Robinson) 619/298-2233 • 7pm-2am, from 2pm Fri-Sun, clsd Tue • lesbians/ gay men • dancing/DJ • Latin night Sat • wheelchair access

**Fiesta Cantina** 142 University Ave 619/298-2500 • noon-2am, from 10am wknds • lesbians/ gay men • Mexican restaurant & bar

**Gossip Grill** 1440 University Ave (at Normal) 619/260-8023 • 2pm-close • mostly women • also restaurant • patio • wheelchair access • gay-owned

**The Hole in the Wall** 2820 Lytton St (at Rosecrans) 619/996-9000 • 4pm-2pm, from noon Sun • mostly gay men

**No 1 Fifth Ave (no sign)** 3845 5th Ave (at University) 619/299-1911 • noon-2am • mostly gay men • neighborhood bar • videos nights • patio

**Redwing Bar & Grill** 4012 30th St (at Lincoln, North Park) 619/281-8700 • 11am-2am • mostly gay men • neighborhood bar • patio

**Soul Kiss** • mostly women • dancing/DJ • multiracial • weekly hip hop parties • check soulkisssd.com for details

**SRO Lounge** 1807 5th Ave (btwn Elm & Fir) 619/232-1886 • 10am-2am • mostly gay men • cocktail lounge • transgender-friendly

## Nightclubs

**Numbers** 3811 Park Blvd (at University) 619/294-7583 • popular • mostly gay men • ladies night Sat • dancing/DJ • karaoke • theme nights • patio • wheelchair access

**Rich's** 1051 University Ave (at Vermont) 619/295-2195 • popular • open Wed-Sun • mostly gay men • ladies night Th • dancing/DJ • theme nights

## Cafes

**Babycakes** 3766 5th Ave (at Robinson) 619/296-4173 • 9am-11pm, till midnight Fri-Sat • beer/ wine • patio

**The Big Kitchen** 3003 Grape St (at 30th) 619/234-5789 • 8am-2pm • wheelchair access • women-owned

**Claire de Lune** 2906 University Ave 619/688-9845 • 6am-10pm, till midnight Fri-Sat

**Extraordinary Desserts** 2929 5th Ave 619/294-2132 • also store in Little Italy: 1430 Union, 619/249-7001 • the name says it all

**Gelato Vero** 3753 India St 619/295-9269 • 7am-midnight • great desserts (yes, the gelato is truly delicious) & coffee

**Twiggs** 4590 Park Blvd (at Madison Ave, University Heights) 619/296-0616 • 7am-11pm

## Restaurants

**2GOOD2B** 204 N El Camino Real #H, Encinitas 619/942-4663 • 7am-8pm, till 3pm Sun, where everything is delicious, without gluten, corn or soy

**Adams Avenue Grill** 2201 Adams Ave (at Mississippi) **619/298–8440** • 8am–11pm • bistro • plenty veggie • beer/wine • wheelchair access • gay-owned

**Arrivederci** 3845 4th Ave 619/299–6282 • lunch & dinner

**Baja Betty's** 1421 University Ave (at Normal St) **619/269–8510** • 11am–midnight, till 1am Fri-Sat • popular • lesbians/gay men • Mexican • some veggie • patio • wheelchair access

**Bamboo Lounge** 1475 University Ave (at Herbert St) **619/291–8221** • 4pm–midnight, till 1am wknds • sushi

**Cafe 222** 222 Island Ave 619/236–9902 • 7am-2pm • great brkfst

**Cody's La Jolla** 8030 Girard Ave (at Coast Blvd S), La Jolla 858/459–0040 • brkfst & lunch daily • contemporary California cuisine • live music

**The Cottage** 7702 Fay (at Klein), La Jolla 858/454–8409 • 7:30am-3pm, dinner June-Sept

**Crazee Burger** 4201 30th St (at Howard) **619/282–6044** • 11am-9pm, till 11pm Fri, till 10pm Sat • handcrafted burgers

**Crest Cafe** 425 Robinson (btwn 4th & 5th) 619/295–2510 • 7am-midnight • some veggie • wheelchair access

**El Camino** 2400 India St (at Kalmia, in Little Italy) **619/685–3881** • dinner nightly, Sun brunch • kitschy Mexican • live music • full bar

**Hash House A Go Go** 3628 5th Ave 619/298–4646 • brkfst, lunch & dinner, clsd Mon • great brkfst

**Hillcrest Brewing Company** 1458 University Ave (at Normal St) 619/269–4323 • 3pm-midnight • lesbians/gay men • world's first gay brewery

**Jimmy Carter's Mexican Cafe** 3172 5th Ave (at Spruce) 619/295–2070 • 7am-9pm

**Juniper and Ivy** 2228 Kettner Blvd 619/269–9036 • bar from 4pm, creative space with outdoor dining and famous Top Chef alum

**Kous Kous** 3940 4th Ave, Ste 110 (beneath Martinis on Fourth) **619/295–5560** • 5pm-11pm • Moroccan

**Lips** 3036 El Cajon Blvd 619/295–7900 • 5pm-close, Sun gospel brunch, clsd Mon • "the ultimate in drag dining" • Bitchy Bingo Wed • celeb impersonation Th • DJ wknds

**Luna Grill** 350 University 619/296–5862 • 11am-10pm • near East & Mediterranean • plenty veggie/vegan

**Martinis Above Fourth** 3940 4th Ave, Ste 200 (btwn Washington & University) **619/400–4500** • open 5pm, from 4pm Fri-Sat, clsd Sun • also cabaret lounge • outdoor bar • gay-owned

**The Mission** 3795 Mission Blvd (at San Jose), Mission Beach **858/488–9060** • 7am-3pm

**The Prado** 1549 El Prado (in Balboa Park) 619/557–9441 • lunch & dinner • Latin/Italian fusion

**Roberto's Taco Shop** 2744 El Cajon Blvd

619/584–0377 • 8am-11:30pm • the best rolled tacos & guacamole • multiple locations

**Rudford's** 2900 El Cajon Blvd (at Kansas St) 619/282–8423 • 24hrs • popular homestyle cooking

**Rustic Root** 535 5th Ave 619/232–1747 • Gaslamp's only rooftop restaurant

**Rustic Root** 535 5th Ave 619/232–1747 • Gaslamp's only rooftop restaurant

**Saigon on Fifth** 3900 5th Ave, Ste 120 619/220–8828 • 11am-3am • Vietnamese

**Salt & Cleaver** 3805 5th Ave 619/756–6677 • 11:30am-11pm, till 1am Fri Sat • a new dining concept based on the ancient art of sausage making

**South Park Abbey** 1946 Fern St (at Grape St) **619/696–0096** • 3pm-1:30am, from 9am Sat-Sun, till midnight Sun-Mon, clsd Tue

**Uptown Tavern** 1236 University Ave (at Richmond) **619/241–2710** • 4pm-2am, from 10:30 am wknds

**Urban Mo's** 308 University Ave (at 3rd) **619/491-0400** • 9am-2am, 10am-midnight Sun • popular • lesbians/ gay men • some veggie • 3 full bars )• patio • wheelchair access

**Waffle Spot** 1333 Hotel Circle S (at King's Inn) **619/297-2231** • 7am-2pm

**West Coast Tavern** 2895 University Ave **619/295-1688** • lunch & dinner • upscale • also lounge

## ENTERTAINMENT & RECREATION

**Diversionary Theatre** 4545 Park Blvd #101 (at Madison) **619/220-0097 (BOX OFFICE #)**, **619/220-6830** • LGBT theater

**Ocean Beach** I-8 West to Sunset Cliffs Blvd • very dog-friendly

**Torrey Pines Beach State Park ("Blacks Beach")** • popular nude beach, head north for the gay area

## BOOKSTORES

**Traveler's Depot** 1655 Garnet Ave (btwn Jewell & Ingraham) **858/483-1421** • 10am-6pm, 11am-5pm wknds • guides, maps & more

## RETAIL SHOPS

**Auntie Helen's** 4127 30th St (at Lincoln) **619/584-8438** • 10am-6pm, 11am-5pm Sun-Mon • thrift shop benefits PWAs • wheelchair access

**Flesh Skin Grafix** 1155 Palm Ave, Imperial Beach **619/424-8983** • tattoos • piercing

**Mankind** 3425 5th Ave (at Upas St) **619/497-1970** • 11am-10pm, noon-6pm Sun • books, sex toys & videos

## PUBLICATIONS

**The Bottomline** 3314 4th Ave **619/291-6690** • bi-weekly • news, entertainment & listings • covers San Diego & Palm Springs

**San Diego LGBT Weekly** 1850 5th Ave (at Fir) **619/450-4288**

**San Diego PIX** 1010 University Ave **877/727-5446**

## EROTICA

**Pleasures & Treasures Adult/ Leather Shop** 2525 University Ave (at Arnold) **619/822-4280** • 11am-11pm, till 6pm Sun • gay-owned

**Romantix Adult Superstore** 1407 University Ave (at Richmond) **619/299-7186**

# SAN FRANCISCO

San Francisco is divided into 7 geographical areas:
SF—Overview
SF—Castro & Noe Valley
SF—South of Market
SF—Polk Street Area
SF—Downtown & North Beach
SF—Mission District
SF—Haight, Fillmore, Hayes Valley

## SF—Overview

### INFO LINES & SERVICES

**AA Gay/ Lesbian** 1821 Sacramento St **415/674-1821** • check www.aasf.org for meeting times

**The Center for Sex & Culture** 1349 Mission St (btwn 10th & 11th St) **415/902-2071** • very queer-friendly classes, workshops, gatherings, events, readings & more

**Crystal Meth Anonymous** **415/835-4747**

**GLBT Hotline of San Francisco** **415/355-0999** • 5pm-9pm Mon-Fri • peer-counseling • info

**LYRIC (Lavender Youth Recreation/ Information Center)** 127 Collingwood (btwn 18th & 19th) **415/703-6150** • peer-run support line for LGBT youth under 24

**The San Francisco LGBT Community Center** 1800 Market St (at Octavia) **415/865-5555** • noon-10pm, from 9am Sat, clsd Sun • cybercenter • cafe • classes • child care & more

**Women's Building** 3543 18th St (btwn Valencia & Guerrero) **415/431-1180** • 9am-5pm Mon-Fri, till 6pm Sat • social/ support groups • housing & job listings • beautiful murals

### NIGHTCLUBS

**Trannyshack** • occasional drag events, check trannyshack.com for info

### RESTAURANTS

**Beach Chalet Brewery & Restaurant** 1000 Great Hwy (at Fulton St) **415/386-8439** • located above the Golden Gate Park Visitor's Center

### ENTERTAINMENT & RECREATION

**Baker Beach** Lincoln Blvd at Bowley, in the Presidio • popular nude beach

**Bay Area Derby Girls** • SF Bay Area's female roller derby league • visit www.bayareaderbygirls.com for events

**Brava!** 2781 24th St (btwn York & Hampshire) **415/641-7657** • theater w/ culturally diverse performances by women • wheelchair access

**Castro Theatre** 429 Castro (at Market) **415/621-6120** • art house cinema • many LGBT & cult classics • live organ evenings

**Cruisin' the Castro Tours** tour meets at the rainbow flag at Harvey Milk Plaza (corner of Castro & Market) **415/255-1821** • "a TOP city tour & walking w/ pride since 1989! Diverse, fun, informative & NO hills"

➤**Frameline** **415/703-8650** • LGBT media arts foundation • sponsors annual SF Int'l LGBT Film Festival in June

**The Intersection for the Arts** 925 Mission St #109 **415/626-2787** • San Francisco's oldest alternative arts space (since 1965!) w/ plays, art exhibitions, live jazz, literary series, performance art & much more

**Local Tastes of the City Tours** **415/665-0480, 888/358-8687** • explore history & culture of local neighborhoods as "we eat our way through San Francisco"

**The Marsh** 1062 Valencia (at 22nd St) **415/826-5750, 415/282-3055** • queer-positive theater

**National AIDS Memorial Grove** Golden Gate Park (on corner of Middle Drive East & Bowling Green Dr) **415/765-0497, 888/294-7683** • located in a lush, historic dell in Golden Gate Park • guided tours available 9am-noon every 3rd Sat • wheelchair access

**QComedy Gay Comedy Showcase** **415/533-9133** • see website for locations • popular • lesbians/ gay men • cover charge (sliding scale) • see www.qcomedy.com for location

**Steve Silver's Beach Blanket Babylon** 678 Beach Blanket Babylon Ave (formerly Green St) (btwn Powell & Columbus, in Club Fugazi) **415/421-4222** • the USA's longest running musical revue & wigs that must be seen to be believed • very popular • 21+ except Sun

**Thanks Babs, the Day Tripper** **702/370-6961** • tours & getaways • full service concierge for San Francisco & Bay Area • it's like having a lesbian aunt in Northern California!

**Theatre Rhinoceros** 1360 Mission St #200 **800/838-3006, 415/552-4100** • LGBT theater

**Victorian Home Walks** **415/252-9485** • custom-tailored walking tours w/ San Francisco resident • gay-owned

**Yerba Buena Center for the Arts** 701 Mission St (at 3rd St) **415/978-2787** (**BOX OFFICE**) • annual season includes wide variety of contemporary dance, theater & music • also film theater & gallery

## PUBLICATIONS

**BAR (Bay Area Reporter)** **415/861-5019** • the weekly LGBT newspaper

**Bay Times** **415/503-1386** • popular • good Bay Area resource listings

# SF—Castro & Noe Valley

## ACCOMMODATIONS

**Edwardian San Francisco** 1668 Market St (btwn Franklin & Gough) **415/864-1271, 888/864-8070** • gay-friendly • hot tub • jacuzzi • some shared baths • nonsmoking

**Inn on Castro** 321 Castro St (btwn 16th & 17th) **415/861-0321** • lesbians/ gay men • B&B known for its hospitality & friendly atmosphere • full brkfst • nonsmoking • WiFi • gay-owned

**The Parker Guest House** 520 Church St (at 17th) **415/621-3222, 888/520-7275** • popular • gay/straight • guesthouse complex w/ gardens • steam spa • nonsmoking • WiFi • gay-owned

**The Willows Inn** 710 14th St (at Church) **415/431-4770, 800/431-0277** • lesbians/ gay men • "amenities, comfort, great location" • nonsmoking • WiFi • lesbian & gay-owned

## BARS

**13 Licks** 456 Castro St (at Q Bar) **415/864-2877** • 9pm-2am Tue only • popular • mostly women • neighborhood bar • dancing/DJ • sidewalk patio • wheelchair access

**440 Castro** 440 Castro St **415/621-8732** • noon-2am • popular • mostly gay men • neighborhood bar • leather • bears • women genuinely welcome

**Beaux** 2344 Market St (at Castro) • 2pm-2am • mostly men • dancing/DJ

**Blackbird** 2124 Market St **415/503-0630** • 3pm-2am • gay/ straight • neighborhood bar • gay-owned

**The Cafe** 2369 Market St (at Castro) **415/861-3846** • 5pm-2am, from 3pm Sat-Sun • popular • lesbians/ gay men • dancing/DJ • young crowd

**Harvey's** 500 Castro St **415/431–4278** • 11am-11pm, 9am-2am wknds • popular • lesbians/ gay men • neighborhood bar • occasional drag performers • also restaurant • wheelchair access

**Hi Tops** 2247 Market St **415/551–2500** • noon-2am, from 10am Sun • lesbians/ gay men • food served

**The Lookout** 3600 16th St (at Market) **415/431–0306** • 3:30pm-2am, from 12:30pm wknds • mostly gay men • bar food • DJ most nights

**Martuni's** 4 Valencia St (at Market) **415/241–0205** • 4pm-2am • gay/ straight • piano bar & lounge • great martinis

**The Mint** 1942 Market St (at Buchanan) **415/626–4726** • noon-2am • lesbians/ gay men • popular karaoke bar nights • also sushi restaurant • food served till 11pm (till midnight wknds)

**The Mix** 4086 18th St **415/431–8616** • 3pm-2am, from 8am wknds • mostly gay men • neighborhood bar • heated patio

**Moby Dick** 4049 18th St (at Hartford) • 2pm-2am, from noon wknds • mostly gay men • neighborhood bar • videos

**Pilsner Inn** 225 Church St (at Market) **415/621–7058** • 10am-2am • popular • mostly gay men • neighborhood bar • great patio

**Q Bar** 456 Castro St **415/864–2877** • 4pm-2am, from 2pm wknds • popular • mostly gay men, more women Tue • neighborhood bar • dancing/DJ • sidewalk patio • wheelchair access

**Swirl** 572 Castro St (at 19th) **415/864–2262** • 1pm-8pm, till 9pm Fri-Sat wine bar & wine store

## Cafes

**Cafe Flore** 2298 Market St (at Noe) **415/621–8579** • 7am-2am • popular • lesbians/ gay men • some veggie • full bar • great patio • WiFi

**Duboce Park Cafe** 2 Sanchez St (at Duboce) **415/621–1108** • 7am-8pm • outdoor seating

**Eureka! Cafe** 451 Castro St (at Market St) **415/355–9110** • 8am-8pm, from 9am wknds, till 6pm Sun • third wave Blue Bottle Coffee; Organic Ice Cream; SF made product, outdoor seating • wheelchair access

**Samovar Tea Lounge** 498 Sanchez St (at 18th St) **415/626–4700** • 10am-10pm • tea culture from around the world

## Restaurants

**Anchor Oyster Bar** 579 Castro St (at 19th) **415/431–3990** • 11:30am-10pm, from 4pm Sun • lesbians/ gay men • beer/ wine • women-owned

**Catch** 2362 Market St **415/431–5000** • lunch & dinner, wknd brunch • seafood

**Chow** 215 Church St (at Market) **415/552–2469** • 8am-11pm, till midnight wknds • popular • patio

**Cove Cafe** 434 Castro St **415/626–0462** • 8am-9pm, till 10pm Fri-Sat • some veggie • wheelchair access

**Eric's Chinese Restaurant** 1500 Church St (at 27th St) **415/282–0919** • 11am-9pm • popular

**Firewood Cafe** 4248 18th St (at Diamond St) **415/252–0999** • 11am-11pm • rotisserie chicken, pastas, oven-fired pizzas, salads

**Hot Cookie** 407 Castro St **415/621–2350** • 11am-1am • hot cookies!

**Kasa Indian Eatery** 4001 18th St (at Noe) **415/621–6940** • 11am-10pm, till 11pm Fri-Sat • plenty veggie

**La Mediterranée** 288 Noe (at Market) **415/431–7210** • 11am-10pm, till 11pm Sat-Sun • beer/ wine

**Mama Ji's** 4415 18th St **415/626–4416** • 9:30am-9:30pm, great Dim sum in the Castro

**Orphan Andy's** 3991 17th St **415/864–9795** • 24hrs • diner • gay-owned

**Poesia Osteria Italiana** 4072 18th St (at Collingwood) **415/252–9325** • dinner nighly • Italian • great food & full bar

**The Sausage Factory** 517 Castro St **415/626–1250** • 11:30am-midnight • lesbians/ gay men • pizza & pasta • some veggie • beer/ wine

**Takara Sushi** 4243 18th St (at Diamond) **415/626–7864** • lunch & dinner, clsd Tue • lesbians/ gay men • cont'l/ Japanese

**Woodhouse Fish Co** 2073 Market St (at 14th) **415/437–2722** • noon-9:30pm • New England clam shack-style seafood • also 1914 Fillmore St

**Zuni Cafe** 1658 Market St (at Franklin) **415/552–2522** • lunch & dinner, clsd Mon • popular • upscale SF classic spot • full bar

## Entertainment & Recreation

**Castro Country Club** 4058 18th St (at Hartford) **415/552–6102** • alcohol- & drug-free space • cafe

**GLBT History Museum** 4127 18th St (at Castro) **415/621-1107** • 11am-7pm, noon-5pm Sun, clsd Tue • one of the world's largest collections of GLBT archival materials

**Pink Triangle Park** near Market & Castro • "in remembrance of LGBT victims of the Nazi regime"

## BOOKSTORES

**Aardvark Books** 227 Church St **415/552-6733** • 10:30am-10:30pm, mostly used • good LGBT section

**Books, Inc** 2275 Market St **415/864-6777** • 10am-10pm • LGBT section • readings • wheelchair access

## RETAIL SHOPS

**HRC Action Center & Store** 575 Castro St **415/431-2200** • 10am-8pm, till 7pm Sun • Human Rights Campaign merchandise & info

**Kenneth Wingard** 2319 Market St (btwn Castro & Noe) **415/431-6900** • modern & affordable home furnishings, decor & clothing

**Rolo** 2351 Market St **415/431-4545** • 11am-8pm, till 7pm Sun • designer labels

**See Jane Run Sports** 3910 24th St (at Noe) **415/401-8338** • 11am-7pm, 10am-6pm Sat, 11am-6pm Sun • women's athletic apparel

## GYMS & HEALTH CLUBS

**SF Fitness Castro** 2301 Market St **415/348-6377** • day passes available

# SF—South of Market

## ACCOMMODATIONS

**Holiday Inn Civic Center** 50 8th St (at Market) **415/626-6103, 877/252-1169** • gay-friendly • pool • small pets ok • WiFi • wheelchair access

**The Mosser Hotel** 54 4th St (btwn Market & Mission) **415/986-4400, 800/227-3804** • gay/straight • 1913 landmark hotel • some shared baths • nonsmoking • kids ok • also restaurant • SF cuisine • full bar

**The Westin San Francisco Market Street** 50 3rd St **415/974-6400, 888/627-8561** • gay-friendly • hip hotel w/ spectacular views • sauna • kids ok • nonsmoking

## BARS

**Club OMG** 43 6th St **415/896-6453** • 6pm-2am • gay bollywood events • gay/straight • dancing/DJ

**The Eagle Tavern** 398 12th St (at Harrison) **415/626-0880** • noon-2am • mostly gay men • popular • leather • occasional women's leather events • live music • patio

**Mecca 2.0** 181 3rd St (at W Hotel) • upscale lesbian event in San Francisco, happening every 3rd Friday from 6-9 pm in the UPSTAIRS bar of the W Hotel

## NIGHTCLUBS

**Asia SF** 201 9th St (at Howard) **415/255-2742** • 10pm-close Wed-Sat • popular • gay/straight • dancing/DJ • mostly Asian American • theme nights • go-go boys • cover charge • also Cal-Asian restaurant w/ en-drag dinner service

**BeatBox** 314 11th St **415/500-2675** • gay/straight • dancing/DJ • theme nights

**Bootie SF** 375 11th St (at Harrison, at DNA Lounge) **415/626-1409 (DNA INFO LINE)** • 9pm-3am Sat, • gay-friendly • dancing/DJ • mashups, bootlegs, bastard pop • cover charge

**Cat Club** 1190 Folsom St (at 8th) **415/703-8965** • gay/straight • dancing/DJ • hosts many one-night clubs & events

**The Crib SF** 715 Harrison St (at 3rd) • 9:30pm-2am Th only • lesbians/ gay men • dancing/DJ • younger crowd • 18+ • cover

**Endup** 401 6th St (at Harrison) **415/646-0999 (INFO LINE), 415/357-0827** • gay/ straight • dancing/DJ • multiracial • theme nights • popular Sun mornings

**Fever** 401 6th St (at Harrison, at Endup) • 11pm-11am Fri only • mostly gay men • dancing/DJ

**Go BANG!** 399 9th St (at The Stud) • 1st Sat only • lesbians/ gay men • underground 70s-80s disco

**Honey Soundsystem** • check site for events, local DJ collectiv • mostly men • dancing/DJ collective • bears

**Oasis** 298 11th St **415/595-3725** • 4pm-2am • mostly gay men • dancing/DJ • live shows • drag shows

**The Stud** 399 9th St (at Harrison) **415/863-6623** • 5pm-2am • popular • lesbians/ gay men • dancing/DJ • theme nights

**UHAUL SF** 314 11th St (at Beatbox) • mostly women • dancing/DJ • check site for event dates

## Restaurants

**Ame** 689 Mission St (at 3rd St, in St Regis Hotel) **415/284–4040** • lunch & dinner • full bar • reservations recommended

**Ananda Fuara** 1298 Market St (at 9th) **415/621–1994** • 8am-8pm, till 3pm Wed, clsd Sun • vegetarian

**Anchor & Hope** 83 Minna St (at 2nd St) **415/501–9100** • lunch Mon-Fri, dinner nightly • seafood

**Don Ramon's Mexican Restaurant** 225 11th St (btwn Howard & Folsom) **415/864–2700** • lunch Tue-Fri, dinner nightly, clsd Mon • some veggie • full bar

**Fringale** 570 4th St (btwn Bryant & Brannan) **415/543–0573** • lunch Tue-Fri & dinner nightly • French bistro • wheelchair access

**Rocco's Cafe** 1131 Folsom St (at 7th) **415/554–0522** • brkfst & lunch daily, dinner Wed-Sat only

**The Slanted Door** 1 Ferry Building #3 **415/861–8032** • popular • Vietnamese • full bar • reservations recommended

**Ted's** 1530 Howard St (at 11th) **415/552–0309** • 6am-6pm, 8am-5pm wknds • excellent deli sandwiches

**Tu Lan** 8 6th St (at Market) **415/626–0927** • lunch & dinner, clsd Sun • Vietnamese • some veggie • dicey neighborhood but delicious (& cheap) food

## Retail Shops

**Dandelion** 55 Potrero Ave (at Alameda St) **415/436–9500, 888/548–1968** • 10am-7pm, till 6pm Fri-Sat, noon-5pm Sun • gay-owned

**Mr S Leather & Fetters USA San Francisco** 385 8th St (at Harrison) **415/863–7764, 800/746–7677** • 11am-7pm • erotic goods • custom leather • latex

**Stompers** 323 10th St (at Folsom) **415/255–6422, 888/BOOTMAN** • 11am-6pm, noon-4pm Sun, clsd Mon

## Gyms & Health Clubs

**SF Fitness** 1001 Brannan St (at 9th) **415/348–6377** • popular • day passes available

## Erotica

**Good Vibrations** 899 Mission St (at 5th St) **415/513–1635, 800/289–8423** • 10am-9pm, till 11pm Fri-Sat • popular • clean, well-lighted sex toy store • wheelchair access

# SF—Polk Street Area

## Accommodations

**The Phoenix Hotel** 601 Eddy St (at Larkin) **415/776–1380, 800/248–9466** • gay-friendly • 1950s-style motor lodger • fave of celebrity rockers • pool • kids ok • WiFi

## Bars

**The Cinch** 1723 Polk St (at Clay) **415/776–4162** • 9am-2am, from 6am wknds • mostly gay men • neighborhood bar • patio • lots of pool tables & no attitude • DJ Th-Sat • drag shows Fri & Sun • WiFi • wheelchair access

**Edinburgh Castle** 950 Geary St (at Polk) **415/885–4074** • 5pm-2am • mostly straight Scottish pub w/ single malts & authentic fish & chips • live bands

**Gangway** 841 Larkin St (btwn Geary & O'Farrell) **415/776–6828** • 8am-2am • mostly gay men • dive neighborhood bar

**Lush Lounge** 1092 Post (at Polk) **415/771–2022** • 3pm-2am, from 1pm wknds • gay/ straight • wheelchair access

## Nightclubs

**Divas** 1081 Post St (at Larkin) **415/474–3482** • 7am-2am • mostly gay men • neighborhood bar • dancing/DJ • multiracial • transsexuals, transvestites & their admirers • drag shows

## Cafes

**La Boulange de Polk** 2310 Polk St (at Green St) **415/345–1107** • 7am-7pm • French bakery & cafe • outdoor seating • Parisian down to the attitude

## Restaurants

**Street** 2141 Polk St (btwn Broadway & Vallejo) **415/775–1055** • dinner, clsd Mon • incredible hamburgers

## Bookstores

**Books Inc Opera Plaza** 601 Van Ness Ave (at Turk) **415/776–1111** • 8:30am-9pm • independent • LGBT section • many readings

## Erotica

**Good Vibrations** 1620 Polk St (btwn Sacramento & Clay) **415/345–0400** • 10am-9pm, till 10pm Fri-Sat • clean, well-lighted sex toy store

# SF—Downtown & North Beach

## ACCOMMODATIONS

**Adante Hotel** 610 Geary St (at Jones) 415/673–9221, 888/423–0083 • gay/ straight • in Union Square/ Theater District • kids ok • nonsmoking • wheelchair access

**Andrews Hotel** 624 Post St (btwn Taylor & Jones) 415/563–6877, 800/926–3739 • gay-friendly • Victorian hotel • also restaurant • Italian • nonsmoking • WiFi

**Argonaut Hotel** 495 Jefferson St (at Hyde) 415/563–0800, 800/790–1415 • gay-friendly • boutique hotel in Fisherman's Wharf • pets ok • nonsmoking • wheelchair access

**Cartwright Hotel** 524 Sutter St (at Powell) 415/421–2865 • gay-friendly • B&B-inn on Union Square

**Executive Hotel Vintage Court** 650 Bush St (at Powell) 415/392–4666, 888/388–3932 • gay-friendly • nonsmoking • WiFi • also world-famous 5-star Masa's restaurant • French • wheelchair access

**Galleria Park Hotel** 191 Sutter St (at Kearny) 415/781–3060, 800/792–9639 • gay/ straight • boutique hotel • kids ok • WiFi • nonsmoking • wheelchair access

**Grand Hyatt San Francisco** 345 Stockton St (at Sutter) 415/398–1234 • gay-friendly • restaurant & lounge • gym

**Handlery Union Square Hotel** 351 Geary St (at Powell) 415/781–7800, 800/995–4874 • gay-friendly • steps from Union Square • pool • WiFi • wheelchair access

**Handlery Union Square Hotel** 351 Geary St (at Powell) 415/781–7800, 800/995–4874 • gay-friendly • steps from Union Square • pool • WiFi • wheelchair access

**Harbor Court Hotel** 165 Steuart St (btwn Howard & Mission) 415/882–1300, 866/792–6283 • gay-friendly • in the heart of the Financial District • gym • pool • pets ok • WiFi • wheelchair access

**Hilton San Francisco Financial District** 750 Kearny St (at Clay) 415/433–6600, 800/424–8292

**Hotel Adagio** 550 Geary St (at Shannon) 415/775–5000, 800/228–8830 • gay-friendly • hotel • kids ok • wheelchair access

**Hotel Carlton** 1075 Sutter (at Larkin) 415/673–0242, 800/922–7586 • gay-friendly • also Saha restaurant (Arabic-fusion)

**Hotel Diva** 440 Geary (at Mason) 415/885–0200, 800/553–1900 • gay-friendly • hip hotel • also gym • nonsmoking • WiFi

**Hotel Fusion** 140 Ellis St (at Powell St) 415/568–2525, 866/753–4244 • gay/ straight • nonsmoking • kids ok • WiFi • wheelchair access

**Hotel Griffon** 155 Steuart St (at Mission) 415/495–2100, 800/321–2201 • gay/ straight • WiFi • also restaurant • bistro/ cont'l • wheelchair access

**Hotel Mark Twain** 345 Taylor St (at Ellis) 415/673–2332, 877/854–4106 • gay-friendly • also Fish & Farm restaurant • wheelchair access

**Hotel Metropolis** 25 Mason St (at Eddy) 415/775–4600, 877/628–4412 • gay-friendly • near Union Square shopping • WiFi

**Hotel Nikko San Francisco** 222 Mason St (at Ellis) 415/394–1111, 866/645–5673 • gay-friendly • pool • health club & spa • nonsmoking • also restaurant • wheelchair access

**The Hotel Rex** 562 Sutter St (at Powell) 415/433–4434, 800/433–4434 • gay-friendly • full bar • wheelchair access

**Hotel Triton** 342 Grant Ave (at Bush) 415/394–0500, 800/800–1299 • gay/ straight • designer theme rooms • kids/ pets ok • WiFi • wheelchair access

**Hotel Union Square** 114 Powell St (at Ellis) 415/397–3000, 800/553–1900 • gay-friendly • 1930s art deco lobby • WiFi

**Hotel Vitale** 8 Mission St (at Steuart) 415/278–3700, 888/890–8688 • gay-friendly • 4-star, full-service waterfront luxury hotel • rooftop spa • restaurant & bar • nonsmoking • WiFi • wheelchair access

**Hotel Zetta** 55 5th St 415/543–8555 • gay/straight • WiFi • gym & restaurant on-site

**Hyatt Regency San Francisco** 5 Embarcadero Center (at California) 415/788–1234, 800/233–1234 • gay-friendly • luxury waterfront hotel • WiFi

**The Inn at Union Square** 440 Post St (at Powell) 415/397–3510, 800/288–4346 • gay-friendly • complimentary breakfast and wine and cheese daily • WiFi

**Kensington Park Hotel** 450 Post St 415/788–6400 • gay-friendly • on Union Square • nonsmoking • WiFi • also Farallon Restaurant

**Nob Hill Hotel** 835 Hyde St (btwn Bush & Sutter) 415/885-2987, 877/662-4455 • gay/ straight • European-style hotel • jacuzzi • nonsmoking • kids ok • also restaurant • wheelchair access

**Petite Auberge** 863 Bush St (at Taylor) 415/928-6000, 800/365-3004 • gay-friendly • B&B • kids ok • nonsmoking

**Prescott Hotel** 545 Post St (btwn Taylor & Mason) 415/563-0303, 866/271-3632 • gay-friendly • small luxury hotel • nonsmoking • WiFi

**Sir Francis Drake Hotel** 450 Powell St (at Sutter) 415/392-7755, 800/795-7129 • gay-friendly • 1928 landmark • also restaurant & Starlight Room • WiFi

**Vertigo Hotel** 940 Sutter St (at Leavenworth) 415/885-6800, 888/444-4605 • gay/ straight • boutique hotel • nonsmoking • WiFi • wheelchair access

## BARS

**Aunt Charlie's Lounge** 133 Turk St (at Taylor) 415/441-2922 • 10am-midnight, till 2am Fri- Sat • mostly gay men • neighborhood bar • drag shows wknds

**Bourbon & Branch** 501 Jones St (at O'Farrell) 415/931-7292 • gay/ straight • in Prohibition-era speakeasy • drinks are worth the price • reservations required

## CAFES

**Caffe Trieste** 601 Vallejo St 415/392-6739 • get a taste of the real North Beach (past & present)

**Sugar Cafe** 679 Sutter St (at Taylor) 415/441-5678 • 10am-2am, from 8am wknds • cafe by day, cocktails by night • food served • WiFi

## RESTAURANTS

**The Buena Vista** 2765 Hyde St (at Beach) 415/474-5044 • 9am-2am, from 8am wknds • the restaurant that introduced Irish coffee to America

**Le Colonial** 20 Cosmo Pl (btwn Taylor & Jones) 415/931-3600 • dinner nightly, wknd brunch • Vietnamese • full bar

**Mario's Bohemian Cigar Store Cafe** 566 Columbus Ave (at Union) 415/362-0536 • 10am-close • great foccacia sandwiches • some veggie • beer/ wine • WiFi

## ENTERTAINMENT & RECREATION

**Rrazz Room** 222 Mason (at Nikko Hotel) 415/394-1189, 800/380-3095 • gay/ straight • cabaret w/ world-class performers • wheelchair access

**Sunday's A Drag@The Starlight Room** 450 Mason St (at Sutter) 415/395-8595 • Sun brunch • noon & 2:30pm drag shows

## BOOKSTORES

**Book Passage** 1 Ferry Bldg #42 415/835-1020 • 10am-8pm, from 8am Sat, 10am-7pm Sun-Mon • independent

**City Lights Bookstore** 261 Columbus Ave (at Pacific) 415/362-8193 • 10am-midnight • historic beatnik bookstore • many progressive titles • LGBT section • whole floor for poetry

## RETAIL SHOPS

**Dragonfly Ink** 490 Post St #1701 415/550-1445 • tattoo studio • woman-owned

## SEX CLUBS

**Power Exchange** 220 Jones St 415/487-9944 • play space open to hetero, gay, bi, trans, men & women

## EROTICA

**Good Vibrations** 189 Kearny St (at Sutter) 415/653-1364 • 11am-8pm, till 6pm Sun • popular • clean, well-lighted sex toy store • wheelchair access

# SF—Mission District

includes Bernal Heights

## ACCOMMODATIONS

**The Inn San Francisco** 943 S Van Ness Ave (btwn 20th & 21st) 415/641-0188, 800/359-0913 • gay-friendly • Victorian mansion • hot tub • some shared baths • kitchens • fireplaces • patio • nonsmoking • WiFi

**Noe's Nest B&B** 1257 Guerrero St (btwn 24th & 25th Sts) 415/821-0751 • gay-friendly • WiFi • nonsmoking • kids ok

## BARS

**El Rio** 3158 Mission St (at Cesar Chavez) 415/282-3325 • 5pm-close Mon-Th, from 3pm wknds • popular • gay/ straight • frequent women's events • neighborhood bar • multiracial • live shows • patio

**Nihon** 1779 Folsom St (at 14th St) 415/552-4400 • 6pm-close, clsd Sun • gay/ straight • whiskey lounge • dancing/DJ • also Japanese restaurant

**Phone Booth** 1398 S Van Ness Ave (at 25th) 415/648-4683 • 1pm-2am • lesbians/ gay men • neighborhood/dive bar

**Virgil's Sea Room** 3152 Mission St (at Precita) 415/829-2233 • 4pm-2am, from 2pm wknds • gay/straight, lesbian-owned

**Wild Side West** 424 Cortland, Bernal Heights (at Wool) **415/647-3099** • 2pm-2am • gay/ straight • neighborhood bar • patio • magic garden • wheelchair access

**Zeitgeist** 199 Valencia St (at Duboce) **415/255-7505** • 9am-2am • divey biker bar & beer garden • food served

## NIGHTCLUBS

**Hard French** 3158 Mission (at El Rio) • 2pm-8pm 1st Sat only • lesbians/ gay men • soul dance party • food served

**The Make-Out Room** 3225 22nd St (at Mission) **415/647-2888** • 6pm-2am • gay/ straight • dancing/DJ

**Mango** 3158 Mission (at El Rio) **415/339-8310** • 3pm-8:30pm 4th Sat March-Nov • women only • dancing/DJ • multiracial • food served • cover

**Mighty** 119 Utah St (at 15th St) **415/762-0151** • gay-friendly • dancing/DJ • call for events

**Stay Gold** 161 Erie St (at Mission, at Public Works) • 10:30pm last Wed only • lesbians/ gay men • dancing/DJ

**Sundance Saloon** 550 Barneveld Ave (at space550, 2 blocks off Bayshore Blvd at Industrial) **415/820-1403** • 5pm-10:30pm Sun (lessons at 5:30pm) & 6:30pm-10:30pm Th (lessons at 7pm) • lesbians/ gay men • dancing/DJ • country/ western • gay-owned • cover

## CAFES

**Dolores Park Cafe** 501 Dolores St (at 18th St) **415/621-2936** • 7am-8pm • outdoor seating overlooking Dolores Park • live music Fri

**Farleys** 1315 18th St (at Texas St, Potrero Hill) **415/648-1545** • 6:30am-9:30pm, from 7:30am wknds • coffeehouse • live music some nights

**The Revolution Cafe** 3248 22nd St (btwn Mission & Bartlett) **415/642-0474** • 9am-1am • live music

**Tartine Bakery** 600 Guerrero St (at 18th St) **415/487-2600** • 8am-7pm, from 9am Sun • French bakery w/ a line out the door

## RESTAURANTS

**Aslam's Rasoi** 1037 Valencia St (at 21st) **415/695-0599** • 5pm-11pm • Indian & Pakistani

**Delfina** 3621 18th St (at Dolores) **415/552-4055** • 5:30pm-10pm • popular • excellent Tuscan cuisine • full bar • reservations required • patio (summers)

**El Farolito** 2779 Mission St (at 24th) **415/824-7877** • popular • 10am-3am • delicious, cheap burritos & more

**Farina** 3560 18th St (at Guerrero) **415/565-0360** • dinner nightly, Sun brunch • Italian

**Just For You** 722 22nd St (at 3rd St) **415/647-3033** • 7:30am-3pm • popular • lesbians/ gay men • Southern brkfst • some veggie • women-owned

**Luna Park** 694 Valencia St (at 18th) **415/553-8584** • lunch & dinner, wknd brunch

**Moki's Sushi & Pacific Grill** 615 Cortland Ave (at Moultine) **415/970-9336** • dinner nightly

**Pauline's Pizza Pie** 260 Valencia St (btwn 14th & Duboce) **415/552-2050** • 5pm-10pm, clsd Sun-Mon • popular • gourmet pizza • beer/ wine

**Picaro** 3120 16th St (at Valencia) **415/431-4089** • 5pm-10pm, from 9:30am wknds • Spanish tapas bar • beer/ wine • wheelchair access

**Pork Store Cafe** 3122 16th St (at Valencia) **415/626-5523** • 8am-4pm daily & 7pm-3am Fri-Sat • popular • American/ diner food • great brkfsts • also 1451 Haight St, 415/864-6981

**Range** 842 Valencia St (btwn 19th & 20th Sts) **415/282-8283** • dinner nightly • popular • California contemporary • full bar

**Slow Club** 2501 Mariposa (at Hampshire) **415/241-9390** • lunch Mon-Fri, dinner Mon-Sat, wknd brunch • full bar • wheelchair access

## ENTERTAINMENT & RECREATION

**Dolores "Beach"** Church & 19th St (at the top corner of Dolores Park) • popular "beach" in Dolores Park • crowded on sunny days

## BOOKSTORES

**Dog Eared Books** 900 Valencia St (at 20th) **415/282-1901** • 10am-10pm, till 8pm Sun • new & used • good LGBT section

**Modern Times Bookstore** 2919 24th St (at Alabama) **415/282-9246**

## RETAIL SHOPS

**Black & Blue Tattoo** 381 Guerrero St (at 16th St) **415/626-0770** • noon-7pm • queer-, gender-fluid-, trans- & POC-friendly • women-owned

**Body Manipulations** 3234 16th St (btwn Guerrero & Dolores) **415/621-0408** • noon-7pm, from 2pm Mon-Th • piercing (walk-in basis) • jewelry

**The Scarlet Sage** 1193 Valencia St (near 23rd St) 415/821-0997 • 11am-6pm • spiritual & metaphysical emporium • lesbian-owned

### EROTICA

**Good Vibrations** 603 Valencia St (at 17th St) 415/522-5460, 800/289-8423 • 10am-9pm, till 11pm Fri-Sat • popular • clean, well-lighted sex toy store • wheelchair access

## SF—Haight, Fillmore, Hayes Valley

### ACCOMMODATIONS

**The Buchanan** 1800 Sutter St (at Buchanan) 415/921-4000 • gay-friendly • in Japantown • restaurant & bar • nonsmoking • WiFi

**The Chateau Tivoli B&B** 1057 Steiner St (at Golden Gate) 415/776-5462, 800/228-1647 • gay-friendly • historic San Francisco B&B • nonsmoking • WiFi

**Hayes Valley Inn** 417 Gough St (at Hayes) 415/431-9131, 800/930-7999 • gay/straight • European-style pension • shared baths • close to opera & symphony • nonsmoking • WiFi

**Hotel Del Sol** 3100 Webster St (at Greenwich) 415/921-5520, 877/433-5765 • popular • gay/ straight • pool • nonsmoking • wheelchair access • WiFi

**Hotel Drisco** 2901 Pacific Ave (at Broderick) 415/346-2880, 800/634-7277 • gay-friendly • 1903 hotel in Pacific Heights • kids ok • nonsmoking

**Hotel Kabuki** 1625 Post St (at Laguna) 415/922-3200, 800/533-4567 • gay-friendly • in the heart of Japantown • wheelchair access

**Inn at the Opera** 333 Fulton St (at Franklin) 415/863-8400, 866/729-7182 • gay-friendly • restaurant on site • WiFi • wheelchair access

**Jackson Court** 2198 Jackson St (at Buchanan) 415/929-7670 • gay-friendly • 19th-c brownstone mansion • nonsmoking • kids ok • WiFi

**The Laurel Inn** 444 Presidio Ave (at Sacramento) 415/567-8467, 800/552-8735 • gay-friendly • hotel • in Pacific Heights • nonsmoking • kids/ pets ok

**Metro Hotel** 319 Divisadero St (at Haight) 415/861-5364 • gay-friendly • European-style pension • WiFi

**Queen Anne Hotel** 1590 Sutter St (at Octavia) 415/441-2828, 800/227-3970 • gay-friendly • wood-burning fireplaces • kids ok • nonsmoking • WiFi • gay-owned • (mention Damron for discount)

**Stanyan Park Hotel** 750 Stanyan St (at Waller) 415/751-1000 • gay-friendly • restored Victorian hotel listed on the Nat'l Register of Historic Places • kids ok • completely nonsmoking • WiFi • wheelchair access

### BARS

**Rickshaw Stop** 155 Fell St (btwn Van Ness & Franklin) 415/861-2011 • Wed-Sat only, Cockblock 2nd Sat • popular hipster bar, nightclub (live bands) & restaurant+

**Trax** 1437 Haight St (at Masonic) 415/864-4213 • noon-2am • mostly gay men • neighborhood bar

### NIGHTCLUBS

**Cockblock** 155 Fell St (at Rickshaw Shop) • 10pm-2am 2nd Sat • queer dance party for lezzies, the happy gays, you & your friends • multiracial

**Underground SF** 424 Haight St (at Webster) 415/745-1921 • 10pm-2am, clsd Sun • gay/ straight • dancing/DJ • alternative • theme nights • call for events • more gay Sat

### CAFES

**Blue Bottle Coffee Company** 315 Linden St (at Gough St) 510/653-3394 • 7am-6pm, from 8am wknds • popular • organic coffee & treats from kiosk in front of artists' workshop—wonderful hidden treat

### RESTAURANTS

**Absinthe Brasserie & Bar** 398 Hayes St (at Gough) 415/551-1590 • lunch & dinner, bar till 2am Fri-Sat, clsd Mon • upscale SF classic

**Alamo Square Seafood Grill** 803 Fillmore (at Grove) 415/440-2828 • dinner only

**Burma Superstar** 309 Clement St 415/387-2147 • lunch & dinner • Burmese food that will rock your world

**Eliza's** 2877 California (at Broderick) 415/621-4819 • lunch Mon-Wed, dinner nightly • excellent Chinese food

**Ella's** 500 Presidio Ave (at California) 415/441-5669 • brkfst & lunch Mon-Fri, popular wknd brunch

**Garibaldi's** 347 Presidio Ave (at Sacramento) 415/563-8841 • lunch weekdays, dinner nightly • Mediterranean • full bar • wheelchair access • gay-owned

**Greens** Fort Mason, Bldg A (near Van Ness & Bay) 415/771-6222 • lunch Tue-Sat, dinner Mon-Sat, Sun brunch • gourmet vegetarian • spectacular view of the Golden Gate Bridge

**Memphis Minnie's BBQ** 576 Haight St **415/864-7675** • 11am-10pm, till 9pm Sun, clsd Mon

**Nopa** 560 Divisadero St (at Hayes) **415/864-8643** • dinner 6pm-1am, bar from 5pm • urban rustic

**Patxi's Chicago Pizza** 511 Hayes St (at Octavia St) **415/558-9991** • 11am-10pm, clsd Mon • Chicago-style deep dish pizza • also thin crust

**Suppenküche** 601 Hayes (at Laguna) **415/252-9289** • dinner, Sun brunch • German cuisine served at communal tables • beer/ wine • gay-owned

**Thep-Phanom** 400 Waller St (at Fillmore) **415/431-2526** • 5:30pm-10:30pm • popular • excellent Thai food (worth the wait!) • beer/ wine

## BOOKSTORES

**The Booksmith** 1644 Haight St **415/863-8688** • cool independent • big-name author readings

## RETAIL SHOPS

**Cold Steel America** 1783 Haight St **415/621-7233** • noon-8pm • piercing & tattoo studio

**Flight 001** 525 Hayes St (btwn Octavia & Laguna) **415/487-1001, 877/354-4481** • 11am-7pm, till 6pm Sun • way cool travel gear

**Timbuk 2 Store** 506 Hayes St **415/252-9860** • 11am-7pm, noon-6pm Sun, messenger-style bags & backpacks

## GYMS & HEALTH CLUBS

**Kabuki Springs & Spa** 1750 Geary Blvd (at Fillmore) **415/922-6000** • 10am-9:45pm • traditional Japanese bath w/ extensive menu of spa services

# San Jose

## INFO LINES & SERVICES

**AA Gay/ Lesbian** 274 E Hamilton Ave, Ste D, Campbell **408/374-8511** • 24hr helpline • check www.aasanjose.org for meetings

**Billy DeFrank LGBT Community Center** 938 The Alameda **408/293-3040** • 3pm-9pm, from 10am Wed, clsd Sat-Mon • wheelchair access

## ACCOMMODATIONS

**Hotel De Anza** 233 W Santa Clara St **408/286-1000, 800/843-3700** • gay-friendly • art deco gem • nonsmoking • Italian restaurant • wheelchair access

**Moorpark Hotel** 4241 Moorpark Ave **408/864-0300, 877/740-6622** • gay-friendly • hotel in heart of Silicon Valley • pool • also bar & restaurant • wheelchair access

## BARS

**The Caravan Lounge** 98 S Almaden Ave **408/995-6220** • 11am-2am, from 6am Fri-Sun • gat/straight • neighborhood bar • karaoke

**Mac's Club** 39 Post St (btwn 1st & Market) **408/288-8221** • noon-2am • mostly men • neighborhood bar • patio

**Renegades** 501 W Taylor St (at Coleman Ave) **408/275-9902** • 2pm-2am • mostly gay men • neighborhood bar • leather • patio

## NIGHTCLUBS

**Splash** 65 Post St (at 1st) **408/292-2222** • 4pm-2am ,from 3pm Sun • mostly gay men • dancing/DJ • karaoke • videos • gay-owned

## RESTAURANTS

**Pasta Pomodoro** 1205 The Alameda (at Race) **408/292-9929** • Italian

**Vin Santo** 1346 Lincoln Ave **408/920-2508** • dinner nightly, clsd Mon • Northern Italian • wine bar

## ENTERTAINMENT & RECREATION

**Tech Museum of Innovation** 201 S Market St (at Park Ave) **408/294-8324** • 10am-5pm • IMAX Dome Theater • a must-see for digital junkies

## EROTICA

**Leather Masters** 969 Park Ave (at Race St) **408/293-7660** • noon-8pm, clsd Sun-Mon • handmade leather clothes • rubber/ fetishwear • electrical/ medical gear, etc

**Pleasures from the Heart** 1565 Winchester Blvd, Campbell **408/871-1826** • 11am-10pm, 1pm-7pm Sun • intimate apparel, toys & gifts • women-owned

# San Luis Obispo

## INFO LINES & SERVICES

**GALA/ Gay & Lesbian Alliance of the Central Coast** 1060 Palm St (at Santa Rosa St) **805/541-4252** • 8am-noon & 1pm-5pm , clsd wknds

## ACCOMMODATIONS

**The Madonna Inn** 100 Madonna Rd **805/543-3000, 800/543-9666** • gay-friendly • one-of-a-kind theme rooms • food served • pool

**The Palomar Inn** 1601 Shell Beach Rd, Shell Beach **888/384-4004** • gay/ straight • motel • nonsmoking • WiFi

**Sycamore Mineral Springs Resort** 1215 Avila Beach Dr **805/595-7302, 800/234-5831** • gay-friendly • hot mineral spring spa • integrative retreat center • also award-winning restaurant

## BARS

**Fuel Dock** 900 Main St, Morro Bay **805/772-8478** • gay-friendly • live music on Sun

**Gaslight Lounge** 2143 Broad St **805/543-4262** • gay-friendly dive bar

**Legends** 899 Main St, Morro Bay **805/772-2525** • gay-friendly

**The Library** 723 Higuera St **805/542-0199** • gay-friendly • dancing/DJ • wheelchair access

## CAFES

**Linnaea's Cafe** 1110 Garden St (near Marsh) **805/541-5888** • 6:30am-11pm • plenty veggie • WiFi • live entertainment

**Outspoken Cafe** 1422 Monterey St (at California) **805/788-0885** • 7am-4pm, clsd wknds • cafe & juice bar • lesbian-owned

## RESTAURANTS

**Big Sky Cafe** 1121 Broad St (btwn Higuera & Marsh Sts) **805/545-5401** • 7am-10pm, 8am-9pm Sun-Th • plenty veggie/vegan

**High Street Deli** 350 High St **805/541-4738** • 7am-7pm, 8am-3pm Sun

**Novo** 726 Higuera St **805/543-3986** • lunch & dinner • great outdoor seating

**Vieni Vai** 690 Higuera St **805/544-5282** • lunch & dinner, Sun brunch • Italian

## ENTERTAINMENT & RECREATION

**Pirate's Cove Beach** 404 Front St, Avila Beach • gay/straight • nude beach

## BOOKSTORES

**Coalesce Bookstore** 845 Main St, Morro Bay **805/772-2880** • 10am-5:30pm, 11am-4pm Sun • LGBT section • women-owned

**Volumes of Pleasure** 1016 Los Osos Valley Rd, Los Osos **805/528-5565** • 10am-6pm, clsd Sun-Mon • wheelchair access • lesbian-owned

## PUBLICATIONS

**GALA News & Reviews** **805/541-4252** • news & events for Central California coast

# San Rafael

see Marin County

# San Ramon

see East Bay

# Santa Ana

see Orange County

# Santa Barbara

see also Ventura

## INFO LINES & SERVICES

**Pacific Pride Foundation** 126 E Haley St #A-11 **805/963-3636** • 9am-5pm Mon-Fri

## ACCOMMODATIONS

**Canary Hotel** 31 W Carrillo **805/884-0300, 866/999-5401** • gay-friendly

**Inn of the Spanish Garden** 915 Garden St (at Carrillo) **805/564-4700, 866/564-4700** • gay/straight • luxury hotel • pool • nonsmoking • kids ok • wheelchair access

**Old Yacht Club Inn** 431 Corona Del Mar Dr **805/962-1277, 800/676-1676** • gay-friendly • only B&B on beach • full brkfst • nonsmoking • WiFi

## BARS

**Reds Wine Bar** 211 Helena Ave **805/966-5906** • 2pm-10pm, till 2am Th-Sat, clsd Mon • food served • live music • WiFi

## NIGHTCLUBS

**Wildcat Lounge** 15 W Ortega St **805/962-7970** • gay/straight • more gay Sun • popular • dancing/DJ

## CAFES

**Our Daily Bread** 2700 De La Vina St **805/966-3894** • 6am-3pm, 7am-2pm wknds• bakery/cafe

## RESTAURANTS

**Joe's Cafe** 536 State St **805/966-4638** • 7:30am-11pm

**The Natural Cafe** 508 State St **805/962-9494** • 11am-9pm

**Opal Restaurant & Bar** 1325 State St (at Sola St) **805/966-9676** • lunch (Mon-Sat) & dinner nightly • full bar

**Sojourner Cafe** 134 E Canon Perdido (at Santa Barbara) **805/965-7922** • 11am-10pm, till 11pm Th-Sat • plenty veggie • beer/wine • wheelchair access

## ENTERTAINMENT & RECREATION

**Santa Barbara Mission** 2201 Laguna St **805/682-4713** • the "queen of the missions" • take a self-guided tour btwn 9am-4:30pm daily & find out why

## BOOKSTORES

**Chaucer's Books** 3321 State St (at Las Positas Rd, Loreto Plaza) **805/682–6787** • 9am–9pm, till 6pm Sun • popular •

## EROTICA

**The Riviera Adult Superstore** 4135 State St (at Hwy 154 intersection) **805/967–8282** • 10am–midnight • pride items • community resources

# Santa Clara

## ACCOMMODATIONS

**Avatar Hotel** 4200 Great America Pkwy **408/235–8900, 800/586–5691** • gay/ straight • nonsmoking • hotspot in Silicon Valley • WiFi • wheelchair access

**Biltmore Hotel & Suites** 2151 Laurelwood Rd (at Montague Expwy) **408/988–8411, 800/255–9925** • gay-friendly • pool • also restaurant & gym • nonsmoking • WiFi

# Santa Cruz

## INFO LINES & SERVICES

**AA Gay/ Lesbian** 5732 Soquel Dr, Soquel **831/475–5782 (AA#)** • call or visit www.aasantacruz.org for meetings

**The Diversity Center** 1117 Soquel Ave (at Cayuga) **831/425–5422** • open daily • call for events • WiFi

## ACCOMMODATIONS

**Chaminade Resort & Spa** 1 Chaminade Ln (at Soquel Ave) **831/475–5600, 800/283–6569** • gay-friendly • pool • nonsmoking • wheelchair access

**Dream Inn** 175 W Cliff Dr **831/426–4330, 866/774–7735** • gay/ straight • restaurant • pool & hot tub • WiFi • wheelchair access

## NIGHTCLUBS

**Blue Lagoon** 923 Pacific Ave **831/423–7117** • 3:30pm–2am • gay-friendly • dancing/DJ • alternative • transgender-friendly • videos • live bands • wheelchair access

## RESTAURANTS

**Betty Burgers** 505 Seabright Ave (at Murray) **831/423–8190** • 10am–10pm • retro burger joint • outdoor seating • some veggie

**Cafe Limelight** 1016 Cedar St (at Locust St) **831/425–7873** • lunch & dinner, clsd Mon • European • transgender-friendly • wheelchair access • gay-owned

**Cilantros Mexican Restaurant** 1934 Main St (in Town Center strip mall), Watsonville **831/761–2161** • lunch & dinner

**Crepe Place** 1134 Soquel Ave (at Seabright, across from Rio Theater) **831/429–6994** • 11am–midnight, from 9am Sat-Sun • live music • full bar • garden patio • wheelchair access

**Saturn Cafe** 145 Laurel St (at Pacific) **831/429–8505** • 10am–3am • vegetarian diner • lesbian-owned

**Silver Spur** 2650 Soquel Dr **831/475–2725** • 6am–3pm, clsd Sun

## ENTERTAINMENT & RECREATION

**Bonny Doon Beach** Hwy 1 at Bonny Doon Rd (at milepost 27.6, N of Santa Cruz) • gay/ straight • park in paved parking lot • nude side of beach to the north

## BOOKSTORES

**Bookshop Santa Cruz** 1520 Pacific Ave **831/423–0900** • 9am–10pm • cafe • wheelchair access

## GYMS & HEALTH CLUBS

**Kiva Retreat House Spa** 702 Water St (at Ocean) **831/429–1142** • noon–11pm, till midnight Fri-Sat • check for women-only & men-only hours

## EROTICA

**Frenchy's Cruzin Books & Video** 3960 Portola Dr (at 41st Ave) **831/475–9221** • arcade, adult novelties, lingerie & DVDs

# Santa Rosa

see Sonoma County

# Saratoga

## RETAIL SHOPS

**Vine Life** 14572-A Big Basin Way **408/872–1500** • 11am–5pm • wine, cards & gifts

# Sausalito

see Marin County

# Sebastopol

see also Russian River & Sonoma County

# Sonoma County

see also Russian River

## INFO LINES & SERVICES

**AA Meetings in Sonoma County** **707/544–1300 (AA#), 800/224–1300** • call or visit www.sonomacountyaa.org for meetings

**Sonoma County Tourism** 707/522–5800, 800/576-6662 • Sonoma County, located 30 miles from San Francisco, provides a genuine, independent, and adventurous wine country experience, featuring more than 425 wineries, 100-plus organic farms, and 55 miles of stunning Pacific coast • for a free visitors guide or information on hotels, wineries, events, spas, attractions and dining in Sonoma County, visit www.sonomacounty.com

## Accommodations

**An Inn 2 Remember** 171 W Spain St (at First St W), Sonoma 707/938-2909 • gay-friendly • located in Wine Country • whirlpool baths & fireplaces • free use of bikes • nonsmoking • WiFi

**Beltane Ranch** 11775 Sonoma Hwy (Hwy 12), Glen Ellen 707/996-6501 • gay-friendly • 1892 New Orleans-style ranch house

**Best Western Dry Creek Inn** 198 Dry Creek Rd, Healdsburg 707/433-0300, 800/222-5784 • gay/ straight • near wineries • pool, gym steam & sauna • pets ok • WiFi

**Camellia Inn** 211 North St (at Fitch), Healdsburg 707/433-8182, 800/727-8182 • gay-friendly • Italianate Victorian • full brkfst • pool • nonsmoking • WiFi

**The Gaige House** 13540 Arnold Dr, Glen Ellen 707/935-0237, 800/935-0237 • gay-friendly • boutique hotel in the Wine Country • pool • WiFi

**Grape Leaf Inn** 539 Johnson St, Healdsburg 707/433-8140, 866/433-8140 • gay-friendly • Queen Anne Victorian • full brkfst • WiFi

**Hyatt Vineyard Creek Hotel** 170 Railroad St (at Third St), Santa Rosa 707/284-1234 • gay-friendly • resort • pool • kids/ pets ok • WiFi • seafood restaurant • wheelchair access

**Madrona Manor** 1001 Westside Rd, Healdsburg 707/433-4231, 800/258-4003 • gay-friendly • full brkfst • pool • nonsmoking • some rooms ok for kids • also restaurant • wheelchair access

**Magliulo's Rose Garden Inn** 681 Broadway (at Andrieux), Sonoma 707/996-1031 • gay-friendly • WiFi • wheelchair access

**Sonoma Chalet** 18935 5th St W, Sonoma 707/938-3129, 800/938-3129 • gay-friendly • B&B inn & cottages • hot tub

**Sonoma's Best Guest Cottages** 1190 E Napa St (at 8th St E), Sonoma 707/933-0340, 800/291-8962 • gay-friendly • vacation cottages • kids/ pets ok • WiFi

## Cafes

**A' Roma Roasters** 95 5th St (Railroad Square), Santa Rosa 707/576-7765 • 6am-close, from 7am Sat-Sun • lesbians/ gay men • live music wknds • wheelchair access • lesbian-owned

**Coffee Catz** 6761 Sebastopol Ave #300 (in Gravenstein Station), Sebastopol 707/829-6600 • 7am-6pm, till 10pm Wed (open mic), till 10pm Fri-Sat (live bands) • garden • WiFi

**Screamin' Mimi's** 6902 Sebastopol Ave (intersection of Hwy 12 & 116), Sebastopol 707/823-5902 • espresso drinks & homemade ice cream

**Sonoma's Best** 1190 E Napa St (at 8th St E), Sonoma 707/996-7600 • 7:30am-6pm, 8am-5pm Sun • local products—cheese, wine, olive oils & more—all under one roof

## Restaurants

**Fig Cafe & Wine Bar** 13690 Arnold Dr, Glen Ellen 707/938-2130 • dinner nightly, Sun brunch

**Mom's Apple Pie** 4550 Gravenstein Hwy N, Sebastopol 707/823-8330 • pie worth stopping for on your way to & from Russian River!

**Singletree Inn** 165 Healdsburg Ave, Healdsburg 707/433-8263 • 7am-3pm • good brkfsts • famous BBQ sandwiches (including tofu) • some veggie • local wines • outdoor seating • lesbian-owned

**Slice of Life** 6970 McKinley St, Sebastopol 707/829-6627 • 11am-9pm, from 9am Sat-Sun, clsd Mon • vegan & vegetarian

## Entertainment & Recreation

**Out In The Vineyard** 707/495-9732 • LGBT luxury wine event & tour company • gay-owned

**River's Edge Kayak & Canoe Company** 707/433-7247 • river excursions • lesbian-owned

## Retail Shops

**Grower's Collective Tasting Room** 707/996-1364 • noon-5:30pm, clsd Tue-Th, open wknds only in winter

**Milk & Honey** 123 N Main St, Sebastopol 707/824-1155 • 11am-7pm • transgender-friendly • goddess- & woman-oriented crafts • cafe

EROTICA

**Secrets Santa Rosa** 3301 Santa Rosa Ave (at Todd), Santa Rosa **707/542-8248**

## Springville

ACCOMMODATIONS

**Great Energy** PO Box 473, 93265 **559/539-2382** • lesbians/ gay men • retreat in foothills of Sierra Nevada mtns • pool • hiking • kids ok • woman-owned

## Stockton

see also Modesto

NIGHTCLUBS

**Paradise Club** 10100 N Lower Sacramento Rd (near Grider) **209/477-4724** • 6pm-2am, from 3pm Sun • lesbians/ gay men • dancing/DJ • live shows • young crowd

EROTICA

**Suzie's Adult Superstores** 3126 E Hammer Ln **209/952-6900** • 24hrs

## Sunnyvale

see also San Jose

ACCOMMODATIONS

**Wild Palms Hotel** 910 E Fremont Ave (at Wolfe Ave) **408/738-0500, 800/538-1600** • gay-friendly • pool • hot tub • kids ok • WiFi • wheelchair access

## Tiburon

see Marin County

## Twentynine Palms

see Joshua Tree Nat'l Park

## Ukiah

BARS

**Perkins St Lounge** 228 E Perkins St **707/462-0327** • 3pm-2am • gay-friendly • dancing/DJ • live shows • karaoke

## Upland

EROTICA

**Sensations Love Boutique** 1656 W Foothill Blvd (at Mountain) **909/985-1654**

## Vacaville

INFO LINES & SERVICES

**Solano Pride Center** 1234 Empire St #1560, Fairfield **707/398-3463** • call for meeting times

## Vallejo

includes Benicia

BARS

**Town House Cocktail Lounge** 401-A Georgia St (at Marin) **707/553-9109** • 1pm-midnight, from 10am Sat-Sun • gay/ straight • neighborhood bar • gay-owned

BOOKSTORES

**Bookshop Benicia** 856 Southampton Rd, Benicia **707/747-5155** • 10am-7pm, till 6pm wknds • wheelchair access

## Ventura

see also Santa Barbara

INFO LINES & SERVICES

**AA Gay/ Lesbian** 805/389-1444 (AA#), 800/990-7750

BARS

**Paddy McDermott's** 2 W Main St (at Ventura) **805/652-1071** • 2pm-2am • lesbians/ gay men • dancing/DJ • food served • live shows • karaoke • beer busts

EROTICA

**Three Star Books** 359 E Main St **805/653-9068** • 24hrs

## Victorville

BARS

**Ricky's** 13728 Hesperia Rd #12 **760/951-5400** • 6pm-2am, clsd Mon • gay/ straight • dancing/DJ • food served • karaoke • wheelchair access

## Walnut Creek

see East Bay

## Yosemite Nat'l Park

ACCOMMODATIONS

**The Ahwahnee Hotel** Yosemite Valley Floor **866/875-8456 (RESERVATIONS)** • gay-friendly • pool • non-smoking • also restaurant

**Highland House B&B** 3125 Wild Dove Ln (at Jerseydale Rd), Mariposa **209/966-3737** • gay-friendly • B&B near Yosemite & Sierra Nat'l Forest • kids ok

**The Homestead** 41110 Rd 600, Ahwahnee 559/683–0495, 800/483–0495 • gay-friendly • cottages, suite & 2-bdrm house nestled under the oaks on 160 acres • close to restaurants, golf, hiking & biking • kitchens • fireplaces • nonsmoking • WiFi • kids ok

**June Lake Villager** 2640 Hwy 158 (2.5 miles W of Hwy 395), June Lake 760/648–7712, 800/655–6545 • gay-friendly • 20 minutes from Yosemite • jacuzzi • nonsmoking • kids/pets ok • women-owned

**Queen's Inn by the River** 41139 Hwy 41, Oakhurst 559/683–4354 • gay/ straight • private patios & decks • some fireplaces • garden w/ river view • nonsmoking • WiFi • wheelchair access • lesbian-owned

**Tenaya Lodge at Yosemite** 1122 Hwy 41, Fish Camp 559/683–6555, 888/514–2167 • gay-friendly • resort w/ spa services • restaurant • pets ok • pool

**Yosemite View Lodge** 11136 Hwy 140, El Portal 209/379–2681, 888/742–4371 • gay-friendly • 3 pools • lounge & 2 restaurants • wheelchair access

**Yosemite's Apple Blossom Inn B&B** 559/642–2001, 888/687–4281 • gay-friendly • B&B • 20 minutes from south entrance of Yosemite Nat'l Park • hot tub • kids/ pets ok • nonsmoking • wheelchair access

# COLORADO

## Aspen

### ACCOMMODATIONS

**Aspen Mountain Lodge** 311 W Main St 970/925–7650, 800/362–7736 • gay-friendly • full brkfst • après-ski wine & cheese • kids/pets ok • hot tub • pool • nonsmoking

**Hotel Aspen** 110 W Main St 970/925–3441, 800/527–7369 • gay-friendly • mountain brkfst • après-ski wine & cheese • hot tub • pool • nonsmoking • kids/ pets ok

**Hotel Lenado** 200 S Aspen St 970/925–6246, 800/321–3457 • gay-friendly • full brkfst • hot tub • full bar

**St Moritz Lodge** 334 W Hyman Ave 970/925–3220, 800/817–2069 • gay-friendly • pool • hot tub/ steam • nonsmoking • WiFi • gay-owned

### RESTAURANTS

**Jimmy's** 205 S Mill St (at Hopkins) 970/925–6020 • 5:30pm-11pm, Sun brunch • also bar from 4:30pm • patio

**Syzygy** 308 E Hopkins Ave 970/925–3700 • seasonal • 6pm-10pm, bar till 2am • some veggie • live jazz • wheelchair access

### BOOKSTORES

**Explore Booksellers & Bistro** 221 E Main St (at Aspen) 970/925–5336, 800/562–7323 • 10am-7pm • also nutritarian restaurant • WiFi • wheelchair access

## Beaver Creek

### ACCOMMODATIONS

**Beaver Creek Lodge** 26 Avondale Ln (at Village Rd) 970/845–9800, 800/525–7280 • gay-friendly • nonsmoking • also restaurant w/ mtn views & fire pits • pool • WiFi • wheelchair access

## Boulder

### INFO LINES & SERVICES

**Out Boulder** 2132 14th St (at Pine) 303/499-5777 • LGBT resource center

### ACCOMMODATIONS

**The Briar Rose B&B** 2151 Arapahoe Ave (at 22nd St) 303/442–3007, 888/786–8440 • gay-friendly • full organic brkfst • nonsmoking • WiFi

### CAFES

**Walnut Cafe** 3073 Walnut St (at 30th) 303/447–2315 • 7am-3:30pm • popular • plenty veggie • patio • wheelchair access • women-owned

### ENTERTAINMENT & RECREATION

**Boulder Area Bicycle Adventures** 303/918–7062 • bike tours of Boulder & annual LGBT ride in June • lesbian-owned

## Colorado Springs

(includes Manitou Springs)

### ACCOMMODATIONS

**Blue Skies Inn B&B** 402 Manitou Ave (at Mayfair), Manitou Springs 719/685–3899, 800/398–7949 • gay/ straight • Civil Unions • full brkfst • gazebo hot tub • WiFi • kids ok • wheelchair access

**Blue Skies Inn B&B** 402 Manitou Ave (at Mayfair), Manitou Springs 719/685–3899, 800/398–7949 • gay/ straight • Civil Unions • full brkfst • gazebo hot tub • WiFi • kids ok • wheelchair access

**Old Town Guesthouse** 115 S 26th St 719/632–9194, 888/375–4210 • gay-friendly • full brkfst • nonsmoking • WiFi • wheelchair access

**Pikes Peak Paradise** 236 Pinecrest Rd, Woodland Park **719/687-6656, 800/728-8282** • gay-friendly • mansion w/ view of Pikes Peak • full brkfst • hot tub • fireplaces • nonsmoking • pets/kids ok • WiFi • gay-owned

## BARS

**Club Q** 3430 N Academy Blvd (at N Carefree) **719/570-1429** • 3pm-2am, till 4am Fri-Sat • mostly men • ladies night 3rd Fri • neighborhood bar • dancing/DJ • karaoke • live entertainment • strippers • food served • 18+ • wheelchair access • gay-owned

## RESTAURANTS

**Dale Street Bistro Cafe** 115 E Dale (at Nevada) **719/578-9898** • lunch and dinner, clsd Mon • some veggie • full bar

# Denver

## INFO LINES & SERVICES

**Gay/ Lesbian AA** 303/322-4440

**The GLBT Center of Colorado (The Center)** 1301 E Colfax **303/733-7743** • 10am-8pm Mon-Fri, from noon Sat • extensive resources & support groups • wheelchair access

## ACCOMMODATIONS

**The Brown Palace** 321 17th St (at N Broadway) **303/297-3111, 800/321-2599** • gay-friendly • sun in every room • WiFi • restaurant & spa

**Capitol Hill Mansion B&B** 1207 Pennsylvania St (at 12th) **303/839-5221, 800/839-9329** • gay-friendly • B&B • full brkfst • hot tub • nonsmoking • kids ok • WiFi • gay-owned

**Castle Marne B&B** 1572 Race St (at 16th Ave) **303/331-0621, 800/926-2763** • gay-friendly • 1889 mansion on Nat'l Register of Historic Places • hot tubs on private balconies • WiFi

**The Curtis-a DoubleTree by Hilton** 1405 Curtis St **303/571-0300, 800/525-6651** • gay-friendly • hip hotel • WiFi • also restaurant

**Hotel Monaco** 1717 Champa St (at 17th) **303/296-1717, 800/990-1303** • gay-friendly • gym • spa • nonsmoking • WiFi • also Italian restaurant • pets ok

**The Oxford Hotel** 1600 17th St **303/628-5400, 800/228-5838** • gay-friendly • health club & spa • also 2 restaurants, art deco lounge • WiFi

## BARS

**Aqua Lounge** 1417 Krameria (btwn 14th & Colfax) **720/287-0584** • 4pm-2am • lesbians/ gay men • piano bar • WiFi

**Barker Lounge** 475 Santa Fe Dr (at 5th St) **303/778-0545** • 3pm-2am, from noon Fri-Sun • mostly gay men • neighborhood bar • patio w/ bar • dogs welcome

**The Beauty Bar** **720/542-8024** • 5pm-2am , from 7pm Sat, clsd Sun-Mon • gay/ straight • dancing/DJ • shows

**Black Crown Piano Lounge** 1446 S Broadway **720/353-4701** • 4pm-midnight, till 2am Fri-Sat, from 11am Sat-Sun • mostly gay men • tapas menu • game room

**Blush & Blu** 1526 E Colfax (btwn Humboldt & Franklin) **303/830-8437** • 11am-2am •popular • lesbians/ gay men • WiFi • wheelchair access • lesbian-owned

**Broadways** 1027 Broadway (at 11th Ave) **303/623-0700** • 2pm-2am, from noon Sat-Sun • lesbians/ gay men • neighborhood bar • cool mix of folk • karaoke • WiFi

**Charlie's** 900 E Colfax Ave (at Emerson) **303/839-8890** • 11am-2am • popular • mostly gay men • country bar & house music room • dancing/DJ • country/ western • wheelchair access

**The Compound/Basix** 145 Broadway (at 2nd Ave) **303/722-7977** • 7am-2am • popular • mostly gay men • neighborhood bar • dancing/DJ Fri-Sat

**Dazzle** 930 Lincoln St (btwn 9th & 10th Aves) **303/839-5100** • from 4pm Sun-Th, from 11am Fri, also Sun brunch • gay-friendly • jazz club & restaurant • live music

**Denver Eagle** 3600 Blake St (at 36th) **303/291-0250** • 4pm-2am • mostly men • bears • never a cover charge • wheelchair access • gay-owned

**El Chapultepec** 1962 Market St (at 20th) **303/295-9126** • 9am-2am • popular • gay-friendly • live jazz & blues since 1951 • 1-drink minimum per set • cover

**El Potrero** 4501 E Virginia Ave, Glendale **303/388-8889** • gay/ straight • Mexican restaurant from 3pm• Latino gay bar late, clsd Mon-Tue

**R&R Denver** 4958 E Colfax Ave (at Elm St) **303/320-9337** • 3pm-2am, from 1pm Fri, from 11am wknds • lesbians/ gay men • neighborhood bar

**X Bar** 629 E Colfax Ave **303/832-2687** • 3pm-2am, from noon Sun • lesbians/ gay men • dancing/DJ

## NIGHTCLUBS

**Beta Nightclub** 1909 Blake St (btwn 19th & 20th) **303/383–1909** • gay/ straight • more gay Th • dancing/DJ • cover charge

**Climax Sunday at Club Vinyl** 1082 Broadway **303/832–8628** • 4pm–2am Sun (May-Sept only) • dancing/DJ • great rooftop patio

**First Friday/ Babes Around Denver** 3500 Walnut St (at 35th, at Tracks) **303/475–4620** • 6pm–2am, 1st Fri only • mostly women • dancing/DJ

**Hip Chicks Out** • mostly women • roving monthly • check www.hipchicksout.com

**La Rumba** 99 W 9th Ave (at Broadway) **303/572–8006** • gay-friendly • salsa dancing & lessons Th & Sat • more gay for Lipgloss Fri (Brit-pop & indie music) • cover

**Lannie's Clocktower Cabaret** 16th St Mall at Arapahoe (in historic D&F Tower) **303/293–0075** • gay-friendly • upscale cabaret w/ variety of acts weekly, including drag & burlesque

**Tracks** 3500 Walnut St (at 36th) **303/863–7326** • 9pm–2am, clsd Sun-Wed • gay/ straight • women's night 1st Fri • dancing/DJ • drag shows

## CAFES

**City, O City** 206 E 13th Ave (at Sherman) **303/831–6443** • 7am–2am, from 8am wknds, vegetarian/ vegan • also bar

**Common Grounds** 1550 17th St **303/296–9248** • 6:30am–10pm, till 9pm Sun

**Jelly Cafe** 600 E 13th Ave (at Pearl) **303/831–6301** • 7am–3pm • a whole lotta Jelly filled fun

**The Market at Larimer Square** 1445 Larimer Sq (btwn 14th & 15th) **303/534–5140** • 6am–11pm, till midnight Fri-Sat, till 10pm Sun

**Paris on the Platte** 1553 Platte St (at 15th) **303/455–2451** • 7am–2am, soups, salads, sandwiches • live music • WiFi

## RESTAURANTS

**Annie's Cafe & Bar** 3100 E Colfax (at St Paul) **303/355–8197** • 7am–10pm, from 8am Sat, till 8pm Sun • popular • comfort food and cocktails • some veggie

**The Avenue Grill** 630 E 17th Ave (at Washington) **303/861–2820** • 11am–11pm, till midnight Fri-Sat, till 10pm Sun

**Banzai Sushi** 6655 Leetsdale Dr (E of Colorado Blvd) **303/329–3366** • lunch Mon-Fri, dinner nightly

**Barricuda's** 1076 Ogden St (at E 11th) **303/860–8353** • 10am–2am • also dive bar

**Beatrice & Woodsley** 38 S Broadway **303/777–3505** • one of America's top restaurants • reservations suggested

**Benny's Restaurante y Tequila Bar** 301 E 7th Ave (at Grant St) **303/894–0788** • lunch & dinner • patio

**The Corner Office Restaurant & Martini Bar** 1405 Curtis St (at Curtis Hotel) **303/825–6500** • 6am-midnight, till 2am Fri-Sat • groovy Sun disco brunch

**Devil's Food** 1020 S Gaylord St (at E Tennessee) **303/733–7448** • 7am-10pm, till 4pm Sun-Mon • yummy desserts

**Duo** 2413 W 32nd Ave (at Zuni) **303/477–4141** • dinner nightly, wknd brunch • hip, organic, creative American • full bar

**Euclid Hall Bar & Kitchen** 1317 14th St **303/595–4255** • 11:30am-1am-, till 2am Fri-Sat • American tavern focuses on high quality and innovative pub food

**Fruition** 1313 E 6th Ave **303/831–1962** • 5pm-10pm, till 8pm Sun • contemporary French

**Hamburger Mary's** 700 E 17th Ave (at Washington St, across from JR's bar) **303/832–1333** • 11am-2am, from 10am Sun • popular • dancing/DJ • karaoke • drag shows

**Il Vicino** 550 Broadway **303/861–0801** • 11am-10pm • pizza

**The Populist** 3163 Larimer **720/432–3163** • New American small plates, clsd Sun-Mon

**Steuben's** 523 E 17th Ave **303/830–1001** • 11am-11pm, till midnight Fri, 10am-midnight Sat • American comfort food served up hip • patio • full bar

**Sunny Gardens** 6460 E Yale Avenue **303/691–8830** • Chinese • plenty veggie/ vegan

**Thai Pot Cafe** 1550 S Colorado Blvd (at E Florida) **303/639–6200** • lunch & dinner

**Tom's Home Cookin'** **303/388–8035** • 11am-3pm, clsd Sat-Sun • Southern comfort food • wheelchair access • gay-owned

**Vesta Dipping Grill** 1822 Blake St (near 18th St) **303/296–1970** • 5pm-10pm Sun-Th, till 11pm Fri-Sat • upscale

**WaterCourse Foods** 837 E 17th Ave (at Clarkson) **303/832–7313** • 7am-9pm, till 10pm Fri-Sat • vegetarian/ vegan

**Wazee Supper Club** 1600 15th St (at Wazee) 303/623–9518, 303/825–3199 (PIZZA DELIVERY) • 11am-2am, noon-midnight Sun • classic comfort food • full bar • wheelchair access

ENTERTAINMENT & RECREATION

**Rocky Mountain Rainbeaus** 303/863–7739 • all-inclusive, all-levels, high-energy square dance club

BOOKSTORES

**Tattered Cover Book Store** 2526 Colfax Ave (at Elizabeth St) 303/322-7727, 800/833–9327 • 9am-9pm, 10am-6pm Sun • independent • cafe • also 1628 16th St, 303/436-1070 • wheelchair access

PUBLICATIONS

**Out Front Colorado** 303/778–7900 • statewide bi-weekly LGBT newspaper • since 1976

## Durango

ACCOMMODATIONS

**Leland House B&B** 721 E 2nd Ave 970/385–1920 • gay-friendly • full brkfst • nonsmoking • WiFi • wheelchair access

**Mesa Verde Far View Lodge** 1 Navajo Hill, Mesa Verde National Park 602/331–5210, 800/449–2288 • gay-friendly • camping • RV hookups • inside nat'l park at 8250' elevation • full brkfst • nonsmoking • WiFi

**Rochester Hotel** 721 E 2nd Ave 800/664–1920 • gay-friendly • popular • newly renovated 1892 house decorated in Old West motif • full brkfst • nonsmoking • kids/pets ok • wheelchair access

RESTAURANTS

**Palace Restaurant** 505 Main Ave (at 5th St) 970/247-2018 • 11am-10pm, clsd Sun in winter, full bar • patio • gay-owned

## Estes Park

ACCOMMODATIONS

**Stanley Hotel** 333 Wonderview Ave 800/976–1377, 970/577-4000 • gay-friendly • pool • restaurant • WiFi the inspiration for Stephen King's The Shining

## Fort Collins

INFO LINES & SERVICES

**The Center Northern Colorado** 400 Remington St #100 970/221-3247 • 9-11am Fri social

ACCOMMODATIONS

**Archer's Poudre River Resort** 33021 Poudre Canyon Hwy, Bellvue 970/881–2139, 888/822-0588 • gay-friendly • cabins, tents, RV hookups • lesbian-owned

## Grand Junction

RESTAURANTS

**Leon's Taqueria** 505 30th Rd 970/242–1388 • 11am-9pm

## Hotchkiss

ACCOMMODATIONS

**Leroux Creek Inn & Vineyards** 12388 3100 Rd 970/872–4746 • gay-friendly • Southwestern-style adobe on 54 acres • full brkfst

RESTAURANTS

**North Fork Valley Restaurant & Thirsty Parrot Pub** 140 W Bridge St 970/872-4215 • 11am-8pm • American/ Mexican

## Pueblo

BARS

**Pirate's Cove** 105 Central Plaza (off 1st & Union) 719/543-2683 • 4pm-2am, call for Sun hrs, clsd Mon • lesbians/gay men • neighborhood bar • wheelchair access

## Stratton

ACCOMMODATIONS

**Claremont Inn & Winery** 800 Claremont St (off exit 419, I-70) 719/348-5125, 888/291–8910 • gay/ straight • 2 hours from Denver • full brkfst • commitment ceremonies • WiFi • gay-owned

## Vail

RESTAURANTS

**Larkspur Restaurant & Market** 458 Vail Valley Dr (in the Golden Peak Lodge) 970/754-8050 • lunch & dinner • fine dining • also bar • patio • ski-in/ out • wheelchair access

**Sweet Basil** 193 E Gore Creek Dr 970/476-0125 • lunch & dinner • some veggie • full bar • wheelchair access

## Westcliffe

### RESTAURANTS

**Westcliffe Wine Mine** 109 N 3rd St (at Main St) **719/783-2490** • call for hours • older crowd • wheelchair access • lesbian-owned

# CONNECTICUT

## Bethel

### CAFES

**Molten Java** 213 Greenwood Ave **203/739-0313** • 6am-9pm, till 10pm Fri-Sat, 8am-8pm Sat-Sun • live entertainment • lesbian-owned

### RESTAURANTS

**Bethel Pizza House** 206 Greenwood Ave **203/748-1427** • 11am-11pm, till midnight Fri-Sat

## Bridgeport

### RESTAURANTS

**Bloodroot Restaurant & Bookstore** 85 Ferris St (at Harbor Ave) **203/576-9168** • lunch Tue & Th-Sat, dinner Tue-Sat, brunch only Sun, clsd Mon • feminist vegetarian • patio • wheelchair access • women-owned

### EROTICA

**Romantix Adult Superstore** 410 North Ave **203/332-7129**

## Bristol

### EROTICA

**Amazing** 167 Farmington Ave **860/582-9000**

## Colebrook

### ACCOMMODATIONS

**Rock Hall Luxe Lodging** 19 Rock Hall Rd **860/379-2230** • gay/straight • resort-style lodging in an Addison Mizner manor house & estate • pool • nonsmoking • WiFi

## Danbury

### ACCOMMODATIONS

**Maron Hotel & Suites** 42 Lake Ave Extension (off I-84) **203/791-2200, 866/811-2582** • gay-friendly • kids/pets ok • WiFi • wheelchair access

### RESTAURANTS

**Sesame Seed** 68 W Wooster St **203/743-9850** • lunch & dinner, clsd Sun, Mediterranean/Italian • funky decor • plenty veggie

**Thang Long** 56 Padanaram Rd (near North Street Shopping Center) **203/743-6049** • lunch & dinner • Vietnamese • bring your own bottle

## Enfield

### EROTICA

**Bookends** 44 Enfield St/Rte 5 **860/745-3988**

## Hartford

### INFO LINES & SERVICES

**Hartford Gay & Lesbian Health Collective** 1841 Broad St (at New Britain Ave) **860/278-4163** • 9am-5pm, till 9pm Th, clsd wknds

**True Colors** 30 Arbor St (at Capital Ave) **860/232-0050, 888/565-5551** • support & mentoring for LGBT youth

### ACCOMMODATIONS

**Butternut Farm** 1654 Main St, Glastonbury **860/633-7197** • gay/straight • 18th-c house furnished w/ antiques • full brkfst • WiFi

**Inn at Kent Falls** 107 Kent Cornwall Rd, Kent **860/927-3197** • gay/straight • 1 hr from Hartford • pool • kids ok • nonsmoking • WiFi • wheelchair access • gay-owned

**The Mansion Inn** 139 Hartford Rd (at Main St), Manchester **860/646-0453** • gay-friendly • B&B • full brkfst • in-room fireplaces

### BARS

**Chez Est** 458 Wethersfield Ave (at Main St) **860/525-3243** • 3pm-1am, till 2am Fri-Sat • popular • lesbians/gay men • dancing/DJ • food served • karaoke • drag shows

### NIGHTCLUBS

**Vine Symmetry** 70 Union Pl **860/384-8574** • 9pm-12:30pm • check facebook.com/VineSymmetry page for upcoming parties • mostly gay men • dancing/DJ

### CAFES

**Tisane Tea & Coffee Bar** 537 Farmington Ave (at Kenyon) **860/523-5417** • 8am-1am, till 2am Sat • food served • karaoke • WiFi • also bar • women's night 1st Sun

RESTAURANTS

**Arugula** 953 Farmington Ave, West Hartford **860/561-4888** • lunch & dinner, clsd Mon • Mediterranean • reservations recommended • wheelchair access

**Firebox** 539 Broad St **860/246-1222** • 11:30am-10:30pm, 4:30pm-8:30pm Sun, clsd Mon • contemporary American

**Peppercorns Grill** 357 Main St **860/547-1714** • lunch Mon-Fri, dinner nightly, clsd Sun • Northern Italian

**Pond House Cafe** 1555 Asylum Ave, W Hartford **860/231-8823** • lunch & dinner Tue-Sat, wknd brunch • bring your own bottle • patio • wheelchair access

**Trumbull Kitchen** 150 Trumbull St (at Pearl St) **860/493-7417** • lunch Mon-Sat, dinner nightly • global cuisine/ tapas

ENTERTAINMENT & RECREATION

**Real Art Ways** 56 Arbor St **860/232-1006** • contemporary art • cinema • performance • also lounge • WiFi

RETAIL SHOPS

**MetroStore** 493 Farmington Ave (at Sisson Ave) **860/231-8845** • 8:30am-8pm, till 5:30pm Tue, Wed & Sat, clsd Sun • magazines • travel guides • DVD rentals • leather & more

EROTICA

**Very Intimate Pleasures** 100 Brainard Rd (exit 27, off I-91) **860/246-1875**

## Mystic

ACCOMMODATIONS

**House of 1833 B&B Resort** 72 N Stonington Rd **860/536-6325, 800/367-1833** • gay-friendly • full brkfst • pool • kids ok • nonsmoking • WiFi • gay-owned

**The Mare's Inn B&B** 333 Colonel Ledyard Hwy, Ledyard **860/572-7556** • gay-friendly • full brkfst • nonsmoking • wheelchair access • lesbian-owned

**Mermaid Inn of Mystic** 2 Broadway **860/536-6223, 877/692-2632** • lesbians/ gay men (all welcome) • B&B w/ village location & river views • full brkfst • kids ok • nonsmoking • WiFi • lesbian-owned

**The Old Mystic Inn** 52 Main St (at Rte 27), Old Mystic **860/572-9422** • gay-friendly • full brkfst • nonsmoking • WiFi • gay-owned

## New Haven

INFO LINES & SERVICES

**New Haven Pride Center** 84 Orange , West Haven **203/387-2252** • events • meetings • resources • library • movies • wheelchair access

ACCOMMODATIONS

**Linden Point House** 30 Linden Point Rd, Stony Creek **203/481-0472** • gay-friendly • WiFi • kids/ pets ok

**Omni New Haven Hotel at Yale** 155 Temple St (at Chapel) **203/772-6664, 800/843-6664** • gay-friendly • WiFi • wheelchair access

BARS

**168 York St Cafe** 168 York St **203/789-1915** • 3pm-1am, till 2am Fri-Sat • lesbians/ gay men • also restaurant • dinner Mon-Sat, Sun brunch • patio • gay-owned

**The Bar** 254 Crown St (at College) **203/495-8924** • 11:30am-1am, from 5pm Mon-Tue • gay/ straight • more gay Tue • dancing/DJ • pizza • wheelchair access

**Partners** 365 Crown St (at Park St) **203/776-1014** • 8pm-1am, till 2am Fri-Sat, from 5pm Fri • lesbians/ gay men • dancing/DJ • karaoke

NIGHTCLUBS

**Empire Nightclub** 169 East St **203/498-2484** • 9pm-4am, clsd Sun-Wed • gay/ straight • more gay Sat • 18+ • dancing/DJ • drag shows • wheelchair access

CAFES

**Atticus Bookstore/ Cafe** 1082 Chapel St (at York St) **203/776-4040** • 7am-9pm

RESTAURANTS

**116 Crown** 116 Crown St **203/777-3116** • upscale tapas • great mixed drinks

**Beachhead** 3 Cosey Beach Ave, East Haven **203/469-5450** • 4pm-close, from 1pm Sun • seafood • Italian • patio • live music

**Bentara** 76 Orange St **203/562-2511** • lunch Mon-Sat, dinner nightly • Malaysian • plenty veggie

**Claire's Corner Copia** 1000 Chapel St (at College St) **203/562-3888** • 8am-9pm, till 10pm Fri-Sat • vegetarian • WiFi • wheelchair access

**Mezcal** 14 Mechanic St (at Lawrence) **203/782-4828** • lunch Tue-Sun, dinner nightly • authentic Mexican

**Miya Sushi** 58 Howe St (at Chapel St) 203/777–9760 • lunch & dinner, clsd Sun-Mon

**Soul de Cuba** 238 Crown St 203/498–2822 • lunch & dinner • full bar

EROTICA

**Very Intimate Pleasures** 170 Boston Post Rd, Orange 203/799–7040

## New London

BARS

**O'Neill's Brass Rail** 52 Bank St 860/443–6203 • 1pm-1am, till 2am Fri-Sat • mostly gay men • karaoke • drag shows • WiFi

## Norwalk

INFO LINES & SERVICES

**Triangle Community Center** 618 West Ave 203/853–0600 • activities • newsletter • call for info

## Westport

ENTERTAINMENT & RECREATION

**Sherwood Island State Park Beach** left to gay area

# DELAWARE

## Rehoboth Beach

INFO LINES & SERVICES

**Camp Rehoboth Community Center** 37 Baltimore Ave 302/227–5620 • 9am-5:30pm Mon-Fri, 10am-4pm wknds • drop-in community center • support groups • magazine w/ extensive listings • HIV testing & counseling

**Gay & Lesbian AA** 302/856–6452 • noon Th

ACCOMMODATIONS

**At Melissa's B&B** 36 Delaware Ave (btwn 1st & 2nd) 302/227–7504, 800/396–8090 • gay/ straight • 1 block from beach • nonsmoking • WiFi • women-owned

**Bellmoor Inn** 6 Christian St (at Delaware) 866/227–5800, 800/425–2355 • gay-friendly • upscale inn & spa • pool

**Bewitched & BEDazzled B&B** 67 Lake Ave (at Rehoboth Ave) 302/226–3900, 866/732–9482 • gay/ straight • hot tub • nonsmoking • WiFi • wheelchair access • lesbian-owned

**Cabana Gardens B&B** 20 Lake Ave (at 3rd St) 302/227–5429 • gay/ straight • lake & ocean views • deck • pool • nonsmoking • gay-owned

**Canalside Inn** Canal at 6th 302/226–2006, 866/412–2625 • gay/ straight • pool • hot tub • WiFi • nonsmoking • wheelchair access • gay-owned

**The Homestead at Rehoboth B&B** 35060 Warrington Rd (at Old Landing Rd) 302/226–7625 • gay-friendly • small dogs ok • nonsmoking • WiFi • wheelchair access • lesbian-owned

**Lazy L at Willow Creek** 16061 Willow Creek Rd (at Hwy 1), Lewes 302/644–7220 • gay/ straight • full brkfst • pool • hot tub • very pet friendly • WiFi • lesbian-owned

**The Lighthouse Inn B&B** 20 Delaware Ave (at 1st St) 302/226–0407 • seasonal • gay/ straight • also apt (weekly rental) • nonsmoking • kids/ pets ok • gay-owned

**Rehoboth Guest House** 40 Maryland Ave (btwn 1st & 2nd Sts) 302/227–4117, 800/564–0493 • lesbians/ gay men • near boardwalk & beach • nonsmoking • WiFi • gay-owned

**The Royal Rose Inn** 41 Baltimore Ave (at 1st St) 302/226–2535 • gay/ straight • sundeck • gay-owned

**Silver Lake Guest House** 20388 Silver Lake Dr (at Robinson Dr) 302/226–2115, 800/842–2115 • lesbians/ gay men • near Poodle Beach • nonsmoking • lakefront • ocean views • WiFi • gay-owned

BARS

**The Blue Moon** 35 Baltimore Ave (btwn 1st & 2nd) 302/227–6515 • 6pm-2am, clsd Jan • popular • lesbians/ gay men • live music • drag shows • also restaurant

**Dogfish Head Brewings & Eats** 320 Rehoboth Ave (at 4th) 302/226–2739 • gay-friendly • micro-brewery • wood-grilled food • live music wknds

**The Pond Bar & Grill** 3 S 1st St (near Rehoboth Ave) 302/227–2234 • 11am-1am • gay-friendly • neighborhood bar • food served • karaoke • live music

**Rigby's Bar & Grill** 404 Rehoboth Ave (at State St) 302/227–6080 • 3pm-1am, from 10am Sun

NIGHTCLUBS

**Ladies 2000** 856/869–0193 • seasonal parties • check www.ladies2000.com for events

### CAFES

**The Coffee Mill** 127B Rehoboth Ave **302/227-7530** • 7am-11pm, till 5pm (off-season) • WiFi • lesbian-owned

**Honey's Farm Fresh** 329 Savannah Rd, Lewes **302/644-8400** • 8am-3pm, clsd Tue-Wed

**Lori's Cafe** 39 Baltimore Ave (at 1st) **302/226-3066** • seasonal, call for hours • also sandwiches • courtyard • lesbian-owned

### RESTAURANTS

**Aqua Grill** 57 Baltimore Ave **302/226-9001** • seasonal • deck • full bar

**Back Porch Cafe** 59 Rehoboth Ave **302/227-3674** • lunch & dinner • Sun brunch • seasonal • live shows • full bar • wheelchair access

**Buttery** 102 2nd St, Lewes **302/645-7755** • lunch, dinner, Sun brunch • fine dining in elegant Victorian • reservations suggested

**The Cultured Pearl** 301 Rehoboth Ave (2nd flr) **302/227-8493** • dinner only • pan-Asian/sushi • cocktail lounge

**Dos Locos** 208 Rehoboth Ave (across from Fire Company) **302/227-3353** • 11:30am-10pm, till 11pm Fri-Sat • popular • Mexican • full bar

**Eden** 23 Baltimore Ave **302/227-3330** • dinner Tue-Sat • seasonal • wine list & martini bar • wheelchair access

**Espuma** 28 Wilmington Ave **302/227-4199** • 5pm-10pm, clsd Mon • modern Mediterranean • full bar

**Fins** 243 Rehoboth Ave **302/226-3467** • dinner nightly, lunch Sat-Sun • fish house • raw bar

**Go Fish!** 24 Rehoboth Ave **302/226-1044** • 11:30am-9:30pm (in-season) • authentic British fish & chips

**Hobos Restaurant & Bar** 56 Baltimore Ave **302/226-2226** • from 11am (in-season)

**Iguana Grill** 52 Baltimore Ave **302/727-5273** • lunch & dinner (summers) • Southwestern • full bar • patio

**Jerry's Seafood** 108 2nd St, Lewes **302/645-6611** • lunch & dinner daily • "home of the crab bomb"

**Mariachi** **302/227-0115** • 11am-9pm, till 11pm Fri-Sat • Mexican-Latin American • wheelchair access

**Purple Parrot Grill** 134 Rehoboth Ave **302/226-1139** • lunch & dinner daily, brunch Sun • karaoke & drag shows wknds • wheelchair access

**Seafood Shack** 42 1/2 Baltimore Ave (at 1st St) **302/227-5881** • patio seating • live music wknds

### ENTERTAINMENT & RECREATION

**Cape Henlopen State Park Beach** 42 Cape Henlopen Dr, Lewes **302/645-8983** • 8am-sunset

**Gordon Pond State Park/ North Shores** S end of Cape Henlopen State Park (at jetty S of watch tower) • popular women's beach • 20-minute walk from boardwalk • by car follow the shoreline road to State Park entrance

**Poodle Beach** S of boardwalk at Queen St • popular gay beach

### BOOKSTORES

**Proud Bookstore** 149 Rehoboth Ave (at Village of the Sea Shops) **302/227-6969** • 10am-5pm, till 10pm summer

### RETAIL SHOPS

**Leather Central** 36983 Rehoboth Ave **302/227-0700** • leather uniforms, toys, accessories

### PUBLICATIONS

**Letters from Camp Rehoboth** **302/227-5620** • newsmagazine w/ events & entertainment listings

## Wilmington

### NIGHTCLUBS

**Crimson Moon Tavern** 1909 W 6th St (at Union St) **302/654-9099** • 6pm-2am, from 7pm Sat, clsd Sun-Tue • mostly gay men • dancing/DJ • videos

### RESTAURANTS

**Eclipse** 1020 Union St **302/658-1588** • lunch Mon-Fri, dinner nightly • upscale

**The Green Room** 11th & Market St (at Hotel Dupont) **302/594-3154** • brkfst, lunch & dinner, Sun brunch • full bar • live music

**Mrs Robino's** 520 N Union St (at Pennsylvania) **302/652-9223** • 11am-9pm, till 10pm Fri-Sat • family-style Italian • full bar • wheelchair access

## DISTRICT OF COLUMBIA

### Washington

#### INFO LINES & SERVICES

**Triangle Club** 202/659-8641 • site for various 12-step groups • call for times

#### ACCOMMODATIONS

**Beacon Hotel & Corporate Quarters** 1615 Rhode Island Ave NW (at 17th) 202/296-2100, 800/821-4367 • gay-friendly • restarurant & bar • wheelchair access

**The Carlyle Suites Hotel** 1731 New Hampshire Ave NW (btwn R & S Sts) 202/234-3200, 800/964-5377 • gay/ straight • WiFi • gym • also restaurant & bar • wheelchair access

**Donovan House** 1155 14th St NW (at Massachusetts Ave NW) 202/737-1200 • gay/ straight • stylish hotel • rooftop bar

**Embassy Suites Hotel at the Chevy Chase Pavilion** 4300 Military Rd NW (at Wisconsin) 202/362-9300 • gay-friendly • pool • gym • wheelchair access

**Hamilton Crowne Plaza Hotel** 14th & K St, NW 202/682-0111, 800/263-9802 • gay-friendly • offers a special women's floor, catering to the female business traveler • kids/ pets ok • wheelchair access

**Hotel George** 15 E St NW 202/347-4200, 800/546-7866 • gay-friendly • WiFi • pets ok

**Hotel Helix** 1430 Rhode Island Ave NW 202/462-9001, 800/706-1202 • gay-friendly • full-service boutique hotel • also Helix Lounge • nonsmoking • WiFi • wheelchair access

**Hotel Monaco Washington DC** 700 F St NW (at 7th) 202/628-7177, 800/649-1202 • gay-friendly • boutique hotel • kids/ pets ok • WiFi • wheelchair access

**Hotel Palomar** 2121 P St NW (at 21st St) 202/448-1800, 866/866-3070 • gay-friendly • in Dupont Circle • gym • WiFi • pool • restaurant • wheelchair access

**Hotel Rouge** 1315 16th St NW (at Rhode Island) 202/232-8000, 800/738-1202 • gay-friendly • • kids/ pets ok • also restaurant & bar • WiFi • wheelchair access

**Kalorama Guest House** 2700 Cathedral Ave NW (off Connecticut Ave) 202/328-0860, 800/974-9101 • gay/ straight • near Nat'l Zoo & Washington Cathedral • nonsmoking • WiFi

**Morrison-Clark Historic Hotel & Restaurant** 1015 L St NW (at Massachusetts Ave NW) 202/898-1200, 800/322-7898 • gay-friendly • hotel in 2 Victorian town houses • very popular restaurant • WiFi

**The River Inn** 924 25th St NW (at K St) 202/337-7600, 888/874-0100 • gay-friendly • suites w/ kitchen • gym • WiFi • also Dish + Drinks restaurant • wheelchair access

**Savoy Suites Hotel** 2505 Wisconsin Ave NW (near Georgetown) 202/337-9700, 800/944-5377 • gay-friendly • also restaurant • WiFi • wheelchair access

**Topaz Hotel** 1733 N St NW (at Massachusetts Ave NW) 202/393-3000, 800/775-1202 • gay-friendly • boutique hotel • kids/ pets ok • also restaurant & bar WiFi • wheelchair access

#### BARS

**The Black Cat** 1811 14th St NW (at the Black Cat) 202/667-4490 • gay/ straight • many queer events • live music • dance parties • also cafe

**DC Eagle** 3701 Benning Rd NE 202/347-6025 • 4pm-2am, till 3am Fri-Sat, 2pm-2am Sun • popular • mostly gay men • leather • wheelchair access

**DIK Bar/ Windows** 1637 17th St NW (at R St NW, upstairs) 202/328-0100 • 4pm-2am • mostly gay men • aka Dupont Italian Kitchen • dancing/DJ • karaoke • older crowd

**The Fireplace** 2161 P St NW (at 22nd St) 202/293-1293 • 1pm-2am, till 3am Fri-Sat • mostly gay men • neighborhood bar • multiracial • videos • wheelchair access

**JR's** 1519 17th St NW (at Church) 202/328-0090 • 4pm-2am, till 3am Fri, 1pm-3am Sat, 1pm-2am Sun • popular • mostly gay men • neighborhood bar • food served • videos • young crowd

**Larry's Lounge** 1840 18th St NW (at T St) 202/483-1483 • 4pm-1am, till 2am Fri-Sat • lesbians/ gay men • neighborhood bar • patio • wheelchair access • gay-owned

**Mr Henry's Capitol Hill** 601 Pennsylvania Ave SE (at 6th St) 202/546-8412 • 11:30am-11:30pm • gay-friendly • multiracial • also restaurant • nonsmoking • wheelchair access

**Nellie's Sports Bar** 900 U St NW (at 9th) 202/332-6355 • 5pm-midnight, 3pm-2am Fri, from 11am wknds • mostly gay men

**Number Nine** 1435 P St NW (at 15th St NW) 202/986-0999 • 5pm-close, from 3pm wknds • lesbians/ gay men • neighborhood bar

**POV Roof Terrace Bar** 515 15th Street NW (at Alexander Hamilton Pl) **202/661–2400** • 11am-2am • gay-friendly • pricey cocktails • superior views of the White House & Lincoln Memorial • tapas served

**UpRoar Lounge & Restaurant** 639 Florida Ave NW **202/462–4464** • 5pm-midnight, till 2am wknds • mostly gay men • bears • food served

**Wisdom** 1432 Pennsylvania Ave SE **202/543–2323** • 6pm-12:30, till 3am Fri-Sat 10pm Sun, clsd Mon • gay/ straight • bar food served

## NIGHTCLUBS

**Bachelors Mill** 1104 8th St SE (downstairs at Back Door Pub) **202/546–5979** • 11am-3am Th-Sat only • lesbians/ gay men • popular • dancing/DJ • mostly African American • live shows • karaoke • wheelchair access

**Chief Ike's Mambo Room** 1725 Columbia Rd NW (at Ontario Rd) **202/332–2211** • 4pm-2am, till 3am Fri, 6pm-3am Sat gay-friendly • dancing/DJ • food served• wheelchair access

**Cobalt/ 30 Degrees Lounge** 1639 R St NW (at 17th) **202/232–4416** • 5pm-2am, till 3am Fri-Sat • mostly gay men • dancing/DJ • live shows • drag shows • videos

**Delta Elite** 3734 10th St NE (at Perry St NE, in Brookland) **202/529–0626** • midnight-4am Fri-Sat only • ladies night Fri • dancing/DJ • mostly African American

**Lure** 1639 R St NW (at 17th, at Cobalt) **202/232–4416** • 10pm 3rd Sat only • mostly women • dancing/DJ

**Mixtape** • 2nd Sat only • alternative queer dance party • venue changes, check mixtapedc.com for info

**She Rex** 1725 Columbia Rd NW (at Ontario Rd, at Chief Ike's) **202/332–2211** • 2nd Fri only • mostly women • dancing/DJ • queer party featuring all music by women • wheelchair access

**Town Danceboutique** 2009 8th St NW (at U St NW) **202/234–8696** • 9pm-4am Fri-Sat • popular • mostly gay men • dancing/DJ • bears Fri • drag shows • 18+ Fri

## CAFES

**Cosi** 1647 20th St NW **202/332–6364** • 7am-11pm, till midnight Fri-Sat, 8am-10pm Sun • full bar from 4pm • popular • make your own s'mores • WiFi

**Hello Cupcake** 1361 Connecticut Avenue NW **202/861–2253** • 10am-7pm, till 9pm Fri-Sat, 11am-6pm Sun • cupcakes!

**Jolt 'n' Bolt** 1918 18th St NW (at Florida) **202/232–0077** • 7am- 8:30pm • popular • patio

**Soho Tea & Coffee** 2150 P St NW (at 21st St) **202/463–7646** • 7am-11pm • WiFi • patio • wheelchair access

## RESTAURANTS

**18th & U Duplex Diner** 2004 18th St NW (at Ave U) **202/265–7828** • 6pm-11pm, till 12:30am Tue-Wed, till 1:30am Fri-Sat • American comfort food • full bar

**2 Amys Pizza** 3715 Macomb St NW **202/885–5700** • lunch & dinner Tue-Sun, dinner only Mon • wheelchair access

**Acadiana** 901 New York Ave NW **202/408–8848** • lunch Mon-Fri, dinner nightly, brunch Sun • Cajun • great bourbon selection • reservations recommended

**Annie's Paramount Steak House** 1609 17th St NW (at Corcoran) **202/232–0395** • 10am-11:30pm, till 1am Th & Sun, 24hrs Fri-Sat • full bar • wheelchair access

**Banana Cafe & Piano Bar** 500 8th St SE (at E St) **202/543–5906** • 11am-10:30pm, till 11pm Fri-Sat • Puerto Rican/ Cuban food • some veggie • famous margaritas • gay-owned

**Bar Pilar** 1833 14th St NW (at Swann St) **202/265–1751** • dinner nightly, Sun brunch • new American

**Beacon Bar & Grill** 1615 Rhode Island Ave NW (at 17th, at Beacon Hotel) **202/872–1126** • brkfst, lunch & dinner • popular Sun brunch • patio

**Busboys & Poets** 2021 14th St NW (at V St) **202/387–7638** • 8am-midnight, till 2am Fri-Sat, 10am-midnight Sun • also bookstore • live jazz & poetry • WiFi • wheelchair access

**Cafe La Ruche** 1039 31st St **202/965–2684** • dinner, Sun brunch • French • patio

**Cafe Saint Ex/ Gate 54** 1847 14th St NW **202/265–7839** • lunch, dinner, Sun brunch • modern American • also Gate 54 club downstairs • popular Th dance party • gay-friendly

**Dupont Italian Kitchen & Bar** 1637 17th St NW (at R St) **202/328–3222, 202/328–0100** • 11am-11pm, bar 4pm-2am • some veggie • wheelchair access

**Floriana** 1602 17th St NW (at Q St NW) **202/667–5937** • dinner nightly • Italian • full bar • patio • gay-owned

**Food For Thought** 1811 14th St NW (at the Black Cat) **202/667-4490** • 8pm-1am, 7pm-2am Fri-Sat • gay-friendly • mostly vegan/veggie • also live music • readings • indie/punk • young crowd • wheelchair access

**Guapo's** 4515 Wisconsin Ave NW (at Albemarle) **202/686-3588** • lunch & dinner • Mexican • some veggie • full bar • wheelchair access

**Jaleo** 480 7th St NW (at E St) **202/628-7949** • lunch & dinner • tapas • full bar • Sevillanas dancers Wed • wheelchair access

**Java Green Eco Cafe** 1020 19th St NW **202/775-8899** • 8am-8pm, 10am-6pm Sat, clsd Sun • organic cafe • plenty veggie/vegan

**Level One** 1639 R St NW (at 17th) **202/745-0025** • dinner nightly, wknd brunch

**Logan Tavern** 1423 P St NW **202/332-3710** • lunch & dinner, wknd brunch • American comfort food • also bar • gay-owned

**Occidental Grill** 1475 Pennsylvania Ave NW (btwn 14th & 15th) **202/783-1475** • lunch Mon-Sat, dinner nightly, clsd Sun • upscale • political player hangout

**Perry's** 1811 Columbia Rd NW (at 18th) **202/234-6218** • 5:30pm-10:30pm, till 11:30pm wknds, popular drag Sun brunch • contemporary American & sushi • full bar • roof deck

**Pizza Paradiso** 2003 P Street NW **202/223-1245** • 11am-11pm, till midnight wknds • Gluten-Free Crust

**Posto** 1515 14th St NW **202/332-8613** • dinner nightly • terrific Italian

**Rasika** 633 D St NW **202/637-1222** • lunch Mon-Fri, dinner Mon-Sat, clsd Sun • Indian • wheelchair access

**Rice** 1608 14th St NW (at 'Q') **202/234-2400** • lunch & dinner • Thai

**Rocklands** 2418 Wisconsin Ave NW (at Calvert) **202/333-2558** • 11am-10pm, till 9pm Sun • BBQ & take-out

**Sala Thai** 1301 U St NW (at 13th) **202/462-1333** • lunch & dinner • some veggie

**Smoke & Barrell** 2471 18th St NW **202/319-9353** • beer, bbq & bourbon

**Thaitanic** 1326 14th St NW (at Rhode Island Ave) **202/588-1795** • lunch & dinner • Thai • plenty veggie

**Zaytinia** 701 9th Street NW (at G St) **202/638-0800** • lunch & dinner • Greek/Mediterranean • plenty veggie

## ENTERTAINMENT & RECREATION

**Anecdotal History Tours** 301/294-9514 • gay-friendly • variety of guided tours • by appt only

**Bike & Roll Washington DC** 1100 Pennsylvania Ave NW (off 12th St, at Old Post Office Pavilion) **202/842-2453** • 9am-6pm • tour the nation's capital on bike!

**Capital Bikeshare** 877/430-2453 • look for the red bikes at parking stations around the city • join for 24hrs or longer

**Hillwood Museum & Gardens** 4155 Linnean Ave NW (at Tilden St NW) **202/686-5807** • 10am-5pm Tue-Sat • Fabergé, porcelain, furniture & more • reservations required

**National Museum of Women in the Arts** 1250 New York Ave **202/783-5000, 800/222-7270**

**Phillips Collection** 1600 21st St NW (at Q St) **202/387-2151** • clsd Mon • America's first museum of modern art • near Dupont Circle

**Washington Mystics** 202/266-2277, 877/324-6671 • check out the Women's Nat'l Basketball Association while you're in DC

## BOOKSTORES

**Kramerbooks & Afterwords Cafe & Grill** 1517 Connecticut Ave NW (at Q St) **202/387-1400** • 7:30am-1am, 24hrs wknds • also cafe & bar • live music • wheelchair access

## RETAIL SHOPS

**Universal Gear** 1529 14th St NW (btwn P & Q) **202/319-0136** • 11am-10pm, till midnight Fri-Sat • casual, club, athletic & designer clothing

## PUBLICATIONS

**Metro Weekly** 202/638-6830 • LGBT newsmagazine • extensive club listings

**Washington Blade** 202/747-2077 • LGBT newspaper

## EROTICA

**Bite the Fruit** 1723 Connecticut Ave NW (btwn R & S Sts) **202/299-0440** • 11am-11pm, till 18pm Sun • provocative apparel and furnishings for sexually curious and adventurous adults

# FLORIDA

## Statewide

### PUBLICATIONS

**Ambush Mag** 504/522–8047 • LGBT newspaper for the Gulf South (TX through FL)

**HOTSPOTS! Magazine** 954/928–1862 • "South Florida's largest gay publication"

**She Magazine, "The Source for Women"** 954/354–9751 • "The hippest & hottest source for women of the rainbow community"

## Boynton Beach

see also West Palm Beach

## Bradenton

see also Sarasota

## Clearwater

see also Dunedin, New Port Richey, Port Richey & St Petersburg

### ACCOMMODATIONS

**Holiday Inn Select** 3535 Ulmerton Rd (Rte 688 W) 727/577–9100, 888/465–4329 • gay-friendly • pool • restaurant & lounge • wheelchair access • WiFi

### BARS

**Pro Shop Pub** 840 Cleveland St (at Prospect) 727/447–4259 • 1pm-2am • popular • mostly gay men • neighborhood bar • bears • gay-owned

### RETAIL SHOPS

**Skinz** 2027 Gulf to Bay Blvd (aka State Rd 60, at Hercules Rd) 727/441–8789 • 10am-6pm, clsd Sun • men's & women's swimwear, gymwear & clubwear

## Cocoa

### BARS

**The Ultra Lounge** 407 Brevard Ave, Cocoa Village 321/690–0096 • 6pm-2am, from 4pm wknds • mostly gay men • neighborhood bar

## Daytona Beach

### ACCOMMODATIONS

**The August Seven Inn** 1209 S Peninsula Dr (at Silver Beach) 386/248–8420 • gay-friendly • 1 block from ocean • full brkfst • WiFi

**Mayan Inn** 103 S Ocean Ave 855/952–3224 • gay-friendly • pool • kids ok • WiFi • wheelchair access

**The Villa B&B** 801 N Peninsula Dr 386/248–2020 • gay-friendly • hot tub • pool • nudity • nonsmoking • gay-owned

### BARS

**Garbo's Lounge** 2842 S Ridgewood Ave, South Daytona 386/214-7599 • 3pm-2am • lesbians/gay men • dancing/DJ • drag shows • food served

**Streamline Lounge** 140 S Atlantic Ave (at Streamline Hotel) 386/258–6937 • 11am-3am (penthouse lounge) • gay-friendly • dancing/DJ • live entertainment • game room

### CAFES

**Java Joint & Eatery** 2201-E N Oceanshore Blvd, Flagler Beach 386/439–1013 • 7am-2pm

### RESTAURANTS

**Anna's Trattoria** 304 Seabreeze Blvd 386/239–9624 • 5pm-10pm, clsd Sun-Mon • Italian • beer/wine

**Frappes North** 123 W Granada Blvd (at S Yonge St), Ormond Beach 386/615–4888 • lunch Tue-Fri, dinner nightly, clsd Sun • patio • full bar • wheelchair access

### PUBLICATIONS

**Watermark** 407/481–2243 • bi-weekly LGBT newspaper for Central FL

## Dunedin

see also St Petersburg

### NIGHTCLUBS

**Blur Nighclub** 325 Main St 727/736–0206 • 8pm-2am, clsd Sun-Mon • mostly gay men • dancing/DJ • karaoke • drag shows

## Fort Lauderdale

### INFO LINES & SERVICES

**Lambda South Inc** 1306 E Las Olas Blvd • meeting space for LGBT in recovery • wheelchair access

**The Pride Center at Equality Park** 2040 N Dixie Hwy, Wilton Manors 954/463–9005 • 10am-10pm, noon-5pm wknds • outreach • wheelchair access

### ACCOMMODATIONS

**Alhambra Beach Resort** 3021 Alhambra St 954/525–7601, 877/309–4014 • gay/straight • motel • close to gay beach • pool • nonsmoking • WiFi • gay-owned

**The Deauville Hotel** 2916 N Ocean Blvd (Oakland Park Blvd & A1A) 954/568–5000 • gay-friendly • pool • non-smoking • wheelchair access

**Ed Lugo Resort** 2404 NE 8th Ave (Wilton Manors) **954/275-8299** • gay-friendly • pool • WiFi • gay-owned

**Island Sands Inn** 2409 NE 7th Ave **954/990-6499** • gay/ straight • pool • WiFi • gay-owned

**Marriott Harbor Beach Resort** 3030 Holiday Dr **954/525-4000, 800/222-6543** • gay-friendly • pool • also restaurant & spa • private beach access

**The Royal Palms Resort & Spa** 717 Breakers Ave **954/564-6444, 800/237-7256** • mostly gay men • nonsmoking • WiFi • gay-owned

## BARS

**13 Even** 2037 Wilton Dr **954/565-8550** • 4pm-11pm, till 1am Fri-Sat, 11am-10pm Sun • lesbians/gay men • wine bar & beer garden • tasty small plates

**Alibi** 2266 Wilton Dr (at NE 4th Ave) **954/565-2526** • 11am-2am, till 3am Fri-Sat • lesbians/ gay men • nonsmoking • food served • videos • WiFi • wheelchair access

**Beach Betty's** 625 Dania Beach Blvd (at Fronton Blvd), Dania **954/921-9893** • noon-3am • mostly women • neighborhood bar • dancing/DJ • live music • karaoke • lesbian-owned

**Cloud 9 Lounge** 7126 Stirling Rd, Davie **954/499-3525** • 7am-4am, from noon Sun • mostly women • multiracial clientele • live shows • drag shows • live bands

**Gym Sports Bar** 2287 Wilton Dr **954/368-5318** • 4pm-3am, from noon wknds • mostly gay men • neighborhood sports bar

**Infinity Lounge** 2184 Wilton Dr **754/223-3619** • 3pm-2am, mostly gay men

**J's Bar** 2780 Davie Blvd **954/581-8400** • 9am-2am, till 3am Fri-Sat, from noon Sun • lesbians/ gay men • neighborhood bar • dancing/DJ

**The Manor Complex** 2345 Wilton Dr, Wilton Manors **954/626-0082** • 11am-11pm • lesbians/ gay men • also Epic nightclub • also restaurant & cafe

**Matty's Video Bar** 2033 Wilton Dr **954/900-3973** • 2pm-2am, from noon wknds • mostly gay men

**Mona's** 502 E Sunrise Blvd (at 5th Ave) **954/525-6662** • noon-2am, till 3am wknds • mostly gay men • neighborhood bar • karaoke

**Monkey Business** 2740 N Andrews Ave **954/514-7819** • 7am-2am • mostly gay men • neighborhood bar • theme nights • cabaret • drag shows

**Naked Grape** 2163 Wilton Dr (at NE 20th St), Wilton Manors **954/563-5631** • 4pm-midnight, 2pm-1am Fri-Sat, clsd Sun-Mon • gay-friendly • wine bar

**Noche Latina Saturday** 2345 Wilton Dr (at Manor Complex), Wilton Manors **954/626-0082** • 11pm Sat • mostly gay men • dancing/DJ • multiracial

**Progress Bar** 2440 Wilton Dr, Wilton Manors **954/533-4916** • 4pm-2am, 2pm-3am Fri-Sat, from 1pm Sun • lesbians/gay men, more women Th • dancing/DJ

**Ramrod** 1508 NE 4th Ave (at 16th St) **954/763-8219** • 3pm-2am, till 3am wknds • popular • mostly gay men • leather/ levi cruise bar • patio • also LeatherWerks leather store

**Scandals** 3073 NE 6th Ave, Wilton Manors **954/567-2432** • noon-2am • mostly men • patio • dancing • country/ western • older crowd • wheelchair access

**Smarty Pants** 2400 Oakland Park Blvd **954/561-1724** • 9am-2am, till 3am Sat, noon-2am Sun • popular • mostly gay men • neighborhood bar • food served • karaoke • drag shows • wheelchair access

## NIGHTCLUBS

**Hunter's** 2232 Wilton Dr, Wilton Manors **954/630-3556** • 4pm-2am, from 2pm Sat, from noon Sun, till 3am wknds • mostly gay men • dancing/DJ • live shows • karaoke • drag shows • T-dance Sun • gay-owned

## CAFES

**Cafe Emunah** 3558 N Ocean Blvd **954/561-6411** • 11am-10pm, clsd Fri, sunset-1am Sat • kosher, kabbalistic cafe & teabar • food served

**Java Boys** 2230 Wilton Dr, Wilton Manors **954/564-8828** • 7am-11pm • WiFi

**Jimmies Chocolates & Cafe** 148 N Federal Hwy, Dania Beach **954/921-0688** • bistro w/ fresh fare & wine

**Oscar's Tea Room and Gift Shop** 1201 NE 26th St #101, Wilton Manors • 11am-10pm, till 6pm Sun, clsd Mon-Tue • authentic English Tea Room • gay-owned

**Storks** 2505 NE 15th Ave (at NE 26th St, Wilton Manors) **954/567-3220** • 6:30am-midnight • ladies night Mon • patio • wheelchair access

## RESTAURANTS

**La Bonne Crêpe** 815 E Las Olas Blvd **954/761–1515** • 7am-9:30pm, till 11:30pm Fri-Sat • patio

**Canyon** 1818 E Sunrise Blvd **954/765–1950** • Southwestern • full bar

**Courtyard Cafe** 2211 Wilton Dr **954/563–2499** • 7am-11pm, 24hrs Th-Sat • gay-owned

**Dapur, Asian Tapas and Lounge** 1620 N Federal Hwy **954/306–2663** • lunch weekday & dinner nightly

**Flip Flops** 3051 NE 32nd Ave **954/567–1672** • 11am-9pm, till 10pm Fri-Sat • casual waterfront dining

**The Floridian** 1410 E Las Olas Blvd **954/463–4041** • 24hr diner • wheelchair access

**Fuego Latino Cuban** 1417 E Commercial Blvd **954/351–7754** • 11am-10pm, till 11pm Fri-Sat, from noon Sun • beer/wine

**Galanga** 2389 Wilton Dr, Wilton Manors **954/202–0000** • dinner nightly, lunch weekdays • Thai • also sushi

**Humpy's** 2244 Wilton Dr, Wilton Manors **954/566–2722** • 11am-10pm, till 2am Th-Sat • pizza & panini

**J Marks Restaurant** 1245 N Federal Hwy **954/390–0770** • 11am-10pm, till 11pm Fri-Sat • full bar • gay-owned

**Kitchenetta** 2850 N Federal Hwy **954/567–3333** • dinner nightly, clsd Mon • wheelchair access

**La Bamba** 4245 N Federal Hwy **954/568–5662** • more gay Mon night

**Lester's Diner** 250 State Rd 84 **954/525–5641** • 24hrs • popular • more gay late nights • wheelchair access

**Lips** 1421 E Oakland Park Blvd (at Dixie Hwy) **954/567–0987** • 6pm-close, Sun brunch, clsd Mon • "the ultimate in drag dining" • karaoke

**Mason Jar Cafe** 2980 N Federal Hwy **954/568–4100** • 11:30am-3pm Mon-Fri, dinner nightly • upscale comfort food • gay-owned

**Mind Your Manors Bar & Grill** 2045 Wilton Dr, Wilton Manors **754/223–2172** • 11:30am-10pm

**Mojo** 4140 N Federal Hwy **954/568–4443** • open 4pm, clsd Sun • live shows • full bar

**Le Patio** 2401 NE 11th Ave **954 /530–4641** • comfort food • lesbian–owned

**PL8 Kitchen** 210 SW 2nd St **954/524–1818** • lunch & dinner, till 2am wknds • small plates

**Rosie's Bar & Grill** 2449 Wilton Dr, Wilton Manors **954/563–0123** • 11am-11pm • popular • full bar

**SAIA** 999 N Fort Lauderdale Beach Blvd **954/302–5252** • authentic Asian cuisine

**Scarfone's Coal Fired Pizza** 2150 Wilton Dr **954/533–0577** • 11:30mam-10:30pm, till 11:30pm Th-Sat, clsd Mon

**Sublime** 1431 N Federal Hwy **954/539–9000** • 5:30pm-10pm, clsd Mon • vegan/ vegetarian

**Tequila Sunrise Mexican Grill** 4711 N Dixie Hwy **954/938–4473** • 11:30am-10pm, till 11pm Th-Sat, 1pm-10pm Sun • live shows

**Tropics Cabaret & Restaurant** 2000 Wilton Dr (at 20th) **954/537–6000** • lunch & dinner, Sun brunch, till 3am Sat • also piano bar • gay-owned • wheelchair access

## ENTERTAINMENT & RECREATION

**Sebastian Beach** • more lesbians on the far north end of the beach

## BOOKSTORES

**Pride Factory** 850 NE 13th St **954/463–6600** • 10am-9pm, 11am-7pm Sun

## RETAIL SHOPS

**GayMartUSA** 2240 Wilton Dr (at NE 6th Ave) **954/630–0360** • 10am-midnight

**Out of the Closet** 2097 Wilton Dr, Wilton Manors **954/358–5580** • 10am-7pm, till 6pm Sun

**To The Moon** 2205 Wilton Dr (at 6th Ave), Wilton Manors **954/564–2987** • 10am-11pm • pride gifts, cards & candy candy candy!

## GYMS & HEALTH CLUBS

**Island City Health & Fitness** 2270 Wilton Dr, Wilton Manors **954/318–3900** • 5am-11pm, 8am-8pm wknds

## EROTICA

**Fetish Factory** 855 E Oakland Park Blvd **954/563–5777** • noon-9pm, noon-6pm Sun

**Hustler Hollywood** 1500 E Sunrise Blvd (at NE 15th Ave) **954/828–9769**

# Fort Myers

## INFO LINES & SERVICES

**Gay AA Lambda Drummers** 3049 McGregor Blvd (at St John the Apostle MCC) **239/275–5111 (AA#)** • 8pm Tue & Sat in social hall • wheelchair access

## ACCOMMODATIONS

**The Resort on Carefree Blvd** 3000 Carefree Blvd (at Cleveland Ave) **239/731–6366** • mostly women • homes & RV lots • pool • gym • kids/ pets ok • older crowd • nonsmoking • woman-owned

## BARS

**The Office Pub** 3704 Cleveland Ave (at Grove) **239/936–3212** • noon-2am • mostly gay men • neighborhood bar • bears • theme nights

**Rascals** 3758 Cleveland Ave (at US 41) **239/931-9976** • noon-2am • mostly gay men • dancing/DJ • drag shows • karaoke

**Rascals** 3750 Cleveland Ave (at US 41 & Collier), Fort Myers **239/931–9976** • noon-2am • lesbians/gay men • dancing/DJ • karaoke • drag shows

**Tubby's City Hangout** 4810 Vincennes St, Cape Coral **239/541–3540** • 2pm-2am • mostly gay men • karaoke • live shows • gay-owned

## NIGHTCLUBS

**The Bottom Line (TBL)** 3090 Evans Ave (at Hanson) **239/337–7292** • 2pm-2am • lesbians/ gay men • more women wknds • dancing/DJ • live shows • karaoke • videos • wheelchair access

## RESTAURANTS

**McGregor Grill** 15675 McGregor Blvd, Ste 24 **239/437–3499** • 11:30am-2am, from 4pm Sun • pub fare • some outdoor dining • also full bar • gay-owned

**The Oasis** 2260 Dr Martin Luther King Blvd **239/334–1566** • breakfast, lunch & dinner • beer/ wine • wheelchair access • women-owned

# Gainesville

## INFO LINES & SERVICES

**Free to Be AA** 3131 NW 13th St (The Pride Center) **352/372–8091 (AA#)** • 7:30pm Sun, LGBT AA group

**Pride Community Center** 3131 NW 13th St #62 **352/377–8915** • 3pm-7pm, noon-4pm Sat, clsd Sun

## BARS

**The University Club** 18 E University Ave (enter rear) **352/378–6814** • 5pm-2am, from 9pm Sat, till 11pm Sun • lesbians/ gay men • 3 levels • young crowd • dancing/DJ • karaoke • live shows • patio • wheelchair access

## ENTERTAINMENT & RECREATION

**Ponte Vedra LGBT Beach** • Go N from Gainesville on Waldo Rd to N 301, then E on I-10. I-10 becomes 95. Go S on 95, then take a left. Go E onto Butler Blvd, which ends at A1A. Turn right onto A1A & then drive 5 to 7 minutes looking for Guana Boat Landing parking lot on the right. Park in a parking lot or get ticketed

## BOOKSTORES

**Wild Iris Books** 22 SE 5th Ave Ste D **352/375–7477** • 1pm-9pm, till 5pm Sat, clsd Sun-Mon • feminist/ LGBT

# Hollywood

## EROTICA

**Pleasure Emporium** 1321 S 30th Ave **954/927–8181**

# Islamorada

## ACCOMMODATIONS

**Casa Morada** 136 Madeira Rd **305/664–0044, 888/881–3030** • gay-friendly • luxury all-suite hotel w/ private island • pool • pets ok • women-owned

**Lookout Lodge Resort** 87770 Overseas Hwy (at Plantation Blvd) **305/852–9915, 800/870–1772** • gay-friendly • waterfront resort • kids/ pets ok • nonsmoking • WiFi

# Jacksonville

## INFO LINES & SERVICES

**Free to Be LGBT AA** 634 Lomax St **904/399–8535 (AA#)** • 6:30pm Mon

**Women's Center of Jacksonville** 5644 Colcord Ave **904/722–3000**

## ACCOMMODATIONS

**Comfort Inn Oceanfront** 1515 N 1st St, Jacksonville Beach **904/241–2311, 800/654–8776** • gay-friendly • pool • fitness center • restaurant & Tiki bar

**Hilton Garden Inn Jacksonville JTB/ Deerwood Park** 9745 Gate Pkwy (at Southside Blvd) **904/997–6600, 877/782–9444** • gay-friendly • 15 minutes to beach • pool • jacuzzi • kids ok • WiFi • wheelchair access

**Spring Hill Suites Jacksonville** 4385 Southside Blvd (at J Turner Butler Blvd) **904/997–6650, 888/287–9400** • gay-friendly • pool • kids ok • nonsmoking • WiFi

## Bars

**Bo's Coral Reef** 201 5th Ave N (at 2nd St), Jacksonville Beach **904/246-9874** • 2pm-2am • lesbians/ gay men • neighborhood bar • dancing/DJ • live shows

**In Cahoots** 711 Edison Ave (btwn Riverside & Park) **904/353-6316** • 6pm-2am, clsd Mon • mostly gay men • dancing/DJ • multiracial • karaoke • drag shows • wheelchair access

**The Metro** 859 Willow Branch Ave **904/388-8719** • 2pm-2am, till 4am Fri-Sat • popular • lesbians/ gay men • dancing/DJ • drag shows • 18+ • wheelchair access

**The New Boot Rack Saloon** 4751 Lenox Ave (at Cassat Ave) **904/384-7090** • 3pm-2am • mostly gay men • country/ western • WiFi • beer/ wine • patio • wheelchair access

**Park Place Lounge** 931 King St (at Post) **904/389-6616** • noon-2am • lesbians/ gay men • neighborhood bar • dancing/DJ • wheelchair access

## Restaurants

**Al's Pizza** 1620 Margaret St, Ste 201 **904/388-8384** • 11am-10pm, till 11pm Fri-Sat, noon-9pm Sun • in Riverside/ Little 5 Points area

**Biscotti's** 3556 Saint Johns Ave (Talbot Ave) **904/387-2060** • 10:30am-10pm, till midnight Fri-Sat, from 8am Sat-Sun • popular • killer desserts • women-owned

**Bistro Aix** 1440 San Marco Blvd **904/398-1949** • 11am-10pm, till 11pm Fri, 5pm-11pm Sat, 5pm-9pm Sun • upscale French bistro

**European Street Cafe** 2753 Park St (at King) **904/384-9999** • 10am-10pm • salads • beer/ wine • patio • wheelchair access • gay-owned

**Mossfire Grill** 1537 Margaret St **904/355-4434** • lunch & dinner • Southwestern • full bar

# Key West

## Info Lines & Services

**Gay & Lesbian Community Center** 513 Truman Ave **305/292-3223** • many meetings & groups • WiFi

**Keep It Simple (Gay/ Lesbian AA)** **305/296-8654 (AA #)** • 8pm Mon-Sat, 5:30pm Sun

➤**Key West Business Guild** **305/294-4603, 800/535-7797** • see ad in front color section

## Accommodations

**Alexander Palms Court** 715 South St (at Vernon) **305/296-6413, 800/858-1943** • gay-friendly • pool • private patios • wheelchair access • gay-owned

**Alexander's Guest House** 1118 Fleming St (at Frances) **305/294-9919, 800/654-9919** • lesbians/ gay men • pool • nudity • WiFi • wheelchair access • gay-owned

**Ambrosia House Tropical Lodging** 615 & 618-622 Fleming St (at Simonton) **305/296-9838** • gay-friendly • pool • hot tub

**Andrews Inn** Zero Whalton Ln (at Duval) **305/294-7730, 888/263-7393** • gay-friendly • pool • kids ok • nonsmoking • WiFi

**The Artist House** 534 Eaton St (at Duval) **305/296-3977, 800/582-7882** • gay/ straight • nonsmoking

**Avalon B&B** 1317 Duval St (at United) **305/294-8233, 800/848-1317** • gay-friendly • swimming • near beach • sundeck • WiFi

**Cypress House & Guest Studios** 601 Caroline (at Simonton) **305/294-6969, 800/525-2488** • gay-friendly • guesthouse • 1888 Grand Conch mansion • pool • sundeck • WiFi • wheelchair access

**The Grand Guesthouse** 1116 Grinnell St **305/294-0590, 888/947-2630** • lesbians/ gay men • in converted rooming house built in 1880s for cigar workers • nonsmoking • WiFi • gay-owned

**Heartbreak Hotel** 716 Duval St (near Petronia) **305/296-5558** • gay/ straight • kitchens • lesbian & gay-owned

**Heron House Court** 412 Frances St (at Eaton) **800/932-9119** • gay-friendly • full brkfst • swimming • nonsmoking • WiFi • wheelchair access

**Key West Harbor Inn B&B** 219 Elizabeth St (at Greene) **305/296-2978, 800/608-6569** • lesbians/ gay men • pool • hot tub • nonsmoking • WiFi

**Knowles House B&B** 1004 Eaton St (at Grinnell) **305/296-8132, 800/352-4414** • gay/ straight • restored 1880s Conch house • pool • nudity • nonsmoking • gay-owned

**La Te Da** 1125 Duval St (at Catherine) **305/296-6706, 877/528-3320** • popular • lesbians/ gay men • full brkfst • nonsmoking • pool • restaurant & 3 bars • WiFi • gay-owned

**Marquesa Hotel** 600 Fleming St (at Simonton) **305/292-1919, 800/869-4631** • gay-friendly • 2 pools • also restaurant • full bar • nonsmoking • WiFi • wheelchair access

**The Mermaid & the Alligator—A Key West B&B** 729 Truman Ave (at Windsor Ln) **305/294-1894, 800/773-1894** • gay/ straight • full brkfst • pool • nonsmoking • WiFi • gay-owned

**Pilot House Guest House** 414 Simonton St (at Eaton) **305/293-6600, 800/648-3780** • gay/ straight • Victorian mansion in Old Town • pool • nudity • nonsmoking • WiFi • wheelchair access

**Seascape Inn** 420 Olivia St (at Duval) **305/296-7776, 800/765-6438** • gay-friendly • pool • hot tub • WiFi • nonsmoking

**Simonton Court Historic Inn & Cottages** 320 Simonton St (at Caroline) **305/294-6386, 800/944-2687** • gay-friendly • built in 1880s • pool • nonsmoking • WiFi

**The Southenmost Inn** 525 United St (at Duval) **305/292-1450, 800/749-6696** • gay/ straight • 2 hot tubs • pool • sundeck • nonsmoking • WiFi • also bar & restaurant • wheelchair access

**Tropical Inn** 812 Duval St (near Petronia) **305/294-9977, 888/611-6510** • gay-friendly • also cottage suites • hot tub • pool • sundeck • WiFi

### BARS

**The 801 Bourbon Bar** 801 Duval St (at Petronia) **305/294-4737** • 10am-4am, from noon Sun • lesbians/ gay men • neighborhood bar • dancing/DJ • popular drag shows • Sun bingo

**Bobby's Monkey Bar** 900 Simonton St (at Olivia) **305/294-2655** • noon-4am • mostly gay men • neighborhood bar • WiFi • wheelchair access

**Bourbon Street Pub** 724 Duval St (at Petronia) **305/293-9800** • 11am-4am, from noon Sun • mostly gay men • popular • garden bar w/ pool & hot tub • wheelchair access

**Garden of Eden** 224 Duval St **305/296-4565** • 10am-4am, from noon Sun • gay/ straight • clothing-optional sun bathing • dancing/DJ • live music

**Hog's Breath Saloon** 400 Front St **305/296-4222** • gay-friendly • food • music

**La Te Da** 1125 Duval St (at Catherine) **305/296-6706** • lesbians/ gay men • 3 bars (piano bar & cabaret) & restaurant • wheelchair access • gay-owned

### NIGHTCLUBS

**Aqua** 711 Duval St **305/294-0555** • 3pm-2am • lesbians/ gay men • dancing/DJ • drag shows • karaoke • wheelchair access • lesbian-owned

**Bottle Cap Lounge** **305/296-2807** • noon-4am • gay/ straight • dancing/ DJ

### CAFES

**Croissants de France** 816 Duval St **305/294-2624** • bakery 7:30am-6pm, restaurant open till 10pm • beer/ wine • patio

### RESTAURANTS

**Antonia's Restaurant** 615 Duval St (at Southard) **305/294-6565** • lunch & dinner • popular • Italian • full bar

**Azur** 425 Grinnell St **305/292-2987** • Mediterranean

**Blue Heaven** 729 Thomas St **305/296-8666** • great brkfst, also lunch & dinner • live entertainment

**Bo's Fish Wagon** 801 Caroline (at William) **305/294-9272** • lunch & dinner • popular • "seafood & eat it"

**Cafe Sole** 1029 Southard St (at Frances) **305/294-0230** • dinner nightly, Sun brunch • romantic • candlelit backyard

**Camille's** 1202 Simonton (at Catherine) **305/296-4811** • brkfst, lunch & dinner • bistro • hearty brkfst

**El Meson de Pepe** 410 Wall St (in Mallory Sq) **305/295-2620** • lunch & dinner • Cuban • live music

**The Flaming Buoy Filet Co** 1100 Packer St (at Virginia) **305/295-7970** • open daily at 6pm • wheelchair access

**Grand Cafe Key West** 314 Duval St **305/292-4740** • lunch & dinner

**Half Shell Raw Bar** 231 Margaret St **305/294-7496** • 11am-10pm • waterfront

**Hurricane Hole** **305/294-8025, 305/294-0200** • 10am-10pm • dockside bar

**Jack Flats** 509 Duval St **305/294-7955** • 11am-2am • wheelchair access

**Kelly's Caribbean Bar Grill & Brewery** 301 Whitehead St (at Caroline) **305/293-8484** • lunch & dinner • full bar • owned by actress Kelly McGillis

**La Trattoria Venezia** 524 Duval St (at Fleming) **305/296-1075** • 5pm-10:30pm • full bar

**Lobos Mixed Grill** 5 Key Lime Sq (south of Southard St) **305/296-5303** • 11am-6pm • sandwiches • plenty veggie • beer/ wine

**Louie's Backyard** 700 Waddell Ave (at Vernon) **305/294-1061** • 11:30am-1am • popular • fine cont'l dining

**Mangia Mangia** 900 Southard St (at Margaret St) **305/294-2469** • dinner only • fresh pasta • beer/ wine • patio

**Mangoes** 700 Duval St (at Angela) **305/292-4606** • lunch & dinner, bar till 1am • "Floribbean" cuisine • full bar • patio • wheelchair access

**Michaels** 532 Margaret St **305/295-1300** • dinner only • steakhouse

**New York Pasta Garden** 1075 Duval St (Duval Square) **305/292-1991** • 11am-10pm

**Nine One Five** 915 Duval St **305/296-0669** • dinner only • tapas • full bar

**Sarabeth's** 530 Simonton St **305/293-8181** • 8am-9pm • American

**Seven Fish** 632 Olivia St (at Elizabeth) **305/296-2777** • 6pm-10pm, clsd Tue • popular

**Six Toed Cat** 832 Whitehead St **305/294-3318** • brkfst & lunch

**Square One** 1075 Duval St (at Truman) **305/296-4300** • 4pm-11pm • full bar • wheelchair access

## ENTERTAINMENT & RECREATION

**Fort Zachary Taylor Beach** • more gay to the right

**Gay & Lesbian Trolley Tour** **305/294-4603** • 10:50am Sat • check out all of the gay hotspots & historical points • look for rainbow-decorated trolley

**Island Ceremonies** **305/304-0806, 305/745-8886** • commitment ceremonies in the Keys w/ Captain Lynda • woman-owned

**Moped Hospital** 601 Truman **866/296-1625** • forget the car—mopeds are a must for touring the island

**Venus Charters** Garrison Bight Marina **305/304-1181** • snorkeling • light-tackle fishing • dolphin-watching • personalized excursions • lesbian-owned

## BOOKSTORES

**Key West Island Books** 513 Fleming St (at Duval) **305/294-2904** • 10am-9pm, till 6pm Sun • new & used rare books • LGBT section

## RETAIL SHOPS

**In Touch Gay Pride Store** 706-A Duval St (at Angela) **305/294-1995** • 9am-9pm • gay gifts

## GYMS & HEALTH CLUBS

**Key West Island Gym** 1119 White St **305/295-8222** • gay-owned

## EROTICA

**Fairvilla Megastore** 520 Front St **305/292-0448** • 9am-midnight • clean, well-lighted adult store w/ emphasis on couples

**Leather Master** 418 Appelrouth Ln **305/292-5051** • 11am-10pm, noon-8pm Sun • custom leather, toys & more

# Lake Worth

see also **West Palm Beach**

## INFO LINES & SERVICES

**Compass LGBT Community Center** 201 N Dixie Hwy **561/533-9699** • 9am-9pm, till 7pm Fri, 3pm-7pm Sat • wheelchair access

## BARS

**The Bar** 2211 N Dixie Hwy **561/370-3954** • 2pm-2am, noon-midnight Sun • lesbians/ gay men • neighborhood bar • dancing/DJ • karaoke • lesbian-owned

**The Mad Hatter Bar & Grill** 1532 N Dixie Hwy (16th Ave) **561/547-8860** • 1pm-2am, noon-midnight Sun • mostly men • neighborhood bar • older crowd • gay-owned

## CAFES

**Mother Earth Sanctuary Cafe & Healing Center** **561/460-8647** • 8am-7pm, till 10pm Fri-Sat • fair trade • organic beans • cash only

## RESTAURANTS

**The Cottage** 522 Lucerne Ave **561/586-0080** • dinner only • also bar • wheelchair access

# Largo

## BARS

**Quench Lounge** 13284 66th St N **727/754-5900** • 2pm-2am • mostly gay men • dancing/DJ • karaoke • shows

# Marathon

## ACCOMMODATIONS

**Tropical Cottages** 243 61st St Gulf **305/743-6048** • gay-friendly • outdoor hot tub • pets ok • nonsmoking

## ENTERTAINMENT & RECREATION

**Bahia Honda State Park & Beach** 12 miles S of Marathon

# Melbourne

## ACCOMMODATIONS

**Crane Creek Inn B&B** 907 E Melbourne Ave **321/768-6416** • gay/ straight • full brkfst • pool • hot tub • dogs ok • WiFi

# MIAMI

**Miami is divided into 3 geographical areas:Miami—OverviewMiami—Greater MiamiMiami—Miami Beach/ South Beach**

## Miami—Overview

### INFO LINES & SERVICES

➤**Greater Miami CVB** 305/539-3000, 800/933-8448 • plan your Miami vacation! • see ad on inside back cover

**LGBT Visitor Center** 1130 Washington Ave, 1st flr N (at 11th St), Miami Beach 305/397-8914 • 9am-6pm, 11am-4pm wknds

**Switchboard of Miami** 305/358-1640 • 24hrs • gay-friendly info & referrals for Dade County

### ENTERTAINMENT & RECREATION

**Sailboat Charters of Miami** 3400 Pan American Dr (at S Bayshore Dr) 305/772-4221 • lesbians/ gay men • private sailing charters aboard all-teakwood 46-foot clipper to Bahamas & the Keys

## Miami—Greater Miami

### BARS

**The Dugout** 3215 NE 2nd Ave (at NE 32nd St) 305/438-1117 • 5pm-3am, clsd Mon-Tue • mostly gay men

**Eros Lounge** 8201 Biscayne Blvd 305/754-3444 • 4pm-3am, till midnight Sun-Mon • mostly gay men • neighborhood bar • karaoke • drag shows • monthly ladies night

### NIGHTCLUBS

**Azucar** 2301 SW 32nd Ave (at Coral Wy) 305/443-7657 • lesbian&gay men • 10:30pm-5am Th-Sat, clsd Mon-Wed • women's night Fri • dancing/DJ • Latina cliente • drag shows

**Discotekka** 950 NE 2nd Ave (at Metropolis Nightclub) 305/371-3773 • after hours Sat only • mostly gay men • dancing/DJ • 18+

**Space Miami** 34 NE 11th St (at NE 1st Ave) 305/375-0001 • gay-friendly • dancing/DJ • popular club w/ int'l visiting DJs

### CAFES

**Gourmet Station** 7601 Biscayne Blvd (at NE 71st St) 305/762-7229 • 8am-9pm, till 8pm Fri, clsd Sat-Sun

### RESTAURANTS

**Area 31** 270 Biscayne Blvd Way (at the Epic Hotel) 305/424-5234 • brkfst, lunch & dinner • seafood • amazing view • wheelchair access

**Cafeina** 297 NW 23rd St (W of Miami Ave) 305/438-0792 • 5pm-3am Th-Fri, from 9pm Sat, clsd Sun-Wed • tapas • also gallery, bands, events

**Habibi's Grill** 93 SE 2nd St (at NE 1st Ave) 786/425-2699 • 11am-8pm, clsd Sun • Lebanese/ Mediterranean • plenty veggie

**Jimmy's East Side Diner** 7201 Biscayne Blvd 305/754-3692 • 7am-4pm • wheelchair access

**Joey's** 2506 NW 2nd Ave 305/438-0488 • lunch & dinner, clsd Sun • Italian • patio

**The Magnum Lounge & Restaurant** 709 NE 79th St 305/757-3368 • 6pm-midnight, bar open 5pm-2am, clsd Mon • neighborhood bar • piano bar • reservations recommended

**Michy's** 6927 Biscayne Blvd (at NE 69th) 305/759-2001 • dinner only • "luxurious comfort food"

**Ortanique on the Mile** 278 Miracle Mile (at Salzedo), Coral Gables 305/446-7710 • lunch Mon-Fri, dinner nightly • Caribbean • full bar

**Ristorante Fratelli Milano** 213 SE 1st St (at 2nd Ave) 305/373-2300 • 11am-10pm • homemade Italian • wheelchair access

**Royal Bavarian Schnitzel Haus** 1085 NE 79th St 305/754-8002 • 5pm-11pm • German fare

**Soyka** 5556 NE 4th Ct 305/759-3117 • lunch & dinner, wknd brunch • full bar

**UVA 69** 6900 Biscayne Blvd (at NE 69th St) 305/754-9022 • 11am-11pm, 8am-midnight wknds • European bistro & lounge • patio

**Wynwood Kitchen & Bar** 2550 NW 2nd Ave 305/722-8959 • 5:30pm-midnight • Latin • great art

### ENTERTAINMENT & RECREATION

**Awarehouse Miami** 550 NW 29th St 305/576-4004 • artsy venue w/ live music, art shows & more

### BOOKSTORES

**Lambda Passages Bookstore** 7545 Biscayne Blvd (at NE 76th) 305/754-6900 • 11am-9pm, noon-6pm Sun • LGBT/ feminist

## Miami—Miami Beach/ South Beach

### ACCOMMODATIONS

**The Angler's** 660 Washington Ave 305/534-9600, 866/729-8800 • gay/ straight • luxury boutique resort • restaurant & lounge • pool • WiFi

**Beachcomber Hotel** 1340 Collins Ave (at 13th St) 305/531–3755, 888/305–4683 • gay-friendly • nonsmoking • WiFi

**Beacon South Beach Hotel** 720 Ocean Dr 305/674-820, 800/997–9814 • gay/straight • cont'l brkfst • WiFi

**Blue Moon Hotel** 944 Collins Ave 305/673–2262 • gay-friendly • pool • also bar

**The Cardozo Hotel** 1300 Ocean Dr 305/535–6500, 800/782–6500 • gay-friendly • restaurant • Gloria Estefan's plush hotel • kids ok • WiFi • wheelchair access

**The Century** 140 Ocean Dr 305/674–8855, 877/659–8855 • gay-friendly • nonsmoking • WiFi • wheelchair access

**Chesterfield Hotel, Suites & Day Spa** 855 Collins Ave 305/531–5831, 877/762–3477 • gay/ straight • super stylish hotel

**Circa 39 Hotel** 3900 Collins Ave (at 39th St) 305/538–4900, 877/824–7223 • gay-friendly • pool • lounge • WiFi • wheelchair access

**The Colony Hotel** 736 Ocean Dr (at 7th St) 305/673–0088 • gay-friendly • bistro • oceanfront • WiFi • wheelchair access

**Delano Hotel** 1685 Collins Ave 305/672–2000, 800/697–1791 • gay-friendly • food served • pool • kids ok • wheelchair access

**The European Guesthouse** 721 Michigan Ave (btwn 7th & 8th) 305/673–6665 • lesbians/ gay men • B&B • full brkfst • pool • WiFi • gay-owned

**The Hotel** 801 Collins Ave 305/531–2222, 877/843–4683 • gay-friendly • restaurant & bar • pool • nonsmoking • WiFi • wheelchair access

**Hôtel Gaythering** 1409 Lincoln Rd 786/284-1176
• mostly gay men • Miami Beach's only "straight friendly" hotel • bar & coffee shop

**Hotel Ocean** 1230–38 Ocean Dr 305/672–2579 • popular • gay/ straight • great location • pets ok • WiFi • wheelchair access

**The King & Grove Tides** 1220 Ocean Dr (at 12th St) 305/604–5070, 305/503–3268 • gay/ straight • private beach area • pool • WiFi • also La Marea restaurant

**The National Hotel** 1677 Collins Ave 305/532–2311, 800/327–8370 • gay/ straight • pool • kids ok • restaurant & lounge • WiFi • wheelchair access

**Penguin Hotel** 1418 Ocean Dr 305/534–9334 • lesbians/ gay men • full restaurant • kids ok • wheelchair access

**The Raleigh, Miami Beach** 1775 Collins Ave (at Ocean Front) 305/534-6300, 800/848–1775 • gay-friendly • pool • restaurant & bars • kids/ pets ok • WiFi • wheelchair access

**SoBeYou** 1018 Jefferson Ave 305/534–5247, 877/599–5247 • gay/ straight • nonsmoking • WiFi • wheelchair access • lesbian-owned

**South Seas** 1751 Collins Ave 305/538–1411, 800/345–2678 • gay-friendly • clean & basic • beach access • pool • WiFi

**The Winterhaven** 1400 Ocean Dr 305/531–5571 • gay/ straight • ocean views • also bar • WiFi • wheelchair access

## BARS

**Palace Bar & Grill** 1200 Ocean Dr (at 12th St) 305/531–7234 • 10am-1am, till 2am Fri-Sat • lesbians/ gay men • also restaurant • drag shows

## NIGHTCLUBS

**Pandora Events** 305/975–6933 • monthly women's parties • locations rotate so check website: www.pandoraevents.com

**Score** 1437 Washington Ave 305/535–1111 • lounge opens 3pm, dance club 10pm-5am Tue & Th-Sat • popular • lesbians/ gay men • drag shows • karaoke • videos

**Twist** 1057 Washington Ave (at 11th) 305/538–9478 • 1pm-5am • popular • mostly gay men • 7 bars • dancing/DJ • karaoke • drag shows • go-go boys • wheelchair access

## CAFES

**News Cafe** 800 Ocean Dr (at 8th St) 305/538–6397 • 24hrs • also gift shop and bar

## RESTAURANTS

**11th Street Diner** 1065 Washington (at 11th) 305/534–6373 • 24hrs • full bar

**B&B: Burger & Beer Joint** 1766 Bay Rd (at 18th St) 305/672–3287 • lunch & dinner • the name says it all

**Balans** 1022 Lincoln Rd (btwn Michigan & Lennox) 305/534–9191 • 8am-midnight

**Big Pink** 157 Collins (at 2nd St) 305/532–4700 • 8am-midnight, open late wknds • "real food for real people"

**Juice & Java** 1346 Washington Ave (at 14th St) 305/531–6675 • 9am-9pm, 10am-6pm Sun, • healthy fast food • wheelchair access

**Larios on the Beach** 820 Ocean Dr (at 8th) 305/532–9577 • 11:30am-midnight • Cuban • wheelchair access

**Nexxt Cafe** 700 Lincoln Rd (at Euclid Ave) 305/532–6643 • 11:30am-11pm, till midnight Fri-Sat

**Something Special, a Lesbian Venture** 305/696–8826 • women only • 6pm-10pm, clsd Mon-Tue • vegetarian • lesbian-owned

**Spiga** 1228 Collins Ave (at 12th St) 305/534–0079 • dinner only • tasty homemade pastas

**Sushi Rock Cafe** 1351 Collins Ave (at 14th) 305/532–2133 • noon-midnight • popular

### ENTERTAINMENT & RECREATION

**Fritz's Skate & Bike** 1620 Washington Ave 305/532–1954

**The Gay Beach/ 12th St Beach** 12th St & Ocean

**Haulover Beach Park** AIA S of Sunny Isle Blvd, North Miami Beach • popular nude beach

**Lincoln Rd** Lincoln Rd (btwn Bay Rd & Collins Aves) • pedestrian mall that embodies the rebirth of South Beach

**South Beach Bike Tours** 305/673–2002 • half-day bike tour of Art Deco district • gay-owned

### RETAIL SHOPS

**Perfect Gifts South Beach** 723 Lincoln Rd (at Meridian Ave) 305/397–8097 • 10am-11pm • unique gifts

### GYMS & HEALTH CLUBS

**Crunch** 1259 Washington Ave 305/674–8222

## Mt Dora

### ACCOMMODATIONS

**Adora Inn** 352/735–3110 • gay/ straight • full brkfst • kids 8+ ok • nonsmoking • WiFi • gay-owned

## Naples

**see also Fort Myers**

### BARS

**Bambusa Bar & Grill** 600 Goodlette Rd N (at 5th Ave N) 239/649–5657 • 4pm-midnight • gay-friendly • neighborhood bar • karaoke Sat • also restaurant • videos • gay-owned

### CAFES

**Sunburst Cafe** 2340 Pine Ridge Rd (at Airport Pulling Rd) 239/263–3123 • 7am-3pm • wheelchair access

### RESTAURANTS

**Caffe dell'Amore** 1400 Gulf Shore Blvd N (at Banyan Blvd) 239/261–1389 • dinner only • clsd Sun in summer • Italian • beer/ wine • reservations required • wheelchair access • gay-owned

**The Real Macaw** 3275 Bayshore Dr 239/732–1188 • occasionally have gay events

## Ocala

### BARS

**Copa/ Tropix** 2330 S Pine Ave 352/351–5721 • 2pm-2am • mostly gay men • dancing/DJ • drag shows • food served

**The Pub** 14 NW 5th St 352/857–7256 • 8pm-2am • mostly gay men • neighborhood bar

## Orlando

### INFO LINES & SERVICES

**GLBT Community Center of Central Florida** 946 N Mills Ave 407/228–8272 • 9am-9pm, noon-5pm Sat-Sun

### ACCOMMODATIONS

**B Resort & Spa** 1905 Hotel Plaza Blvd, Lake Buena Vista, DC 407/828–2828 • gay/straight • restaurants • pool • WiFi • wheelchair access

**Eo Inn & Spa** 227 N Eola Dr (at Robinson) 407/481–8485, 888/481–8488 • gay/ straight • boutique hotel • nonsmoking • sundeck • hot tub • WiFi • cafe on-site

**Four Points by Sheraton Studio City** 5905 International Dr (at Kirkman) 407/351–2100, 866/716–8105 • gay-friendly • bar & restaurant • pool • WiFi • wheelchair access

**Grand Bohemian Hotel Orlando** 325 S Orange Ave 407/313–9000, 888/213–9110 • gay-friendly • luxury hotel • pool • kids ok • nonsmoking • WiFi • wheelchair access

**Hyatt Residency Grand Cypress** 1 Grand Cypress Blvd 407/239–1234 • gay-friendly • 1,500 acre resort • private lake • horseback riding • golf • pool • WiFi • wheelchair access

**The Parliament House Resort** 410 N Orange Blossom Tr 407/425–7571 • lesbians/ gay men • pool • restaurant • wheelchair access • also 6 bars • multiracial • live shows • dancing/DJ • young crowd • gay-owned

**The Point Orlando Resort** 7389 Universal Blvd • gay-friendly • all-suite luxury boutique hotel, gym, bar & grill • pool • wheelchair access

**Rick's B&B** PO Box 22318, 32830 **407/414–7751** • mostly gay men • full brkfst • pool • nudity • patio • WiFi • gay-owned

**Wyndham Orlando Resort** 8001 International Dr **407/351–2420** • gay-friendly • villa surrounded by gardens • pools • wheelchair access

## BARS

**Bear's Den** 410 N Orange Blossom Tr (at Parliament House) **407/425–7571** • 6pm-2am, from noon wknds • mostly gay men • country/ western • levi/ leather • strippers • piano • also restaurant

**Club Revere** 6603 International Dr (at Sand Lake Rd) **407/770–6004** • mostly gay men • huge club with outdoor pool bar • live shows • wheelchair access • WiFi

**Copper Rocket** 106 Lake Ave (at 17-92), Maitland **407/645–0069** • 4pm-2am • gay-friendly • also restaurant • wheelchair access

**Hank's** 5026 Edgewater Dr (at Lee Rd) **407/291–2399** • noon-2am • mostly gay men • neighborhood bar • beer/ wine • patio • wheelchair access

**Stonewall Bar** 741 W Church St (at Glenn Ln) **407/373–0888** • 5pm-2am • mostly gay men • dancing/DJ • karaoke • wheelchair access • gay-owned

## NIGHTCLUBS

**Parliament House Resort** 410 N Orange Blossom Tr **407/425–7571** • 10:30am-3am • lesbians/ gay men • 6 bars • dancing/DJ • multiracial • live shows • videos • also restaurant • wheelchair access • gay-owned

**Pulse Orlando** 1912 S Orange Ave (at Kaley St) **407/649–3888** • 9pm-2am, clsd Sun • mostly gay men • dancing/DJ • theme nights • drag shows • 18+

**Southern Nights** 375 S Bumby Ave (at South St) **407/412–5039** • 4pm-2:30am, from 9pm Sun-Mon • lesbians/ gay men •

## CAFES

**Pom Pom's** 67 N Bumby Ave **407/894–0865** • 11am-5am, 24hrs Fri-Sat • tea & sandwiches

**White Wolf Cafe & Antique Shop** 1829 N Orange Ave (at Princeton) **407/895–9911** • 7am-9pm, till 10pm Fri-Sat, 8am-3pm Sun • beer/ wine • wheelchair access

## RESTAURANTS

**Dandelion Communitea Cafe** 618 N Thornton Ave (at Colonial) **407/362–1864** • 11am-10pm, till 3pm Mon, till 5pm Sun • vegetarian/ vegan • beer/ wine

**Dexter's Thornton Park** 808 E Washington St **407/648–2777** • lunch & dinner • also Winter Park & Lake Mary locations

**Ethos Vegan Kitchen** 601-B New York Ave (at Fairbanks) **407/228–3898** • 11am-10pm, 10am-3pm Sun • WiFi • wheelchair access

**Funky Monkey Wine Company** **407/427–1447** • 5pm-11pm • sushi • drag shows weekly

**Garden Cafe** 810 W Colonial Dr (at Westmoreland) **407/999–9799** • 11am-10pm, from noon wknds • clsd Mon • vegetarian Chinese • wheelchair access

**Hamburger Mary's Orlando** 110 W Church St (at Garland) **321/319–0600** • 11am-midnight, till 1am Th-Sat • full bar • live shows • karaoke • wheelchair access • gay-owned

**Houston's** 215 South Orlando Ave, Winter Park **407/740–4005** • lunch & dinner • upscale American • wheelchair access

**Hue** 629 E Central Blvd (at N Summerlin Ave) **407/849–1800** • lunch & dinner • new American • full bar

**Loving Hut** 2101 E Colonial Dr (at Palm Dr) **407/894–5673** • 11am-9pm, from 3pm Sun, clsd Tue • vegetarian/ vegan • wheelchair access

**The Rainbow Cafe** at Parliament House **407/425–7571** • 7am-11pm • lesbians/ gay men

## BOOKSTORES

**Mojo** 930 N Mills Ave (at E Marks St) **407/896–0204** • 1pm-8pm, 3pm-6pm Sun • LGBT

## RETAIL SHOPS

**A Comic Shop** 114 South Semoran Blvd, Winter Park **407/332–9636** • 11am-7pm, till 9pm Wed, till midnight Fri-Sat

**Fairvilla's Sexy Things** 7631 International Blvd **407/826–1627** • gifts • adult toys • clothing

## PUBLICATIONS

**Hotspots** 954/928–1862 • weekly entertainment guide

**Watermark** PO Box 533655 32853 **407/481–2243** • bi-weekly LGBT newspaper for Central FL

## EROTICA

**Fairvilla Megastore** 1740 N Orange Blossom Tr **407/425–6005** • 9am-2am

## Palm Beach

### ACCOMMODATIONS

**The Chesterfield Hotel** 363 Coconut Row
**561/659-5800** • gay-friendly • pool • jacuzzi

### RESTAURANTS

**Ta-boo** 221 Worth Ave **561/835-3500** •
11:30am-10pm, till 11pm Fri-Sat • cont'l •
wheelchair access

## Panama City

### ACCOMMODATIONS

**Casa de Playa** 20304 Front Beach Rd,
Panama City Beach **850/381-1351** • lesbians/
gay men • guesthouse • steps from Gulf of
Mexico • jacuzzi • pool • nonsmoking • patios
• gay-owned

**Wisteria Inn** 20404 Front Beach Rd, Panama
City Beach **850/234-0557** • gay/ straight •
tropical inn • hot tub • pool • nonsmoking

### BARS

**Splash Bar** 6520 Thomas Dr, Panama City
Beach **850/236-3450** • 6pm-2am, till 4am Th-
Sat • mostly gay men • 18+ • drag shows •
also pride shop • wheelchair access • gay-
owned

### NIGHTCLUBS

**Fiesta Room** 110 Harrison Ave (at Beach Dr)
**850/763-1755** • 3pm-3am • popular •
lesbians/ gay men • dancing/DJ • drag shows •
wheelchair access

## Pensacola

### INFO LINES & SERVICES

**GLBT AA Group** 716 9th Ave (at Jackson)
**850/433-4191 (AA#)** • 6pm Sun

### BARS

**The Cabaret** 101 S Jefferson St
**850/607-2020** • 3pm-3am • lesbians/ gay
men • live shows • karaoke • wheelchair
access

**The Round-Up** 560 E Heinberg St
**850/433-8482** • 2pm-3am • popular • mostly
gay men • neighborhood bar • videos • patio
• wheelchair access

### NIGHTCLUBS

**Emerald City** 406 E Wright St (at Alcaniz)
**850/433-9491** • 3pm-3am, dance club from
9pm, clsd Tue • popular • lesbians/ gay men •
dancing/DJ • live shows • 18+ • patio •
wheelchair access

### CAFES

**End of the Line Cafe** 610 E Wright St
**850/429-0336** • 10am-10pm, 11am-5pm Sun,
clsd Mon • vegetarian cafe • live bands • art •
WiFi • wheelchair access

## Pompano Beach

### RESTAURANTS

**J Marks Restaurant** 1490 NE 23th St (at
Federal Hwy/ US1) **954/782-7000** • 11am-
10pm, till 11pm Fri-Sat • live music wknds •
full bar • gay-owned

### EROTICA

**Exxxit Video** 1833 E Sample Rd
**954/783-6570**

## Sarasota

### INFO LINES & SERVICES

**Gay AA** 7225 N Lockwood Ridge Rd (in
Pierce Hall, Church of the Trinity MCC)
**941/355-0847 (CHURCH #)** • 7pm Sun & 7pm
Th

### ACCOMMODATIONS

**The Cypress** 621 Gulfstream Ave S
**941/955-4683** • gay-friendly • B&B inn • full
brkfst • nonsmoking • WiFi

**Turtle Beach Resort** 9049 Midnight Pass
Rd **941/349-4554** • gay-friendly • pool •
nonsmoking • WiFi • wheelchair access

### NIGHTCLUBS

**Throb** 2201 Industrial Blvd **941/358-6969** •
3pm-2am, till 9pm Mon,Th & Sun • mostly gay
men • dancing/DJ • drag shows • gay-owned

### RESTAURANTS

**Caragiulos** 69 S Palm Ave **941/951-0866** •
lunch & dinner • Italian-American

## South Beach

see **Miami Beach/ South Beach**

## St Augustine

see also **Jacksonville**

### ACCOMMODATIONS

**Alexander Homestead** 14 Sevilla St
**904/826-4147, 888/292-4147** • gay-friendly •
Victorian inn • full brkfst • WiFi

**Casa Monica** 95 Cordova St **904/827-1888,
888/213-8903** • gay-friendly • restaurant &
piano bar • gym • pool • kids ok • wheelchair
access

**The Inn at Camachee Harbor** 201 Yacht Club Dr (at May St) **904/825–0003, 800/688–5379** • gay-friendly • restaurant & bar • WiFi

**Our House B&B** 7 Cincinnati Ave **904/347–6260** • gay/ straight • full brkfst • WiFi • gay-owned

## RESTAURANTS

**Collage** 60 Hypolita St **904/829–0055** • dinner nightly • "artful global dining" • reservations required

# St Petersburg

see also Tampa

## ACCOMMODATIONS

**Bay Palms Waterfront Resort** 4237 Gulf Blvd, St Petersburg Beach **727/360–7642, 800/257–8998** • gay-friendly • pool • nonsmoking • WiFi • kids/ pets ok

**Boca Ciega B&B** **727/381–2755** • women only • B&B in private home • pool • lesbian-owned

**Changing Tides Cottages** 225 Boca Ciega Dr, Madeira Beach **727/397–7706** • gay/ straight • rental cottages • WiFi • lesbian-owned

**Cordova Inn** 253 2nd Ave N (at 2nd St) **727/822–7500, 800/735–6607** • gay/ straight • kids ok

**Dicken's House B&B** 335 8th Ave NE **727/822–8622, 800/381–2022** • gay/ straight • pool • full brkfst • WiFi • gay-owned

**Flamingo Resort** 4601 34th St South **727/321–5000** • mostly gay men • pool • hotel with 6 theme bars & restaurant • live shows • WiFi • wheelchair access

**The Hotel Zamora** 3701 Gulf Blvd **727/456–8900** • gay/straight • new Mediterranean boutique luxury with a great rooftop bar • restaurant on site • pool

**La Veranda B&B** 111 5th Ave N **727/224–1057** • gay/ straight • 1 block from the beach • women-owned

**Postcard Inn on the Beach** 6300 Gulf Blvd **727/367–2711, 800/237–8918** • gay-friendly • pool • restaurant • WiFi

## BARS

**Enigma** 1110 Central Ave **727/235-0867** • noon-3am • gay/straight • dancing/DJ • karaoke

**Oar House** 4807 22nd Ave S **727/327–1691** • 9am-2am, from 11am Sun • lesbians/ gay men • neighborhood bar • karaoke

**A Taste for Wine** 241 Central Ave (at 2nd St N) **727/895–1623** • 4pm-9pm, till midnight Fri-Sat, clsd Mon • occasional lesbian events • women-owned

## RESTAURANTS

**Bella Brava** 204 Beach Dr NE **727/895–5515** • new world trattoria

**Central Avenue Oyster Bar** 249 Central Ave **727/897–9728** • 11am-midnight

**Parkshore Grill** 300 Beach Dr NE **727/896–3463** • local favorite

**Sea Porch Cafe** 3400 Gulf Blvd (at Don Cesar Hotel) **727/360–1884** • beach views

**Sea Salt** 183 2nd Ave N **727/873–7964** • fine dining

**Skyway Jack's** 2795 34th St S **727/867–1907** • 5am-3pm • Southern cooking (diner-style)

## ENTERTAINMENT & RECREATION

**Bedrocks Beach/ Sunset Beach** W Gulf Blvd (at S end of Treasure Island, Sunset Beach) • popular park

**Dali Museum** 1 Dali Blvd **727/823–3767, 800/442–3254** • soak in the brilliance as you are surrounded by an unparalleled collection of works by renowned artist Salvador Dalí. Enjoy an afternoon wandering through the awe-inspiring building and interactive gardens then grab a bite of authentic Spanish cuisine at Café Gala

**Fort DeSoto Park** Pinellas Bayway S • beautiful gay beach

# Tampa

see also St Petersburg

## ACCOMMODATIONS

**Don Vicente de Ybor Inn** 1915 Republica de Cuba **813/241–4545, 866/206–4545** • gay/ straight • cafe & bar

**Gram's Place Hostel** 3109 N Ola Ave **813/221–0596** • gay/ straight • nudity • kids ok • nonsmoking • WiFi

**Hampton Inn & Suites** 1301 East 7th Ave **813/247–6700** • gay/ straight • WiFi • pool • wheelchair access

**Hyatt Regency** 211 N Tampa St **813/225–1234** • gay/ straight • pool • restaurant & bar • WiFi • wheelchair access

**Sawmill Camping Resort** 21710 US Hwy 98, Dade City **352/583–0664** • mostly gay men • theme wknds w/ entertainment • RV hookups • cabins • tent spots • dancing • karaoke • pool • nudity • gay-owned

## Bars

**Baxter's** 1519 S Dale Mabry (at W Neptune) **813/258-8830** • noon-3am • mostly gay men • neighborhood bar • karaoke • wheelchair access

**Body Shop Bar** 14905 N Nebraska **813/971-3576** • 3pm-3am • mostly gay men • neighborhood bar • karaoke • gay-owned

**Bradley's on 7th** 1510 E 7th Ave, Ybor City **831/241-2723** • 4pm-3am • mostly gay men • dancing/DJ • drag shows

**Centro Cantina** 1600 E 8th Ave **813/241-8588** • 11am-9pm, till 2am Fri-Sat 8 gay/straight • Tex Mex • great balcony

**City Side** 3703 Henderson Blvd (at Dale Mabry) **813/350-0600** • 11am-3am • lesbians/gay men • dancing/DJ • neighborhood bar • karaoke • WiFi • patio

## Nightclubs

**The Castle** 2004 N 16th St **813/247-7547** • 10:30pm-3am, clsd Tue-Wed • mixed gay/straight • dancing/DJ • theme nights

**Crowbar** 1812 N 17th St **813/241-8600** • 10pm-3am • mixed gay/straight • dancing/DJ • live shows • karaoke

**Liquid** 1502 E 7th Ave **813/248-6104** • 4pm-3am, from 7pm Sat, clsd Mon • mostly gay men • dancing/DJ • drag shows

**Southern Nights** 1401 E 7th Ave **813/599-8625** • 8pm-3am, from 4pm Fri-Sat, clsd Sun-Tue • lesbians/gay men • dancing/DJ • drag shows

**Southern Nights** 1401 E 7th Ave **813/599-8625** • 8pm-3am, from 4pm Fri-Sat, clsd Sun-Tue • lesbians/gay men • dancing/DJ • drag shows

**Steam Fridays** 1507 E 7th Ave (at the Honey Pot) **813/247-4663** • 10pm Fri only • mostly gay men • dancing/DJ • 18+ • 3 flrs

## Cafes

**Joffrey's Coffee** 1600 E 8th Ave **813/247-4600** • 7am-10pm, till midnight wknds • WiFi

**Sacred Grounds Cafe** 4819 E Busch Blvd (at Hyaleah Rd) **813/983-0837** • 6pm-midnight, till 2am Fri-Sat • lesbians/gay men • live music, poetry, performance • WiFi

**Tre Amici** 1907 19th St N **813/247-6964** • 8am-5pm, till 11pm Th, clsd Sun • cafe & wine bar

## Restaurants

**Bernini** 1702 E 7th Ave **813/248-0099** • lunch Mon-Fri, dinner nightly • Italian

**Columbia** 2117 E 7th Ave **813/248-4961** • 11am-close, from noon Sun • Cuban & Spanish

**Crabby Bill's** 401 Gulf Blvd, Indian Rocks Beach **727/595-4825** • inexpensive seafood joint

**Gaspar's Grotto** 1805 E 7th Ave **813/248-5900** • 11am-3am • live shows • karaoke • WiFi • patio

**Hamburger Mary's** **813/241-6279** • 11am-11pm • live music • karaoke * wheelchair acess • gay-owned

**JJ's Cafe & Bar** 1601 E 7th Ave (at N 16th St) **813/247-4125** • 11am-10pm, till 2:30am wknds

**The Laughing Cat** 1820 N 15th St **813/241-2998** • Italian • wheelchair access

**The Queen's Head** 2501 Central Ave, St Petersburg **727/498-8584** • 4:30pm-2am, from noon wknds, clsd Mon • European • full bar

## Entertainment & Recreation

**Picnic Island** Picnic Island Blvd (across from the military base, on E side) • gay beach at end of park

## Retail Shops

**King Corona Cigars** 1523 E 7th Ave **888/248-3812** • local, handmade cigars • also cafe & bar

**The MC Film Festival** 1901 N 15th St (at 8th Ave) **813/247-6233** • LGBT pride gift store

## Publications

**Watermark** **813/655-9890, 877/926-8118** • bi-weekly LGBT newspaper for Central FL

# West Palm Beach

## Accommodations

**Grandview Gardens B&B** 1608 Lake Ave (at Palm) **561/833-9023** • gay-friendly • pool • nonsmoking • WiFi • wheelchair access • gay-owned

**Hotel Biba** 320 Belvedere Rd **561/832-0094** • mid-century chic motor lodge

**Scandia Lodge** 625 S Federal Hwy (at 6th Ave), Lake Worth **561/586-3155** • gay/straight • pool • pets ok • nonsmoking

## Bars

**Fort Dix** 6205 Georgia Ave (at Colonial) **561/533-5355** • noon-3am, till 4am Fri-Sat • mostly gay men • neighborhood dive bar • dancing/DJ wknds • patio • wheelchair access

**HG Rooster's** 823 Belvedere Rd (btwn Parker & Lake) **561/832-9119** • 3pm-3am, till 4am Fri-Sat • popular • mostly gay men • neighborhood bar • drag shows • karaoke • food served • wheelchair access

## NIGHTCLUBS

**Respectable Street** 518 Clematis St **561/832-9999** • 9pm-3am, till 4am Fri-Sat, clsd Sun-Tue • gay-friendly • dancing/DJ • alternative • retro & new wave nights • live music

## RESTAURANTS

**Rhythm Cafe** 3800-A S Dixie Hwy **561/833-3406** • 6pm-10pm, clsd Mon • some veggie • beer/wine

**Thai Bay** 1900 Okeechobee Blvd (in Palm Beach Market Pl) **561/640-0131** • lunch & dinner, clsd Sun

## ENTERTAINMENT & RECREATION

**MacArthur Beach** Singer Island, N Palm Beach

## BOOKSTORES

**Changing Times Bookstore** 911 Village Blvd #806 (at Palm Beach Lakes) **561/640-0496** • 10am-7pm, till 5pm Sat-Sun • community bulletin board • wheelchair access

## RETAIL SHOPS

**Eurotique** 814 Northlake Blvd, North Palm Beach **561/684-2302** • 10am-8pm, till 6pm Sat, noon-5pm Sun • leather • books • videos

## Wilton Manors

**see Fort Lauderdale**

## Winter Haven

### BARS

**Old Man Frank's** 1005 S Lake Howard Dr (at Central) **863/294-9179** • 11am-2am, from noon-midnight Sun • gay-friendly • on the lake • food served • smoking allowed • wheelchair access

## GEORGIA

## Athens

### ACCOMMODATIONS

**Ashford Manor B&B** 5 Harden Hill Rd (at Main St), Watkinsville **706/769-2633** • gay-friendly • pool • nonsmoking • WiFi • gay-owned

### BARS

**The Globe** 199 N Lumpkin St (at Clayton) **706/353-4721** • 11am-2am, till midnight Sun • gay-friendly • 40 single-malt scotches • also restaurant

### NIGHTCLUBS

**Forty Watt Club** 285 W Washington St (at Pulaski) **706/549-7871** • call for events• gay-friendly • alternative • live music • wheelchair access

### CAFES

**Jittery Joe's Coffee** 297 E Broad St (at Jackson) **706/613-7449** • 7am-11pm, from 8am wknds • WiFi • gallery • wheelchair access

### RESTAURANTS

**The Grit** 199 Prince Ave **706/543-6592** • 11am-10pm, great wknd brunch 10am-3pm • ethnic vegetarian • wheelchair access

## Atlanta

### INFO LINES & SERVICES

**Galano Club** 585 Dutch Valley Rd (at Monroe) **404/881-9188** • meetings throughout the day • LGBT recovery club • call for meeting times

### ACCOMMODATIONS

**The Georgian Terrace Hotel** 659 Peachtree St NE (at Ponce de Leon) **404/897-1991, 800/651-2316** • gay-friendly • "Atlanta's only historic luxury hotel" • hosted Gone w/ the Wind world-premier reception in 1939 • pool • kids ok • WiFi • wheelchair access

**Glenn Hotel** 110 Marietta St NW (at Spring) **404/521-2250, 888/717-8851** • gay/straight • boutique hotel • also restaurant & rooftop lounge • WiFi

**Hotel Indigo** 683 Peachtree St NE (at 3rd) **404/874-9200, 800/863-7818** • cozy, stylish no-frills hotel • workout room • also restaurant • WiFi

**Le Méridien Atlanta Perimeter Hotel**
111 Perimeter Center W (at Ashford
Dunwoody Rd) **770/396–6800** • gay-friendly •
pool • nonsmoking • WiFi • also restaurant •
wheelchair access

**Stonehurst Place Bed & Breakfast** 923
Piedmont Ave NE (at 8th St) **404/881–0722,
877/285–2246** • gay/ straight • in 1896
shingle-style house furnished w/ antiques • full
brkfst • nonsmoking • WiFi • lesbian-owned

**W Atlanta Midtown** 188 14th St NE (at
Juniper St NE) **404/892–6000** • gay/ straight •
stylish hotel • WiFi • pool • convenient
location

## BARS

**Amsterdam** 502 Amsterdam Ave NE
**404/892–2227** • 11:30am-close • mostly gay
men • dancing/DJ • food served • video &
sports bar

**Atlanta Eagle** 306 Ponce de Leon Ave NE
(at Argonne) **404/873–2453** • 7pm-3am, from
5pm Sat, clsd Sun • popular • mostly gay men
• dancing/DJ • bears • leather • also leather
store • gay-owned

**Blake's on the Park** 227 10th St (at
Piedmont) **404/892–5786** • 3pm-3am, from
1pm Fri-Sun, till midnight Sun • lesbians/ gay
men • karaoke • drag shows

**Bulldogs** 893 Peachtree St NE (btwn 7th &
8th) **404/872–3025** • 4pm-3am, 12:30pm-
midnight Sun • mostly gay men • African-
American clientele

**Burkhart's Pub** 1492–F Piedmont Ave NE
(at Monroe, in Ansley Square) **404/872–4403**
• 4pm-3am, from 2pm wknds, till midnight
Sun • lesbians/ gay men • neighborhood bar •
food served • karaoke • live shows • patio •
wheelchair access

**The Daiquiri Factory** 889 W Peachtree St
(at 7th) **404/881–8188** • 11am-2:30am •
lesbians/ gay men • the name says it all

**Eddie's Attic** 515–B N McDonough St (at
Trinity Place), Decatur **404/377–4976** • 5pm-
close Mon-Th, till 2am Fri-Sat, open 1 hr
before showtime Sun • gay/ straight •
occasional lesbian hangout • live music •
open mic & comedy • restaurant • rooftop
deck

**Felix's on the Square** 1510-G Piedmont Ave
NE (Ansley Square) **404/249–7899** • 2pm-
2:30am, from noon Sat, 12:30pm-midnight
Sun • mostly gay men • food served • karaoke
• wheelchair access

**Friends on Ponce** 736 Ponce de Leon NE
(at Ponce de Leon Pl) **404/817–3820** • 2pm-
3am, from noon Sat, till midnight Sun •
rooftop patio • WiFi • wheelchair access

**The Hideaway** 1544 Piedmont Ave NE #124
(at Monroe, in Ansley Mall) **404/874–8247** •
2pm-2am Mon-Th, till 3am Fri-Sat, 12:30pm-
midnight Sun • mostly men • neighborhood
bar • wheelchair access

**Mary's** 1287B Glenwood Ave (at Flat Shoals)
**404/624–4411** • 5pm-3am, clsd Sun-Mon •
lesbians/ gay men • friendly neighborhood •
dancing/DJ • karaoke • videos • wheelchair
access

**Mixx** 1492–B Piedmont Ave NE (at Monroe,
in Ansley Square) **404/228–4372** • 4pm-2am,
till 3am Fri-Sat, clsd Sun • mostly gay men •
neighborhood bar • dancing/DJ wknds •
karaoke • bears • food served

**My Sister's Room** 66 12th Street NE
**678/705–4585** • 8pm-close, clsd Sun-Tue •
popular • mostly women • live music • also
restaurant • younger crowd • patio

**My Sister's Room** 66 12th Street NE
**678/705–4585** • 8pm-close, clsd Sun-Tue •
popular • mostly women • live music • also
restaurant • younger crowd • patio

**Opus I** 1086 Alco St NE (at Cheshire Bridge)
**404/634–6478** • 11am-3am, 12:30pm-
midnight Sun • mostly gay men •
neighborhood bar • wheelchair access

**Oscar's Video Bar** 1510-C Piedmont Ave NE
(in Ansley Mall) **404/815–8841** • 2pm-2:30am,
clsd Sun • mostly gay men • drag shows

**Sister Louisa's Church of the Living
Room & Ping Pong Emporium** 466
Edgewood Ave SE **404/522-8275** • 5pm-3am
• lesbians/gay men • Church, as it's commonly
called, is a quirky spot loaded with tongue-in-
cheek (sac)religious art, killer organ karaoke
Wed and super-gay patio parties

## NIGHTCLUBS

**Girls in the Night** • women's parties &
events around Atlanta • check local listings or
girlsinthenight.com

**The Heretic** 2069 Cheshire Bridge Rd (at
Piedmont) **404/325–3061** • 9am-3am, clsd
Sun, till 11pm Mon-Tue • mostly gay men •
dancing/DJ • wheelchair access

**Ladies at Play** 79 Poplar St (at Fairlie St) •
monthly women's dance party • check
ladiesatplay.com for details • mostly women •
dancing/DJ • multiracial

**Traxx** 866/602–5553 • dance parties & events around Atlanta • mostly gay men • dancing/DJ • mostly African American • live shows

**Traxx Girls Parties** 888/935–8729 • weekly women's dance parties • check traxxgirls.com for info

**Wild Mustang/ Jungle** 2115 Faulkner Rd NE (off Cheshire Bridge Rd NE) 404/844–8800 • 10pm-3am, clsd Sun • lesbians/ gay men • dancing/DJ • also Stars of the Century (drag shows) Mon 11pm • cover charge

## CAFES

**Apache Cafe** 64 3rd St NW 404/876–5436 • food served • poetry readings • events • gallery • multiracial

**Aurora Coffee** 468 Moreland Ave 404/523–6856 • 6:30am-9pm, from 7am wknds

**Intermezzo** 1845 Peachtree Rd NE 404/355–0411 • 7:30am-2am • classy cafe • plenty veggie • full bar • great desserts

## RESTAURANTS

**Apres Diem** 931 Monroe Dr #C-103 404/872–3333 • 11:30am-midnight, till 2am Fri-Sat, from 11am wknds, brunch Sat-Sun • French bistro • live jazz Wed • full bar

**Aria** 490 E. Paces Ferry 404/233–7673 • dinner only, clsd Sun

**Aurum** 915 Peachtree St (at 8th St) 404/815–9426 • 9pm-2am, till 3am wknds • gay/ straight • lounge

**Bacchanalia/ Star Provisions/ Quinones** 1198 Howell Mill Rd NW 404/365–0410 • dinner only, clsd Sun • upscale • American

**Buckhead Diner** 3073 Piedmont Rd NE 404/262–3336 • lunch Mon-Sun, dinner nightly, Sun brunch • upscale diner fare

**Cafe Sunflower** 2140 Peachtree Rd NW (at Bennett St NW) 404/352–8859 • lunch & dinner, clsd Sun • vegetarian

**The Colonnade** 1879 Cheshire Bridge Rd NE 404/874–5642 • dinner nightly, lunch wknds • traditional Southern

**Cowtippers** 1600 Piedmont Ave NE (at Monroe) 404/874–3751 • 11am-11pm, till midnight Fri-Sat • steak house • transgender-friendly • wheelchair access

**Ecco** 40 7th St NE 404/347–9555 • 5:30pm-10pm, till 11pm Fri-Sat, till 10pm Sun • Italian • reservations recommended • wheelchair access

**Einstein's** 1077 Juniper St (at 12th) 404/876–7925 • 11am-11pm, till midnight Fri-Sat, from 9am Sun, wknd brunch • popular • some veggie • full bar • patio • wheelchair access • reservations accepted

**The Flying Biscuit Cafe** 1655 McLendon Ave (at Clifton) 404/687–8888 • 7am-10pm • popular • healthy brkfst all day • plenty veggie • beer/ wine • wheelchair access • multiple locations

**Fresh To Order** 860 Peachtree St NE (at 7th St NE) 404/593–2333 • 11am-10pm, brunch Sun from 10am • healthy fast food • patio

**Frogs** 931 Monroe Dr NE 404/607–9967 • 11am-10pm, till 11pm wknds • Mexican

**Gilbert's Cafe & Bar** 219 10th St NE (at Piedmont Ave) 404/872–8012 • dinner Tue-Sat, wknd brunch, food till 2am, bar till 3am, till midnight Sun

**Hobnob** 1551 Piedmont Ave NE (at Monroe) 404/968–2288 • 11am-11pm, till 3pm Sun • wheelchair access

**Joe's On Juniper** 1049 Juniper St NE 404/875–6634 • 11am-2am, till midnight Sun • American

**Las Margaritas** 1842 Chesire Bridge Rd 404/873–4464 • lunch & dinner • Latin fusion • wheelchair access

**The Lobby at Twelve** 361 17th St 404/961–7370 • brkfst, lunch & dinner • upscale American • reservations recommended

**Majestic Diner** 1031 Ponce de Leon Ave (at Highland) 404/875–0276 • 24hrs • popular diner right from the '50s w/ cantankerous waitresses included • at your own risk • some veggie • wheelchair access

**Mi Barrio Restaurante Mexicano** 571 Memorial Dr SE 404/223–9279 • lunch Tue-Sat, dinner nightly, clsd Sun • full bar • wheelchair access

**Murphy's** 997 Virginia Ave NE (at N Highland Ave) 404/872–0904 • 11am-10pm, till midnight Fri-Sat, from 8am wknds • popular • plenty veggie • wheelchair access

**No Más! Cantina** 180 Walker St 404/574–5678 • lunch & dinner daily, wknd brunch • Mexican • also huge furniture & gift store • gay-owned

**Pastries A Go Go** 235 Ponce De Leon Place (at Commerce), Decatur 404/373–3423 • 7:30am-4pm, clsd Tue • delicious baked goods • wheelchair access

**R Thomas Deluxe Grill** 1812 Peachtree Rd NW (btwn 26th & 27th) **404/872-2942, 404/881-0246** • 24hrs • popular • beer/ wine • healthy Californian/ juice bar • plenty veggie • wheelchair access

**Ria's Bluebird Cafe** 421 Memorial Dr (at Cherokee) **404/521-3737** • 8am-3pm • very popular • gourmet brunch in quaint old diner in Grant Park • plenty veggie • everything made from scratch • wheelchair access • woman-owned

**Roxx Tavern & Diner** 1824 Cheshire Bridge Rd NE (at Manchester) **404/892-4541** • lunch & dinner, Sun brunch • patio • wheelchair access

**Sawicki's** 250 W Ponce De Leon Ave, Decatur **404/377-0992** • 11am-7pm, till 8pm Fri-Sat, noon-5pm Sun • deli • great sandwiches

**The Shed at Glenwood** 475 Bill Kennedy Way **404/835-4363** • dinner nightly, Sun brunch • also bar

**Swan Coach House** 3130 Slaton Dr NW **404/261-0636** • 11am-2:30pm, clsd Sun • also gift shop & art gallery

**Table 1280** 1280 Peachtree St NE (at Woodruff Arts Center) **404/897-1280** • lunch & dinner, wknd brunch, clsd Mon • upscale American & tapas

**TWO urban licks** 820 Ralph McGill Blvd **404/522-4622** • dinner nightly, brunch Sun • great grill • full bar • live blues • reservations recommended

**The Vortex** 438 Moreland Ave NE (at Euclid) **404/688-1828** • 11am-midnight, till 3am wknds • biker ambiance • great burgers • 18+

**Watershed** 1820 Peachtree St **404/809-3561** • 11am-10pm, Sun brunch • wine bar • also gift shop • owned by Emily Saliers of the Indigo Girls • wheelchair access

## ENTERTAINMENT & RECREATION

**AIDS Memorial Quilt/ NAMES Project** 204 14th St **404/688-5500** • visit The Quilt at the foundation offices

**Ansley Park Playhouse** 1545 Peachtree St **404/941-7453** • some LGBT-themed productions

**Atlanta Rollergirls** • Atlanta's female roller derby league • visit www.atlantarollergirls.com for events

**Joining Hearts, Inc** Piedmont Park Pool **678/318-1446** • great dance/ pool party in July • wheelchair access • wheelchair access 100% of every dollar raised donated to our beneficiaries

**Little 5 Points, Moreland & Euclid Ave** S of Ponce de Leon Ave • hip & funky area w/ too many restaurants & shops to list

**Martin Luther King, Jr Center for Non–Violent Social Change** 449 Auburn Ave NE **404/526-8900** • 9am-5pm daily • includes King's birth home, the church where he preached in the '60s & his gravesite

**Publix on Ponce** 1001 Ponce de Leon Ave • supermarket • dyke cruising territory

## BOOKSTORES

**Brushstrokes/ Capulets** 1510 Piedmont Ave NE (near Monroe) **404/876-6567** • 10am-10pm, till 11pm Fri-Sat • LGBT variety store • gay-owned

**Charis Books & More** 1189 Euclid Ave NE (at Moreland) **404/524-0304** • 11am-7pm, noon-8pm Sun • feminist • wheelchair access

## RETAIL SHOPS

**The Boy Next Door** 1447 Piedmont Ave NE (btwn 14th & Monroe) **404/873-2664** • 10am-8pm, noon-6pm Sun • clothing

**The Junkman's Daughter** 464 Moreland Ave NE (at Euclid) **404/577-3188** • 11am-7pm, till 8pm Fri, till 9pm Sat, from noon Sun • hip stuff • wheelchair access

## PUBLICATIONS

**David Atlanta** **404/418-8901** • gay entertainment magazine w/ extensive nightlife calendar, maps & directory

**Fenuxe** **404/835-2016** • the voice of Atlanta's Gay Community

**Georgia Voice** **404/815-6941** • bi-weekly LGBT publication

## GYMS & HEALTH CLUBS

**Gravity Fitness** 2201 Faulkner Rd (off Cheshire Bridge Rd) **404/486-0506** • day passes available

**Urban Body Fitness** 500 Amsterdam Ave **404/885-1499**

## EROTICA

**Inserection** 1739 Cheshire Bridge Rd **404/262-9113**

**Southern Nights Videos** 2205 Cheshire Br Rd (at Woodland Ave NE) **404/728-0701** • 24hrs

**Starship** 2275 Cheshire Bridge Rd **404/320-9101, 800/215-1053** • 24hrs • many locations in Atlanta

## Augusta

### ACCOMMODATIONS

**The Executive Inn** 1238 Gordon Hwy
**706/722-1155** • gay/straight • in the
Metropolis Complex of bars • WiFi

**Metropolis Complex** 1250 Gordon Hwy
**706/722-1155** • gay/straight • resort complex
on 12 acres of beautifully landscaped grounds
featuring 2 motels, 2 bars and an RV Park

### BARS

**Capri Lounge** 1238 Gordon Hwy **706/724-3351** • 5pm-11pm, later on the wknds •
gay/straight • retro piano bar

**Edge** 1258 Gordon Hwy **706/828-7400** •
8pm-close Th-Sat only • mostly gay men

## Cherry Log

### ACCOMMODATIONS

**Fox Mountain Camp & Artist Retreat** 350
Black Ankle Way **404/502-3538** • women-
only • camping • live music

## Dewy Rose

### ACCOMMODATIONS

**The River's Edge** 2311 Pulliam Mill Rd
**706/213-8081** • mostly gay men • cabins •
camping • RV • live shows • pool • nudity •
nonsmoking • wheelchair access

## Lake Lanier

### ENTERTAINMENT & RECREATION

**Gay Cove** btwn Athens Park Rd & Frank
Boyd Rd (Channel Marker 21) • a rainbow
rendezvous for the pleasure-boating crowd—
look for the rainbow flag

## Savannah

### INFO LINES & SERVICES

**First City Network** 307 E Harris St
**912/236-2489** • complete info & events line •
social group • also newsletter

### ACCOMMODATIONS

**The Azalea Inn & Gardens** 217 E
Huntingdon St (at Abercorn St)
**912/236-6080, 800/582-3823** • gay-friendly •
19th-c Italianate • vintage gardens • pool • full
Southern brkfst • nonsmoking • WiFi

**Catherine Ward House Inn** 118 E
Waldburg St (at Abercorn) **912/234-8564,
800/327-4270** • gay/straight • Victorian
Italianate • full brkfst • WiFi

**The Galloway House** 107 E 35th St
**912/658-4419** • gay/straight • furnished apts
• cont'l brkfst

**Kehoe House** 123 Habersham St
**912/232-1020, 800/820-1020** • gay-friendly •
full brkfst • WiFi

**Mansion on Forsyth Park** 700 Drayton St
**912/238-5158, 888/213-3671** • gay-friendly •
restored Victorian mansion in historic district •
pool • nonsmoking • WiFi • wheelchair access

**Statesboro Inn** 106 S Main, Statesboro
**912/489-8628, 800/846-9466** • gay-friendly •
full brkfst • WiFi

**Thunderbird Inn** 611 W Oglethorpe Ave (at
MLK Blvd) **912/232-2661, 866/324-2661** •
gay-friendly • motel • kids ok • nonsmoking •
WiFi • gay-owned

### BARS

**Chuck's Bar** 305 W River St **912/232-1005** •
8pm-1am, clsd Sun • gay/ straight •
neighborhood bar • young crowd • student &
artist hangout

### NIGHTCLUBS

**Club One** 1 Jefferson St (at Bay)
**912/232-0200** • 5pm-3am, till 2am Sun •
lesbians/ gay men • dancing/DJ • food served •
live shows Th-Sun • karaoke • drag shows
• dancers • videos

### CAFES

**Joe's Homemade Café & Bakery** 5515
Waters Ave (at 70th St) **912/349-0251**
• 8:30am-5:30pm, 11am-4pm Sat, clsd Sun •
gay-owned

**The Sentient Bean** 13 E Park Ave (at Bull
St) **912/232-4447** • 7am-10pm • food served
• vegetarian/ vegan • shows at night

**Wright Square Cafe** 21 W York St
**912/238-1150** • 7:30am-5pm, from 9am Sat,
clsd Sun • large chocolate selection • patio

### RESTAURANTS

**The 5 Spot** 4430 Habersham St
**912/777-3021**
• 8am-11pm, till 10pm Sun • modern
American menu with full bar

**B Matthews** 325 E Bay St **912/233-1319** •
8am-9pm, till 10pm Fri-Sat, till 3pm Sun •
casual bistro • wheelchair access

**Bar Food** 4523 Habersham St **912/355-5956**
• 4pm-1am, clsd Sun • full bar • WiFi •
wheelchair access • gay-owned

**Casbah** 20 E Broughton St **912/234–6168** • dinner nightly • Moroccan • also entertainment

**Churchill's Pub** 13 W Bay St **912/232–8501** • 5pm-1am

**Clary's Cafe** 404 Abercorn (at Jones) **912/233–0402** • 7am-4pm, from 8am Sat-Sun • country cookin'

**The Distillery** 416 W Liberty St **912/236–1772** • 11am-1am, till 3am Fri-Sat, noon-9pm Sun • wheelchair access

**Fannie's on the Beach** 1613 Strand Ave (at Silver Ave), Tybee Island **912/786–6109** • noon-11pm, till 2am wknds • dancing/DJ • live shows

**Firefly Cafe** 321 Habersham St **912/234–1971** • 11am-9pm, till 9:30pm Fri-Sat, 9am-3pm Sun • wheelchair access

**Green Truck Neighborhood Pub** 2430 Habersham St **912/234–5885** • 11am-11pm, clsd Sun-Mon • beer/ wine • wheelchair access • gay-owned

**Local 11 Ten** 1110 Bull St **912/790–9000** • dinner nightly • upscale dining in a restored 1950s bank • also Perch rooftop bar

**Mellow Mushroom** 11 W Liberty St **912/495–0705** • 11am-10pm • pizza & beer • wheelchair access

**Olde Pink House** 23 Abercorn St **912/232–4286** • upscale Southern dining upstairs, cozy bar downstairs • live jazz

**Rocks on the Roof** 102 W Bay St (on the roof of The Bohemian Hotel) **912/721–3900** • 7am-10pm, till 11pm wknds • fantastic views of river & historic district

**Soho South Cafe** 12 W Liberty St **912/233–1633** • 11am-4pm daily • eclectic

ENTERTAINMENT & RECREATION

**Savannah Walks, Inc** **912/238–9255, 888/728–9255** • walking tours of downtown Savannah

## Washington

RESTAURANTS

**Talk of the Town** 10 West Public Sq **706/678–7661** • 11am-2pm • gay-owned

# HAWAII

**Please note that cities are grouped by islands:**
**Hawaii (Big Island)**
**Kauai**
**Maui**
**Molokai**
**Oahu (includes Honolulu)**

# HAWAII (BIG ISLAND)

## Captain Cook

ACCOMMODATIONS

**Aloha Guest House** 84–4780 Mamalahoa Hwy **808/328–8955, 800/897–3188** • gay/ straight • full organic brkfst • nudity • nonsmoking • WiFi • wheelchair access • gay-owned

**Areca Palms Estate B&B** **808/323–2276, 800/545–4390** • gay-friendly • full brkfst • nonsmoking

**Horizon Guest House** **808/938–7822** • gay/ straight • full brkfst • pool • nonsmoking • WiFi • wheelchair access • gay-owned

**Ka'awa Loa Plantation** 82-5990 Napoopoo Rd 96704 **808/323–2686** • gay/ straight • plantation-style B&B • nonsmoking • WiFi • gay-owned

**Kealakekua Bay B&B** **808/328–8150, 800/328–8150** • gay/ straight • Mediterranean-style villa • nonsmoking • kids ok • also 2-bdrm guesthouse

**South Kona Hideaway** 83-5399 Middle Keei Rd (at Mamalahoa Hwy ) **808/339–7265, 303/808–4408** • gay/ straight • WiFi • two rental suites tucked away in the coffee farms • lesbian -owned

## Hilo

ACCOMMODATIONS

**Aloha Healing Women** 14-4817 Kapoha Kai St **808/936–6067, 877/850–2250** • women only • all-inclusive holistic healing retreats • full brkfst • pool • accupuncture • women-owned

RESTAURANTS

**Cafe Pesto** 308 Kamehameha Ave **808/969–6640** • lunch & dinner • pizzas, salads, pastas • on the waterfront • also at Kawaihae Shopping Center 808/882–1071

## ENTERTAINMENT & RECREATION

**Best of Hilo Adventures Tours** 1477 Kalanianaole Ave **808/987-3905** • lesbian-owned

**Richardson Beach** at end of Kalanianaole Ave (Keaukaha)

**Sun and Sea Hawaii** 224 Kamehameha Ave (at Kalakaua Ave) **808/934-0902** • LGBT snorkel rental & tour company • women's party producers • lesbian-owned

# Honaunau-Kona

## ACCOMMODATIONS

**Dragonfly Ranch Healing Arts Center** 1 1/2 miles down City of Refuge Rd **808/328-2159** • gay/ straight • hot tub • nonsmoking • eco-spa • luxuriously rustic upscale treehouse

# Kailua-Kona

## INFO LINES & SERVICES

**Gay AA** 808/329-1212

## ACCOMMODATIONS

**1st Class B&B Kona Hawaii** 77–6504 Kilohana St **808/329-8778, 888/769-1110** • gay-friendly • ocean views • full brkfst • nonsmoking • WiFi

**Holualoa Inn** 76-5932 Mamalahoa Hwy **808/324-1121** • gay-friendly • luxury B&B near Kona Beach • WiFi • women owned

**KonaLani Hawaiian Inn & Coffee Plantation** 76-5917 Hookahi St **808/324-0793** • lesbians/ gay men • full brkfst • condo rentals • nonsmoking • gay-owned

**Royal Kona Resort** 75–5852 Ali'i Dr **808/329-3111, 800/222-5642** • gay-friendly • pool • private beach • bar • live shows • WiFi • wheelchair access

## BARS

**The Mask-querade** 75–5660 Kopiko St **808/329-8558** • noon-2am • lesbians/ gay men • neighborhood bar • dancing/DJ • live shows • karaoke • Mon ladies night • gay-owned

**My Bar** 74-5606 Luhia St (btwn Kaiwi & Eho St) **808/331-8789** • 11am-2am, from 10am wknds • gay-friendly • karaoke

## RESTAURANTS

**Agnes' Portuguese Bake Shop** 46 Hoolai St **808/262-5367** • 6am-6pm, till 2pm Sun, clsd Mon

**Buzz's Original Steak House** 413 Kawailoa Rd **808/261-4661** • across from beach, great Mai Tais

**Huggo's** 75-5828 Kahakai Rd (on Kailua Bay) **808/329-1493** • dinner only • waterfront dining • also bar • live entertainment • patio

**Moke's Bread & Breakfast** 27 Ho'olai St **808/261-5565** • 6:30am-3pm, clsd Tue, great brkfst

## BOOKSTORES

**Kona Stories** 78-6831 Ali'i Dr #142 (in the Keauhou Shopping Ctr) **808/324-0350** • bookstore that hosts PFLAG meetings & other LGBT groups

## RETAIL SHOPS

**The Wright Gallery** 73-5590 Kauhola St **808/333-6572** • 10am-5pm, clsd Mon • gay-owned

# Kamuela

## ACCOMMODATIONS

**Aaah the Views Bed & Breakfast** 66-1773 Alaneo St **808/885-3455** • gay/ straight • magnificent view of Mauna Kea's summit • kids ok • WiFi

# Na'alehu

## ACCOMMODATIONS

**Margo's Corner** near South Point **808/929-9614** • gay-friendlyl • cottage & 4 campsites • kids ok • WiFi

# Pahoa

## ACCOMMODATIONS

**Aloha Inn Hawaii** **808/965-2211** • mostly women • cooking & massage available • nonsmoking • wheelchair access • lesbian-owned

**Coconut Cottage B&B** **808/965-0973, 866/204-7444** • gay/ straight • centrally located btwn Hilo & Volcanoes Nat'l Park • gay-owned

**Green Fire Productions** 14-4707 Ewa Ln (Kapoho Beach Estates) **808/965-1733** • women only • artesiian ocean pond • nonsmoking • lesbian-owned

**Hawaiian Retreat** 14-234 Papaya Farm Rd **808/640-2157** • gay/ straight • kids/ pets ok • organic farm & orchard • WiFi

**Kalani** **808/965-7828, 800/800-6886** • gay/ straight • coastal wellness retreat & spa • pool • nudity • nonsmoking • WiFi • food served • wheelchair access

**Pamalu—Hawaiian Country House**
808/965-0830 • gay/ straight • secluded
country retreat • pool • kids ok if family rents
whole house • nonsmoking • WiFi • gay-
owned

**Rainbow Retreat Center** 808/965-9011 •
gay/ straight • large no-chemical pool • kids/
pets ok • nonsmoking • limited wheelchair
access • lesbian-owned

### ENTERTAINMENT & RECREATION

**Kehena Beach** off Hwy 137 (trailhead at 19-
mile marker phone booth) • lava rock trail to
clothing-optional black-sand beach

## Volcano Village

### ACCOMMODATIONS

**The Artist Cottage at Volcano Garden
Arts** 19-3834 Old Volcano Rd (at Wright Rd)
808/985-8979 • gay-friendly • kids/ pets ok •
WiFi

**The Chalet Kilauea Collection** 19-4178
Wright Rd 808/967-7786, 800/937-7786 •
gay-friendly • hot tub • nonsmoking • WiFi

**Hale Ohia Cottages** 808/967-7986,
800/455-3803 • gay/ straight • WiFi • gay-
owned

**Kulana Artist Sanctuary For the
Creatively & Spiritually Inclined**
808/985-9055 • mostly women • artist retreat
• camping, cabins & guest rooms available •
no smoking, drugs or alcohol • kid sometimes
ok • women-owned

### CAFES

**Ono Cafe** 19-3834 Old Volcano Rd (at Wright
St, at Volcano Garden Arts) 808/985-8979 •
11am-3pm

# KAUAI

## Anahola

### ACCOMMODATIONS

**Mahina Kai Ocean Villa** 4933 Aliomanu Rd
808/822-9451, 800/337-1134 • gay/ straight •
pool • hot tub • nudity • nonsmoking • WiFi •
gay-owned

## Hanalei

### NIGHTCLUBS

**Tahiti Nui** 5-5134 Kuhio Hwy (near Hanalei
Center) 808/826-6277 • 11am-2am, 4pm-
11pm Sun • gay-friendly • dancing/DJ • live
music most nights • karaoke • also restaurant
• Italian/ local • wheelchair access

## Kapaa

### ACCOMMODATIONS

**17 Palms Kauai** 808/246-6799,
888/725-6799 • gay/ straight • 2 secluded
cottages 200 steps from beach • kids ok •
nonsmoking • WiFi • wheelchair access • gay-
owned

**Fern Grotto Inn** 4561 Kuamoo Rd (at Kuhio
Hwy) 808/821-9836, 808/822-4845 • gay/
straight • cottages on the banks of the Wailua
River • kids ok • nonsmoking

**Plantation Hale Suites** 525 Aleka Loop
808/822-4941, 800 /775-4253 • gay-friendly •
in Kauai's scenic Royal Coconut Coast.Large
one bedroom condos with kitchens and full
daily maid service • pool • mention DAMRON
for a 10% discount off our best available rate •
wheelchair access • gay-run

### RESTAURANTS

**Eggbert's** 4-484 Kuhio Hwy (in Coconut
Plantation Marketplace) 808/822-3787 •
7am-1pm • light fare until 6pm Mon-Sat •
wheelchair access

**Mema** 4-369 Kuhio Hwy (in shopping
center) 808/823-0899 • lunch Mon-Fri, dinner
nightly • Thai & Chinese • BYOB • wheelchair
access

## Lihue

### ACCOMMODATIONS

**Kauai Beach Resort** 4331 Kauai Beach Dr
808/245-1955, 866/536-7676 • gay-friendly •
pools• also restaurant/ bar • non-smoking •
WiFi

## Puunene

### RESTAURANTS

**Roy's Poipu Bar & Grill** 2360 Kiahuna
Plantation Dr (in Poipu Shopping Ctr)
808/742-5000 • 5:30pm-10pm

## Wailua

### RESTAURANTS

**Caffe Coco** 4-369 Kuhio Hwy 808/822-7990
• lunch Tue-Fri, dinner nightly, clsd Mon • art
gallery • live music • patio • BYOB •
wheelchair access

## Waimea

### ACCOMMODATIONS

**Aston Waimea Plantation Cottages**
808/338-1625, 877/997-6667 • gay-friendly •
swimming • kids ok • WiFi

# MAUI

## INFO LINES & SERVICES

**Both Sides Now** • all-inclusive LGBT community organization • resources • events

# Hana

## ACCOMMODATIONS

**Hana Accommodations** 808/248–7868, 800/228–4262 • gay/ straight • studios & tropical cottages • nonsmoking • kids ok • gay-owned

# Kaanapali

## ACCOMMODATIONS

**The Royal Lahaina Resort** 2780 Kekaa Dr 808/661–3611, 800/222–5642 • gay-friendly • full-service resort • pool • wheelchair access

# Kihei

## ACCOMMODATIONS

**Eva Villa** 815 Kumulani Dr 808/874–6407, 800/884–1845 • gay-friendly • B&B • near Wailea beaches • hot tub • pool • WiFi • kids over 12 yrs ok • wheelchair access

➤**Maui Sunseeker LGBT Resort** 551 S Kihei Rd (at Wailana Place) 808/879–1261 • lesbians/ gay men • ocean views • pool • nudity allowed • nonsmoking • WiFi • gay-owned

**Tutu Mermaids on Maui B&B** 2840 Umalu Pl 808/874–8687, 800/598–9550 • gay/ straight • jacuzzi • pool • near beach • nonsmoking • WiFi • lesbian-owned

## BARS

**Diamond's Ice Bar & Grill** 1279 S Kihei Rd 808/874–9299 • 11am-2am, from 7am Sun • gay-friendly local bar • food served • live shows

## NIGHTCLUBS

**Ambrosia Martini Lounge** 1913 S Kihei Rd #H (in Kihei Kalama Village) 808/891–1011 • 6pm-2am • gay/straight • dancing/DJ • wheelchair access

## CAFES

**Cafe at La Plage** 2395 S Kihei Rd (at Kam Beach I) 808/875–7668 • 7am-5pm, till 3pm Sun • WiFi • wheelchair access

## RESTAURANTS

**Jawz Tacos** 41 E Lipoa St (in the Lipoa Center) 808/874–8226 • 11am-9pm • fresh fish tacos • wheelchair access

**Stella Blues Cafe** 1279 S Kihei Rd (in Azeka II Shopping Center) 808/874–3779 • 7:30am-11pm • live music • wheelchair access

## EROTICA

**The Love Shack** 1913 S Kihei Rd (in Kalama Vlg) 808/875–0303 • intimate apparel

# Kula

## ACCOMMODATIONS

**The Upcountry B&B** 4925 Lower Kula Rd (at Copp St) 808/878–8083 • gay-friendly • nonsmoking • WiFi • wheelchair access

# Lahaina

## RESTAURANTS

**Betty's Beach Cafe** 505 Front St 808/662–0300 • 8am-10pm, fmore gay at bar till midnight

**Lahaina Coolers** 180 Dickenson St 808/661–7082 • 8am-1am • patio • wheelchair access

# Makawao

## ACCOMMODATIONS

**Aloha Cottage** 808/575–9228, 800/782–6105 • rental cottage • WiFi • designed for comfort, style, charm & seclusion • outdoor soaking tub • lesbian -owned

**Hale Ho'okipa Inn B&B** 32 Pakani Pl 808/572–6698, 877/572–6698 • gay-friendly • restored Hawaiian plantation home • nonsmoking • WiFi • volunteer-on-vacation program and Real Estate licensed agent • woman-owned

## RESTAURANTS

**Casanova Restaurant & Deli** 1188 Makawao Ave 808/572–0220 • lunch & dinner • Italian • full bar till 2am • gay-friendly • ladies night Wed • live music

# Makena

## ENTERTAINMENT & RECREATION

**Little Beach at Makena** • lesbians/ gay men • Pilani Hwy S to Wailea, right at Wailea Ike Dr, left on Wailea Alanui Dr to public beach, then take trail up hill at right end of beach

## Wailuku

### ACCOMMODATIONS

**Maalaea Kai Condo** 70 Hauoli St (Maalaea Village) 562/212–3312 • gay-friendly • oceanfront 2-bdrm condo • WiFi

# MOLOKAI

## Kaunakakai

### RESTAURANTS

**Kanemitsu Bakery & Coffee Shop** 79 Ala Malama St 808/553–5855 • 5:30am-5pm, clsd Tue • great sweet bread

# OAHU

## Haleiwa

### ACCOMMODATIONS

**Kelea Surf Spa** 949/492–7263 • women only • surf spa & yoga on Oahu's North Shore • open during spring only • 18+

## Honolulu

### INFO LINES & SERVICES

**Gay/ Lesbian AA** 310 Pa`okalani Ave, Room 203A 808/946–1438 • 7pm & 8pm Sat

### ACCOMMODATIONS

**Aqua Palms Waikiki** 1850 Ala Moana Blvd (at Kalia & Ena) 808/947–7256, 866/406–2782 • gay-friendly • kids ok • nonsmoking • WiFi • wheelchair access

**Aston Waikiki Circle Hotel** 2464 Kalakaua Ave (at Uluniu St, Waikiki) 808/923–1571, 877/997–6667 • gay-friendly • kids welcome • nonsmoking • WiFi

**Hotel Renew** 129 Paoakalani Ave (at Lemon Rd, Waikiki) 808/687–7700, 888/485–7639 • gay-friendly • nonsmoking • WiFi

**Waikiki Grand Hotel** 134 Kapahulu Ave 808/923–1814, 808/923–1511 • gay/ straight • rentals above Hula's Bar • pool • nonsmoking • women-owned

### BARS

**Bacchus Waikiki** 408 Lewers St 808/926–4167 • noon-2am • lesbians/ gay men • neighborhood bar

**Chiko's Tavern** 930 McCully St (at Algaroba St) 808/949–5440 • 5pm-2am • gay/straight • neighborhood bar • food served • karaoke

**In Between** 2155 Lau'ula St (off Lewers, across from Planet Hollywood, Waikiki) 808/926–7060 • noon-2am • mostly gay men • neighborhood bar • karaoke

**Lo Jax** 2256 Kuhio Ave, 2nd flr (at Seaside, Waikiki) 808/922–1422 • noon-2am • lesbians/ gay men • neighborhood/ sports bar • food served • WiFi

**Tapa's Restaurant & Lanai Bar** 407 Seaside, 2nd flr (at Kuhio Ave) 808/921–2288 • 9am-2am • gay/ straight • lanai bar • karaoke • also restaurant • East-West fusion • gay-owned

**Wang Chung's** 2424 Koa Ave (at Kaiulani) 808/921–9176 • 5pm-2am • lesbians/ gay men • karaoke • wheelchair access

### NIGHTCLUBS

**District** 1349 Kapiolani Blvd 808/949–1349 • 9pm-4am • gay/ straight • dancing/DJ • mostly Asian American • wheelchair access

**Fusion Waikiki** 2260 Kuhio Ave, 2nd flr (at Seaside) 808/924–2422 • 10pm-4am, from 8pm Fri-Sat • mostly gay men • dancing/DJ • transgender-friendly • live shows • karaoke Mon-Tue • drag shows • videos

**Hula's Bar & Lei Stand** 134 Kapahulu Ave (2nd flr of Waikiki Grand Hotel) 808/923–0669 • 10am-2am • popular • mostly gay men • dancing/DJ • food served • live shows • videos • young crowd • weekly catamaran cruise • WiFi

### CAFES

**Kala Ena Bistro** 1888 Kalakaua Ave, C106 (in Waikiki Landmark Building) 808/979–2299 • 9am-2pm & 5pm-9pm, clsd Sun & Sat only dinner • full bar • WiFi • gay-owned

**Leonard's Bakery** 933 Kapahulu Ave 808/737–5591 • 5:30am-9pm, till 10pm Fri-Sat • irresistible malasadas & doughnuts

**Mocha Java Cafe** 1200 Ala Moana Blvd (in Ward Center) 808/591–9023 • 8am-9pm, till 6pm Sun • WiFi • outdoor seating • wheelchair access

### RESTAURANTS

**Alan Wong's** 1857 S King St (at Pumehana St) 808/949–2526 • dinner only • upscale, romantic Hawaiian dining

**Arancino di Mare** 2552 Kalakaua Ave (in Waikiki Beach Marriott) 808/931–6273 • brkfst, lunch & dinner • Italian

**Cafe Sistina** 1314 S King St 808/596–0061 • lunch Mon-Fri, dinner nightly • northern Italian • some veggie • full bar • wheelchair access

**Cha Cha Cha** 342 Seaside Ave **808/923–7797**
• lunch & dinner • Mexican • happy hour

**Cheeseburger in Paradise** 2500 Kalakaua
Blvd **808/923–3731** • 7am-11pm • full bar

**Chef Chai** 1009 Kapiolani Blvd **808/585-0011**
• 4pm-10pm

**Eggs 'n' Things** 343 Saratoga Rd (at
Kalakaua Ave) **808/926–3447** • 6am-2pm,
5pm-10pm

**House Without A Key** 2199 Kalia Rd (at
Lewers St, at Halekulani Hotel) **808/923-2311**
• 7am-9pm • stunning sunset views •
Hawaiian music nightly

**Hula Grill** 2335 Kalakaua Ave (in Outrigger
Hotel) **808/923-4852**

**La Cucaracha** 2446 Koa Ave **808/924–3366**
• noon-11pm • Mexican • full bar

**Liliha Bakery** 515 N Kuakini St (at Liliha St)
**808/531-1651** • open 24hrs, till 8m Sun, clsd
Mon • diner fare & baked goods • wheelchair
access

**Lulu's** 2586 Kalakaua Ave **808/926–5222** •
7am-2am • full bar • live shows

**Rock Island Cafe** 131 Kaiulani Ave (off
Kalakaua, in King's Village Waikiki)
**808/923-8033** • old-fashioned soda fountain

**Tiki's Grill & Bar** 2570 Kalakaua Ave (in
ResortQuest Hotel) **808/923-8454**

### ENTERTAINMENT & RECREATION

**Diamond Head Beach** • gay/ straight •
take road from lighthouse to beach • some
nude sunbathing

**Girls Who Surf** 1020 Auahi St, Bldg 4, Ste 4
(Ward Shopping Ctr) **808/772-4583** • surf
lessons for all levels • everyone welcome

**Honolulu Gay/ Lesbian Cultural
Foundation** 1670 Makaloa St #204
**808/675-8428** • last wknd of May annual
Honolulu Rainbow Film Festival • art exhibits
• concerts • plays

**Rainbow Sailing Charters** **808/347-0235** •
lesbians/ gay men • day & overnight sailing
adventures • whale-watching • sunset cocktail
cruises • weddings • lesbian-owned

### PUBLICATIONS

**Expression Magazine** **808/393-7994** •
monthly glossy LGBT magazine

### EROTICA

**Suzie's Secrets** 1370 Kapiolani Blvd
**808/949-4383** • 24hrs

## Windward Coast

### ACCOMMODATIONS

**Ali'i Bluffs Windward B&B** 46–251 Ikiiki St,
Kane'ohe **808/235–1124** • gay/ straight • pool
• nonsmoking • WiFi • gay-owned

**Ali'i Bluffs Windward B&B** 46–251 Ikiiki St,
Kane'ohe **808/235–1124** • gay/ straight • pool
• nonsmoking • WiFi • gay-owned

# IDAHO

## Statewide

### PUBLICATIONS

**Diversity Newsmagazine** 208/336–3870 •
statewide LGBT newspaper • monthly •
http://www.tccidaho.org/DiversityNews2.htm

## Boise

### INFO LINES & SERVICES

**The Community Center** 305 E 37th St,
Garden City **208/336-3870** • volunteer staff

### ACCOMMODATIONS

**Hotel 43** 981 W Grove St (at 10th & Front)
**800/243–4622** • gay/ straight • upscale
boutique hotel in the heart of downtown •
restaurant & bar • WiFi

**The Modern Hotel & Bar** 1314 W Grove St
**208/424–8244, 866/780–6012** • gay-friendly •
refurbished 1960's Travelodge & restaurant,•
pets ok • WiFi

### BARS

**The Lucky Dog** 2223 W Fairview Ave (at
23rd) **208/333-0074** • 2pm-2am, from noon
wknds • mostly gay men • neighborhood bar •
patio • WiFi

**Neurolux** 111 N 11th St (at W Idaho)
**208/343-0886** • 1pm-2am • gay-friendly •
dancing/DJ • live music

### NIGHTCLUBS

**The Balcony Club** 150 N 8th St #226 (at
Idaho) **208/336-1313** • 4pm-2am • lesbians/
gay men • popular • dancing/DJ • karaoke •
theme nights • wheelchair access • gay-owned

### CAFES

**Flying M Coffeehouse** 500 W Idaho St (at
5th St) **208/345-4320** • 6:30am-11pm, from
7:30am wknds, till 6pm Sun • WiFi

**River City Coffee** 5517 W State St
**208/853-9161** • 6am-5pm, till 4pm Sun

RESTAURANTS

**Lucky 13 Pizza** 3662 S Eckert Rd
**208/344-6967** • 11am-9pm, till 10pm wknds

ENTERTAINMENT & RECREATION

**The Flicks** 646 Fulton St **208/342-4222** •
opens 4pm, from noon Fri-Sun • 4 movie
theaters • food served • beer/ wine • patio •
wheelchair access

**Visual Arts Collective** 3638 Osage St
**208/424-8297** • noon-6pm Sat, performance
and music venue in Garden City with a full bar

BOOKSTORES

**Crone's Cupboard** 712 N Orchard
**208/333-0831** • 10am-7pm, clsd Sun-Mon •
Wiccan • New Age • feminist/ lesbian books &
art

RETAIL SHOPS

**The Record Exchange** 1105 W Idaho St (at
11th) **208/344-8010** • 9am-9pm, till 7pm Sun
• gifts • music • also cafe & live music

EROTICA

**The O!Zone** 1615 Broadway Ave (at Howe)
**208/395-1977** • noon-7pm, till 5pm Sun

**Pleasure Boutique** 5022 Fairview Ave (at
Orchard) **208/433-1161**

**Vixen Video** 5777 W Overland Rd
**208/672-1844** • 10am-2am • gay-owned

## Coeur d'Alene

see also Spokane, Washington

ACCOMMODATIONS

**The Clark House on Hayden Lake** 5250 E
Hayden Lake Rd, Hayden Lake **208/772-3470,
800/765-4593** • gay-friendly • mansion on a
wooded 12-acre estate • full brkfst • also fine
dining • hot tub • nonsmoking • WiFi • gay-
owned

## Lava Hot Springs

see also Pocatello

ACCOMMODATIONS

**Aura Soma Lava** 196 E Main St
**208/776-5800, 800/757-1233** • gay/ straight •
pool • also retail store

## Moscow

INFO LINES & SERVICES

**Inland Oasis LGBTA Center** 1320 S
Mountain View Rd **208/596-4449** • HIV
testing • youth group & more

BOOKSTORES

**Bookpeople** 521 S Main (btwn 5th & 6th)
**208/882-2669** • 9:30am-6:30pm, till 8pm Fri-
Sat • general

## Nampa

CAFES

**Flying M Coffee Garage** 1314 2nd St S
**208/467-5533** • 7am-11pm, till 6pm wknds •
entertainment

## Pocatello

NIGHTCLUBS

**Club Charleys** 331 E Center St **208/232-9606**
• 5pm-2am, clsd Sun • lesbians/ gay men •
dancing/DJ • live shows • karaoke • drag
shows • wheelchair access

CAFES

**Main St Coffee & News** 234 N Main St
(btwn Lander & Clark) **208/234-9834** •
6:30am-4pm, from 8am Sat, from 9am Sun

## Twin Falls

CAFES

**Annie's Lavender & Coffee Cafe** 591
Addison Ave W (at 8th St) **208/736-2003** •
6am-5pm, seasonal wknd hrs • wheelchair
access

RESTAURANTS

**Pizza Planet** 720 Main St (at 8th St), Buhl
**208/543-8560** • 11am-8pm, till 9pm Fri-Sat

# ILLINOIS

## Alton

see also St Louis, Missouri

NIGHTCLUBS

**Bubby & Sissy's** 602 Belle St (at 6th)
**618/465-4773** • 3pm-2am, till 3am Fri-Sat,
clsd Mon • lesbians/ gay men • dancing/DJ •
drag shows • karaoke • food served •
wheelchair access

## Arlington Heights

see Chicago

## Bloomington

CAFES

**Coffee Hound** 407 N Main St **309/827-7575**
• 6:30am-6pm, 8am-5pm Sun • WiFi

**Kelly's Bakery & Cafe** 113 N Center St **309/820-1200** • 7am-6pm, till 2pm Sat, clsd Sun • wheelchair access

## Blue Island

**see also Chicago**

NIGHTCLUBS

**Club Krave** 13126 S Western Ave (at Grove) **708/597-8379** • 8pm-2am, till 3am Fri-Sat, from 6pm Mon • lesbians/ gay men • neighborhood bar • dancing/DJ • transgender-friendly • karaoke • drag shows • WiFi • wheelchair access

## Bradley

EROTICA

**Slightly Sinful** 101 N Kinzie Ave (at Broadway) **815/937-5744**

## Carbondale

INFO LINES & SERVICES

**AA Lesbian/ Gay** 618/549-4633

## Champaign/ Urbana

ACCOMMODATIONS

**Sylvia's Irish Inn** 312 W Green St, Urbana **217/384-4800** • gay-friendly • full brkfst • nonsmoking • WiFi

BARS

**Mike 'N Molly's** 105 N Market St (at University), Champaign **217/355-1236** • 4pm-2am • gay-friendly • live music • dancing/DJ • beer garden

NIGHTCLUBS

**Chester Street** 63 Chester St (at Water St), Champaign **217/356-5607** • 5pm-2am • lesbians/ gay men • dancing/DJ • drag show Sun • gay-owned

CAFES

**Aroma Cafe** 118 N Neil St, Champaign **217/356-3200** • 7am-10pm, from 8am wknds

**Cafe Kopi** 109 N Walnut (at University), Champaign **217/359-4266** • 7am-midnight • espresso bar with sandwiches • WiFi

**Espresso Royale** 602 E Daniel St (at 6th St), Champaign **217/328-1112** • 7am-midnight

**Pekara Bakery & Bistro** 116 N Neil St, Champaign **217/359-4500** • 7am-8pm, from 8am Sun

RESTAURANTS

**Boltini Lounge** 211 N Neil St, Champaign **217/378-8001** • 4pm-2am, from 6pm Sat, clsd Sun • also full bar • upscale

**The Courier Cafe** 111 N Race St, Urbana **217/328-1811** • 7am-11pm

**Dos Reales** 1407 N Prospect Ave, Champaign **217/351-6879** • 11am-10pm • Mexican • wheelchair access

**Farren's Pub & Eatery** 308 N Randolph St, Champaign **217/359-6977** • 11am-9pm, till 10pm Fri, from noon wknds • full bar

**Fiesta Cafe** 216 S 1st St (at E Clark), Champaign **217/352-5902** • 11am-11pm, bar till 1am • Mexican • gay-owned

**The Great Impasta** 156C Lincoln Sq, Urbana **217/359-7377** • 11am-9pm, till 10pm Fri, 5pm-10pm Sat • music • wheelchair access

**Radio Maria** 119 N Walnut St, Champaign **217/398-7729** • 4pm-2am, wknd brunch • eclectic Mexican cuisine

**Silvercreek** 402 N Race St, Urbana **217/328-3402** • lunch & dinner, brunch Sun • live music

BOOKSTORES

**Jane Addams Book Shop** 208 N Neil St (S of Main), Champaign **217/356-2555** • 10am-7pm, till 5pm Sat-Sun • LGBT & women's sections

GYMS & HEALTH CLUBS

**Refinery** 2302 W John St, Champaign **217/355-4444** • gay-friendly

# CHICAGO

**Chicago is divided into 5 geographical areas:**
**Chicago—Overview**
**Chicago—North Side**
**Chicago—Boystown/ Lakeview**
**Chicago—Near North**
**Chicago—South Side**

## Chicago—Overview

**includes some listings for Greater Chicagoland; please check individual cities like Oak Park as well**

INFO LINES & SERVICES

**AA/ New Town Alano Club** 909 W Belmont Ave, 2nd flr (btwn Clark & Sheffield) **773/529-0321** • call for meeting times or check,www.newtownalanoclub.org

**Affinity** 6400 S Kimbark (at church) **773/324–0377** • nonprofit "serving Chicago's black lesbian & bisexual women's community" through "education, social & community collaborations"

**The Center on Halsted** 3656 N Halsted St (at Waveland) **773/472–6469** • 8am-9pm • LGBT center • theater • gym • technology center

## ACCOMMODATIONS

**Chicago Women's Residence** 1957 S Spaulding Ave (at S 21st) **773/542–9126** • women only • furnished rooms in women's residence • WiFi • please call ahead • lesbian-owned

## NIGHTCLUBS

**Doll House Entertainment** 312/927–1144 • women's parties at clubs around the city • www.facebook.com/DollHouseChicago

## ENTERTAINMENT & RECREATION

**360 Chicago** 875 N Michigan Ave (in John Hancock Center) **312/751–3681** • soars 1,000 feet above Lake Michigan and the city's majestic skyline to offer visitors the most breathtaking views of downtown Chicago, the lakefront and four neighboring states

**Artemis Singers** 773/764–4465 • lesbian feminist chorus

**Chicago Neighborhood Tours** 312/819-5363 • the best way to make the Windy City your kind of town

**Heartland Cafe** 7000 N Glenwood Ave (in Rogers Park) **773/465–8005** • cafe w/ full bar, theater, radio show • lots of live music including performers popular on women's music circuit

**Leather Archives & Museum** 6418 N Greenview Ave **773/761–9200** • 11am-7pm Th-Fri, till 5pm Sat-Sun • membership required (purchase at door)

**Second City** 1616 N Wells St (at North) **312/337–3992, 312/337–3992** • gay-friendly • legendary comedy club • call for reservations

## PUBLICATIONS

**Nightspots** 773/871–7610 • weekly LGBT nightlife magazine

**Windy City Times** 773/871–7610 • weekly LGBT newspaper & calendar guide

# Chicago—North Side

## ACCOMMODATIONS

**House 5863 B&B** 5863 N Glenwood (at Admore) **773/682–5217** • gay/ straight • nonsmoking • WiFi • gay-owned

**Lang House B&B** 7421 N Sheridan Rd (at Jarvis) **773/764–9851** • gay/straight • on the Lake Michigan beach block • WiFi • gay-owned

## BARS

**The Anvil** 1137 W Granville (E of Broadway) **773/973–0006** • 9am-2am • mostly gay men • neighborhood bar • videos

**Big Chicks** 5024 N Sheridan (btwn Foster & Argyle) **773/728–5511** • 4pm-2am, from 3pm wknds • lesbians/ gay men • neighborhood bar • dancing/DJ • videos • patio • Sun BBQ • WiFi • wheelchair access

**The Call** 1547 W Bryn Mawr (at Clark) **773/334–2525** • 4pm-2am • lesbians/ gay men • dancing/DJ • country/ western • drag shows • videos • wheelchair access

**Crew** 4804 N Broadway St (at Lawrence) **773/784–2739** • 11:30am-midnight, 11am-2am Fri-Sat • lesbians/ gay men • sports bar & grill • videos • patio

**The Glenwood** 6962 N Glenwood Ave (at Morse) **773/764–7363** • 3pm-2am, from noon Sun • lesbians/ gay men • neighborhood sports bar • wheelchair access

**Green Mill** 4802 N Broadway Ave (at Lawrence) **773/878–5552** • noon-4am • gay/ straight • noted jazz venue • hosts the Uptown Poetry Slam

**In Fine Spirits** 5420 N Clark St (at Rascher Ave) **773/334–9463** • 4pm-midnight, 3pm-2am Fri-Sat • wine bar • patio • food served • also wine store

**Joie de Vine** 1744 W Balmoral Ave (at Paulina St) **773/989–6846** • 5pm-2am, till 3am Sat • mostly women • wine bar • patio • WiFi • wheelchair access • lesbian-owned

**Marty's** 1511 W Balmoral Ave (at Clark) **773/321–7481** • 5pm-2am • gay-friendly • upscale wine & martini bar • food served

**Scot's** 1829 W Montrose Ave (at Damen) **773/528–3253** • 3pm-2am, 1pm-3am Sat, from 11am Sun • mostly gay men • neighborhood bar

**The Sofo Tap** 4923 N Clark St (at W Argyle) **773/784–7636** • 5pm-2am, from 3pm Fri, from noon wknds • mostly gay men • video bar • backyard beer garden • wheelchair access

**Spyner's Pub** 4623 N Western Ave (at W Eastwood) 773/784-8719 • 11am-2am, till 3am Sat • mostly women • neighborhood bar • karaoke

**Touché** 6412 N Clark St (at Devon) 773/465-7400 • 5pm-4am, 3pm-5am Sat, noon-4am Sun • popular • mostly gay men • leather

### NIGHTCLUBS

**Atmosphere** 5355 N Clark St (at W Balmoral Ave) 773/784-1100 • 6pm-2am, till 3am Sat, from 3pm Sat-Sun, clsd Mon • lesbians/gay men • dancing/DJ • male dancers • drag shows • WiFi • gay-owned

### CAFES

**Coffee Grind** 5256 N Broadway St (btwn Berwyn & Foster) 773/784-1305 • 7am-9pm, from 8am wknds • WiFi • wheelchair access

**KOPI: A Traveler's Cafe** 5317 N Clark St 773/989-5674 • 8am-11pm • food served • wheelchair access

**Metropolis Coffee** 1039 W Granville Ave (at Kenmore) 773/764-0400 • 6:30am-8pm, from 7:30am Sat-Sun • popular • WiFi

### RESTAURANTS

**A Taste of Heaven** 5401 N Clark St 773/989-0151 • brunch, dinner and delicious. savory and sweet items • gay-owned

**Andie's** 5253 N Clark (btwn Berwyn & Farragut) 773/784-8616 • 11am-11pm • eastern Mediterranean • full bar • wheelchair access

**Anteprima** 5316 N Clark St (at Summerdale) 773/506-9990 • dinner nightly • Italian • wheelchair access

**Deluxe Diner** 6349 N Clark St (at Devon) 773/743-8244 • 24hr diner

**Fat Cat** 4840 N Broadway (at Lawrence Ave) 773/506-3100 • 4pm-2am, from 11am wknds • full bar

**Fireside** 5739 N Ravenswood (at Rosehill) 773/561-7433 • 11am-4am, till 5am Sat, 10am-4am Sun • Cajun & pizza • patio • full bar

**Hamburger Mary's/ Attic** 5400 N Clark St (at Balmoral) 773/784-6969 • 11:30am-midnight, till 2am Wed-Sun, from 10:30am wknds • full bar • karaoke • drag shows • wheelchair access

**Hot Woks Cool Sushi** 30 S Michigan Ave (at Madison) 312/345-1234 • 11am-9pm • sushi/ Thai

**Jin Ju** 5203 N Clark St (at Summersdale) 773/334-6377 • dinner only, clsd Mon • Korean • also bar • wheelchair access

**Pauline's** 1754 W Balmoral (at Ravenswood) 773/561-8573 • 7am-3pm • hearty brkfsts • wheelchair access

**Svea Restaurant** 5236 N Clark (btwn Berwyn & Farragut) 773/275-7738 • 7am-2pm, till 3pm wknds • Swedish/ American comfort food • wheelchair access

**Tedino's** 5335 N Sheridan Rd (at Broadway) 773/275-8100 • 11am-midnight, from 3pm Mon • popular • pizza • full bar • wheelchair access

**Thai Pastry & Restaurant** 4925 N Broadway St, Unit E (at Argyle) 773/784-5399 • 11am-10pm, till 11pm Fri-Sat • wheelchair access

**Tweet** 5020 N Sheridan Rd (at Argyle) 773/728-5576 • 9am-3pm • brkfst & brunch • cash only • WiFi

### ENTERTAINMENT & RECREATION

**Hollywood /Osterman Beach** at Hollywood & Sheridan Sts • popular • "the" gay beach

### BOOKSTORES

**Women & Children First** 5233 N Clark St (at Foster) 773/769-9299 • 11am-7pm, till 9pm Wed-Fri, 10am-7pm Sat, 11am-6pm Sun • wheelchair access • women-owned

### RETAIL SHOPS

**Enjoy, An Urban General Store** 4727 N Lincoln Ave (Lincoln Square) 773/334-8626 • 10am-7pm, till 6pm Sun • cards & gifts • lesbian-owned

**Leather 6410** 6410 N Clark St (at Devon, btwn Jackhammer & Touché) 773/508-0900 • noon-8pm, till 3am Th, 4am Fri-Sat, 2pm-10pm Sun • gay-owned

### GYMS & HEALTH CLUBS

**Cheetah Gym** 5248 N Clark St (at Foster) 773/728-7777, 866/961-6840

### EROTICA

**Early to Bed** 5044 N Clark St 773/271-1219 • clsd Mon • transgender-friendly • 18+ • lesbian-owned

**Tulip Sex Toy Gallery** 1480 W Berwyn (at Clark) 773/275-6110, 877/708-8547 • noon-10pm, till 7pm Sun • sex toys for women • lesbian-owned

# Chicago—Boystown/ Lakeview

## ACCOMMODATIONS

**Best Western Plus Hawthorne Terrace**
3434 N Broadway St (at Hawthorne Pl)
773/244-3434, 888/860-3400 • gay-friendly •
in heart of Chicago's gay community • WiFi •
wheelchair access

**City Suites Hotel** 933 W Belmont Ave (btwn
Clark & Sheffield) 773/404-3400,
800/248-9108 • gay-friendly • European style
• nonsmoking rooms available • WiFi

**Hotel Lincoln** 1816 N Clark St 312/254-4700
• gay/straight • great location and fabulous
rooftop restaurant & bar • pets OK

**Majestic Hotel** 528 W Brompton Ave (at
Addison) 773/404-3499, 800/727-5108 • gay-
friendly • romantic 19th-c atmosphere •
nonsmoking • WiFi

**The Willows** 555 W Surf St (at Broadway)
773/528-8400, 800/787-3108 • gay/straight •
nonsmoking • WiFi

## BARS

**3160** 3160 N Clark St (at Belmont)
773/327-5969 • 3pm-2am, noon-3am Sat,
11am-2am Sun • lesbians/ gay men •
neighborhood bar • live shows • piano •
cabaret • wheelchair access

**Beat Kitchen** 2100 W Belmont (btwn Hoyne
& Damen) 773/281-4444 • 4pm-2am, from
11:30am Sat-Sun, till 3am Sat • gay-friendly •
live bands • also grill • some veggie •
wheelchair access

**Blues** 2519 N Halsted St (at Lill Ave)
773/528-1012, / • 8pm-2am, till 3am Sat •
gay-friendly • classic Chicago blues spot

**Bobby Love's** 3729 N Halsted St (at
Waveland) 773/525-1200 • 3pm-2am, from
noon wknds, till 3am Sat • lesbians/ gay men •
neighborhood bar • karaoke • wheelchair
access

**Cell Block** 3702 N Halsted St (at Waveland)
773/665-8064 • 2pm-3am • mostly gay men •
leather • also back bar wknds from 10pm •
wheelchair access

**Charlie's Chicago** 3726 N Broadway St
(btwn Waveland & Grace) 773/871-8887 •
3pm-4am, till 5am Sat • mostly gay men •
dancing/DJ • country/ western • karaoke • club
music after 1am

**The Closet** 3325 N Broadway St (at
Buckingham) 773/477-8533 • 4pm-4am,
noon-5am Sat, till 4am Sun • popular •
lesbians/ gay men • neighborhood video bar •
karaoke

**D.S. Tequila Company** 3352 N Halsted St
(at Roscoe) 773/697-9127 • 5pm-2am, noon-
3am wknds • gay/ straight • good burgers &
tacos

**Elixir** 3452 N Halsted St (at Cornelia)
773/975-9244 • 6pm-close • mostly gay men
• swank cocktails

**Little Jim's** 3501 N Halsted St (at Cornelia)
773/871-6116 • noon-4am, till 5am Sat •
popular • mostly gay men • neighborhood bar

**The Lucky Horseshoe Lounge** 3169 N
Halsted St (at Briar) 773/404-3169 • 3pm-
2am, 1pm-3am Sat • mostly gay men •
neighborhood bar

**Minibar** 3341 N Halsted St (at Roscoe)
773/871-6227 • 5pm-2am, from 11am wknds
• lesbians/ gay men • food served •
wheelchair access

**The North End** 3733 N Halsted St (at Grace)
773/477-7999 • 2pm-2am, from 11am Fri-Sun
• mostly gay men • neighborhood sports bar •
wheelchair access

**Progress Bar** 3359 N Halsted 773/697-9268
• 4pm-2am, from 3pm Fri, 2pm-3am sat, from
1pm Sun • lesbians/gay men • dancing/DJ

**Replay** 3439 N Halsted (btwn Cornelia &
Newport) 773/975-9244 • noon-2am, till 3am
Sat • mostly gay men • neighborhood bar •
queer arcade & great beer garden

**Roscoe's** 3354-56 N Halsted St (at W
Roscoe) 773/281-3355 • 4pm-2am, from 3pm
Fri, from 2pm Sat • lesbians/ gay men • food
served • neighborhood bar • dancing/DJ •
live/drag shows • karaoke • patio •

**Scarlet** 3320 N Halsted St (at Aldine)
773/348-1053 • 6pm-2am, from 2pm wknds •
mostly gay men • DJ/dancing

**Sidetrack** 3349 N Halsted St (at Roscoe)
773/477-9189 • 3pm-2am, till 3am Sat •
popular • lesbians/ gay men • upscale video
bar • wheelchair access

## NIGHTCLUBS

**Berlin** 954 W Belmont (at Sheffield)
773/348-4975 • 5pm-4am, from10pm Tues,
clsd Mon • popular • lesbians/ gay men •
dancing/DJ • transgender-friendly • live shows
• wheelchair access

**Circuit/Rehab** 3641 N Halsted St (at Addison) 773/325-2233 • 9pm-4am, till 5am Sat, clsd Mon-Wed • mostly gay men • dancing/DJ • multiracial • Latin nights Th & Sun (T-dance)

**Hydrate** 3458 N Halsted St (at Cornelia) 773/975-9244 • 8pm-4am, till 5am Sat, opens earlier in summer • popular • gay/ straight • dancing/DJ • drag shows

**Planet Earth** 3534 W Belmont (at Late Bar) 773/267-5283 • 10pm-5am Sat • gay/ straight • dancing/DJ • New Wave

**Seven** 3206 N Halsted 872/206-2052 • 9pm-2am, till 3am sat, clsd Sun-Wed • gay/straight • dancing/DJ

**Smart Bar** 3730 N Clark St (downstairs at the Metro) 773/549-0203 • 10pm-4am, till 5am Sat, clsd Mon-Tue • gay-friendly • dancing/DJ • popular • theme nights

## CAFES

**The Coffee & Tea Exchange** 3311 N Broadway St 773/528-2241 • 7am-8pm, till 7pm Sat, 9am-6pm Sun • fair-trade coffee & tea

## RESTAURANTS

**Angelina Ristorante** 3561 N Broadway St (at Addison) 773/935-5933 • 5pm-10pm, wknd brunch • Italian • full bar • wheelchair access

**Ann Sather's** 909 W Belmont Ave (at Sheffield) 773/348-2378 • 7am-3pm, till 4pm Sat-Sun • Swedish diner & Boystown fixture

**Cesar's** 2924 N Broadway (at Oakdale) 773/296-9097 • 11am-11pm, till midnight Fri-Sat, till 8pm Sun • "home of the killer margaritas"

**Chicago Diner** 3411 N Halsted St (at Roscoe) 773/935-6696 • 11am-10pm, from 10am wknds, till 11pm Fri-Sat • hip & vegan • beer/ wine & organic booze

**Halsted's Bar & Grill** 3441 N Halsted St (btwn Newport & Cornelia) 773/348-9696 • dinner nightly, brunch wknds • neighborhood sports bar • gay-owned

**Home Bistro** 3404 N Halsted St (at Roscoe, btwn Addison & Belmont) 773/661-0299 • dinner only, clsd Mon • upscale American • bring your own bottle • wheelchair access

**Horizon Cafe** 3805 N Broadway St (corner w/ Halsted & Grace) 773/883-1565 • 7am-9pm, till 10pm Fri-Sat • diner • brkfst anytime

**J Parker** 1816 N Clark St (at Hotel Lincoln) 312/254-4747 • 5pm-1am, from 4pm Fri-Sun • most spectacular views in all of Chicago • cocktail bar and small plate menu

**Joy's Noodles & Rice** 3257 N Broadway St (at Melrose) 773/327-8330 • 11am-10pm, till 11pm Fri-Sat • Thai • patio • BYOB • wheelchair access

**Kanok** 3422 N Broadway St (at W Hawthorne Pl) 773/529-2525 • 4pm-10:30pm • sushi/ Asian • BYOB • wheelchair access

**Kit Kat Lounge & Supper Club** 3700 N Halsted St (at W Waveland Ave) 773/525-1111 • 5:30pm-2am, brunch Sun (seasonal) • drag cabaret some nights • gay-owned

**Kitsch'n On Roscoe** 2005 W Roscoe (at Damen) 773/248-7372 • 8:30am-3pm, dinner served in summer • comfort food for hipsters • full bar

**Las Mananitas** 3523 N Halsted St (at Cornelia) 773/528-2109 • 11am-11pm, till midnight Fri-Sat • strong margaritas • wheelchair access

**Melrose Restaurant** 3233 N Broadway St 773/327-2060 • 24hrs, great food

**Mon Ami Gabi** 2300 N Lincoln Park W (at Belden) 773/348-8886 • dinner only • French bistro

**Nookie's Tree** 3334 N Halsted St (at Roscoe) 773/248-9888 • 7am-midnight, 24hrs wknds • popular • BYOB • wheelchair access

**Orange** 2413 N Clark St 773/549-7833 • 8am-3pm • popular brunch spot

**Panino's Pizzeria** 3702 N Broadway (at Waveland) 773/472-6200 • 11:30am-11pm, till 10pm Sun • full bar • wheelchair access

**Pick Me Up Cafe** 3408 N Clark St (at Roscoe) 773/248-6613 • 11am-2am,till 4am Fri, till 5am Sat • brkfst all day

**Pie Hole Pizza** 3477 N Broadway 773/525-8888 • 11am-midnight, till 3am Fri-Sat

**Pingpong** 3322 N Broadway St 773/281-7575 • 5pm-midnight, noon-10pm Sun • Asian fusion • patio • wheelchair access

**The Raw Bar & Grill** 3720 N Clark St (at Waveland) 773/348-7291 • 11am-2am, till 3am Sat • seafood • lounge • live shows • wheelchair access

**Stella's Diner** 3042 N Broadway St 773/472-9040 • 7am-10pm

**Sushisamba Rio** 504 N Wells St (at W Illinois) **312/595–2300** • lunch & dinner, popular brunch • glitzy lounge atmosphere • wheelchair access

**Taverna 750** 750 W Cornelia Ave (at Halsted) **773/904–7466** • 5:30-late, Sun brunch • shared plates tapas inspired food menu • full bar • wheelchair access

**Yoshi's Cafe** 3257 N Halsted St (at Melrose) **773/248–6160** • dinner Tue-Sun, also Sun brunch • Asian-inspired French • wheelchair access

## Bookstores

**Unabridged Books** 3251 N Broadway St (at Aldine) **773/883–9119** • 10am-9pm, till 7pm wknds • popular • LGBT section

## Retail Shops

**Brown Elephant** 5404 N Clark St **773/271–9382** • 11am-6pm, all purchases benefit Howard Brown general health center; also in Lakeview and Oak Park

**Uncle Fun** 1338 W Belmont (at Racine) **773/477–8223** • heaven for kitsch lovers

## Erotica

**Batteries Not Included** 3420 N Halsted St (at Newport) **773/935–9900** • 11am-midnight, till 1am Fri, 10am-2am Sat

**The Pleasure Chest** 3436 N Lincoln Ave (at Newport) **773/525–7152, 800/525–7152** • clsd Sun

**Tulip Sex Toy Gallery** 3459 N Halsted St (btwn Newport & Cornelia) **773/975–1515, 877/708–8547** • noon-10pm, till midnight Fri-Sat • lesbian-owned

# Chicago—Near North

## Accommodations

**ACME Hotel Company Chicago** 15 E Ohio St (at State St) **312/894–0900** • gay-friendly • gym • kids ok • WiFi • wheelchair access

**Allegro Chicago** 171 W Randolph St (at LaSalle) **312/236–0123, 866/672–6143** • gay-friendly • Kimpton hotel • upscale lounge & restaurant • live shows • kids/pets ok • WiFi • wheelchair access

**Chicago Getaway Hostel** 616 W Arlington Pl (at Geneva Terr) **773/929–5380** • gay-friendly • in a trendy university area Lincoln Park • nonsmoking • WiFi

**Dana Hotel & Spa** 660 N State St (at Erie) **312/202–6000, 888/301–7946** • gay-friendly • rooftop lounge & Asian steakhouse • smoke free rooms • wheelchair access

**Flemish House of Chicago** 68 E Cedar St (btwn Rush & Lake Shore Dr) **312/664–9981** • gay/ straight • B&B, studios & apts in greystone row house • nonsmoking • WiFi • gay-owned

**Gold Coast Guest House B&B** 113 W Elm St (btwn Clark & LaSalle) **312/337–0361** • gay-friendly • nonsmoking • WiFi • women-owned

**The Hotel Burnham** One W Washington St (at State) **312/782–1111, 866/690–1986** • gay-friendly • Chicago landmark • nonsmoking • WiFi • wheelchair access

**Hotel Indigo Chicago Gold Coast** 1244 N Dearborn Pkwy (btwn Goethe & Division) **312/787–4980, 866/521–6950** • gay-friendly • gym • WiFi • restaurant & lounge • wheelchair access

**Hotel Monaco** 225 N Wabash (at S Water & Wacker Pl) **312/960–8500, 800/397–7661** • gay-friendly • 4-star luxury hotel • gym • restaurant • WiFi

**Millennium Knickerbocker Hotel** 163 E Walton Pl (Michigan Ave) **312/751–8100, 800/621–8140** • gay-friendly • restaurant • martini bar • gym • right off Magnificent Mile • wheelchair access

**Palmer House Hilton** 17 E Monroe St (at State St) **312/726–7500** • gay-friendly • pool • fitness center • shopping arcade • business center

**W Chicago—Lakeshore** 644 N Lake Shore Dr (at Ontario) **312/943–9200** • gay-friendly • overlooking Lake Michigan • pool • nonsmoking • WiFi • also restaurant & bar • wheelchair access

## Bars

**Davenport's** 1383 N Milwaukee (in Wicker Park) **773/278–1830** • 7pm-midnight, till 2am Fri-Sat, till 11pm Sun, clsd Tue • cabaret • piano bar

**Downtown** 440 N State (at Illinois) **312/464–1400** • 3pm-2am, till 3am Sat • mostly gay men • live shows • cabaret • professional crowd • videos

**Slippery Slope** 2357 N Milwaukee Ave **773/799–8504** • 8pm-2am • gay/straight • dancing/DJ • dive bar more gay on the 3rd Th

## Nightclubs

**Baton Show Lounge** 436 N Clark St (btwn Illinois & Hubbard) **312/644–5269** • showtimes at 8:30pm, 10:30pm, 12:30am, clsd Mon-Tue • lesbians/ gay men • drag shows • reservations recommended • wheelchair access • since 1969!

**Chances Dances** 2011 W North Ave (at Damen, at Subterranean) • 3rd Mon 10pm-2am • lesbians/ gay men • dancing/DJ • also 2nd Tue at Danny's • 1959 W Dickens Ave • check chancesdances.org for other events

**Underground Wonder Bar** 710 N Clark St (at Huron) 312/266-7761 • 5pm-late • gay-friendly • live music • multiracial cliente

## CAFES

**Earwax Cafe** 1561 N Milwaukee Ave (in Wicker Park) 773/772-4019 • 11am-5pm, till 8pm wknds • food served • some vegan • wheelchair access

## RESTAURANTS

**Blackbird** 619 W Randolph St (at Des Plaines) 312/715-0708 • lunch Mon-Fri, dinner nightly, clsd Sun

**Catch 35** 35 W Wacker Dr (at Dearborn) 312/346-3500, 312/346-3535 • lunch Mon-Fri, dinner nightly • steak & seafood

**Fireplace Inn** 1448 N Wells St (at North Ave) 312/664-5264, 312/664-5264 • lunch & dinner • famous for their ribs • patio • full bar open late

**Girl and the Goat** 809 W Randolph St 312/492-6262 • 4:30pm-11pm, clsd Mon-Wed • fun foods, craft beers, and making wine in a rustic and bad ass environment • lesbian-owned

**Hot Chocolate** 1747 N Damen Ave (in Wicker Park) 773/489-1747 • lunch, dinner & dessert, wknd brunch, clsd Mon • full bar • wheelchair access

**Ina's** 1235 W Randolph St (at Racine) 312/226-8227 • brkfst & lunch • full bar

**Kiki's Bistro** 900 N Franklin St (at Locust) 312/335-5454 • lunch Mon-Fri, dinner nightly, clsd Sun • French • full bar

**Lou Mitchell's** 565 W Jackson Blvd (at Jefferson) 312/939-3111 • great brkfst

**Manny's** 1141 S Jefferson St (at Roosevelt) 312/939-2855 • 6am-8pm, clsd Sun • killer corned beef

**Nacional 27** 325 W Huron (at N Orleans) 312/664-2727 • dinner nightly, clsd Sun • Nuevo Latino • also lounge open late

**Park Grill** 11 N Michigan Ave (in Millennium Park) 312/521-7275 • 11am-10pm • classic American • seasonal outdoor dining

**Parthenon Restaurant** 314 S Halsted St (near W Jackson) 312/726-2407 • 11am-midnight • full bar • "best gyros in Chicago" • wheelchair access

**Shaw's Crab House** 21 E Hubbard St (at State St) 312/527-2722 • lunch & dinner • live music • full bar • wheelchair access

**Topolobampo/ Frontera Grill** 445 N Clark St (btwn Illinois & Hubbard) 312/661-1434 • lunch & dinner, Sat brunch (Frontera only), clsd Sun-Mon • Mexican

**Vermilion** 10 W Hubbard St (at State) 312/527-4060 • lunch Mon-Fri, dinner nightly • Latin-Indian fusion • full bar • patio • wheelchair access

## BOOKSTORES

**After-Words New & Used Books** 23 E Illinois St (btwn State & Wabash) 312/464-1110 • 10:30am-10pm, till 11pm Fri-Sat, noon-7pm Sun • WiFi • cards • stationery • women-owned

**Quimby's Bookstore** 1854 W North Ave (at Wolcott, in Wicker Park) 773/342-0910 • noon-9pm, 11am-10pm Sat, noon-6pm Sun • alternative literature & comics • wheelchair access

## RETAIL SHOPS

**Flight 001** 1133 N State St (at Elm) 312/944-1001 • 11am-7pm, till 6pm Sun • way cool travel gear

## GYMS & HEALTH CLUBS

**Cheetah Gym** 1934 W North Ave (at Damen, in Wicker Park) 773/394-5900

# Chicago—South Side

## BARS

**Club Escape** 1530 E 75th St (at Stoney Island Ave) 773/667-6454 • 4pm-2am, till 3am Sat • lesbians/ gay men • dancing/DJ • drag shows • mostly African American • food served • women's night Th

**Inn Exile** 5758 W 65th St (at Menard, near Midway Airport; 1 mile W of Midway hotel center at 65th & Cicero) 773/582-3510 • 8pm-2am, till 3am Sat • mostly gay men • dancing/DJ • videos • WiFi • wheelchair access

**Jeffery Pub** 7041 S Jeffery Blvd (at 71st) 773/363-8555 • noon-4am, till 5am Sat, clsd Mon • popular • lesbians/ gay men • dancing/DJ • mostly African American • drag shows • wheelchair access

## BOOKSTORES

**57th St Books** 1301 E 57th St, Hyde Park (at Kimbark St) 773/684-1300 • 10am-8pm • LGBT section

**Powell's Bookstore** 1218 S Halsted St (at W Roosevelt) **312/243-9070** • 9am-9pm, 10am-6pm Sun • popular • wheelchair access • other location: 1501 E 57th St, 773/ 955-7780

## Decatur

### RESTAURANTS

**Robbie's Grill** 122 N Merchant St **217/423-0448** • 11am-10pm, till 3am Sat, clsd Sun • full bar

### EROTICA

**Romantix Adult Superstore** 2015 N 22nd St **217/362-0105**

## Elk Grove Village

see also Chicago

## Elkhart

### CAFES

**Bluestem Bake Shop** 107 Governor Oglesby St **217/947-2222** • 9am-4pm, clsd Mon, Wed & Sat

## Forest View

### BARS

**Forest View Lounge** 4519 S Harlem Ave (at 46th St) **708/484-3067** • 11am-midnight, till 2am wknds, clsd Sun • mostly women • neighborhood bar • home of the large Marge volcano burgers • beer garden • live shows

## Galesburg

### EROTICA

**Romantix Adult Superstore** 595 N Henderson St (at Losey) **309/342-7019**

## Joliet

### INFO LINES & SERVICES

**Community Alliance & Action Network** 68 N Chicago St #401 (at Jefferson) **815/726-7906** • by appointment • LGBT community center

### NIGHTCLUBS

**Maneuvers & Co** 118 E Jefferson (at Chicago) **815/727-7069** • 8pm-2am, till 3am Fri-Sat • lesbians/ gay men • more women Tue • dancing/DJ • transgender-friendly • drag shows • frequent events • patio

## Monticello

### RESTAURANTS

**The Brown Bag** 212 W Washington St **217/762-9221** • 9am-7pm, till 8pm Tue & Fri, till 4pm Sat, clsd Sun

## Normal

### CAFES

**Coffeehouse & Deli** 114 E Beaufort St **309/452-6774** • 7am-10pm • vegetarian/ vegan • WiFi

## O'Fallon

### RESTAURANTS

**The Mansion** 1680 Mansion Wy (at Lakepointe Center Dr) **618/624-0629** • 5pm-9pm Tue-Th, till 10pm Fri-Sat • steakhouse • wheelchair access • gay-owned

## Oak Park

see Berwyn & Chicago

## Ottawa

### EROTICA

**Brown Bag Video** 3042 N State Rte 71 (at I-80, exit 93) **815/313-4125** • 24hrs

## Peoria

### ACCOMMODATIONS

**Hotel Pere Marquette** 501 Main St **309/637-6500, 800/447-1676** • gay-friendly • buffet brkfst • WiFi

### CAFES

**One World** 1245 W Main St (at University) **309/672-1522** • 7am-11pm, from 8am wknds • WiFi • wheelchair access

### RESTAURANTS

**Two 25** 225 NE Adams St (at Mark Twain Hotel) **309/282-7777** • lunch Mon-Fri, dinner nightly, clsd Sun

### EROTICA

**Swingers World** 335 SW Adams (at Harrison) **309/676-9275**

## Quincy

### NIGHTCLUBS

**Irene's Cabaret** 124 N 5th St (at Washington Park, enter rear) 217/222–6292 • 10pm-2:30am,9pm-3:30am Fri-Sat, clsd Sun-Tue • lesbians/ gay men • dancing/DJ • multiracial • karaoke • drag shows • wheelchair access • gay-owned

## Rockford

### NIGHTCLUBS

**The Office Niteclub** 513 E State St (btwn 2nd & 3rd) 815/965-0344 • noon-2am • popular • lesbians/ gay men • dancing/DJ • live shows • karaoke • drag shows • male & female strippers • videos

### RESTAURANTS

**Lucerne's Fondue & Spirits** 845 N Church St (at Whitman) 815/968-2665 • 5pm-11pm, clsd Mon • reservations required • full bar • wheelchair access

**Maria's** 828 Cunningham St (at Corbin) 815/968–6781 • 4:30pm-9pm, clsd Sun-Mon • Italian • full bar

## Springfield

### INFO LINES & SERVICES

**The Phoenix Center** 109 E Lawrence Ave 217/528-5253 • 8:30am-4:30pm, clsd wknds

### ACCOMMODATIONS

**The State House Inn** 101 E Adams St (at First St) 217/528-5100 • gay-friendly • kids/ pets ok • WiFi • wheelchair access

### BARS

**The Station House** 304–306 E Washington (btwn 3rd & 4th Sts) 217/525-0438 • 4pm-3am, from noon wknds, till midnight Sun • lesbians/ gay men • neighborhood bar • karaoke • dancing/DJ • wheelchair access

### RETAIL SHOPS

**New Age Tattoos & Body Piercings** 2915 S MacArthur Blvd 217/546-5006 • 11am-8pm, till 6pm Sun

## INDIANA

## Bloomington

### BARS

**The Back Door** 207 S College Ave (down the alley), IN 812/333–3123 • 4pm-2am, from 7pm Fri-Sun • lesbians /gay men • dancing/DJ • drag shows • karaoke

### CAFES

**Rachael's Cafe** 300 E 3rd St 812/330–1882 • 8am-9pm, till 7pm Sun • live shows

**Soma Coffee House** 322 E Kirkwood Ave (below Laughing Planet) 812/331–2770 • 7am-11pm, from 8am Sun • WiFi

### RESTAURANTS

**Laughing Planet Cafe** 322 E Kirkwood Ave (enter on Grant) 812/323–2233 • 11am-9pm • vegan/veggie • outdoor seating

**Village Deli** 409 E Kirkwood 812/336–2303 • 7am-9pm, 8am-9pm wknds

### ENTERTAINMENT & RECREATION

**BloomingOut** WFHB 91.3 & 98.1 & 100.7 & 106.3FM 812/325–7870 & 323–1200 • 6pm Th, "your midwest queer connection"

### RETAIL SHOPS

**Athena Gallery** 116 N Walnut 812/339–0734 • 10:30am-7pm, till 8:30pm Fri, noon-5pm Sun • clothing, drums, incense, gifts, etc • wheelchair access

## Elkhart

**see South Bend**

## Evansville

### NIGHTCLUBS

**Someplace Else** 930 Main St (at Sycamore) 812/424-3202 • 4pm-3am • lesbians/ gay men • dancing/DJ • drag shows • karaoke • patio

### EROTICA

**Boudoir Noir** 4605 Washington Ave 812/401–7399 • 10am-midnight, noon-10pm Sun

## Fort Wayne

### INFO LINES & SERVICES

**Gay/ Lesbian AA** 501 W Berry St (at Plymouth church) 260/423–9424 • 2nd Tue at 6:30pm, 1pm every Sun

## NIGHTCLUBS

**After Dark/Babylon** 112 E Masterson Ave 260/456-6235 • noon-3am, 6pm-12:30am Sun • mostly gay men • dancing/DJ • karaoke • drag shows • male strippers • wheelchair access • gay-owned

**Babylon** 112 E Masterson Ave 260/247-5092 • 8pm-3am Fri-Sat only • mostly gay men • dancing/DJ • karaoke • patio

## CAFES

**Firefly** 3523 N Anthony Blvd 260/373-0505 • 6:30am-8pm, from 8am wknds • live entertainment • WiFi

## RESTAURANTS

**The Loving Cafe** 7605 Coldwater Rd 260/489-8686 • 10am-8pm, clsd Sun • vegetarian/vegan • wheelchair access

## RETAIL SHOPS

**Boudoir Noir** 512 W Superior St 260/420-0557 • 10am-midnight, noon-8pm Sun • gifts • sex toys • leather

# Gary

**see also Chicago, Illinois**

## EROTICA

**Romantix Adult Superstore** 8801 W Melton Rd/ US 20 (at Ripley Rd) 219/938-2194 • 24hrs

# Goshen

**see also South Bend**

## CAFES

**The Electric Brew** 136 S Main St 574/533-5990 • 6am-10pm, noon-7pm Sun • "Goshen's original coffeehouse" • live music

# Hammond

## BARS

**Dick's R U Crazee?** 1221 E 150th St 219/852-0222 • 8pm-3am, from 7pm wknds • mostly gay men • neighborhood bar • karaoke • drag shows

# Hebron

## EROTICA

**The Lion's Den Adult Superstore** 18010 Colorado St (exit 240, off I-65) 219/696-1276 • 24hrs

# Indiana Dunes

## ACCOMMODATIONS

**The Gray Goose Inn B&B** 350 Indian Boundary Rd (at I-95), Chesterton 219/926-5781, 800/521-5127 • gay/ straight • full brkfst • WiFi • nonsmoking rooms available

# Indianapolis

## INFO LINES & SERVICES

**AA Gay/ Lesbian** 317/632-7864 • various LGBT meeting • check web (www.indyaa.org) for meeting times & locations

## ACCOMMODATIONS

**The Alexander** 333 S Delaware St 855/200-3002 • gay-friendly • boutique-style art hotel

**The Fort Harrison State Park Inn** 5830 N Post Rd 317/638-6000 • gay-friendly • luxury inn in historic Fort Harrison in NE Indianapolis • nonsmoking

**Stone Soup Inn** 1304 N Central Ave (at 13th St) 317/639-9555, 866/639-9550 • gay/ straight • in the heart of the historic Old Northside • WiFi

**Sycamore Knoll B&B** 10777 Riverwood Ave, Noblesville 317/776-0570 • gay/ straight • 1886 estate near the White River • gardens & apple orchard • full brkfst • nonsmoking • WiFi • lesbian-owned

**The Villa** 1456 N Delaware St (at 15th) 317/916-8500 , 866/626-8500 • gay/ straight • spa and restaurant • WiFi

**Wyndham Indianapolis West** 2544 Executive Dr (off Airport Expy) 317/248-2481, 800/444-2326 • gay-friendly • seasonal pool • fitness center • WiFi in lobby, restaurant & lounge

## BARS

**501 Eagle** 501 N College (at Michigan St) 317/632-2100 • 5:30pm-3am, from 7:30pm Sat, 4pm-12:30am Sun • popular • mostly gay men • dancing/DJ • bears • leather

**Downtown Olly's** 822 N Illinois St (at St Clair) 317/636-5597 • open 24hrs • mostly men • sports & video bar • karaoke • brkfst, lunch, dinner

**Metro Nightclub & Restaurant** 707 Massachusetts Ave (at College) 317/639-6022 • 3pm-3am, from 1pm wknds • popular • lesbians/ gay men • neighborhood bar • piano bar • karaoke • patio • also restaurant • wheelchair access

**Noah Grant's Grill House & Raw Bar** 65 S 1st St (at W Oak St), Zionsville **317/732-2233** • 4pm-close, clsd Mon • gay-friendly • wine bar & bistro • serving lunch & dinner, Sun brunch • patio

**Zonie's Closet** 1446 E Washington St (at Arsenal) **317/266-0535** • 3pm-2am, cld Mon-Tue • gay/straight • dancing/DJ • karaoke • drag shows

## NIGHTCLUBS

**Greg's** 231 E 16th St (at Alabama) **317/638-8138** • 4pm-3am • mostly gay men • drag shows • county/western • patio • wheelchair access

**Talbott Street** 2145 N Talbott St (at 22nd St) **317/931-1343** • 9pm-2am Fri-Sat • gay/straight • dancing/DJ • drag shows • theme nights

## CAFES

**Bee Coffee** 5510 Lafayette Rd (at 56th St) **317/280-1236** • 6am-5pm, 7am-3pm Sat, clsd Sun

**Cornerstone Coffeehouse** 651 E 54th St (at N College Ave, Broad Ripple) **317/726-1360** • 6am-10pm, from 7am Sat, till 9pm Sun • food served • full bar • WiFi

**Earth House Collective** 237 N East St **317/636-4060** • 11am-9pm, clsd Sun • coffeehouse • also art, music & classes • WiFi

**Henry's on East Street** 627 N East St **317/951-0335** • 7am-7pm, till 9pm Fri, from 8am wknds • popular • gay-owned

**Hubbard & Cravens** 4930 N Pennsylvania St (in Broad Ripple) **317/251-5161** • 6am-7pm, 7am-3pm Sun • food served • WiFi

**Hubbard & Cravens** 4930 N Pennsylvania St (in Broad Ripple) **317/251-5161** • 6am-7pm, 7am-3pm Sun • food served • WiFi

**Monon Coffee Company** 920 E Westfield Blvd (at Guilford) **317/255-0510** • 6:30am-8pm, till 10pm Fri, from 7am Sat, 8am-8pm Sun

## RESTAURANTS

**Adobo Grill** 110 E Washington **317/822-9990** • lunch Fri-Sun, dinner nightly • Mexican • full bar • wheelchair access

**BARcelona** 201 N Delaware St **317/638-8272** • 11am-11pm • also full bar • tapas

**Bazbeaux Pizza** 329 Massachusetts Ave **317/636-7662** • lunch & dinner

**Cafe Zuppa** 320 N Meridian St (at New York St) **317/634-9877** • 7am-2:30pm, Sun brunch buffet

**English Ivy's** 944 S Alabama (at 10th) **317/822-5070** • 11am-3am from 10am wknds • also full bar • WiFi • wheelchair access

**India Garden** 830 Broad Ripple Ave (btwn Carrollton & Guilford) **317/253-6060** • lunch & dinner • Indian • wheelchair access • also 207 N Delaware St, 317/634-6060

**King David Dogs** 15 N Pennsylvania St • great hot dogs

**La Piedad** 6524 Cornell Ave **317/475-0988** • lunch & dinner • Mexican

**Mama Carolla's** 1031 E 54th St (at Winthrop) **317/259-9412** • dinner only, clsd Sun-Mon • traditional Italian

**Naked Tchopstix** 6253 N College Ave (in Broad Ripple) **317/252-5555** • lunch & dinner • popular • Korean, Japanese, Chinese cuisine • also sushi bar

**Oakley's Bistro** 1464 W 86th St (at Ditch Rd) **317/824-1231** • lunch & dinner, clsd Sun-Mon • popular • gourmet cont'l • reservations suggested • wheelchair access

**Pancho's Taqueria** 7023 Michigan Rd (at Westlane) **317/202-9015** • 11am-9pm • popular • authentic Mexican • wheelchair access

**Sawasdee** 1222 W 86th St (at Ditch Rd) **317/844-9451** • lunch Mon-Sat, dinner nightly • Thai • some veggie • wheelchair access

**Three Sisters Cafe** 6360 N Guilford Ave (at Main St) **317/257-5556** • 8am-9pm, till 3pm Sun • plenty veggie & vegan • popular Sun brunch

**Usual Suspects** 6319 Guilford Ave (at Broad Ripple) **317/251-3138** • 5pm-10pm, till 11pm Fri-Sat, till 9pm Sun, clsd Mon • eclectic • full bar • patio

**Yats** 659 Massachusetts Ave (at Walnut) **317/686-6380** • 11am-9pm, till 10pm Fri-Sat, till 7pm Sun • Cajun • also 5363 N College Ave & 8352 E 96th St • wheelchair access

## ENTERTAINMENT & RECREATION

**Indiana Fever** 1 Conseco Ct (in Conseco Fieldhouse) **317/917-2500** • check out the Women's Nat'l Basketball Association while you're in Indianapolis

**Indy Indie Artist Colony** 26 E 14th St **317/295-9302** • noon-5pm Th-Sat • largest artist community in the city with 72 artist live/work spaces

### BOOKSTORES

**Bookmamas** 9 S Johnson Ave (at E Washington St, in Irvington) **317/375-3715** • open Wed-Sat • call for hours • used bookstore

### RETAIL SHOPS

**All My Relations** 7218 Rockville Rd **317/227-3925** • noon-6pm, till 7pm Wed-Th, 10am-6pm Sat • New Age/ metaphysical store • also classes

**Metamorphosis** 828 Broad Ripple Ave (at Carrollton) **317/466-1666** • 1pm-9pm, till 5pm Sun • tattoo & piercing parlor

### PUBLICATIONS

**Nuvo** **317/254-2400** • Indy's alternative weekly

**The Word** **317/632-8840** • LGBT newspaper

## Lafayette

### INFO LINES & SERVICES

**Pride Lafayette, Inc** 640 Main St #218 **765/423-7579** • community center 6pm-8pm, 5pm-9pm wknds • support/ social activities

### EROTICA

**Fantasy East** 2315 Concord Rd (at Teal) **765/474-2417** • 10am-1am

## Marion

### EROTICA

**After Dark** 1311 W Johnson St **765/662-3688** • 10am-11pm, till midnight Fri-Sat, noon-10pm Sun

## Michigan City

### ACCOMMODATIONS

**Duneland Beach Inn & Restaurant** 3311 Pottawattomie Trail (at Duneland Beach Dr) **219/874-7729, 800/423-7729** • gay-friendly • also restaurant/ bar • 1 block away from Lake Michigan & private beach • 60 miles from Chicago

**Tryon Farm Guest House** 1400 Tryon Rd (at Hwy 212) **219/879-3618** • gay-friendly • full brkfst • hot tub • kids/ pets ok • nonsmoking • WiFi • women-owned

## Mishawaka

**see also South Bend**

### ACCOMMODATIONS

**The Beiger Mansion** 317 Lincolnway E **574/255-6300, 800/437-0131** • gay-friendly • B&B in 4-level neo-classical limestone mansion • pool • nonsmoking • WiFi • gay-owned

## New Albany

**see also Louisville, KY**

### NIGHTCLUBS

**Pride Bar & Lounge** 504 State St **812/329-0519** • 4pm-1am, till 3am Fri-Sat, till midnight Sun • lesbians/gay men • dancing/DJ • karaoke • patio

## Noblesville

**see Indianapolis**

## Richmond

### EROTICA

**Exotic Fantasies** 12 S 11th St **765/935-5827** • 9am-midnight, till 2am Fri-Sat

## South Bend

### ACCOMMODATIONS

**Innisfree B&B** 702 W Colfax **574/283-0740** • gay-friendly • 1892 Queen Anne minutes from Notre Dame • full brkfst • nonsmoking

### BARS

**Jeannie's Tavern** 621 S Bendix (at Ford St) **574/288-2962** • 2pm-2am • gay-friendly • neighborhood bar • transgender-friendly • gay-owned

**Vickies Inc** 112 W Monroe St (at S Michigan St) **574/232-4090** • 2pm-2am • gay/ straight • neighborhood bar • transgender-friendly • food served • football party every Sat in season • gay-owned

### ENTERTAINMENT & RECREATION

**GLBT Resource Center of Michiana** **574/254-1411** • 5pm-8pm Mon & 11am-2pm Sat

### EROTICA

**Romantix Adult Superstore** 2715 S Main St (at Eckman St) **574/291-1899**

## Terre Haute

### NIGHTCLUBS

**Zimmarss Nightclub** 1500 Locust St (at 15th St) 812/232-3026 • 8pm-3am, 7pm-12:30am Sun, clsd Mon-Tue • lesbians/ gay men • dancing/DJ • transgender-friendly • drag shows • strippers • gay-owned

## Valparaiso

### ACCOMMODATIONS

**Inn at Aberdeen** 3158 S State Rd 2 219/465-3753, 866/761-3753 • gay-friendly • 1880s Queen Anne • full brkfst • nonsmoking • WiFi • wheelchair access

## IOWA

## Statewide

### PUBLICATIONS

**The ACCESSline** 712/560-1807 • the Heartland's LGBT newspaper

## Ames

### RESTAURANTS

**Lucullan's Italian Grill** 400 Main St (at Burnett) 515/232-8484 • dinner Tue-Sun • some veggie • full bar

### EROTICA

**Romantix Adult Superstore** 117 Kellogg St (at Lincoln Wy) 515/232-7717 • 9am-4am

## Burlington

### ACCOMMODATIONS

**Arrowhead Motel** 2520 Mt Pleasant St 319/752-6353 • gay-friendly • kids ok • WiFi • nonsmoking • wheelchair access • gay-owned •

### BARS

**Steve's Place** 852 Washington St (at Central Ave) 319/754-5868 • 9am-2am, clsd Sun • gay/ straight • full meun • wheelchair access • gay-owned

## Cedar Falls

see also Waterloo

## Cedar Rapids

### NIGHTCLUBS

**Belle's Basix** 3916 1st Ave NE (btwn 39th & 40th) 319/363-3194 • 4pm-2am • lesbians/ gay men • transgender-friendly • dancing/DJ • drag shows • gay/ lesbian-owned

### CAFES

**Blue Strawberry** 118 2nd St SE 319/247-2583 • 6:30am-5:30pm, 8am-2pm Sun

### ENTERTAINMENT & RECREATION

**CSPS Arts Center** 1103 3rd St SE 319/364-1580 • galleries • concerts • plays • many LGBT events

## Council Bluffs

see also Omaha, Nebraska

### RESTAURANTS

**Dixie Quick's** 157 W Broadway 712/256-4140 • lunch & dinner, brunch from 9am wkds, clsd Mon • Southern • reservations recommended

## Davenport

### ACCOMMODATIONS

**Hotel Blackhawk** 200 East 3rd St 563/322-5000, 888/525-4455 • gay-friendly • newly renovated • bowling alley on-site

### BARS

**Mary's on 2nd** 832 W 2nd St (btwn Warren & Brown) 563/884-8014 • 4pm-2am • lesbians/ gay men • neighborhood bar • dancing/DJ • occasional live shows • videos • patio • wheelchair access

### NIGHTCLUBS

**Connections** 822 W 2nd St (at Brown) 563/322-1121 • 5pm-2am • lesbians/ gay men • dancing/ DJ • drag shows • karaoke

## Des Moines

### ACCOMMODATIONS

**Hotel Fort Des Moines** 1000 Walnut St (at 10th St) 515/243-1161, 800/532-1466 • gay-friendly • full brkfst • pool • hot tub • kids ok • gym • nonsmoking • WiFi • wheelchair access

**The Renaissance Savery Hotel** 401 Locust St (at 4th) 515/244-2151, 800/514 • gay-friendly • pool • kids ok • restaurant • WiFi • wheelchair access

## Bars

**The Blazing Saddle** 416 E 5th St (btwn Grand & Locust) **515/246-1299** • 2pm-2am, from noon wknds • mostly gay men • dancing/DJ • leather • drag shows • WiFi • wheelchair access

**Buddy's Corral** 418 E 5th St (btwn Grand & Locust) **515/244-7140** • noon-2am, from 10am Sat • gay-friendly • karaoke

## Nightclubs

**The Garden** 112 SE 4th St **515/243-3965** • 8pm-2am, 5pm-midnight Sun, clsd Mon-Tue • lesbians/gay men • more women Th • dancing/DJ • live shows • karaoke • videos • patio • young crowd • wheelchair access

**Le Boi Bar** 508 Indianola Ave (at 7th) **515/284-1074** • 8pm-2am, 3pm-midnight Sun, clsd Mon-Tue • lesbians/gay men • dancing/DJ • drag shows

## Cafes

**Drake Diner** 1111 25th St (btwn University & Cottage Grove) **515/277-1111** • 7am-11pm • try the cake shake • full bar • patio • wheelchair access

**Java Joe's** 214 4th St (at Court Ave) **515/288-5282** • 7am-11pm, till midnight Th-Sat, till 10pm Sun• live shows • WiFi • wheelchair access

**Ritual Cafe** 1301 E Locust St **515/288-4872** • 7am-7pm, till 11pm Fri-Sat, clsd Sun • live music

**Zanzibar's Coffee Adventure** 2723 Ingersoll Ave (at 28th St) **515/244-7694** • 6:30am-8pm, till 9pm Fri-Sat, 8am-6pm Sun • wheelchair access

## Restaurants

**Cafe di Scala** 644 18th St (at Woodland) **515/244-1353** • dinner Th-Sat only • Italian • beer/wine • wheelchair access

## Retail Shops

**Liberty Gifts** 333 E Grand Ave, Ste 105 (entrance on E 4th St) **515/508-0825** • 10am-8pm, 11am-7pm Sun• pride store

## Erotica

**Gallery Book Store** 1000 Cherry St (at 10th) **515/244-2916**

**Romantix Adult Superstore** 2020 E Euclid Ave (at Delaware) **515/266-7992** • 24hrs

# Dubuque

## Cafes

**Cafe Manna Java** 700 Locust St (Roshek Building) **563/588-3105** • 7am-9pm, 8pm-2am Sun • WiFi • full bar • lesbian-owned

# Iowa City

## Info Lines & Services

**AA Gay/ Lesbian** 500 N Clinton (at church) **319/338-9111 (AA#)** • 5pm Sun

**Women's Resource & Action Center** 130 N Madison St (at Market) **319/335-1486** • 9am-5pm, clsd wknds • community center • support groups • counseling • wheelchair access

## Bars

**Deadwood Tavern** 6 S Dubuque St **319/351-9417** • 11am-2am • popular • gay-friendly • neighborhood bar • college crowd • wheelchair access

**Studio 13** 13 S Linn St (in the alley btwn Linn & Dubuque Sts) **319/338-7185** • 7pm-2am, clsd Mon lesbians/gay men • dancing/DJ • drag shows Fri & Sun • 19+ • gay-owned

## Restaurants

**The Mill** 120 E Burlington St **319/351-9529** • lunch & dinner, wknd brunch • popular Americana music venue

## Entertainment & Recreation

**Old Capitol City Roller Girls** • Iowa City's own female roller derby league • facebook.com/oldcapitolcityrollergirls

## Bookstores

**Prairie Lights Bookstore** 15 S Dubuque St (at Washington) **319/337-2681, 800/295-2665** • 9am-9pm, till 6pm Sun • also cafe & wine bar • wheelchair access

## Retail Shops

**New Pioneer Co-op & Bakehouse** 22 S Van Buren (at Washington) **319/338-9441** • 7am-11pm • health food store & deli • wheelchair access • also Coralville location at 1101 2nd St

## Erotica

**Romantix Adult Superstore** 315 Kirkwood Ave (at Gilbert) **319/351-9444** • 8am-4am

# Sioux City

## Erotica

**Romantix Adult Superstore** 511 Pearl St **712/277-8566** • 8am-4am, noon-2am Sun

## Waterloo

### ACCOMMODATIONS

**Stella's Guesthouse & Gardens** 324 Summit Ave (at Chicago) **319/232-2122** • lesbians/ gay men • full brkfst • hot tub • clothing-optional • shared baths • nonsmoking • gay-owned

### NIGHTCLUBS

**Kings & Queens Knight Club** 304 W 4th St (at Jefferson) **319/232-3001** • 6:30pm-2am, clsd Sun-Mon • gay-friendly • dancing/DJ • transgender-friendly • drag shows • young crowd • wheelchair access

## KANSAS

## Statewide

### PUBLICATIONS

**The Liberty Press** 316/652-7737 • Kansas statewide LGBT newspaper

## Kansas City

**see also Kansas City, Missouri**

## Lawrence

### NIGHTCLUBS

**Granada** 1020 Massachusetts (at 11th) **785/842-1390** • hours vary • gay/ straight • dancing/DJ • live bands • wheelchair access

**Jazzhaus** 926-1/2 Massachusetts St **785/749-3320, 785/749-1387** • 8pm-2am • gay-friendly • live music • karaoke • WiFi

### CAFES

**Henry's** 11 E 8th St (btwn Massachusetts St & New Hampshire St) **785/331-3511** • 7am-2am • cafe downstairs • bar from 5pm upstairs • WiFi

**Java Break** 17 E 7th St (at New Hampshire) **785/749-5282** • 24hrs • sandwiches • desserts • gay-owned

### RESTAURANTS

**Merchants Pub & Plate** 746 Massachusetts St (at 8th) **785/843-4111** • 11am-midnight, till 2am Th-Sat • serving rich Midwestern harvest with over 30 craft beers • wheelchair access

### BOOKSTORES

**The Dusty Bookshelf** 708 Massachusetts St **785/749-4643** • 10am-8pm, till 10pm Fri-Sat, noon-6pm Sun • used books • feminist & LGBT section • gay-owned

## Manhattan

### BOOKSTORES

**The Dusty Bookshelf** 700 N Manhattan Ave **785/539-2839** • 10am-8pm, till 6pm Sat, noon-5pm Sun • feminist & LGBT section • gay-owned

## Overland Park

### ACCOMMODATIONS

**Hawthorn Suites** 11400 College Blvd **913/826-6167** • gay-friendly • pool • jacuzzi • WiFi • wheelchair access

## Topeka

### INFO LINES & SERVICES

**Freedom Group AA** 3916 SW 17th St (at Gage, at St David's church) **785/272-9483** • 8pm Fri

### BARS

**Skivies** 921 S Kansas Ave (near 10th St) **785/234-0482** • 3pm-2am • mostly gay men • neighborhood bar • dancing/DJ • drag shows • country/ western • gay-owned

## Wichita

### INFO LINES & SERVICES

**One Day at a Time Gay AA** 156 S Kansas Ave (at MCC, enter on English) **316/684-3661** • 8pm Tue & Th

### ACCOMMODATIONS

**Hawthorn Suites** 2405 N Ridge Rd **316/729-5700** • gay-friendly • kids/ small pets ok • brkfst buffet • WiFi • wheelchair access •

### BARS

**Club Boomerang** 1400 E 1st **316/262-2412** • 5pm-2am, clsd Mon-Wed • lesbians/gay men • dancing/DJ • drag shows • karaoke

**J's Lounge** 513 E Central Ave (at N Emporia St) **316/262-1363** • 4pm-2am • lesbians/ gay men • cabaret • live shows • karaoke • patio • wheelchair access • "an upscale dive"

**Rain Cafe & Lounge** 518 E Douglas (btwn St Francis & Emporia) **316/261-9000** • 11am-2am, from 10:30am Sun • full menu till 9pm • lesbians/ gay men • dancing/DJ Fri-Sat • Karaoke Th • DJ on wknds

**The Store** 3210 E Osie **316/683-9781** • 2pm-2am • mostly women • men welcome • neighborhood bar

## CAFES

**The Vagabond** 614 W Douglas Ave 316/303–1110 • 7am-2am • theme nights • art gallery • also bar • WiFi

## RESTAURANTS

**Moe's Sub Shop** 2815 S Hydraulic St (at Wassall) 316/524–5511 • 11am-8pm, clsd Sun

**Oh Yeah! China Bistro** 3101 N Rock Rd 316/425–7700 • lunch & dinner • wheelchair access

**Old Mill Tasty Shop** 604 E Douglas Ave (at St Francis) 316/264–6500 • 11am-3pm, from 8am Sat, clsd Sun • old-fashioned soda fountain • some veggie

**River City Brewing Company** 150 N Mosley St 316/263–2739 • 11am-10pm, till 2am wknds • live music

**Riverside Cafe** 739 W 13th St (at Bitting) 316/262–6703 • 6am-8pm, till 2pm Sun

## ENTERTAINMENT & RECREATION

**Cabaret Oldtown Theatre** 412 1/2 E Douglas Ave (at Topeka) 316/265–4400 • edgy, kitschy productions

**Mosley Street Melodrama** 234 N Mosley St (btwn 1st & 2nd Sts) 316/263–0222 • melodrama, homestyle buffet & full bar!

**Wichita Arts** 334 N Mead 316/462–2787 • promotes visual & performing arts • ArtScene publication has extensive cultural calendar

## PUBLICATIONS

**The Liberty Press** 316/652–7737 • statewide LGBT newspaper

## EROTICA

**Fetish Lingerie** 2150 S Broadway St (btwn E Clark & E Kinkaid Sts) 316/264–7800 • 11:30-7pm, clsd Sun-Mon • all sizes available

**Patricia's** 6143 W Kellogg (at Dugan) 316/942–1244 • 9am-1am, from noon-10pm Sun

# KENTUCKY

## Covington

**see also Cincinnati, Ohio**

## BARS

**Bar 32** 701 Bakewell St (at 7th St) 859/431–7011 • 3pm-1am, from 1pm Sun • gay-friendly • neighborhood bar • dancing/DJ • live shows • karaoke • food served

**Rosie's Tavern** 643 Bakewell St (at 7th St) 859/291–9707 • 3pm-2:30am • gay/ straight • neighborhood bar • lesbian-owned

# Lexington

## INFO LINES & SERVICES

**Gay/ Lesbian AA** 530 E High St (at Woodland Church) 859/225–1212 (AA#) • 8pm Wed • also 7:30pm Fri at 205 E Short St (church)

**GLSO Pride Center of the Bluegrass** 389 Waller Ave #100 859/253–3233 • 10am-3pm Mon-Fri

## ACCOMMODATIONS

**Hyatt Regency Lexington** 401 W High St 859/253–1234 • gay-friendly • pool • bar & restaurant • wheelchair access

**Ramada Limited** 2261 Elkhorn Rd (off I-75) 859/294–7375, 800/272–6232 • gay-friendly • pool • WiFi • nonsmoking • wheelchair access

## BARS

**The Bar Complex** 224 E Main St (at Esplanade) 859/255–1551 • 4pm-midnight, till 2am wknds • popular • lesbians/ gay men • dancing/DJ • drag shows • live shows • WiFi • wheelchair access

**Crossings** 117 N Limestone St 859/233–7266 • 4pm-2am • mostly gay men • neighborhood bar • live shows • karaoke • wheelchair access

**Soundbar** 208 S Limestone 859/523–6338 • 4:30pm-close • gay/ straight • dancing/DJ • karaoke

## CAFES

**Third Street Stuff** 257 N Limestone 859/255–5301 • 6:30am-11pm, from 8am Sun, salads & sandwiches • also funky boutique

## RESTAURANTS

**Alfalfa Restaurant** 141 E Main St 859/253–0014 • lunch & dinner, brunch wknds • healthy multi-ethnic • plenty veggie • folk music wknds

**Natasha's Bistro & Bar** 112 Esplanade (at Main St) 859/259–2754 • lunch & dinner, clsd Sun • eclectic dining • plenty veggie • also live theater & music

## BOOKSTORES

**Joseph-Beth** 161 Lexington Green Circle (at Nicholasville Rd) 859/273–2911, 800/248–6849 • 9am-10pm, till 11pm Fri-Sat, 11am-9pm Sun • also cafe • WiFi • wheelchair access

**Sqecial Media** 371 S Limestone St (btwn Pine & Winslow) 859/255–4316 • 10am-8pm, noon-6pm Sun • also pride items

## PUBLICATIONS

**LinQ** 859/253–3233 • local news & calendar

## Louisville

### Info Lines & Services

**Gay AA** 1432 Highland Ave **502/587–6225** • 4:30pm Sun & 6pm Mon

### Accommodations

**21c Museum Hotel Louisville** 700 W Main St **502/217–6300, 877/217–6400** • gay-friendly • boutique hotel w/ museum • also Proof on Main restaurant

**The Brown Hotel** 335 W Broadway (at 4th) **502/583–1234, 888/387–0498** • gay-friendly • WiFi • nonsmoking • also restaurant & bar

**Columbine B&B** 1707 S 3rd St (near Lee St) **502/635–5000, 800/635–5010** • gay-friendly • 1896 Greek Revivial mansion • full brkfst • nonsmoking • WiFi • gay-owned

**Galt House Hotel & Suites** 140 N 4th St (at W Main) **502/589–5200, 800/843–4258** • gay-friendly • waterfront hotel

**Inn at the Park** 1332 S 4th St (at Park Ave) **502/638–0045** • gay-friendly • restored mansion • full brkfst • nonsmoking • WiFi

### Bars

**The Levee** 1005 W Market, Jeffersonville, IN **812/284–4759** • 4pm-3am • gay/ straight • neighborhood bar • dancing/DJ • karaoke • WiFi • 2 minutes from downtown Louisville

**Magnolia Bar** 1398 S 2nd St (at Magnolia) **502/637–9052** • 2pm-4am • gay-friendly • neighborhood/dive bar

**Purrswaytions** 2235 S Preston St **502/409–8487** • 2pm-1am, till 4am Fri-Sat • lesbians/gay men • karaoke

**Teddy Bears Bar & Grill** 1148 Garvin Pl (at St Catherine) **502/589–2619** • 11am-4am, from 1pm Sun • mostly gay men • neighborhood bar • wheelchair access

**Tryangles** 209 S Preston St (at Market) **502/583–6395** • 4pm-4am, from 1pm Sun • mostly gay men • karaoke Tue • wheelchair access

### Nightclubs

**The Connection Complex** 120 S Floyd St (at Market) **502/585–5752** • 8pm-4am, till 2am Mon-Wed • popular • lesbians/ gay men • dancing/DJ • piano bar & cabaret • videos • wheelchair access

### Cafes

**Days Espresso & Coffee** 1420 Bardstown Rd (at Edenside) **502/456–1170** • 6:30am-10pm, till 11pm Fri-Sat • WiFi • wheelchair access • lesbian-owned

### Restaurants

**Cafe Mimosa** 1543 Bardstown Rd (at Stevens Ave) **502/458–2233** • lunch & dinner • Vietnamese, Chinese & sushi

**El Mundo** 2345 Frankfort Ave **502/899–9930** • 11:30am-10pm, full bar till 2am Th-Sat, clsd Sun-Mon • popular • Mexican • wheelchair access

**Havana Rumba** 4115 Oechsli Ave (off State Hwy 1447) **502/897–1959** • lunch & dinner • Cuban

**Jack Fry's** 1007 Bardstown Rd **502/452–9244** • lunch & dinner • steak/ Southern • live jazz • wheelchair access

**Mayan Cafe** 813 E Market St **502/566–0651** • lunch Mon-Fri, dinner nightly, clsd Sun • Mayan/ Mexican

**Porcini** 2730 Frankfort Ave (at Bayly) **502/894–8686** • dinner nightly, clsd Sun • Italian

**Proof on Main** 702 W Main St (at 7th, at 21c Hotel) **502/217–6360** • brkfst & lunch Mon-Fri, dinner nightly • upscale • modern American w/ Tuscan influence

**Ramsi's Cafe on the World** 1293 Bardstown Rd **502/451–0700** • 11am-1am, till 2am Fri-Sat, Sun brunch • eclectic menu • wheelchair access

**Vietnam Kitchen** 5339 Mitscher Ave **502/363–5154** • clsd Wed, Vietnamese • plenty veggie • wheelchair access

**Zen Garden** 2240 Frankfort Ave **502/895–9114** • lunch & dinner, clsd Sun • Asian • vegetarian • wheelchair access

### Entertainment & Recreation

**Pandora Productions** PO Box 4185 40204 **502/216–5502** • LGBT-themed productions

**Rudyard Kipling** 422 W Oak St (btwn 4th & Garvin) **502/636–1311** • live music & theater, also restaurant, open wknds

### Bookstores

**Carmichael's** 1295 Bardstown Rd (at Longest Ave) **502/456–6950** • 8am-9pm, till 10pm Fri-Sat • LGBT section

### Publications

**The Community Letter** • LGBT newspaper

### Erotica

**Romantix Adult Superstore** 933 Winchester Rd (at Liberty Rd) **859/252–0357** • 24hrs

## Newport

### see also Cincinnati, Ohio

BARS

**The Crazy Fox Saloon** 901 Washington Ave (at 9th) **859/261–2143** • 3pm-2:30am • gay/ straight • friendly neighborhood bar • patio

## Paducah

EROTICA

**Romantix Adult Superstore** 243 Brown (at Irvin Cobb Dr) **270/442–5584**

# LOUISIANA

## Statewide

PUBLICATIONS

**Ambush Mag** 504/522–8049 • oldest LGBT newspaper for the Gulf South (Texas through Florida)

## Baton Rouge

INFO LINES & SERVICES

**Freedom of Choice/ Gay AA** 7747 Tom Dr (at MCC) **225/930–0026 (AA#)** • 8pm Th & Sat

BARS

**George's Place** 860 St Louis **225/387–9798** • 3pm-2am, from 5pm Sat, clsd Sun • popular • lesbians/ gay men • neighborhood bar • videos • karaoke • male strippers Fri • wheelchair access

**Hound Dogs** 668 Main St (at 7th) **225/344–0807** • 2pm-2am, from 4pm Mon-Tue, from noon Sun • lesbians/ gay men • neighborhood bar • wheelchair access

NIGHTCLUBS

**Splash** 2183 Highland Rd **225/242–9491** • 9pm-2am, clsd Sun-TWed• popular • lesbians/ gay men • dancing/DJ • drag shows • 18+ • wheelchair access

RESTAURANTS

**Drusilla Seafood** 3482 Drusilla Ln (at Jefferson Hwy) **225/923–0896, 800/364–8844** • 11am-10pm

**Mestizo** 2323 Acadian Thruway (just off I-10) **225/387–2699** • lunch & dinner • Louisiana-Mexican fusion

**Ralph & Kacoo's** 6110 Bluebonnet Blvd (off I-10 & Perkins) **225/766–2113** • 11am-9:30pm, till 10:30pm Fri-Sat • Cajun • full bar • wheelchair access

PUBLICATIONS

**Ambush Mag** 504/522–8049 • LGBT newspaper for the Gulf South (TX through FL)

EROTICA

**Grand Cinema Station** 10732 Florida Blvd 225/272-2010

## Breaux Bridge

ACCOMMODATIONS

**Maison des Amis** 111 Washington St (at Bridge St) **337/507–3399** • gay-friendly • charming 1870 residence overlooking legendary Bayou Teche • full brkfst • WiFi

## Lafayette

INFO LINES & SERVICES

**AA Gay/ Lesbian** 115 Leonie St **337/991–0830 (AA#)** • call for times & locations

## Lake Charles

ACCOMMODATIONS

**Aunt Ruby's B&B** 504 Pujo St (at Hodges) **337/430–0603** • gay/ straight • full brkfst • WiFi

NIGHTCLUBS

**Crystal's** 112 E Broad (at Ryan) **337/433–5457** • 9pm-2am, till 4am Fri • lesbians/ gay men • dancing/DJ • country/ western • drag shows • wheelchair access

RESTAURANTS

**Pujo St Cafe** 901 Ryan St (at Pujo) **337/439–2054** • 11am-9pm, till 10pm Fri-Sat, clsd Sun • full bar • gay-owned

## Metairie

see New Orleans

## Monroe

### BARS

**The Corner Bar** 512 N 3rd St (at Pine) 318/329–0046 • 9pm-2am, clsd Sun-Wed • lesbians/ gay men • neighborhood bar • multiracial • live shows • karaoke • drag shows • 18+ • gay-owned

### NIGHTCLUBS

**Club Pink** 1914 Roselawn Ave 318/654–7030 • 7pm-2am • lesbians/ gay men • dancing/DJ • karaoke • 18+ • wheelchair access • gay-owned

## Natchitoches

### ACCOMMODATIONS

**Chez des Amis B&B** 910 Washington St (btwn Texas & Pavie) 318/352–2647 • gay/ straight • full brkfst • nonsmoking • WiFi • gay-owned

**Judge Porter House B&B** 321 Second St 318/527–1555, 800/441–8343 • gay/ straight • full brkfst • nonsmoking • WiFi • gay-owned

## New Orleans

### INFO LINES & SERVICES

**AA Lambda Center** 1024 Elysian Fields Ave 504/838–3399 (GENERAL AA OFFICE #) • daily meetings • call for schedule

**LGBT Community Center of New Orleans** 504/945–1103 • noon-8pm, noon-6pm Fri-Sat • call first • wheelchair access

### ACCOMMODATIONS

**1896 O'Malley House B&B** 120 S Pierce St (at Canal St) 504/488–5896, 866/226–1896 • gay/ straight • nonsmoking • WiFi • gay-owned

**5 Continents B&B** 1731 Esplanade Ave (at Claiborne) 504/324–8594, 800/997–4652 • gay/ straight • B&B • full brkfst • kids/ pets ok • WiFi • gay-owned

**Aaron Ingram Haus** 1012 Elysian Fields Ave (btwn N Rampart & St Claude) 504/949–3110 • gay/ straight • guesthouse • apts • courtyard • WiFi • gay-owned

**Andrew Jackson Hotel** 919 Royal St (btwn St Philip & Dumaine) 504/561–5881, 800/654–0224 • gay-friendly • historic inn • WiFi • nonsmoking

**Antebellum Guest House** 1333 Esplanade Ave (at Marais St) 504/943–1900 • gay/ straight • full brkfst • clothing-optional • nonsmoking • WiFi • gay-owned

**Ashton's B&B** 2023 Esplanade Ave (at Galvez) 504/942–7048, 800/725–4131 • gay-friendly • quiet location • WiFi

**Auld Sweet Olive B&B** 2460 N Rampart St (at Spain) 504/947–4332, 877/470–5323 • gay/ straight • popular • kids 13+ ok • nonsmoking • WiFi

**B&W Courtyards B&B** 2425 Chartres St (btwn Mandeville & Spain) 504/324–3396, 800/585–5731 • gay-friendly • hot tub • nonsmoking • WiFi • gay-owned

**Biscuit Palace Guest House** 730 Dumaine (btwn Royal & Bourbon) 504/525–9949 • gay-friendly • 1820s Creole mansion • B&B & apts • in the French Quarter • kids ok • WiFi • wheelchair access

**Bon Maison Guest House** 835 Bourbon St (btwn Lafitte's & Bourbon Pub) 504/561–8498 • gay/ straight • nonsmoking • gay-owned

**Bourbon Orleans Hotel** 717 Orleans (at Bourbon St) 504/523–2222, 866/513–9744 • gay-friendly • swimming • WiFi • nonsmoking • also restaurant & 2 bars

**The Burgundy B&B** 2513 Burgundy St (at St Roch) 504/261–9477 • gay/ straight • near French Quarter • clothing-optional hot tub • nonsmoking • WiFi • gay-owned

**Bywater B&B** 1026 Clouet St 504/944–8438 • gay-friendly • fireplace • nonsmoking • kids/ pets ok • WiFi • lesbian & gay-owned

**Canal Street Inn** 3620 Canal St (at Telemachus) 504/483–3033 • gay/ straight • nonsmoking • WiFi

**Chez Palmiers B&B** 1744 N Rampart St (at St Anthony) 504/208–7044, 504/729–8686 • gay/ straight • nonsmoking • kids 13+ ok • WiFi • gay-owned

**The Chimes B&B** 1146 Constantinople St (in Garden District) 504/899–2621, 504/453–2183 • gay-friendly • 1876 home • nonsmoking • WiFi • kids/ pets ok w/ approval

**The Cornstalk Hotel** 915 Royal St 504/523–1515, 800/759–6112 • gay-friendly • kids ok • WiFi

**Elysian Guest House** 1008 Elysian Fields Ave (at Rampart St) 504/324–4311 • gay-friendly • hot tub • nonsmoking • WiFi • gay-owned

**The Frenchmen Hotel** 417 Frenchmen St (where Esplanade, Decatur & Frenchmen intersect) 504/948–2166, 800/831–1781 • gay/ straight • spa • pool • kids ok • nonsmoking • WiFi • wheelchair access

**The Green House Inn** 1212 Magazine St (at Erato) **504/525–1333, 800/966–1303** • lesbians/gay men • 1840s guesthouse • gym • hot tub • pool • nonsmoking • pets ok • WiFi • gay-owned

**Harrah's Casino** 228 Poydras St **504/533–6000, 800/847–5299** • gay-friendly • restaurants & lounges • wheeelchair access

**Hotel Monteleone** 214 Royal St (at Iberville) **504/523–3341, 800/535–9595** • gay-friendly • deluxe historic hotel • rumored to be haunted • pool • WiFi

**Kerlerec House** 928 Kerlerec St (at Dauphine St) **504/944–8544** • gay/straight • 1 block from the French Quarter • hot tub • gardens • kids ok • nonsmoking • WiFi • gay-owned

**La Dauphine, Residence des Artistes** 2316 Dauphine St (btwn Mandeville & Marigny) **504/948–2217** • gay/straight • B&B • nonsmoking • WiFi • gay-owned

**La Maison Marigny B&B on Bourbon** 1421 Bourbon St (at Esplanade) **504/948–3638, 800/570–2014** • gay-friendly • on the quiet end of Bourbon St • nonsmoking • WiFi • gay-owned

**Lafitte Guest House** 1003 Bourbon St (at St Philip) **504/581–2678, 800/331–7971** • gay/straight • elegant French manor house • nonsmoking • kids ok • WiFi

**Lamothe House Hotel** 621 Esplanade Ave (btwn Royal & Chartres) **504/947–1161, 800/367–5858** • gay/straight • popular • jacuzzi • pool • kids ok • nonsmoking • WiFi • straight & gay-owned

**Maison de Ville** 727 Toulouse St **504/324–4888** • gay/straight • historic property with southern elegance located in the heart of the French Quarter • WiFi

**Maison Dupuy Hotel** 1001 Toulouse St **504/586–8000, 800/535–9177** • gay-friendly • luxury boutique hotel • fine dining restaurant • swimming pool • hot tub • WiFi

**Mentone B&B** 1437 Pauger St (at Kerlerec) **504/943–3019** • gay-friendly • suite in Victorian in the Faubourg Marigny district • nonsmoking • WiFi • women-owned

**The Olivier House Hotel** 828 Toulouse (at Bourbon) **504/525–8456** • gay-friendly • pool • kids/pets ok • WiFi • wheelchair access

**Pierre Coulon Guest House** **504/943–6692, 877/943–6692** • gay-friendly • quiet apt patio • nonsmoking • WiFi

**Royal Street Courtyard** 2438 Royal St (at Spain) **504/943–6818, 888/846–4004** • gay/straight • suites in 1850s guesthouse • hot tub • pets ok • WiFi • gay-owned

**W New Orleans—French Quarter** 316 Chartres St **504/581–1200, 877/WHOTELS (RESERVATIONS ONLY)** • gay-friendly • pool • WiFi • also restaurant • wheelchair access

## BARS

**700 Club** 700 Burgundy (at St Peter) **504/561–1095** • noon-4am • lesbians/gay men • videos • food served • wheelchair access

**Big Daddy's** 2513 Royal St (at Franklin) **504/948–6288** • 24hrs • lesbians/gay men • neighborhood bar • wheelchair access

**Bourbon Pub & Parade** 801 Bourbon St (at St Ann) **504/529–2107** • 24hrs • popular • lesbians/gay men • dancing/DJ • theme nights • Sun T-dance • drag shows/strippers • videos • 18+ • WiFi

**Cafe Lafitte in Exile/ The Balcony Bar** 901 Bourbon St (at Dumaine) **504/522–8397** • 24hrs • popular • mostly gay men • dancing/DJ • live shows • videos

**Country Club** 634 Louisa St (at Royal) **504/945–0742** • 11am-1am • popular • gay/straight • food served • karaoke • swimming • volleyball • nude sunbathing • WiFi • not your father's country club!

**Cutter's** 706 Franklin Ave (at Royal) **504/948–4200** • 3pm-3am, from 11am wknds • lesbians/gay men • neighborhood bar • live music • WiFi • wheelchair access

**The Double Play** 439 Dauphine (at St Louis) **504/523–4517** • 24hrs • mostly gay men • neighborhood bar • transgender-friendly

**The Four Seasons** 3229 N Causeway Blvd (at 18th), Metairie **504/832–0659** • 3pm-close • mostly gay men • neighborhood bar • live music & shows in summer • patio • also the Out Back Bar summers • gay-owned

**The Friendly Bar** 2301 Chartres St (at Marigny) **504/943–8929** • 11am-close • popular • mostly gay men • neighborhood bar • wheelchair access • women-owned

**Good Friends Bar** 740 Dauphine (at St Ann) **504/566–7191** • 1pm-4am, 24hrs wknds • mostly gay men • neighborhood bar • karaoke Tue • wheelchair access • also Queens Head Pub upstairs Fri-Sun, popular piano sing-along 4pm-8pm

**GrandPre's** 834 N Rampart (at Dumaine) **504/267-3615** • noon-2am * lesbians/gay men • neighborhood bar • drag shows • patio • wheelchair access

**Napoleon's Itch** 734 Bourbon (at St Ann) **504/237-4144** • noon-2am, till 4am Fri-Sat • popular • lesbians/gay men • wine & martini bar

**Rawhide 2010** 740 Burgundy St (at St Ann) **504/525-8106** • 1pm-5am • mostly gay men • neighborhood bar • dancing/DJ • leather crowd

**The Spotted Cat Music Club** 623 Frenchmen St • 4pm-2am • gay-friendly • excellent live jazz • dancing • wheelchair access

**Tubby's Golden Lantern** 1239 Royal St (at Barracks) **504/529-2860** • 8am-2am • mostly gay men • neighborhood bar • karaoke • drag shows

## NIGHTCLUBS

**Oz** 800 Bourbon St (at St Ann) **504/593-9491** • 24hrs • popular • mostly gay men • dancing/DJ • drag shows • live shows • videos • young crowd • wheelchair access

## CAFES

**Cafe Rose Nicaud** 632 Frenchmen St (btwn Royal & Chartres) **504/949-3300** • 7am-7pm • WiFi

**CC's Coffee House** 941 Royal St **504/581-6996** • 7am-9pm • WiFi

**Croissants d'Or** 617 Ursulines St **504/524-4663** • 6am-3pm, clsd Tue • delicious pastries • wheelchair access

**The Orange Couch** 2339 Royal St **504/267-7327** • 7am-10pm • ultra mod cafe • live music • WiFi • wheelchair access

**Royal Blend Coffee & Tea House** 621 Royal St **504/523-2716** • 6am-8pm, till midnight wknds • on a quiet, hidden courtyard • also salads & sandwiches

**Z'otz** 8210 Oak St **504/861-2224** • 7am-1am • coffee shop & art space • live entertainment

## RESTAURANTS

**13 Monaghan's** 517 Frenchmen St **504/942-1345** • 11am-4am • brkfst, lunch & dinner all the time • some veggie • full bar • wheelchair access

**Acme Oyster House** 724 Iberville St (at Royal) **504/522-5973** • 11am-10pm, till 11pm wknds • long line moves quickly, worth the wait!

**Angeli on Decatur** 1141 Decatur St (at Gov Nicholls) **504/566-0077** • 11am-2am, till 4am Fri-Sat • pizza • WiFi • wheelchair access

**Brennan's** 417 Royal St (at Conti) **504/525-9711** • brkfst, lunch & dinner • upscale • reservations recommended

**Cafe Amelie** 912 Royal St (in Princess of Monaco Courtyard) **504/412-8965** • lunch & dinner, Sun brunch, clsd Mon-Tue • Creole

**Cafe Negril** 606 Frenchmen St (at Chartres St) **504/944-4744** • dinner, clsd Sun-Mon, Caribbean • live music • dancing/DJ • woman-owned • wheelchair access

**Casamento's** 4330 Magazine St (at Napoleon Ave) **504/895-9761** • lunch, dinner Th-Sat, clsd Sun-Mon (also clsd June-Aug) • best oyster loaf in city • wheelchair access

**Clover Grill** 900 Bourbon St (at Dumaine) **504/598-1010** • 24hrs • popular • diner fare

**Commander's Palace** 1403 Washington Ave (at Coliseum St, in Garden District) **504/899-8221** • lunch Mon-Fri, dinner nightly, jazz brunch wknds • popular • upscale Creole • dress code • reservations required • wheelchair access

**Coquette** 2800 Magazine St (at Washington Ave) **504/265-0421** • lunch Wed-Sat, dinner Mon-Sat • wheelchair access

**The Court of Two Sisters** 613 Royal St **504/522-7261** • daily jazz brunch buffet 9am-3pm, dinner nightly • Creole

**Dante's Kitchen** 736 Dante St (at River Rd) **504/861-3121** • dinner nightly, wknd brunch, clsd Tue • Cajun • wheelchair access

**EAT New Orleans** 900 Dumaine St (at Dauphine) **504/522-7222** • lunch & dinner, Sun brunch, clsd Mon • Cajun/Creole homecooking • some veggie

**Elizabeth's** 601 Gallier St **504/944-9272** • 8am-2:30pm & 6pm-10pm, clsd for dinner Sun • one of the best brunch's in the city

**Feelings Cafe** 2600 Chartres St (at Franklin Ave) **504/945-2222** • dinner Th-Sun, also Sun brunch • Creole • piano bar • courtyard • wheelchair access

**Fiorella's Cafe** 45 French Market Pl (at Gov Nicholls & Ursulines) **504/553-2155** • noon-midnight, till 2am Fri-Sat • awesome Fried Chicken

**Gott Gourmet Cafe** 3100 Magazine St (at 8th St) **504/373-6579** • 11am-9pm, 8am-5pm wknds

**Gumbo Shop** 630 St Peter St (at Chartres) **504/525-1486** • award-winning gumbo

**Herbsaint** 701 St Charles Ave **504/524-4114** • lunch & dinner, bistro menu afternoons, clsd Sun • French/Southern

**Marigny Brasserie** 640 Frenchmen St **504/945-4472** • lunch Mon-Fri, dinner nightly, wknd brunch • French

**Meauxbar Bistro** 942 N Rampart St (at St Philip) **504/569-9979** • 6pm-10pm, clsd Sun-Mon

**Mike's On The Avenue** 628 St Charles Ave (in the Lafayette Hotel) **504/523-7600** • lunch & dinner • great views of St Charles Ave • wheelchair access

**Mona Lisa** 1212 Royal St (at Barracks) **504/522-6746** • 11am-10pm, from 5pm Mon-Th • Italian • some veggie • beer/wine • gay-owned • wheelchair access

**Mona's** 504 Frenchmen St **504/949-4115** • 11am-10pm, till 11pm Fri-Sat, noon-9pm Sun • cheap Middle Eastern eats

**Moon Wok** 800 Dauphine St **504/523-6910** • 11am-9pm, till 10pm Fri-Sat • Chinese

**Napoleon House** 500 Chartres St **504/524-9752** • lunch daily, dinner only Mon, clsd Sun • po' boys & muffulettas • wheelchair access

**Olivier's** 204 Decatur St **504/525-7734** • 5pm-10pm • Creole • wheelchair access

**Orleans Grapevine** 718-720 Orleans Ave **504/523-1930** • 4pm-10:30pm, till 11:30pm Fri-Sat • wine bar & bistro • wheelchair access

**Phillips** 733 Cherokee St (at Maple) **504/865-1155** • 4pm-2am • wheelchair access • gay-owned

**Praline Connection** 542 Frenchmen St (at Chartres) **504/943-3934** • 11am-10pm • soul food

**Restaurant August** 301 Tchoupitoulas St (at Gravier St) **504/299-9777** • lunch Mon-Fri, dinner nightly • upscale French/Mediterranean • wheelchair access

**Sammy's Seafood** 627 Bourbon St (across from Pat O' Brien's) **504/525-8442** • 11am-11pm • Cajun/Creole

**Stanley** 547 St Ann St (at Chartres) **504/587-0093** • 7am-10pm • upscale diner fare

**Stella** 1032 Chartres St (at Ursulines Ave) **504/587-0091** • dinner nightly • upscale global fusion cuisine • wheelchair access

**The Upperline Restaurant** 1413 Upperline St **504/891-9822** • dinner Wed-Sun • Creole • fine dining • full bar • wheelchair access

## ENTERTAINMENT & RECREATION

**Big Easy Rollergirls** • New Orleans' female roller derby league • visit www.bigeasyrollergirls.com for events

**Cafe du Monde** 800 Decatur St (at St Ann, corner of Jackson Square) **504/525-4544, 800/772-2927** • till you've had a beignet—fried dough, powdered w/ sugar, that melts in your mouth—you haven't been to New Orleans & this is "the" place to have them 24hrs a day • wheelchair access

**Haunted History Tour** **504/861-2727, 888/644-6787** • guided 2-1/2-hour tours of New Orleans' most famous haunts, including Anne Rice's former home • other tours available

**Mardi Gras World** 1380 Port of New Orleans Pl **504/361-7821** • tour this year-round Mardi Gras float workshop

**Pat O'Brien's** 718 St Peter St (btwn Bourbon & Royal) **504/525-4823, 800/597-4823** • gay-friendly • more than just a bar—come for the Hurricane, stay for the kitsch • wheelchair acess

**Preservation Hall** 726 St Peter St (btwn Bourbon & Royal) **504/522-2841, 888/946-5299** • 8pm-midnight, set begins at 8:30pm • come & hear the music that started jazz: New Orleans-style jazz! • cover charge

**St Charles Streetcar** St Charles St (at Canal St) **504/248-3900** • it's not named Desire, but you should still ride it, Blanche, if you want to see the Garden District

## BOOKSTORES

**FAB -Faubourg Marigny Art & Books** 600 Frenchmen St (at Chartres) **504/947-3700** • 1pm-11pm • LGBT books & art

**Garden District Book Shop** 2727 Prytania St (at Washington) **504/895-2266** • 10am-6pm, till 4pm Sun

**Kitchen Witch Cook Books** 631 Toulouse St (at Royal St) **504/528-8382** • 10am-7pm, clsd Tue • cookbooks from rare to campy

## RETAIL SHOPS

**Angela King Gallery** 241 Royal St **504/524-8211** • lesbian-owned

**Bourbon Pride** 909 Bourbon St (at Dumaine) **504/566-1570** • 10am-8pm, till 11pm wknds • LGBT cards • gifts

**Hit Parade** 741 Bourbon St **504/524-7700** • 3pm-11pm, 11am-2am Fri-Sat, 11am-midnight Sun • gift and clothing store

## PUBLICATIONS

**Ambush Mag** 504/522-8049 • LGBT newspaper for the Gulf South (TX through FL)

## EROTICA

**Mr Binky's** 107 Chartres St (off Canal St) 504/302-2095 • 24hrs

# Shreveport

## ACCOMMODATIONS

**Twenty-Four Thirty-Nine Fairfield** 2439 Fairfield Ave 318/424-2424, 877/251-2439 • gay-friendly • WiFi • pets ok

## BARS

**Korner Lounge II** 800 Louisiana Ave (near Cotton) 318/222-9796 • 3pm-2am • mostly gay men • neighborhood bar • karaoke

## NIGHTCLUBS

**Central Station** 1025 Marshall St (btwn Fairfield & Creswell) 318/222-2216 • 5pm-close, till 4am Fri-Sat • popular • lesbians/ gay men • dancing/DJ • country/western wknds • drag shows Fri • transgender-friendly • wheelchair access

## EROTICA

**Fun Shop Too** 9434 Mansfield Rd 318/688-2482 • clsd Sun-Mon • adult, novelty & gag gifts • toys

# Slidell

## BARS

**Billy's** 2600 Hwy 190 W **985/847-1921** • 6pm-1am • lesbians/ gay men • neighborhood bar • drag shows • karaoke • WiFi

# MAINE

# Aroostook County

## ACCOMMODATIONS

**Magic Pond Wildlife Sanctuary & Guest House** Blaine 215/287-4174 • lesbians/gay men • nonsmoking • lesbian-owned

# Augusta

### includes Hallowell

## ACCOMMODATIONS

**Annabessacook Farm** 192 Annabessacook Rd, Winthrop **207/377-3276** • popular • gay/ straight • restored 1810 farmhouse • full brkfst • WiFi

**Maple Hill Farm Inn** Hallowell 207/622-2708, 800/622-2708 • gay/ straight • Victorian farmhouse on 130 acres • full brkfst • sauna & hot tub • nonsmoking • WiFi • wheelchair access • gay-owned

## RESTAURANTS

**Slates** 167 Water St (Franklin), Hallowell **207/622-9575, 207/622-4104** • lunch Tue-Fri, dinner Mon-Sat, brunch wknds • also bakery • live shows Mon

# Bangor

## BOOKSTORES

**Pro Libris Bookshop** 10 3rd St (at Union) 207/942-3019 • 10am-6pm, clsd Sun-Mon • new & used

# Bar Harbor

## ACCOMMODATIONS

**Aysgarth Station** 20 Roberts Ave (at Cottage St) 207/288-9655 • gay-friendly • 10-minute drive from Acadia • cats on premises • nonsmoking • WiFi

**Manor House Inn** 106 West St (near Bridge St) 207/288-3759, 800/437-0088 • open April-Oct • gay-friendly • 1887 Victorian mansion • full brkfst • some rooms w/ whirlpools • nonsmoking • WiFi

## RESTAURANTS

**Mama DiMatteo's** 34 Kennebec Pl (at Firefly Ln) 207/288-3666 • 4:30pm-10pm • upscale casual dining • full bar • gay-owned

## ENTERTAINMENT & RECREATION

**ImprovAcadia** 15 Cottage St (2nd flr) 207/288-2503 • May-Oct • live improvised theater

# Bath

## ACCOMMODATIONS

**The Inn at Bath** 969 Washington St (at North St) 207/443-4294, 800/423-0964 • gay/ straight • 1810 Greek Revival B&B • full brkfst • jacuzzi • nonsmoking • wheelchair access

# Boothbay Harbor

## ACCOMMODATIONS

**Sur La Mer Inn** 18 Eames Rd, PO Box 663, 04538 207/633-7400, 207/380-6400 • gay-friendly • seasonal luxury oceanfront B&B • nonsmoking • kids ok • gay-owned

**Topside Inn** 60 McKown St 207/633-5404, 888/633-5404 • gay/straight • WiFi • full brkfst • gay-owned

## Brunswick

### BOOKSTORES

**Gulf of Maine Books** 134 Maine St (at Pleasant) **207/729-5083** • 9:30am-5:30pm, clsd Sun • alternative

## Bucksport

### ACCOMMODATIONS

**Williams Pond Lodge B&B  207/460-6064** • gay/ straight • WiFi • gay-owned

## Corea

### ACCOMMODATIONS

**The Black Duck Inn on Corea Harbor 207/963-2689** • gay/ straight • restored farmhouse • also cottages • full brkfst • nonsmoking • WiFi • gay-owned

## Deer Isle

### RESTAURANTS

**Fisherman's Friend** 5 Atlantic Ave, Stonington **207/367-2442** • seasonal • 11am-9pm, till 10pm Fri-Sat

## Dexter

### ACCOMMODATIONS

**Brewster Inn** 37 Zion's Hill Rd (at Dexter St) **207/924-3130** • gay-friendly • historic mansion • full brkfst • kids ok • nonsmoking • WiFi • wheelchair access

## Farmington

### BOOKSTORES

**Devany, Doak & Garrett Booksellers** 193 Broadway (at High St) **207/778-3454** • 10am-5pm, till 5:30pm Th, till 6:30pm Fri, 9am-5pm Sat, noon-3pm Sun • LGBT section

## Freeport

### ACCOMMODATIONS

**The Royalsborough Inn** 1290 Royalsborough Rd, Durham **207/353-6372, 800/765-1772** • gay-friendly • full brkfst • spa services • massage • also alpaca farm • nonsmoking • kids ok • conference room for 20 • WiFi

### RESTAURANTS

**Harraseeket Lunch & Lobster Co** 36 Main St (at Harraseeket Rd), S Freeport **207/865-4888, 207/865-3535** • lunch & dinner • open May-Oct

## Greenville

### ACCOMMODATIONS

**Greenville Inn at Moosehead Lake** 40 Norris St **207/695-2206, 888/695-6000** • gay/straight • private suites, cottages & historic inn rooms, full brkfst, one block from town and lake • also restaurant • WiFi • lesbian owned

## Kennebunkport

### ACCOMMODATIONS

**Hidden Pond Maine** 354 Goose Rocks Rd **207/967-9050, 888/967-9050** • gay-friendly • pool • great restaurant • nonsmoking • WiFi

**White Barn Inn & Spa** 37 Beach Ave **207/967-2321** • gay-friendly • pool • restaurant • nonsmoking • WiFi

### RESTAURANTS

**Nunan's Lobster Hut** 9 Mills Rd **207/967-4362** • seasonal

## Kittery

**see Portsmouth, New Hampshire**

## Lewiston

### EROTICA

**Paris Adult Book Store** 297 Lisbon St (at Chestnut) **207/783-6677, 800/581-6901**

## Naples

### ACCOMMODATIONS

**Lambs Mill Inn** Lambs Mill Rd (1/2 mile off Rte 302) **207/693-6253** • gay/ straight • 1860s farmhouse • full brkfst • nonsmoking • WiFi • lesbian-owned

## Newcastle

### ACCOMMODATIONS

**The Tipsy Butler B&B** 11 High St **207/563-3394** • gay-friendly • on the Damariscotta River • full brkfst • nonsmoking • WiFi

## Ogunquit

### ACCOMMODATIONS

**2 Village Square Inn Ogunquit** 14 Village Square Ln (at Main St) **207/646-5779** • open May-Oct • mostly gay men • Victorian w/ ocean views • heated pool • nonsmoking • WiFi • gay-owned

**Abalonia Inn** 268 Main St (at Berwick Rd) **207/646-7001** • gay/ straight • salt water pool • WiFi  gay-owned

**Beauport Inn** 339 Clay Hill Rd, Cape Neddick 207/361–2400 • gay/straight • full brkfst • WiFi • pool • complimentary bikes • lesbian-owned

**Beaver Dam Campground** 551 School St, Rte 9, Berwick 207/698–2267 • gay-friendly • campground on 20-acre spring-fed pond • pool • kids/ pets ok • women-owned

**Belm House Vacation Units** 207/641–2637 • lesbians/ gay men • apt rentals • hot tub • kids/ dogs ok • WiFi • gay-owned

**Black Boar Inn** 277 Main St (at Ogunquit Rd) 207/646–2112 • lesbians/ gay men • kids ok • nonsmoking • weekly rentals only • gay-owned

**Leisure Inn** 73 School St (at Main St) 207/646–2737 • gay-friendly • nonsmoking • WiFi • seasonal

**Meadowmere Resort** 74 S Main St (at Rte 1) 207/646–9661, 800/633–8718 • gay-friendly • pool • health club & spa • kids ok • nonsmoking • WiFi • wheelchair access

**Moon Over Maine B&B** Berwick Rd 207/646–6666 • lesbians/ gay men • hot tub • nonsmoking • WiFi • gay-owned

**Ogunquit Beach Inn** 67 School St 207/646–1112 • lesbians/ gay men • 5 minutes walk to beach • WiFi • gay-owned

**The Ogunquit Inn** 17 Glen Ave 207/646–3633, 866/999–3633 • clsd Nov-March • lesbians/ gay men • Victorian B&B • nonsmoking • WiFi • gay-owned

**OgunquitCottages.com** 25 Mill St, N Reading, MA 01864 207/646–3840, 978/664–5813 • lesbians/ gay men • weekly rentals • seasonal (June-Sept) • near bars & beach • nonsmoking • pets/ kids ok • gay-owned

**Old Village Inn** 250 Main St (at Berwick Rd) 207/646–7088 • gay-friendly • 1880s B&B • ocean views • kids/ pets ok • nonsmoking • WiFi • also restaurant • seafood • upscale

**Rockmere Lodge B&B** 150 Stearns Rd 207/646–2985, 800/646–2985 • gay/ straight • Maine shingle cottage • near beach • nonsmoking • gay-owned

**Yellow Monkey Guest Houses & Motel** 280 Main St 207/646–9056 • gay/ straight • seasonal • fitness room • kids/ pets ok • wheelchair access • gay-owned

## BARS

**Front Porch Cafe** 9 Shore Rd (at Beach St) 207/646–4005 • lunch & dinner (seasonal) • gay/ straight • piano bar upstairs • full menu

## NIGHTCLUBS

**Maine Street** 195 Main St/ US Rte 1 207/646–5101 • 5pm-1am, T-dance from 3pm wknds • popular • lesbians/ gay men • dancing/DJ • karaoke • cabaret • food served • gay-owned

**Women's T Dance** 195 Main St/ US Rte 1 (at Maine Street nightclub) 207/646–5101 • monthly, call for dates • popular • mostly women • dancing/DJ

## CAFES

**Bread & Roses** 246 Main St 207/646–4227 • 7am-7pm, seasonal

## RESTAURANTS

**Amore Breakfast** 309 Shore Rd 207/646–6661, 866/641–6661 • 7am-1pm • seasonal

**Angelina's Ristorante** 655 Main St 207/646–0445 • dinner • Italian

**Backyard Coffeehouse & Eatery** Rte 1 207/251–4554 • 7am-8pm • women-owned

**Beachfire Bar & Grill** 658 Main St 207/646–8998 • dinner nightly, wknd brunch • outdoor fire pit

**Clay Hill Farm** 220 Clay Hill Rd (off Logging Rd), Cape Neddick (York) 207/361–2272 • dinner only • seafood • some veggie • also piano bar

**Five-0** 50 Shore Rd 207/646–5001 • popular • 5pm-midnight • martini bar & restaurant • full bar

**Jonathan's** 92 Bourne Ln 207/646–4777 • dinner nightly • steak/ seafood • full bar • entertainment • wheelchair access

**The Lobster Shack** 110 Perkins Cove Rd 207/646–2941 • 11am-9pm • gluten-free chowder

**La Pizzeria** 239 Main St 207/646–1143 • lunch & dinner • open April-Dec • some veggie • beer/ wine • gay-owned

**Wild Blueberry Cafe & Bistro** 82 Shore Rd 207/646–0990 • brkfst, lunch & dinner, jazz brunch 10am-1pm Sun

## ENTERTAINMENT & RECREATION

**Ogunquit Playhouse** 10 Main St 207/646–5511 (BOX OFFICE), 207/646–2402 • summer theater • some LGBT-themed productions

## Portland

### ACCOMMODATIONS

**The Chadwick B&B** 140 Chadwick St
207/774–5141, 800/774–2137 • gay/ straight •
full brkfst • WiFi • gay-owned

**The Inn at St John** 939 Congress St
207/773–6481, 800/636–9127 • gay/ straight •
kids/ pets ok • nonsmoking • WiFi • gay-
owned

**The Inn by the Sea** 40 Bowery Beach Rd,
Cape Elizabeth 207/799–3134, 800/888–4287
• gay-friendly • pool • kids/ pets ok •
nonsmoking • wheelchair access • also
restaurant

**Mercury Inn** 146 Pine St (at Neal St)
207/956–6670 , 844/730–7800 • gay-friendly •
full brkfst • nonsmoking • WiFi

**The Percy Inn** 15 Pine St (at Longfellow
Square) 207/871–7638, 888/417–3729 • gay-
friendly • nonsmoking • WiFi

**The Pomegranate Inn** 49 Neal St (at Carroll
St) 207/772–1006, 800/356–0408 • gay-
friendly • full brkfst • private garden •
nonsmoking • WiFi

**Sea View Inn** 65 W Grand Ave (at Atlantic
Ave), Old Orchard Beach 207/934–4180,
800/541–8439 • gay/ straight • oceanfront
motel • pool • patio • kids/ pets ok • gift shop
• WiFi • nonsmoking • wheelchair access

**Wild Iris Inn** 273 State St (at Grant St)
207/775–0224, 800/600–1557 • gay-friendly •
nonsmoking • WiFi • kids ok • women-owned

**Wolf Cove Inn** 5 Jordan Shore Dr, Poland
Spring 207/998–4976 • gay-friendly • on the
shores of Tripp Lake • WiFi • pets ok

### BARS

**Blackstones** 6 Pine St (off Longfellow
Square) 207/775–2885 • 4pm-1am, from 3pm
wknds • mostly gay men • neighborhood bar •
leather 3rd Sat • theme nights • wheelchair
access

### NIGHTCLUBS

**Styxx** 3 Spring St (at Center St) 207/828–0822
• 7pm-1am, from 4pm Th-Sat, clsd Mon •
popular • lesbians/ gay men • more women
Th • dancing/DJ • live shows • theme nights •
drag shows • gay-owned

### CAFES

**Coffee by Design** 43 Washington Ave (at
Oxford St) 207/879–2233 • 8am-5pm, clsd
wknds

### RESTAURANTS

**Becky's** 390 Commercial St (at High St)
207/773–7070 • 4am-10pm • great brkfst &
chowdah • wheelchair access

**Grace** 15 Chestnut St 207/828–4422 • fine
dining in renovated old church

**Katahdin** 27 Forest Ave 207/774–1740 •
5pm-11pm, clsd Sun-Mon • American menu •
full bar

**Portland & Rochester Public House** 118
Preble St 207/773–2000 • 3pm-1am, bistro &
pub in the Bayside neighborhood

**Street & Co** 33 Wharf St (btwn Dana &
Union) 207/775–0887 • 5:30pm-9:30pm, till
10pm Fri-Sat • popular • seafood • beer/ wine
• wheelchair access

**Walter's Cafe** 2 Portland Sq (at Union)
207/871–9258 • lunch & dinner, dinner nightly
• seafood/ pasta • some veggie • wheelchair
access

### BOOKSTORES

**Longfellow Books** 1 Monument Way
207/772–4045 • 9am-7pm, till 6pm Sat,
9:30am-5pm Sun • LGBT section

### RETAIL SHOPS

**The Corner General Store** 154 Middle St
(at Market) 207/253–5280 • 8am-1am • great
wine selection

**Emerald City** 564 Congress St 207/774–8800
• 10am-6pm, First Friday Art Walk • gifts, pride
items & more • gay-owned

### EROTICA

**Condom Sense** 424 Fore St (at Union)
207/871–0356, 877/871–0356 • 10am-8pm, till
9pm Th, till 10pm Fri-Sat, till 6pm Sun •
condoms, lube, massage oils, novelties, etc

## Richmond

### ENTERTAINMENT & RECREATION

**Kennebec Tidewater Charters** Kennebec
River & Casco Bay 207/737–4695,
866/347–4874 • guided fishing & kayak trips •
scenic coastal tours • women-owned

## Rockland

### ACCOMMODATIONS

**Captain Lindsey House Inn** 5 Lindsey St
207/596–7950, 800/523–2145 • gay-friendly •
19th-c Maine sea captain's home •
nonsmoking • WiFi • wheelchair access

**The Old Granite Inn** 546 Main St
207/594-9036, 800/386-9036 • gay-friendly •
1880s stone guesthouse • full brkfst •
nonsmoking • WiFi

## Rockport

### RESTAURANTS

**Chez Michel** 2530 Atlantic Hwy (at Rte 1),
Lincolnville 207/789-5600 • dinner Wed-Sun
• full bar • some veggie

**Lobster Pound** Rte 1, Lincolnville Beach
207/789-5550 • 11:30am-8pm • May-Oct •
full bar • patio • wheelchair access

## Tenants Harbor

### ACCOMMODATIONS

**Eastwind Inn** 207/372-6366, 800/241-8439
• clsd Dec-April • gay-friendly • rooms & apts
• full brkfst • pets ok

## Upper Kennebec Valley

### ACCOMMODATIONS

**The Sterling Inn B&B** 1041 US Route 201,
Caratunk 207/672-3333 • gay-friendly •
mention Damron for special rates • many
outdoor activities groups discounts • WiFi •
kids/pets ok • gay-owned

## Western Mtns

### ACCOMMODATIONS

**Mountain Village Farm B&B** 164 Main St,
Kingfield 04947 207/265-2030 • gay-friendly
•working farm & B&B • full brkfst •
nonsmoking • WiFi • women owned

## York Harbor

### RESTAURANTS

**York Harbor Inn** 480 York St 207/363-5119,
800/343-3869 • lunch Mon-Sat, dinner
nightly, Sun brunch • also the Cellar Pub •
also lodging

# MARYLAND

## Annapolis

### INFO LINES & SERVICES

**AA Gay/ Lesbian** 199 Duke of Gloucester St
(at St Anne's Parish) 410/268-5441 • 8pm
Tue

### ACCOMMODATIONS

**Two-O-One B&B** 201 Prince George St (at
Maryland Ave) 410/268-8053 • gay/ straight •
English country house • full brkfst •
nonsmoking • WiFi • gay-owned

### RESTAURANTS

**Cafe Sado** 205 Tackle Cir (at Castle Marina
Rd), Chester 410/604-1688 • lunch & dinner
• sushi/ Asian fusion

## Baltimore

### INFO LINES & SERVICES

**AA Gay/ Lesbian** 410/663-1922 • call for
times and locations

**Gay, Lesbian, Bisexual & Transgender
Community Center of Baltimore** 1000
Cathedral St 3rd Fl (Waxter Building
) 410/777-8145 • many groups & services

### ACCOMMODATIONS

**Abacrombie Fine Food &
Accommodations** 58 W Biddle St (at
Cathedral) 410/244-7227, 888/922-3437 •
gay/ straight • 1880s town house •
nonsmoking • also restaurant

**Hotel Monaco Baltimore** 2 N Charles St
443/692-6170, 888/752-2636 • gay/staight •
also restaurant • wiFi • wheelchair access

**Lord Baltimore Hotel** 20 W Baltimore St
410/539-8400, 855/539-1928 • gay/ straight •
historic, landmark hotel • restaurant • WiFi •
wheelchair access

**Pier 5 Hotel** 711 Eastern Ave (at President)
410/539-2000, 866/583-4162 • gay/ straight •
full brkfst • restaurant • WiFi • wheelchair
access

**Scarborough Fair B&B** 801 S Charles St
410/837-0010, 877/954-2747 • gay-friendly •
gay-owned

### BARS

**Club Bunns** 608 W Lexington St (at Greene
St) 410/234-2866 • 5pm-2am, 7pm-1am Sun
• lesbians/ gay men • dancing/DJ • multiracial
• live shows • female strippers Sat

**The Gallery Bar & Studio Restaurant**
1735 Maryland Ave (at Lafayette)
410/539-6965 • 6pm-1am • lesbians/ gay
men • African-American clientele • dinner
Mon-Fri • wheelchair access

**Grand Central** 1001 N Charles St (at Eager)
410/752-7133 • 4pm-close • popular •
lesbians/ gay men • dancing/DJ • occasional
women's night on Sat unstairs at the Loft •
karaoke • drag shows • 21+

**Jay's on Read** 225 W Read St 410/225–0188 • 4pm-1am • mostly gay men • piano bar

**Leon's** 870 Park Ave (at Chase) 410/539–4993, 410/539–4850 • 4pm-2am • lesbians/gay men • neighborhood bar • WiFi • wheelchair access • also Singer's restaurant

**Mixers** 6037 Belair Rd (at Glenarm Ave) 410/483–6011 • 5pm-2am • lesbians/gay men • neighborhood bar • dancing/DJ • karaoke • live shows

**The Rowan Tree** 1633 S Charles St (at E Heath) 410/468–0550 • 11am-2am • gay/straight • karaoke • "where diversity is our name"

**Ziascoz** 1313 E Pratt St (at Eden) 410/276–5790 • 7pm-2am • gay/straight • neighborhood bar • karaoke • mostly African American

## NIGHTCLUBS

**Club 1722** 1722 N Charles St (at Lafayette) 410/547–8423 • afterhours club • Fri-Sat only, 2am-close • gay/straight • dancing/DJ • multiracial • 18+ • BYOB • dress code

**Club Orpheus** 1003 E Pratt St 410/276–5599 • gay/straight • Fri-Sat goth/fetish party

**The Paradox** 1310 Russell St (at Ostend) 410/837–9110 • 11pm-5am, midnight-6am Sat • popular • gay/straight • more gay 3rd Sat • dancing/DJ • multiracial • food served • live shows • videos • wheelchair access

## CAFES

**Station North Arts Cafe** 1816 N Charles St 410/625–6440 • 8am-3pm, from 10am Sat, clsd Sun • also art gallery • events

## RESTAURANTS

**Aldos** 306 S High St 410/727–0700 • dinner nightly • Italian

**Alonso's** 415 W Cold Spring Ln (at Keswick Rd) 410/235–3433 • 4pm-10:30pm, from 11:30am Fri-Sat • pizza & burgers • full bar • wheelchair access

**Cafe Hon** 1002 W 36th St (at Roland) 410/243–1230 • 11am-10pm, from 9am-close wknds • wheelchair access

**The Dizz** 300 W 30th St 443/869–5864 • 10am-2am • full bar

**Golden West Cafe** 1105 W 36th St 410/889–8891 • brkfst, lunch & dinner • New Mexican • also bar • live bands

**Jerry D's Seafood** 7804 Harford Rd, Parkville 410/668–1299 • 11am-8pm, till 9:30 Fri-Sat, 10am-6pm Sun, best local crabs around

**Mount Vernon Stable & Saloon** 909 N Charles St (btwn Eager & Read) 410/685–7427 • 11:30am-midnight, till 1am Fri-Sat, Sun brunch • also bar

**Trinidad Gourmet** 418 E 31st St 410/243–0072 • 7am-8:30pm, clsd Sun • Caribbean • delicious & inexpensive

**Woodberry Kichen** 2010 Clipper Park Rd #126 410/464–8000 • dinner nightly • organic & sustainable • full bar • wheelchair access

**XS Baltimore** 1307 N Charles St 410/468–0002 • 7am-midnight, till 2am Fri-Sat • sushi restaurant, cafe & lounge

## ENTERTAINMENT & RECREATION

**The Charm City Kitty Club** 3134 Eastern Ave (at Creative Alliance) 410/276–1651 • performing arts cabaret for lesbian, dyke, bisexual, trans women & allies

## BOOKSTORES

**Read Street Books** 229 W Read St 410/669–4103 • 11am-7pm, noon-6pm Sun, clsd Mon • women's bookstore • also cafe

## PUBLICATIONS

**Baltimore OUTloud** 410/244–6780

**Gay Life** 410/837–7748 • LGBT newspaper

## EROTICA

**Chained Desires** 136 W Read St 410/528–8441 • 11am-8pm, till 9pm Fri-Sat, clsd Mon • custom leather crafts & apparel • adult toys

**Sugar** 1001 W 36th St (at Roland) 410/467–2632 • 11am-close • lesbian-owned sex toy shop • transgender-friendly

# Hagerstown

## NIGHTCLUBS

**The Lodge** 21614 National Pike, Boonsboro 301/591–4434 • 9pm-2am, clsd Sun-Th • mostly gay men • dancing/DJ • drag shows • gay-owned

# Keedysville

## ACCOMMODATIONS

**Inn at Red Hill** 4936 Red Hill Rd (at Rte 67/340) 301/730–2620 • gay/straight • just a morning drive from DC and Baltimore • WiFi • lesbian-owned

## Laurel

### Bars

**PW's Sports Bar & Grill** 9855 N Washington Blvd (at Whiskey Bottom Rd) **301/498-4840** • 9am-2am, till midnight Sun-Mon • lesbians/ gay men • sports bar • food served • drag shows • karaoke • WiFi • gay-owned

## Princess Anne

### Accommodations

**The Alexander House Booklovers B&B** 30535 Linden Ave (at corner of Beckford) **410/651-5195** • gay-friendly • literary-themed B&B • full brkfst • nonsmoking

## Rock Hall

### Accommodations

**Tallulah's on Main** 5750 Main St (at Sharp St) **410/639-2596** • gay/ straight • small suite hotel • kids ok • nonsmoking • wheelchair access • gay-owned

## Snow Hill

### Accommodations

**River House Inn** 201 E Market St (at Green St) **410/632-2722** • gay-friendly • pool • WiFi • gay-owned

## MASSACHUSETTS

## Amherst

**see also Northampton**

### Bookstores

**Amherst Books** 8 Main St **413/256-1547, 800/503-5865** • 6:30am-9pm, till 5pm Sun • independent • LGBT section

## Barre

### Accommodations

**Jenkins Inn & Restaurant** **978/355-6444, 800/378-7373** • gay-friendly • full brkfst • restaurant • full bar • nonsmoking • WiFi • gay-owned

## Berkshires

### Accommodations

**The B&B at Howden Farm** 303 Rannapo Rd, Sheffield **413/229-8481** • gay/ straight • 250-acre working farm • near river • full brkfst • nonsmoking • some shared baths • gay-owned

**The Barrington** 281 Main St (at Church), Great Barrington **413/528-6159** • gay-friendly • kids 10+ ok • WiFi • gay-owned

**Gateways Inn** 51 Walker St (at Church St), Lenox **413/637-2532, 888/492-9466** • gay-friendly • full brkfst • also bar & restaurant • nonsmoking

**Guest House at Field Farm** 554 Sloan Rd, Williamstown **413/458-3135** • gay-friendly • transgender-friendly • nonsmoking • pool • WiFi

**River Bend Farm B&B** 643 Simonds Rd, Williamstown **413/458-3121** • gay-friendly • restored 1770s home • shared baths • seasonal • well-behaved kids ok • nonsmoking

**The Rookwood Inn** 11 Old Stockbridge Rd (at Walker St/ Rte 183), Lenox **413/637-9750, 800/223-9750** • gay/ straight • Victorian inn near Tanglewood & skiing • full brkfst • kids ok • nonsmoking • WiFi • women-owned

**The Thaddeus Clapp House** 74 Wendell Ave, Pittsfield **413/499-6840, 888/499-6840** • gay-friendly • full brkfst • nonsmoking

**Topia Inn** 10 Pleasant St (at Rte 8), Adams **413/743-9600, 888/868-6742** • gay-straight • nonsmoking • WiFi • wheelchair access • eco-friendly B&B • organic gourmet brkfst • kids ok • lesbian-owned

**Windflower Inn** 684 S Egremont Rd, Great Barrington **413/528-2720, 800/992-1993** • gay-friendly • gracious country inn • full brkfst • pool • nonsmoking • WiFi • kids ok

### Restaurants

**Allium Restaurant + Bar** 42 Railroad St (at Main), Great Barrington **413/528-2118** • 5pm-9pm, till 10pm Fri-Sat • bar open late

**Cafe Lucia** 80 Church St (at Tucker), Lenox **413/637-2640** • dinner only, clsd Mon, seasonal

**Church Street Cafe** 65 Church St (at Franklin), Lenox **413/637-2745** • lunch & dinner, seasonal • American bistro • some veggie

**Mezze Bistro + Bar** 777 Cold Spring Rd, Williamstown **413/458-0123** • 5pm-9pm, till 10pm Fri-Sat, seasonal hrs

### Entertainment & Recreation

**Tanglewood** 197 Rte 183, Lenox **888/266-1200** • live music venue • summer home of the Boston Symphony/ Pops

**Williamstown Theatre Festival** just E of Rte 2 & Rte 7 junction, Williamstown **413/597-3400, 413/458-3200** • call for season calendar

# Boston

## INFO LINES & SERVICES

**Gay AA** 12 Channel St #604 617/426-9444 (AA#)

**GLBT Helpline** 617/267-9001, 888/340-4528 • 6pm-11pm

## ACCOMMODATIONS

**463 Beacon St Guest House** 463 Beacon St 617/536-1302 • gay-friendly • nonsmoking • WiFi • gay- & straight-owned

**Beacon Hill Hotel & Bistro** 25 Charles St (at Chestnut St) 617/723-7575 • gay/ straight • bistro onsite • WiFi

**Chandler Inn** 26 Chandler St (at Berkeley) 617/482-3450, 800/842-3450 • gay-friendly • European-style hotel • centrally located • nonsmoking

**The Charles Hotel** 1 Bennett St (at Eliot), Cambridge 617/864-1200, 800/882-1818 • gay-friendly • in Harvard Square • also restaurants & bar

**Clarendon Square Inn** 198 W Brookline St (btwn Tremont & Columbus) 617/536-2229 • gay/ straight • restored Victorian town house • hot tub • kids ok • fireplaces • nonsmoking • WiFi • gay-owned

**The College Club** 44 Commonwealth Ave (at Berkeley St) 617/536-9510 • gay-friendly • B&B in Back Bay • some shared baths • kids ok • nonsmoking • WiFi

**Encore B&B** 116 W Newton St (at Tremont) 617/247-3425 • gay-friendly • 19th-c town house in Boston's historic South End • nonsmoking • gay-owned

**Fifteen Beacon Hotel** 15 Beacon St (at Somerset) 617/670-1500, 877/982-3226 • gay-friendly • in 1903 Beaux Arts bldg • kids/ pets ok

**Hotel 140** 140 Clarendon St (at Stuart St) 617/585-5600, 800/714-0140 • gay/ straight • boutique hotel • near Copley Square • nonsmoking • wheelchair access • women-owned

**Hotel Onyx** 155 Portland St (at Causeway) 617/557-9955, 866/660-6699 • gay-friendly • kids/ pets ok • WiFi • nonsmoking

**The Liberty Hotel** 215 Charles St (at Cambridge St) 617/224-4000, 866/507-5245 • gay-friendly • in the former Charles St Jail • full brkfst • nonsmoking • WiFi • wheelchair access

**Nine Zero Hotel** 90 Tremont St (at Bosworth) **617/772–5800, 866/646–3937** • gay-friendly • luxury hotel • full brkfst • jacuzzi • kids/ pets ok • nonsmoking • wheelchair access

**Oasis Guest House** 22 Edgerly Rd (at Westland) **617/267–2262, 800/230–0105** • popular • gay/ straight • Back Bay location • some shared baths • nonsmoking • WiFi • wheelchair access • gay-owned

**The Verb Hotel** 1271 Boylston St **855/695–6678** • gay/straiught • great Fenway location, restaurant & bar on site • WiFi

**Whitman House Inn** 17 Worcester St (at Norfolk St), Cambridge **617/945–5350, 617/913–6189** • gay/ straight • nonsmoking • WiFi • gay-owned

## BARS

**Bella Luna Restaurant & Milky Way Lounge** 284 Amory St, Jamaica Plain **617/524–3740** • 6pm-1am • gay/ straight • food served • theme nights • live music

**Boston Ramrod** 1254 Boylston St (at Ipswich, 1 block from Fenway Park) **617/266–2986** • noon-2am • popular • mostly gay men • bears • leather • dress code Fri-Sat • dancing/DJ • videos • game room • wheelchair access

**Cathedral Station** 1222 Washington St **617/338–6060** • 2pm-2am, from noon wknds, sports bar & pub

➤**Club Cafe Restaurant, Nightclub & Cabaret** 209 Columbus Ave (at Berkeley St) **617/536–0966** • 11am-2am, incredible Sunday brunch buffet along with lunch other days • popular • lesbians/ gay men •Th ladies night • dancing/DJ • karaoke • piano bar • live shows • videos • 3 bars • wheelchair access

**Dyke Night** 284 Amory St (at Milky Way Lounge), Jamaica Plain **617/524–3740** • check www.dykenight.com for events • mostly women • dancing/DJ

**Jacque's** 79 Broadway (at Stuart) **617/426–8902** • 11am-midnight, from noon Sun • mostly gay men • popular • drag cabaret • cover charge

**Ryles** 212 Hampshire St (at Cambridge St, in Inman Square), Cambridge **617/876–9330** • gay/ straight • live shows • great wknd jazz brunch

**Sister Sorel/ Tremont 647** 647 Tremont (at W Brookline) **617/266–4600** • gay/straight • dinner only, wknd pajama brunch • patio • wheelchair access

**Trophy Room** 26 Chandler St (at Chandler Inn) **617/482–3450** • noon-2am, Sat-Sun brunch • gay/straight • American bistro & bar

## NIGHTCLUBS

**dbar** 1236 Dorchester Ave (at Hancock St), Dorchester **617/265–4490** • 5pm-midnight, till 2am wknds • gay/ straight • also restaurant • dinner nightly

**Dyke Night Productions** • special events in various locations • mostly women • dancing/DJ • live shows • younger crowd • wheelchair access • check www.dykenight.com for info

**Epic Saturday** 15 Lansdowne St (House of Blues) **888/693–2583** • 10:30pm Sat only • mostly gay men • dancing/DJ

**Machine** 1254 Boylston St (at Park, below Boston Ramrod) **617/536–1950** • 10pm-2am • popular • mostly gay men • women's night 2nd Sat • dancing/DJ • go-go boys • wheelchair access

**The Middle East & ZuZu** 472 Massachusetts Ave (in Central Square), Cambridge **617/864–3278** • 11am-1am, till 2am wknds • gay-friendly • alternative • live music • young crowd • cover charge • also restaurant

**Midway Cafe** 3496 Washington St (at William), Jamaica Plain **617/524–9038** • gay/ straight • mostly women Th • dancing/DJ • theme nights • karaoke • live shows

➤**Napoleon Cabaret** 209 Columbus Ave (at Club Cafe) **617/536–0966** • nightly piano & vocals • also restaurant • wheelchair access

## CAFES

**1369 Cafe** 757 Massachusetts Ave (in Central Square), Cambridge **617/576–4600** • 7am-11pm • also 1369 Cambridge St (Inman Square), 617/576-1369

**Berkeley Perk** 69 Berkeley St (at Chandler) **617/426–7375** • 6:30am-5pm, from 7:30am Sat, clsd Sun • food served • wheelchair access • gay-owned

**Diesel Cafe** 257 Elm St (in Davis Square), Somerville **617/629–8717** • 6am-11pm, from 7am wknds • pool tables • lesbian-owned • wheelchair access

**Fiore's Bakery** 55 South St (at Bardwell), Jamaica Plain **617/524–9200** • 7am-7pm, from 8am wknds • some vegan • gay-owned

**Francesca's** 564 Tremont St (at Clarendon) **617/482–9026** • 8am-11pm • wheelchair access

**South End Buttery** 314 Shawmut Ave (at Union Park St) **617/482-1015** • cupcakes! also brkfst, lunch & dinner • full bar • wheelchair access

**True Grounds** 717 Broadway (at Boston Ave), Somerville **617/591-9559** • 7am-9pm, 8am-7pm wknds • live shows • WiFi • wheelchair access

## Restaurants

**BarLola** 160 Commonwealth Ave (at Dartmouth) **617/266-1122** • 4pm-midnight • tapas lounge • flamenco performed Sun • gay-owned

**Casa Romero** 30 Gloucester St (at Commonwealth) **617/536-4341** • dinner • Mexican • also bar

**Charlie's Sandwich Shoppe** 429 Columbus Ave (at Pembroke St) **617/536-7669** • great brkfst, clsd Sun • wheelchair access

**City Girl Cafe** 204 Hampshire St (at Inman), Cambridge **617/864-2809** • noon-10pm, from 10am Sat-Sun, clsd Mon • Italian • great sandwiches • lesbian-owned

➤**Club Cafe** 209 Columbus Ave (adjacent to Club Cafe) **617/536-0966** • dinner & Sun brunch • popular • some veggie • also 3 bars • piano • videos • wheelchair access

**Ecco** 107 Porter St **617/561-1112** • 4pm-midnight, from noon Sun, Sun gay event night 8pm

**Johnny D's Restaurant & Music Club** 17 Holland St (in Davis Square), Somerville **617/776-2004** • dinner nightly, lunch Th-Sun • live music • wheelchair access

**My Thai Cafe** 3 Beach St, 2nd flr (at Washington) **617/451-2395** • 11am-10pm, till 11pm Fri-Sat • Asian • vegetarian/ vegan

**Rabia's** 73 Salem St (at Cross St) **617/227-6637** • 11am-10:30pm • fine Italian • wheelchair access

**Ristorante Lucia** 415 Hanover St (at Harris) **617/367-2353** • lunch & dinner • great North End pasta • wheelchair access

**Stella** 1525 Washington St (at W Brookline) **617/247-7747** • dinner & Sun brunch, full bar till 2am • also cafe 7am-3pm • WiFi • wheelchair access

**Sweet Cheeks Q** 1381 Boylston St **617/266-1300** • 11:30am-11pm • American south north of the Mason Dixon • lesbian owned

**Trattoria Pulcinella** 147 Huron Ave (at Concord), Cambridge **617/491-6336** • 5pm-10pm • fine Italian

**Veggie Planet** 47 Palmer St (at Club Passim), Cambridge **617/661-1513** • 11:30am-10:30pm • live music venue nights

## Entertainment & Recreation

**Boston Derby Dames** • Boston's first & only women's flat-track roller derby league • visit www.bostonderbydames.com for events

**Freedom Trail** **617/357-8300** • start at the Visitor Information Center in Boston Common (at Tremont & West Sts), the most famous cow pasture & oldest public park in the US, then follow the red line to some of Boston's most famous sites

**Jamaica Pond** • great girl-watching

**New Repertory Theatre** 321 Arsenal St, Watertown **617/923-8487 (BOX OFFICE), 617/923-7060**

**Urban AdvenTours** 103 Atlantic Ave (at Richmond St) **617/670-0637, 800/979-3370** • guided bike tours of Boston & bike rentals

## Bookstores

**Calamus Bookstore** 92-B South St **617/338-1931, 888/800-7300** • 9am-7pm, noon-6pm • complete GLBT bookstore

**Trident Booksellers & Cafe** 338 Newbury St (off Mass Ave) **617/267-8688** • 8am-midnight • good magazine browsing • also restaurant • beer/ wine • WiFi • wheelchair access

## Publications

**Bay Windows 617/464-7280** • LGBT newspaper

**The Rainbow Times 413/282-8881, 617/444-9618** • bi-weekly LGBT news magazine for MA, northern CT & southern VT

## Erotica

**Good Vibrations** 308 Harvard St ((rear entrance)), Brookline **617/264-4400** • 10am-9pm, till 10pm Th-Sat • clean, well-lighted sex toy store • workshops & events • wheelchair access

**Hubba Hubba** 2 Ellery St, Cambridge **617/492-9082** • fetish gear

## Brookline

see Boston

## Cambridge

see Boston

## Cape Cod

**see also Provincetown listings**

### INFO LINES & SERVICES

**Gay/ Lesbian AA** 508/775-7060 • call for info

### ACCOMMODATIONS

**The Colonial House Inn & Restaurant** 277 Main St, Rte 6A (at Strawberry Ln), Yarmouthport 508/362-4348, 800/999-3416 • gay-friendly • dinner & light brkfst included • pool • jacuzzi • also restaurant & lounge • nonsmoking • WiFi • wheelchair access

**Lamb & Lion Inn** 2504 Main St (Rte 6A), Barnstable 508/362-6823, 800/909-6923 • gay-friendly • pool • pets ok • WiFi

**White Swan B&B** 146 Manomet Point Rd, Plymouth 508/224-3759 • gay-friendly • in 200-year-old farmhouse • open year-round • at mouth of Cape Cod • nonsmoking • WiFi

**Woods Hole Passage** 186 Woods Hole Rd, Falmouth 508/548-9575, 800/790-8976 • gay-friendly • full brkfst • non-smoking • WiFi

## Chelsea

**see Boston**

## Easthampton

### NIGHTCLUBS

**The Platinum Pony** 30 Cottage St • 5pm-10pm Mon, till midnight Wed-Th, till 2am Fri, from 3pm Sat, 10am-10pm Sun, clsd Tue • lesbians/gay men • full menu • dancing/DJ • check www.theplatinumpony.com for free shuttle service from Northampton

## Greenfield

### ACCOMMODATIONS

**Brandt House** 29 Highland Ave 413/774-3329, 800/235-3329 • gay-friendly • 16-rm estate on hill • full brkfst • kids ok • nonsmoking • WiFi

### RESTAURANTS

**Hope & Olive** 44 Hope St 413/774-3150 • lunch & dinner, clsd Mon

### BOOKSTORES

**World Eye Bookshop** 156 Main St (at Miles St) 413/772-2186 • 9:30am-6:30pm, 9am-5pm Sat, 11am-4pm Sun • general • LGBT section • community bulletin board • women-owned

## Haverhill

### BARS

**Phoenix** 103 Washington St (2nd Fl of Chit Chat Lounge) 978/374-9710 • 5pm-1am, till 2am Fri, clsd Mon-Tue • lesbians/gay men * dancing/DJ

**Phoenix** 103 Washington St (2nd Fl of Chit Chat Lounge) 978/374-9710 • 5pm-1am, till 2am Fri, clsd Mon-Tue • lesbians/gay men * dancing/DJ

### CAFES

**Wicked Big Cafe** 19 Essex St (at Wingate) 978/556-5656 • 7am-5pm, 8am-3pm Sat, 9am-2pm Sun • coffee house w/ excellent food • WiFi • wheelchair access • lesbian-owned

## Lenox

**see Berkshires**

## Lynn

### BARS

**Fran's Place** 776 Washington St (at Sagamore) 781/598-5618 • 3pm-1am • lesbians/ gay men • dancing/DJ • also sports bar • wheelchair access

## Martha's Vineyard

### ACCOMMODATIONS

**Martha's Vineyard Surfside Motel** 7 Oak Bluffs Ave, Oak Bluffs 508/693-2500, 800/537-3007 • gay-friendly • non-smoking • jacuzzis • pets ok • WiFi • wheelchair access

**The Shiverick Inn** 5 Pease's Pt Wy, Edgartown (at Pent Ln) 508/627-3797, 800/723-4292 • gay/ straight • full brkfst • nonsmoking • WiFi • gay-owned

### RESTAURANTS

**The Black Dog Tavern** Beach St Extension #21 (at Water St) 508/693-9223 • brkfst, lunch & dinner, seasonal • wheelchair access

### BOOKSTORES

**Bunch of Grapes** 44 Main St (at Center St), Vineyard Haven 508/693-2291, 800/693-0221 • 9am-6pm, 11am-5pm Sun • some LGBT titles & magazines

## New Bedford

### BARS

**Le Place** 20 Kenyon St (at Belleville Ave) 508/990-1248 • 2pm-2am • popular • lesbians/ gay men • karaoke • dancing/DJ • women-owned

## Newton

see Boston

## North Adams

see Berkshires

## Northampton

see also Amherst

### ACCOMMODATIONS

**The Hotel Northampton** 36 King St (near Bridge St) **413/584–3100, 800/547–3529** • gay-friendly • gym • cafe & historic tavern • nonsmoking • WiFi • wheelchair access

**Starlight Llama Solar B&B** 940 Chesterfield Rd, Florence **413/584–1703** • gay/straight • award winning green inn

### NIGHTCLUBS

**Diva's** 492 Pleasant St (at Conz St) **413/586–8161** • 9pm-2am, clsd Sun-Mon • lesbians/ gay men • dancing/DJ • live music • theme nights • 18+ Tue-Fri

**Pearl Street** 10 Pearl St (at Main) **413/586–8686** • 7pm-1am • gay/ straight • dancing/DJ • live music • young crowd

### CAFES

**Haymarket Cafe** 185 Main St **413/586–9969** • 7am-10pm, till 11pm Fri-Sat, from 8am Sun • popular • also restaurant • wheelchair access

### RESTAURANTS

**Bela** 68 Masonic St **413/586–8011** • noon-8:30pm, clsd Sun-Mon • vegetarian • wheelchair access • lesbian-owned • cash only

**Blue Heron Restaurant** 112 N Main St, Sunderland **413/665–2102** • 4pm-9pm, till 10pm Fri-Sat, clsd Sun- Mon • fine dining • 10 minutes out of town • lesbian-owned

**Bueno Y Sano** 134 Main St (at Center St) **413/586–7311** • 11am-10pm, till 9pm Sun • Mexican

**The Old Creamery Co-op** 445 Berkshire Tr, Cummington **413/634–5560** • 7am-7:30pm • delicious, quality, homemade deli and bakery foods; abundant fresh produce, try the Spicy Maddow (hint hint) • lesbian-owned

**Paul & Elizabeth's** 150 Main St (in Thorne's Marketplace) **413/584–4832** • lunch & dinner, Sun brunch • seafood • plenty veggie • beer/ wine • wheelchair access

### ENTERTAINMENT & RECREATION

**The Iron Horse** 20 Center St (at Main) **413/586–8686** • 5:30pm-close • restaurant & bar • live music • all ages • nonsmoking

### RETAIL SHOPS

**Oh My A Sensuality Shop** 122 Main St (at Center) **413/584–9669** • noon-7pm, till 8pm Fri-Sat, noon-5pm Sun • informative, helpful & intimate sex toy store

## Provincetown

see also Cape Cod listings

### INFO LINES & SERVICES

**Provincetown Business Guild** **508/487–2313**

### ACCOMMODATIONS

**A Secret Garden Inn** 300–A Commercial St **508/487–9027** • lesbians/ gay men • kids ok • nonsmoking

**Admiral's Landing** 158 Bradford St (btwn Conwell & Pearl) **508/487–9665, 800/934–0925** • lesbians/gay men • WiFi • nonsmoking • lesbian-owned

**Aerie House & Beach Club** 184 Bradford St (at Miller Hill) **508/487–1197, 800/487–1197** • lesbians/ gay men • hot tub • sundeck • WiFi • gay-owned

**Anchor Inn Beach House** 175 Commercial St (at Winthrop) **508/487–0432, 800/858–2657** • gay/ straight • nonsmoking • private beach • wheelchair access • lesbian & straight-owned/ run

**Atlantic Light Inn** 11 Pearl St (at Bradford) **508/487–0302** • gay/straight • hot tub • nonsmoking • WiFi • gay owned

**Bayberry Accommodations** 16 Winthrop St (at Commercial) **508/487–4605, 800/422–4605** • lesbians/ gay men • hot tub • nonsmoking • WiFi • gay-owned

**Bayshore** 493 Commercial St (at Howland) **508/487–9133** • gay/ straight • apts • private beach • kitchens • pets ok • WiFi • nonsmoking • lesbian-owned

**Beaconlight Guest House** 12 Winthrop St (at Bradford) **508/487–9603, 800/696–9603** • mostly gay men • WiFi • nonsmoking • parking • gay-owned

**Benchmark Inn** 6–8 Dyer St **508/487–7440, 888/487–7440** • lesbians/ gay men • nonsmoking • WiFi • wheelchair access • gay-owned

**Boatslip Resort** 161 Commercial St **508/487–1669, 877/786–9662** • popular • mostly gay men • resort • pool • seasonal • also several bars • popular T-dance • gay-owned

**The Bradford Carver House** 70 Bradford St 508/487-0728, 800/826-9083 • lesbians/ gay men • restored mid-19th-c home • centrally located • nonsmoking • WiFi • gay-owned

**Bradford House & Motel** 41 Bradford St (at Conant) 508/487-0173 • gay-friendly • near town center • 1 block from the beach • wheelchair access • women-owned

**Brass Key Guesthouse** 67 Bradford St (at Carver) 508/487-9005, 800/842-9858 • popular • mostly gay men • hot tub • pool • nonsmoking • pets ok • WiFi • wheelchair access • gay-owned

**Carpe Diem Guesthouse & Spa** 12 Johnson St 508/487-4242, 800/487-0132 • lesbians/ gay men • also cottage • full German brkfst • hot tub • nonsmoking • WiFi • gay-owned

**Chicago House** 6 Winslow St (at Bradford) 508/487-0537, 800/733-7869 • lesbians/ gay men • rooms & apts • hot tub • some shared baths • nonsmoking • WiFi • gay-owned

**Christopher's by the Bay** 8 Johnson St (at Commercial) 508/487-9263 • lesbians/ gay men • Victorian guesthouse • some shared baths • patio • nonsmoking • gay-owned

**Crown & Anchor** 247 Commercial St 508/487-1430 • lesbians/ gay men • pool • nonsmoking • WiFi • also bars • cabaret • gay-owned

**Crowne Pointe Historic Inn & Shui Spa** 82 Bradford St 508/487-6767, 877/276-9631 • lesbians/ gay men • full brkfst • heated pool • nonsmoking • WiFi • wheelchair access • gay-owned

**Designer's Dock** 349 Commercial St 508/776-5746, 800/724-9888 • gay/ straight • weekly condos in town & on beach • June-Sept • kitchens • WiFi • gay-owned

**Eben House** 90 Bradford St 508/487-0386 • lesbians/ gay men • nonsmoking • WiFi • parking • fireplaces

**Enzo** 186 Commercial St (at Court) 508/487-7555 • gay/ straight • WiFi • Italian restaurant & piano bar on premises

**Gifford House Inn** 11 Carver St 508/487-0688, 800/434-0130 • lesbians/ gay men • seasonal • WiFi • also several bars & restaurant • gay-owned

**The Inn at Cook Street** 7 Cook St (at Bradford) 508/487-3894, 888/266-5655 • gay-friendly • nonsmoking • women-owned

**Inn at the Moors** 59 Provincelands Rd 508/487-1342, 800/842-6379 • gay-friendly • motel • across from Nat'l Seashore Province Lands • seasonal • nonsmoking • WiFi • pool • lesbian-owned

**John Randall House** 140 Bradford St (at Center) 508/487-3533, 800/573-6700 • lesbians/ gay men • kids ok • nonsmoking • WiFi • gay-owned

**Land's End Inn** 22 Commercial St 508/487-0706, 800/276-7088 • gay/ straight • nonsmoking • WiFi

**Lotus Guest House** 296 Commercial St (at Standish) 508/487-4644, 888/508-4644 • lesbians/ gay men • seasonal • decks • garden • teens ok • WiFi • lesbian & gay-owned

**Moffett House** 296-A Commercial St (at Ryder) 508/487-6615, 800/990-8865 • lesbians/ gay men • gay-owned

**Prince Albert Guest House** 164-166 Commercial St (at Central) 508/487-1850 • mostly gay men • Victorian • nonsmoking • WiFi • gay-owned

**Provincetown Hotel at Gabriel's** 102 Bradford St 508/487-3232 • popular • lesbians/ gay men • full brkfst • nonsmoking • sundecks • kids/ pets ok • WiFi • lesbian & gay-owned

**Ravenwood Guest House** 462 Commercial St (at Cook) 508/487-3203 • lesbians/ gay men • also apts & cottage • nonsmoking • private beach • wheelchair accessible cottage • lesbian-owned

**The Red Inn** 15 Commercial St (at Point) 508/487-7334, 866/473-3466 • gay-friendly • historic B&B • nonsmoking • wheelchair access • gay-owned

**Revere Guesthouse** 14 Court St (btwn Commercial & Bradford) 508/487-2292, 800/487-2292 • lesbians/ gay men • nonsmoking • gay-owned

**Rose & Crown Guest House** 158 Commercial St (at Central) 508/487-3332 • gay/ straight • lesbian-owned

**Rose Acre** 5 Center St (at Commercial) 508/487-2347 • women only • suites • also apts & cottage • nonsmoking • parking • open May-Oct • WiFi • women-owned

**Sage Inn & Lounge** 336 Commercial St 508/487-6424 • gay/ straight • WiFi • wheelchair access

**Salt House Inn** 6 Conwell St (at Railroad) 508/487-1911 • lesbians/ gay men • B&B • nonsmoking • WiFi • sundeck • gay-owned

**Sandcastle Resort and Club** 929 Commercial St 508/487–9300 • gay/ straight • beachfront resort w/ kitchen facilities & private bath in every room pool • WiFi

**Snug Cottage** 178 Bradford St 508/487–1616, 800/432–2334 • gay/ straight • nonsmoking • WiFi • gay-owned

**Somerset House** 378 Commercial St (at Pearl) 508/487–0383, 800/575–1850 • lesbians/ gay men • Victorian mansion • nonsmoking • WiFi • gay-owned

**Sunset Inn** 142 Bradford St (at Center) 508/487–9810, 800/965–1801 • lesbians/ gay men • some shared baths • seasonal • clothing-optional sundeck • nonsmoking • WiFi • gay-owned

**Surfside Hotel & Suites** 543 Commercial (at Kendall Ln) 508/487–1726, 800/421–1726 • gay/ straight • waterfront hotel • lots of amenities • private beach • pool • nonsmoking • WiFi • kids/ pets ok • gay-owned

**The Tucker Inn** 12 Center St (at Bradford) 508/487–0381, 800/477–1867 • lesbians/ gay men • full brkfst • pets ok • WiFi • also cottage • nonsmoking • gay-owned

**The Waterford** 386 Commercial St (at Pearl) 508/487–6400, 800/487–0784 • gay/ straight • deck w/ full bar • also restaurant • WiFi

**Watermark Inn** 603 Commercial St 508/487–0165 • gay/ straight • kids ok • nonsmoking • WiFi

**Watership Inn** 7 Winthrop St (at Commercial St) 508/487–0094, 800/330–9413 • mostly gay men • sundeck • WiFi • gay-owned

**White Wind Inn** 174 Commercial St (at Winthrop) 508/487–1526, 888/449–9463 • lesbians/ gay men • WiFi • gay-owned

**Women Innkeepers of Provincetown** PO Box 573, 02657 • women-owned accommodations in Provincetown • see ad in front color section

## Bars

**The Boatslip Resort** 161 Commercial St 508/487–1669, 877/786–9662 • seasonal • popular • lesbians/ gay men • T-dance 4pm daily during season • young crowd • swimming • outdoor/ waterfront grill

**Governor Bradford** 312 Commercial St (at Standish) 508/487–2781 • 11am-1am, from noon Sun • gay-friendly • "drag karaoke" Sat (nightly in season) • also restaurant in summer

**PiedBar** 193–A Commercial St (at Court St) 508/487–1527 • seasonal May-Oct, noon-1am • popular • lesbians/ gay men • dancing/DJ • more women Fri-Sat • wheelchair access

**Porchside Lounge** 11 Carver St (in the Gifford House) 508/487–0688 • 5pm-1am • mostly gay men • neighborhood bar • also restaurant

**Shipwreck Lounge** 10 Carver St (at Bradford) 508/487–1472 • lesbians/ gay men • upscale lounge • outdoor seating w/ fire pit

**Wave Video Bar** 247 Commercial St (in the Crown & Anchor) 508/487–1430 • 11am-1am • lesbians/ gay men • neighborhood bar • karaoke • T-dance Sun

### NIGHTCLUBS

**Atlantic House (The "A-House")** 6 Masonic Pl 508/487–3169 • 10pm-1am • popular • mostly gay men • neighborhood bar • 3 bars • dancing/DJ • theme parties

**Club Purgatory** 9-11 Carver St (at Bradford St, in the Gifford House) 508/487–8442 • opens 7pm, from 9pm Sun (in season) • lesbians/ gay men • dancing/DJ

**Girl Power** 193–A Commercial St (at The PiedBar) • Provincetown events for women • check www.provincetownforwomen.com for events • see ad in front color section

**Paramount** in the Crown & Anchor 508/487–1430 • 10:30pm-1am (seasonal) • popular • lesbians/ gay men • dancing/DJ • live shows • drag shows • cabaret

### CAFES

**Post Office Cafe Cabaret** 303 Commercial St (upstairs) 508/487–3892 • 8am-11pm, seasonal hours • some veggie

### RESTAURANTS

**Bayside Betsy's** 177 Commercial St 508/487–6566 • brkfst , lunch & dinner, bar till 10pm • on waterfront • wheelchair access

**Big Daddy's Burritos** 205 Commercial St 508/487–4432 • 11am-10pm (May-Oct) • Tex-Mex, burritos, veggie wraps, salads & nachos

**Bubala's by the Bay** 183–185 Commercial 508/487–0773 • lunch & dinner • popular • seasonal • patio

**Ciro & Sal's** 4 Kiley Ct (btwn Bangs St & Lovett's Ct) 508/487–6444 • dinner from 5:30pm • Northern Italian • reservations recommended

**Fanizzi's** 539 Commercial St (at Kendall Lane) 508/487–1964 • popular • lunch & dinner • some veggie • full bar • on the water • wheelchair access

**Front Street Restaurant** 230 Commercial St 508/487–9715 • 6pm-10:30pm, bar till 1am • bistro beer/ wine • seasonal

**Lobster Pot** harborside (at 321 Commercial St) 508/487–0842 • 11:30am-10pm (April-Nov) • "a Provincetown tradition" • wheelchair access

**The Mews Restaurant & Cafe** 429 Commercial St (at Bangs St) 508/487–1500 • dinner • seasonal Sun brunch • popular • off-season live shows • wheelchair access • waterfront dining

**Napi's Restaurant** 7 Freeman St 508/487–1145, 800/571–6274 • dinner • lunch Oct-April • int'l/ seafood • plenty veggie • wheelchair access

**The Red Inn** 15 Commercial St (at Point) 508/487–7334, 866/473–3466 • dinner nightly, brunch Th-Sun, clsd Jan-April • reservations a must • full bar

**Relish** 93 Commercial St 508/487–8077 • yummy baked goods • pick up a sandwich on the way to the beach!

**Spiritus Pizza** 190 Commercial St 508/487–2808 • noon-2am • popular • great espresso shakes & late-night hangout for a slice

### ENTERTAINMENT & RECREATION

**Art House Theatre & Cafe** 214 Commercial St 508/487–9222

**Art's Dune Tours** 4 Standish St 508/487–1950, 800/894–1951 • day trips, sunset tours & charters through historic sand dunes & Nat'l Seashore Park • kids ok • gay-owned

**Dolphin Fleet Whale Watch** 305 Commercial St 508/240–3636, 800/826–9300 • gay-friendly • 3-hr day & evening cruises • full galley & bar on board • wheelchair access

**Herring Cove Beach**

**Ptown Bikes** 42 Bradford 508/487–8735 • 9am-6pm • rentals • gay-owned

**Spaghetti Strip** • nude beach • 1.5 miles south of Race Point Beach

### RETAIL SHOPS

**HRC Action Center & Store** 209-211 Commercial St 508/487–7736 • Human Rights Campaign merchandise & info

**Recovering Hearts** 4 Standish St 508/487–4875 • 10am-11pm (in summer), call for off-season hours • recovery • LGBT & New Age books • wheelchair access

➤**Womencrafts** 376 Commercial St (at Pearl St) **508/487-2501** • 11AM - 9PM (summer hours) please call for off-season hours • women-crafted Jewelry, Pottery, Glass, Porcelain, Mosaics, Photographs, Sculpture, Books, CDs, and DVDs. Open since 1976, representing over 100 women from the USA and Canada • lesbian -owned

## PUBLICATIONS

**Provincetown Banner** 167 Commercial St **508/487-7400** • newspaper

**Provincetown Magazine** **508/487-1000** • seasonal • Provincetown's oldest weekly magazine

## GYMS & HEALTH CLUBS

**Mussel Beach Health Club** 35 Bradford St (btwn Montello & Conant) **508/487-0001** • 6am-9pm, till 8pm in winter

**Provincetown Gym** 82 Shank Painter Rd (at Winthrop) **508/487-2776**

## Quincy

see also Boston

## Somerville

see Boston

## Springfield

## BARS

**Pure** 234 Chestnut St (E of Main) **413/205-1483** • 1pm-2am • mostly gay men • neighborhood bar • food served • wheelchair access

## NIGHTCLUBS

**Oz Nightclub** 397 Dwight St (at Taylor) **413/732-4562** • 9pm-2am, from 7pm Fri-Sat, clsd Sun-Mon • neighborhood bar • dancing/DJ • karaoke

**The X Room** 395 Dwight St **413/732-4562** • 7pm-2am, from 2pmTh-Sun • mostly gay men • dancing/DJ • strippers/ nude dancers

**The X Room** 395 Dwight St **413/732-4562** • 7pm-2am, from 2pmTh-Sun • mostly gay men • dancing/DJ • strippers/ nude dancers

## Taunton

## BARS

**Bobby's Place** 62 Weir St (at Route 44, 138 & 140, at Taunton Green) **508/824-9997** • 5pm-1am, from 2am Fri-Sat, from 2pm Sun • lesbians/ gay men • dancing/DJ • food served • karaoke • drag shows

## Williamstown

see Berkshires

## Worcester

## BARS

**MB Lounge** 40 Grafton St (at Franklin) **508/799-4521** • 5pm-2am, from 3pm wknds • lesbians/ gay men • neighborhood bar • WiFi • wheelchair access • gay-owned

## RETAIL SHOPS

**Glamour Boutique** 850 Southbridge St, Auburn **508/721-7800** • large-size dresses, wigs, etc

# MICHIGAN

## Statewide

## PUBLICATIONS

**Out Post** **313/702-0272** • bi-weekly nightlife guide for SE Michigan

## Ann Arbor

## INFO LINES & SERVICES

**The Jim Toy Community Center** 319 Braun Ct **734/995-9867** • LGBT resource center, HIV testing 5pm-7pm Sun

**Lesbian/ Gay AA** **734/482-5700**

## BARS

**\'aut\ Bar** 315 Braun Ct (at Catherine) **734/994-3677** • 4pm-2am, from 11am Sat, 10 am Sun • popular • lesbians/ gay men • also restaurant (dinner & wknd brunch) • American/ Mexican • patio • wheelchair access

## NIGHTCLUBS

**The Necto** 516 E Liberty (at Maynard) **734/994-5436** • 9pm-2am • gay/ straight • dancing/DJ • videos • young crowd • 18+ • theme nights • gay night Fri

## CAFES

**Cafe Verde** 214 N Fourth Ave (at Catherine St) **734/994-9174** • 7am-9:30pm, 9am-8pm Sun • fair trade & organic coffee & tea • also soups, sandwiches & salads

## RESTAURANTS

**Dominick's** 812 Monroe St (at Tappan Ave) **734/662-5414** • 10am-10pm, clsd Sun • Italian • beer/ wine • wheelchair access

**The Earle** 121 W Washington (at Ashley) 734/994-0211 • 5:30pm-9pm, till 11pm Fri-Sat, 5pm-8pm Sun • cont'l • some veggie • beer/ wine • wheelchair access

**Mani Osteria & Bar** 341B E Liberty 734/769-6700 • 11:30am-10pm, from 4pm wknds, clsd Mon • great pizza

**Seva** 2541 Jackson Ave (at 5th Ave) 734/662-1111 • 11am-9pm, from 10am wknds • vegetarian • also cafe & wine bar

**Zingerman's Delicatessen** 422 Detroit St (at Kingsley) 734/663-3354, 888/636-8162 • 7am-10pm • also ship food worldwide

### ENTERTAINMENT & RECREATION

**The Ark** 316 S Main St (btwn William & Liberty) 734/761-1818, 734/761-1800 • gay-friendly • concert house • women's music shows

### BOOKSTORES

**Common Language** 317 Braun Ct (at 4th) 734/663-0036 • 11am-10pm, till midnight Fri-Sat, till 7pm Sun • LGBT • wheelchair access

**Crazy Wisdom Books & Tea Room** 114 S Main St (btwn Huron & Washington) 734/665-2757 • 11am-9pm, till 11pm Fri-Sat, 11am-8pm Sun • holistic & metaphysical • live music

### RETAIL SHOPS

**People's Food Cooperative** 216 N Fourth Ave (at Catherine St) 734/994-9174 • 8am-10pm, full-service, natural foods grocery featuring organic, local and fair trade products

## Battle Creek

### NIGHTCLUBS

**Partners** 910 North Ave (at Morgan) 269/964-7276 • 7pm-2am, clsd Mon • lesbians/ gay men • dancing/DJ • karaoke • wheelchair access

### EROTICA

**Romantix Adult Superstore** 690 W Michigan Ave (at Grand) 269/964-3070

## Bay City

### BARS

**Malickey's Pub** 501 S Madison 989/414-6667 • 11:30am-1:30am • gay/ straight • theme nights

## Bellaire

### ACCOMMODATIONS

**Applesauce Inn B&B** 7296 S M-88 231/533-6448 • gay-friendly • B&B in 100-year-old farmhouse • dog-friendly • WiFi • nonsmoking

**Bellaire B&B** 212 Park St (at Antrim) 231/533-6077, 800/545-0780 • gay/ straight • stately 1879 home • full brkfst • nonsmoking • WiFi • gay-owned

## Detroit

### INFO LINES & SERVICES

**Affirmations Community Center** 290 W 9 Mile Rd (at Planavon), Ferndale 800/398-4297 • 9am-9pm, clsd Sun • helpline line 4pm-9pm

**Helpline** 800/398-4297 • 4pm-9pm Tue-Sat • support & resources line

### ACCOMMODATIONS

**The Atheneum Suite Hotel** 1000 Brush Ave (at Lafayette) 313/962-2323, 800/772-2323 • gay-friendly • restaurant & lounge • gym • WiFi • wheelchair access

**Detroit Marriott at the Renaissance Center** 400 Renaissance Center Dr 313/568-8000, 800/228-9290 • gay-friendly • wheelchair access

**Honor & Folly** 2138 Michigan Ave (above Slows BBQ) • gay/ straight • WiFi • design-focused B&B with cooking classes, bike rentals and goods made by local designers and artisantisan

### BARS

**Centaur Bar** 2233 Park Ave (at W Montcalm St) 313/963-4040 • 4pm-2am • gay/ straight • sports bar • food served

**Club Gold Coast** 2971 E 7 Mile Rd (at Conant) 313/366-6135 • 7pm-2am • popular • mostly gay men • dancing/DJ • male dancers nightly • WiFi • wheelchair access

**Gigi's** 16920 W Warren (at Clayburn, enter rear) 313/584-6525 • noon-2am, from 2pm wknds • mostly gay men • dancing/DJ • transgender-friendly • drag shows • gay-owned

**Menjo's** 928 W McNichols Rd (at Hamilton) 313/863-3934 • 1pm-2am, popular happy hour • mostly gay men • dancing/DJ • karaoke • live shows • videos • young crowd

**Pronto** 608 S Washington (at 6th St), Royal Oak 248/544-7900 • 11am-2am • popular • lesbians/ gay men • patio • also restaurant

**Soho** 205 W 9 Mile (at Woodward), Ferndale **248/542-7646** • 4pm-close, from 6pm wknds • lesbians/ gay men • karaoke • swank cocktail lounge

**The Woodward Video Bar & Grill** 6426 Woodward Ave (at Milwaukee, rear entrance) **313/872-0166** • 2pm-2am • mostly gay men • DJ Th-Sun • karaoke • videos

## NIGHTCLUBS

**Escape** 19404 Sherwood (at 7 Mile) **313/892-1765** • 10pm-5am • lesbians/ gay men • neighborhood bar • drag shows • grill menu • gay-owned

**Inferno Detroit** 1641 Middlebelt Rd (btwn Michigan Ave & Cherry Hill Rd), Inkster **734/729-0345** • 8pm-2am Th-Sun • lesbians/ gay men • dancing/DJ • drag shows • karaoke

**Leland City Club** 400 Bagley St (at Leland Hotel) **313/962-2300** • 10pm-4:30am Fri-Sat • gay-friendly • dancing/DJ • goth/ alternative • 18+

**Luna** 1815 N Main St (at 12 Mile), Royal Oak **248/589-3344** • from 9pm, clsd Sun-Tue • gay-friendly • dancing/DJ • theme nights

**Temple** 2906 Cass Ave (btwn Charlotte & Temple) **313/832-2822** • 1pm-2am • mostly gay men • dancing/DJ • transgender-friendly • mostly African American • popular wknds • wheelchair access

## CAFES

**Avalon International Breads** 422 W Willis (at Cass) **313/832-0008** • 6am-6pm, clsd Sun-Mon • lesbian-owned

**Coffee Beanery Cafe** 28557 S Woodward Ave (S of 12 Mile), Berkley **248/336-9930** • 7am-11pm • WiFi

**Five 15** 515 S Washington St, Royal Oak **248/515-2551** • 11am-8pm till 6pm Sun, 10am-9:30pm Fri-Sat • Drag Bingo Th-Sat• performances • art shows • WiFi • gay-owned

## RESTAURANTS

**Amici's** 3249 12 Mile Rd (at Gardner Ave), Berkley **248/544-4100** • gourmet pizza & martinis

**Atlas Global Bistro** 3111 Woodward Ave (at Charlotte) **313/831-2241** • lunch & dinner • Sun brunch • American/ int'l • upscale

**Cacao Tree Cafe** 204 W 4th St, Royal Oak **248/336-9043** • 9am-9pm • gourmet raw food/ vegan

**Cass Cafe** 4620 Cass Ave (at Forest) **313/831-1400** • 11am-2am, 5pm-1am Sun • plenty veggie • full bar • WiFi

**Coach Insignia** 200 Renaissance Ctr, 71st Fl **313/567-2622** • dinner, clsd Sun • steakhouse

**Como's** 22812 Woodward (at 9 Mile), Ferndale **248/548-5005** • 11am-2am, till 4am Fri-Sat • Italian • full bar • patio • wheelchair access

**Elwood Bar & Grill** 300 Adams (at Brush, by Comerica Park) **313/962-2337** • 11am-8pm, till 2pm Mon, clsd Sun (unless there's a Tiger's game) • Art Deco diner

**Inn Season** 500 E 4th St (at Knowles), Royal Oak **248/547-7916** • lunch & dinner • Sun brunch • clsd Mon • organic vegetarian/ vegan

**La Dolce Vita** 17546 Woodward Ave (at McNichols) **313/865-0331** • lunch & dinner, Sun brunch, clsd Mon • lesbians/ gay men • Italian • plenty veggie • full bar • patio • wheelchair access

**Mercury Burger & Bar** 2163 Michigan Ave **313/964-5000** • 11am-11pm

**One-Eyed Betty's** 175 W Troy, Ferndale **248/808-6633** • 4pm-2am, from 9am wknds • many beers on tap • gay-owned

**Red Star** 13944 Michigan Ave, Dearborn **313/581-1451** • Chinese • plenty veggie/ vegan

**Roast** 1128 Washington Ave (at State St) **313/961-2500** • dinner nightly • steakhouse

**Seva** 66 E Forest **313/974-6661** • 11am-9pm, till 11pm Fri-Sat • vegetarian

**Sweet Lorraine's Cafe & Bar** 29101 Greenfield Rd (at 12 Mile), Southfield **248/559-5985** • 11am-10pm, till midnight Fri-Sat • popular • modern American • wheelchair access

**Traffic Jam & Snug** 511 W Canfield St (at SE corner of 2nd Ave) **313/831-9470** • 11am-10:30pm, till midnight Fri-Sat, till 9pm Sun • eclectic • plenty veggie • also full bar, bakery, dairy & brewery • wheelchair access

**Vivio's** 2460 Market St (at Napoleon St) **313/393-1711** • lunch & dinner, clsd Sun • Italian, famous bloody marys & steamed pot o' mussels• full bar • wheelchair access

**Wolfgang Puck Grille** 1777 3rd St (at the MGM Grand Hotel) **313/465-1648** • 5pm-10pm, 9am-2pm Sat-Sun, clsd Mon-Tue

## ENTERTAINMENT & RECREATION

**Charles H Wright Museum of African American History** 315 E Warren Ave (at Cass) **313/494-5800**

**Detroit Derby Girls** 37637 Five Mile Rd #311, Livonia • visit www.detroitrollerderby.com for events

**Motown Historical Museum** 2648 W Grand Blvd 313/875–2264 • come see where the Motown Sound began • guided tours & gift shop

### Retail Shops

**Royal Oak Tattoo** 820 S Washington Ave (at Lincoln), Royal Oak 248/398–0052 • tattoo & piercing studio

### Publications

**Between the Lines** 734/293–7200 • statewide LGBT weekly

**Metra Magazine** PO Box 71844, Madison Heights 48071 248/543–3500 • covers IN, IL, MI, OH, PA, WI & Ontario, Canada

### Erotica

**Noir Leather** 124 W 4th St (btw S Main St & S Washington), Royal Oak 248/541–3979 • 11am-9pm, till 10pm Fri-Sat, noon-7pm Sun • wheelchair access

## Douglas

see Saugatuck

## Flint

### Bars

**Pachyderm Pub** G–1408 E Hemphill Rd (btwn I–475 & Saginaw St), Burton 810/744–4960 • 3pm-2am, from 5pm wknds • lesbians/ gay men • also restaurant • dancing/DJ • karaoke • male dancers • multiracial • transgender-friendly • patio • WiFi • gay-owned

### Cafes

**The Good Beans Cafe** 328 N Grand Traverse (at 1st Ave) 810/237–4663 • 7:30am-4pm, till 9pm Th-Fri, open some wknds • espresso & pastries • live shows • WiFi • gay-owned • wheelchair access

## Frankfort

### Accommodations

**Wayfarer Lodgings** 1912 S Scenic Hwy (M-22) 231/352–9264, 800/735–8564 • gay-friendly • cottages • near Frankfort, Lake Michigan & Betsie River • kids/pets ok • nonsmoking • WiFi

## Glen Arbor

### Accommodations

**Duneswood** at Sleeping Bear Dunes Nat'l Lakeshore 231/668–6789 • women only • located in northern MI • nonsmoking • lesbian-owned

## Grand Rapids

### Info Lines & Services

**Lesbian/ Gay Network of W Michigan** 343 Atlas Ave SE (behind Spirit Dreams in Eastown) 616/458–3511 • 11am-5:30pm, clsd wknds • lounge • library • evening social groups

### Accommodations

**Radisson Riverfront Hotel** 270 Ann St NW (at Turner Ave) 616/363–9001, 800/395–7046 • gay-friendly • nonsmoking • pool • wheelchair access • WiFi

### Bars

**Apartment Lounge** 33 Sheldon NE (at Library) 616/451–0815 • 1pm-2am, from noon wknds • mostly gay men • neighborhood bar • sandwiches served • wheelchair access

**Diversions** 10 Fountain St NW (at Division) 616/451–3800 • 8pm-2am • popular • lesbians/ gay men • dancing/DJ • karaoke • 18+ • videos • wheelchair access

### Nightclubs

**Rumors Nightclub** 69 S Division Ave (at Oakes St) 616/454–8720 • 4pm-2am • mostly gay men • women's night Fri • dancing/DJ • karaoke • male strippers • wheelchair access

### Restaurants

**Brandywine** 1345 Lake Dr SE (in East Town) 616/774–8641 • 7am-8pm, from 7:30am Sat, 8am-2:30pm Sun

**Cherie Inn** 969 Cherry St SE (at Lake Dr) 616/458–0588 • 7am-3pm, from8am wknds, clsd Mon • some veggie • wheelchair access

**Gaia Cafe** 209 Diamond Ave SE (at Cherry St) 616/454–6233 • 8am-8pm, till 3pm wknds, clsd Mon • vegetarian

### Entertainment & Recreation

**Grand Raggidy Roller Girls** 616/752–8475 • Grand Rapids' female roller derby league

## Honor

### Accommodations

**Labrys Wilderness Resort** 231/882–5994 • women only • cabins in Sleeping Bear Dunes Nat'l Lakeshore • lesbian-owned

## Kalamazoo

### INFO LINES & SERVICES

**Kalamazoo Gay/ Lesbian Resource Center** 629 Pioneer St **269/349-4234** • 9am,-5pm, clsd wknds • educational/ support groups • youth group • hotline

## Lansing

### BARS

**Esquire** 1250 Turner St (at Clinton) **517/487-5338** • 3pm-2am • lesbians/ gay men • neighborhood bar • karaoke

### NIGHTCLUBS

**Spiral** 1247 Center St (at Clinton) **517/371-3221** • 8pm-2am, clsd Mon-Tue • mostly gay men • dancing/DJ • theme nights • shows • videos • 18+ • wheelchair access

### BOOKSTORES

**Everybody Reads** 2019 E Michigan Ave **517/346-9900** • 11am-7pm, 10am-4pm Sun • cool general bookstore • also coffeehouse

## Marquette

### ACCOMMODATIONS

**The Landmark Inn** 230 N Front St (at Ridge St) **906/228-2580, 888/752-6362** • gay-friendly • historic boutique hotel overlooking Lake Superior • restaurant & bar • gym • nonsmoking • WiFi • kids ok

## Owendale

### ACCOMMODATIONS

**Windover Resort** 3596 Blakely Rd **989/375-2586** • women only • seasonal private resort • campsites & RV hookups • pool

## Petoskey

### ACCOMMODATIONS

**Coach House Inn** 1011 N US 31 (at Mitchell) **231/347-8281, 877/347-8088** • gay-friendly • basic amenities • WiFi • nonsmoking • gay-owned

## Pontiac

### BARS

**Liberty Bar** 85 N Saginaw **248/758-0771** • 11:30am-2am, from 2pm wknds • lesbians/ gay men • dancing/DJ • food served

## Port Huron

### NIGHTCLUBS

**Seekers** 3301 24th St (btwn Oak & Little) **810/985-9349** • 7pm-2am • lesbians/ gay men • dancing/DJ • drag shows

## Saugatuck

### ACCOMMODATIONS

**Beechwood Manor Inn & Cottage** 736 Pleasant St (at Allegan) **269/857-1587, 877/857-1587** • gay/ straight • full brkfst • nonsmoking • WiFi • gay-owned

**Bella Vita Spa & Suites** 119 Butler St **269/857-8482** • gay-friendly • upscale, modern suites overlooking downtown Saugatuck • also day spa • WiFi

**The Belvedere Inn & Restaurant** 3656 63rd St **269/857-5777, 877/858-5777** • gay-friendly • full brkfst •

**The Bunkhouse B&B at Campit** **269/543-4335, 877/226-7481** • lesbians/ gay men • cabins • private baths • access to Campit Resort amenities (see listing below) • pool • nonsmoking • WiFi

**Campit Outdoor Resort** 6635 118th Ave, Fennville **269/543-4335, 877/226-7481** • lesbians/ gay men • campsites • RV hookups • separate women's area • pool • seasonal • pets ok • WiFi • membership required • lesbian & gay-owned

**Douglas House B&B** 41 Spring St (at Wall St), Douglas **269/857-1119** • gay/ straight • near gay beach • gay-owned • open April-Oct

**The Dunes Resort** 333 Blue Star Hwy, Douglas **269/857-1401** • lesbians/ gay men • motel & cottages • transgender-friendly • pool • food served • women's wknds in April, June & Oct • dancing/DJ • live shows • pets ok • wheelchair access • gay-owned

**Hidden Garden Cottages & Suites** 247 Butler St **269/857-8109, 888/857-8109** • gay-friendly • cottages & suites • nonsmoking • WiFi

**Hillby Thatch Cottages** 1438-1440 71st St, Glenn **847/864-3553** • gay/ straight • kitchens • fireplaces • kids ok • nonsmoking • woman-owned

**J Paules Fenn Inn** 2254 S 58th St, Fennville 269/561–2836, 877/561–2836 • gay-friendly • full brkfst • kids/ pets ok • nonsmoking

**The Kingsley House B&B** 626 West Main St, Fennville 269/561-6425, 866/561-6425 • gay-friendly • full brkfst • nonsmoking • WiFi • gay-owned

**Kirby House** 294 Center St (at Blue Star Hwy) 269/857–2904, 800/521–6473 • gay/ straight • full brkfst • pool • nonsmoking • WiFi • gay-owned

**Maple Ridge Cottages** 713-719 Maple 269/857–5211 (Pines #) • gay/ straight • quaint cottages • hot tub • nonsmoking • gay-owned

**The Park House Inn B&B** 888 Holland St 269/857-4535, 866/321-4535 • gay-friendly • B&B in one of Saugatuck's oldest residences • full brkfst • nonsmoking • WiFi • also cottage

**The Pines Motor Lodge & Cottages** 56 Blue Star Hwy (at Center St), Douglas 269/857–5211 • gay/ straight • newly renovated boutique retro motel • nonsmoking • also retro gift gallery • WiFi • gay-owned

**The Spruce Cutter's Cottage** 6670 126th Ave (at Blue Star Hwy & M–89), Fennville 269/543-4285, 800/493-5888 • gay/ straight • full brkfst • gay-owned

### BARS

**Dunes Disco** 333 Blue Star Hwy (at the Dunes Resort) 269/857–1401 • 9am-2am • lesbians/ gay men • dancing/DJ • transgender-friendly • cabaret • patio • gay-owned

### CAFES

**Uncommon Grounds** 127 Hoffman (at Water) 269/857–3333 • 6:30am-10pm • coffee & juice bar • WiFi

### RESTAURANTS

**Back Alley Pizza Joint** 22 Main St (at Center), Douglas 269/857–7277 • 11am-10pm, till 11pm Fri-Sat • fresh grinder bread daily

**Everyday People Cafe** 11 Center St (at Main), Douglas 269/857-4240 • call for hours • wheelchair access

**Marro's Italian** 147 Water St (at Mason St) 269/857-4248 • dinner only, clsd Mon-Tue, nightclub till 2am Fri-Sat

**Monroe's Cafe-Grille** 302 Culver St (at Griffith) 269/857–1242 • 8am-9pm, clsd Nov-March • great brkfst

**Phil's Bar & Grille** 215 Butler St (at Mason) 269/857–1555 • 11:30am-10pm, till 11pm Fri-Sat • patio

**Scooters** 322 Culver St (at Griffith) 269/857–1041 • noon-9pm, till 10pm wknds, clsd Tue • great pizza

**The White House Bistro** 149 Griffith (at Mason) 269/857–3240 • 4pm-10pm, 9am-midnight Sat, 9am-9pm Sun • live music

**Wicks Park** 449 Water St 269/857–2888 • dinner nightly • live music wknds • wheelchair access

**Wild Dog Grill** 24 W Center St (at Spring), Douglas 269/857–2519 • dinner nightly, from noon wknds, clsd Mon-Tue

### ENTERTAINMENT & RECREATION

**Earl's Farm Market** 1630 Blue Star Hwy, Fennville 269/227–2074 • 8am-9pm May-Oct only • pick your own berries! • gay-owned

**Oval Beach** consult local map for driving directions, Douglas • popular beach on Lake Michigan

**Tulip Time Festival** Holland 800/822–2770

### RETAIL SHOPS

**Amaru Leather** 322 Griffith St (at Hoffman St) 269/857–3745 • "original & custom creations in leather by two resident designers"

**Groovy! Groovy! Retro Gift Gallery** 56 Blue Star Hwy (at Center St), Douglas 269/857–5211 • seasonal hours • antiques, funky gifts & goods • gay-owned

**Hoopdee Scootee** 133 Mason (at Butler) 269/857–4141 • seasonal • clothing • gifts

**Saugatuck Drug Store** 201 Butler St (at Mason) 269/857–2300 • seasonal • old-fashioned corner drug store, including actual soda fountain!

### GYMS & HEALTH CLUBS

**Pump House Gym** 6492 Blue Star Hwy (at 135th) 269/857–7867 • day passes

## South Haven

### ACCOMMODATIONS

**Yelton Manor B&B** 140 North Shore Dr (at Dyckman) 269/637–5220 • gay/ straight • full brkfst • nonsmoking • WiFi • wheelchair access

## St Ignace

### ACCOMMODATIONS

**Budget Host Inn & Suites** 700 N State St 906/643-9666, 800/872-7057 • gay-friendly • pool • facing harbor of Lake Huron & across from ferries to Mackinac Island • WiFi • kids/ pets ok • wheelchair access

## Traverse City

### ACCOMMODATIONS

**Neahtawanta Inn** 1308 Neahtawanta Rd (at Peninsula Dr) **231/223–7315, 800/220–1415** • gay-friendly • swimming • sauna • nonsmoking • WiFi • wheelchair access

### NIGHTCLUBS

**Side Traxx** 520 Franklin St (at E 8th) **231/935–1666** • 5pm-2am • lesbians/ gay men • dancing/DJ • videos • gay-owned

### BOOKSTORES

**The Bookie Joint** 124 S Union St (btwn State & Front) **231/946–8862** • noon-6pm, clsd Sun • pride gifts • used books

## Union Pier

### ACCOMMODATIONS

**Blue Fish Guest House & Cottage** 10234 Community Hall Rd **269/469–0468 x112** • gay/ straight • cottages & guesthouses available • some shared baths • nonsmoking • kids/ pets ok • gay-owned

**Fire Fly Resort** 15657 Lakeshore Rd **269/469–0245** • gay/ straight • 1- & 2–bdrm units • kitchens • nonsmoking • gay-owned

## Ypsilanti

see also Ann Arbor

# MINNESOTA

## Duluth

see also Superior, Wisconsin

### ACCOMMODATIONS

**The Olcott House B&B Inn** 2316 E 1st St (at 23rd Ave) **218/728–1339, 800/715–1339** • gay-friendly • nonsmoking • WiFi • gay-owned

### BARS

**Duluth Flame** 28 N 1st Ave W **218/727–2344** • 3pm-2:30am • lesbians/ gay men • dancing/DJ • live entertainment • karaoke • drag shows

### CAFES

**Amazing Grace Bakery & Cafe** 394 Lake Ave S **218/723–0075** • 7am-9pm, till 10pm Fri-Sat • live shows • plenty veggie/vegan • WiFi

**Jitters** 102 W Superior St **218/720–6015** • 7am-7pm, 8am-5pm Sat, 9am-1pm Sun • WiFi

### RESTAURANTS

**At Sara's Table Chester Creek Cafe** 1902 E 8th St (at 19th) **218/724–6811** • 7am-8pm • live music • WiFi • wheelchair access • women-owned

## Lanesboro

### ACCOMMODATIONS

**Stone Mill Hotel & Suites** 100 E Beacon St (at Parkway Ave) **507/467–8663, 866/897-8663** • gay/ straight • WiFi • non-smoking • wheelchair access • gay-owned

## Mankato

### CAFES

**The Coffee Hag** 329 N Riverfront Dr **507/387–5533** • 7am-10pm, till 11pm Fri-Sat • veggie menu • live shows • wheelchair access • women-owned

## Minneapolis/ St Paul

### INFO LINES & SERVICES

**AA Intergroup** 952/922-0880

**OutFront Minnesota** 310 E 38th St #204, Minneapolis **612/822–0127, 800/800–0350** • info line w/ 24hr pre-recorded visitor info

**Quatrefoil Library** 1220 East Lake St, Minneapolis **612/729–2543** • 7pm-9pm, 10am-5pm Sat, 1pm-5pm Sun • LGBT library & resource center

### ACCOMMODATIONS

**The Depot Renaissance Minneapolis** 225 3rd Ave S, Minneapolis **612/375–1700, 866/211-4611** • gay-friendly • bar & restaurant • ice rink and water park

**Graves 601 Hotel** 601 1st Ave N (at 6th St N), Minneapolis **612/677–1100, 866/523–1100** • gay-friendly • WiFi • gym • restaurant & bar

**Hotel 340** 340 Cedar St **651/280–4120** • gay-friendly • boutique hotel on the upper 3 floors of the Saint Paul Athletic Club • pool • WiFi

**Le Meridien Chambers** 901 Hennepin Ave, Minneapolis **612/767–6900, 800/543–4300** • gay-friendly • art-filled hotel •restaurant & bar • WiFi • kids/ pets ok • wheelchair access

**Namaste Cafe** 2512 Hennepin Ave S, Minneapolis **612/827–2496** • 11am-10pm, full bar, great Indian & Napali food

**Water Street Inn** 101 S Water St, Stillwater **651/439-6000** • gay-friendly • full brkfst • WiFi • wheelchair access • also restaurant & pub

## Bars

**19 Bar** 19 W 15th St (at Nicollet Ave), Minneapolis **612/871-5553** • 3pm-2am, from 1pm wknds • mostly gay men • neighborhood bar • wheelchair access

**Bev's Wine Bar** 250 3rd Ave N #100 (at Washington Ave), Minneapolis **612/337-0102** • 4:30pm-1am • gay-friendly • food served • patio • wheelchair access

**Brass Rail** 422 Hennepin Ave (at 4th), Minneapolis **612/332-7245** • noon-2am • popular • mostly gay men • karaoke • videos • wheelchair access

**Bryant Lake Bowl** 810 W Lake St (near Bryant), Minneapolis **612/825-3737** • 8am-2am • gay-friendly • bowling alley • also theater • restaurant • plenty veggie/ vegan • wheelchair access

**Camp Bar** 490 N Robert St (at 9th St), St Paul **651/292-1844** • 4pm-2am • mostly gay men • dancing/DJ • karaoke • male dancers • videos • also restaurant • wheelchair access

**Jetset** 115 N First St (at 1st Ave N), Minneapolis **612/339-3933** • 5pm-close, from 6pm Sat, clsd Sun-Mon • lesbians/ gay men • dancing/DJ • karaoke • nonsmoking

**Lush Food Bar** 990 Central Ave (at Spring St), Minneapolis • 8am-2am, clsd Mon• lesbians/ gay men • dancing/DJ • cabaret • drag shows • food served, brunch everyday till 2pm

**The Town House** 1415 University Ave W (at Elbert), St Paul **651/646-7087** • 2pm-2am, from noon wknds • popular • lesbians/ gay men • dancing/DJ • food served • karaoke • drag shows • piano bar • women-owned

## Nightclubs

**Gay 90s** 408 Hennepin Ave (at 4th St S), Minneapolis **612/333-7755** • 8am-2am (dinner Wed-Sun) • popular • mostly gay men • dancing/DJ • multiracial • karaoke • drag shows Wed-Sun • 18+ • wheelchair access

**Ground Zero** 15 NE 4th St (at Hennepin), Minneapolis **612/378-5115** • 10pm-2am Th-Sat only • gay/ straight • more gay Sat for Bondage-A-Go-Go • dancing/DJ • live shows • wheelchair access

**Kitty Cat Klub** 315 14th Ave SE (at SE University Ave) **612/331-9800** • gay-friendly • lounge w/ eclectic decor • food served • live bands

**The Saloon** 830 Hennepin Ave (at 9th), Minneapolis **612/332-0835** • noon-2am, from 11am Sun • lesbians/ gay men • dancing/DJ • food served • young crowd • wheelchair access • gay-owned

## Cafes

**Black Dog Coffee & Wine Bar** 308 Prince St (at Broadway), St Paul **651/228-9274** • 7am-10pm, till 11pm Fri-Sat, 8am-8pm Sun • food served • beer & wine

**Blue Moon** 3822 E Lake St, Minneapolis **612/721-9230** • 7am-10pm, from 8am wknds • WiFi • lesbian-owned

**Cahoots** 1562 Selby Ave (at Snelling), St Paul **651/644-6778** • 6:30am-10:30pm, from 7am wknds • coffee bar • WiFi • wheelchair access

**Moose & Sadie's** 212 3rd Ave N (at 2nd St), Minneapolis **612/371-0464** • 7am-8pm, 9am-2pm wknds • WiFi • wheelchair access

**Uncommon Grounds** 2809 Hennepin Ave (at W 28th St), Minneapolis **612/872-4811** • noon-midnight, till 1am Fri-Sat • outdoor seating

**The Urban Bean** 3255 Bryant Ave S (at 33rd), Minneapolis **612/824-6611** • 6:30am-11pm, from 7:30am Sun • patio • WiFi • wheelchair access

**Wilde Roast Cafe** 65 Main St SE (at Hennepin Ave), Minneapolis **612/331-4544** • 7am-10pm • beer/ wine • wheelchair access • gay-owned

## Restaurants

**Al's Breakfast** 413 14th Ave SE (at 4th), Minneapolis **612/331-9991** • 6am-1pm, from 9am Sun • popular • great hash

**Barbette** 1600 W Lake St (at Irving), Minneapolis **612/827-5710** • 8am-1am, till 2am Fri-Sat • French/ American • women-owned

**Birchwood Cafe** 3311 E 25th St, Minneapolis **612/722-4474** • 7am-9pm, from 8am Sat, 9am-8pm Sun • veggie/ vegan • WiFi • wheelchair access

**Brasa Premium Rotisserie** 600 E Hennepin, Minneapolis **612/379-3030** • 11am-9pm, till 10pm Fri-Sat • beer/ wine • wheelchair access

**French Meadow** 2610 Lyndale Ave S, Minneapolis **612/870-7855** • 6:30am-9pm, till 10pm Fri-Sat• organic & local • plenty veggie/ vegan • beer/ wine

**Hard Times Cafe** 1821 Riverside Ave, Minneapolis **612/341-9261** • 6am-4am • vegan/vegetarian • punk rock ambiance • WiFi

**Hell's Kitchen** 80 9th St S, Minneapolis **612/332-4700** • 7:30am-10pm, till 2am Fri-Sat• great brkfst & free music wknds 11am-2pm

**Loring Kitchen & Bar** 1359 Willow St, Minneapolis **612/843-0400** • 11am-11pm, till 1am Fri-Sat, from 9am Sat-Sun • delicious food w/ an enticing bar • gay-owned

**Lucia's Restaurant & Wine Bar** 1432 W 31st St, Minneapolis **612/825-1572** • lunch & dinner, clsd Mon • wheelchair access

**Monte Carlo** 219 3rd Ave N, Minneapolis **612/333-5900** • lunch & dinner, bar till 1am • wheelchair access

**Murray's** 26 S 6th St (at Hennepin), Minneapolis **612/339-0909** • lunch Mon-Fri, dinner nightly • steak & seafood

**Nye's Polonaise** 112 E Hennepin Ave, Minneapolis **612/379-2021** • 4pm-2am, from 11am Fri-Sat • piano bar • live polka & bands • full bar

**Psycho Suzi's Motor Lounge** 2519 Marshall St NE, Minneapolis **612/788-9069** • 11am-2am • pu-pu's & pizza • live music • wheelchair access

**Punch Neapolitan Pizza** 704 Cleveland Ave S, St Paul **651/696-1066** • 11am-9:30pm • wheelchair access • also at 210 E Hennepin Ave

**Red Stag Supperclub** 509 1st Ave NE (at 5th St), Minneapolis **612/767-7766** • 11am-2am, from 9am Sat-Sun • live music • wheelchair access

**Restaurant Alma** 528 University Ave SE, Minneapolis **612/379-4909** • dinner nightly, organic New American

**Seward Cafe** 2129 E Franklin Ave, Minneapolis **612/332-1011** • 7am-3pm, 8am-4pm wknds • vegetarian/vegan • wheelchair access

**Toast Wine Bar & Cafe** 415 N 1st St (in the Heritage Landing Bldg) **612/333-4305** • 5pm-11pm, till midnight Fri-Sat

### ENTERTAINMENT & RECREATION

**Calhoun 32nd Beach** 3300 E Calhoun Pkwy (33rd & Calhoun Blvd), Minneapolis **612/230-6400**

**Minnesota RollerGirls** • MN's female roller derby league • visit www.mnrollergirls.com for events

### RETAIL SHOPS

**The Rainbow Road** 109 W Grant St (at LaSalle), Minneapolis **612/872-8448** • 10am-10pm • LGBT • wheelchair access

### PUBLICATIONS

**Lavender Magazine** **612/436-4660, 877/515-9969** • LGBT newsmagazine for IA, MN, ND, SD, WI

**Minnesota Women's Press** 970 Raymond Ave #201, St Paul **651/646-3968** • newspaper

**Scene** **612/886-3151** • LGBTQA Twin Cities publication

### EROTICA

**Fantasy Gifts** 1437 University Ave, St Paul **651/256-7484** • noon-8pm, clsd Sun-Tue

**The Smitten Kitten** 3010 Lyndale Ave S, Minneapolis **612/721-6088, 888/751-0523** • 11am-9pm, noon-7pm Sun • transgender-friendly • lesbian-owned

## Moorhead

**see also Fargo, North Dakota**

### CAFES

**Atomic Coffee & Wine Bar** 805 30th Ave S **218/477-6161** • 6:30am-11pm, 7:30am-8pm Sun

# MISSISSIPPI

## Biloxi

### BARS

**Club Veaux** 834 Howard Ave **228/207-3271** • 4pm-4am • mostly gay men • dancing/DJ • drag shows

**Just Us Lounge** 906 Division St (at Caillavet) **228/374-1007** • 24hrs • lesbians/gay men • neighborhood bar • live shows • dancing/DJ • drag shows • go-go boys • karaoke

## Jackson

### INFO LINES & SERVICES

**Lambda AA** 5400 Old Canton Rd (at Saint Phillips Episcopal Church) **601/856-5337** • 6:30pm Mon

## BARS

**Jack's Construction Site (JC's)** 425 N Mart Plaza **601/362–3108** • 5pm-2am, from 7pm Wed & Fri-Sat, clsd Mon • mostly gay men • more women Wed & Fri • neighborhood bar • BYOB • WiFi

**Metro Reloaded** 4670 Hwy 80 West • 10:30pm-6am Sat & Sun • dancing/DJ • ladies night Fri, boys night Sat

**Metro Reloaded** 4670 Hwy 80 West • 10:30pm-6am Sat & Sun • dancing/DJ • ladies night Fri, boys night Sat

## Natchez

### ACCOMMODATIONS

**Historic Oak Hill Inn B&B** 409 S Rankin St (at Orleans St) **601/446–2500, 601/446–8641** • antebellum mansion near the Mississippi • nonsmoking • WiFi • gay-owned

**Mark Twain Guesthouse** 25 Silver St **601/446–8023** • above Under the Hill Saloon

### BARS

**Under the Hill Saloon** 25 Silver St **601/446–8023** • 10am-close • gay-friendly • neighborhood bar • live music • WiFi

# MISSOURI

## Branson

see also **Springfield & Eureka Springs, Arkansas**

## Cape Girardeau

### NIGHTCLUBS

**Independence Place** 5 S Henderson St (at Independence, at Holiday Happenings) **573/334–2939** • 8:30pm-1:30am, from 7pm Fri-Sat, clsd Sun • lesbians/ gay men • dancing/DJ • transgender-friendly • drag shows

## Columbia

### BARS

**The Arch & Column Pub** 1301 Business Loop 70 E (at College) **573/441–8088** • 5:30pm-1:30am, clsd Sun clsd Sun • mostly men • neighborhood bar • karaoke • wheelchair access • gay-owned

### CAFES

**Ernie's Cafe** 1005 E Walnut St (at 10th) **573/874–7804** • 6:30am-2pm

**Uprise Baker/ RagTag Cinema** 10 Hitt St (Broadway) **573/443–4359, 573/441–8504** • 5pm-close, from 2pm wknds • independent & alternative cinema • also theater, music & dance • food served • beer & wine

### RESTAURANTS

**Main Squeeze** 28 S 9th St (at Cherry St) **573/817–5616** • 10am-8pm, till 5pm Sun • local organic ingredients • vegetarian • WiFi • wheelchair access

### BOOKSTORES

**The Peace Nook** 804 C East Broadway (btwn 8th & 9th) **573/875–0539** • 10am-9pm, noon-6pm Sun • LGBT section • books • pride products

### EROTICA

**Bocomo Bay** 1122–A Wilkes Blvd **573/443–0873** • smoke shop too

## Hannibal

### ACCOMMODATIONS

**Garden House B&B** 301 N 5th St (at Bird) **573/221–7800, 866/423–7800** • gay-friendly • WiFi • nonsmoking • gay-owned

**Rockcliffe Mansion B&B** 1000 Bird St (at 10th St) **573/221–4140, 877/423–4140** • gay-friendly • guilded-age Mansion built in 1898 on a limestone bluff • nonsmoking • WiFi • gay-owned

### RESTAURANTS

**LaBinnah Bistro** 207 N 5th St (at Center) **573/221–7800** • dinner only, clsd Mon • in a Victorian home • beer/ wine • gay-owned

## Joplin

### INFO LINES & SERVICES

**Joplin Pride Center (Gay Lesbian Center)** **401/595-0061** • a community center & clearinghouse for gay & lesbian events in the greater Joplin, MO area

## Kansas City

see also **Kansas City & Overland Park, Kansas**

### INFO LINES & SERVICES

**The LIKEME Lighthouse** 3909 Main St • noon-8pm, till 6pm • Sun LGBT community center founded by country music star, Chely Wright

**Live & Let Live AA** 3901 Main St #211 (at 39th) **816/531–9668** • 6pm daily, noon Sun

## ACCOMMODATIONS

**Hotel Phillips** 816/221–7000, 800/433–1426 • gay-friendly • art deco landmark in downtown KC

**Q Hotel & Spa** 560 Westport Rd (at Mill St) **816/931–0001, 800/942–4233** • gay-friendly • in Westport district • WiFi • wheelchair access

**The Raphael** 325 Ward Pkwy (at Wornall Rd) 816/756–3800, 800/821–5343 • gay-friendly • WiFi • also restaurant

**Southmoreland on the Plaza** 116 E 46th St (at Main St) **816/531–7979** • gay-friendly • 1913 B&B • full brkfst • veranda • nonsmoking

## BARS

**Buddies** 3715 Main St (at 37th) 816/561–2600 • 6am-3am, clsd Sun, mostly gay men, neighborhood bar

**Missie B's/ Bootleggers** 805 W 39th St (at SW Trafficway) 816/561–0625 • noon-3am • lesbians/ gay men • neighborhood bar • dancing/DJ • transgender-friendly • live shows • karaoke • drag shows

**Sidekicks** 3707 Main St (at 37th) **816/931–1430** • 1pm-3am, from 4pm Sun, clsd Mon • lesbians/ gay men • dancing/DJ • country/ western • drag shows • wheelchair access

## CAFES

**Broadway Cafe** 4106 Broadway (at Westport) **816/531–2432** • 7am-9pm • food served • nonsmoking • also 412 Washington

## RESTAURANTS

**Beer Kitchen** 435 Westport Rd (at Pennsylvania) 816/389–4180 • 11am-3am, from 10am wknds • gastro pub • live music

**Bistro 303** 303 Westport Rd 816/753–2303 • open 3pm, from 11am Sat-Sun • patio • wheelchair access • gay-owned

**Blue Bird Bistro** 1700 Summit St (at W 17th St) **816/221–7559** • 7am-10pm, 10am-2pm Sun • organic fare • wheelchair access

**Cafe Trio/ Starlet Lounge** 4558 Main St 816/756–3227 • 11am-10pm. till 11pm Sat, 4pm-9pm Sun • piano bar • gay-owned

**Chubby's** 3756 Broadway St (at 38th) 816/931–2482 • open 24hrs • popular late nights • diner fare • wheelchair access

**Classic Cup Cafe** 301 W 47th St (at Central) 816/753–1840 • brkfst, lunch, dinner, Sun brunch • great appetizers • wheelchair access

**Grand Street Cafe** 4740 Grand St (at 47th St) **816/561–8000** • lunch & dinner, Sun brunch • patio seating • nonsmoking • wheelchair access

**Hamburger Mary's KC** 101 Southwest Blvd (at Baltimore Ave) **816/842–1919** • 11am-1:30am, clsd Mon • full bar• theme nights • karaoke • live entertainment • food served • juicy burgers w/ a side of camp

**Le Fou Frog** 400 E 5th St (at Oak St) 816/474–6060 • dinner only • French bistro

**McCoy's Public House** 4057 Pennsylvania Ave 816/960–0866 • 11am-3am, till midnight Sun • huge patio

**The Mixx** 4855 Main St (at W 48th) **816/756–2300** • lunch & dinner • fast & healthy • huge selection of salads • wheelchair access

**Tannin Wine Bar** 816/842–2660 • 11:30am-1:30am, from 4pm wknds • wine & cheese flights • full dinner menu • patio seating

**YJ's Snack Bar** 128 W 18th St (at W Baltimore Ave) **816/472–5533** • 8am-10pm, 24hrs Th-Sat • inexpensive • wheelchair access

## ENTERTAINMENT & RECREATION

**First Fridays Art Walk** Crossroads District (Baltimore & 20th) 816/994–9325 • 5pm-10pm 1st Fri • art gallery walk • also live music & vendors

**Kansas City Roller Warriors** 816/809–8496 • KC's female roller derby league • visit kcrollerwarriors.com for events

**Nelson-Atkins Museum** 4525 Oak St 816/751–1278 • American Indian galleries

## EROTICA

**Erotic City** 8401 E Truman Rd (off I–435, at Alice Ave) 816/252–3370

# Osage Beach

## ACCOMMODATIONS

**Utopian Inn** 1962 Alcorn Hollow Rd, Roach 573/347–3605 • lesbians/ gay men • 3 bdrm rental on a lake • kids/ small pets ok • nonsmoking • gay-owned

# Overland

## EROTICA

**Patricia's** 10210 Page Ave (E of Ashby) 314/423–8422

## Springfield

### INFO LINES & SERVICES

**AA Gay/ Lesbian** 518 E Commercial St 417/823–7125 (AA #) • 6pm Sat • nonsmoking

**Gay & Lesbian Community Center of the Ozarks** 518 E Commercial St 417/869–3978 • many groups • newsletter • wheelchair access

### BARS

**Martha's Vineyard** 219 W Olive St (at S Patton) 417/864–4572 • 5pm-1:30am, from 2pm Sun, clsd Mon • lesbians/ gay men • neighborhood bar • dancing/DJ • drag shows • Th women's night • patio • wheelchair access • cover charge wknds

**Mud Lounge** 321 E Walnut 417/865–6964 • 4pm-1:30am, clsd Sun • food served

### NIGHTCLUBS

**Mix Ultralounge** 1221 E Saint Louis St 417/866–7166 • 5pm-1:30am, from 3pm Sun • lesbians/gay men • dancing/DJ • karaoke

### CAFES

**Mudhouse** 323 South Ave 417/832–1720 • 7am-midnight, 9am-8pm Sun • food served

### BOOKSTORES

**Renaissance Books & Gifts** 1337 E Montclair St 417/883–5161 • 10am-6:30pm, noon-5pm Sun • women's/ alternative • wheelchair access

### EROTICA

**Patricia's** 1918 S Glenstone (at E Cherokee) 417/881–8444

## St Louis

### ACCOMMODATIONS

**A St Louis Guesthouse** 1032 Allen Ave (at Menard) 314/773–1016 • mostly gay men • located in historic Soulard district • hot tub (nudity ok) • nonsmoking • WiFi • gay-owned

**Brewers House B&B** 1829 Lami St (at Lemp) 314/771–1542, 888/767–4665 • lesbians/ gay men • 1860s home • jacuzzi • pets ok • nonsmoking • WiFi • gay-owned

**The Cheshire** 6300 Clayton Rd 314/647–7300 • gay/ straight • pool • WiFi

**Dwell 912 B&B** 912 Hickory St (at S 9th St) 314/599–3100 • gay-friendly • nonsmoking • WiFi • gay-owned

**Grand Center Inn** 3716 Grandel Sq (at N Grand Blvd) 314/533–0771 • gay/ straight • WiFi • nonsmoking • gay-owned

### BARS

**Bar: PM** 7109 S Broadway (at Blow St) 314/835–7251 • 5pm-1:30am • lesbians/gay men • dancing/DJ • drag/live shows

**Cicero's** 6691 Delmar Blvd (at Kingsland Ave), University City 314/862–0009 • 11am-12:30am, till 11pm Sun • gay/ straight • Italian restaurant • live music venue

**Club Escapades** 133 W Main St (at 2nd), Belleville, IL 618/222–9597 • 6pm-2am, clsd Sun-Tue • lesbians/ gay men • dancing/DJ • drag shows • food served • karaoke • live shows • WiFi

**Erney's 32 Degree** 4200 Manchester Ave (at Boyle) 314/652–7195 • 7pm-3am, clsd Mon • mostly gay men • dancing/DJ

**Grey Fox Pub** 3503 S Spring (at Potomac) 314/772–2150 • 2pm-1:30am, noon-midnight Sun • lesbians/ gay men • neighborhood bar • drag shows • transgender-friendly • patio

**Hummel's Pub** 7101S Broadway (at Blow St) 314/353–5080 • 11am-1am, from 2pm Mon • lesbians/ gay men • neighborhood bar • full menu • karaoke • lesbian-owned

**I Don't Know Bar** 102 Evans Lane 314/521-9990 • 10am-1am, clsd Sun • lesbians/gay men

**Just John** 4112 Manchester Ave 314/371–1333 • 3pm-3am, from noon-1am Sun • lesbians/ gay men • neighborhood bar • dancing/DJ Fri-Sat • drag shows • karaoke • videos

**Keypers Piano Bar** 2280 S Jefferson (at Shenandoah) 314/664–6496 • 1pm-1:30am, 2pm-midnight Sun, patio • lesbians/ gay men • piano bar • food served • patio

**Meyer's Grove** 4510 Manchester Ave 314/932–7003 • 4pm-1:30pm, till midnight Sun • lesbians/ gay men • drag shows

**Rehab Lounge** 4052 Chouteau Ave (at Boyle) 314/652–3700 • 11:30am-1:30am • gay/ straight • neighborhood bar • also restaurant

**Rosie's Place** 4573 Laclede Ave 314/361–6423 • 11am-1:30am • gay/ straight • neighborhood bar

**Soulard Bastille** 1027 Russell Blvd (at Menard) 314/664–4408 • 11am-1:30am • mostly gay men • neighborhood bar

**Sub Zero Vodka Bar** 308 N Euclid Ave 314/367–1200 • 11:30am-1:30am • gay/ straight • full menu includes sushi and burgers

## NIGHTCLUBS

**Atomic Cowboy** 4140 Manchester Ave (btwn Kentucky & Talmadge) 314/775-0775 • 11am-3am, from 5pm Sat-Sun • gay/ straight • dancing/DJ • live shows • burlesque • also Fresh-Mex Mayan grill • art lounge • WiFi • patio

**Attitudes** 4100 Manchester Ave (at S Sarah) 314/534-0044 • 7pm-3am, clsd Mon • popular • lesbians/ gay men • dancing/DJ • drag shows • karaoke

**The Back Door** 9212 St Charles Rock Rd ( lower level of O.T.Saloon, enterance is at rear of building) 314/426-9990 • open 6pm, clsd Mon-Tue • mostly women • dancing/DJ • karaole

**Bubby & Sissy's** 602 Belle St (at 6th St), Alton, IL 618/465-4773 • 3pm-2am, till 3am Fri-Sat • lesbians/ gay men • dancing/DJ • live shows • karaoke • drag shows • food served • wheelchair access

**Honey** 4170 Manchester Rd 314/932-1211 • 6pm-3am, clsd Mon • gay/straight • dancing/DJ

## CAFES

**Coffee Cartel** 2 Maryland Plaza (at Euclid) 314/454-0000 • 24hrs • popular • food served • WiFi • wheelchair access

**MoKaBe's** 3606 Arsenal (at S Grand) 314/865-2009 • 8am-midnight, from 9am Sun • popular • plenty veggie • occasional shows • wheelchair access

**Soulard Coffee Garden Cafe** 910 Geyer Ave (btwn 9th & 10th) 314/241-1464 • 6:30am-4pm, from 8am wknds • food served • WiFi • wheelchair access

## RESTAURANTS

**Billie's Diner** 1802 S Broadway 314/621-0848 • 5am-2:30pm, midnight-1:30pm wknds • wheelchair access

**Cafe Osage** 4605 Olive St 314/454-6868 • 7am-2pm, till 5pm Th-Sat, from 9am Sun

**City Diner** 3139 S Grand Blvd 314/772-6100 • 7am-11pm, 24hrs Fri-Sat, till 10pm Sun • wheelchair access

**Dressel's** 419 N Euclid (at McPherson) 314/361-1060 • 11am-1am, till midnight Sun • great Welsh pub food • full bar • live shows • wheelchair access

**Eleven Eleven Mississippi** 1111 Mississippi 314/241-9999 • lunch Mon-Fri, dinner nightly, clsd Sun • wine country bistro

**Joanie's Pizza** 2101 Menard St 314/865-1994 • 11am-11pm, till midnight wknds

**Majestic Cafe** 4900 Laclede Ave (at Euclid) 314/361-2011 • 6am-10pm, bar till 1:30am • Greek-American diner fare • wheelchair access

**Mango** 1101 Lucas Ave 314/621-9993 • 11am-10pm, bar till 1:30am Fri-Sat, 4pm-9pm Sun • Latin American/ Peruvian

**Meskerem** 3210 S Grand Blvd 314/772-4442 • lunch & dinner • Ethiopian • plenty veggie

**Mojo Tapas** 3117 S Grand Blvd (at Arsenal St) 314/865-0500 • 4pm-11pm, full bar till 1:30am

**Molly's in Soulard** 816 Geyer Ave 314/241-6200 • 11am-9pm, full bar till 1:30am • old-world New Orleans charm • live music • huge patio

**Pappy's Smokehouse** 3106 Olive St 314/535-4340 • 11am-8pm, till 4pm Sun • excellent BBQ

**Rue 13** 1311 Washington 314/588-7070 • 5pm-3am, clsd Sun-Mon • sushi • full bar • dancing/DJ • burlesque

**Ted Drewes Frozen Custard** 6726 Chippewa (at Jameson) 314/481-2652, 314/481-2124 • 11am-10pm • seasonal • a St Louis landmark • also 4224 S Grand Blvd, 314/352-7376 • wheelchair access

**Three Monkey's** 153 Morgan Ford Rd 314/772-9800 • 11am-1:30am

**Tony's** 410 Market St (at Broadway) 314/231-7007 • dinner only, clsd Sun-Mon • Italian fine dining • reservations advised • wheelchair access

**Van Goghz** 3200 Shenandoah (at Compton) 314/865-3345 • 11am-11pm, till 1:30am Fri-Sat, 9:30am-3pm Sun • also bar • WiFi • wheelchair access

**Vin de Set** 2017 Chouteau Ave (at S 21st St) 314/241-8989 • lunch & dinner, dinner only wknds, clsd Mon • rooftop bar & bistro • wheelchair access

**The Wild Flower Restaurant & Bar** 4590 Laclede Ave (at Euclid) 314/367-9888 • lunch & dinner, bar till 1:30am, clsd Tue, Sun brunch • wheelchair access

## BOOKSTORES

**Left Bank Books** 399 N Euclid Ave (at McPherson) 314/367-6731 • 10am-10pm, 11am-6pm Sun • popular • feminist & LGBT titles • also at 321 N 10th St

## RETAIL SHOPS

**CheapTRX** 3209 S Grand Blvd (at Wyoming St) 314/664-4011 • alternative shopping • body piercing • tattoos • wheelchair access

### PUBLICATIONS

**Vital Voice** 314/256–1196 • bi-weekly news & features publication

### EROTICA

**Patricia's** 3552 Gravois Ave (at Grand) 314/664–4040 • 10am-10pm, till midnight Fri-Sat • fetish clothes • toys • videos

## MONTANA

### Billings

#### BARS

**The Loft** 1123 1st Ave N (at 12th) 406/259–9074 • 10am-2am • lesbians/ gay men • dancing/DJ • karaoke • shows • wheelchair access

#### EROTICA

**Big Sky Books** 1203 1st Ave N (at 12th St) 406/259–0051 • 9am-3am, 10am-2am Sun

**The Victorian** 2019 Minnesota Ave (at 21st) 406/245–4293 • noon-midnight, clsd Sun-Mon • fireplace & piano • HIV testing

### Bozeman

#### ACCOMMODATIONS

**Lehrkind Mansion Inn** 719 N Wallace Ave 406/585–6932 • gay/ straight • full brkfst • hot tub • nonsmoking • WiFi • gay-owned

#### CAFES

**The Nova Cafe** 312 E Main St (at Rouse Ave) 406/587–3973 • 7am-2pm

### Butte

#### RESTAURANTS

**Four Seasons** 3030 Elm St 406/723–3888 • 11am-9:30pm, from noon wknds • Chinese

**Matt's Place** 2339 Placer St (btwn Montana & Rowe) 406/782–8049 • 11:30am-7pm, clsd Sun-Mon • classic soda-fountain diner

**Pork Chop John's** 2400 Harrison Ave 406/782–1783 • 10:30am-10:30pm, clsd Sun • also 8 W Mercury, 406/782-0812

**Uptown Cafe** 47 E Broadway 406/723–4735 • lunch weekdays & dinner nightly • bistro • full bar • wheelchair access

### Great Falls

#### INFO LINES & SERVICES

**LGBTQ Center** 600 Central Ave #323 406/290–7338 • 3pm-7pm, 9am-1pm Wed, 2pm-6pm Sun

### Missoula

#### INFO LINES & SERVICES

**KISMIF Gay/ Lesbian AA** 405 University Ave (at church) 406/543–0011 • 7pm Mon

**Western Montana Gay/ Lesbian Community Center** 127 N Higgins Ave #202 406/543–2224 • LGBT resource center • call for hours

#### BARS

**The Oxford** 337 N Higgins Ave (at Pine) 406/549–0117 • popular • gay-friendly • 8am-2am • 24hr cafe & casino

#### CAFES

**The Catalyst** 111 N Higgins 406/542–1337 • 8am-3pm

#### RESTAURANTS

**Montana Club** 2620 Brooks 406/543–3200 • 6am-10pm, till 11pm Fri-Sat, casino open till 2am • full bar • wheelchair access

#### BOOKSTORES

**Fact & Fiction** 220 N Higgins 406/721–2881 • 9am-6pm, 10am-5pm Sat, noon-4pm Sun • many LGBT titles • wheelchair access

#### RETAIL SHOPS

**Jeannette Rankin Peace Center** 519 S Higgins Ave 406/543–3955 • 10am-6pm, noon-4pm Sun • fair trade gift store • peace resource center • events

### Swan Valley

#### ACCOMMODATIONS

**Holland Lake Lodge** 1947 Holland Lake Rd (at Hwy 83) 406/754–2282, 877/925–6343 • gay-friendly • resort w/ lakefront cabins • full brkfst • hot tub • kids ok • WiFi • restaurant & bar • wheelchair access • gay-owned

# NEBRASKA

## Lincoln

### INFO LINES & SERVICES

**Rainbow Group Gay/ Lesbian AA** 2325 S 24 St (at Sewell, at St Matthew's) **402/438–5214** • 7:30pm Mon & Fri

### BARS

**Panic** 200 S 18th St (at N St) **402/435–8764** • 4pm-1am, from 1pm wknds • lesbians/ gay men • live shows • WiFi • patio • wheelchair access • gay-owned

### NIGHTCLUBS

**Karma** 226 S 9th St (btwn M & N Sts) **402/261–6756** • 4pm-2am • lesbians/gay men • dancing/DJ • live shows • drag shows • 19+

### ENTERTAINMENT & RECREATION

**No Coast Derby Girls** • Lincoln's female roller derby league • visit www.nocoastderbygirls.com for events

## Omaha

### INFO LINES & SERVICES

**AA Gay/ Lesbian** 851 N 74th St (at Presbyterian Church) **402/556–1880** • 8:15pm Fri

### ACCOMMODATIONS

**Castle Unicorn** 57034 Deacon Rd (at Hwy 34 & I-29), Pacific Jct, IA **712/527–5930** • gay/ straight • medieval-style B&B • full brkfst • hot tub • WiFi • nonsmoking • patio • gay-owned

**The Cornerstone Mansion Inn** 140 N 39th St (at Dodge) **402/558–7600, 888/883–7745** • gay-friendly • fireplaces • brkfst served • nonsmoking • WiFi

### NIGHTCLUBS

**Flixx Lounge** 1019 S 10th St **402/408–1020** • 5pm-1am • mostly men • dancing/DJ • cabaret • drag shows

**The Max** 1417 Jackson St (at 15th St) **402/346–4110** • 4pm-2am • popular • mostly gay men • dancing/DJ Wed-Sun • drag shows • strippers patio • wheelchair access • cover charge Fri-Sat

### RESTAURANTS

**The Boiler Room** 1110 Jones St **402/916–9274** • dinner only, clsd Sun • full bar • wheelchair access

**California Tacos & More** 3235 California St **402/342–0212** • 11am-9pm, clsd Sun • beer/ wine • wheelchair access

**The Flatiron Cafe** 1722 St Marys Ave **402/345–7477** • dinner only, clsd Sun • full bar • wheelchair access

**M's Pub** 422 S 11th St **402/342–2550** • 11am-1am, from 5pm Sun • full bar • wheelchair access

**McFoster's Natural Kind Cafe** 302 S 38th St **402/345–7477** • lunch & dinner • vegetarian • full bar • wheelchair access

### ENTERTAINMENT & RECREATION

**Omaha Rollergirls** • Omaha's female roller derby league • visit www.omaharollergirls.org

# NEVADA

## Carson City

### ACCOMMODATIONS

**West Walker Motel** 106833 Hwy 395, Walker, CA **530/495–2263** • gay-friendly • WiFi • kids/ pets ok • in Toiyabe Nat'l Forest near West Walker River • women-owned

## Lake Tahoe

see Lake Tahoe, California

## Las Vegas

### INFO LINES & SERVICES

**Alcoholics Together** 900 E Karen, 2nd flr #A-202 (at Sahara, in Commercial Center) **702/598–1888** • 12:15pm & 8pm daily • call for other meeting times

**The Gay/ Lesbian Community Center of Southern Nevada** 401 S Maryland Pkwy **702/733–9800** • 11am-7pm, clsd wknds

### ACCOMMODATIONS

**Delano** 3950 Las Vegas Blvd S **702/632–9444** • gay-friendly • not downtown but great property

**El Cortez** 600 Fremont St (at 7th St) **702/385–5200, 800/634–6703** • gay-friendly • recently renovated, old-style Vegas glamour on Fremont St

**Paris, Las Vegas Resort & Casino** 3655 Las Vegas Blvd S **702/946–7000, 800/630–7933** • gay-friendly • also restaurants, bars, spas • LGBT honeymoon packages • see ad in front color section

**Vdara Hotel & Spa** 2600 W Harmon Ave **702/590–2767, 866/745–7767** • gay-friendly • pool • non-smoking

## BARS

**Badlands Saloon** 953 E Sahara #22 (in Commercial Center) **702/792–9262** • 24hrs • mostly gay men • neighborhood bar • dancing/DJ • country/ western • wheelchair access • gay-owned

**Bastille on 3rd** 1402 S 3rd St (at Imperial) **702/385–9298** • 24hrs • mostly gay men • neighborhood bar • in the Arts District

**Charlie's Las Vegas** 5012 S Arville St (at Tropicana) **702/876–1844** • popular • mostly gay men • dancing/DJ • country/ western • dance lessons 7pm-9pm Mon, Th-Sat • drag shows • wheelchair access

**Club Metro** 1000 E Sahara Ave **702/629–2368** • 4pm-5am • mostly gay men, 3rd Sat women's party • ultra-lounge and dance club •

**Flex** 4347 W Charleston (at Arville) **702/385–3539, 702/878–3355** • 24hrs • lesbians/ gay men • dancing/DJ • drag shows • strippers • wheelchair access

**Freezone** 610 E Naples **702/794–2300** • 24hrs • lesbians/ gay men • women's night Sun• neighborhood bar • dancing/DJ • transgender-friendly • drag shows Fri-Sat • karaoke • young crowd • also restaurant • gay-owned

**Goodtimes** 1775 E Tropicana Ave (at Spencer, in Liberace Plaza) **702/736–9494** • 24hrs • mostly gay men • neighborhood bar • dancing/DJ karaoke Wed • wheelchair access

**The Las Vegas Eagle** 3430 E Tropicana (at Pecos) **702/458–8662** • 24hrs • mostly gay men • leather • DJ Wed & Fri

**Las Vegas Lounge** 900 E Karen Ave (at Maryland Pkwy) **702/737–9350** • 24hrs • gay-friendly • neighborhood bar • mostly transgender

**Phoenix Bar & Lounge** 4213 W Sahara Ave **702/826–2422** • noon-4am • lesbians/ gay men • karaoke • wheelchair access • gay-owned

**The Spotlight Lounge** 975 E Sahara (at Commercial Center's entrance) **702/431–9775** • 24hrs • mostly gay men • neighborhood bar • Wifi

## NIGHTCLUBS

**Don't Tell Mama** 517 Fremont St #A (downtown) **702/207–0788** • 8pm-3am, clsd Mon • mostly gay men • great piano bar • wheelchair access

**Downtown Cocktail Room** 111 Las Vegas Blvd S **702/880–3696** • gay/straight • speakeasy with a warm bohemian-chic décor

**Insert Coins** 512 Fremont St **702/477–2525** • lesbian/gay men • 8pm-close, clsd Mon-Tue • dancing/DJ • arcade • gay-owned

**The Light Las Vegas** 3950 Las Vegas Blvd S (Mandalay Bay Las Vegas) **702/693–8300** • open Wed, Fri-Sat • gay/straight • dancing/DJ • nightclub by Cirque du Soleil

**Piranha** 4633 Paradise Rd (at Naples) **702/791–0100** • opens 10pm nightly • lesbians/ gay men • dancing/DJ • wheelchair access

**QueerKat** • check www.LesbiansInVegas.com for events • popular • mostly women • dancing/DJ • multiracial

**Revolution Lounge** 3400 Las Vegas Blvd S (at the Mirage) **702/791–7111** • 10pm-4am, clsd Tue • gay-friendly • psychedelic Beatles-influenced décor • gay night Sun

**Share Nighclub and Ultra Lounge** 4636 Wynn Rd **702/258–2681** • 6pm-2am, till 4am Mon, Th-Sat • mostly gay men • dancing/DJ

## CAFES

**Inspire News Cafe** 107 Las Vegas Blvd S **702/750–0017** • also rooftop lounge

## RESTAURANTS

**Bootlegger Bistro** 7700 S Las Vegas Blvd (btwn Windmill & Robindale) **702/736–4939** • 24hrs • a Vegas classic • Italian • musical entertainment nightly

**Border Grill** 3950 Las Vegas Blvd S (at the Mandalay Bay Resort & Casino) **702/632–7403** • 11:30am-close • Mexican • full bar • patio

**Chicago Joe's** 820 S 4th St (at Gass Ave) **702/382–5637** • 11am-10pm, from 5pm Sat, clsd Sun-Mon • old-school Italian • in downtown arts district

**Cupcakery** 7175 W Lake Mead **702/835–0060**

**Eat** 707 Carson (at 7th) **702/534–1515** • 8am-3pm, till 2pm wknd • the place for brkfst & lunch • lesbian-owned

**The Egg & I** 4533 W Sahara Ave (near Arville) **702/364–9686** • popular • 6am-3pm • wheelchair access

**Firefly** 3900 Paradise Rd #A **702/369–3971** • 11am-2am • tapas • also bar • wheelchair access

**Go Raw** 2381 E Windmill Ln 702/450-9007 • 8am-8pm, till 5pm Sun • organic vegan • also juice bar • also at 2910 Lake East Dr, 702/254-5382

**Grand Lux Cafe** 3355 Las Vegas Blvd S (at the Venetian) 702/414-3888 • open 24hrs • generous portions

**Lindo Michoacan** 2655 E Desert Inn Rd (near Eastern) 702/735-6828 • 11am-11pm, till midnight wknds • popular • Mexican

**Lotus of Siam** 953 E Sahara Ave #A-5 (in Commercial Center) 702/735-3033 • lunch Mon-Fri, dinner nightly • Thai • wheelchair access

**Mingo Kitchen & Lounge** 1017 S First St #180 (in the heart of the Arts District) 702/685-0328 • 11am-10pm, from 5pm Mon & Sat, till midnight Tue-Sat, from 11am-6pm Sun • gay owned

**Mon Ami Gabi** 3655 Las Vegas Blvd S (at Paris Las Vegas) 702/944-4224 • 7am-11pm • outdoor seating • wheelchair access

**Park on Fremont** 506 Fremont St 702/834-3160 • great outdoor comfort food dining

**The Perch** 707 Fremont St (in the Container Park) 702/854-1418 • fabulous, not fussy menu

**Society Cafe Encore** 3121 Las Vegas Blvd S (at Encore) 702/248-3463 • 7am-11pm, till 1am wknds • upscale American

**Stir Krazy Mongolian Gril** 4503 Paradise Rd (across from the Hard Rock ) 702/998-9994 • 11:30am-9pm, till 10pm Fri-Sat • Asian Cuisine Stir-Fry • gay-owned

## ENTERTAINMENT & RECREATION

**18b Arts District** bounded by Commerce St, Hoover Ave, Fourth St and Las Vegs Blvd (at Charleston and Colorado Ave) • mix of galleries, one-of-a-kind stores, and restaurants just a short walk or bus ride from Fremont St, aslo sponsor 1st Fridat festival

**Cupid's Wedding Chapel** 827 Las Vegas Blvd S (1 block N of Charleston) 702/598-4444, 800/543-2933 • commitment ceremonies • "Have the Vegas wedding you've always dreamed of!"

**Erotic Heritage Museum** 3275 Industrial Rd 702/369-6442 • 6pm-10pm Wed-Th, 3pm-midnight Fri, from noon wknds, clsd Mon-Tue

**Frank Marino's Divas Las Vegas** 3535 Las Vegas Blvd S (at the Imperial Palace) 702/794-3261, 888/777-7664 • show at 7:30pm • the biggest drag show in town: Frank Marino & friends impersonate the divas, from Joan Rivers to Tina Turner

**Onyx Theatre** 953 E Sahara Ave # 16A (at Maryland Pkwy) 702/732-7225 • alternative films & performances

**Sin City Rollergirls** • Vegas' female roller derby league • visit www.sincityrollergirls.com for events

**Thanks Babs, the Day Tripper** 702/370-6961 • tours, shows, attractions & getaways • full service concierge for Las Vegas, state of NV, & the Southwest • it's like having a lesbian aunt in Las Vegas!

**Viva Las Vegas Wedding Chapel** 1205 Las Vegas Blvd 800/574-4450 • gay-owned

## BOOKSTORES

**Get Booked** 4640 S Paradise Rd #15 (at Naples) 702/737-7780 • 10am-midnight, till 2am Fri-Sat • LGBT

## RETAIL SHOPS

**Glamour Boutique II** 714 E Sahara Ave #104 (at S 6th St) 702/697-1800, 866/692-1800 • clsd Sun • large-size dresses, wigs, etc

**Teazled** 6955 N Durango Dr #1115-123 702/823-1399 • lesbian-owned card shop

## PUBLICATIONS

**Las Vegas Night Beat** 702/369-8441 • monthly news & entertainment magazine

**QVegas** 702/650-0636 • monthly LGBT news & entertainment magazine

## GYMS & HEALTH CLUBS

**The Las Vegas Athletic Club** 2655 S Maryland Pkwy 702/734-5822 • day passes

## SEX CLUBS

**The Studios** 5150 S Pecos Rd 702/443-3732 • play space open to hetero, gay, bi, trans, men & women • free for women & trans people

## EROTICA

**Bare Essentials Fantasy Fashions** 4029 W Sahara Ave (near Valley View Blvd) 702/247-4711 • exotic/ intimate apparel • toys • gay-owned

**Rancho Adult Entertainment Center** 4820 N Rancho Dr (at Lone Mtn) 702/645-6104 • 24hrs

## Laughlin

**see Bullhead City, Arizona**

## Reno

### Accommodations

**Boomtown Hotel & Casino** 2100 Garson Rd, Verdi **775/345-6000, 800/648-3790** • gay-friendly •great live shows • restaurant • wheelchair access

**Silver Legacy Resort & Casino** 407 N Virginia St **775/325-7401, 800/687-8733** • gay-friendly • pool • restaurant & bar

**Whitney Peak Hotel** 255 N Virginia St **775/398-5400** • gay/straight • downtown Reno's only non-gaming, non-smoking boutique hotel

### Bars

**Cadillac Lounge** 1114 E 4th St (at Sutro) **775/324-7827** • noon-2am • lesbians/ gay men • neighborhood bar

**Chapel Tavern** 1099 S Virginia St (at Vassar) **775/324-2244** • 2pm-4am, from 10am wknds • gay/straight • patio

**Five Star Saloon** 132 West St (at 1st) **775/329-2878** • 5pm-5am, from 1pm Sat • gay/ straight • neighborhood bar • dancing/DJ • wheelchair access

**The Patio** 600 W 5th St (btwn Washington & Ralston) **775/323-6565** • 11am-2am • lesbians/ gay men • neighborhood bar • live shows • karaoke

### Restaurants

**4th Street Bistro** 3065 W 4th St **775/323-3200** • dinner nightly, clsd Sun-Mon • upscale • extensive wine list

**Brasserie Saint James** 901 S Center St **775/348-8888** • 11am-11pm, till 1am Fri-Sat, full bar • great roof deck

**The Daily Bagel** 495 Morill Ave # 102 **775/786-1611** • 6:30am-2pm, till 3pm Wed-Fri, 8am-2pm, Sat, clsd Sun

**Old Granite Street Eatery** 243 S Sierra St **775/622-3222** • 11am-11pm, from 10am wknds, full bar

**Pneumatic Diner** 501 W 1st St (in Truckee River Apts, 2nd flr) **775/786-8888 x106** • 11am-10pm, from 8am Sun • vegetarian

### Entertainment & Recreation

**Brüka Theatre** 99 N Virginia St **775/323-3221** • alternative theater & performance space

### Bookstores

**Sundance Books** 1155 W 4th St #106 (at Keystone) **775/786-1188** • 9am-9pm, 9am-5pm wknds • independent

### Publications

**Reno Gay Page** **775/453-4058** • monthly • bar & resource listings • community events • arts & entertainment

### Erotica

**Suzie's** 195 Kietzke Ln (at E 2nd St) **775/786-8557** • 24hrs

## Winnemucca

### Bars

**Cheers** 320 S Bridge St, Winnemuca **775/623-2660** • 9am-close • gay-friendly • neighborhood bar

# NEW HAMPSHIRE

## Concord

### Accommodations

**Idleday Guest Rooms** 180 W Parish Rd **603/520-6886, 603/753-6113** • women only • secluded setting on river • nonsmoking

## Manchester

### Accommodations

**Radisson Hotel Manchester** 700 Elm St **603/625-1000, 800/395-7046** • gay-friendly • food served • pool • kids/ pets ok • WiFi • wheelchair access

### Bars

**The Breezeway** 14 Pearl St **603/621-9111** • 4pm-1am • lesbians/ gay men • neighborhood bar • dancing/DJ • theme nights • cabaret • drag shows • gay-owned

**Doogie's Bar & Grill** 37 Manchester St **603/232-0732** • 4pm-1am • mostly gay men • neighborhood bar • food served • dancing/DJ • patio • wheelchair access

**Element Lounge** 1055 Elm St **603/627-2922** • 3pm-1am, from noon Sun,clsd Mon • lesbians/ gay men • dancing/DJ • food served • karaoke • drag shows

## Nashua

### Accommodations

**Radisson Hotel** 11 Tara Blvd **603/888-9970** • gay-friendly • pool • WiFi • wheelchair access

## Newfound Lake

### ACCOMMODATIONS

**The Inn on Newfound Lake** 1030 Mayhew Tpke Rte 3–A, Bridgewater **603/744-9111, 800/745-7990** • gay/ straight • private beach on cleanest lake in NH • also renowned restaurant • full bar • nonsmoking • WiFi • gay-owned

## Portsmouth

### ACCOMMODATIONS

**Ale House Inn** 121 Bow St (at Market St) **603/431-7760** • gay-friendly • WiFi • gay-owned

**The Hotel Portsmouth** 40 Court St **603/433-1200**

### CAFES

**Breaking New Grounds** 14 Market Square **603/436-9555** • 6:30am-11pm • espresso shakes • WiFi

### RESTAURANTS

**The Mombo** 66 Marcy St (at State St) **603/433-2340** • dinner only, clsd Sun-Mon • wheelchair access

## White Mtns

### ACCOMMODATIONS

**Beal House** 2 W Main St, Littleton **603/444-2661** • gay-friendly • WiFi • restaurant

**Highlands Inn** 240 Valley View Lane, Bethlehem **603/869-3978, 877/LES-B-INN (537-2466)** • Women only • 100 acres • full brkfst • outdoor & indoor spas • pool • 100 mtn acres • special events • concerts • kids/ pets ok • non-smoking • WiFi • wheelchair access • ignore No Vacancy sign • lesbian-owned

**The Horse & Hound Inn** 205 Wells Rd, Franconia **603/823-5501, 800/450-5501** • gay-friendly • 1840s fully restored lodge stye • full brkfst • nonsmoking • WiFi • also restaurant • gay-owned

**The Inn at Bowman** 1174 Rte 2 (Presidential Hwy), Randolph **603/466-5006** • gay/ straight • swimming • hot tub • nonsmoking • wheelchair access • gay-owned

**Inn at Crystal Lake** 2356 Eaton Rd (at Rte 16), Eaton **603/447-2120, 800/343-7336** • gay/ straight • full brkfst • also restaurant • kids age 12+ ok • dogs ok • WiFi • gay-owned

**The Notchland Inn** 2 Morey Rd, Hart's Location **603/374-6131, 800/866-6131** • gay/ straight • full brkfst • other meals available • nonsmoking • also cottages • gay-owned

**The Sunny Grange B&B** 1354 Rte 175 (Mad River Rd), Campton **603/726-5555, 877/726-5553** • gay-friendly • full brkfst • kids ok • nonsmoking • WiFi

**Wildcat Inn & Tavern** Rte 16A, Jackson Village **603/383-4245, 855/532-7727** • gay-friendly • full brkfst • also tavern & dining room • nonsmoking

**Wyatt House Country Inn** 3046 White Mountain Hwy, N Conway **603/356-7977, 800/527-7978** • gay/ straight • full brkfst • WiFi • lesbian-owned

### RESTAURANTS

**Polly's Pancake Parlor** 672 Rte Sugar Hill Rd (exit 38 off 93 N), Sugar Hill **603/823-5575** • 7am-2pm, till 3pm wknds, clsd winters

**The Red Parka Steakhouse & Pub** Rte 302, Glen **603/383-4344** • open from 3pm, also bar

### ENTERTAINMENT & RECREATION

**Reel North Fly Fishing** **603/858-4103** • casting lessons • half & full day river trips • lesbian-owned/run

# NEW JERSEY

## Statewide

### PUBLICATIONS

**Out in Jersey** 743 Hamilton Ave, Trenton 08629 **609/213-9310** • bimonthly glossy magazine for all of New Jersey's LGBT community

## Asbury Park

### ACCOMMODATIONS

**Empress Hotel** 101 Asbury Ave **732/774-0100** • gay-friendly • swimming • WiFi • also Empress Lobby Lounge on wknds

### BARS

**Georgie's** 812 5th Ave (at Main) **732/988-1220** • 2pm-2am • lesbians/ gay men • neighborhood bar • food served • karaoke • drag shows

### NIGHTCLUBS

**Paradise** 101 Asbury Ave (at Ocean Ave) **732/988-6663** • 4pm-2am, from 2pm Sat, from noon Sun • lesbians/ gay men • dancing/DJ • 2 dance flrs • live shows • piano bar • tiki/ pool bar in summer

RESTAURANTS

**Moonstruck** 517 Lake Ave (at Grand) **732/988-0123** • dinner only, clsd Mon-Tue • also bar • live music wknds

## Atlantic City

ACCOMMODATIONS

**The Carisbrooke Inn** 105 S Little Rock Ave, Ventnor **609/822-6392** • gay-friendly • on a beach block • nonsmoking • WiFi

**Tropicana Casino & Resort** 2831 Boardwalk (at Brighton) **609/340-4000, 800/345-8767** • gay-friendly • pool • oceanview rooms

BARS

**Rainbow Room** 55 S Bellevue Ave **609/317-4593** • 6pm-2am • mostly gay men • neighborhood bar

NIGHTCLUBS

**Club 11** 123 S Indiana Ave (at Claridge Hotel) **609/416 0110** • 9pm-2am Sun till 3am Fri Sat, 6pm-Midnight Mon, clsd Tu-Th • lesbians/gay men • dancing/DJ

RESTAURANTS

**Dock's Oyster House** 2405 Atlantic Ave **609/345-0092** • 5pm-10pm, till 11pm Fri-Sat • wheelchair access

**White House Sub Shop** 2301 Arctic Ave (at Mississippi) **609/345-1564** • 10am-8pm, till 9pm Fri-Sat

## Camden

ENTERTAINMENT & RECREATION

**The Walt Whitman House** 30 Mickle Blvd (btwn S 3rd & S 4th Sts) **856/964-5383** • the last home of America's great & controversial poet

## Cape May

ACCOMMODATIONS

**Congress Hall** 251 Beach Ave **609/884-8421, 888/944-1816** • gay-friendly • pool • WiFi

**Cottage Beside the Point** **609/204-0549, 609/898-0658** • gay/ straight • studio • kids ok • nonsmoking • lesbian-owned

**Highland House** 131 N Broadway (at York) **609/898-1198** • gay-friendly • B&B • kids/ pets ok • gazebo • nonsmoking • gay & straight-owned

**The Virginia Hotel** 25 Jackson St (btwn Beach Dr & Carpenter's Ln) **609/884-5700, 800/732-4236** • gay-friendly • WiFi • also The Ebbitt Room restaurant • seafood/ cont'l

BARS

**The King Edward Room** 301 Howard St (at The Chalfonte Hotel) **609/884-8409** • 3pm-1am summer only • mostly gay men

## Hammonton

NIGHTCLUBS

**Club Revolution**
19 N Egg Harbor Rd (at Orchard Ave) **609/561-2525** • 6pm-midnight Th, from 7pm Fri-Sat, 6pm-midnight Sun • lesbians/gay men • dancing/DJ • shows • tiki bar/patio • lesbian-owned

## Highland Park

INFO LINES & SERVICES

**Pride Center of New Jersey** 85 Raritan Ave (at S 1st Ave) **732/846-2232** • info line • meeting space for various groups

## Hoboken

BARS

**Maxwell's Tavern** 1039 Washington St **201/653-7777** • 11am-10pm, till 11pm Fri-Sat • full bar

## Jamesburg

RESTAURANTS

**Fiddleheads** 27 E Railroad Ave **732/521-0878** • lunch & dinner, Sun brunch, clsd Mon-Tue • upscale bistro • BYOB

## Jersey City

INFO LINES & SERVICES

**Hudson Pride Connections** 32 Jones St **201/963-4779** • "serving the LGBT communities & all people living w/ HIV, since 1993"

ACCOMMODATIONS

**Hyatt Regency Jersey City** 2 Exchange Pl (on the Hudson) **201/645-4712, 201/469-1234** • gay-friendly • luxury waterfront hotel • short ride to NYC • pool • nonsmoking • WiFi

## Linden

### BARS

**Duval Bar & Lounge** 9 Cedar Ave **908/290-3535** • 6pm-2am, till 3am Th-Sat, clsd Sun-Mon • lesbians/gay men, more women Th • danicng/DJ • food served • karaoke

## Lodi

### RESTAURANTS

**Penang Malaysian & Thai Cuisine** 334 N Main St (at Garibaldi Ave) **973/779-1128** • 11am-11pm • full bar • gay-owned

## Morristown

### INFO LINES & SERVICES

**GAAMC (Gay Activist Alliance in Morris County)** 21 Normandy Hts Rd (at Columbia Rd, Unitarian Fellowship) **973/285-1595** • info line 7:30pm-9pm, also recorded info • also women's network

## New Brunswick

### BARS

**The Den** 700 Hamilton St (at Douglas), Somerset **732/545-7354** • 8pm-2am Wed-Sat only • popular • mostly gay men • dancing/DJ wknds • multiracial • live shows • wheelchair access

### RESTAURANTS

**The Frog & the Peach** 29 Dennis St (at Hiram Square) **732/846-3216** • lunch Mon-Fri, dinner nightly • full bar • upscale • wheelchair access

**Sophie's Bistro** 700 Hamilton St (at Douglas), Somerset **732/545-7778** • dinner nightly, lunch Tue-Fri, clsd Mon • patio

**Stage Left** 5 Livingston Ave (at George) **732/828-4444** • popular • expensive • full bar • patio • wheelchair access • gay-owned

## River Edge

### NIGHTCLUBS

**Feathers** 77 Kinderkamack Rd (at Grand) **201/342-6410** • 9pm-2am, till 3am Sat, clsd Mon-Tue • mostly gay men • dancing/DJ • karaoke • live shows • videos • young crowd • wheelchair access

## NEW MEXICO

## Albuquerque

includes Bernalillo, Corrales, Placitas & Rio Rancho

### INFO LINES & SERVICES

**AA Gay/ Lesbian** 505/266-1900 (AA#) • 7pm Mon & Th

**Common Bond Info Line** 505/891-3647 • 24hrs • covers LGBT community

### ACCOMMODATIONS

**Adobe Nido** 1124 Major Ave NW (at 12th St & Candilaria NW) **505/344-1310, 866/435-6436** • gay-friendly • B&B • also aviary • nonsmoking • WiFi

**Bottger Mansion of Old Town B&B** 110 San Felipe (at Central Ave) **505/243-3639, 800/758-3639** • transgender-friendly • WiFi

**Brittania & W E Mauger Estate B&B** 701 Roma Ave NW (at 7th) **505/242-8755, 800/719-9189** • gay-friendly • full brkfst • nonsmoking • WiFi

**Casa Manzano B&B** 103 Forest Rd 321 (at State Rte 55), Tajique **505/384-9767** • gay/ straight • full brkfst • nonsmoking • kids/ pets ok • wheelchair access

**Casas de Suenos** 310 Rio Grande Blvd SW (btwn York & Alhambra) **505/247-4560, 800/665-7002** • gay/ straight • spacious casitas • full brkfst • kids ok • nonsmoking • WiFi

**La Casita B&B** 317 16th St NW (at Lomas Blvd) **505/242-0173** • gay-friendly • adobe guesthouse • nonsmoking • WiFi

**Golden Guesthouses** 2645 Decker NW (at Glenwood) **505/344-9205, 888/513-GOLD** • lesbians/ gay men • individual & shared units • nonsmoking • lesbian-owned

**The Nativo Lodge** 6000 Pan American Fwy NE **505/798-4300, 888/628-4861**

**Sheraton Albuquerque Airport Hotel** 2910 Yale Blvd SE (at Gibson) **505/843-7000, 800/325-3535** • gay-friendly • 4-star hotel • pool • also restaurant

### BARS

**Albuquerque Social Club** 4021 Central Ave NE (at Morningside, enter rear) **505/262-1088** • 3pm-2am, noon-midnight Sun • popular • lesbians/ gay men • dancing/DJ • private club

**Sidewinders Ranch** 8900 Central SE (at Wyoming) **505/554-2078** • 4pm-2am, till midnight Sun, clsd Mon & Wed • mostly gay men • dancing/DJ • country/western • karaoke • wheelchair access

### NIGHTCLUBS

**Effex** 420 Central SW (at 5th) **505/842-8870** • 9pm-2am Th-Sat • lesbians/gay men • dancing/DJ

### CAFES

**Java Joe's** 906 Park Ave SW **505/765-1514** • 6:30am-3:30pm • coffee & pastries • monthly art shows

### RESTAURANTS

**Artichoke Cafe** 424 Central Ave SE (at Arno St) **505/243-0200** • lunch Mon-Fri, dinner nightly • bistro • plenty veggie • wheelchair access

**Cafe Cubano at Laru Ni Hati** 3413 Central Ave NE (btwn Tulane & Amherst) **505/255-1575** • 10am-9pm, till 8pm Sat, noon-5pm Sun, clsd Mon • cigars • cheap Cuban food • also unisex hair salon • gay-owned

**Copper Lounge** 1504 Central Ave SE (at Maple) **505/242-7490** • 11am-2am, clsd Sun • pizza, burgers • full bar • wheelchair access

**El Patio** 142 Harvard St SE (at Central) **505/268-4245** • 11am-9pm • popular • young crowd • beer/wine • plenty veggie • wheelchair access

**El Pinto** 10500 4th St NW (at Roy Ave) **505/898-1771** • lunch & dinner, Sun brunch • Mexican

**Flying Star Cafe** 3416 Central Ave SE (2 blocks W of Carlisle) **505/255-6633** • 6am-10pm, till 11pm Fri-Sat • plenty veggie • WiFi • wheelchair access

**Frontier** 2400 Central Ave SE (at Cornell) **505/266-0550** • 5am-1am • good brkfst burritos

**The Original Garcia's Kitchen** 1113 4th St NW (at Mountain) **505/247-9149** • 7am-9pm • awesome little down home place • wheelchair access

**Romano's Macaroni Grill** 2100 Louisiana NE (at Winrock Mall) **505/881-3400** • 11am-10pm • Italian • wheelchair access

**Sadie's Cocinita** 6230 4th St NW (near Osuna) **505/345-5339** • 11am-10pm, 10am-9pm Sun • popular • New Mexican • wheelchair access

**Zinc Wine Bar & Bistro** 3009 Central Ave NE (at Dartmouth) **505/254-9462** • lunch & dinner, brunch wknds • live music • reservations recommended

### ENTERTAINMENT & RECREATION

**Bio Park Botanic Garden** 2601 Central Ave NW (at New York Ave) **505/768-2000** • an oasis in the desert: native & exotic plants, butterflies

**Duke City Derby** • Albuquerque's female roller derby league • visit www.dukecityderby.com for events

### BOOKSTORES

**Page One** 5850 Eubank Blvd NE #B41 **505/294-2026, 800/521-4122** • 9am-9pm, till 6pm Sun • "New Mexico's largest independent bookstore"

### EROTICA

**Castle Megastore** 5110 Central Ave SE (at San Mateo) **505/262-2266**

**Self Serve** 3904-B Central Ave SE (at Morningside) **505/265-5815** • noon-7pm, till 8pm Fri, till 6pm Sun • erotica store & sexuality resource center • lesbian-owned

## Chimayo

### ACCOMMODATIONS

**Casa Escondida B&B** **505/351-4805** • gay-friendly • full brkfst • hot tub • kids/pets ok w/ approval • nonsmoking • WiFi

## Cloudcroft

### RETAIL SHOPS

**Off The Beaten Path** 100 Glorietta Ave (at 1st) **575/682-7284** • eclectic gifts • original artwork • wheelchair access • lesbian-owned

## Farmington

### ACCOMMODATIONS

**Quality Inn** 1901 E Broadway **505/325-3700, 877/424-6423** • gay-friendly • kids/pets ok • WiFi • wheelchair access

## Las Cruces

### ACCOMMODATIONS

**Hotel Encanto de Las Cruces** 705 S Telshor Blvd **575/522-4300, 866/383-0443**

### RETAIL SHOPS

**Spirit Winds Gifts & Cafe** 2260 S Locust St (at Thomas Dr) **575/521-0222** • 7:30am-7pm, 8am-6pm Sun • live music some wknds • food served • patio • WiFi • wheelchair access

## Madrid

### BARS

**Mineshaft Tavern** 2846 State Hwy 14
**505/473-0743** • 11:30am-close • gay-friendly
• live shows • also restaurant • some veggie

### CAFES

**Java Junction** 2855 State Hwy 14
**505/438-2772** • 7am-4pm, till 5pm wknds •
WiFi • also giftshop & B&B

## Ojo Caliente

### RESTAURANTS

**Mesa Vista Cafe** 35323 Hwy 285
**505/583-2245** • 8am-9pm • wheelchair
access

## Ramah

### ACCOMMODATIONS

**El Morro RV Park, Cabins & Cafe** 4018
Hwy 53 **505/783-4612** • gay/ straight • in Zuni
Mtns • full brkfst • nonsmoking • WiFi • also
cafe • lesbian-owned

## Santa Fe

### INFO LINES & SERVICES

**AA Gay/ Lesbian** 1601 S St Francis Dr
**505/982-8932** • 6pm Mon • also 6pm Tue at
Friendship Club, 1915 Rosina St

### ACCOMMODATIONS

**Bishop's Lodge Resort & Spa** 1297
Bishops Lodge Rd **505/983-6377,**
**800/731-2240** • gay-friendly • on 450 acres •
kids/ pets ok • pool • hot tub • nonsmoking •
wheelchair access • WiFi

**Dragonfly Canyon Retreat** Glorieta
**505/757-2991** • gay/ straight • 3-bdrm casita
• near Pecos Wilderness • nonsmoking • also
women's retreats • lesbian-owned

**El Farolito B&B** 514 Galisteo St (at Paseo
de Peralta) **505/988-1631, 888/634-8782** •
gay/ straight • adobe compound w/ romantic,
private casitas • kids ok • nonsmoking • WiFi •
gay-owned

**Four Kachinas Inn** 512 Webber St
**505/982-2550, 800/397-2564** • gay/ straight •
courtyard • kids ok • nonsmoking • WiFi •
wheelchair access • gay-owned

**Hacienda Nicholas** 320 E Marcy St
**505/986-1431, 888/284-3170** • gay/ straight •
adobe home • full brkfst • teens/ pets ok •
nonsmoking • WiFi • wheelchair access

**Inn at Vanessie** 427 W Water St
**505/984-1193, 800/646-6752** • gay-friendly •
historic adobe inn • nonsmoking • kids/ pets
ok • WiFi • wheelchair access • also restaurant
& live music club

**The Inn of the Five Graces** 150 E DeVargas
St **505/992-0957 , 866/992-0957** • gay-
friendly • guest rooms and suites are each
individual, mysterious & deeply luxurious

**Inn of the Turquoise Bear B&B** 342 E
Buena Vista St (at Old Santa Fe Tr)
**505/983-0798** • lesbians/ gay men • B&B in
historic Witter Bynner estate • nonsmoking •
WiFi • gay-owned

**Inn on the Alameda** 303 E Alameda (at
Canyon Rd) **505/984-2121, 888/984-2121** •
gay-friendly • afternoon wine reception • hot
tubs • WiFi • wheelchair access

**Las Palomas** 460 W San Francisco St
**505/982-5560, 877/982-5560** • gay-friendly •
luxury hotel 3 blocks from Plaza • kids ok •
nonsmoking • WiFi • wheelchair access

**The Madeleine Inn** 106 Faithway St
**505/982-3465, 888/877-7622** • gay/ straight •
Queen Anne Victorian • full brkfst • hot tub •
kids ok • nonsmoking • WiFi • also spa

**New Mexico Women's Guesthouse,
Retreat & Healing Center** PO Box 130,
Serafina 87569 **575/421-2533** • women only •
guesthouses on 1,000-acre wildlife refuge •
healing workshops • hot tub • nonsmoking •
lesbian-owned

**Rosewood Inn of the Anasazi** 113
Washington Ave **505/988-3030, 888/767-3966**
• gay-friendly • luxury hotel 1/2 block from
Plaza • kids ok • WiFi • nonsmoking •
wheelchair access • also restaurant

### RESTAURANTS

**Anasazi Restaurant** 113 Washington Ave (at
Inn of the Anasazi) **505/988-3030** • brkfst,
lunch, dinner & wknd brunch • wheelchair
access

**Cafe Pasqual's** 121 Don Gaspar Ave (at
Water St) **505/983-9340, 800/722-7672** •
brkfst, lunch, dinner & Sun brunch • popular •
Southwestern • some veggie • beer/ wine •
wheelchair access

**The Compound Restaurant** 653 Canyon
Rd (at Delgado) **505/982-4353** • lunch Mon-
Sat, dinner nightly • upscale • Southwestern •
nonsmoking • patio • reservations
recommended • wheelchair access

**Cowgirl BBQ** 319 S Guadalupe St (at Aztec)
**505/982-2565** • 11am-11pm, till midnight Fri-
Sat • great margaritas • plenty veggie

**El Farol** 808 Canyon Rd **505/983–9912** • Spanish/tapas • live music

**Geronimo** 724 Canyon Rd (at Camino del Monte Sol) **505/982–1500** • dinner nightly • eclectic gourmet • full bar 11am-11pm • wheelchair access

**Harry's Roadhouse** 96 Old Las Vegas Hwy **505/989–4629** • 7am-9:30pm • outdoor seating • popular brunch

**Pink Adobe** 406 Old Santa Fe Trl **505/983–7712** • steak & seafood • also Dragon Room bar

**Santacafe** 231 Washington Ave **505/984–1788** • lunch & dinner • New American • some veggie • full bar • wheelchair access

**Tune Up Cafe** 1115 Hickox St (at Cortez) **505/983–7060** • 7am-10pm, from 8am wknds • New Mexican • some veggie • beer/wine • wheelchair access

### ENTERTAINMENT & RECREATION

**Ten Thousand Waves** 3451 Hyde Park Rd (4 miles out of town) **505/982–9304** • Japanese health spa & lodging • clothing-optional • kids ok

**Wise Fool New Mexico** 2778 Agua Fria Unit D (at Siler Rd) **505/992–2588** • women & kids circus art classes, workshops & performances • social justice theatre & puppetry • check local listings for upcoming events & info

### BOOKSTORES

**Downtown Subscription** 376 Garcia St (at Acequia Madre) **505/983–3085** • 7am-6pm • newsstand • coffee shop • wheelchair access

### RETAIL SHOPS

**The Ark** 133 Romero St (at Agua Fria) **505/988–3709** • 10am-6pm, 11am-5pm Sun • spiritual

## Silver City

### ACCOMMODATIONS

**Gila House Hotel & Gallery** 400 N Arizona **575/313–7015** • gay-friendly • also Gallery 400

### RESTAURANTS

**Diane's Restaurant & Bakery** 510 N Bullard **575/538–8722** • 7am-6pm, 8am-3pm Sun • beer/wine

## Taos

### ACCOMMODATIONS

**Adobe & Stars B&B** 584 State Hwy 150 (at Valdez Rim Rd) **575/776–2776, 800/211–7076** • gay/straight • full brkfst • nonsmoking • WiFi • wheelchair access • woman-owned

**Casa Benavides B&B** 137 Kit Carson Rd (at Paseo del Pueblo Sur) **575/758–1772, 800/552–1772** • gay-friendly • fireplaces • hot tubs • extensive gardens • full brkfst • nonsmoking • kids ok • WiFi • wheelchair access

**Casa Gallina** 613 Callejon Rd **575/758–2306** • gay/straight • charming guesthouse in quiet, pastoral setting • nonsmoking • wheelchair access • gay-owned

**Dobson House** 484 Tune Dr **575/776–5738** • gay-friendly • luxury suites • N of Taos • full brkfst • solar-powered eco-resort • nonsmoking

**Dreamcatcher B&B** 416 La Lomita Rd (at Valverde) **575/758–0613** • gay-friendly • near Taos Plaza • full brkfst • hot tub • nonsmoking • WiFi • wheelchair access

**The Historic Taos Inn** 125 Paseo del Pueblo Norte (at Bent St) **575/758–2233, 888/518–8267** • gay-friendly • several adobe houses date from the 1800s • pueblo-style fireplaces • also restaurant & bar

**San Geronimo Lodge** 1101 Witt Rd (off Kit Carson) **575/751–3776, 800/894–4119** • popular • gay/straight • full brkfst • pool • hot tub • massage available • kids/pets ok • nonsmoking • WiFi • wheelchair access

### RESTAURANTS

**Sabroso** 470 State Hwy 150, Arroyo Seco **575/776–3333** • 5pm-10pm • American & Mediterranean • also full bar • patio • wheelchair access

### ENTERTAINMENT & RECREATION

**Llama Trekking Adventures** **800/758–5262** • day hikes & multiday llama treks in Sangre de Cristo Mtns & Rio Grande Gorge

## Truth or Consequences

### ACCOMMODATIONS

**The Belair Inn** 705 N Date St (at 7th Ave) **575/894–8977** • gay/straight • "retro 1950s motel w/ 21st-century amenities" • nonsmoking • WiFi

# NEW YORK

## Adirondack Mtns

### ACCOMMODATIONS

**The Cornerstone Victorian** 3921 Main St (Rte 9), Warrensburg **518/623-3308** • gay-friendly • gourmet brkfst

**The Doctor's Inn** 304 Trudeau Rd (at Bloomingdale Ave), Saranac Lake **607/316-6455** • gay-friendly • Adirondack guesthouse • nonsmoking

**King Hendrick Motel** 1602 State Rte 9, Lake George **518/792-0418, 866/521-6883** • gay-friendly • swimming • WiFi • nonsmoking • small pets ok • wheelchair access

**Secluded Retreat Cabin** Lake Luzerne **518/361-2375** • lesbians/ gay men • nonsmoking • secluded, rustic cabin • women-owned

**Tea Island Resort** 3020 Lake Shore Dr, Lake George **518/668-2776** • gay-friendly • chalets, cottages & suites

## Albany

**see Capital District**

## Binghamton

### INFO LINES & SERVICES

**AA Gay/ Lesbian** 607/722-5983

### BARS

**Merlin's** 73 Court St **607/722-1022** • 4pm-1am , till 3am Fri-Sat • lesbians/ gay men • neighborhood bar • dancing/DJ • live shows • karaoke • patio

**Squiggy's** 34 Chenango St (at Court) **607/722-2299** • 6pm-midnight, till 2am Fri-Sat, from 8pm Sat, clsd Sun • lesbians/ gay men • neighborhood bar • dancing/DJ Fri-Sat • karaoke

### CAFES

**Lost Dog Cafe** 222 Water St (at Henry) **607/771-6063** • 11:30am-10pm, till 11pm Fri-Sat, clsd Sun • popular • some veggie • beer/ wine • live shows • wheelchair access

### RESTAURANTS

**The Whole in the Wall** 43 S Washington St **607/722-5138** • 11:30am-9pm, clsd Sun-Mon • plenty veggie/ vegan

## Buffalo

### INFO LINES & SERVICES

**Lesbian/ Gay AA** 18 Trinity Pl (at AIDS Comm Svc) **716/852-7743** • 8pm Mon & Wed

**Pride Center of Western NY** 206 S Elmwood Ave **716/852-7743** • meetings, resources & more

### ACCOMMODATIONS

**The Mansion on Delaware** 414 Delaware Ave **716/886-3300** • gay/ straight • WiFi • wheelchair access

### BARS

**Cathode Ray** 26 Allen St (at N Pearl) **716/884-3615** • 1pm-4am • mostly gay men • neighborhood bar • wheelchair access

**Fugazi** 503 Franklin St (near Allen St) **716/881-3588** • 5pm-2am • gay/ straight • intimate cocktail lounge • videos

**The Underground** 274 Delaware Ave (at Johnson) **716/853-0092** • noon-4am • mostly gay men • neighborhood bar • dancing/DJ • karaoke

### NIGHTCLUBS

**Club Marcella** 622 Main St **716/847-6850** • 10pm-4am, clsd Mon-Wed • lesbians/ gay men • dancing/DJ • drag shows • wheelchair access

### CAFES

**Cafe 59** 62 Allen St **716/883-1880** • 8am-10pm, till midnight Fri, 10am-11pm Sat, noon-9pm Sun • WiFi • gay-owned

### RESTAURANTS

**Allen Street Hardware Cafe** 245 Allen St (at College) **716/882-8843** • from 5pm daily • full bar • live music • art

**Anchor Bar** 1047 Main St **716/886-8920, 716/884-4083** • 11am-10pm, till midnight Fri-Sat

**Atmosphere 62** 62 Allen St (at Franklin) **716/881-0062** • from 4pm Wed-Sat • full bar

**Mothers** 33 Virginia Pl (at Virginia St) **716/882-2989** • 4pm-4am, full bar

**Rue Franklin** 341 Franklin St (at W Tupper) **716/852-4416** • 5:30pm-10pm, clsd Sun-Mon • upscale, contemporary French

**Tempo** 581 Delaware Ave (at Allen St) **716/885-1594** • dinner only, clsd Sun • upscale Italian/ American

**Towne Restaurant** 186 Allen St **716/884-5128** • 7am-5am, clsd Sun • Greek

## ENTERTAINMENT & RECREATION

**Babeville** 341 Delaware Ave (at W Tupper) **716/852–3835** • Ani Di Franco's rehabbed church performance space • also Hallwalls Arts Center

**Buffalo United Artists** 119 Chippewa (btwn Delaware & Elmwood) **716/886–9239** • gay-themed theater company

## BOOKSTORES

**Talking Leaves** 3158 Main St (btwn Winspear & Hertel Aves) **716/837–8554** • 10am-6pm, till 8pm Wed-Th, clsd Sun • also 951 Elmwood Ave

## PUBLICATIONS

**Outcome Buffalo** 495 Linwood Ave **716/228–8828** • monthly

## EROTICA

**Elmwood Books Adult Mart** 1871 Elmwood Ave, Kenmore **716/874–1045** • 24hrs • women receive 20% off Wed

**Video Liquidators** 1770 Elmwood Ave **716/874–7223** • 24hrs

# Capital District

includes Albany, Cohoes, Salem, Schenectady & Troy

## INFO LINES & SERVICES

**Capital District Lesbian/ Gay Community Center** 332 Hudson Ave, Albany **518/462–6138** • social & human service programs • also Rainbow Cafe 6pm-9pm, clsd Sat

**Holding Our Own** 373 Central Ave, Albany **518/462–2871** • community center • call for hours

## ACCOMMODATIONS

**The Morgan State House** 393 State St, Albany **518/427–6063, 888/427–6063** • gay-friendly • 1800s town house • nonsmoking • WiFi

## BARS

**Clinton Street Pub** 159 Clinton St, Schenectady **518/377–8555** • 11am-close, from 8am Sat, from noon Sun • lesbians/ gay men • neighborhood bar • dancing/DJ • live shows • karaoke

**Oh Bar** 304 Lark St (at Madison), Albany **518/463–9004** • 2pm-4am • lesbians/ gay men • neighborhood bar • multiracial • karaoke • videos • wheelchair access

**Waterworks Pub** 76 Central Ave (btwn Lexington & Northern), Albany **518/465–9079** • 1pm-4am • popular • mostly gay men • neighborhood bar • dancing/DJ wknds • garden bar • food served • karaoke • 18+ • wheelchair access

## NIGHTCLUBS

**Fuze Box** 12 Central Ave, Albany **518/703–8937** • 8pm-4am Th-Sat • gay/ straight • dancing/DJ • live shows • swing dancing • gay-owned

## RESTAURANTS

**Bomber's Burrito Bar** 258 Lark St, Albany **518/463–9636** • 11am-2am, till 3am wknds • plenty veggie • gay-owned

**Bomber's Burrito Bar** 447 State St, Schenectady **518/374–3548** • 11am-2am, till 3am wknds • plenty veggie • gay-owned

**El Loco Mexican Cafe** 465 Madison Ave (btwn Lark & Willett), Albany **518/436–1855** • lunch Wed-Sat, dinner nightly, clsd Mon • healthy Tex-Mex • full bar

**Midtown Tap & Tea Room** 289 New Scotland Ave, Albany **518/435–0202** • 11am-10pm, from 4pm Sat, clsd Mon • wheelchair access lesbian-owned

**Yono's** 25 Chapel St (at Sheridan), Albany **518/436–7747** • 5:30pm-10pm, clsd Sun-Mon • full bar • live music • wheelchair access

## ENTERTAINMENT & RECREATION

**Albany All Stars** Albany • Albany's female roller derby league

## RETAIL SHOPS

**Romeo's Gifts** 299 Lark St (at Madison), Albany **518/434–4014** • noon-9pm, till 5pm Sun

# Catskill Mtns

## INFO LINES & SERVICES

**Wise Woman Center** 845/246–8081 • women only • workshops • correspondence courses • newsletter

## ACCOMMODATIONS

**Beds on Clouds** 5320 Main St/ Rte 23 (at CR21), Windham **518/734–4692** • gay/ straight • 1854 mansion features suites & famous artwork • woman-owned

**Bradstan Country Hotel** 1561 Rte 17-B, White Lake **845/583–4114** • gay-friendly • also cottages • piano bar & cabaret from 9pm-1am Fri-Sat

**Country Suite** Rte 23, Windham
518/734–4079 • B&B • Victorian-style
farmhouse • full brkfst • nonsmoking • kids ok
• lesbian-owned

**Cuomo's Cove** 33 Cumo's Cove Rd (at South
St), Windham 518/734–5903, 800/734–5903 •
gay-friendly • nonsmoking • women-owned

**ECCE B&B** 19 Silverfish Rd, Barryville
845/557–8562, 888/557–8562 • gay/ straight •
above Upper Delaware River • full brkfst • WiFi
• nonsmoking • gay-owned

**Fairlawn Inn** 7872 Main St, Hunter
518/263–5025 • gay-friendly • kids/ pets ok •
WiFi • gay-owned

**Kate's Lazy Meadow Motel** 5191 Rte 28,
Mt Tremper 845/688–7200 • gay-friendly •
love shack owned by Kate Pierson of the B-52s
• WiFi • nonsmoking

**The Roxbury, Contemporary Catskill
Lodging** 2258 County Hwy 41 (at Bridge St),
Roxbury 607/326–7200 • gay/ straight • hip
country motel • kids ok • nonsmoking • WiFi •
wheelchair access • gay-owned

**Village Green** 845/679–0313 • B&B • gay-
owned

### BARS

**Public Restaurant & Lounge** 2318 City
Hwy 41 (Bridge St), Roxbury 607/326–4026 •
5pm-9pm, till midnight Fri-Sat, clsd Mon-Tue •
gay-friendly

### RESTAURANTS

**Catskill Rose** 5355 Rte 212, Mt Tremper
845/688–7100 • 5pm-close Th-Sun • some
veggie • full bar • patio • also lodging

### BOOKSTORES

**Golden Notebook** 29 Tinker St, Woodstock
845/679–8000 • 11am-6pm, till 7pm Fri-Sat •
LGBT section • wheelchair access

## Cherry Creek

### ACCOMMODATIONS

**The Cherry Creek Inn** 1022 West Rd (CR68)
(at Center Rd) 716/296–5105 • gay-friendly •
B&B • full brkfst • in wine & Amish country •
kids ok

## Cooperstown

### ACCOMMODATIONS

**Cobblescote on the Lake** 6515 State Hwy
80 607/437–1146 • gay-friendly • spectacular
views at refurbished waterfront resort • food
served • gay-owned

## Corning

### ACCOMMODATIONS

**Black Sheep Inn** 8329 Pleasant Valley Rd
(Rte 54), Hammondsport 607/569–3767,
877/274–6286 • gay/ straight • full brkfst •
nonsmoking • WiFi

**Rufus Tanner House B&B** 60 Sagetown
Rd, Pine City 607/732–0213, 800/360–9259 •
gay/ straight • full brkfst • hot tub •
nonsmoking • WiFi • wheelchair access

## Croton-on-Hudson

### ACCOMMODATIONS

**Alexander Hamilton House** 49 Van Wyck St
914/271–6737 • gay/ straight • full brkfst •
pool • nonsmoking • kids/ pets ok • WiFi

## Findley Lake

### ACCOMMODATIONS

**Blue Heron Inn** 10412 Main St (at
Shadyside Rd) 716/769–7852 • gay-friendly •
B&B • full brkfst • kids ok • nonsmoking

## Fire Island

see also Long Island

### INFO LINES & SERVICES

**AA** 631/654–1150 • call for meeting times

### ACCOMMODATIONS

**Dune Point Guesthouse** 631/597–6261,
631/560–2200 (CELL) • lesbians/ gay men • hot
tub • kids/ pets ok • nonsmoking • wheelchair
access • lesbian & gay & straight-owned/ run

**Grove Hotel** Dock Walk, Cherry Grove
631/597–6600 • mostly gay men • pool •
nudity • nonsmoking room available •
wheelchair access • gay-owned

**Hotel Ciel** Harbor Walk 631/597–6500 •
mostly gay men • swimming • also restaurant
• wheelchair access

**The Madison Fire Island Pines** 22 Atlantic
Walk 631/597–6061 • mostly gay men •
guesthouse w/ full amenities • pool •
nonsmoking • WiFi • gay-owned

### BARS

**Blue Whale** Harbor Walk, The Pines
631/597–6500 • seasonal • lesbians/ gay men
• popular • dancing/DJ • popular Low Tea
dance • also restaurant • wheelchair access

**Cherry's On the Bay** 158 Bayview Walk, Cherry Grove **631/597-7859** • seasonal • noon-4am • popular • lesbians/gay men • dancing/DJ • piano bar • live shows • drag shows • also restaurant • patio

**Pines Bistro & Martini Bar** 36 Fire Island Blvd, The Pines **631/597-6862** • seasonal, opens 6pm

**Sip • n • Twirl** 36 Fire Island Blvd, The Pines **631/597-3599** • seasonal • noon-4am • mostly gay men • dancing/DJ

NIGHTCLUBS

**Ice Palace** Bayview Walk, Cherry Grove **631/597-6600** • hours vary • popular • lesbians/gay men • dancing/DJ • drag shows • wheelchair access

**The Pavilion** Harbor Walk, The Pines **631/597-6500** • seasonal • noon-8am Fri-Sun only • lesbians/gay men • popular • dancing/DJ • popular High Tea dance • wheelchair access

CAFES

**Cultured Elephant** Harbor Walk, The Pines **631/597-6500** • coffee, smoothies, cocktails & food

RESTAURANTS

**Cherry Grove Pizza** Dock Walk (under the GroveHotel), Cherry Grove **631/597-6766** • seasonal • 11am-10pm

**Marina Meat Market** Harbor Walk, The Pines **631/597-6588** • great sandwiches

**Pines Pizza** 36 Fire Island Blvd, The Pines **631/597-3597** • seasonal, 11am-11pm

**Sand Castle** 140 Lewis Walk, Cherry Grove **631/597-4174** • seasonal • lunch & dinner • also bar

ENTERTAINMENT & RECREATION

**Cherry Grove Beach** • lesbians/gay men • nude beach

**Invasion of the Pines** The Pines dock (July 4th wknd) • come & enjoy the annual fun as boatloads of drag queens from Cherry Grove arrive to terrorize the posh Pines

GYMS & HEALTH CLUBS

**Pool Deck** Harbor Walk, The Pines • noon-5pm, till 10pm Fri-Sun • DJ wknds

## Geneva

ACCOMMODATIONS

**Belhurst** 4069 Rte 14 S (near Snell Rd) **315/781-0201** • gay-friendly • in historic castle overlooking Seneca Lake • fireplaces • also restaurant

## Glens Falls

ACCOMMODATIONS

**Glens Falls Inn** 25 Sherman Ave **646/743-9365** • gay-friendly • B&B in Victorian • full brkfst • WiFi • woman-owned

## Hamptons

see Long Island—Suffolk/ Hamptons

## Hudson Valley

Hudson Valley includes Catskill, High Falls, Highland, Hudson, Hyde Park, Kinderhook, Kingston, New Paltz, Poughkeepsie, Rhinebeck & Saugerties

ACCOMMODATIONS

**Barclay Heights B&B** 158 Burt St (at Trinity Place), Saugerties **845/246-3788** • gay-friendly • full brkfst • cozy Victorian cottage • nonsmoking

**The Country Squire B&B** 251 Allen St (at 3rd), Hudson **518/822-9229** • gay/ straight • restored Queen Anne • kids ok • nonsmoking • WiFi

**Hotel Tivoli** 53 Broadway,, Tivoli **845/757-2100** • gay/straight • amazing design, restaurant and pets ok

**Hudson City B&B** 326 Allen St (at Rte 9-G/ 3rd St), Hudson **518/822-8044** • gay/ straight • 18th-c Victorian in antique district • WiFi • kids/ small pets ok • gay-owned

**Van Schaack House** 20 Broad St (at Albany Rd), Kinderhook **518/758-6118** • gay-friendly • B&B • full brkfst • nonsmoking • gay-owned

RESTAURANTS

**Armadillo Bar & Grill** 97 Abeel St, Kingston **845/339-1550** • lunch wknds, dinner nightly, clsd Mon • full bar • patio

**Rock & Rye** 215 Hugenot St (behind conference center), New Paltz **845/255-7888** • 5pm-close, Sun brunch 11am-3pm, clsd Mon

**Terrapin** 6426 Montgomery St, Rhinebeck **845/876-3330** • lunch & dinner • bistro & bar • patio

**The Would Restaurant** 120 North Rd (off Rte 9 W), Highland **845/691-9883** • dinner nightly, clsd Sun-Mon • some veggie • full bar • patio • gay-owned

ENTERTAINMENT & RECREATION

**Dia:Beacon Riggio Galleries** 3 Beekman St (at Rte 9D), Beacon **845/440-0100** • modern art museum

## Ithaca

### INFO LINES & SERVICES

**AA Gay/ Lesbian** 607/273–1541

### ACCOMMODATIONS

**Juniper Hill B&B** 16 Elm St (at Main St), Trumansburg **607/387–3044, 888/809–1367** • gay-friendly • full brkfst • nonsmoking • WiFi • gay-owned

**Noble House Farm** 215 Connecticut Hill Rd, Newfield **607/277–4798** • gay-friendly • near gorges & wine tours • kids/ pets ok • nonsmoking • wheelchair access • lesbian-owned

**William Henry Miller Inn** 303 N Aurora St (at E Buffalo St) **607/256–4553, 877/256–4553** • gay-friendly • full brkfst • pets ok • kids over 12 ok • WiFi • nonsmoking

### CAFES

**Sarah's Patisserie** 200 Pleasant Grove Rd (at Hanshaw Rd) **607/257–4257** • 10am-6pm, clsd Sun-Mon • lesbian-owned

### ENTERTAINMENT & RECREATION

**Out Loud Chorus** 607/280–0374

## Jamestown

### ACCOMMODATIONS

**Fairmount Motel** 138 W Fairmount (Rte 394) **716/763–9550** • gay-friendly • near Chautauqua Institution • kids ok • WiFi • gay-owned

### BARS

**Sneakers** 100 Harrison (at Institute) **716/484–8816** • 3pm-2am, clsd Mon • lesbians/ gay men • wheelchair access

### ENTERTAINMENT & RECREATION

**The Lucille Ball/ Desi Arnaz Center** 2 W 3rd St (at Main) **716/484–0800, 877/582–9326** • for those who love Lucy

## Little Falls

### CAFES

**Piccolo Cafe** 365 Canal Pl **315/823–9856** • lunch Tue-Fri, dinner Wed-Sun, clsd Mon

## LONG ISLAND

**Long Island is divided into 2 geographical areas:**
**Long Island—Nassau**
**Long Island—Suffolk/ Hamptons**
**see also Fire Island**

## Long Island – Nassau

### INFO LINES & SERVICES

**Long Island GLBT Center** 400 Garden City Plaza #110, Garden City **516/323–0011** • Long Island GLBT services network

### NIGHTCLUBS

**Pure Silk** Westbury **516/474–1707** • 4pm-9pm Sun only • monthly party • check puresilkproductions.com • mostly women • dancing/DJ

### RESTAURANTS

**RS Jones** 153 Merrick Ave (off Sunrise), Merrick **516/378–7177** • dinner, clsd Mon • Tex-Mex • women-owned

### ENTERTAINMENT & RECREATION

**Pride for Youth Coffeehouse** 2050 Bellmore Ave, Bellmore **516/679–9000** • 7:30pm-11:30pm Fri • ages 13-20 • live music

## Long Island – Suffolk/ Hamptons

### INFO LINES & SERVICES

**The Center at Bay Shore** 34 Park Ave, Bay Shore **631/665–2300** • drop-in lounge w/ cybercenter • events

**The Hamptons GLBT Center** 44 Union St, Sag Harbor **831/899–4950** • Long Island GLBT services network

### ACCOMMODATIONS

**The Atlantic** 1655 Country Rd 39, Southampton **631/283–6100** • gay-friendly • pool • jacuzzi • kids/ pets ok • wheelchair access

**East Hampton Village B&B** 172 Newtown Ln (at McGuirk St), East Hampton **631/324–1858** • gay/ straight • lovely turn-of-the-century home • nonsmoking • WiFi

**Hermosa Lodge** 78 Mecox Rd, Water Mill **774/893–3262** • gay/straight • full brkfst • Pool • WiFi •

**Mill House Inn** 31 N Main St (at Newtown Lane), East Hampton **631/324–9766** • gay-friendly • full brkfst • nonsmoking • kids/ dogs ok • WiFi • wheelchair access

**Stirling House B&B** 104 Bay Ave, Greenport 631/477–0654, 800/551–0654 • gay-friendly • full brkfst • jacuzzi • nonsmoking • WiFi • gay-owned

**Sunset Beach** 35 Shore Rd, Shelter Island 631/749–2001 • gay-friendly • seasonal • food served

### RESTAURANTS

**Babette's** 66 Newtown Ln, East Hampton 631/329–5377 • seasonal • brkfst, lunch & dinner • healthy • plenty veggie • woman-owned

### ENTERTAINMENT & RECREATION

**Fowler Beach** Southampton

## Middletown

### ACCOMMODATIONS

**Best Western Inn at Hunt's Landing** 120 Rtes 6 & 209, Matamoras, PA 570/491–2400, 800/528–1234 • gay-friendly • pool • gym • restaurant & bar • WiFi

## Montgomery

### ACCOMMODATIONS

**The Borland House B&B** 130 Clinton St 845/457–1513 • gay-friendly • full brkfst • nonsmoking • WiFi

# NEW YORK CITY

**New York City is divided into 9 geographical areas:**
NYC—Overview
NYC—Soho, Greenwich & Chelsea
NYC—Downtown
NYC—Midtown
NYC—Uptown
NYC—Brooklyn
NYC—Queens
NYC—Bronx
NYC—Staten Island

## NYC—Overview

### INFO LINES & SERVICES

**AA Gay/ Lesbian Intergroup** at Lesbian/ Gay Community Center 212/647–1680

**LGBT Community Center** 208 W 13th (at 7th Ave) 212/620–7310 • 9am-11pm • many group meetings & resources • museum • wheelchair access

### ENTERTAINMENT & RECREATION

**Before Stonewall: A Lesbian & Gay History Tour** meet: Washington Square Arch (at Big Onion Walking Tours) 212/439–1090

**Gotham Girls Roller Derby** 888/830–2253 • NYC's female roller derby league

**New York Liberty** Madison Square Garden, New York 212/465–6766 • check out the Women's Nat'l Basketball Association while you're in New York

### PUBLICATIONS

**Gay City News** 646/452–2500 • LGBT newspaper • weekly

**Get Out Magazine** 646/761–3325 • content from the hottest gay and gay-friendly spots in New York

**GO Magazine** 888/466–9244 • the nation's most widely distributed, free, lesbian publication • "cultural road map for the city girl" • listings, features, entertainment, style, fitness & more

**MetroSource** 212/691–5127 • LGBT lifestyle magazine & resource directory

**Next Magazine** • entertainment & nightlife paper

**Odyssey Magazine** 323/874–8788 • dish on NYC's club scene

**Velvetpark Magazine** 347/881–1025, 888/616–1989 • quarterly lesbian/ feminist glossy w/ focus on the arts

### SEX CLUBS

**Submit** 718/789–4053 • monthly • women & trans play party • takes place in Park Slope, Brooklyn, call for exact location

## NYC—Soho, Greenwich & Chelsea

### INFO LINES & SERVICES

**Audre Lorde Project** 147 W 24th St 212/463–0342 • 1pm-7pm Tue-Th only • LGBT center for people of color • transgender welcoming

### ACCOMMODATIONS

**Ace Hotel** 20 W 29th St (at Broadway) 212/679–2222 • gay-friendly • hip hotel near Flatiron District

**Chelsea Pines Inn** 317 W 14th St (btwn 8th & 9th Aves) 212/929–1023, 888/546–2700 • gay/ straight • WiFi • gay-owned

**The Chelsea Savoy Hotel** 204 W 23rd St (at 7th Ave) 212/929–9353, 866/929–9353 • gay/ straight • kids ok • WiFi • wheelchair access

**Chelsea Star Hotel** 300 W 30th St (at 8th Ave) 212/ 244–7827, 877/ 827–6969 • gay/ straight • WiFi

**Crosby Street Hotel** 79 Crosby St (at Spring) 212/226–6400 • gay-friendly • each of the 86 rooms are one-of-a-kind, afternoon tea served, bar, restaurant and gym • WiFi

**Eventi** 851 6th Ave (at 30th St) 212/564–4567, 866/996–8396 • gay-friendly • pets ok

**The GEM Hotel Chelsea** 300 W 22nd St (at 8th Ave) 212/675–1911 • gay/ straight • WiFi • wheelchair access • see ad in front color section

**The GEM Hotel SoHo** 135 E Houston St (btwn 1st & 2nd Aves) 212/358–8844 • gay/ straight • WiFi • wheelchair access • see ad in front color section

**Gershwin Hotel** 7 E 27th St (at 5th Ave) 212/545–8000 • gay-friendly • artsy hotel w/ model's floor dorms & rooms • art gallery • WiFi

**Hotel 17** 225 E 17th St 212/475–2845 • gay-friendly • "East Village chic" budget hotel • shared baths

**Incentra Village House** 32 8th Ave (at W 12th St) 212/206–0007 • gay/straight • nonsmoking • WiFi • wheelchair access

**The Jade Hotel** 52 W 13th St (at 6th Ave) 212/375–1300 • gay-friendly

**The Jane** 113 Jane St (at Hudson River Pk) 212/924–6700 • gay/ straight • inspired by luxury train cabins • some shared baths • WiFi

**Soho Grand Hotel** 310 W Broadway (at Canal St) 212/965–3000, 800/965–3000 • gay-friendly • big, glossy, over-the-top hotel • WiFi • wheelchair access

**The Standard Hotel** 848 Washington St (at W 13th) 212/645–4646, 877/550–4646 • gay-friendly • ultra-modern, luxe hotel straddling the High Line • pool • WiFi

**Tribeca Grand** 2 Ave of the Americas 212/519–6600 • gay/ straight • WiFi • pets ok

**Washington Square Hotel** 103 Waverly Pl (at MacDougal St) 212/777–9515, 800/222–0418 • gay-friendly • on historic Washington Square Park • also North Square restaurant & lounge • WiFi

**Wyndham Garden Hotel Chelsea** 37 W 24th St 212/243–0800 • gay-friendly • WiFi • wheelchair access

## BARS

**Arrow Bar** 85 Ave A (btwn 5th & 6th) 212/673–1775 • 4pm-close • gay/ straight • dancing/DJ • theme nights

**Barracuda** 275 W 22nd St (at 8th Ave) 212/645–8613 • 4pm-4am • popular • mostly gay men • live DJs • drag shows

**Beauty Bar** 231 E 14th St (at 3rd Ave) 212/539–1389 • 5pm-4am, from 7pm wknds • gay/ straight • dancing/DJ

**The Boiler Room** 86 E 4th St (at 2nd Ave) 212/254–7536 • 4pm-4am • mostly gay men • neighborhood bar • WiFi

**Boots & Saddle** 100A 7th Ave S (at Christopher) 212/633–1986 • 1pm-4am • mostly gay men • neighborhood bar • drag shows • karaoke

**Cake Shop** 152 Ludlow St (btwn Stanton & Rivington) 212/253–0036 • 9am-2am, till 4am wknds • gay-friendly • cafe/ bakery by day, punk bands at night

**Cubbyhole** 281 W 12th St (at 4th St) 212/243–9041 • 4pm-4am, from 2pm wknds • lesbians/ gay men • neighborhood bar

**Eastern Bloc** 505 E 6th St (at Ave A) 212/777–2555 • 7pm-4am • popular • lesbians/ gay men • trendy lounge w/ DJ • go-go boys Th-Sat • wheelchair access

**G Lounge** 225 W 19th St (at 7th Ave) 212/929–1085 • 4pm-4am • mostly gay men • lounge • live DJs • gay-owned

**Gym Sports Bar** 167 8th Ave (btwn 18th & 19th) 212/337–2439 • 4pm-close, from 1pm wknds • mostly gay men • neighborhood sports bar

**Henrietta Hudson** 438 Hudson (at Morton) 212/924–3347 • 4pm-4am, from 2pm wknds • mostly women • neighborhood bar • dancing/DJ • wheelchair access

**Julius'** 159 W 10th St 212/243-1928 • 11am-2am, till 4am wknds • mostly gay men • neighborhood bar • food served

**Marie's Crisis** 59 Grove St (at 7th Ave) • 4pm-4am • lesbians/ gay men • piano bar from 9:30pm

**The Monster** 80 Grove St (at W 4th St, Sheridan Square) 212/924–3558 • 4pm-4am, from 2pm wknds • popular • mostly gay men • dancing/DJ • piano bar & cabaret • T-dance Sun • wheelchair access

**Nowhere** 322 E 14th St (btwn 1st & 2nd) 212/477–4744 • 3pm-4am • lesbians/ gay men • transgender-friendly • neighborhood bar

**Phoenix** 447 E 13th (at Ave A) 212/477–9979 • 3pm-4am • lesbians/ gay men • neighborhood bar • patio

**The Rust Knot** 425 West St (at 11th St) 212/645–5668 • 4pm-2am, from 2pm wknds • gay/ straight • LGBT Sunday Tea dance called Scissor Sundays • bar food served • wheelchair access

**Stonewall Inn** 53 Christopher St (at 7th Ave) **212/488-2705** • 2pm-4am • lesbians/gay men, more women Fri • neighborhood bar • dancing/DJ • drag shows

## NIGHTCLUBS

**Bar 13** 35 E 13th St (btwn Broadway & 5th Ave) **212/979-6677** • 5pm-4am, till midnight Mon • gay/ straight • check local listings for gay events

**Big Apple Ranch** 39 W 19th St, 5th flr (btwn 5th & 6th, at Dance Manhattan) • 8pm-1am Sat only • lesbians/gay men • dancing/DJ • country/western • two-step lessons • beer & wine only • cover charge

**Boys Night Out** 369 W 46th St (at the Ritz) • Th only, mostly gay men, younger crowd

**Happy Ending** 302 Broome St (at Forsyth) **212/334-9676** • 7pm-4am, from 10pm Tues, clsd Sun-Mon • gay/ straight • theme nights

**Hot Rabbit** 80 Grove St (at W 4th, at the Monster) • 10pm Fri only • queer dance party • lots of girls

**Penthaus Fridays** 760 8th Ave (btwn 46th & 47th, at the Copa) • 11pm Fri • mostly men • rooftop dancing & cocktails • younger crowd

**Pyramid** 101 Ave A (at 7th St) **212/228-4888** • gay/ straight • dancing/DJ • theme nights

**Sea Tea** leaves from Pier 40 (West Side Hwy at Houston St) **212/675-2971** • 6pm-10pm Sun (June-Sept) • mostly gay men • dancing/DJ • professional • multiracial • buffet • live shows • gay-owned • cover

**Sweet Fox** 92 2nd Ave (at Lit Lounge) • 10pm Th only • lesbians/gay men • dancing/DJ

## RESTAURANTS

**7A** 109 Ave A (at 7th St) **212/475-9001** • 24hrs • great fake meat & tasty mimosas!

**Agave** 140 Seventh Ave (btwn 10th St & Charles) **212/989-2100** • noon-close • popular brunch • Southwestern

**Angelica Kitchen** 300 E 12th St (at 1st Ave) **212/228-2909** • 11:30am-10:30pm • vegetarian/vegan

**Awash** 338 E 6th (btwn 1st & 2nd Aves) **212/982-9589** • 11am-11pm • Ethiopian

**Benny's Burritos** 113 Greenwich (at Jane) **212/633-9210** • 11am-11pm, till midnight Fri-Sat • cheap & huge

**Big Gay Ice Cream Shop** 125 E 7th St (at 1st Ave) **212/533-9333** • 1pm-midnight • also Big Gay Ice Cream Truck from May-Oct

**Blossom** 187 9th Ave (at 21st) **212/627-1144** • lunch Fri-Sun, dinner nightly • gourmet vegan

**Blue Ribbon** 97 Sullivan St (at Spring St) **212/274-0404** • 4pm-4am • chef hangout • wheelchair access

**Cowgirl Hall of Fame** 519 Hudson St (at W 10th) **212/633-1133** • lunch, dinner, wknd brunch

**Crispo** 240 W14th St (at 7th) **212/229-1818** • dinner only, great caramelized cauliflower & carbonara

**East of Eighth** 254 W 23rd St (at 8th) **212/352-0075** • lunch & dinner, bar open late

**Elmo** 156 7th Ave (at 20th St) **212/337-8000** • lunch & dinner, also lounge

**Intermezzo** 202 8th Ave (at 21st St) **212/929-3433** • noon-11pm, till 4pm Sun • Italian • great wknd brunch

**LaVagna** 545 E 5th St (btwn Aves A & B) **212/979-1005** • dinner only • Italian • some veggie

**Lucky Cheng's** 95 Delancey St (at Ludlow) **212/995-5500** • 5:30pm-midnight • popular • Asian/ fusion • full bar • drag shows • karaoke

**The Meatball Shop** 200 9th St **212/257-4363** • 6pm-midnight, till 1am Fri-Sat, also on 84 Stanton, 64 Greenwich & 170 Bedford

**The Noho Star** 330 Lafayette St (at Bleecker) **212/925-0070** • 8am-midnight, from 10:30am wknds • eclectic European & Chinese

**Omai** 158 9th Ave (at 19th St) **212/633-0550** • dinner nightly • Vietnamese

**Philip Marie** 569 Hudson St (at 11th St) **212/242-6200** • noon-11pm, clsd Mon • New American dining • outside seating

**Red Bamboo** 140 W 4th St (at MacDougal) **212/260-1212** • noon-midnight • vegetarian/vegan

**Sacred Chow** 227 Sullivan St (btwn W 3rd St & Bleecker) **212/337-0863** • 11am-10pm, till 11pm Fri-Sat • gourmet vegan • juice & smoothie bar • baked goods • kosher • wheelchair access

**Sigiri** 91 1st Ave (btwn 5th & 6th Sts) **212/614-9333** • lunch & dinner • Sri Lankan

**Trattoria Pesce Pasta** 262 Bleecker St (at 6th Ave) **212/645-2993** • noon-midnight

**Veselka** 144 2nd Ave (at 9th St) **212/228-9682** • 24hrs • Ukrainian • great pierogi

## ENTERTAINMENT & RECREATION

**Chelsea Classics** 260 W 23rd St (btwn 7th & 8th, at Clearview Cinema) 212/691–5519 • Th night only • drag diva Hedda Lettuce hosts camp movies

**Dixon Place** 161 Chrystie St (at Delancey) 212/219–0736 • many gay-themed productions • also HOT Festival of queer performance in July

**High Line** Gansevoort & W 30th St (btwn 9th & 11th Ave) 212/500–6035 • elevated railway converted to beautiful urban park

**La Mama** 74 E 4th St 212/475–7710 • experimental theater

**Leslie/ Lohman Gay Art Foundation & Gallery** 26 Wooster St (btwn Grand & Canal) 212/431–2609 • noon-6pm, clsd Sun-Mon

**PS 122** 150 1st Ave (at E 9th St) 212/477–5829, 212/352–3101 (TICKETS) • it's rough, it's raw, it's real New York performance art

**WOW Cafe Theatre** 59-61 E 4th St, 4th flr (btwn 2nd Ave & Bowery) 917/725–1482 • open Th-Sat • women & trans theater

## BOOKSTORES

**Bluestockings Bookstore** 172 Allen St (btwn Stanton & Rivington) 212/777–6028 • 11am-11pm • fairtrade cafe • nightly readings • activist center • performances • live music

## RETAIL SHOPS

**Flight 001** 96 Greenwich Ave (btwn Jane & 12th) 212/989–0001, 877/354–4481 • 11am-8pm, noon-6pm Sun • way cool travel gear

## EROTICA

**Babeland** 43 Mercer St (btwn Broome & Grande) 212/966–2120 • 11am-10pm, till 7pm Sun

**Babeland** 94 Rivington (btwn Orchard & Ludlow) 212/375–1701 • noon-10pm • owned by women

**Pleasure Chest** 156 7th Ave S (at Charles) 212/242–2158 • 10am-midnight

# NYC—Downtown

## ACCOMMODATIONS

**Gild Hall, A Thompson Hotel** 15 Gold St (at Platt) 212/232–7700, 212/232–7800 (RESERVATIONS) • gay/straight • high-tech boutique hotel • also restaurant & lounge • wheelchair access

## RESTAURANTS

**La Flaca** 384 Grand St 646/692–9259 • noon-4am • Mexican • full bar

# NYC—Midtown

## ACCOMMODATIONS

**Archer** 45 W 38th St 212/719-4100, 855/437-9100 • gay/straight • filled with quirky, curated luxuries • restaurant and rooftop bar

**Chambers Hotel** 15 W 56th St (at 5th Ave) 212/974–5656, 866/204–5656 • gay-friendly • upscale boutique hotel • fabulous art collection

**Comfort Inn - Midtown West** 442 W 36th St (btwn 9th & 10th) 212/714–6699 • gay-friendly • WiFi • wheelhair access

**Distrikt Hotel** 342 W 40th St (at 9th Ave) 646/831–6780 , 888/444–5610 • gay-friendly • WiFi • upscale boutique hotel

**The GEM Hotel Midtown West** 449 W 36th St (at 10th Ave) 212/967–7206 • gay/ straight • WiFi • wheelchair access • see ad in front color section

**Hotel 57** 130 E 57th St (at Lexington) 212/753–8841, 800/497–6028 • gay-friendly • nonsmoking • WiFi • wheelchair access

**The Hotel Metro** 45 W 35th St (at 5th Ave) 212/947–2500, 800/356–3870 • gay-friendly • WiFi • wheelchair access

**Hudson Hotel** 356 W 58th St (at 9th) 512/554–6000, 800/697–1791 • magical hotel w/ trendy bars

**Ink48** 653 11th Ave (at 48th St) 212/757–0088, 877/843–8869 • gay-friendly • WiFi • luxe hotel in former printing house

**Ivy Terrace** 230 E 58th St 516/662–6862 • private studio rental • terrace • nonsmoking • women-owned

**The MAve** 61 Madison Ave (at 27th St) 212/532-7373 • gay-friendly • WiFi • pets ok

**The Out NYC** 510 W 42nd S 212/947–2999, 855/568-8692 • lesbians/ gay men • NYC's first straight-friendly urban resort • restaurant & club on-site

**The Pod Hotel** 230 E 51st Street (near 2nd Ave) 212/355–0300, 800/742–5945 • gay-friendly • nonsmoking • WiFi • compact rooms • rooftop lounge • wheelchair access

**Room Mate Grace** 125 W 45th St (near Sixth Ave) 212/354–2323 • gay-friendly • swimming pool nonsmoking • WiFi • wheelchair access

**The Strand** 33 W 37th St 212/448–1024 • gay-friendly • WiFi

**Travel Inn** 515 W 42nd St (at 10th Ave) 212/695–7171, 800/869–4630 • gay-friendly • outdoor pool • wheelchair access

**The Tuscany** 120 E 39th St (at Park Ave) 212/686–1600, 877/WHOTELS (RESERVATIONS ONLY) • gay/ straight • WiFi • also Parisian-style cafe-bar • wheelchair access

## BARS

**9th Avenue Saloon** 656 9th Ave (at 46th St) 212/307–1503 • noon-4am • mostly gay men • neighborhood bar • karaoke

**Atlas Social Club** 753 9th Ave (btw 59th & 51) 212/262–8527 • 4pm-4am, decorated like an old school boxing gym

**Bar Centrale** 324 W 46th St (at 8th Ave) 212/581–3130 • 5pm-close • gay/ straight • neighborhood bar • celebs a-plenty

**Bar Tini Ultra Lounge** 642 10th Ave (at 45th) 917/388–2897 • 4pm-4am • mostly gay men • theme nights

**Don't Tell Mama** 343 W 46th St (at 9th Ave) 212/757–0788 • 4pm-4am • popular • gay-friendly • young crowd • piano bar & cabaret • cover + 2-drink minimum for cabaret • call for shows

**Evolve** 221 E 58th St (at 2nd Ave) 212/355–3395 • 4pm-4am • mostly gay men • trangender parties

**Flaming Saddle's Saloon** 793 9th Ave 212/713–0481 • 4pm-2am, from 2pm Sat-Sun • lesbians/ gay men • dancing/Dj • country western

**HK Hell's Kitchen** 523 9th Ave (at 39th St) 212/913–9092 • swank lounge • also restaurant • theme nights

**Industry** 355 W 52nd St (at 9th Ave) 646/476–2747 • 4pm-4am • mostly gay men

**Posh Bar & Lounge** 405 W 51st St (at 9th Ave) 212/957–2222 • 3pm-4am • mostly gay men • neighborhood bar • popular happy hour • theme nights • DJ nightly

**The Ritz** 369 W 46th St (btwn 8th & 9th Aves) 212/333–2554 • 4pm-4am • mostly gay men • dancing/DJ • great place for a drink pre- or post- theater • frag shows

**Therapy** 348 W 52nd St (at 9th) 212/397–1700 • 5pm-4am • lesbians/ gay men • live shows • cabaret • food served

**Uncle Charlie's** 139 E 45th St (btwn 3rd & Lexington) 212/661–9097 • 4pm-4am • mostly gay men • mostly Asian • open mic Fri-Sun • karaoke • piano bar

## NIGHTCLUBS

**BPM** 516 W 42nd S 212/239–2999 • 10pm-4am • mostly gay men • dancing/DJ • live shows • cabaret • drag shows

**Escuelita** 301 W 39th St (at 8th Ave) 212/631–0588 • 10pm-5am, more women Fri , clsd Mon & Wed • mostly gay men • dancing/DJ • drag shows • Latino/a • cover • 18+

**Girlnation** 531 Hudson St (at Charles St, at Budhu Lounge) 212/391–8053 • check facebook.com/girlnationnyc1 for events • mostly women • popular lounge party • dancing/DJ

**LoverGirl NYC** 60 E 2nd Ave (btwn 3rd & 4th at Bonafide) 212/252–3397 • 10:30pm-4am Sat • mostly women • dancing/DJ • multiracial • live shows • cover charge

## RESTAURANTS

**44 & X Hell's Kitchen** 622 10th Ave (at 44th St) 212/977–1170 • lunch & dinner • American comfort food • wheelchair access • gay-owned

**44 1/2** 626 10th Ave (btwn 44 & 45) 212/399–4450 • 5:30pm-close, brunch wknds • wheelchair access • gay-owned

**A Voce** 41 Madison Ave (at 26th) 212/545–8555 • lunch Mon-Fri, dinner nightly • Italian • reservations recommended

**Arriba Arriba** 762 9th Ave (at 51st) 212/489–0810 • noon-midnight, till 1am wknds • Mexican • great margaritas

**Bamboo 52** 344 W 52nd St (btwn 8th & 9th Aves) 212/315–2777 • noon-4am, from 4pm Sun • sushi • also sake bar • garden

**Bann** 350 W 50th St (btwn 8th & 9th Aves) 212/582–4446 • lunch Mon-Fri, dinner nightly • Korean

**Lips** 227 E 56th St (at 3rd Ave) 212/675–7710 • 6pm-midnight, till 1:30am Fri-Sat, gospel brunch Sun, clsd Mon • Italian/ American • served by queens

**Market Cafe** 496 9th Ave (at 38th St) 212/967–3892 • lunch & dinner, wknd brunch • great food • gay-owned

**Vynl** 754 9th Ave (at 51st St) 212/974–2003 • 11am-11pm • also bar • also at 102 8th Ave

## ENTERTAINMENT & RECREATION

**Ars Nova** 511 W 54th St (at 10th Ave) 212/489–9800 • many gay-themed productions

**Empire State Building** 350 5th Ave (btwn 33rd & 34th) • spectacular views of the city • visit day or night

**Sex & the City Hotspots Tour** 5th Ave, in front of the Pulitzer Fountain (at 58th St) 212/913–9780 • 3 hours • reservations a must!

## EROTICA

**Eve's Garden** 119 W 57th St #1201 (btwn 6th & 7th) 212/757-8651 • 11am-7pm, clsd Sun • women's sexuality boutique

# NYC—Uptown

## ACCOMMODATIONS

**710 Guest Suites** 710 St Nicholas Ave (at 145th) 212/491-5622 • gay-friendly • modern, chic apt suites

**BB Lodges** 1598 Lexington Ave (btwn 101st & 102nd) 917/345-7914 • gay/ straight • private rooms w/ private kitchens • nonsmoking • WiFi • gay-owned

**Harlem Renaissance House** 212/226-1590 • gay/ straight • in heart of Harlem's Striver Row District • kids ok • nonsmoking • WiFi • gay-owned

**Hotel Newton** 2528 Broadway (btwn 94th & 95th) 212/678-6500, 800/643-5553 • gay/ straight • hotel on Upper West Side • nearest to Columbia University • wheelchair access

**Mount Morris House B&B** 12 Mount Morris Park W (at 121st St) 917/478-6214 • gay/ straight • private suites & apartments in 1888 historic Manhattan Mansion • WiFi • gay-owned

## BARS

**Brandy's Piano Bar** 235 E 84th St (at 2nd Ave) 212/650-1944 • 4pm-4am • lesbians/ gay men • piano bar from 9:30pm

**Cava Wine Bar** 185 W 80th St (at Amsterdam) 212/724-2282 • 5:30pm-2am, from 3:30pm Sun • gay-friendly • also tapas

**Suite** 992 Amsterdam (at 109th St) 212/222-4600 • 5pm-4am • mostly gay men • friendly neighborhood bar • karaoke • drag shows

## RESTAURANTS

**Billie's Black** 271 W 119th St (at St Nicholas Ave ) 212/280-2248 • noon-midnight, till 4am Fri-Sat • soul food • also full bar • live music Th-Fri • karaoke • gay-owned

**Joanne Trattoria** 70 W 68th St (btw Columbus & Central Park W), New York 212/721-0068

## EROTICA

**Pleasure Chest** 1150 2nd Ave (at E 60th) 212/355-6909 • 10am-10pm, till midnight Th-Sat

# NYC—Brooklyn

## INFO LINES & SERVICES

**Audre Lorde Project** 85 S Oxford St 718/596-0342 • 1pm-7pm Tue-Th only • LGBT center for people of color • transgender welcoming • events, resources, HIV services

**Lesbian Herstory Archives** 484 14th St 718/768-3953 • exists to gather & preserve records of lesbian lives & activities • wheelchair access

## ACCOMMODATIONS

**Hotel Le Bleu** 370 4th Ave 718/625-1500, 866/427-6073 • gay-friendly • WiFi • cont'l bkfst

**Hotel Le Jolie** 235 Meeker Ave 718/625-2100, 866/526-4097 • gay-friendly • WiFi • cont'l bkfst •

**South Slope Green B&B** 452A 17th St (at 8th Ave) 347/721-6575 • gay/ straight • nonsmoking • WiFi • lesbian-owned

## BARS

**The Abbey** 536 Driggs Ave (btwn N 7th & 8th), Williamsburg 718/599-4400 • 3pm-4am • gay/ straight • neighborhood dive bar

**Alligator Lounge** 600 Metropolitan Ave (at Lorimer) 718/599-4440 • 3pm-4am, from 1pm wknds • gay/ straight • free pizza from 6pm • karaoke Th

**Branded Saloon** 603 Vanderbilt Ave (at Bergen) 718/484-8704 • gay/ straight • neighborhood bar • live shows • karaoke • gay-owned

**Excelsior** 390 5th Ave (btwn 6th & 7th) 718/832-1599 • 6pm-4am, from 2pm wknds • lesbians/ gay men • patio

**Ginger's Bar** 363 5th Ave (btwn 5th & 6th Sts, in Park Slope) 718/788-0924 • 5pm-4am, from 2pm wknds • lesbians/ gay men • neighborhood bar • patio • occasional live shows • lesbian-owned

**Metropolitan** 559 Lorimer St (at Metropolitan Ave), Williamsburg 718/599-4444 • 3pm-4am • lesbians/ gay men • comfy neighborhood bar w/ 2 fireplaces & patio • more women Wed • WiFi

**This N That** 108 N 6th St (at Berry), Williamsburg 718/599-5959 • 4pm-4am • lesbians/ gay men • neighborhood bar

**This n' That** 108 N 6th St 718/599-5959 • 4pm-4am • gay/ lesbian • dancing/DJ • live shows

## NIGHTCLUBS

**Club Langston** 1073 Atlantic Ave (btwn Franklin & Classon) 718/622-5183 • 11pm-4am Th-Sun • mostly gay men • mostly African American • theme nights

**Glasslands Gallery** 289 Kent Ave, Williamsburg (btwn S 1st & S 2nd) 718/599-1450 • performance, art & dance space

**Hot Rabbit Brooklyn** 22 Wyckoff Ave (at Radio Bushwick) • 10pm Sat only • queer dance party • lots of girls

## CAFES

**Outpost** 1014 Fulton St (at Downing) 718/636-1260 • 7:30am-midnight, 9am-11pm wknds • lesbians/gay men • art gallery • young, artsy crowd • also beer/wine • gay-owned

## RESTAURANTS

**Alma** 187 Columbia St (at Degraw) 718/643-5400 • dinner nightly, wknd brunch • upscale Mexican • outdoor rooftop seating w/ view of Manhattan • also B61 Bar downstairs

**Bogota Latin Bistro** 141 5th Ave (at St John's Pl) 718/230-3805 • dinner nightly, wknd brunch, clsd Tue • live music • gay-owned

**ChipShop** 383 5th Ave (at 6th St) 718/244-7746 • noon-10pm, till 11pm Th-Sat, from 11am wknds • home of the famous fried Twinkie!

**home made** 293 Van Brunt St (btwn Pioneer & King) 347/223-4135 • dinner & wknd brunch • lesbian-owned

**Johnny Mack's** 1114 8th Ave (btwn 11th & 12th) 718/832-7961 • 4pm-2am, from noon wknds

**Krescendo** 364 Atlantic Ave • famed chef Elizabeth Falkner makes pizza

**Melt** 440 Bergen St (btwn 5th & Flatbush) 718/230-5925 • dinner nightly, brunch wknds, clsd Mon

**Santa Fe Grill** 62 7th Ave (at Lincoln) 718/636-0279 • 5pm-close, from noon wknds • also bar

**Superfine** 126 Front St (at Pearl St) 718/243-9005 • 11:30am-3am, 2pm-11pm Sat, 11am-10pm Sun, clsd Mon • relaxed atmophere • live shows • also bar • lesbian-owned

**Tandem** 236 Troutman St (btwn Wilson & Knickerbocker, in Bushwick) 718/386-2369 • 6pm-4am • also full bar • occasional gay parties

## ENTERTAINMENT & RECREATION

**The Elizabeth A. Sackler Center for Feminist Art of the Brooklyn Museum** 200 Eastern Pkwy (at the Brooklyn Museum, at Washington Ave) 718/638-5000

**Galapagos Art Space** 16 Main St (at Water St) 718/222-8500 • performance & art space • occasional gay parties

**Ova the Rainbow** 59 Montrose Ave (at The Spectrum) • monthly queer dance party • transgender-friendly

**The Spectrum** 59 Montrose Ave • queer performance space

## EROTICA

**Babeland** 462 Bergen St (at 5th Ave) 718/638-3820 • noon-9pm, till 7pm Sun

# NYC—Queens

## BARS

**Albatross** 36-19 24th Ave (at 37th), Astoria 718/204-9045 • 6pm-4am • gay/straight • neighborhood bar • more gay wknds • gay-owned

**Hombres Lounge** 85-25 37th Ave #206, Jackson Heights 718/930-0886 • 5pm-4pm • mostly gay men • neighborhood bar • karaoke

**The Pop Bar** 12-21 Astoria Blvd (at 14th St) 718/204-8313 • 7pm-4am • gay/straight • live shows

**Sorry Not Sorry Restaurant Bar & Lounge** 70-15 Austin St, Forest Hills 718/263-7743 • 4pm-4am • gay/straight • dancing/DJ • food served

**True Colors** 79-15 Roosevelt Ave (btwn 79th & 80th Sts, Jackson Hts) 718/672-7505 • 4pm-4am • mostly gay men • neighborhood bar • dancing/DJ • multiracial

## NIGHTCLUBS

**Bum Bum Bar** 6314 Roosevelt Ave 718/651-4145 • 10pm-4am Th-Sun • lesbians/gay men • dancing/DJ • mostly Latina

**Evolution** 76-19 Roosevelt Ave (at 77th St), Jackson Hts 718/457-3939 • 5pm-4am • lesbians/gay men • dancing/DJ • mostly Latino/a • drag shows

## RESTAURANTS

**Monika's Cafe Bar** 3290 36th St, Astoria 718/204-5273 • 10am-2am, till 4am Fri-Sat, Th gay night • Th gay night & great brunch menu

## NYC—Bronx

### NIGHTCLUBS

**El Morocco/ Escandalo** 3534 Broadway (at 145th St) **646/479–2361, 212/939–0909** • Wed, Fri, Sat & Sun, gay Latin night • mostly men • dancing/DJ • multiracial

## Nyack

### NIGHTCLUBS

**Barz** 327 Rte 9 W **845/353–4444** • 8pm-4am, from 3pm Sun, clsd Sun-Mon • lesbians/ gay men • dancing/DJ • alternative • karaoke

## Orange County

### EROTICA

**Exotic Gifts & Videos** 658 Rte 211 E (exit 120, off Rte 17), Middletown **845/692–6664**

## Rochester

### INFO LINES & SERVICES

**Gay Alliance of the Genesee Valley (GAGV)** 875 E Main St, 5th flr **585/244–8640** • events • education • SAGE & youth services

### ACCOMMODATIONS

**Silver Waters Bed & Breakfast** 8420 Bay St (at Lummis), Sodus Point **315/483–8098** • gay/ straight • full brkfst • gay-owned

### BARS

**140 Alex Bar & Grill** 140 Alexander St (at Broadway) **585/256–1000** • 4pm-2am, from 2pm Sun • lesbians/ gay men • neighborhood bar • also restaurant • dancing/DJ • live shows • karaoke • drag shows • gay-owned

**Avenue Pub** 522 Monroe Ave (at Goodman) **585/244–4960** • 4pm-2am • popular • mostly gay men • neighborhood bar • dancing/DJ • patio

### NIGHTCLUBS

**Tilt Nightclub** 444 Central Ave **585/232–8440** • 10pm-2:30am Th-Sat • gay/ straight • dancing/DJ • drag shows

**Vertex** 169 N Chestnut St **585/232–5498** • 10pm-2am Wed-Sat • gay/ straight • dancing/DJ • goth club

### CAFES

**Little Theatre Cafe** 240 East Ave **585/258–0400** • 5pm-10pm, till 11pm Fri-Sat, till 8pm Sun • popular • beer/ wine • soups • salads • live jazz • wheelchair access • art gallery

### RETAIL SHOPS

**Equal Grounds** 750 South Ave (at Caroline) **585/256–2362** • 7am-midnight, from 10am wknds • LGBT gifts & books • also coffeehouse

**Outlandish** 274 N Goodman St (in the Village Gate) **585/760–8383** • 11am-9pm, noon-5pm Sun • videos • pride items • books • toys • gay-owned

### PUBLICATIONS

**Empty Closet** **585/244–8640** • LGBT newspaper • resource listings

## Saratoga Springs

### ACCOMMODATIONS

**The Inn at Round Lake** 14 Covel Ave (at Burlington), Round Lake **518/899–4914** • gay-friendly • Victorian B&B • pool • nonsmoking • WiFi • gay-owned

**The Mansion** 801 Rte 29, Rock City Falls **518/885–1607, 888/996–9977** • gay-friendly • 1860 Victorian mansion • full brkfst • fireplaces • nonsmoking • wheelchair access • gay-owned

### BARS

**Desperate Annie's** 12 Caroline St (off Broadway) **518/587–2455** • 4pm-close • gay-friendly • neighborhood bar

### RESTAURANTS

**Esperanto** 6 1/2 Caroline St (off Broadway) **518/587–4236** • 11:30am-close • doughboys!

**Little India** 60 Court St **518/583–4151** • lunch & dinner • tasty & authentic Indian food • beer/ wine only

## Seneca Falls

### RETAIL SHOPS

**WomanMade Products** 91 Fall St **315/568–9364** • 10am-6pm, till 4pm wknds • lesbian & feminist T-shirts • crafts

## Sharon Springs

### ACCOMMODATIONS

**American Hotel** 192 Main St **518/284–2105** • gay/ straight • 1847 Nat'l Register hotel • kids ok • also restaurant & bar • WiFi • wheelchair access • gay-owned

**Edgefield** 153 Washington St **518/284–3339** • gay/ straight • full brkfst • nonsmoking • gay-owned

**The TurnAround Spa Lodge** 105 Washington St 518/284-9708 • lesbians/ gay men • small hotel & health spa • full brkfst • hot tub • food served • nonsmoking • kids ok • clsd Nov-April • lesbian- & gay-owned

## Syracuse

### INFO LINES & SERVICES

**AA Gay/ Lesbian** 315/463-5011 (AA#) • call for meeting schedule

### BARS

**Rain Lounge** 103 N Geddes St 315/218-5951 • 4pm-2:30am • mostly gay men • neighborhood bar • multiracial • transgender-friendly • videos • gay-owned

**Wolf's Den** 617-619 Wolf St 315/560-5637 • 4pm -2am, till midnight Sun-Tue, from noon Sun for brunch • lesbians/gay men • neighborhood bar • karaoke

### NIGHTCLUBS

**Trexx** 319 N Clinton St (exit 18, off Rte 81) 315/474-6408 • 8pm-2am, till 4am Fri-Sat, clsd Sun-Wed • mostly gay men • dancing/DJ • drag shows • videos • 18+ • wheelchair access

### RESTAURANTS

**Cafe Mira** 14 Main St, Adams 315/232-4470 • open 5pm Wed-Sat only • wheelchair access • lesbian-owned

## Utica

### NIGHTCLUBS

**That Place** 216 Bleecker St (at Genesee) • 9pm-2am Th & Sat • popular • mostly gay men • dancing/DJ • young crowd • wheelchair access

## Watertown

### BARS

**Clueless** 545 Arsenal St 315/782-9006 • 8pm-2am Th-Sat • mostly gay men • neighborhood bar • dancing/DJ • videos

## Westchester

### BARS

**B Lounge** 4 Broadway , Valhalla 914/437-5093 • 5pm-1am, till 4am Wed-Fri, 8pm-4am Sat, 6pm-1am Sun • lesbians/ gay men • dancing/DJ • karaoke

## White Plains

### INFO LINES & SERVICES

**The LOFT** 252 Bryant Ave 914/948-2932, 914/948-4922 (HELPLINE) • LGBT community center • call for hours • also newsletter

# NORTH CAROLINA

## Asheville

### INFO LINES & SERVICES

**Lambda AA** 9 Swan St (at Cathedral of All Souls Episcopal Church) 828/254-8539 (AA#), 800/524-0465 • 7pm Mon & Wed, 8pm Fri

### ACCOMMODATIONS

**1889 WhiteGate Inn & Cottage** 173 E Chestnut St 828/253-2553, 800/485-3045 • gay/ straight • 3-course brkfst • nonsmoking • WiFi • gay-owned

**The 1900 Inn on Montford** 296 Montford Ave 828/254-9569, 800/254-9569 • gay-friendly • full brkfst • kids/ pets ok • nonsmoking • WiFi

**27 Blake Street** 27 Blake St 828/252-7390 • gay/ straight • private entrance in Victorian home • gardens • nonsmoking • WiFi • woman-owned

**Biltmore Village Inn** 119 Dodge St (at Irwin) 828/274-8707, 866/274-8779 • gay-friendly • nonsmoking • WiFi • gay-owned

**Cedar Crest Inn** 674 Biltmore Ave 828/252-1389 , 877/251-1389 • gay/ straight • full brkfst • gay-owned

**Compassionate Expressions Mtn Inn & Healing Sanctuary** 828/683-6633 • mostly women • cabins & rooms w/ a view of Blue Ridge Mtns • spa services • commitment ceremonies • nonsmoking • wheelchair access • women-owned

**The Heron House** 828/575-9229 • women only • 3 acres in peaceful Riceville Valley, 15 minutes from downtown •l esbian-owned

**Mountain Laurel B&B** 139 Lee Dotson Rd, Fairview 828/628-9903, 828/712-6289 (CELL) • lesbians/ gay men • full brkfst • nonsmoking • kids ok • WiFi • lesbian-owned

**North Lodge on Oakland B& B** 84 Oakland Rd (at Victoria Rd) 828/252-6433, 800/252-3602 • gay-friendly • nonsmoking • WiFi • gay-owned

**Rainbows End** 23 Deaver St (at Reynolds) 253/732-0458 • mostly women • guest room in private home • shared baths • lesbian-owned

**The Tree House** 190 Tessie Ln, Black Mountain **828/669-3889** • mostly women • transgender-friendly • nonsmoking • lesbian/trans-owned

## BARS

**O Henry's/ The Underground** 237 Haywood St **828/254-1891** • 4pm-2am • mostly gay men • Underground from 10pm Fri-Sat only • dancing/DJ

**Tressa's** 28 Broadway **828/254-7072** • 4pm-2:30am, from 6pm Sat, clsd Sun-Mon • gay/straight • jazz/cigar bar • dancing/DJ • live shows

## NIGHTCLUBS

**Scandals** 11 Grove St (at Patton) **828/252-2838** • 10pm-3am Th-Sun • lesbians/gay men • dancing/DJ • drag shows • videos • 18+ • private club • wheelchair access

## CAFES

**Biltmore's** 67 Biltmore Ave **828/252-1500** • 8am-6pm, clsd Sun • wheelchair access

**Edna's of Asheville** 870 Merrimon Ave **828/255-3881** • 6am-10pm • beer/wine • WiFi • private club • wheelchair access • gay-owned

## RESTAURANTS

**Avenue M** 791 Merrimon Ave (at Graclyn Rd) **828/350-8181** • 5pm-late, 10am-2:30pm & 5pm-9pm Sun • full bar

**Barley's Taproom & Pizzeria** 42 Biltmore **828/255-0504** • 11:30am-2am, till midnight Sun

**Charlotte Street Grill & Pub** 157 Charlotte St **828/252-2948** • noon-2am • WiFi • lesbian-owned

**Early Girl Eatery** 8 Wall St **828/259-9292** • brkfst & lunch daily, dinner Tue-Sun, wknd brunch • Southern • local ingredients

**Firestorm Cafe & Books** 610 Haywood Rd **828/255-8115** • 10am-11pm, clsd Sun • vegetarian • WiFi • worker-owned

**Laughing Seed Cafe** 40 Wall St (at Haywood) **828/252-3445** • 11:30am-9pm, till 10pm Fri-Sat, Sun brunch from 10am, clsd Tue • vegetarian/ vegan • beer/ wine • patio • wheelchair access

**Table** 48 College St **828/254-8980** • 11am-2:30pm & 5:30pm-11pm, Sun brunch, clsd Tue • moderately priced New American

**Tupelo Honey Cafe** 12 College St **828/255-4404** • 9am-10pm • "Southern homecookin' w/ an uptown twist" • woman-owned

## ENTERTAINMENT & RECREATION

**LaZoom Tours** 90 Biltmore Ave **828/225-6932** • city-wide comedy tours of Asheville, afternoons & evenings • BYOB

## BOOKSTORES

**Malaprop's Bookstore/ Cafe** 55 Haywood St (at Walnut) **828/254-6734, 800/441-9829** • 9am-9pm, till 7pm Sun

## RETAIL SHOPS

**Jewels That Dance: Jewelry Design** 63 Haywood St **828/254-5088** • 10:30am-6pm, clsd Sun • gay-owned

## EROTICA

**BedTyme Stories** 2334 Hendersonville Rd, Arden **828/684-8250**

**Va Va Voom** 36 Battery Park Ave **828/254-6329** • women's lingerie, toys, etc

# Blowing Rock

## ACCOMMODATIONS

**Blowing Rock Victorian Inn** 242 Ransom St (at US 321) **828/295-0034** • gay-friendly • full brkfst • pets ok • nonsmoking • WiFi • gay-owned

# Brevard

## ACCOMMODATIONS

**Ash Grove Mountain Cabins & Camping** 749 E Fork Rd **828/885-7216** • gay/straight • camping & cabins • nonsmoking • WiFi • gay-owned

# Charlotte

## INFO LINES & SERVICES

**Acceptance Group Gay/ Lesbian AA** 2830 Dorcester Pl (at St. Paul United Methodist Church) **704/377-0244, 877/233-6853** • 8pm Fri

## ACCOMMODATIONS

**VanLandingham Estate** 2010 The Plaza (at Belvedere) **704/334-8909, 888/524-2020** • gay-friendly • full brkfst • nonsmoking • WiFi • gay-owned

## BARS

**The Bar At 316** 316 Rensselaer Ave (at South Blvd) **704/910-1478** • 5pm-2am, from 3pm Sun • popular • lesbians/ gay men • neighborhood bar • private club

**Petra's Piano Bar** 1917 Commonwealth Ave (at Thomas) **704/332-6608** • 5pm-2am, clsd Mon • gay/straight • live shows • karaoke • WiFi

**Sidelines Sports Bar & Billiards**
704/525–2608 • 4pm-2am, from noon wknds • gay-friendly • neighborhood bar • food served • WiFi • private club • wheelchair access • gay-owned

## NIGHTCLUBS

**Cathode Azure Club** 1820 South Blvd (near East Blvd) 704/823–6066 • 7pm-2am, from noon Sun • mostly gay men • dancing/DJ • drag shows

**L4 Lounge** 2906 Central Ave 704/567–2158 • 7pm-midnight Wed-Th, 9pm-2:30am fri-Sat, clsd Sun-Tue • mostly womens • dancing/DJ • live shows • food served

**The Nickel Bar** 704/916–9389 • 9pm-2am, from 5pm Sun, clsd Mon-Wed • lesbians/ gay men • dancing/DJ • mostly African American

**Scorpio's** 2301 Freedom Dr (at Berryhill Rd) 704/373–9124 • 9pm-3am Wed & Fri-Sun • lesbians/ gay men • dancing/DJ • multiracial • 18+ • private club • wheelchair access

**UpStage** 3306 N Davidson St (at E 36th St) 704/430-4821 • gay/ straight • performing arts and creative events

## CAFES

**Amelie's French Bakery** 2424 N Davidson St 704/376–1781 • open 24hrs • soup & sandwiches, & of course pastries!

**Smelly Cat Coffee** 514 E 36th St 704/374–9656 • 7am-10pm, till 1am Fri-Sat

## RESTAURANTS

**300 East** 300 East Blvd (at Cleveland) 704/332–6507 • 11am-10pm, till 11pm Fri-Sat, Sun brunch • full bar • wheelchair access

**Alexander Michael's** 401 W 9th St (at Pine) 704/332–6789 • lunch & dinner, clsd Sun • pub fare • full bar

**Cosmos Cafe** 300 N College (at 6th) 704/372–3553 • 11am-2am, clsd Sun • also martini lounge

**Dish** 1220 Thomas Ave (at Central) 704/344–0343 • 11am-10pm, till 11pm Fri-Sat, clsd Sun • comfort food • patio

**Lupie's Cafe** 2718 Monroe Rd (near 5th St) 704/374–1232 • 11am-10pm,from noon Sat, clsd Sun • homestyle cookin' • some veggie

## ENTERTAINMENT & RECREATION

**One Voice Chorus** PO Box 9241 28299 • LGBT chorus

## BOOKSTORES

**Paper Skyscraper** 330 East Blvd (at Euclid Ave) 704/333–7130 • 10am-7pm, till 6pm Sat, noon-5pm Sun • books • funky gifts • wheelchair access

**White Rabbit Books** 920 Central Ave (at E 10th) 704/377–4067 • 10am-9pm, noon-6pm Sun • LGBT • books • magazines • T-shirts • DVDs • novelties

## RETAIL SHOPS

**The Bag Lady** 1710 Kenilworth Ave (at East Blvd) 704/338–9778 • books & gifts • events

## PUBLICATIONS

**Q Notes** 704/531–9988 • bi-weekly LGBT newspaper for North Carolina

# Fayetteville

## EROTICA

**Cupid's Boutique** 137 N Reilly Rd (at Morganton) 910/860–7716

**Fort Video & News** 4431 Bragg Blvd (near 401 overpass) 910/868–9905 • 24hrs

**Priscilla McCall's** 3800 Sycamore Dairy Rd (at Bragg Blvd) 910/860–1776

# Greensboro

## INFO LINES & SERVICES

**Live & Let Live AA** 617 N Elm St (at Presbyterian Church) 336/854–4278 (AA#) • 8pm Tue • also Free Spirit, 8pm Sat, 2105 W Market St (at Episcopal Church)

## ACCOMMODATIONS

**Biltmore Greensboro Hotel** 111 W Washington St (at Elm St) 336/272–3474, 800/332–0303 • gay/ straight • fully restored historic hotel • gym • WiFi • kids/ pets ok • wine & cheese tastings • nonsmoking • gay-owned

**O Henry Hotel** 624 Green Valley Rd (at Benjamin Pkwy) 336/854–2000, 800/965–8259 • gay-friendly • pool • full brkfst • afternoon tea • bar/ restaurant popular w/ local gay community • wheelchair access

## BARS

**The Q** 708 W Market St 336/272–2587 • 4pm-close, from 9pm Sat, from 7pm Sun • lesbians/ gay men • more women Sun • neighborhood bar • DJ • karaoke • 18+ • WiFi • patio

## NIGHTCLUBS

**Chemistry** 2901 Spring Garden St 336/617–8571 • 8pm-2:30am, from 5pm Fri & Sun • mostly gay men • dancing/DJ • drag shows • karaoke

# Hickory

## NIGHTCLUBS

**Club Cabaret** 101 N Center St (at 1st Ave) 828/322–8103 • 8pm-2am, from 9pm Fri-Sat, clsd Mon-Wed • lesbians/ gay men • dancing/DJ • live shows • WiFi • private club • wheelchair access

## CAFES

**Taste Full Beans** 29 2nd St NW 828/325–0108 • 7am-5:30pm, till 2:30 Sat, clsd Sun • art exhibits • gay-owned

# Jacksonville

## EROTICA

**Priscilla McCall's** 113–A Western Blvd 910/355-0765

# Little Switzerland

## ACCOMMODATIONS

**La Petite Chalet** 38 Orchard Ln (at Hwy 226A) 888/828–1654 • gay/ straight • located on the Blue Ridge Parkway of North Carolina midway between Asheville & Blowing Rock • gay-owned

# Mooresville

## RESTAURANTS

**Pomodoro's Italian American Cafe** 168 Norman Station Blvd 704/663–6686 • 11am-10pm, till 11pm Fri-Sat • beer/ wine • wheelchair access • gay-owned

# Raleigh/Durham/Chapel Hill

## INFO LINES & SERVICES

**Common Solutions Gay/ Lesbian AA** Crownwell Bldg, East Campus (at Duke University), Durham 919/286–9499 (AA#) • 6:30pm Mon

**LGBT Center of Raleigh** 324 S Harrington St, Raleigh 919/832-4484 • social & educational activities, services & groups

## ACCOMMODATIONS

**Heartfriends Inn B&B** 4389 Siler City/Snow Camp Rd (at Ed Clapp Rd), Siler City 919/663-1707, 877/679-0980 • gay/ straight • WiFi • women-owned • wheelchair access

**The King's Daughters Inn** 204 N Buchanan Blvd, Durham 919/354–7000, 877/534–8534 • gay-friendly • complimentary bikes

## BARS

**Fifteen** 317 W Morgan St #113, Raleigh 919/615–2758 • 5pm-2am • lesnbians/gay men • DJ/dancing •piano bar

**Flex** 2 S West St (at Hillsborough), Raleigh 919/832-8855 • 5pm-close, from 2pm Sun • popular • mostly gay men • karaoke • drag shows • private club

**Hibernian Restaurant & Pub** 311 Glenwood Ave (at W Lane St), Raleigh 919/833–2258 • 11am-2am • gay-friendly • live music

## NIGHTCLUBS

**Above & Beyond Ultra Nightclub** 2526 Hillsborough Rd #301, Raleigh 919/813–2582 • 10pm-2am Fri, till 3:30am Sat • lesbians/gay men • dancing/DJ • drag shows

**The Bar** 711 Rigsbee Ave, Durham 919/956–2929 • 4pm-2am, from 2pm wknds, clsd Mon-Tue • lesbians/ gay men • dancing/DJ • deck • karaoke • private club • wheelchair access • lesbian-owned

**Legends/ View** 330 W Hargett St (at S Harrington St), Raleigh 919/831–8888 • 5pm-2:30am • lesbians/ gay men • dancing/DJ • strippers • drag shows • young crowd • private club • wheelchair access

**The Pinhook** 117 W Main St, Durham 991/667–1100 • 5pm-2am, 6pm-midnight Sun • gay/ straight • live music • patio

## CAFES

**Bean Traders** 105-249 W NC Hwy 54, Durham 919/484-2499 • 6am-8pm, from 8am wknds

**Caffe Driade** 1215 E Franklin St #A (at Elizabeth St), Chapel Hill 919/942-2333 • 7am-11pm • live music • also beer & wine served

**Third Place** 1811 Glenwood Ave (at W Whitaker Mill Rd), Raleigh 919/834-6566 • 6am-7pm • also sandwiches & salads

## RESTAURANTS

**Blu Seafood & Bar** 2002 Hillsborough Rd (at 9th St), Durham 919/286–9777 • lunch & dinner, clsd Sun

**The Borough** 317 W Morgan St, Raleigh 919/832-8433 • 4pm-2am • also bar • WiFi

**Crooks Corner** 610 Franklin St (at Merritt Mill Rd), Chapel Hill 919/929–7643 • dinner nightly, Sun brunch, clsd Mon • Southern • full bar • patio • wheelchair access

**Elmo's Diner** 776 9th St (in the Carr Mill Mall), Durham **919/416-3823** • 6:30am-10pm

**Five Star** 511 W Hargett St (at West St), Raleigh **919/833-3311** • 5:30pm-2am • Asianfusion • sexy ambiance for cocktails & nibbles

**Humble Pie** 317 S Harrington St (at Martin), Raleigh **919/829-9222** • 5pm-11pm, bar open late, brunch only Sun • small plates

**Irregardless Cafe** 901 W Morgan St (at Hillsborough), Raleigh **919/833-8898** • lunch Tue-Fri, dinner Tue-Sat, Sun brunch, clsd Mon • plenty veggie • live music • dancing Sat

**Lantern** 423 W Franklin St, Chapel Hill **919/969-8846** • dinner nightly, clsd Sun • Asian • also cocktail lounge till 2am

**The Mad Hatter's Bakeshop & Cafe** 1802 W Main St (at Broad), Durham **919/286-1987** • 7am-9pm, 8am-3pm Sun • awesome cakes & baked goods • WiFi

**The Pit** 328 W Davie St (at S Dawson), Raleigh **919/890-4500** • 11am-10pm, till 11pm wknds • upscale BBQ

**Rue Cler** 401 E Chapel Hill St (at Mangum St), Durham **919/682-8844** • lunch & dinner, wknd brunch • French

**Solas** **919/755-0755** • dinner, Sun brunch • upscale dining • dress code • also rooftop lounge & nightclub

**Spotted Dog** 111 E Main St (at N Greensboro St), Carrboro **919/933-1117** • 11:30am-midnight, clsd Mon • full bar • plenty veggie

**Sunrise Biscuit Kitchen** 1305 E Franklin St, Chapel Hill **919/933-1324** • great brkfst • drive-thru only

**Vivace** 4209 Lassiter Mill Rd #115 (at Pamlico Dr), Raleigh **919/787-7747** • lunch & dinner, Sun brunch • Italian • patio seating • full bar

## ENTERTAINMENT & RECREATION

**Carolina Rollergirls** • NC's female roller derby league • visit carolinarollergirls.com for events

## BOOKSTORES

**Internationalist Books & Community Center** 101 Lloyd St, Carrboro **919/942-1740** • 11am-8pm, noon-6pm Sun • progressive/ alternative • cooperatively run • nonprofit • readings & events

**Quail Ridge Books** 3522 Wade Ave (at Ridgewood Center), Raleigh **919/828-1588, 800/672-6789** • 9am-9pm • LGBT section

**The Regulator Bookshop** 720 9th St (btwn Hillsborough & Perry), Durham **919/286-2700** • 10am-9pm, noon-6pm Sun

## EROTICA

**Castle Video & News** 1210 Capitol Blvd, Raleigh **919/836-9189** • 24hrs

**Cherry Pie** 1819 Fordham Blvd, Chapel Hill **919/928-0499** • 10am-midnight • adult toys

**Frisky Business Boutique** 1720 New Raleigh Hwy, Durham **919/957-4441** • adult toys • also classes

# Washington

## CAFES

**Back Water Jack's Tiki Bar** 1052 E Main St (at Havens St) **252/975-1090** • lunch & dinner, clsd Mon • also bar • wheelchair access

# Wilmington

## ACCOMMODATIONS

**Best Western Coastline Inn** 503 Nutt St **910/763-2800** • gay/ straight • kids ok • nonsmoking • wheelchair access • WiFi • gay-owned

**Rosehill Inn B&B** 114 S 3rd St (at Dock St) **910/815-0250, 800/815-0250** • gay-friendly • WiFi

**The Taylor House Inn** 14 N 7th St **910/763-7581, 800/382-9982** • gay/ straight • romantic 1905 house • full brkfst • nonsmoking • kids ok

## BARS

**Costello's** 211 Princess St (btwn 2nd & 3rd) **910/470-9666** • 7pm-2am, from 5pm Fri • mostly gay men, more women Mon • piano bar • videos • private club • wheelchair access • gay-owned

## NIGHTCLUBS

**Ibiza** 118 Market St (rear) **910/251-1301** • 8pm-3am Wed-Sun only • mostly gay men • dancing/DJ • more women Th • karaoke • drag shows • strippers • young crowd • private club • wheelchair access • gay-owned

## ENTERTAINMENT & RECREATION

**Cinematique** 310 Chestnut St (at Thalian Hall) **910/343-1640** • classic, foreign & notable films

## NORTH DAKOTA

### Fargo

#### INFO LINES & SERVICES

**The Fargo Moorhead Pride Collective and Community Center** 1105 1st Ave S 218/287–8034 • referrals • support • social groups • check www.pridecollective.com for events

#### ACCOMMODATIONS

**The Hotel Donaldson** 101 Broadway 701/478–1000, 888/478–8768 • gay/ straight • restaurant & bar • WiFi

#### CAFES

**Atomic Coffee** 701/478–6160 • 7am-11pm, 8pm-10pm Sun • food served • plenty veggie/ vegan • WiFi

#### RESTAURANTS

**Fargo's Fryn' Pan** 300 Main St (at 4th) 701/293–9952 • 24hrs • popular • wheelchair access

**Mom's Kitchen** 1322 Main St 701/235–4460 • 6am-10pm • full bar

#### RETAIL SHOPS

**Zandbroz Variety** 420 N Broadway 701/239–4729 • 9am-8pm, noon-5pm Sun • books & gifts

#### EROTICA

**Romantix Adult Superstore** 417 N Pacific Ave 701/235–2640 • 9am-3am

### Grand Forks

#### EROTICA

**Romantix Adult Superstore** 102 S 3rd St (at Kittson) 701/772–9021

### Minot

#### EROTICA

**Risque's** 1514 S Broadway 701/838–2837

## OHIO

### Statewide

#### PUBLICATIONS

**Outlook** 614/268–8525 • statewide LGBT newsweekly • good resource pages

### Akron

#### INFO LINES & SERVICES

**AA Intergroup** 330/253–8181 (AA#)

**Akron Pride Center** 895 N Main St 330/252–1559 • call for meeting schedule

#### BARS

**Adams Street Bar** 77 N Adams St (at Upson) 330/434–9794 • 5pm-2am, from 6:30pm wknds • popular • mostly gay men • piano bar Wed • dancing/DJ Fri-Sat • food served • strippers • WiFi

**Cocktails** 33 W Mapledale Ave 330/376–2625 • 11am-2:30am • mostly gay men • videos • drag king show Mon • Daddy's leather bar upstairs wknds

**The Office Bistro & Lounge** 778 N Main St (at Cuyahoga Falls Ave) 330/376–9550 • 11am-2:30am • gay-friendly • bi-sexual friendly • neighborhood bistro & lounge • multiracial • WiFi • wheelchair access

**Tear-Ez** 360 S Main St (near Exchange St) 330/376–0011 • 11am-2:30am, from noon Sun • lesbians/ gay men • neighborhood bar • drag shows Th & Sun • WiFi • wheelchair access

#### NIGHTCLUBS

**Interbelt** 70 N Howard St (near Perkins & Main) 330/253–5700 • 9pm-2:30am • lesbians/ gay men • dancing/DJ • live shows • videos • patio

**Square** 820 W Market St (near Portage Path) 330/374–9661 • 5pm-2:30am, from 8pm Sat, from 7pm Sun • mostly gay men • dancing/DJ • karaoke • wheelchair access • gay-owned

#### CAFES

**Angel Falls Coffee Company** 792 W Market St (btwn S Highland & Grand) 330/376–5282 • 7am-10pm • lunch & desserts • patio • WiFi • wheelchair access • gay-owned

#### RESTAURANTS

**Aladdin's Eatery** 782 W Market St (at Grand) 330/535–0110 • 11am-10pm • Middle Eastern

**Bricco** 1 W Exchange St (at S Main St) 330/475–1600 • 11am-midnight, till 1am Fri-Sat, 4pm-9pm Sun • Italian • also bar • gay-owned

**Bruegger's Bagels** 1821 Merriman Rd 330/867–8394 • 6am-4pm

## Athens

### ACCOMMODATIONS

**SuBAMUH (Susan B Anthony Memorial UnRest Home) Womyn's Land Trust** PO Box 5853, 45701 740/448–6424 • women only • cabins & camping • summer workshops • swimming • hot tub • nonsmoking • lesbian-owned

## Bowling Green

### BARS

**Uptown Downtown Sports Grill** 162 N Main St 419/352–9310 • 4pm-2:30am, from 3pm wknds • gay/straight • gay Tue night • drag shows

## Brunswick

see also Akron & Cleveland

### RESTAURANTS

**Pizza Marcello** 67–A Pearl Rd (near Boston Rd) 330/225–1211 • 3pm-close, from noon wknds • Italian

## Cincinnati

### INFO LINES & SERVICES

**AA Gay/ Lesbian** 328 W McMillan St (enter at 445 Herman St), Corryville 513/351–0422 (AA#) • 8pm Wed • call for locations of wknd meetings

### ACCOMMODATIONS

**Cincinnatian Hotel** 601 Vine St (at 6th St) 513/381–3000, 800/942–9000 • gay-friendly • restaurant & lounge • kids ok • nonsmoking • WiFi • wheelchair access

**Crowne Plaza** 5901 Pfeiffer Rd (at I-71) 513/793–4500, 800/468–3597 • gay-friendly • pool • kids ok • WiFi • wheelchair access

**First Farm Inn** 2510 Stevens Rd, Petersburg, KY 859/586–0199 • gay-friendly • 20 minutes from Cincinnati • small weddings • full brkfst • WiFi • nonsmoking • wheelchair access

**Millennium Hotel Cincinnati** 150 W 5th St 513/352–2100, 800/876–2100 • gay-friendly • outdoor rooftop pool & sundeck • WiFi • wheelchair access

**Weller Haus B&B** 319 Poplar St, Bellevue, KY 859/391–8315, 800/431–4287 • gay-friendly • jacuzzis • nonsmoking • WiFi

### BARS

**Below Zero Lounge** 1120 Walnut St (at E Central Pkwy) 513/421–9376 • 6pm-2am • dancing/DJ • live music • karaoke • dancing/DJ • drag shows • WiFi

**Junkers Tavern** 4158 Langland St (at Chase) 513/541–5470 • 9am-1am • gay-friendly • neighborhood bar • karaoke • live bands

**The Main Event** 835 Main St (at 9th) 513/421–1294 • 6am-2:30am, from 11am Sun • gay/ straight • neighborhood bar

**Milton's** 301 Milton St (at Sycamore) 513/784–9938 • 4pm-2:30am • gay-friendly • neighborhood bar

**Shooters** 927 Race St (at Court) 513/381–9900 • 4pm-2:30am • mostly gay men • dancing/DJ • country/ western • more women Th • karaoke Wed

**Simon Says** 428 Walnut St (at 5th) 513/381–7577 • 11am-2:30am, from 1pm Sun • popular • mostly gay men • professional • neighborhood bar • wheelchair access

### NIGHTCLUBS

**The Cabaret** 1122 Walnut St (at E Central Pkwy) 513/284–2050 • 10pm-2am Th-Sun • mostly gay men • drag shows

**The Dock** 603 W Pete Rose Wy (near Central) 513/241–5623 • 10pm-3am, till 4am Fri-Sat, clsd Mon-Wed • popular • lesbians/ gay men • multiracial • dancing/DJ • drag shows • live shows • 19+ • volleyball court • wheelchair access

### CAFES

**College Hill Coffee Co** 6128 Hamilton Ave (at North Bend Rd) 513/542–2739 • 6:30am-6:30pm, till 10pm Fri, 8:30am-10pm Sat, till 4pm Sun, clsd Mon • live music Sat • WiFi • wheelchair access

### RESTAURANTS

**Boca** 3200 Madison Rd (at Brazee St), Oakley 513/542–2022 • dinner Tue-Sat, clsd Sun • full bar • patio • wheelchair access

**Honey** 4034 Hamilton Ave (at Blue Rock) 513/541–4300 • dinner & Sun brunch, clsd Mon, casual fine dining • wheelchair access

**The Loving Hut** 6227 Montgomery Rd (at Woodmont) 513/731–2233 • 11am-7pm, clsd Sun-Mon • vegetarian/ vegan

**Melt Eclectic Deli** 4165 Hamilton Ave (at Lingo St) 513/681–6358 • 11am-9pm, 10am-3pm Sun

**Myra's Dionysus** 121 Calhoun St (at Dennis St) **513/961–1578** • 11am-10pm, till 11pm Fri-Sat, from 5pm Sun • diverse menu • plenty veggie

**Tucker's** 1637 Vine St (at Green) **513/721–7123** • great brkfst hole-in-wall • vegan too • wheelchair access

## ENTERTAINMENT & RECREATION

**Ensemble Theatre of Cincinnati** 1127 Vine St (at 12th) **513/421–3555**

**Know Theatre** 1120 Jackson St (at Central Pkwy) **513/300–5669** • contemporary multicultural theater

**Ohio Lesbian Archives** 3416 Clifton Ave (at Clifton United Methodist Church) **513/256–7695** • call first for appt

## RETAIL SHOPS

**Park & Vine** 1202 Main St **513/721–7275** • eco-friendly merchandise

**Pink Pyramid** 907 Race St (btwn 9th & Court) **513/621–7465** • noon-9pm, till 11pm Fri-Sat, 1pm-7pm Sun • pride items • also leather

## PUBLICATIONS

**CNKY Scene** **513/309–9729** • LGBT publication

# Cleveland

## INFO LINES & SERVICES

**AA Gay/ Lesbian** 6600 Detroit Ave (at LGBT Center) **216/241–7387, 800/835–1935**

**LGBT Community Center** 6600 Detroit Ave **216/651–5428** • 1pm-8pm, clsd wknds • wheelchair access

## ACCOMMODATIONS

**Clifford House** 1810 W 28th St (at Jay) **216/589–0121** • gay/ straight • 1868 historic brick home • near downtown • nonsmoking • WiFi • gay-owned

**Radisson Hotel Cleveland—Gateway** 651 Huron Rd (at Prospect) **216/377–9000, 800/967–9033** • gay-friendly • also restaurant • kids ok • WiFi • wheelchair access

**Stone Gables B&B** 3806 Franklin Blvd (at W 38th) **216/961–4654, 877/215–4326** • gay/ straight • full brkfst • jacuzzi • kids/ pets ok • WiFi • wheelchair access • gay-owned

## BARS

**ABC The Tavern** 1872 W 25th St **216/861–3857** • 4pm-2:30am, from noon wknds • gay-friendly dive bar w/ great food

**The Hawk** 11217 Detroit Ave (at 112th St) • noon-2:30am • neighborhood bar • wheelchair access

**Now That's Class** 11213 Detroit Ave (at 112th St) **216/221–8576** • 4pm-close • gay-friendly • punk & metal bands • food served • plenty veggie/ vegan • wheelchair access

**Paradise Inn** 4488 State Rd (Rte 94, at Rte 480) **216/741–9819** • 11am-2:30am • lesbians/ gay men • neighborhood bar • lesbian-owned

**Twist** 11633 Clifton (at 117th St) **216/221–2333** • 11:30am-2:30am, from noon Sun • popular • lesbians/ gay men • neighborhood bar • dancing/DJ • professional crowd

**Vibe** 11633 Lorain Ave (at W 117th St) **216/476–1970** • 5pm-2:30am, from 3pm Sat • lesbians/ gay men • neighborhood bar • live shows • karaoke • patio

## CAFES

**Grumpy's Cafe** 2621 W 14th St **216/241–5025** • 7am-9pm, till 3pm Sun-Mon

**Gypsy Beans & Baking Co** 6425 Detroit Ave (at W 65th St, next to Cleveland Public Theatre) **216/939–9009** • 7am-9pm, till 11pm Fri-Sat • popular • fresh-baked gourmet pastries, soups, sandwiches • WiFi • wheelchair access

**Lucky's Cafe** 777 Starkweather Ave (at Professor Ave) **216/622–7773** • 7am-9pm, 8am-3pm wknds, popular wknd brunch • cafe & bakery • outdoor seating • WiFi • woman-owned • wheelchair access

**Phoenix Coffee** 2287 Lee Rd (at Essex), Cleveland Heights **216/932–8227** • 6am-10pm, till 11pm Fri, from 7am Sat, 7am-7pm Sun • great sandwiches • WiFi • patio • wheelchair access

## RESTAURANTS

**Ali Baba** 12021 Lorain Ave (at W 120th St) **216/251–2040** • 5pm-10pm Th-Sat • popular • the best Middle Eastern food you'll have outside the Middle East • vegan/veggie • BYOB • woman-owned

**Bar Cento** 1948 W 25th St (at Lorain Ave) **216/274–1010** • 4:30pm-2am, from noon Sat • great pizza • beer/ wine • patio • wheelchair access

**Battiste & Dupree Cajun Grill & Bar** 1992 Warrensville Ctr Rd (at Wyncote) **216/381–3411** • lunch & dinner, clsd Sun-Mon • wheelchair access

**Cafe Tandoor** 2096 S Taylor Rd (at Cedar), Cleveland Heights **216/371–8500** • lunch & dinner, 3pm-9pm Sun • Indian • plenty veggie • wheelchair access

**The Coffee Pot** 12415 Madison Ave (at Robin), Lakewood **216/226–6443** • 6am-4pm, till 3pm Sat, till 2pm Sun, clsd Mon • diner • woman-owned

**Crop Bistro** 2537 Lorain Ave (at 25th) **216/696–2767** • lunch Tue-Fri, dinner nightly, clsd Mon • innovative American

**Diner on Clifton** 11637 Clifton Blvd (at W 117th St) **216/521–5003** • 7am-11pm

**Flying Fig** 2523 Market Ave (at W 25th St) **216/241–4243** • lunch & dinner, wknd brunch

**The Greenhouse Tavern** 2038 E 4th St **216/241–5025** • 11am-11pm, till 1am Fri-Sat • organic and environmentally friendly

**Hecks** 2927 Bridge Ave (at W 30th) **216/861–5464, 800/677–8592** • lunch & dinner, brunch Sun • popular • gourmet burgers • wheelchair access

**Hodge's** 668 Euclid Ave **216/771–4000** • 11am-11pm, from 4pm wknds • global comfort food

**The Inn on Coventry** 2785 Euclid Heights Blvd (at Coventry), Cleveland Heights **216/371–1811** • 7am-2pm, 8am-2:30pm wknds • homestyle • popular Bloody Marys • some veggie • full bar • wheelchair access • women-owned

**Johnny Mango World Cafe & Bar** 3120 Bridge Ave (btwn Fulton & W 32nd, in Ohio City) **216/575–1919** • 11am-10pm, till 11pm Fri-Sat • healthy world food • juice bar • also full bar till 1am

**Latitude 41N** 5712 Detroit Ave (at W 58th St, Detroit Shoreway) **216/961–0000** • 8am-9pm, till 10pm Fri, till 3pm Sun • restaurant & cafe • WiFi • wheelchair access • lesbian-owned

**Lolita** 900 Literary Rd (at Professor Ave, in Tremont) **216/771–5652** • 5pm-11pm, till 1am Fri-Sat, 4pm-9pm Sun, clsd Mon • popular • upscale cont'l • full bar

**Luchita's** 3456 W 117th St (at Governor) **216/252–1169** • lunch & dinner, clsd Mon • popular • Mexican • full bar

**Luxe** 6605 Detroit Ave (at W 65th St) **216/920–0600** • 5pm-midnight, lounge till 2am • gourmet comfort food • also lounge • live music • wheelchair access

**Momocho** 1835 Fulton Rd (at Woodbine Ave) **216/694–2122** • 5pm-close, from 4pm Sun • modern Mexican • also bar • wheelchair access

**My Friend's Deli & Restaurant** 11616 Detroit Ave (at W 117th) **216/221–2575** • 24hrs • beer/ wine • WiFi

**Pearl of the Orient** 19300 Detroit Rd (in Beachcliff Market Sq), Rocky River **440/333–9902** • lunch & dinner • pan-Asian • some veggie • also restaurant on East Side • wheelchair access

**Tommy's** **216/321–7757** • 9am-9pm, till 10pm Fri, 7:30am-10pm Sat • plenty veggie • great milkshakes • WiFi • wheelchair access

## ENTERTAINMENT & RECREATION

**Rock & Roll Hall of Fame** 1100 Rock & Roll Blvd (at E 9th & Lake Erie) **216/781–ROCK** • even if you don't like rock, stop by & check out IM Pei's architectural gift to Cleveland

## BOOKSTORES

**Loganberry Books** 13015 Larchmere Blvd, Shaker Heights **216/795–9800** • 10am-6pm, till 8:30pm Wed-Th, noon-4pm Sun • used & rare books • woman-owned

**Mac's Backs** 1820 Coventry Rd (next to Tommy's), Cleveland Heights **216/321–2665** • 10am-9pm, till 10pm Fri-Sat, 11am-8pm Sun • great new & used • 3 floors • reading series • some LGBT titles

## RETAIL SHOPS

**The Dean Rufus House of Fun** 1422 W 29th St (at Detroit) **216/348–1386** • 1pm-midnight, till 2:30am Fri-Sat, clsd Mon • clothing • DVDs

**Torso** 11520 Clifton Blvd (at Warren), Lakewood **216/862–3987** • 11am-9pm, till 5pm Sun, clsd Mon • clothing • gay-owned

## PUBLICATIONS

**Gay People's Chronicle** **216/916–9338** • Ohio's largest bi-weekly LGBT newspaper w/ extensive listings

## EROTICA

**Adult Mart** 16700 Brookpark Rd (at W 150th) **216/267–9019**

**Rocky's Entertainment & Emporium** 13330 Brookpark Rd (at W 130th) **216/267–4659**

# Columbus

## INFO LINES & SERVICES

**AA Gay/ Lesbian** 614/253-8501, 800/870-3795 (IN OH)

**Stonewall Columbus Community Center/ Hotline** 1160 N High St (at E 4th Ave) 614/299-7764 • 9am-5pm, clsd wknds • wheelchair access

## ACCOMMODATIONS

**The Blackwell** 2110 Tuttle Park Pl (at Lane Ave) 614/247-4000, 866/247-4000 • gay-friendly • on OSU campus • also restaurant

**Harrison House B&B** 313 W 5th Ave (at Neil Ave) 614/421-2202, 800/827-4203 • gay-friendly • nonsmoking • WiFi • kids/pets ok • woman-owned

**The Lofts** 55 E Nationwide Blvd (at High St) 614/461-2663, 800/735-6387 • gay-friendly • boutique hotel

**The Westin Columbus** 310 S High St (at Main) 614/223-3800, 800/937-8461 • gay-friendly • beautiful old 100+ year old hotel, great location • also restaurant

## BARS

**Cavan Irish Pub** 1409 S High St (at Jenkins) 614/725-5502 • 2pm-2:30am, from noon wknds • gay-friendly • shows • karaoke

**Club Diversity** 863 S High St (at Whittier) 614/224-4050 • 4pm-midnight, till 2:30am Fri, noon-2:30am Sat • lesbians/ gay men • piano bar Fri-Sat

**Level Dining Lounge** 614/754-7111 • 11am-2:30am • gay/ straight • restaurant w/ great bar • dancing/DJ • karaoke • wheelchair access

**Slammers** 202 E Long St (at N 5th St) 614/221-8880 • 11am-12:30am, till 2:30am Fri-Sat, from 4pm wknds, clsd Mon-Tue • mostly women • dancing/DJ • food served • WiFi • wheelchair access

**The South Bend Tavern** 126 E Moler St (at 4th St) 614/444-3386 • noon-2:30am • lesbians/ gay men • neighborhood bar • drag shows Sat • wheelchair access

**The Toolbox Saloon** 744 Frebis Ave 614/670-8113 • noon-2:30am • mostly gay men • neighborhood bar • dancing/DJ• drag shows

**Union Cafe** 782 N High St (at Hubbard) 614/421-2233 • 11am-2:30am • popular • lesbians/ gay men • video bar • also restaurant • plenty veggie • WiFi • wheelchair access

## NIGHTCLUBS

**Axis** 775 N High St (at Hubbard) 614/291-4008 • 10pm-2:30am Fri-Sat only • popular • mostly gay men • dancing/DJ • also Pump cabaret lounge • drag shows • 18+ • wheelchair access • gay-owned

**Wall Street** 144 N Wall St (at Spring St) 614/464-2800 • 9pm-2:30am, from 10pm Wed, 8pm-midnight Th, clsd Mon-Tue • popular • lesbians/ gay men • more women Fri-Sat • dancing/DJ • country/ western Th • wheelchair access

## CAFES

**Cup O Joe Cafe** 627 S 3rd St (at Sycamore) 614/221-1563 • 6am-10pm, till 11pm Fri-Sat, from 7am wknds, till 10pm Sun • food served • WiFi • wheelchair access

## RESTAURANTS

**Alana's Food & Wine** 2333 N High St (at Patterson ) 614/294-6783 • from 5pm, clsd Sun-Tue • host many special events

**Banana Leaf** 816 Bethel Rd (at Olentangy River Rd) 614/459-4101 • 11:30am-9:30pm • vegetarian/ vegan Indian • wheelchair access

**Betty's** 680 N High St 614/228-6191 • 11am-2am • plenty veggie • also bar

**Blue Nile** 2361 N High St (at W Patterson) 614/421-2323 • lunch & dinner, clsd Mon • Ethiopian

**Cap City Diner** 1299 Olentangy River Rd (at W 5th) 614/291-3663 • 11am-10pm, till 11pm Fri-Sat, till 9pm Sun

**Lemongrass** 641 N High (at Russell) 614/224-1414 • lunch & dinner, clsd Sun-Mon • popular • Asian cuisine • reservations advised

**Northstar Cafe** 951 N High St (at W 2nd Ave) 614/298-9999 • 9am-10pm • popular • plenty veggie

**Surly Girl Saloon** 1126 N High St (at W 4th Ave) 614/294-4900 • 11am-2am • plenty veggie • also bar • open mic comedy Wed & punk rock aerobics 6:30 Tue

**Till** 247 King Ave 614/298-9986 • lunch & dinner, wknd brunch • patio

**Tip Top Kitchen & Cocktails** 73 E Gay St (at 3rd St) 614/221-8300 • 11am-2am

**Whole World Bakery & Restaurant** 3269 N High St (at W Como Ave) 614/268-5751 • 11am-8pm, Sun brunch, clsd Mon • vegetarian/vegan • wheelchair access

## ENTERTAINMENT & RECREATION

**Ohio Roller Girls** • Columbus' female roller derby league • visit www.ohiorollergirls.com for events

## BOOKSTORES

**The Book Loft of German Village** 631 S 3rd St (at Sycamore) 614/464-1774 • 10am-11pm, till midnight Fri-Sat • LGBT section

## RETAIL SHOPS

**Hausfrau Haven** 769 S 3rd St (at Columbus) 614/443-3680 • 10am-7pm, noon-5pm Sun • greeting cards • wine • gifts

**Piercology** 190 W 2nd Ave (at Hunter Ave) 614/297-4743 • noon-8pm, 1pm-7pm Sun • body-piercing studio • gay-owned • wheelchair access

**Schmidt's Fudge Haus** 220 E Kossuth St (in Historic German Village) 614/444-2222 • noon-close • old fashioned fudge & candy • gifts

**Torso** 772 N High St (at Warren) 614/421-7663 • 11am-10pm, till 5pm Sun-Mon • clothing • gay-owned

## PUBLICATIONS

**Gay People's Chronicle** 440/986-0051

**Outlook Weekly** 614/268-8525 • statewide LGBT weekly • good resource pages

## EROTICA

**The Garden** 1174 N High St (btwn 4th & 5th Ave) 614/294-2869 • 11am-3am, noon-midnight Sun • adult toys

# Dayton

## INFO LINES & SERVICES

**AA Gay/ Lesbian** 20 W 1st St (off Main, at Christ Episcopal Church) 937/222-2211 • 8pm Sat

**Greater Dayton Lesbian/ Gay Center** 117 E 3rd St 937/274-1776

## ACCOMMODATIONS

**Dayton Marriott** 1414 S Patterson Blvd 937/223-1000, 800/450-8625

## BARS

**Argos Bar** 301 Mabel Ave (near Linden & I-35) 937/252-2976 • 8pm-2:30am • men only • neighborhood bar • leather • gay-owned

**MJ's Cafe** 119 E 3rd St (at S Jefferson) 937/223-3259 • 3pm-2:30am • mostly gay men • dancing/DJ • food served • karaoke • male strippers • deck

**Stage Door** 44 N Jefferson St (at 2nd) 937/223-7418 • 3pm-2:30am • mostly gay men • leather • wheelchair access

## NIGHTCLUBS

**Masque** 34 N Jefferson St (btwn 2nd & 3rd) 937/228-2582 • 8pm-2:30am, till 5am wknds • popular • mostly gay men • dancing/DJ • drag shows • strippers • 18+

## RESTAURANTS

**Cold Beer & Cheeseburgers** 33 S Jefferson St (at 4th St) 937/222-2337 • 11am-close • grill • full bar • wheelchair access

**The Spaghetti Warehouse** 36 W 5th St (at Ludlow) 937/461-3913 • 11am-10pm, till 11pm wknds • more gay Tue w/ Friends of the Italian Opera

## BOOKSTORES

**Books & Co** 4453 Walnut St (in Greene Shopping Ctr) 937/429-2169 • 9am-11pm, till 8pm Sun

## PUBLICATIONS

**Gay Dayton** 937/623-1590 • monthly LGBT publication

# Findlay

## EROTICA

**Findlay Adult Books & Video** 623 Trenton Ave (at I-75, exit 159) 419/422-1301

# Kent

## BARS

**The Zephyr Pub** 106 W Main St (at Water St) 330/678-4848 • 3pm-close • gay-friendly • live shows • karaoke • wheelchair access

# Lima

## NIGHTCLUBS

**Somewhere in Time** 804 W North St (at Baxter) 419/227-7288 • 5pm-2:30am, from 8pm wknds • lesbians/ gay men • dancing/DJ • karaoke • drag shows • male & female strippers

# Logan

## ACCOMMODATIONS

**Glenlaurel—A Scottish Country Inn** 14940 Mt Olive Rd (off State Rte I-80), Rockbridge 740/385-4070, 800/809-7378 • gay/ straight • full brkfst & dinner • hot tub • nonsmoking • wheelchair access

**Inn & Spa at Cedar Falls** 21190 State Rte 374 **740/385-7489, 800/653-2557** • gay/ straight • rooms, log cabins & cottages • fine dining on-site • nonsmoking • WiFi • wheelchair access

**Lazy Lane Cabins** **740/385-3475, 877/225-6572** • gay-friendly • secluded cabins sleep 2-8 • hot tubs • fireplaces • nonsmoking • kids/ pets ok

## Lorain

### BARS

**Tim's Place** 2223 Broadway (btwn 22nd & 23rd) **440/218-2223** • 8pm-2:30am, clsd Mon-Tue • lesbians/gay men • neighborhood bar • dancing/DJ • drag shows • patio • wheelchair access

## Mansfield

### BARS

**Sami's** 178 Wayne St **419/522-1500** • open Fri-Sat • lesbians/gay men • neighborhood bar • dancing/DJ• drag shows

## Marietta

### ACCOMMODATIONS

**Fourth St B&B** **614/638-1187** • gay/ straight • kids ok • nonsmoking • gay-owned

## Monroe

### BARS

**Old Street Saloon** 13 Old St (at Elm St) **513/539-9183** • 8pm-2am Th-Sat, till 1am Wed, clsd Sun-Tue • lesbians/ gay men • neighborhood bar • dancing/DJ • drag shows • karaoke

## Niles

### EROTICA

**Niles Books** 5970 Youngstown Warren Rd (off Rte 46) **330/544-3755**

## Oberlin

### ACCOMMODATIONS

**Hallauer House B&B** 14945 Hallauer Rd **440/774-3400, 877/774-3406** • gay-friendly • eco-friendly historic inn 3 miles S of Oberlin • pool • nonsmoking • WiFi

### RESTAURANTS

**The Feve** 30 S Main St (at College St) **440/774-1978** • 11am-midnight • popular wknd brunch • plenty veggie • full bar from 5pm

**Weia Teia** 9 S Main St (at College St) **440/774-8880** • lunch & dinner • Thai/ Asian fusion • upscale • full bar • some veggie

### BOOKSTORES

**MindFair Books** 13 W College St (shares storefront w/ Ben Franklin) **440/774-6463** • 10am-6pm, till 8pm Fri, noon-5pm Sun

## Sandusky

### NIGHTCLUBS

**Crowbar** 206 W Market St (at Jackson St) **419/624-0109** • 6pm-2:30am, clsd Tue • lesbians/gay men • dancing/DJ • karaoke • gay-owned

### RESTAURANTS

**Mona Pizza Gourmet** 135 Columbus Ave (at Market St) **419/626-8166** • 11am-10pm, till 3am wknds • multiracial • transgender-friendly • gay-owned

## Springfield

### NIGHTCLUBS

**Diesel** 1912-14 Edwards Ave (at N Belmont Ave) **937/324-0383** • 8:30pm-2:30am, clsd Mon-Tue • gay-friendly • dancing/DJ • live shows • karaoke • patio

## Toledo

### INFO LINES & SERVICES

**AA Gay/ Lesbian** 3535 Executive Pkwy (at Unity) **419/380-9862** • 8pm Wed

### ACCOMMODATIONS

**Mansion View Inn** 2035 Collingwood Blvd (at Irving) **419/244-5676** • gay-friendly • 1887 Victorian near downtown • nonsmoking • WiFi

### BARS

**Legends/Mojo** 119 N Erie St **567/315-8333** • 1pm-2:30am, from 11am Fri-Sun • mostly gay men • drag shows

**R House** 5534 Secor Rd (btwn Laskey & Alexis) **419/474-2929** • 4pm-2:30am • mostly gay men • drag shows • patio

### NIGHTCLUBS

**Bretz** 2012 Adams St **419/243-1900** • 10pm-2:30am Th-Sat • lesbians/ gay men • dancing/DJ • karaoke • drag shows • strippers • 18+ • wheelchair access

### BOOKSTORES

**People Called Women** 6060 Reinaissance Pl #F **419/469-8983** • 11am-7pm, clsd Sun-Mon • multicultural • feminist

## Warren

### NIGHTCLUBS

**Club 441** 441 E Market St (at Vine, enter rear) 330/394–9483 • 4pm-2:30am, from 2pm wknds • lesbians/ gay men • dancing/DJ • live shows • wheelchair access

**The Funky Skunk** 143 E Market St (at Park Ave) • 9pm-close • mostly gay men • ladies night Sun • dancing/DJ • drag shows • karaoke

## West Lafayette

### RESTAURANTS

**Lava Rock Grill at Unusual Junction** 56310 US Hwy 36 740/545–9772 • '50s-style diner in restored railroad station • wheelchair access • gay-owned

## Yellow Springs

### RESTAURANTS

**Winds Cafe & Bakery** 215 Xenia Ave (at Cory St) 937/767–1144 • lunch & dinner, Sun brunch, clsd Mon • plenty veggie • full bar • wheelchair access • women-owned

## Youngstown

### BARS

**Mineshaft** 1105 Poland Ave 330/207–6437 • 5pm-midnight, till 2am Fri-Sat, from 3pm Sun • mostly gay men • neighborhood bar • food served

### NIGHTCLUBS

**The Backroom at 76** 5335 76th Dr Unit 2 330/799-4900 • 5:30pm-2pm • lesbians/gay men • drag shows

### CAFES

**The Knox** 110 W Federal Plaza W 330/744–7683 • 11:30am-2:30am • food served • also bar • events, movies, art & more

# OKLAHOMA

## Grand Lake

### ACCOMMODATIONS

**Southern Oaks Resort & Spa** 2 miles S of Hwy 28/ 82 Junction, Langley 918/782–9346, 866/452–5307 • gay-friendly • 19 cabins on 30 acres • pool • hot tub • nonsmoking • gay-owned

### RESTAURANTS

**The Artichoke Restaurant & Bar** 35896 S Hwy 82, Langley 918/782–9855 • 5pm-10pm, clsd Sun-Mon

**Frosty & Edna's Cafe** Highway 28, Langley 918/782–9123 • 6am-9:30pm

**Lighthouse Supper Club** Highway 85 & Main, Ketchum 918/782–3316 • 5pm-9pm, clsd Sun-Tue

## Oklahoma City

### INFO LINES & SERVICES

**AA Live & Let Live** 3405 N Villa 405/947–3834 • 8pm Mon

**Herland Sister Resources** 2312 NW 39th St 405/521–9696 • 1pm-5pm 2nd & 4th Sat • women's resource center w/ books, crafts & lending library • also sponsors monthly events • wheelchair access

### ACCOMMODATIONS

➤**Habana Inn** 2200 NW 39th St (at Youngs) 405/528–2221, 800/988–2221 (RESERVATIONS ONLY) • popular • lesbians/ gay men • resort • pool • nonsmoking • also 3 bars • restaurant • gift shop • wheelchair access

**Hawthorn Suites** 1600 NW Expy (Richmond Square) 405/840-1440, 800/527–1133 • gay-friendly • full brkfst • pool • WiFi

**Waterford Marriott** 6300 Waterford Blvd (at Pennsylvania) 405/848–4782 • gay-friendly • pool • fitness center • also bar & restaurant • nonsmoking • WiFi

### BARS

**Alibi's** 1200 N Pennsylvania (at NW 11th) 405/605–3795 • noon -2am • gay/ straight • neighborhood bar • transgender-friendly • gay-owned

**The Boom** 2218 NW 39th St (at Pennsylvania) 405/601–7200 • 4pm-2am, from 11am Sun, clsd Mon • lesbians/ gay men • neighborhood bar • food served • karaoke • drag shows • WiFi • patio • wheelchair access

**Edna's** 5137 N Classen Blvd (at NW 51st) 405/840–3339 • 2pm-2am, from noon wknds • gay-friendly • neighborhood dive bar • food served

➤**The Finishline** at Habana Inn 405/525–2900 • noon-2am • lesbians/ gay men • neighborhood bar • dancing/DJ • country/ western • poolside bar • wheelchair access

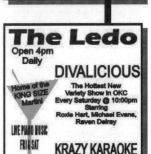

**Hi-Lo Club** 1221 NW 50th St (btwn Western & Classen) **405/843-1722** • noon-2am • lesbians/gay men • neighborhood bar • live bands • drag shows

➤**The Ledo** at Habana Inn **405/525-0730** • 4pm-10:30pm, till 2am Fri-Sat • lesbians/gay men • martini lounge • food served • karaoke • nonsmoking • wheelchair access

**Partners 4 Club** 2805 NW 36th St (at May Ave) **405/602-2030** • 5pm-close, from 7pm Fri-Sat, clsd Mon • popular • mostly women • neighborhood bar • dancing/DJ • karaoke • live shows • patio • wheelchair access

**Partners Too** 2807 NW 36th St (at May Ave) **405/942-2199** • open Wed-Sat • lesbians/gay men • dancing/DJ • patio • wheelchair access

**Tramps** 2201 NW 39th St (at Barnes) **405/521-9888** • noon-2am, from 10am wknds • mostly gay men • drag shows • WiFi • wheelchair access

## NIGHTCLUBS

**Apothecary 39 OKC**
2125 NW 39th St (at Pennsylvania) **405/605-4100** • 5pm-2am • mostly gay men • upbeat jazz • patio • wheelchair access

➤**The Copa** at Habana Inn **405/525-0730** • 9pm-2am, clsd Mon • popular • lesbians/gay men • dancing/DJ • drag shows • karaoke • wheelchair access

**Wreck Room** 2127 NW 39th St (at Pennsylvania) **405/525-7610** • 10pm-close Fri-Sat only • lesbians/gay men • dancing/DJ • live shows • drag shows • young crowd • 18+ after 1am

## CAFES

**The Red Cup** 3122 N Classen Blvd (at NW 30th St) **405/525-3430** • 7am-5pm, till 8pm Th-Fri, from 9am wknds • vegetarian • nonsmoking • WiFi • live music

## RESTAURANTS

**Bricktown Brewery Restaurant** 1 N Oklahoma Ave (at Sheridan) **405/232-2739** • 11am-10pm, till midnight Sat, from noon Sun • full bar

**Cheever's Cafe** 2409 N Hudson Ave (at NW 23rd) **405/525-7007** • 11am-9:30pm, 5pm-10:30pm Sat, brunch Sun • reservations recommended

**Earl's Rib Palace** 216 Johnny Bench Dr, Ste BBQ (in Bricktown) **405/272-9898** • 11am-9pm, till 10pm Fri-Sat, noon-8pm Sun

➤**Gusher's** at Habana Inn **405/525-0730** • 11am-10:30pm, from 9am wknds, till 3:30am Fri-Sat for after-hours brkfst • wheelchair access

**Iguana Bar & Grill** 9 NW 9th St (at N Santa Fe Ave) **405/606-7172** • lunch & dinner • Mexican

**Ingrid's Kitchen** 3701 N Youngs (btwn Penn & May, on NW 36th) **405/946-8444** • 7am-9pm, till 10pm Fri-Sat 9:30am-2pm Sun • German/American bakery, deli & bar • gay-owned

**Pops** 660 W Hwy 66, Arcadia **405/928-7677** • brkfst, lunch & dinner • diner fare • look for the 66-foot tall soda bottle

**Rococo Restaurant & Fine Wine** 2824 N Pennsylvania (at NW 27th St) **405/528-2824** • lunch Mon-Fri, dinner nightly, Sun jazz brunch • full bar

**Someplace Else Deli & Bakery** 2310 N Western Ave **405/524-0887** • 7am-6:30pm, 9:30am-4pm Sat, clsd Sun • popular

**Sushi Neko** 4318 N Western (btwn 42nd & 43rd) **405/528-8862** • 11am-11pm, clsd Sun

**Ted's Cafe Escondido** 8324 S Western Ave (at 84th St) **405/635-8337** • lunch & dinner • popular • Tex-Mex

## ENTERTAINMENT & RECREATION

**First Friday Gallery Walk** from 28th at N Walker to 30th at N Dewey **405/525-2688** • open tour of Paseo Arts District galleries • first Fri-Sat

## BOOKSTORES

**Full Circle Bookstore** 50 Penn Pl, 1900 NW Expwy (in NE corner of 1st level) **405/842-2900, 800/683-7323** • 10am-9pm, noon-5pm Sun • also cafe & coffee bar

## RETAIL SHOPS

➤**Jungle Red** at Habana Inn **405/524-5733** • 1pm-close • novelties • leather • gifts • wheelchair access

## PUBLICATIONS

**The Herland Voice** **405/521-9696** • monthly newsletter for OKC women's community

**Oklahoma Gazette** **405/528-6000** • "Metro OKC's independent weekly"

## EROTICA

**Christie's Toy Box** 7914 N MacArthur **405/720-2453** • multiple locations in OKC

## Tulsa

### INFO LINES & SERVICES

**Dennis R Neill Equality Center** 621 E 4th St (at Kenosha) **918/743-4297** • 3pm-9pm, clsd Sun • many activities & Pride store • wheelchair access

**Gay/ Lesbian AA** 2545 S Yale Ave (at Community of Hope) **918/627-2224** • 5:30pm Sat

### ACCOMMODATIONS

**The Mayo Hotel** 115 W 5th St **918/582-6296** • gay-friendly • luxury hotel • restaurant • WiFi • wheelchair access

**Tulsa Hyatt** 100 E Second St (at 2nd St) **918/582-9000, 800/980-6429** • gay-friendly • restaurant • pool • kids/ pets ok • wheelchair access

### BARS

**Bamboo Lounge** 7204 E Pine **918/836-8700** • noon-2am • mostly gay men • neighborhood bar • dancing/DJ • live shows • karaoke • patio • wheelchair access

**New Age Renegade** 1649 S Main St (at 17th) **918/585-3405** • 4pm-2am • lesbians/ gay men • neighborhood bar • live shows • karaoke • patio

**The Yellow Brick Road** 2630 E 15th St (at Harvard) **918/293-0304** • 1pm-2am • lesbians/ gay men • neighborhood bar • wheelchair access

### NIGHTCLUBS

**Area 18 Bar & Ultra Lounge** 39 E 18th St **918/510-7340** • 6pm-2am, from 8pm Fri-Sat • lesbians/gay men • dancing/DJ • drag shows

**Club Majestic** 124 N Boston (at Brady) **918/584-9494** • 9pm-2am Th-Sun • dancing/DJ • drag/live shows • transgender-friendly • WiFi • wheelchair access • gay-owned

**Rum Runnerz** 822 S Sheridan (at 9th) **918/289-0159** • 4pm-2am • lesbians/ gay men • dancing/DJ • country/ western

### CAFES

**Gypsy's Coffee House** 303 N Cincinnati Ave **918/295-2181** • 7am-10pm, till 2am Fri-Sat, from 10am Sat-Sun • live shows • WiFi

### RESTAURANTS

**Cancun International** 705 S Lewis Ave (at 11th) **918/583-8089** • 11am-9pm, from 10am Sat-Sun, clsd Wed

**Eloté** 514 S Boston Ave **918/582-1403** • 11am-10pm, till 2pm Mon, clsd Sun, fresh Mexican • full bar

**James E McNellie's Public House** 409 E 1st St **918/382-7468** • 11am-2am • great burgers • full bar • wheelchair access

**White Lion Pub** 6927 S Canton Ave (off 71st) **918/491-6533** • 4pm-10pm, clsd Sun-Mon • British-style pub

**Wild Fork** 1820 Utica Square **918/742-0712** • 7am-10pm, clsd Sun • full bar • wheelchair access • women-owned

### ENTERTAINMENT & RECREATION

**Gilcrease Museum** 1400 N Gilcrease Museum Rd **918/596-2700, 888/655-2278** • one of the best collections of Native American & cowboy art in the US

**Philbrook Museum of Art** 2727 S Rockford Rd (1 block E of Peoria, at end of 27th St) **918/324-7941** • clsd Mon • Italian villa built in the '20s oil boom complete w/ kitschy lighted dance flr • the gardens are a must in spring & summer

### PUBLICATIONS

**Urban Tulsa Weekly** **918/592-5550** • "Tulsa Metro's only independent newsweekly"

# OREGON

## Ashland

### INFO LINES & SERVICES

**Gay/ Lesbian AA** 541/732-1850

### ACCOMMODATIONS

**The Arden Forest Inn** 261 W Hersey St (at N Main) **541/488-1496, 800/460-3912** • gay/ straight • full brkfst • nonsmoking • pool • kids 10+ ok • wheelchair access • WiFi • gay-owned

**Ashland Creek Inn** 70 Water St **541/482-3315** • gay-friendly • secluded forest location • kitchens • gourmet brkfst • nonsmoking • gay-owned

**Country Willows B&B Inn** 1313 Clay St (at Siskiyou Blvd) **541/488-1590, 800/945-5697** • gay-friendly • full brkfst • pool • jacuzzi • nonsmoking • WiFi • wheelchair access • gay-owned

**Lithia Springs Resort** 2165 W Jackson Rd (at N Main) **541/482-7128, 800/482-7128** • gay/ straight • full brkfst • natural hot-springs-fed whirlpools in rooms • nonsmoking • WiFi

**Romeo Inn B&B** 295 Idaho St 800/915-8899 • gay-friendly • full brkfst • jacuzzi • pool • nonsmoking • WiFi

### RESTAURANTS

**The Black Sheep Pub & Restaurant** 51 N Main St (on the Plaza) 541/482-6414 • 11:30am-1am • WiFi • woman-owned

**Greenleaf Restaurant** 49 N Main St (on The Plaza) 541/482-2808 • 8am-8pm • creekside dining • beer/ wine

### BOOKSTORES

**Bloomsbury Books** 290 E Main St (btwn 1st & 2nd) 541/488-0029 • 8:30am-9pm, 10am-6pm Sun

### RETAIL SHOPS

**Travel Essentials** 252 E Main St 541/482-7383, 800/258-0758 • 10am-5:30pm, 11am-5pm Sun • luggage • books • accessories

## Bend

### ACCOMMODATIONS

**Dawson House Lodge** 109455 Hwy 97 N, Chemult 541/365-2232, 888/281-8375 • gay-friendly • rustic inn w/ modern amenities • near Crater Lake • nonsmoking • kids/ pets ok • WiFi

## Eugene

### INFO LINES & SERVICES

**Gay/ Lesbian AA** 1166 Oak St (at First Christian Church) 541/342-4113

### ACCOMMODATIONS

**C'est La Vie Inn** 1006 Taylor St (at W 10th) 541/302-3014, 866/302-3014 • gay-friendly • full brkfst • nonsmoking • WiFi

**Valley River Inn** 1000 Valley River Wy 541/743-1000, 800/543-8266 • gay-friendly • pool • also restaurant • nonsmoking • WiFi • wheelchair access

### NIGHTCLUBS

**The Hammered Lamb** 150 W Broadway 541/357-8411 • lesbians/gay men • dancing • food served • drag shows • transgender-friendly • wheelchair access

### RESTAURANTS

**Glenwood Restaurant** 1340 Alder St (at 13th Ave) 541/687-0355 • 7am-9pm

**Keystone Cafe** 395 W 5th Ave (at Lawrence) 541/342-2075 • 7am-3pm • popular brkfst • plenty veggie

### EROTICA

**Spice Adult Emporium** 1166 South A St (at 10th St), Springfield 541/726-6969 • 8pm-midnight, 24hrs Th-Sun

## Grants Pass

### ACCOMMODATIONS

**Rainbows on the Fly** 541/324-0485 • women's land on 40 acres • cabin, campsites, RV hookups • also guided flyfishing • nonsmoking • WiFi • lesbian-owned

**WomanShare** 541/862-2807 • women only • cabins • shared kitchen • bathhouse • hot tub • girls/ pets ok • nonsmoking • lesbian-owned

### CAFES

**Sunshine Natural Foods Cafe** 128 SW H St (btwn 5th & 6th Sts) 541/474-5044 • 9am-6pm, 9:30am-5pm Sat, clsd Sun • vegetarian • also market • WiFi • wheelchair access

## Idleyld Park

### ACCOMMODATIONS

**Umpqua's Last Resort Wilderness RV Park & Campground** 115 Elk Ridge Ln 541/498-2500 • gay/ straight • WiFi • gay-owned

## Jacksonville

### ACCOMMODATIONS

**The TouVelle House** 455 N Oregon St (at E St) 541/899-8938, 800/846-8422 • gay-friendly • 1916 Craftsman • full brkfst • pool • WiFi • nonsmoking

## Port Orford

### ACCOMMODATIONS

**Ocean Breeze Retreat** nr Garrison Lake 541/366-2117 • women only, cottage is tucked in its own oasis of a natural environment, WiFi, lesbian-owned

# Portland

## INFO LINES & SERVICES

**Live & Let Live Club** 1210 SE 7th Ave **503/238-6091** • 12-step meetings

**Q Center** 4115 N Mississippi Ave (at N Mason St) **503/234-7837** • LGBTQ community center • WiFi

**Travel Gay Portland Visitors Center** 800 SW Washington St #M1 • 11am-6pm • free baggage check • tour & lodging info • bar & club guide • maps & more * WiFi

## ACCOMMODATIONS

**The Ace Hotel** 1022 SW Stark St (at 11th) **503/228-2277** • gay/ straight • hip hotel for "cultural influencers on a budget" • nonsmoking • WiFi • kids/ pets ok • wheelchair access

**Hotel deLuxe** 729 SW 15th Ave (at SW Morrison) **503/219-2094, 866/895-2094** • gay-friendly • 1940s Hollywood decor • nonsmoking • WiFi

**Hotel Monaco Portland** 506 SW Washington (at 5th Ave) **503/222-0001, 866/861-9514** • gay-friendly • restaurant • gym • kids/ pets ok • WiFi

**Hotel Vintage Plaza** 422 SW Broadway (at SW Washington) **503/228-1212, 800/263-2305** • popular • gay-friendly • upscale hotel • restaurant & lounge • WiFi • wheelchair access •

**Inn at Northrup Station** 2025 NW Northrup St (at NW 21st) **503/224-0543, 800/224-1180** • gay-friendly • cute, colorful boutique hotel

**Jupiter Hotel** 800 E Burnside **503/230-9200, 877/800-0004** • gay-friendly • boutique hotel • nonsmoking • restaurant & lounge • kids/ pets ok • WiFi • wheelchair access

**The Lion & the Rose** 1810 NE 15th Ave (at NE Schuyler) **503/287-9245, 800/955-1647** • gay/ straight • in 1906 Queen Anne mansion • nonsmoking • WiFi • gay-owned

**The Mark Spencer Hotel** 409 SW Eleventh Ave (near Stark) **503/224-3293, 800/548-3934** • gay-friendly • nonsmoking • kids/ pets ok • WiFi

**McMenamins Crystal Hotel** 303 SW 12th Ave (at Stark) **503/972-2670, 855/205-3930** • gay/ straight • pool • WiFi • also restaurant & bar

**The Nines** 525 SW Morrison St **877/229-9995** • gay-friendly • great art, rooftop deck & bar with vew of the west side

**Portland's White House B&B** 1914 NE 22nd Ave (at NE Hancock St) **503/287-7131, 800/272-7131** • gay/ straight • in 1911 Greek Revival mansion • nonsmoking • WiFi • gay-owned

**Riverplace Hotel** 1510 SW Harbor Way **503/228-3233** • gay-friendly • restaurant & bar • WiFi • pets ok

## BARS

**CC Slaughter's** 219 NW Davis St (at 3rd) **503/248-9135, 888/348-9135** • 3pm-2am • popular • mostly gay men • dancing/DJ • karaoke • videos • also martini lounge • WiFi • wheelchair access

**Chopsticks Express II** 2651 E Burnside St (at NE 26th Ave) **503/234-6171** • noon-2am • gay/ straight • karaoke • young crowd • food served • wheelchair access

**Crush** 1400 SE Morrison (at SE 14th) **503/235-8150** • 4pm-2am, clsd Mon • gay/ straight • wine & martini bar • food served • WiFi • wheelchair access

**Darcelle XV** 208 NW 3rd Ave (at NW Davis St) **503/222-5338** • 6pm-11pm, till 2am Fri-Sat, clsd Sun-Tue • gay/ straight • cabaret • strippers • drag shows • food served • wheelchair access

**Fox & Hounds** 217 NW 2nd Ave (btwn Everett & Davis) **503/243-5530** • 11am-2am • popular • mostly gay men • also restaurant • brunch wknds • wheelchair access

**Hot Flash Portland** 9 NW 2nd Ave (at Barracuda) **503/252-9333** • 6pm-10pm 4th Sat only • "for seasoned lesbians 36+ (& the women who love us!)" • dancing/DJ • cover charge

**JOQ's Tavern** 2512 NE Broadway (at NE 25th Ave) **503/287-4210** • 1pm-2am • mostly gay men • neighborhood bar • food served, wheelchair access

**Moonstar** 7410 NE Martin Luther King Jr Blvd (at NE Lombard St) **503/285-1230** • 11am-1:30am • gay/ straight

**Rotture** 315 SE 3rd Ave (at SE Pine) **503/234-5683** • 9pm-2:30am • gay-friendly • live music venue

**Scandals** 1125 SW Stark St (at SW 12th) **503/227-5887** • noon-2am • mostly gay men • friendly neighborhood bar • karaoke • bands • food served • wheelchair access • gay-owned

**Silverado** 318 SW 3rd Ave (at SW Oak St) **503/224-4493** • 9am-2:30am • mostly gay men • dancing/DJ • strippers • karaoke Mon • food served • wheelchair access • gay-owned

**Vault Martini Bar** 226 NW 12th Ave (btwn 12th & Davis Sts) **503/224-4909** • 4pm-1am, till 2am Thu-Sat, 1pm-10pm Sun • gay/straight • full menu • wheelchair access

## NIGHTCLUBS

**Casey's** 610 NW Couch St (at 6th) **503/505-9468** • 11am-2:30am • lesbians/gay men • dancing/DJ • karaoke

**Embers** 110 NW Broadway (at NW Couch St) **503/222-3082** • 11am-2am • popular • mostly gay men • dancing/DJ • drag shows • also restaurant • wheelchair access

**Holocene** 1001 SE Morrison (at SE 10th) **503/239-7639** • gay/straight • popular dance club • many LGBT theme nights • live music • check local listings

**Under Wonder Lounge** 128 NE Russell **503/284-8686** • 5pm-midnight, open show nights only • transgender-friendly • nonsmoking • gay-owned

## CAFES

**Blend** 2710 N Killingsworth (at Greeley) **503/473-8616** • 7am-6pm, 8am-5pm Sun • WiFi • wheelchair access

**Cup & Saucer Cafe** 3566 SE Hawthorne Blvd (at SE 36th) **503/236-6001** • 7am-9pm • popular w/ lesbians • full menu • vegan-friendly • beer/wine • nonsmoking • wheelchair access

**Elephant's Delicatessen** 115 NW 22nd Ave (at NW Davis) **503/299-6304** • 7am-7:30pm, 9:30am-6:30pm Sun • wheelchair access

**Marco's Cafe & Espresso Bar** 7910 SW 35th (at Multnomah Blvd), Multnomah **503/245-0199** • 7am-9pm, from 8am Sat, 8am-2pm Sun • food served • plenty veggie • beer/wine • wheelchair access

**Pix Pâtisserie** 3402 SE Division St (at SE 34th) **503/232-4407** • 2pm-midnight, noon-2am Fri-Sat • dessert • beer/wine • wheelchair access

**Three Friends Coffeehouse** 201 SE 12th Ave (at Ash) **503/236-6411** • 7am-10pm, from 8am wknds, till 9pm Sun • WiFi • wheelchair access

**Voodoo Doughnut** 22 SW 3rd Ave **503/241-4704** • 24hrs

## RESTAURANTS

**Andina** 1314 NW Glisan St (at 13th Ave) **503/228-9535** • lunch, dinner & tapas • Peruvian • full bar

**Aura Restaurant & Lounge** 1022 W Burnside St (btwn SW 10th & 11th) **503/597-2872** • 5pm-midnight, till 2:30am Fri-Sat, clsd Sun-Tue • also bar • wheelchair access

**Bastas Trattoria** 410 NW 21st (at Flanders) **503/274-1572** • dinner nightly • northern Italian • some veggie • full bar till late • wheelchair access

**Berbati's Pan** 19 SW 2nd Ave (btwn Burnside & Ankeny) **503/226-2122** • 11am-2am, from 3pm Sun-Mon • Greek • full bar • wheelchair access

**Besaw's** 2301 NW Savier (at NW 23rd) **503/228-2619** • 7am-10pm Tue-Fri, from 8am Sat, 8am-3pm Sun-Mon • American • wheelchair access

**Bijou Cafe** 132 SW 3rd St (at Pine St) **503/222-3187** • 7am-2pm, from 8am wknds • popular • plenty veggie • "farm-fresh brkfst" • WiFi • wheelchair access

**Bluehour** 250 NW 13th Ave (at NW Everett St) **503/226-3394** • lunch Sun-Fri, dinner nightly, Sun brunch • extensive wine list • upscale • wheelchair access

**Bread & Ink Cafe** 3610 SE Hawthorne Blvd (at 36th) **503/239-4756** • brkfst, lunch & dinner, packed for brunch on Sun • popular • full bar • WiFi • wheelchair access

**Dot's Cafe** 2521 SE Clinton (at 26th) **503/235-0203** • noon-2am • popular • full bar • eclectic American • plenty veggie • wheelchair access

**Equinox** 830 N Shaver St (at Mississippi) **503/460-3333** • dinner, brunch wknds, clsd Mon • int'l • patio • wheelchair access

**Esparza's Tex-Mex Cafe** 2725 SE Ankeny St (at 28th) **503/234-7909** • 11:30am-10pm • popular • funky • wheelchair access

**Farm Cafe** **503/736-3276** • 5pm-11pm • Northwest cuisine • wheelchair access

**Genie's Cafe** 1101 SE Division St (at 12th) **503/445-9777** • 8am-3pm • brunch • house-infused vodkas • wheelchair access

**Hobo's** 120 NW 3rd Ave (btwn Davis & Couch) **503/224-3285** • 4pm-2:30am • piano bar • some veggie • wheelchair access

**Masu** 406 SW 13th Ave (at Burnside) **503/221-6278** • lunch Mon-Th, dinner nightly • sushi • WiFi • wheelchair access

**Mint** 816 N Russell St **503/284-5518** • 5pm-10pm, till 11pm Fri-Sat, clsd Sun-Mon • fusion food • also 820 Lounge • wheelchair access

**Montage** 301 SE Morrison (at 3rd) 503/234–1324 • lunch Tue-Fri, dinner till 2am, till 4am Fri-Sat • popular • Louisiana-style cookin' • full bar • wheelchair access

**Nicholas'** 318 SE Grand (btwn Oak & Pine) 503/235–5123 • 11am-9pm, from noon Sun • Middle Eastern • wheelchair access

**Nostrana** 1401 SE Morrison 503/234–2427 • lunch Mon-Fri, dinner nightly • fresh, local, wood-fired Italian • wheelchair access

**Old Town Pizza** 226 NW Davis (at NW 3rd) 503/222–9999 • 11:30am-11pm, till midnight Fri-Sat • above Shanghai Tunnels • supposedly home to 100-year-old ghost • wheelchair access

**Oven & Shaker** 1134 NW Everett St 503/241–1600 • 11:30am-midnight

**Paley's Place** 1204 NW 21st Ave (at NW Northrup St) 503/243–2403 • dinner nightly • Northwest cuisine

**Paradox Cafe** 3439 SE Belmont St (at SE 35th) 503/232–7508 • brkfst, lunch & dinner • popular • vegetarian diner • killer Reuben • wheelchair access

**Pour** 2755 NE Broadway (at NE 28th) 503/288–7687 • 4:30pm-11pm, till close Fri-Sat, clsd Sun • wine bar & bistro • wheelchair access

**The Roxy** 1121 SW Stark St (btwn 11th & 12th) 503/223–9160 • 24hrs, clsd Mon • popular • retro American diner • WiFi • wheelchair access

**Santa Fe Taqueria** 831 NW 23rd (at Kearney) 503/220–0406 • 11am-midnight • live entertainment • wheelchair access

**Saucebox** 214 SW Broadway (at Burnside) 503/241–3393 • 5pm-close • pan-Asian • plenty veggie • full bar • DJ • wheelchair access • gay-owned

**Tasty n Sons** 3808 N Williams 503/241–1600 • 9am-10pm, till 11pm Fri-Sat • full bar

**Vita Cafe** 3023 NE Alberta St (btwn 30th & 31st) 503/335–8233 • brkfst, lunch & dinner • mostly vegetarian/vegan • some free-range meat • wheelchair access

**West Cafe** 1201 SW Jefferson St (12th Ave) 503/227–8189 • lunch Mon-Fri, dinner nightly, Sun brunch • "comfort food w/ a twist" • live entertainment • WiFi • wheelchair access

**Yakuza Lounge** 5411 NE 30th Ave (at Killingsworth) 503/450–0893 • 5pm-close, clsd Mon-Tue • Japanese • full bar • wheelchair access

## ENTERTAINMENT & RECREATION

**Gay Skate** 1 SE Spokane St (at Oaks Park Way, at Oaks Rink) 503/233–5777 • 7pm-9pm 3rd Mon only

**Out Dancing** 975 SE Sandy Blvd (at SE Ankeny St & SE 9th Ave) 503/236–5129 • LGBT dance lessons

**Rose City Rollers** • Portland's female roller derby league • visit www.rosecityrollers.com for events

**Sauvie's Island Beach** 25 miles NW (off US 30) • follow Reeder Rd to the Collins beach area, park at the farthest end of the road, then follow path to beach

## BOOKSTORES

**CounterMedia** 927 SW Oak (btwn 9th & 10th) 503/226–8141 • 11am-7pm, noon-6pm Sun • alternative comics • vintage gay books/ periodicals/ erotica

**In Other Words** 14 NE Killingsworth St (at Williams) 503/232–6003 • noon-7pm, clsd Sun-Mon • feminist lit • music • resource center • wheelchair access

**Laughing Horse Bookstore** 12 NE 10th Ave (near Burnside) 503/236–2893 • 11am-7pm, clsd Sun • alternative/ progressive • wheelchair access

**Powell's Books** 1005 W Burnside St (at 10th) 503/228–4651, 800/878–7323 • 9am-11pm • popular • largest new & used bookstore in the world • cafe • readings • wheelchair access

## RETAIL SHOPS

**Fat Fancy** 1013 SW Morrison (btwn 10th & 11th) 503/445–4353 • plus-size clothing boutique • wheelchair access • gay-owned

**Hip Chicks Do Wine** 4510 SE 23rd Ave (SE Holgate & 26th) 503/234–3790 • 11am-6pm

## GYMS & HEALTH CLUBS

**Common Ground Wellness Center** 5010 NE 33rd Ave (at Alberta St) 503/238–1065 • 10am-11pm • gay-friendly • wellness center • call for women's & trans nights • reservations required

## EROTICA

**Fantasy for Adults** 1512 W Burnside (near 15th) 503/295–6969 • 24hrs

**Spartacus Leathers** 300 SW 12th Ave (at Burnside) 503/224–2604

## Salem

### NIGHTCLUBS

**Southside Speakeasy** 3529 Fairview Industrial Dr SE (at Madrona) **503/362–1139** • 11am-2am, from 3:30pm wknds • gay/ straight • neighborhood bar • dancing/DJ • food served • karaoke • drag shows • WiFi • gay-owned

### RESTAURANTS

**Davinci's** 180 High St SE **504/399-1413** • dinner only, clsd Sun • full bar

**Word Of Mouth** 140 NE 17th St **503/930-4285** • 7am-3pm, clsd Mon-Tue

## Sauvie Island

### ENTERTAINMENT & RECREATION

**Collins Beach** take Hwy 30 N from Portland, turn onto "Sauvie Island Bridge" (then take Gillihan Rd to Reeder Rd) • gay/ straight • nude beach • get a parking permit before you go (available at general store at base of Sauvie Island Bridge)

## Silverton

### ACCOMMODATIONS

**The Oregon Garden Resort** 895 W Main St **800/966-6490** • gay-friendly • restaurant & lounge • pool • WiFi

# PENNSYLVANIA

## Abington

### BARS

**Kitchen Bar** 1482 Old York Rd **215/576-9766** • noon-2am, from 8am wknds • gay-friendly • dancing/DJ • food served • live entertainment

### RESTAURANTS

**Vintage Bar & Restaurant** 1116 Old York Rd **215/887-8500** • 11am-2am • wheelchair access

## Allentown

**see also Bethlehem**

### ACCOMMODATIONS

**Grim's Manor B&B** 10 Kern Rd, Kutztown **610/683-7089** • lesbians/ gay men • 200-yr-old stone farmhouse on 5 acres • full brkfst • nonsmoking • gay-owned

### BARS

**Candida's** 247 N 12th St (at Chew) **610/434-3071** • 4pm-2am, from 2pm Fri-Sun • lesbians/ gay men • dancing/DJ • neighborhood bar • food served • karaoke

**Stonewall, Moose Lounge** 28 N 10th St (at Hamilton) **610/432-0215** • 7pm-2am, clsd Sun- Mon • popular • mostly gay men • dancing/DJ • live shows • karaoke • drag shows • male dancers • videos

## Altoona

### NIGHTCLUBS

**Escapade** 2523 Union Ave, Rte 36 **814/946-8195** • 8pm-2am • lesbians/ gay men • dancing/DJ • gay-owned

## Bethlehem

### NIGHTCLUBS

**Diamonz** 1913 W Broad St (at Pennsylvania Ave) **610/865-1028** • 7pm-2am, from 5pm Fri-Sat • mostly women • dancing/DJ • live shows • karaoke • also restaurant • some veggie • wheelchair access

## Bristol

### EROTICA

**Bristol News World** 576 Bristol Pike/ Rte 13 N **215/785-4770**

## Butler

### NIGHTCLUBS

**M&J's Lounge** 124 Mercer St **724/496-8955** • 9pm-midnight Th, 9:30pm-3am Fri-Sat • lesbians/ gay men • neighborhood bar • 18+ •

## Easton

### BARS

**La Pazza** 1251 Ferry St **610/515-0888** • 4pm-closing, clsd Mon • lesbians/gay men • dancing/DJ • food served

## Erie

### NIGHTCLUBS

**The Zone** 133 W 18th St (at Peach) **814/452-0125** • 8pm-2am • lesbians/ gay men • dancing/DJ • food served

### RESTAURANTS

**La Bella** 802 W 18th St **814/456-2244** • 5pm-9pm, clsd Sun-Tue • BYOB • gay-owned

**Pie in the Sky Cafe** 463 W 8th St (at Walnut) 814/459–8638 • lunch & dinner, clsd Sun-Mon • BYOB • reservations recommended • wheelchair access

## PUBLICATIONS

**Erie Gay News  814/456–9833** • covers news & events in the Erie, Cleveland, Pittsburgh, Buffalo & Chautauqua County (NY) region

# Gettysburg

## ACCOMMODATIONS

**Battlefield B&B** 2264 Emmitsburg Rd (at Ridge Rd) 717/334–8804 • gay/ straight • full brkfst • Civil War home • pets/kids ok • WiFi • lesbian-owned • wheelchair access

**The Beechmont Inn B&B** 315 Broadway, Hanover 717/632–3013, 800/553–7009 • gay-friendly • WiFi • wheelchair access

**Sheppard Mansion B&B** 117 Frederick St (at High St), Hanover 717/633–8075, 877/762–6746 • gay/ straight • full brkfst • kids 12 years & up ok • nonsmoking • WiFi • also restaurant & bar

# Harrisburg

## INFO LINES & SERVICES

**LGBT Community Center Coalition of Central PA** 1306 N 3rd St 717/920–9534

## BARS

**Bar 704** 704 N 3rd St 717/234–4226 • 4pm-2am • mostly gay men • neighborhood bar • older crowd • wheelchair access

**The Brownstone Lounge** 412 Forster St (btwn 3rd & 6th) 717/234–7009 • 11am-2am, from 5pm wknds • lesbians/ gay men • neighborhood bar • wheelchair access

## NIGHTCLUBS

**Stallions** 706 N 3rd St (enter rear) 717/232–3060 • 7pm-2am • popular • mostly gay men • dancing/DJ • live shows • karaoke • drag shows • strippers • wheelchair access

# Johnstown

## NIGHTCLUBS

**Lucille's** 520 Washington St (near Central Park) 814/539–4448 • 6pm-2am, clsd Sun-Mon • gay/straight • dancing/DJ • drag shows • strippers • karaoke

# Lancaster

## ACCOMMODATIONS

**Cameron Estate Inn** 1855 Mansion Ln, Mount Joy 717/492–0111, 888/422–6376 • gay/ straight • full brkfst • nonsmoking • restaurant • wheelchair access • gay-owned

**Lancaster Arts Hotel**  300 Harrisburg Ave 717/299–3000, 866/720–2787 • gay-friendly • great restaurant • wheelchair access

## BARS

**Tally Ho** 201 W Orange St (at Water) 717/299–0661 • 8pm-2am • lesbians/ gay men • dancing/DJ • karaoke • drag shows • young crowd

## RESTAURANTS

**The Loft** above Tally Ho bar 717/299–0661 • lunch Mon-Fri, dinner Mon-Sat • contemporary American/ French

# Milford

## ACCOMMODATIONS

**Hotel Fauchere** 401 Broad St (at Catharine St) 570/409–1212 • gay-friendly • historic boutique hotel • full brkfst • also restaurant & bar • nonsmoking • kids/ pets ok • wheelchair access

# New Hope

**see also Lambertville & Sergeantsville, New Jersey**

## ACCOMMODATIONS

**Ash Mill Farm B&B** 5358 York Rd (at Rte 202), Holicong 215/794–5373 • gay-friendly • full brkfst • nonsmoking • WiFi • gay-owned

**The Wishing Well Guesthouse** 144 Old York Rd 215/862–8819 • gay/ straight • nonsmoking • kids ok • gay-owned

## BARS

**Havana** 105 S Main St 215/862–9897 • noon-2am • gay/ straight • concert venue & restaurant • karaoke

**Razz Room** 6426 Lower York Rd (at the Ramada Hotel) 215/862–5221 • gay/ straight • cabaret • dinner served • also hotel

## RESTAURANTS

**Eagle Diner** 6522 Lower York Rd 215/862–5575 • 24hrs • wheelchair access

**Karla's** 5 W Mechanic St 215/862–2612 • noon-10pm, till midnight Fri-Sat, from 11am Sun • some veggie • full bar till 2am

## Erotica

**Le Chateau Exotique** 27 W Mechanic St
215/862–3810 • fetishwear

# Philadelphia

## Info Lines & Services

**William Way LGBT Community Center**
1315 Spruce St (at Juniper) 215/732–2220 •
11am-10pm, noon-5pm wknds

## Accommodations

**Alexander Inn** Spruce (at 12th St)
215/923–3535, 877/253–9466 • gay/ straight •
gym • nonsmoking • WiFi • gay-owned

**The Gables B&B** 4520 Chester Ave
215/662–1918 • gay/ straight • nonsmoking •
WiFi • gay-owned

**The Independent Hotel** 1234 Locust St (at
13th) 215/772–1440 • gay/ straight • boutique
hotel • WiFi • wheelchair access

**Morris House Hotel** 225 S 8th St
215/922–2446 • gay-friendly • nonsmoking •
WiFi • also M Restaurant

**Palomar Philadelphia** 117 S 17th St
215/563–5006, 888/725–1778 • gay-friendly •
WiFi • wheelchair access

## Bars

**Bike Stop** 204-206 S Quince St (btwn 11th &
12th) 215/627–1662 • 4pm-2am, from 2pm
wknds • mostly gay men • DJ • leather (very
leather-women-friendly) • karaoke

**Boxers PHL** 1330 Walnut St 215/735-2977 •
4pm-2am from noon wknds • mostly gay men,
more women on Sun • sports bar

**ICandy** 254 S 12th St (btwn Locust & Spruce)
267/324–3500 • 4pm-2am • mostly gay men •
dancing/DJ • multi-level entertainment
complex

**Khyber Pass Pub** 56 S 2nd St (btwn Market
& Chestnut) 215/238–5888 • 11am-2am •
gay-friendly • food served • live bands •
wheelchair access

**L'Etage** 624 S 6th St (at Bainbridge)
215/592–0656 • 7:30pm-1am, till 2am Fri-Sat,
clsd Mon • gay/ straight • cabaret
• also crepe restaurant downstairs

**North Third** 801 N 3rd (at Brown)
215/413–3666 • 4pm-2am, from 10am wknd
brunch • gay/ straight • also restaurant

**Rosewood** 1302 Walnut St 215/545–1893 •
9pm-2am, from 5pm Fri, clsd Sun-Wed •
mostly gay men • cosy & elegant, easy way to
get into Woodys

**Stir Lounge** 1705 Chancellor St (at
Rittenhouse Sq btwn Walnut & Spruce)
215/732–2700 • 4pm-2am • lesbians/ gay
men • neighborhood bar • dancing/DJ • girl
party 1st Sat

**Tabu Lounge & Sports Bar** 200 S 12th St
215/964–9675 • noon-2am • gay/ straight •
food served • karaoke • gay Latin night 4th Sat

**Tavern on Camac** 243 S Camac St (at
Spruce) 215/545–0900 • 4pm-2am • lesbians/
gay men • dancing/DJ • piano bar • food
served

**Woody's** 202 S 13th St (at Walnut)
215/545–1893 • 4pm-2am • mostly gay men •
dancing/DJ • country/ western • karaoke •
Latin Th • strippers • WiFi • wheelchair access

## Nightclubs

**Bob & Barbara's Lounge** 1509 South St
215/545–4511 • 3pm-2am, from 5pm Sun •
gay/ straight • drag shows Th • live jazz Fri-Sat

**Groove Philly** • mostly women • dancing/DJ
• occasional events by Denise Cohen and the
former staff of Sisters , check
www.groovephilly.com for events

**Ladies 2000** 856/869–0193 • seasonal
parties • check www.ladies2000.com for events

**Voyeur** 1221 St James St (off 13th & Locust)
215/735–5772 • 1am-3am, from 9pm wknds •
mostly gay men • dancing/DJ • live bands •
karaoke • cabaret • private club

## Cafes

**10th Street Pour House** 262 S 10th St (at
Spruce) 215/922–5626 • 6am-2pm, popular
brunch wknds • wheelchair access

**B2 Cafe** 1500 E Passyunk Ave 215/271–5520
• great vegan soft serve ice cream • WiFi

**Capogiro** 119 S 13th St (at Sansom)
215/351–0900 • 7:30am-11:30pm, till 1am Fri-
Sat • gelato

**Capriccio** 110 N 16th St (at Benjamin
Franklin Pkwy) 215/735–9797 • 6:30am-7pm,
8am-8pm wknds

**Cosi** 1128 Walnut St 215/413–1608 • 7am-
11pm

**Green Line Cafe** 4239 Baltimore Ave (at
43rd) 215/222–3431 • 7am-11pm, 8am-8pm
Sun • live shows

## Restaurants

**Bar Ferdinand** 1030 N 2nd St • great tapas
& wine

**Cantina Feliz** 424 S Bethlehem Pike, Fort
Washington 215/646–1320 • 11am-9pm, from
4pm Sat-Sun, till 10pm Fri- Sat

**The Continental** 138 Market St (at 2nd) 215/923–6069 • lunch, dinner, wknd brunch • also bar until 2am

**Geno's Steaks** 1219 S 9th St 215/389-0659 • 24hrs • great cheesesteak • gay-owned

**Honey's** 800 N 4th St 215/925–1150 • 7am-4pm, till 5pm wknds • BYOB

**Knock** 226 S 12th St 215/925–1166 • lunch & dinner, Sun brunch • American • also bar

**Liberties** 705 N 2nd St (at Fairmount) 215/238–0660 • lunch & dinner • full bar till 2am

**Little Nonna's** 1234 Locust (at The Independent Hotel) 215/546-2100 • casual Italian-American • lesbian-owned

**Lolita** 106 S 13th St (at Sansom) 215/546-7100 • 5pm-10pm • upscale Mexican • BYOB

**Mercato** 1216 Spruce St 215/985–2962 • dinner • Italian • BYOB

**Midtown II** 122 S 11th St 215/627–6452 • 24hrs • diner • popular late night • transgender-friendly

**Mixto** 1141 Pine St 215/592–0363 • lunch & dinner, brkfst wknds • Latin American

**My Thai** 2200 South St (at 22nd) 215/985–1878 • 5pm-10pm, till 11pm Fri-Sat • full bar

**New Harmony** 135 N 9th St (at Cherry) 215/627–4520 • 11am-11pm • vegan/Chinese

**Paesano's** 1017 S 9th St 215/440–0371 • 11am-7pm • great sandwiches

**Sabrina's** 910 Christian St 215/574–1599 • 8am-10pm, till 8pm Tue-Th, till 4pm Sun-Mon

**El Vez** 121 S 13th St (at Sansom) 215/928–9800 • lunch Mon-Sat, dinner nightly, Sun brunch • Latin American/Mexican • full bar

**White Dog Cafe** 3420 Sansom St (at Walnut) 215/386–9224 • lunch & dinner, brunch Sun • full bar

## ENTERTAINMENT & RECREATION

**Philly Roller Girls** • Philly's female roller derby league • visit www.phillyrollergirls.com for events

**The Walt Whitman House** 328 Mickle Blvd, Camden, NJ 856/964–5383 • the last home of America's great & controversial poet, just across the Delaware River

## BOOKSTORES

**Philly AIDS Thrift @ Giovanni's Room** 345 S 12th St (at Pine) 215/923–2960 • 11am-8pm,till 9pm Fri-Sat, till 7pm Sun • all proceeds from thrift items to fund local HIV/AIDS organizations

## RETAIL SHOPS

**Philadelphia AIDS Thrift** 710 S 5th St 215/922–3186 • 11am-8pm, till 9pm Fri-Sat, till 7pm Sun

## PUBLICATIONS

**PGN (Philadelphia Gay News)** 215/625–8501 • LGBT newspaper w/ extensive listings

## GYMS & HEALTH CLUBS

**12th St Gym** 204 S 12th St (btwn Locust & Walnut) 215/985–4092 • pool • day passes

## EROTICA

**The Mood** 531 South St 215/413–1930

**Passional Boutique** 317 South St 215/829–4986, 877/826–7738 • noon-10pm • corsets • fetishwear • toys • woman-owned

**Sexploratorium** 317 South St (across from TLA theater) 215/923-1398 • noon-10pm • workshops • gallery

# Pittsburgh

## INFO LINES & SERVICES

**AA Gay/ Lesbian** 412/471–7472 • call for times & location

**Gay/ Lesbian Community Center** 210 Grant St 412/422–0114 • 9am-9pm, noon-6pm Sun

## ACCOMMODATIONS

**Camp Davis** 311 Red Brush Rd, Boyers 724/637–2402 • April-Oct • lesbians/ gay men • cabins, trailer, & campsites • pool • adults 21+ only • 1 hour from Pittsburgh

**The Inn on Negley** 703 S Negley Ave (at Elmer St) 412/661–0631 • gay-friendly • full brkfst • nonsmoking • WiFi • wheelchair access • women-owned

**The Inn on the Mexican War Streets** 604 W North Ave 412/231–6544 • lesbians/ gay men • nonsmoking • WiFi • gay-owned

**Morning Glory Inn B&B** 2119 Sarah St 412/431–1707 • gay-friendly • WiFi • woman-owned

**The Parador Inn** 939 Western Ave 412/231–4800, 877/540–1443 • gay-friendly • WiFi • gay-owned

**The Priory** 614 Pressley St (near Cedar Ave) **412/231–3338, 866/377–4679** • gay-friendly • nonsmoking • kids ok • WiFi • wheelchair access

## Bars

**5801** 5801 Ellsworth Ave (at Maryland) **412/661–5600** • 4pm-2am, from 2pm Sun • lesbians/ gay men • deck • also restaurant • wheelchair access

**The Backdraft Bar & Grill** 3049 Churchview Ave **412/885–1239** • 11am-2am, till midnight Sun • gay/ straight • live bands • karaoke

**Blue Moon Bar & Lounge** 5115 Butler St (in Lawrenceville) **412/781–1119** • 5pm-2am, 4pm-1am Mon • mostly gay men • neighborhood bar • transgender-friendly • go-go dancers

**Cattivo** 146 44th St **412/687–2157** • 4pm-2am Wed-Sun, clsd Mon-Tue • mostly women • dancing/DJ • karaoke • drag shows • food served

**Cruze Bar** 1600 Smallman St (at 16th St) **412/471–1400** • 4pm-2am, clsd Mon • lesbians/ gay men • dancing/DJ • live entertainment • gay-owned

**Images** 965 Liberty Ave (at 10th St) **412/391–9990** • 2pm-2am • mostly gay men • karaoke • videos

**PTown** 4740 Baum Blvd **412/621–0111** • 6pm-2am • lesbians/ gay men • dancing/DJ • strippers • WiFi

**Real Luck Cafe** 1519 Penn Ave (at 16th) **412/471–7832** • 4pm-2am • lesbians/ gay men • neighborhood bar • go-go dancers • food served • wheelchair access • gay-owned

**Remedy** 5121 Butler St, Lawrenceville **412/781–6771** • 4pm-2am, from 12:30pm Sun • gay/ straight • multiracial • neighborhood bar • dancing/DJ • also restaurant upstairs

**Spin Bartini/ Ultra Lounge** 5744 Ellsworth Ave, Shadyside **412/362–7746** • 4pm-2am • gay/ straight • live jazz • wheelchair access

**There Ultra Lounge** 931 Liberty Ave (at Smithfield) **412/642–4435** • 3:30pm-2am, from 7:30pm Sat-Sun • lesbians/ gay men • karaoke • wheelchair access

## Nightclubs

**1226 on Herron** 1226 Herron Ave (at Liberty) **412/682–6839** • 6pm-2am, clsd Mon-Wed • mostly men

**941 Saloon** 941 Liberty Ave (at Smithfield St, 2nd flr) **412/281–5222** • 2pm-2am • lesbians/ gay men • dancing/DJ • karaoke

**The Link** 91 Wendel Rd, Herminie **724/446–7717** • 7pm-2am, clsd Mon • lesbians/ gay men • dancing/DJ • live shows • drag shows • male dancers • food served • patio

## Cafes

**Square Cafe** 1137 S Braddock Ave **412/244–8002** • 7am-3pm, from 8am Sun • live shows monthly • lesbian-owned

**Zeke's Coffee** 6012 Penn Ave **724/201–1671** • 9am-5pm, till 2pm Mon, till 8pm Th, clsd Sun

## Restaurants

**Abay** 130 S Highland Ave (at Baum Blvd) **412/661–9736** • lunch & dinner, clsd Mon • Ethiopian • plenty veggie

**Capri** 6001 Penn Ave (at Highland Ave) **412/363–1250** • 11am-midnight, 6pm-2am Th-Sat • pizza

**Dinette** 5996 Penn Cir S **412/362–0202** • dinner only, clsd Sun-Mon • plates to share, starters & thin-crust pizzas • women-owned

**Dish** 128 S 17th St (at Sarah) **412/390–2012** • 5pm-2am, clsd Sun • Italian • also bar

**Double Wide Grill** 2339 E Carson St (at S 24th St) **412/390–1111** • lunch & dinner, wknd brunch • BBQ • plenty veggie/ vegan

**Eleven** 1150 Smallman St (at 11th) **412/201–5656** • lunch & dinner, Sun brunch

**Harris Grill** 5747 Ellsworth Ave **412/362–5273** • dinner nightly, wknd brunch • full bar

**Kaya** 2000 Smallman St (at 20th) **412/261–6565** • lunch & dinner • Latin/ Caribbean • plenty veggie

**NOLA On the Square** 24 Market Sq **412/471–9100** • 11am-11pm, clsd Sun • live music

**OTB Bicycle Cafe** 2518 East Carson St (at S 26th) **412/381–3698** • 11am-10pm • burgers • plenty veggie • also bar • occasional events

**Pamela's Diner** 60 21st St **412/281–6366** • 7am-3pm, from 8am Sun • also 5 other locations in Pittsburgh • lesbian-owned

**Point Brugge Cafe** 401 Hastings (at Reynolds) **412/441–3334** • lunch & dinner, Sun brunch, clsd Mon • Belgian/ European

**Primanti Brothers** 46 18th St **412/263–2142** • Pittsburgh's iconic sandwich shop • many locations

**Red Oak Cafe** 3610 Forbes Ave (at Lothrop) **412/621–2221** • 7am-7pm, till 5pm Fri, clsd wknds • salads & sandwiches • plenty veggie/vegan

**Spoon** 134 S Highland Ave **412/362–6001** • fresh "farm to table" menu • also lounge

**Zenith** 86 S 26th St **412/481–4833** • 11:30am-8:30pm, Sun brunch 11am-2pm, clsd Mon-Wed • vegetarian/ vegan • also antiques store • wheelchair access

### ENTERTAINMENT & RECREATION

**Andy Warhol Museum** 117 Sandusky St (at General Robinson) **412/237–8300** • 10am-5pm, till 10pm Fri, clsd Mon • is it soup or is it art? see for yourself

**Burgh Bits & Bites Food Tour** **412/209–3370, 800/979–3370** • explore the vivid history & culinary delights of the Steel City

**Pittsburgh Public Market** 2401 Penn Ave **412/281–4505** • the goodness of locally grown produce, fresh-baked goods, handmade crafts

### RETAIL SHOPS

**Slacker** 1321 E Carson St (btwn 13th & 14th) **412/381–3911** • noon-9pm, 11am-6pm Sun • magazines • clothing • leather • wheelchair access

**Who New?** 5156 Butler St **412/781–0588** • noon-6pm, clsd Mon-Tue, open Sun by chance • vintage modern design • gay-owned

### EROTICA

**Adult Mart** 346 Blvd of the Allies **412/261–9119** • 24hrs

## Poconos

### ACCOMMODATIONS

**Rainbow Mountain Resort** 570/223–8484 • lesbians/ gay men • transgender-friendly • swimming • hot tub • WiFi • gay-owned • also restaurant & bar • dancing/DJ Fri-Sat • piano bar • karaoke

**The Woods Campground** 845 Vaughn Acres Ln, Lehighton 610/377–9577 • lesbians/ gay men • 84 campsites • RV spots • also cabins • swimming • 18+ • WiFi

## Reading

### BARS

**The Peanut Bar & Restaurant** 332 Penn St 610/376–8500, 800/515–8500 • 11am-11pm, till midnight Fri-Sat, clsd Sun • a Reading landmark! • non-smoking • WiFi

### RESTAURANTS

**Judy's On Cherry** 332 Cherry St 610/374–8511 • lunch Tue-Fri, dinner Tue-Sat, clsd Sun-Mon • Mediterranean

**The Ugly Oyster** 21 S 5th St (at Cherry) 610/373–6791 • 11:30am-10pm, from noon Sat, clsd Sun • traditional Irish pub (bar open till 2am) • live shows

## Scranton

### BARS

**Twelve Penny Saloon** 3501 Birney Ave, Moosic 570/941–0444 • 6pm-2pm, from 3pm wknds • lesbians/ gay men • neighborhood bar • dancing/DJ • leather • transgender-friendly • food served • karaoke • drag shows • wheelchair access • gay-owned

## State College

### ACCOMMODATIONS

**The Atherton Hotel** 125 S Atherton St (at College Ave) 814/231–2100, 800/832–0132 • gay-friendly • nonsmoking • WiFi • also restaurant & bar • wheelchair access

### BARS

**Chumley's** 100 W College 814/238–4446 • 5pm-2am, from 6pm Sun • popular • lesbians/ gay men • neighborhood bar • wheelchair access

### NIGHTCLUBS

**Indigo** 112 W College Ave 814/234–1031 • 9pm-2am, clsd Mon-Wed • gay/ straight • "Alternative" night Sun • dancing/DJ • young crowd

## Uniontown

### NIGHTCLUBS

**Club 231** 231 Pittsburgh St/ Rte 51 (at Fulton) 724/430–1477 • 9pm-close • mostly men • dancing/DJ • karaoke • drag shows • gay-owned

## Wilkes-Barre

### INFO LINES & SERVICES

**NEPA Rainbow Alliance Resource Center** 67 Public Square, 5th flr, Edwardsville 570/972–2523 • coalition of NE PA's LGBT organizations & businesses • WiFi

## York

### ACCOMMODATIONS

**Yorktowne Hotel** 48 E Market St
717/848–1111 • gay-friendly • restaurant •
WiFi • wheelchair access

### NIGHTCLUBS

**Altland's Ranch** 8505 Orchard Rd, Spring
Grove 717/225–4479 • 8pm-2am Fri-Sat only
• lesbians/ gay men • dancing/DJ • country
western 3rd Fri • karaoke

## RHODE ISLAND

## Coventry

### RESTAURANTS

**Indigo Lounge & Pizzeria** 599 Tiogue Ave
401/615–9600 • 4pm-10pm, till 1am wknds •
live music • karaoke

## Newport

### INFO LINES & SERVICES

**Sobriety First** 135 Pelham St (at Channing
Memorial Church) 401/438–8860 • 8pm Fri

### ACCOMMODATIONS

**Architect's Inn** 2 Sunnyside Pl
401/845–2547, 877/466–2547 • gay-friendly •
WiFi • gay-owned

**Francis Malbone House Inn** 392 Thames
St (at Memorial Blvd) 401/846–0392,
800/846–0392 • gay-friendly • nonsmoking •
WiFi • wheelchair access

**Hilltop Inn** 2 Kay St 800/846–0392 • gay-
friendly • craftsman-style inn • full brkfst •
WiFi • gay-owned

**Hydrangea House Inn** 16 Bellevue Ave
401/846–4435, 800/945–4667 • popular • gay/
straight • full brkfst • near beach •
nonsmoking • WiFi • gay-owned

**The Spring Seasons Inn** 86 Spring St (btwn
Mary St & Touro) 401/849–0004,
877/294–0004 • gay-friendly • full brkfst •
jacuzzi baths • nonsmoking

### RESTAURANTS

**Whitehorse Tavern** 26 Marlborough St (at
Farewell) 401/849–3600 • lunch & dinner, Sun
brunch • upscale dining • nonsmoking • patio

## Pawtucket

### INFO LINES & SERVICES

**Gay & Lesbian AA** 71 Park Place (at Park
Place Congregational Church) 401/438–8860
• 7:30pm Tue

### RESTAURANTS

**Blaze Restaurant** 999 Main St #1113
401/277–2529 • lunch & dinner, clsd Mon •
lesbian-owned

**Garden Grill** 727 East Ave (and of
Blackstone Blvd) 401/454–8951 • 11am-10pm
• vegetarian, vegan & wheat- and gluten-free

## Providence

### ACCOMMODATIONS

**The Dean** 122 Fountain St 401/45–3236 •
gay/straight • historical building has been
elegantly transformed into a 52-room hotel
•coffee shop & bar • karaoke

**Edgewood Manor** 232 Norwood Ave (at
Broad) 401/781–0099 • gay-friendly • 1905
Greek Revival mansion • nonsmoking • WiFi

**Hotel Dolce Villa** 63 De Pasquale Square (at
Atwells) 401/383–7031 • gay/ straight •
boutique hotel • nonsmoking

**The Hotel Providence** 139 Mathewson
401/861–8000, 800/861–8990 • gay/ straight •
Aspire restaurant onsite • WiFi • nonsmoking

**NYLO Hotel** 400 Knight St, Warwick
401/734–4460 • gay/ straight • restaurant &
bar • WiFi • whelchair access

**Renaissance Providence Hotel** 5 Avenue
of the Arts (at Francis) 401/919–5000,
800/468–3571 • gay/ straight • restaurant &
bar • WiFi • nonsmoking

### BARS

**Alleycat** 17 Snow St (at Washington)
401/272–6369 • 3pm-1am, till 2am Fri-Sat •
lesbians/ gay men • neighborhood bar •
videos • gay-owned

**The Providence Eagle** 124 Snow St
401/421–1447 • 3pm-1am, till 2am Fri, from
noon wknds

**The Stable** 125 Washington (at Mathewson)
401/272–6950 • 2pm-1am, till 2am Fri-Sat,
from noon Sat-Sun • lesbians/ gay men •
neighborhood bar • videos • wheelchair
access

**The Village** 373 Richmond St (at Point St) 401/228-7222 • 11am-1am, rill 2am Fri-Sat from 10am wknds, clsd Mon-Tue • lesbians/gay men, more women Fri • dancing/DJ • also restaurant • live shows • wheel chair access

## NIGHTCLUBS

**Club Heat** 71 Richmond St 774/319-2751 • 3pm-1am • mostly gay men • dancing/DJ

**EGO Providence** 73 Richmond St 401/383-1208 • 9pm-1am Th, 10pm-3am Sat • mostly gay men • dancing/DJ • drag show

**Girl Spot** 65 Poe St (at Platforms) 401/781-3121 • Sat only • mostly women • dancing/DJ • live music • 18+ • cover charge

**Mirabar** 15 Elbow St 401/331-6761 • 3pm-1am, till 2am Fri-Sat • mostly gay men • dancing/DJ • live shows • male dancers • wheelchair access

**Platforms Dance Club** 165 Poe St 401/781-3121 • gay/ straight • dancing/DJ • gay night Sat • Salsa Sun • 18+

## CAFES

**Coffee Exchange** 207 Wickenden St 401/273-1198 • 6:30am-11pm • deck

**Nicks on Broadway** 500 Broadway 401/421-0286 • lunch & dinner Wed-Sat, Sun brunch, clsd Mon-Tue

**Pastiche Fine Desserts** 92 Spruce St 401/861-5190 • 8:30am-11pm, 10am-10pm Sun

**White Electric Coffee** 711 Westminster 401/453-3007 • 7am-6:30pm

## RESTAURANTS

**Al Forno** 577 S Main St 401/273-9760 • dinner only, clsd Sun-Mon

**Bacaro** 262 S Water St 401/751-3700 • dinner only, clsd Sun-Mon, Cicchetti (small plates) and wine bar

**Bravo Brasserie** 123 Empire St 401/490-5112 • lunch Tue-Sat, dinner nightly, Sun brunch

**Cafe' Paragon** 234 Thayer St 401/331-6200 • 11am-1am • European Bistro/Café style atmosphere with a full bar

**Caffe Dolce Vita** 59 DePasquale Plaza (at Spruce St) 401/331-8240 • 8am-1am, till 2am wknds, wknd brunch • authentic Italian cafe • patio

**Camille's** 71 Bradford St (at Atwell's Ave) 401/751-4812 • lunch & dinner, clsd Sun • full bar

**CAV** 14 Imperial Pl 401/751-9164 • 11am-10pm, till 1am Fri, wknd brunch • eclectic menu & decor

**Don José Tequilas Mexican** 351 Atwells Ave 401/454-8951 • 11:30-11pm, from 3pm-10pm Mon-Wed, till 1am Fri-Sat

**Fellini Pizzeria** 166 Wickenden St 401/751-6737 • open late • free delivery • lesbian-owned

**Julian's** 318 Broadway (at Vinton) 401/861-1770 • 9am-11pm, bar open till 1am

**Kartabar** 284 Thayer St 401/331-8111 • 11:30am-1am • mixed-Mediterranean, with some American classic

**Local 121** 121 Washington St (at Matthewson St) 401/274-2121 • lunch Tue-Sat, dinner nightly, Sun brunch

**Mill's Tavern** 101 N Main St 401/272-3331 • Mon-Fri happy hour oysters , dinner nightly

## ENTERTAINMENT & RECREATION

**Cable Car Cinema & Cafe** 204 S Main St 401/272-3970 • art-house flicks & free popcorn refills

**WaterFire** Waterplace Park 401/272-3111 • May-Oct only • bonfire installations along the Providence River at sunset

## BOOKSTORES

**Books on the Square** 471 Angell St (at Wayland) 401/331-9097, 888/669-9660 • 9am-9pm, 10am-6pm Sun • some LGBT

## PUBLICATIONS

**Get RI Magazine** 401/226-9033 • GLBT magazine

**Options Magazine** 401/724-5428 • LGBT community magazine

## EROTICA

**Mister Sister** 268 Wickenden St 401/421-6969 • women-oriented • fetishwear • sex toys • classes

# SOUTH CAROLINA

## Blacksburg

### EROTICA

**BedTyme Stories** 145 Simper Rd (I-85, exit 100) **864/839-0007** • 9am-midnight • videos, sex toys, lingerie and more

## Charleston

### INFO LINES & SERVICES

**Acceptance Group (Gay AA)** 45 Moultrie St (at St Barnabus Lutheran Church) **843/723-9633 (AA#)** • 7pm Mon, Th & Sat

### ACCOMMODATIONS

**Aloft Charleston Airport & Convention Center** 4875 Tanger Outlet Blvd (at International Blvd), N Charleston **843/566-7300, 877/462-5638** • gay-friendly • gym • pool • WiFi • wheelchair access

**Charleston Place** 205 Meeting St **843/722-4900, 888/635-2350** • gay-friendly • restaurant

### BARS

**Dudley's on Ann** 42 Ann St (at King St) **843/577-6779** • 4pm-2am • mostly gay men • neighborhood bar • karaoke • gay-owed/ run

### NIGHTCLUBS

**Club Pantheon** 28 Ann St (at King) **843/577-2582** • 10pm-2am Fri-Sun only • mostly gay men • dancing • multiracial • live shows • drag shows • cabaret • 18+ • gay-owned

**Deja Vu II** 4628 Spruill Ave **843/554-5959** • 5pm-2am Th, from 8pm Fri-Sat, clsd Sun-Wed • mostly women • dancing/DJ • live shows • food served • karaoke • private club • wheelchair access • lesbian-owned

### CAFES

**Bear E Patch** 1980-A Ashley River Rd **843/766-6490** • 7am-9pm, 8am-8pm Sat, clsd Sun • wheelchair access

### RESTAURANTS

**82 Queen** 82 Queen St **843/723-7591, 800/849-0082** • lunch & dinner, Sun brunch • Lowcountry cuisine

**Fat Hen** 3140 Maybank Hwy, St Johns Island **843/559-9090** • dinner nightly, Sun brunch • French bistro • seafood

**Fig** 232 Meeting St (near Hasell) **843/805-5900** • 5:30pm-10:30pm, till 11pm Fri-Sat, clsd Sun • local ingredients • full bar • wheelchair access

**High Cotton** 199 E Bay St **843/724-3815** • dinner nightly, lunch Sat, Sun brunch • Southern cuisine • full bar

**Hominy Grill** 843/937-0930 • brkfst, lunch & dinner, wknd brunch

**Joe Pasta** 428 King St (at John) **843/965-5252** • 11:30am-11pm, till midnight Fri-Sat • also full bar

**Melvin's Legendary Bar-B-Que** 538 Folly Rd **843/762-0511** • 10:30am-9pm, clsd Sun • "the #1 cheeseburger in America"

### ENTERTAINMENT & RECREATION

**Historic Charleston Foundation** 40 E Bay St **843/723-1623** • call for info on city walking tours (March-April only)

## Columbia

### INFO LINES & SERVICES

**The Harriet Hancock GLBT Community Center** 1108 Woodrow St (at Millwood) **803/771-7713** • community info • resources & more

**Primary Purpose Gay/ Lesbian AA** 5220 Clemson (in the house behind St Martin's Church) **803/254-5301(AA#)** • 6:30 Tue, 7pm Fri & Sun

### ACCOMMODATIONS

**Holiday Inn Express** 1011 Clemson Frontage Rd **803/419-3558**

### BARS

**Art Bar** 1211 Park St **803/929-0198** • 8pm-2am • gay/ straight • dancing/DJ • karaoke • live music

**Capital Club** 1002 Gervais St **803/256-6464** • 5pm-2am • mostly gay men • neighborhood bar • professional crowd • private club • wheelchair access

### NIGHTCLUBS

**The "L" Word** 625 Frink St (at State St), Cayce **803/794-2111** • 5pm-close • mostly women • dancing/DJ • live shows • karaoke • wheelchair access

**PTS 1109** 1109 Assembly St (at Gervais St) **803/253-8900** • 5pm-2am, till 6am Fri, till 3am Sat-Sun • lesbians/ gay men • dancing/DJ • live shows • WiFi • multiracial • transgender-friendly • private club • gay-owned

## Greenville

### BOOKSTORES

**Out of Bounds** 21 S Pleasantburg Dr **864/239-0106** • 2pm- 8pm, till 6pm Sun, from 11am Fri-Sat • community pride store

## Hilton Head

### ACCOMMODATIONS

**Sonesta Resort Hilton Head Island** 130 Shipyard Dr 843/842–2400, 800/334–1881

## Mrytle Beach

### ACCOMMODATIONS

**Rosewood Manor House B&B, Wedding Venue** 900 Main St, Marion 336/312–9260 • gay/straight • B&B in a 1895 Anabellum private home, 1 hr from Mrytle Beach • WiFi • gay-owned

## Myrtle Beach

### BARS

**Club Ultra Pulse** 2701 S Kings Hwy 843/315–0019 • 4pm-4am • lesbians/ gay men • dancing/DJ • food served • karaoke • drag shows • wheelchair access • gay-owned

**St George** 503 8th Ave N  843/712-1964 • opens 4pm • lesbians/gay men • karaoke

### RESTAURANTS

**Carolina Roadhouse** 4617 N Kings Hwy 843/497–9911 • 11am-10pm

**Mr Fish** 3401 N Kings Hwy 843/839–3474 • 11am-9:30pm • full bar

**Sticky Fingers Smokehouse** 2461 Coastal Grand Cir 843/839–7427 • a chain, but a good one

### ENTERTAINMENT & RECREATION

**Hurl Rock Park** 82 Ave N (at Ocean Blvd , next to the Marriott) • lots of gays and lesbians Fri-Sun

### RETAIL SHOPS

**Kilgor Trouts Music & More** 708 8th Ave N 843/445–2800 • 10am-10pm, till midnight Fri-Sat, clsd Sun, gay pride items

## Rock Hill

### BARS

**Hideaway** 405 Baskins Rd 803/328–6630 • 8pm-2am Th-Sat • lesbians/ gay men • neighborhood bar • drag shows • karaoke • private club

## Spartanburg

### NIGHTCLUBS

**Club South 29** 9112 Greenville Hwy (off I-85 exit 66 or I-26 exit 21a) 864/574–6087 • 9pm-4am Fri-Sat only • mostly gay men • dancing/DJ

## SOUTH DAKOTA

## Murdo

### ACCOMMODATIONS

**Iversen Inn** 108 E 5th St (on I-90 Business Loop) 605/669–2452 • gay-friendly • seasonal • kids/ call for pet policy • WiFi • gay-owned

## Rapid City

### INFO LINES & SERVICES

**The Black Hills Center for Equality** 1102 West Rapid St (at Omaha St) 605/348–3244 • call for hours, clsd Sun • LGBT resource center

## Salem

### ACCOMMODATIONS

**Camp America** 25495 US 81 605/425–9085 • gay-friendly • 35 miles west of Sioux Falls • camping • RV hookups • pool • kids/ pets ok • nonsmoking • WiFi • lesbian-owned

## Sioux Falls

### INFO LINES & SERVICES

**The Center for Equality** 220 S Phillips Ave 605/331–1153 • support groups • counseling • library & more

### NIGHTCLUBS

**Club David** 214 W 10th St (btwn Main & Dakota) 605/274–0700 • 4:30pm-2am • gay/ straight • dancing/DJ • karaoke • drag shows • live music • patio

### EROTICA

**Romantix Adult Superstore** 311 N Dakota Ave (btwn 6th & 7th) 605/332–9316 • 9am-2am, from noon Sun

## Spearfish

### CAFES

**The Bay Leaf Cafe** 126 W Hudson St 605/642–5462 • lunch & dinner • plenty veggie • espresso bar

## TENNESSEE

### Bucksnort

EROTICA

**Miranda's** 4970 Hwy 230 **931/729-2006**

### Chattanooga

BARS

**Chuck's II** 27-1/2 W Main St (at Market) **423/265-5405** • 6pm-1am, till 3am Fri-Sat • lesbians/ gay men • neighborhood bar • dancing/DJ • patio

NIGHTCLUBS

**Alan Gold's** 1100 McCallie Ave (at National) **423/629-8080** • 4:30pm-3am • popular • lesbians/ gay men • dancing/DJ • drag shows • food served • young crowd • wheelchair access

**Images** 6005 Lee Hwy **423/855-8210** • 5pm-3am Th-Sun • lesbians/ gay men • dancing/DJ • drag shows • also restaurant • wheelchair access

EROTICA

**Miranda's** 2025 Broadway **423/266-5956** • 8am-3am, from noon Sun, largest selection of LGBT products in TN

### Cleveland

BARS

**Tbow's Tavern** 1585 Spring Place Rd SE **423/790-7403** • 10am-10pm, till 3am Fri-Sat, noon-6pm Sun • gay/straight •dancing/DJ • food served • live shows • lesbian-owned

### Clifton

ACCOMMODATIONS

**Bear Inn Resort** 2250 Billy Nance Hwy **931/676-5552** • gay/ straight • WiFi • also bar & restaurant • gay-owned

### Gatlinburg

ACCOMMODATIONS

**Big Creek Outdoors** 5019 Rag Mtn Rd, Hartford **423/487-5742, 423/487-3490** • gay/ straight • cabins • camping • horseback riding • kids ok • wheelchair access

**Christopher Place, An Intimate Resort** 1500 Pinnacles Wy, Newport **423/623-6555, 800/595-9441** • gay/ straight • full brkfst • pool • nonsmoking • wheelchair access

**Mountain Vista Cabins** 1805 Shady Grove Rd (at Old Birds Creek Rd), Sevierville **865/712-9897** • lesbians/ gay men • hot tub • well-behaved kids/ pets welcome • nonsmoking • WiFi • woman-owned

**Stonecreek Cabins** **865/429-0400** • gay/ straight • private Smoky Mtn cabins • hot tub • nonsmoking • lesbian-owned

### Johnson City

NIGHTCLUBS

**Fuzzy Holes** 1410 E Main St (at S Broadway St) **423/929-9800** • 8pm-close • gay/ straight • transgender-friendly • sex-positive strip club • food served • BYOB • 18+ • wheelchair access • lesbian-owned • cover charge

**New Beginnings** 2910 N Bristol Hwy **423/282-4446** • 9pm-2am, from 8pm Fri-Sat, clsd Sun-Mon • popular • mostly gay men • dancing/DJ • drag shows • also restaurant • wheelchair access

RETAIL SHOPS

**My Secret Closet** 2910 N Bristol Hwy (inside New Beginnings) **423/282-4446** • 10pm-3am Fri-Sat only • pride gifts

### Knoxville

INFO LINES & SERVICES

**AA Gay/ Lesbian** 2931 Kingston Pike (at Unitarian Church) **865/522-9667 (AA#)** • 7pm Th

**Lesbian Social Group** **865/531-7788** • meet 7pm Wed • call for info

NIGHTCLUBS

**Club XYZ** 1215 N Central **865/637-4999** • 5:30pm-3am, from 9pm Sat, from 7pm Sun • lesbians/ gay men • dancing/DJ • drag shows • karaoke

**The Edge Knox** 7211 Kingston Pike SW (at Cheshire Dr) **865/602-2094** • 5pm-3am • lesbians/ gay men • dancing/DJ • food served • karaoke • drag shows • wheelchair access

# Memphis

## INFO LINES & SERVICES

**AA Intergroup** 1835 Union Ave #302 (at McLean) **901/726-6750** • call for times & locations

**Memphis Gay/ Lesbian Community Center** 892 S Cooper (at Nelson) **901/278-6422** • 2pm-9pm Mon-Fri

## ACCOMMODATIONS

**Madison Hotel** 79 Madison Ave (at Center Ln) **901/333-1200** • gay-friendly • pool

**Talbot Heirs Guesthouse** 99 S 2nd St (btwn Union & Peabody Pl) **901/527-9772, 800/955-3956** • gay-friendly • suites w/ kitchens • funky decor • nonsmoking • kids ok

## BARS

**Dru's Place** 1474 Madison (at McNeil) **901/275-8082** • 11am-midnight, till 3am Fri-Sat, from noon Sun • mostly women • neighborhood bar • dancing/DJ • karaoke • drag shows • beer & set-ups only

**Mollie Fontaine Lounge** 679 Adams Ave (at Orleans) **901/524-1886** • 5pm-2am, clsd Sun-Tue • gay/ straight • food served

**P&H Cafe** 1532 Madison (at Adeline) **901/726-0906** • 3pm-3am, from 5pm Sat, clsd Sun gay/ straight • dive bar • beer/ wine • food served • live shows • karaoke • wheelchair access

## NIGHTCLUBS

**Club Spectrum** 616 Marshall Ave **901/292-2292** • mostly gay men • dancing/DJ

**Venue Entertainment Complex** 3744 Ridgeway St **901/522-8455** • from 10pm Fri-Sat only • lesbians/ gay men • ladies night Fri • mostly African American • dancing/DJ • drag shows • BYOB

## CAFES

**Java Cabana** 2170 Young Ave (at Cooper) **901/272-7210** • 6:30am-10pm, 9am-midnight Fri-Sat, noon-10pm Sun, clsd Mon • poetry readings & live shows • also art gallery • WiFi • wheelchair access

**Otherlands Coffee Bar** 641 S Cooper (at Central) **901/278-4994** • 7am-8pm • live music till 11pm Fri-Sat • plenty veggie • WiFi • also gift shop • wheelchair access

## RESTAURANTS

**Automatic Slim's Tonga Club** 83 S 2nd St (at Union) **901/525-7948** • lunch & dinner, Sun brunch • Caribbean & Southwestern • plenty veggie • full bar • wheelchair access

**Cafe Eclectic** 603 N McLean Blvd (at Faxon Ave) **901/725-1718** • 6am-10pm, 9am-3pm Sun; also Harbortown location

**Cafe Society** 212 N Evergreen St (at Poplar) **901/722-2177** • lunch Mon-Fri, dinner nightly • full bar • wheelchair access

**India Palace** 1720 Poplar Ave (at Lemaster St) **901/278-1199** • lunch & dinner

**Leonard's Pit Barbecue** 5465 Fox Plaza Dr (at Mt Moriah Rd) **901/360-1963** • 11am-9pm, till 2:30pm Sun-Wed• Elvis ordered the pork sandwich at the original Leonard's (now closed), but the food is just as good here!

**Molly's La Casita** 2006 Madison Ave (at N Morrison St) **901/726-1873** • lunch & dinner • Mexican

**Restaurant Iris** 2146 Monroe Ave (at Cooper) **901/590-2828** • dinner Mon-Sat • French/ Creole • upscale • wheelchair access

**RP Tracks** 3547 Walker Ave (at Brister) **901/327-1471** • lunch & dinner, open till 3am • burgers • some veggie

**Saigon Le** 51 N Cleveland (at Jefferson) **901/276-5326** • 11am-9pm, clsd Sun • Chinese/ Vietnamese/ Thai

**Tsunami** 928 S Cooper (at Young) **901/274-2556** • dinner only • Pacific rim cuisine • wheelchair access

## ENTERTAINMENT & RECREATION

**Center for Southern Folklore** 119 S Main St (at Peabody Pl) **901/525-3655** • 11am-5pm, clsd Sun, open later for shows • live music • gallery • cybercafe • food served

**Graceland** 3734 Elvis Presley Blvd **901/332-3322, 800/238-2000** • no visit to Memphis would be complete w/out a trip to see The King

**Memphis Rock 'N Roll Tours** **901/359-3102** • historical tour of Memphis music scene

## RETAIL SHOPS

**Inz & Outz** 553 S Cooper (at Peabody) **901/728-6535** • 10am-8pm, noon-6pm Sun • pride items • books • gifts • wheelchair access

## EROTICA

**Paris Theater** 2432 Summer Ave (at Hollywood) **901/323-2665**

**Romantix Adult Superstore** 2220 E Brooks Rd **901/396-9050**

## Nashville

### INFO LINES & SERVICES

**AA Gay/ Lesbian** 615/831–1050 • call for info

### ACCOMMODATIONS

**The Big Bungalow B&B** 618 Fatherland St (at 7th) **615/256–8375** • gay-friendly • full brkfst • live music • massage available • nonsmoking • WiFi • woman-owned

**Hutton Hotel** 1808 West End Ave (at 19th Ave) **615/340–9333** • gay-friendly • also restaurant • WiFi • fitness center

**Top O' Woodland Historic B&B Inn** 1603 Woodland St (at 16th) **615/228–3868, 888/228–3868** • gay-friendly • also wedding chapel • nonsmoking • WiFi • woman-owned

### BARS

**Canvas Lounge** 1707 Church St **615/320–8656** • 4pm-3am • mostly gay men • dancing/DJ • karaoke

**The Patterson House** 1711 Division St **615/636–7724** • 5pm-3am • gay/straight • food served • great speakeasy vibe

**Stirrup Nashville** 1529 4th Ave S (at Mallory) **615/782–0043** • 4pm-3am, from noon wknds • mostly gay men • multiracial • transgender-friendly • neighborhood bar • food served • patio • wheelchair access

**The Stone Fox** 712 51st Ave N **615/953–1811** • 5pm-3am, from 11am wknds • gay/straight • food served • live music & cheap beer

**Trax** 1501 2nd Ave S (at Carney) **615/742–8856** • noon-3am • mostly gay men • neighborhood bar • karaoke • WiFi

**Tribe** 1517 Church St (at 15th Ave S) **615/329–2912** • 4pm-midnight, till 2am wknds • lesbians/ gay men •popular • live entertainment • upscale • full restaurant • wheelchair access • gay-owned

### NIGHTCLUBS

**Bluebird Cafe** 4104 Hillsboro Pike (nr Warfield Dr) **615/383–1461** • live country music venue

**Lipstick Lounge** 1400 Woodland St (at 14th) **615/226–6343** • 5pm-3am, from 10am Sat-Sun, clsd Mon • mostly women • dancing/DJ • karaoke • live music • lesbian-owned

**Play Dance Bar** 1519 Church St (at 16th Ave) **615/322–9627** • 9pm-3am Wed-Sun • mostly gay men • dancing/DJ • multiracial • transgender-friendly • drag shows • 18+ • wheelchair access

**Vibe** 1713 Church St (at 17th & 18th) **615/329–3838** • afterhours bar • mostly gay men • dancing/DJ • Latina/o clientele • BYOB • patio

### CAFES

**Bongo Java** 2007 Belmont Blvd **615/385–5282** • 7am-11pm, from 8am wknds • coffeehouse • deck • also serves brkfst, lunch & dinner

**Fido** 1812 21st Ave S **615/777–3436** • 7am-11pm, till midnight Fri-Sat, from 8am wknds • also full menu

**Grins Vegetarian Cafe** 2421 Vanderbilt Pl (at 25th Ave) **615/322–8571** • 7am-9pm, till 3pm Fri, clsd wknds

### RESTAURANTS

**Battered & Fried** 1008 Woodland St (at S 10th) **615/226–9283** • lunch & dinner • seafood • full bar • also Wave sushi bar • patio • wheelchair access

**Beyond the Edge** 112 S 11th St **615/226–3343** • 11am-2am • pizza & sandwiches • full bar

**Cafe Coco** 210 Louise Ave (at State) **615/321–2626** • 24hrs • live music • beer/ wine • patio

**Calypso Cafe** 3307 Charlotte Ave **615/321–3878** • 11am-9pm • Caribbean

**Mad Donna's** 1313 Woodland St (at 14th) **615/226–1617** • 11am-10pm, till 11pm Sat, clsd Mon • also lounge • drag bingo Tue

**The Mad Platter** 1239 6th Ave N (at Monroe) **615/242–2563** • lunch Mon-Fri, dinner Wed-Sun • eclectic, local & fresh • wheelchair access

**Pancake Pantry** 1796 21st Ave S (at Wedgewood Ave) **615/383–9333** • 6am-3pm, till 4pm wknds • popular for brkfst

**Rumours Wine & Art Bar** 2304 12th Ave S (at Linden) **615/292–9400** • 5pm-midnight, till 9pm Sun• wheelchair access

**Sky Blue Coffeehouse & Bistro** 700 Fatherland St (at S 7th St) **615/770–7097** • brkfst & lunch

**Sole Mio** 311 3rd Ave S **615/256–4013** • 11am-10pm, till 11pm Fri-Sat, clsd Mon • Italian • wheelchair access

**The Standard at the Smith House** 167 Rosa Parks Ave (at Charlotte) **615/254–1277** • dinner Tue-Sat, clsd Sun-Mon • wheelchair access

**Suzy Wong's House of Yum** 1515 Church St (at 15th Ave S) **615/329–2913** • 5pm-11pm, from 11am Sun • gay-owned

**Watermark** 507 12th Ave S (at Division) **615/254-2000** • dinner nightly, clsd Sun • seafood & more • great wine list • wheelchair access

**Yellow Porch** 734 Thompson Ln (at Bransford Ave) **615/386-0260** • lunch & dinner, clsd Sun • fresh Southern cuisine • wheelchair access

### ENTERTAINMENT & RECREATION

**NashTrash Tours** tours leave from the Farmers Market (900 8th Ave N) **615/226-7300, 800/342-2132** • campy tours of Nashville w/ the Jugg Sisters • ages 13+ • reservations required

### PUBLICATIONS

**Inside Out Nashville** **615/831-1806** • LGBT newspaper & bar guide

**Out & About Newspaper** **615/596-6210** • LGBT newspaper for Nashville, Knoxville, Chattanooga & Atlanta area • monthly

### EROTICA

**Miranda's** 822 5th Ave S **615/256-1310** • 8am-3am, from noon Sun • largest selection of LGBT products in TN

## Smyrna

### NIGHTCLUBS

**Chameleons Lounge** 6528 New Nashville Hwy **615/585-3242** • 5pm-1am, till 3am Fri-Sat, clsd Sun-Mon • lesbians/gay men • drag shows • women-owned

# TEXAS

## Amarillo

### BARS

**212 Club** 212 SW 6th Ave (at Harrison) **806/372-7997** • 3pm-2am • lesbians/gay men • neighborhood bar • dancing/DJ • drag shows • wheelchair access

**Kicked Back** 521 SE 10th Ave (at Buchanan St) **806/418-8971** • 4pm-2am, from 7pm Sun • lesbians/gay men • neighborhood bar • karaoke • lesbian-owned

**R&R** 701 S Georgia St **806/342-9000** • 4pm-2am • gay-friendly • neighborhood bar • wheelchair access • gay-owned

### RESTAURANTS

**Furrbie's** 210 W 6th Ave **806/220-0841** • 11am-7pm, till 3pm Sat, till 4pm Mon, clsd Sun • comfort food • gay-owned

### EROTICA

**Fantasy Gifts & Video** 440 N Lakeside Dr **806/372-6500**

## Arlington

**see also Dallas & Fort Worth**

### INFO LINES & SERVICES

**Tarrant County Lesbian/Gay Alliance** **817/877-5544** • info line • meetings

### NIGHTCLUBS

**The 1851 Club** 931 W Division **682/323-5315** • 3pm-2am • lesbians/gay men • dancing/DJ • drag shows • karaoke • videos • wheelchair access

## Austin

### INFO LINES & SERVICES

**Lambda AA (Live & Let Live)** 6809 Guadalupe St (at Galano Club) **512/444-0071, 512/832-6767 (EN ESPAÑOL)** • 6:30pm & 8pm daily, 10am Sat, 11am Sun

### ACCOMMODATIONS

**Austin Folk House** 506 W 22nd St (at Nueces) **512/472-6700, 866/472-6700** • gay/straight • kids ok • nonsmoking • WiFi • wheelchair access

**Brava House** 1108 Blanco St (at W 12th) **512/478-5034, 866/892-5726** • gay-friendly • close to downtown & 6th Street • nonsmoking • WiFi • lesbian-owned

**Crowne Plaza Hotel Austin** 6121 North IH 35 **512/323-5466**

**Hotel Saint Cecilia** 112 Academy Dr **512/852-2400** • gay-friendly • pool • wheelchair access

**Hotel San Jose** 1316 S Congress Ave **512/852-2350, 800/574-8897** • gay/straight • pool • nonsmoking • kids/pets ok • wheelchair access

**Hotel Van Zandt** 605 Davis St **512/542-5300, 877/202-2191** • gay-friendly • in the thick of the City's hippest nightlife • restaurant & pool

**Kimber Modern** 110 The Circle **512/912-1046** • gay/straight • WiFi • women-owned

**Mt Gainor Inn B&B** 2390 Prochnow Rd (at Mt Gainor Rd), Dripping Springs **512/858-0982, 888/644-0982** • gay/straight • nonsmoking • hot tub • WiFi

**Park Lane Guest House** 221 Park Ln (at Drake) **512/447-7460, 800/492-8827** • gay/straight • full brkfst • pool • also cottage • lesbian-owned/run

**riverbarnsuites** 30 minutes from Austin airport, Kingsbury **512/488-2175** • women only • river resort w/ lots of outdoor activities • swimming • lesbian-owned

**Robin's Nest** 1007 Stewart Cove **512/266-3413** • gay-friendly • on Lake Travis • WiFi

**South Congress Hotel** 1603 S Congress Ave **512/920-6405** • gay-friendly • cool new hotel • restaurant & pool

## BARS

**'Bout Time II** 6607 I-35 N **512/419-9192** • 2pm-3am • lesbians/ gay men • neighborhood bar • DJ/dancing • transgender-friendly • karaoke • WiFi • wheelchair access

**Casino El Camino** 517 E 6th St (at Red River) **512/469-9330** • 4pm-2am • gay-friendly • neighborhood bar • psychedelic punk jazz lounge • great burgers • WiFi • wheelchair access

**Chain Drive** 84 East Ave **512/480-9017** • 2pm-2am • mostly gay men, some women • dancing/DJ • large patio • wheelchair access

**Cheer Up Charlie's** 900 Red River • 4pm-2am • lesbians/gay men • live bands/ shows • also vegan restaurant

**The Jackalope** 404 E 6th **512/472-3663** • 11am-2am • gay/straight • dive bar • food served

## NIGHTCLUBS

**The Belmont** 305 W 6th St **512/457-0300** • gay-friendly • live music venue

**Elysium** 705 Red River (7th St) **512/478-2979** • 9:30pm-2am • gay/ straight • dancing/DJ • '80s Sun • '90s Tue • rest of the week goth, industrial & electronica club

**Highland Lounge** 404 Colorado **512/522-4044** • 7pm-2am • lesbians/ gay men • dancing/DJ • wheelchair access

**Rain** 217-B W 4th St (at Colorado St) **512/494-1150** • 4pm-close, from 3pm Fri-Sun • mostly gay men • dancing/DJ • go-go dancers • wheelchair access

## CAFES

**Austin Java Cafe** 1608 Barton Springs Rd (at Kinney Ave) **512/482-9450** • 7am-11pm, from 8am Sat-Sun • also 1206 Parkway, 512/476-1829 & 300 W 2nd St, 512/481-9400

**Bouldin Creek Coffeehouse** 1900 S 1st St **512/416-1601** • 7am-midnight, from 8am wknds • completely vegetarian menu (brkfst all day) • occasional live music

**Joe's Bakery & Coffee Shop** 2305 E 7th St (at Morelos & Northwestern) **512/472-0017** • 6am-3pm, clsd Mon • Tex-Mex • wheelchair access

**Spider House Patio Bar & Cafe** 2908 Fruth St (at West Dr) **512/480-9562** • 10am-2am • full bar • art & performance • patio

## RESTAURANTS

**Changos** 3023 Guadalupe **512/480-8226** • taqueria, open all day

**Chez Nous** 510 Neches St **512/473-2413** • lunch Tue-Fri, dinner nightly, clsd Mon • wheelchair access

**Chuy's** 1728 Barton Springs Rd **512/474-4452** • 11am-10pm, till 11pm Fri-Sat • Tex-Mex • full bar • wheelchair access

**Corazon at Castle Hill** 1101 W 5th St (at Baylor) **512/476-0728** • lunch weekdays & dinner nightly, clsd Sun • inspired cuisine • some veggie • wheelchair access

**Eastside Cafe** 2113 Manor Rd (at Breeze Terrace) **512/476-5858** • 11:30am-9:30pm, 10am-10pm wknds • some veggie • beer/ wine • wheelchair access

**El Sol y La Luna** 600 E 6th St (at Red River) **512/444-7770** • 11am-10pm, 9am-1pm Fri-Sat, 9am-4pm Sun • great brkfst • live music • wheelchair access • lesbian-owned

**Fonda San Miguel** 2330 W North Loop (at Hancock Rd) **512/459-4121** • dinner only, popular Sun brunch • Mexican • full bar

**Galaxy** 1000 W Lynn **512/478-3434** • 7am-10pm • quick, stylish & tasty

**Guero's** 1412 S Congress (at Elizabeth) **512/447-7688** • 11am-11pm, from 8am wknds • great Mexican & people-watching • outdoor seating • live music outdoors on wknds

**Imperia** 310 Colorado St **512/472-6770** • dinner only • upscale Asian • full bar • wheelchair access

**Jo's Hot Coffee & Good Food** 1300 S Congress Ave (at James) **512/444-3800** • 7am-9pm, till 10pm Sat • "best lazy day outdoor dining scene" • wheelchair access • also 242 W 2nd St, 512/469-9003 • lesbian-owned

**Kenichi** 419 Colorado St **512/320-8883** • dinner nightly • Asian/ sushi • wheelchair access

**Mother's Cafe & Garden** 4215 Duval St (at 43rd) 512/451–3994 • 11:15am-10pm, from 10am wknds • vegetarian • beer/ wine • wheelchair access

**Mr Natural** 1901 E Cesar Chavez St 512/477–5228 • 8am-8pm • vegetarian/ vegan

**Polvos** 2004 S 1st St (at Johanna) 512/441–5446 • 7am-11pm • Mexican • outdoor seating

**Santa Rita Cantina** 1206 W 38th St 512/419–7482 • lunch & dinner, wknd brunch

**Threadgill's** 6416 N Lamar 512/451–5440 • 10am-10pm, till 9pm Sun • great chicken-fried steak • live music Wed • also 301 W Riverside Dr, 512/472-9304 • beer garden • live music

**Wink** 1014 N Lamar Blvd 512/482–8868 • dinner nightly, clsd Sun • upscale • also wine bar • wheelchair access

### ENTERTAINMENT & RECREATION

**Barton Springs** Barton Springs Rd (in Zilker Park) 512/867–3080 • natural swimming hole

**Bat Colony** Congress Ave Bridge (at Barton Springs Dr) • everything's bigger in Texas—including the colony of bats that flies out from under this bridge every evening March-Oct

**Hippy Hollow Park** • gay hangout • nudity permitted

### BOOKSTORES

**Bookpeople** 603 N Lamar Blvd (at 6th) 512/472–5050, 800/853–9757 • 9am-11pm • independent

**BookWoman** 5501 N Lamar Blvd (at Nelray) 512/472–2785 • 10am-8pm, noon-6pm Sun • books • cards • jewelry • music • DVDs • wheelchair access • woman-owned

**MonkeyWrench Books** 110 E North Loop 512/407–6925 • 11am-8pm, from noon wknds • independent, radical bookstore

### RETAIL SHOPS

**Tapelenders** 1114 W 5th St #501 (at Baylor) 512/472–0844 • 10am-10pm, till midnight Fri-Sat • LGBT videos • novelties • gay-owned

### PUBLICATIONS

**Austin Chronicle** 512/454–5766 • Austin's alternative weekly • weekly • has extensive online gay guide (check out www.austinchronicle.com)

### GYMS & HEALTH CLUBS

**Hyde Park Gym** 4125 Guadalupe (at 41st St) 512/459–9174 • 5am-10pm, 7am-7pm Sat, 8am-7pm Sun

**Milk + Honey Spa** 204 Colorado St (at 2nd) 512/236–1115 • 9am-9pm

### EROTICA

**Forbidden Fruit** 108 E North Loop 512/453–8090 • woman-owned & operated

## Bryan

### BARS

**Revolution Cafe & Bar** 211 B S Main St (at 27th) 979/823–4044 • 6pm-2am, from 8pm Sun-Mon, from 4pm Fri • gay-friendly • neighborhood bar • food served • live music • WiFi • wheelchair access

### NIGHTCLUBS

**Halo Bar** 121 N Main St (at William J Bryan Pkwy) 979/823–6174 • 9:30pm-2am Th-Sat • lesbians/ gay men • dancing/DJ • drag shows • karaoke • wheelchair access

## Corpus Christi

### INFO LINES & SERVICES

**Clean & Serene AA** 3026 S Staples (at All Saints Episcopal Church in Pantry Building behind church ) 361/992–8911, 866/672–7029 • 8pm Fri

### ACCOMMODATIONS

**Anthony's By The Sea** 732 S Pearl St, Rockport 361/729–6100, 800/460–2557 • gay/ straight • quiet retreat 4 blocks from water • full brkfst • pool • nonsmoking • wheelchair access • lesbian-owned

**Port Aransas Inn** 1500 S 11th St (at Ave G), Port Aransas 361/749–5937 • gay/ straight • pool • hot tub • WiFi • wheelchair access

### BARS

**The Hidden Door** 802 S Staples St (at Coleman) 361/882–5002 • noon-2am • lesbians/ gay men • neighborhood bar • dancing/DJ • patio • wheelchair access • also the Loft piano bar Fri-Sun • gay-owned

### NIGHTCLUBS

**Triangle Niteclub** 361/903–0977 • 5pm-2am, clsd Mon • lesbians/ gay men • dancing/DJ • drag shows

## Dallas

see also Arlington, Fort Worth

### INFO LINES & SERVICES

**John Thomas Gay/ Lesbian Community Center** 2701 Reagan St (at Brown) 214/528–0144, 214/528–0022 • 9am-9pm, till 5pm Sat, noon-5pm Sun • wheelchair access

**Lambda AA** 2438 Butler #106 214/267–0222

## Accommodations

**Bailey's Uptown Inn** 2505 Worthington St (at Hibernia) 214/720-2258 • gay-friendly • nonsmoking • WiFi

**Hotel ZaZa** 2332 Leonard St (at State) 214/468-8399, 888/880-3244 • gay-friendly • full spa & restaurant

**Lumen** 6101 Hillcrest Ave 214/219-2400, 800/908-1140 • gay-friendly • WiFi • wheelchair access

**MCM Elegante' Hotel and Suites** 2330 W Northwest Hwy 214/358-7846, 877/351-4477 • gay-friendly • pool • WiFi • wheelchair access

**Palomar Dallas** 5300 E Mockingbird Ln 214/520-7969, 888/253-9030 • gay-friendly • pool • WiFi

## Bars

**Alexandre's** 4026 Cedar Springs Rd (at Knight St) 214/559-0720 • 9am-2pm, from 2pm Sun • gay/ straight • live music • karaoke • wheelchair access

**Barbara's Pavillion** 325 Centre St 214/941-2145 • 4pm-2am, from 2pm Sun • mostly gay men • neighborhood bar • karaoke • patio • wheelchair access

**Grapevine** 3902 Maple Ave (at Shelby) 214/522-8466 • 3pm-2am, from 1pm Sun • gay/ straight • classic dive bar • WiFi • wheelchair access

**The Hidden Door** 5025 Bowser Ave (at Mahanna) 214/526-0620 • 7am-2am, from noon Sun • mostly gay men • neighborhood bar • leather • patio • wheelchair access

**JR's Bar & Grill** 3923 Cedar Springs Rd (at Throckmorton) 214/528-1004 • 11am-2am, from noon Sun-Mon • popular • lesbians/ gay men • grill till 4pm • live shows Sun • videos • young crowd • WiFi • wheelchair access

**Pekers** 2615 Oak Lawn Ave, Ste 101 (btwn Fairmount & Brown) 214/528-3333 • 10am-2am • lesbians/ gay men • neighborhood bar • live music • karaoke • drag shows • wheelchair access

**Sue Ellen's** 3014 Throckmorton (at Cedar Springs) 214/559-0707 • 4pm-2am • popular • mostly women • dancing/DJ • live shows/ bands • Sun BBQ (summers) • patio • wheelchair access

**Tin Room** 2514 Hudnall St (at Maple Ave) 214/526-6365 • 10am-2am, from noon Sun • mostly gay men • neighborhood bar • dancing/DJ • male dancers • wheelchair access

**Woody's** 4011 Cedar Springs Rd (btwn Douglas & Throckmorton) 214/520-6629 • 2pm-2am • lesbians/ gay men • live shows • sports bar • videos • nonsmoking upstairs • karaoke • patio • wheelchair access

## Nightclubs

**The Brick/Joe's Dallas** 2525 Wycliff Ave (btwn Maple & Tollway) 214/521-3154 • 4pm-2am, till 4am Fri-Sat, from noon Sat-Sun • lesbians/ gay men • dancing/DJ • multiracial • drag shows

**Kaliente** 4350 Maple Ave (at Hondo) 214/520-6676 • 9pm-2am, clsd Tue • mostly gay men • mostly Latino • dancing/DJ • salsa & Tejano • karaoke • drag shows • wheelchair access

**Marty's Live** 4207 Maple Ave (at Knight St) 214/599-2151 • 1pm-2am • lesbians/ gay men • dancing/DJ • strippers

**Panoptikon** 2911 Main St 214/826-4768 • monthly gothic/electro dance party • gay/ straight

**Round-Up Saloon** 3912 Cedar Springs Rd (at Throckmorton) 214/522-9611 • 3pm-2am, from noon wknds • popular • mostly gay men • dancing/DJ • country/ western • karaoke • dance lessons • patio • wheelchair access

**Station 4** 3911 Cedar Springs Rd (at Throckmorton) 214/526-7171 • 9pm-4am Wed-Sun • popular • lesbians/ gay men • dancing/DJ • drag shows • videos • also Rose Room cabaret • 18+

## Cafes

**Buli** 3908 Cedar Springs Rd 214/528-5410 • 7am-close • WiFi • wheelchair access

**Opening Bell Coffee** 1409 S Lamar St, Ste 012 214/565-0383 • 7am-10pm, from 9am wknds, till midnight wknds • beer/ wine • live music • WiFi

## Restaurants

**Ali Baba Cafe** 1901 Abrams Rd (near La Vista Dr) 214/823-8235 • lunch & dinner • Middle Eastern

**Bangkok Orchid** 331 W Airport Fwy (at N Beltline), Irving 972/252-7770 • lunch & dinner, clsd Mon • ask for Danny • BYOB • wheelchair access • gay-owned

**Black-Eyed Pea** 3857 Cedar Springs Rd (at Reagan) 214/521-4580 • 11am-10pm • wheelchair access

**Blue Mesa Grill** 5100 Belt Line Rd (at Tollway), Addison 972/934-0165 • 11am-10pm • great fajitas • full bar

**Bread Winners** 3301 McKinney Ave 214/754–4940 • 4pm-2am, from 10am wknds • full bar • wheelchair access

**Cafe Brazil** 3847 Cedar Springs Rd 214/461–8762 • open 24hrs

**Cosmic Cafe** 2912 Oak Lawn Ave 214/521–6157 • 11am-10:30pm, till 11pm Fri-Sat, noon-10pm Sun • vegetarian • also yoga & meditation • live events • WiFi

**Cremona Bistro** 2704 Worthington St (at Howell) 214/871–1115 • lunch weekdays & dinner nightly • Italian • full bar • patio • live music

**Dish** 4123 Cedar Springs Rd #110 214/522–3474 • dinner & Sun brunch • full bar • patio • live shows • wheelchair access

**Dream Cafe** 2800 Routh St (in the Quadrangle) 214/954–0486 • 7am-9pm, till 10pm Fri-Sat • plenty veggie • beer/ wine • WiFi • wheelchair access

**Hattie's** 418 N Bishop Ave 214/942–7400 • lunch daily, dinner Tue-Sun • Southern • wheelchair access

**Hibiscus** 2927 N Henderson Ave 214/827–2927 • dinner only, clsd Sun • steak & seafood • wheelchair access

**Hunky's** 3940 Cedar Springs Rd (at Reagan) 214/522–1212 • 11am-10pm, till 11pm Sat, from noon Sun • popular • burgers & salads • beer/ wine • patio • wheelchair access • gay-owned

**Lucky's Cafe** 3531 Oak Lawn 214/522–3500 • 7am-10pm • classic comfort food • great brfkst • wheelchair access

**Mario's** 5404 Lemmon Ave 214/599–9744 • 11am-11pm, Mexican & Salvadorian

**Monica Aca y Alla** 2914 Main St (at Malcolm X) 214/748–7140 • lunch Mon-Fri, dinner Tue-Sun, brunch wknds • popular • contemporary Mexican • full bar • live music wknds • Latin jazz/ salsa • transgender-friendly • wheelchair access

**Naga Kitchen & Bar** 665 High Market St (Victory Park) 214/953–0023 • lunch Mon-Sat, dinner nightly • authentic Thai

**Stephan Pyles** 1807 Ross Ave, Ste 200 214/580–7000 • lunch Mon-Fri, dinner Mon-Sat, clsd Sun • Southwestern cuisine

**Taco Joint** 911 N Peak St 214/826–8226 • 6:30am-2pm, from 8am Sat, clsd Sun • wheelchair access

**Thai Soon** 101 S Coit, Ste 401 (at Belt Line) 972/234–6111 • lunch & dinner • wheelchair access

**Ziziki's** 4514 Travis St, #122 (in Travis Walk) 214/521–2233 • 11am-10pm, Sun brunch • Greek & Italian • full bar • wheelchair access

## ENTERTAINMENT & RECREATION

**Assassination City Derby** 1438 Coliseum Dr • Dallas' female roller derby league • visit www.acderby.com for events

## RETAIL SHOPS

**Tapelenders** 3926 Cedar Springs Rd (at Throckmorton) 214/528–6344 • 9am-midnight • LGBT gifts • gay-owned

## PUBLICATIONS

**Dallas Voice** 214/754–8710 • LGBT newspaper

## EROTICA

**Alternatives** 1720 W Mockingbird Ln (at Hawes) 214/630–7071 • 24hrs

**Leather Masters** 3000 Main St 214/528–3865 • noon-10pm, clsd Sun-Mon • handmade leather clothes • rubber/ fetishwear

# Denison

## BARS

**Good Time Lounge** 2520 Hwy 91 N 903/463–6086 • 7pm-2am Wed-Sun • lesbians/ gay men • karaoke Th & Sun • drag shows • private club

# Denton

## NIGHTCLUBS

**Mable Peabody's Beauty Parlor & Chainsaw Repair** 1125 E University Dr 940/566–9910 • 4pm-2am • lesbians/ gay men • dancing/DJ • live shows • karaoke • drag shows • wheelchair access • lesbian-owned

# El Paso

see also Ciudad Juárez, Mexico

## BARS

**Briar Patch** 508 N Stanton St (at Missouri) 915/577–9555 • noon-2am, from noon wknds • lesbians/ gay men • neighborhood bar • karaoke • patio

**Chiquita's Bar** 310 E. Missouri Ave (at Stanton) 915/351–0095 • 2pm-2am • lesbians/gay men • neighborhood bar • mostly Latino/a • wheelchair access

**Club 101** 201 N Stanton St 915/256–7633 • 8pm-2am Fri-Sat only • lesbians/gay men • dancing/DJ

**Epic** 510 N Stanton St (at Missouri) 915/566-0378 • 9pm-2am, from 6pm Wed-Fri, from 7pm Sun, clsd Mon • lesbians/gay men • dancing/DJ • live bands

### NIGHTCLUBS

**Touch Bar & Nightclub** 800 E San Antonio Ave (at Ochoa) • 3pm-2am • mostly gay men • dancing/DJ • drag shows • videos • patio • wheelchair access

### RESTAURANTS

**The Little Diner** 7209 7th St, Canutillo 915/877-2176 • 11am-8pm, clsd Wed • true Texas fare • beer/wine • wheelchair access

## Eustace

### ACCOMMODATIONS

**Captain's Quarters** PO Box 577 75124 903/802-2771 • gay/straight • cabin rentals

## Fort Worth

**see also Arlington & Dallas**

### INFO LINES & SERVICES

**Tarrant County Lesbian/Gay Alliance** 817/877-5544 • info line • newsletter

### ACCOMMODATIONS

**Hotel Trinity InnSuites Hotel** 2000 Beach St 817/534-4801, 800/989-3556 • gay-friendly • pool • nonsmoking • kids/pets ok • WiFi • wheelchair access

### BARS

**Urban Cowboy Saloon** 2620 E Lancaster Ave 817/744-7765 • 7pm-2am, from 3pm wknds, clsd Mon • lesbians/gay men • neighborhood bar • dancing/DJ • food served • karaoke

### NIGHTCLUBS

**Rainbow Lounge** 651 S Jennings Ave (at Pennsylvania) 817/744-7723 • 9am-2am • mostly gay men • dancing/DJ • drag shows • theme nights • wheelchair access

### ENTERTAINMENT & RECREATION

**National Cowgirl Museum** 1720 Gendy St 817/336-4475, 800/476-3263

## Galveston

### ACCOMMODATIONS

**Hotel Galvez** 2024 Seawall Blvd 409/765-7721, 877/999-3223 • gay-friendly • nonsmoking • WiFi • kids ok • wheelchair access

**Lost Bayou Guesthouse B&B** 1607 Ave L (at 16th) 409/770-0688 • gay-griendly • 1890 Victorian home survived hurricane of 1900 • nonsmoking • kids 10 or over ok • WiFi

### BARS

**23rd Street Station** 1706 23rd St (at O Ave) 409/621-1808 • 10am-midnight • mostly gay men • karaoke • BYOB

**Krave** 2416 Post Office St 409/765-6911 • 4pm-2am, from 2pm wknds • mostly gay men • drag shows • male dancers • deck

**Robert's Lafitte** 2501 Q Ave (at 25th St) 409/765-9092 • 7am-2am, from 10am Sun • mostly gay men • drag shows wknds • patio • wheelchair access

**Splash Bar** 3102 Seawall Blvd 409/497-4176 • 4pm-2am, from noon wknds • lesbians/gay men • dancing/DJ • karaoke • drag shows

**Splash Bar** 3102 Seawall Blvd 409/497-4176 • 4pm-2am, from noon wknds • lesbians/gay men • dancing/DJ • karaoke • drag shows

### CAFES

**Mod Coffee & Tea House** 2126 Post Office St (at 22nd) 409/765-5659 • 7am-10pm • live shows• also art gallery • beer/wine • WiFi

### RESTAURANTS

**Eat Cetera** 408 25th St 409/762-0803 • 11am-7pm, clsd Sun • beer/wine • wheelchair acccess

**Luigi's** 2328 The Strand (at Tremont) 409/763-6500 • dinner only, clsd Sun

**Mosquito Cafe** 628 14th St (at Winnie) 409/763-1010 • 8am-9pm, 8am-9pm Sat, till 3pm Sun, clsd Mon • some veggie • wheelchair access

**The Spot** 3204 Seawall Blvd (at 32nd St) 409/621-5237 • good burgers, great view • also Tiki Bar • wheelchair access

**Star Drug Store** 510 23rd St 409/766-7719 • 9am-3pm • old-fashioned drug store & soda fountain • wheelchair access

## Groesbeck

### ACCOMMODATIONS

**Rainbow Ranch Campground** 1662 LCR 800 254/729-8484, 888/875-7596 • lesbians/gay men • on Lake Limestone • pool • campsites • cabins • nonsmoking • gay-owned

## Gun Barrel City

### BARS

**Garlow's** 308 E Main St **903/887-0853** • 4pm-close • lesbians/gay men • dancing/DJ • drag shows

## Houston

### INFO LINES & SERVICES

**Gay & Lesbian Switchboard Houston** **713/529-3211, 888/843-4564** • 24hr crisis hotline and resource directory

**Lambda AA Center** 1201 W Clay (btwn Montrose & Waugh) **713/521-1243** • wheelchair access

### ACCOMMODATIONS

**Hotel Derek** 2525 W Loop S (at Westheimer) **713/961-3000, 866/292-4100** • gay-friendly • modern, chic hotel

**Hotel Sorella** 800 W Sam Houston Pkwy N **713/973-1600, 866/842-0100** • gay-friendly

**The Houstonian** 111 N Post Oak Ln (near Woodway Dr) **713/680-2626, 800/231-2759** • gay-friendly • urban resort

**La Maison** 2800 Brazos **713/529-3600**, **877/529-3999** • gay/straight • an urban bed and breakfast, a slice of European flavor in the heart of Houston • WiFi • women-owned

**The Lancaster Hotel** 701 Texas Ave **713/228-9500, 800/231-0336** • gay/straight • historic and newly renovated small luxury hotel downtown • restaurant & bar

**Robin's Nest B&B Inn** 4104 Greeley St **713/528-5821, 800/622-8343** • gay-friendly • Montrose Museum District • WiFi

**The Sam Houston** 1117 Prairie St (at Fannin) **832/200-8800** • gay-friendly • boutique hotel • dogs ok • also restaurant & bar • WiFi

### BARS

**Bayou City Bar & Grill** 2409 Grant St (at Hyde Park Blvd) **713/522-2867** • 4pm-2am, clsd Mon • lesbians/gay men * food served • more women Wed

**Blur** 710 Pacific St (at Crocker) **713/529-3447** • 10pm-2am, clsd Mon-Tue • lesbians/gay men • dancing/DJ • 18+

**Club 2020** 2020 Leeland **713/227-9667** • 10pm-4am Sat • lesbians/gay men • women's night Fri • dancing/DJ • mostly African American • hip hop • 18+

**Cockpit Bar & Grill** 101 Airport Blvd **713/640-7139** • 4pm-2am. from 5pm Sat, clsd Sun • gay/straight • lil ol' dive bar by Hobby Airport • WiFi • gay-owned

**Crocker** 2312 Crocker St **713/529-3355** • 11am-2am • mostly gay men • neighborhood bar • karaoke • WiFi

**Guava Lamp** 570 Waugh Dr **713/524-3359** • 4pm-2am, from 2pm Sun • lesbians/gay men • popular Wed for karaoke • WiFi • wheelchair access

**JR's** 808 Pacific (at Grant) **713/521-2519** • noon-2am • popular • mostly gay men • karaoke • drag shows • videos • patio • wheelchair access

**Meteor** 2306 Genesee St (at Fairview) **713/521-0123** • 4pm-2am • mostly gay men • drag shows • wheelchair access • gay-owned

**Michael's Outpost** 1419 Richmond (at Mandell) **713/520-8446** • 3pm-2am, from noon wknds • mostly gay men • neighborhood bar • piano • live entertainment • older crowd

**Pearl Lounge** 4216 Washington **832/740-4933** • mostly women • 5pm-2am, from 3pm wknds • Tue steak night • dancing/DJ wknds • lesbian-owned

**The Room Bar** 4915 FM 2920 Rd #148, Spring **281/907-6866** • 2pm-2am • lesbians/gay men • dancing/DJ • drag shows

**TC's Show Bar** 817 Fairview (at Converse) **713/526-2625** • 10am-2am • lesbians/gay men • neighborhood bar • karaoke • drag shows • transgender-friendly

**Tony's Corner Pocket** 817 W Dallas (btwn Arthur & Crosby) **713/571-7870** • noon-2am • lesbians/gay men • neighborhood bar • karaoke • male dancers • large deck • WiFi

### NIGHTCLUBS

**F Bar Houston** 202 Tuam St **713/522-3227** • 5pm-2am, from 9pm Sat, 3pm Sun, clsd Mon • lesbians/gay men • dancing/DJ • karaoke • live shows

**Numbers** 300 Westheimer (at Taft) **713/526-6551** • gay-friendly • dancing/DJ • 80's Fri • also live music venue • video • young crowd

**Ranch Hill Saloon** 24704 I-45 N, Spring **281/298-9035** • 1pm-2am • lesbians/gay men • neighborhood bar • dancing/DJ • country/western • drag shows • karaoke • wheelchair access • lesbian-owned

**South Beach Nightclub** 810 Pacific 713/521-0107, 713/529-7623 • 9pm-4am Fri-Sat • mostly gay men • dancing/DJ • live shows

## CAFES

**Empire Cafe** 1732 Westheimer Rd 713/528-5282 • 7:30am-10pm, till 11pm Fri-Sat • WiFi • wheelchair access

**Java Java Cafe** 911 W 11th (at Shepherd) 713/880-5282 • 7:30am-3pm, from 8:30am wknds • wheelchair access

**The Path of Tea** 2340 W Alabama St (at Kirby) 713/252-4473 • 10am-9pm, till 11pm Fri-Sat, 1pm-6pm Sun • tea house • wheelchair access

## RESTAURANTS

**Aka Sushi House** 2390 W Alabama St 713/807-7875 • noon-11pm

**Argentina Cafe** 3055 Sage Rd (at Hidalgo St) 713/622-8877 • 9am-9pm, from 10am wknds • wheelchair access

**Baba Yega's** 2607 Grant (at Pacific) 713/522-0042 • 11am-10pm, till 11pm Fri-Sat, from 10am Sun • plenty veggie • full bar • patio • wheelchair access

**Barnaby's Cafe** 604 Fairview (btwn Stanford & Hopkins St) 713/522-0106 • 11am-10pm, till 11pm Fri-Sat • beer/ wine • wheelchair access • multiple locations

**Beaver's** 2310 Decatur (at Sawyer) 713/864-2328 • 11am-10pm, till midnight Sat, clsd Mon • BBQ

**Brasil** 2604 Dunlavy (at Westheimer) 713/528-1993 • 7:30am-midnight • plenty veggie • beer/ wine • wheelchair access

**Chapultepec** 813 Richmond (btwn Montrose & Main) 713/522-2365 • 24hrs • Mexican • full bar • wheelchair access

**El Tiempo Cantina** 1308 Montrose Blvd 713/807-8996 • 11am-9pm, till 10pm Wed-Th, till 11pm Fri-Sat • Mexican seafood • wheelchair access

**House of Pies** 3112 Kirby Dr (btwn Richmond & Alabama) 713/528-3816 • 24hrs • popular • wheelchair access

**Hugo's** 1600 Westheimer Rd (at Mandell) 713/524-7744 • lunch & dinner • Mexican • popular brunch • wheelchair access

**Julia's Bistro** 3722 Main St (at W Alabama) 713/807-0090 • lunch Mon-Fri, dinner Mon-Sat, clsd Sun • Mexican • wheelchair access

**Kelley's Country Cookin'** 8015 Park Pl (at Gulf Fwy) 713/645-6428 • 6am-10pm • great brkfst • wheelchair access

**Mark's American Cuisine** 1658 Westheimer Rd 713/523-3800 • lunch Mon-Fri, dinner nightly • located in renovated 1920s church • wheelchair access

**Ninfa's** 2704 Navigation Blvd (at N Delano St) 713/228-1175 • 11am-11pm • popular • Mexican • some veggie • full bar

**Ruggles Green** 2311 W Alabama 713/533-0777 • 11am-10pm • organic & all-natural American

**Sparrow Bar + Cookshop** 3701 Travis St 713/524-6922 • lunch & dinner Tue-Sat • also bar • patio • wheelchair access • lesbian-owned

## ENTERTAINMENT & RECREATION

**After Hours - Queer Radio With Attitude** KPFT 90.1 FM (also 89.5 Galveston) 713/526-4000, 713/526-5738 (REQUEST LINE) • midnight-3am Sat/Sun • LGBT radio

**Beer Can House** 222 Malone St 713/926-6368 • seasonal; 10am-2pm Wed-Fri • 50,000+ beer cans cover the building!

**Houston Roller Derby** • Houston's female roller derby league • visit ww.houstonrollerderby.com for events

## RETAIL SHOPS

**The Chocolate Bar** 1835 W Alabama St 713/520-8599 • chocolate gifts & yummy desserts

**Hollywood Super Center** 2409 Grant St (at Crocker St) 713/527-8510 • 10am-1am, till 3am Fri-Sat • gifts • T-shirts • novelties

## PUBLICATIONS

**abOUT Magazine** PO Box 667626 713/396-2688 • Texas LGBT entertainment news source

**OutSmart** 713/520-7237 • monthly LGBT newsmagazine

## GYMS & HEALTH CLUBS

**Houston Gym** 1501 Durham Rd (at Washington & Eigel) 713/880-9191 • 5am-10pm, 8am-8pm wknds • gay-owned

## EROTICA

**Eros 1207** 1207 Spencer Hwy (at Allen Genoa) 713/910-0220 • gay-owned

**Loveworks** 25170 I-45 N, Spring 281/292-0070

## Houston

### BARS

**Neon Boots** 11410 Hempstead Rd (in the Historic Esquire Ballroom) **713/677-0828** • 4pm-2am, from noon wknds, till midnight Sun • popular • lesbians/gay men • country western dancing • gay-owned

## Lockhart

### ACCOMMODATIONS

**Lazy J Paradise Campground & Park** 270 Hidden Path (CR 303 and FM 2001) **210/863-9314** • campground w/ RV area catering to the LGBT community • pool • WiFi

## Longview

### NIGHTCLUBS

**Rainbow Members Club (RMC)** 203 S High (at Cotton) **903/753-9393** • 5pm-2am Wed-Sat, from 3pm Sun • lesbians/ gay men • dancing/DJ • private club • wheelchair access

## Lubbock

### INFO LINES & SERVICES

**AA Lambda** 4501 University Ave (at MCC) **806/792-5562** • 8pm Fri

### ACCOMMODATIONS

**LaQuinta Inns & Suites North** 5006 Auburn St (at Winston) **806/749-1600** • gay-friendly • pool • pets ok • gym • nonsmoking • WiFi • wheelchair access • gay-owned

### NIGHTCLUBS

**Club Luxor** 2211 4th St **806/744-3744** • 9pm-2am Fri-Sun • gay/ straight • more gay Fri & Sun • dancing/DJ • karaoke • drag shows • wheelchair access

**Heaven Nightclub** 1928 Buddy Holly Ave (at I-27) **806/762-4466** • 9pm-3am Th-Sun • gay-friendly • dancing/DJ • multiracial • drag shows • 18+ • young crowd

## Marfa

### ACCOMMODATIONS

**El Cosmico** 802 S. Highland Ave **432/729-1950, 877/822-1950** • gay/ straight • vintage trailer, yurt & teepee hotel & campground • WiFi • lesbian-owned

## McAllen

see Rio Grande Valley

## Rio Grande Valley

### BARS

**PBD's** 2908 N Ware Rd (at Daffodil), McAllen **956/682-8019** • 8pm-2am, clsd Mon • mostly gay men • dancing/DJ Th-Sat • drag shows • wheelchair access

## San Antonio

### INFO LINES & SERVICES

**Lambda AA** 319 Camden Rm #4 (Madison Square Presbyterian Church) **210/979-5939** • 8:15pm daily

### ACCOMMODATIONS

**Arbor House Suites B&B** 109 Arciniega (btwn S Alamo & S St Mary's) **210/472-2005, 888/272-6700** • gay/ straight • kids/ pets ok • hot tub • nonsmoking • wheelchair access • gay-owned

**Brackenridge House** 230 Madison (at Beauregard) **210/271-3442, 877/271-3442** • gay-friendly • B&B in historic King William district • pool • hot tub • WiFi

**Emily Morgan Hotel** 705 E Houston St (at Ave E) **210/225-5100, 800/824-6674** • gay-friendly • gym • pets ok • retaurant & bar • WiFi

**Hotel Havana** 1015 Navarro St **210/222-2008** • gay/ straight • also restaurant & lounge • gay-owned

### BARS

**2015 Place** 2015 San Pedro (at Woodlawn) **210/733-3365** • 4pm-2am • mostly gay men • neighborhood bar • patio • karaoke Wed

**The Annex** 330 San Pedro Ave (at Euclid) **210/223-6957** • 2pm-2am • mostly gay men • neighborhood bar • WiFi • wheelchair access

**Electric Company** 820 San Pedro Ave (at W Laurel) **210/212-6635** • 9pm-3am, clsd Mon • lesbians/ gay men, more women Wed & Sun • dancing/DJ • live shows • 18+

**Essence** 1010 N Main Ave (at E Euclid) **210/223-5418** • 2pm-2am • mostly gay men • neighborhood bar • karaoke

**The Flying Saucer** 11255 Huebner Rd #212 (at I-10) **210/696-5080** • 11am-1am, till 2am Th-Sat, noon-midnight Sun • gay-friendly • large beer selection

**Mix** 2423 N St Marys St **210/735-1313** • 5pm-2am, from 7:30pm Sat-Sun, dive bar • gay-friendly dive bar • live music

**One-Oh-Six Off Broadway** 106 Pershing St (at Broadway) **210/820-0906** • noon-2am • lesbians/ gay men • neighborhood bar

**Silver Dollar Saloon** 1818 N Main Ave (at Dewey) 210/227-2623 • 5pm-2am, clsd Mon • lesbians/ gay men • dancing/DJ • country/ western • karaoke

**Sparky's Pub** 1416 N Main Ave (at Evergreen) 210/320-5111 • 3pm-2am • pub atmosphere

## NIGHTCLUBS

**The Bonham Exchange** 411 Bonham St (at 3rd/ Houston) 210/271-3811 • 4pm-2am, from 8pm Sat • popular • in 120-year-old mansion • lesbians/ gay men • dancing/DJ • videos • 18+ • gay-owned

**The Industry** 8021 Pinebrook Dr (at Callaghan) 210/366-3229 • 10pm-2am Th, from 8pm Fri-Sat • gay/ straight • dancing/DJ

## CAFES

**Candlelight Coffeehouse & Wine Bar** 3011 N St Mary's (at Rte 281) 210/738-0099 • 2pm-midnight, wknd brunch 10am-2pm, clsd Mon • live music • WiFi • wheelchair access

## RESTAURANTS

**Chacho's** 7870 Callaghan Rd (at I-10) 210/366-2023 • 24hrs • Mexican • live bands • karaoke • wheelchair access

**Cool Cafe** 12651 Vance Jackson 210/8775/5/20115001 • brkfst, lunch & dinner • Mediterranean

**Giovanni's Pizza & Italian Restaurant** 913 S Brazos (at Guadalupe) 210/212-6626 • 11am-7pm • some veggie

**Guenther House** 129 E Guenther (at S Alamo St) 210/227-1061, 800/235-8186 • 7am-3pm • located in restored Pioneer Flour Mills founding family home

**Lulu's Bakery & Cafe** 918 N Main (at W Elmira) 210/222-9422 • 24hrs • Tex-Mex • wheelchair access

**Luther's Cafe** 1425 N Main Ave (at Evergreen) 210/223-7727 • 11am-3am • great burgers • karaoke • live music • wheelchair access • gay-owned

**Madhatter's Tea House** 320 Beauregard 210/212-4832 • 8am-9pm, till 3pm Sun • BYOB • patio • WiFi • wheelchair access

**El Mirador** 722 S St Mary's St (at Durango Blvd) 210/225-9444 • 6:30am-9pm, till 2pm Sun • Tex-Mex • plenty veggie • beer/ wine • patio • wheelchair access

**Taco Taco Cafe** 145 E Hildebrand 210/822-9533 • 7am-2pm

**WD Deli** 3123 Broadway St 210/828-2322 • 10:30am-5pm, till 4pm Sat, clsd Sun

## ENTERTAINMENT & RECREATION

**Alamo City Rollergirls** 223 Recoleta Rd (at the Rollercade) • San Antonio's female flat track roller derby league • visit www.alamocityrollergirls.com for events

## RETAIL SHOPS

**On Main/ Off Main** 120 W Mistletoe Ave 210/737-2323 • 10am-6pm, till 5pm Sat, clsd Sun • gifts • cards • T-shirts

**ZEBRAZ.com** 1608 N Main Ave (at E Park Ave) 210/472-2800, 800/788-4729 • 9am-midnight, till 10pm Sun-Tue • LGBT dept store

## EROTICA

**Dreamers** 2376 Austin Hwy (at Walzem) 210/653-3538 • 24hrs

# Tyler

## INFO LINES & SERVICES

**Tyler Area Gays/ TAG** 5701 Old Bullard Road #96 • social events & LGBT resources

## ACCOMMODATIONS

**Cross Timber Ranch B&B** 6271 FM 858 (at Hwy 64), Ben Wheeler 903/833-9000, 877/833-9002 • gay/ straight • full brkfst • nonsmoking • WiFi • gay-owned

# Wichita Falls

## BARS

**Krank It Karaoke Kafe** 1400 N Scott Ave (at Old Iowa Park Rd) 940/761-9099 • 8:30pm-2am, from 7pm Fri-Sat, clsd Mon-Tue • gay-friendly • dancing/DJ • 18+ • wheelchair access

# Wimberley

## ACCOMMODATIONS

**Bella Vista** 2121 Hilltop 512/847-6425 • gay/ straight • pool • nonsmoking • gay-owned

## UTAH

### Bryce Canyon

#### ACCOMMODATIONS

**Hatch Station** 177 S Main, Hatch
435/735–4015 • gay-friendly • also restaurant, laundry & convenience store • safe oasis for LGBT travelers in S UT • WiFi • wheelchair access

**The Red Brick Inn of Panguitch B&B** 161 N 100 West (at 200 North), Panguitch
435/690–1048, 866/733–2745 • gay-friendly • full brkfst • kids ok

#### CAFES

**Scoops from the Past** 105 N Main St, Panguitch 435/676–8885 • noon-10pm, till 11pm Fri-Sat, till 6pm Sun • retro ice cream parlor • WiFi

### Moab

#### ACCOMMODATIONS

**Castle Valley Inn** 424 Amber Ln
435/259–6012 • gay-friendly • great views

**Mayor's House B&B** 505 Rose Tree Ln (at 400 E) 435/259–6015, 888/791–2345 • gay-friendly • full brkfst • pool • hot tub • kids ok • nonsmoking • WiFi • gay-owned

**Mt Peale Resort Inn, Lodge & Cabins** 1415 E Hwy 46 (at mile marker 14), Old La Sal 435/686–2284, 888/687–3253 • gay/ straight • B&B & cabins • hot tub • hiking • nonsmoking • WiFi • kids/ pets ok • lesbian-owned

**Red Cliffs Lodge** Hwy 128 (at mile marker 14) 435/259–2002, 866/812–2002 • gay-friendly • resort • on Colorado River • pool • hot tub • kids ok • nonsmoking • wheelchair access

### Park City

#### RESTAURANTS

**Loco Lizard Cantina** 1612 Ute Blvd (in Kimball Jct Shopping Ctr) 435/645–7000 • 11am-10pm, till 11pm Fri-Sat, brunch wknds • Mexican • full bar • transgender-friendly • wheelchair access

### Salt Lake City

#### INFO LINES & SERVICES

**Utah Pride Center** 361 N 300 W, 1st flr 801/539–8800, 888/874–2743 • info • resource center • meetings • coffee shop • programs • youth activity center • much more

#### ACCOMMODATIONS

**Anniversary Inn** 460 S 1000 E (at 400) 435/879–5839, 800/324–4152 • gay-friendly • elaborate, kitschy theme rms • WiFi • women owned

**Hotel Monaco Salt Lake City** 15 W 200 S (at S Main) 801/595–0000, 877/294–9710 • gay-friendly • restaurant & bar • WiFi • gym • kids/ pets ok • wheelchair access

**Parrish Place** 720 E Ashton Ave (at 700 E) 801/832–0970, 855/832–0970 • gay/ straight • Victorian mansion • hot tub • nonsmoking • WiFi

**Peery Hotel** 110 W 300 S 801/521–4300, 800/331–0073 • gay-friendly • kids/pets ok • also 2 restaurants • full bar • nonsmoking • WiFi • wheelchair access

**Under the Lindens** 128 S 1000 E (downtown) 801/355–9808 • mostly gay men • studios • hot tub • nonsmoking • WiFi • commitment ceremonies • mention Damron for discount • gay-owned

#### BARS

**Jam** 751 North 300 West (at Reed Ave) 801/382–8567 • 8pm-2am, clsd Mon-Tue • lesbians/ gay men • neighborhood bar • dancing/DJ • karaoke • WiFi

**Paper Moon** 3737 S State St (at E 3750 S) 801/713–0678 • 3pm-1am, from 6pm Mon, from 7pm Sat, clsd Sun • mostly women • dancing/DJ • karaoke • live music • private club • food served • wheelchair access

**The Sun Trapp** 102 S 600 W (at 100 S) 801/235–6786 • 1pm-2am • lesbians/ gay men • dancing/DJ • country/ western • karaoke • WiFi • wheelchair access

**The Tavernacle Social Club** 201 E 300 South (at 200 E) 801/519–8900 • 5pm-close, from 8pm Sun-Mon • gay-friendly • food • karaoke • "Duelin' Pianos" • nonsmoking • private club

#### NIGHTCLUBS

**Area 51** 451 South 400 West (at 400 S) 801/534–0819 • gay/ straight • dancing/DJ • 80s & goth theme nights Th-Sat only

**Fusion** 540 W 200 South (at Metro Bar) • 9pm-2am Sat only• mostly gay men • dancing/DJ

**Gossip** 579 W 200 S (at 600 W, at Club Sound) 801/328–0255 • 9:30pm-2am Fri only • mostly gay men • dancing/DJ • 18+

**Pachanga at Karamba** 1051 East 2100 South 801/696–0639 • 9pm Sun only • mostly gay men • gay Latin night • dancing/DJ

## CAFES

**Coffee Garden** 878 E 900 S **801/355-3425** • 6am-11pm • light fare • wheelchair access

## RESTAURANTS

**Bambara** 202 S Main St **801/363-5454** • lunch Mon-Fri, brkfst & dinner daily • upscale American

**Blue Plate Diner** 2041 S 2100 E **801/463-1151** • 7am-9pm, till 10pm Fri-Sat

**Cafe Trio Downtown** 680 S 900 E **801/533-8746** • 11am-10pm, Italian

**Cedars of Lebanon** 152 E 200 South (at State St) **801/364-4096** • lunch & dinner • Lebanese • veggie/ vegan-friendly • belly dancers wknds • WiFi

**Citris Grill** 2991 E 3300 South **801/466-1202** • 8am-10pm

**Finn's** 1624 S 1100 East (at Logan) **801/467-4000** • 7:30am-2:30pm

**Fresco Italian Cafe** 1513 S 1500 East **801/486-1300** • dinner nightly • patio

**Himalayan Kitchen** 360 S State St (at 400 S) **801/328-2077** • lunch & dinner, dinner only Sun • Indian/Himalayan • plenty veggie

**Market St Grill** 48 W Market St **801/322-4668** • 11:30-9pm, from 9am Sun • fresh seafood • full bar • wheelchair access

**The Med** 420 E 3300 South **801/493-0100** • lunch & dinner • Mediterranean

**The New Yorker Restaurant** 60 W Market St **801/363-0166** • lunch Mon-Fri, dinner nightly, clsd Sun • fine dining • steak

**Off Trax** 259 W 900 S **801/364-4307** • 7am-7pm, till 3pm Fri, brunch Sun, also from 1am-3am Fri-Sat nights • lesbians/ gay men • WiFi • gay-owned

**Omar's Rawtopia** 2148 Highland Dr **801/486-0332** • noon-8pm, till 9pm Fri-Sat, clsd Sun • raw food

**Red Iguana** 736 W North Temple **801/322-1489** • popular • lunch & dinner • Mexican

**Sage's Cafe** 234 W 900 S **801/322-3790** • lunch & dinner, brkfst wknds • vegan/ vegetarian

**Stoneground** 249 E 400 South **801/364-1368** • 11am-11pm, 5pm-9pm Sun • pizza & more

**Vertical Diner** 2280 S West Temple **801/484-8378** • 10am-9pm • vegetarian/vegan, gltuen-free diner • live shows • full bar • wheelchair access

**Zest Kitchen & Bar** 275 S 200 W **801/433-0589** • 11am-11pm, till 1am Fri-Sat • full cocktail menu, healthy vegetarian, 100% gluten-free kitchen

## ENTERTAINMENT & RECREATION

**Lambda Hiking Club** • hiking & other activities

**Plan-B Theatre Company** 138 West 300 South (at Rose Wagner Performing Arts Center, btwn W Temple & 200 West) **801/355-2787** • at least one LGBT-themed production each season

**Pygmalion Productions Theatre Company** 138 W Broadway (at Rose Wagner Performing Arts Center) **801/355-2787, 888/451-2787** • a "feminine perspective" on theatre

**Tower Theatre** 876 E 900 South **801/321-0310** • alternative films • many LGBT movies

## BOOKSTORES

**Golden Braid Books** 151 S 500 E **801/322-1162** • 10am-9pm, till 6pm Sun • also Oasis Cafe, 8am-9pm, till 10pm wknds • WiFi

**Weller Book Works** 607 Trolley Sq **801/328-2586** • 10am-9pm, noon-5pm Sun

## RETAIL SHOPS

**Cahoots** 878 E 900 S (at 900 E) **801/538-0606** • 10am-9pm • unique gift shop • wheelchair access • gay-owned

## PUBLICATIONS

**Q Salt Lake** **801/649-6663, 800/806-7357** • bi-weekly LGBT newspaper

## EROTICA

**All For Love** 3072 S Main St (at 33rd St S) **801/487-8358** • clsd Sun • lingerie & S/M boutique • transgender-friendly & wheelchair access

**Blue Boutique** 1383 E 2100 South **801/485-2072** • also piercing

**Mischievous** 559 S 300 W (at 6th St S) **801/530-3100** • clsd Sun

# Zion Nat'l Park

## ACCOMMODATIONS

**Canyon Vista Lodge B&B** 2175 Zion Park Blvd (at Hwy 9), Springdale **435/772-3801** • gay-friendly • nonsmoking

**Red Rock Inn** 998 Zion Park Blvd, Springdale **435/772-3139** • gay/ straight • cottages w/ canyon views • full brkfst • hot tub • nonsmoking • wheelchair access • lesbian-owned

**Under The Eaves Inn** 980 Zion Nat'l Park Blvd, Springdale **435/772-3457, 866/261-2655** • gay/straight • romantic 1931 landmark home less than a mile from the park entrance • gay-owned

### Cafes

**Cafe Soleil** 205 Zion Nat'l Park Blvd, Springdale **435/772-0505** • 6am-8pm seasonal • lesbian-owned

# VERMONT

## Statewide

### Info Lines & Services

**Vermont Gay Tourism Association** • Vermont's official organization to promote gay & lesbian travel throughout the state • see www.vermontgaytourism.com

## Brattleboro

### Accommodations

**Nutmeg Inn** 153 Rte 9 W, Wilmington **802/464-3907, 855/868-8634** • gay/ straight • WiFi • wheelchair access • gay-owned

### Bookstores

**Everyone's Books** 25 Elliot St **802/254-8160** • 9:30am-6pm, till 8pm Fri, till 7pm Sat, 11am-5pm Sun • wheelchair access

## Burlington

### Info Lines & Services

**Pride Center** 55 S Champlain St  # 12 **802/860-7812** • drop-in & cybercenter • advocacy & support • events

### Accommodations

**The Inn at Essex** 70 Essex Way, Essex **802/878-1100, 800/727-4295** • gay-friendly • culinary resort • pool • kids/pets ok • WiFi • wheelchair access

**Lang House on Main Street B&B** 360 Main St **802/652-2500, 877/919-9799** • gay-friendly • WiFi • exquisite rooms, gourmet breakfast and personal service, kids ok

**One of a Kind B&B** 53 Lakeview Terrace **802/862-5576** • nonsmoking • 2-rm suite & cottage • WiFi • woman-owned

### Nightclubs

**Metronome/ Nectar's** 188 Main St **802/658-4771, 802/865-4563** • gay-friendly • popular 80s night Sat • live bands • also restaurant

### Cafes

**Muddy Waters** 184 Main St **802/658-0466** • 9am-11pm • coffeehouse, try the white hot chocolate

**Radio Bean Coffeehouse** 8 N Winooski Ave (at Pearl) **802/660-9346** • 8am-midnight, till 2am Th-Sat, 10am-11pm Sun • cool bohemian coffeehouse • live bands & open mic nights

### Restaurants

**Daily Planet** 15 Center St (at College) **802/862-9647** • 4pm-close, also bar till 2am • plenty veggie

**Leunig's Bistro & Cafe** 115 Church St **802/863-3759** • lunch & dinner, gulten free options • lesbian-owned

**Shanty on the Shore** 181 Battery St **802/864-0238** • 11am-9pm • seafood • views of Lake Champlain

**Silver Palace** 1216 Williston Rd **802/864-0125** • 11:30am-9pm, 5pm-9pm Sun• Chinese • full bar

### Retail Shops

**Peace & Justice Store** 60 Lake St (at College St) **802/863-2345** • 10am-6pm, limited hrs in winter • fair trade retail store

## Chester

### Accommodations

**Chester House Inn** 266 Main St **888/875-2205** • gay/ straight • full brkfst • nonsmoking • kids ok • WiFi • wheelchair access • gay-owned

## Jay Peak

### Accommodations

**Phineas Swann B&B** **802/326-4306** • gay/ straight • restored Victorian on Trout River • full brkfst • nonsmoking • WiFi • gay-owned

## Killington

### Accommodations

**Huntington House Inn** 19 Huntington Pl, Rochester **802/767-9140** • gay-friendly • located on the park w/ a restaurant & lounge • WiFi • wheelchair access • gay-owned

**Killlington Mountain Lodge** 2617 Killington Rd **802/772_0972** • gay-friendly • pool • jacuzzi • WiFi • kids ok • wheelchair access

**Salt Ash Inn** 4758 Rte 100A (at Rte 100), Plymouth **802/672-3224** • gay/ straight • 1830s country inn • full brkfst • hot tub • kids/ small pets ok • pool • WiFi • wheelchair access

## Manchester

ACCOMMODATIONS

**Hill Farm Inn** 458 Hill Farm Rd (at Historic Rte 7-A), Arlington **802/375-2269, 800/882-2545** • gay-friendly • full brkfst • nonsmoking • WiFi

CAFES

**Little Rooster Cafe** Rte 7-A (at Hillvale Dr), Manchester Center **802/362-3496** • 7am-2:30pm, clsd Wed (winters)

RESTAURANTS

**Bistro Henry** 1942 Depot St (.5 mile E of Rte 7), Manchester Center **802/362-4982** • dinner only, clsd Mon • Mediterranean • also bar • reservations advised

**Chantecleer** Rte 7-A N, E Dorset **802/362-1616** • call for hours • seasonal

BOOKSTORES

**Northshire Bookstore** 4869 Main St, Manchester Center **802/362-2200, 800/437-3700** • 10am-7pm, till 9pm Fri-Sat

## Marshfield

ACCOMMODATIONS

**Marshfield Inn & Motel** 5630 US Rte 2 **802/426-3383** • gay-friendly • full brkfst • WiFi • lesbian-owned

## Montpelier

RESTAURANTS

**Julio's** 54 State **802/229-9348** • 11:30am-10pm, till 11pm Fri-Sat• Mexican • WiFi

**Sarducci's** 3 Main St **802/223-0229** • 11:30am-9:30pm, from 4:30pm Sun • Italian • some veggie • full bar • wheelchair access

**Wayside Restaurant** 1873 Rte 302 **802/223-6611** • 6:30am-9:30pm • wheelchair access

## Plainfield

ACCOMMODATIONS

**Comstock House** 1620 Middle Rd **802/272-2693** • gay-friendly • overlooks Winooski River Valley • full brkfst • WiFi • gay-owned

## Richmond

RESTAURANTS

**The Kitchen Table Bistro** 1840 W Main St **802/434-8686** • 5pm-9pm, clsd Mon • seasonal menu • local food

## Rutland

ACCOMMODATIONS

**Lilac Inn** 53 Park St, Brandon **802/247-5463, 800/221-0720** • full brkfst • teens/ pets ok • wheelchair access

## Saxtons River

ACCOMMODATIONS

**The Saxtons River Inn** 27 Main St (at Academy Ave) **802/869-2110** • gay-friendly • historic Victorian inn • pub & restaurant • nonsmoking • WiFi • pets ok

## St Johnsbury

ACCOMMODATIONS

**Comfort Inn & Suites** 703 US Rte 5 S (at I-91) **802/748-1500, 800/424-6423** • gay-friendly • pool • hot tub • kids ok • WiFi • wheelchair access

**Fairbanks Inn** 401 Western Ave **802/748-5666** • gay-friendly • motel • pool • kids & pets ok • WiFi • wheelchair access

## Stowe

ACCOMMODATIONS

**Arbor Inn** 3214 Mountain Rd **802/253-4772, 800/543-1293** • gay/ straight • full brkfst • hot tub • pool • nonsmoking • WiFi

**Fitch Hill Inn** 258 Fitch Hill Rd (at Rte 15/100), Hyde Park **802/888-3834, 800/639-2903** • gay/ straight • full brkfst • older kids ok • WiFi • nonsmoking

**The Green Mountain Inn** 18 Main St **802/253-7301, 800/253-7302** • gay-friendly • kids ok • heated pool • hot tub • nonsmoking • WiFi • wheelchair access • 2 restaurants

**Northern Lights Lodge** 4441 Mountain Rd 802/253–8541, 800/448–4554 • gay-friendly • full brkfst • hot tub • pool • sauna • kids/pets ok • WiFi • gay-owned

**The Old Stagecoach Inn** 18 N Main St (at Stowe St), Waterbury 802/244–5056, 800/262–2206 • gay-friendly • historic village inn • full brkfst • kids/pets ok • also full bar

**Timberholm Inn** 452 Cottage Club Rd 802/253–7603, 800/753–7603 • gay/straight • B&B • full brkfst • hot tub • nonsmoking

## Waterbury

### Accommodations

**Grünberg Haus B&B & Cabins** 94 Pine St, Rte 100 S 802/244–7726, 800/800–7760 • gay/straight • Austrian chalet • also cabins May-Oct • full brkfst • fireplace • nonsmoking • WiFi

**Moose Meadow Lodge** 607 Crossett Hill 802/244–5378 • gay/straight • full brkfst • nonsmoking • WiFi • gay-owned

## West Dover

### Accommodations

**Deerhill Inn** 14 Valley View Rd 802/464–3100, 800/993–3379 • gay/straight • inn • pool • teenagers ok • nonsmoking • WiFi • also restaurant

**Inn at Mount Snow** 401 Rte 100 802/464–8388 • gay-friendly • at foot of Mt Snow • • kids ok • nonsmoking • WiFi • gay-owned

**The Inn at Sawmill Farm** 7 Crosstown Rd (at Rte 100) 802/464–8131, 800/493–1133 • gay-friendly • kids/pets ok • nonsmoking • WiFi • wheelchair access

## Windham

### Accommodations

**A Stone Wall Inn** 578 Hitchcock Hill Rd 802/875–4238 • gay/straight • hot tub • WiFi • nonsmoking • gay-owned

## Woodstock

### Accommodations

**The Ardmore Inn** 23 Pleasant St 802/457–3887 • gay-friendly • 1867 Greek Revival • full brkfst • nonsmoking • WiFi

**Deer Brook Inn** 4548 W Woodstock Rd 802/672–3713 • gay-friendly • full brkfst • kids ok • WiFi • gay-owned

**The Lincoln Inn & Restaurant at the Covered Bridge** 2709 W Woodstock Rd 802/457–7052 • gay/straight • on the Ottauquechee River • WiFi • women-owned

**The Woodstocker Inn B&B** 61 River St 802/457–3896 • gay/straight • WiFi

# Virginia

## Alexandria

see also Washington, District of Columbia

### Accommodations

**Crowne Plaza Old Town Alexandria** 901 N Fairfax St 703/683–6000

**Lorien Hotel & Spa** 1600 King St 703/894–3434, 877/956–7436 • gay-friendly • restaurant on-site • kids/pets ok • wheelchair access

**Morrison House** 116 S Alfred St 703/838–8000, 866/834–6628

## Arlington

see also Washington, District of Columbia

### Info Lines & Services

**Arlington Gay/Lesbian Alliance** • monthly meetings • outreach events • check website for schedule: www.agla.org

### Bars

**Freddie's Beach Bar & Restaurant** 555 S 23rd St (at Fern St) 703/685–0555 • 4pm-2am, from 11am Fri, fron 10an wknds for brunch • lesbians/gay men • karaoke • drag show • patio • live bands • food served • wheelchair access

### Cafes

**Java Shack** 2507 N Franklin Rd (at Wilson Blvd & N Barton) 703/527–9556 • 7am-8pm, 8am-6pm Sun

## Cape Charles

### Accommodations

**Cape Charles House B&B** 645 Tazewell Ave (at Fig) 757/331–4920 • gay-friendly • 1912 colonial revival home filled w/ antiques • nonsmoking

**Sea Gate B&B** 9 Tazewell Ave 757/331–2206 • gay-friendly • full brkfst • near beach on quiet, tree-lined street • WiFi • gay-owned

## Charlottesville

### ACCOMMODATIONS

**CampOut** 804/301–3553 • women only • 100-acre rustic campground • nonsmoking • pets ok • wheelchair access • women-owned

**Fiddlestick Lane Guesthouse** 1889 Fiddlestick Ln 434/249–6944 • gay/straight • private home • WiFi • kids ok • gay-owned

**The Inn at Court Square** 410 E Jefferson St 434/295–2800, 866/466–2877 • gay-friendly • restored house w/ period antiques • lunch served Mon-Fri, dinner Fri-Sat • kids ok • nonsmoking • women-owned

### RESTAURANTS

**Escafe** 215 W Water St 434/295–8668 • lunch & dinner • full bar • live music • gay-owned

## Harrisonburg

### CAFES

**Artful Dodger Coffeehouse** 47 W Court Square 540/432–1179 • 8:30am-2am, from 9:30am wknds • DJ • entertainment • also bar • wheelchair access

## Norfolk

### INFO LINES & SERVICES

**Saturday Night Live Gay/ Lesbian AA** 1301 Colley Ave (at First Lutheran Church) 757/625–1953 • 8pm Sat

### ACCOMMODATIONS

**B&B at Historic Page House Inn** 323 Fairfax Ave 757/625–5033, 800/599–7659 • gay-friendly • 1899 mansion • nonsmoking • WiFi

**Tazewell Hotel & Suites** 245 Granby St (at Tazewell St) 757/623–6200 • gay-friendly • kids ok • WiFi • wheelchair access

### BARS

**Hershee Lounge & He Bar** 6117 Sewells Pt Rd (at Norview) 757/853–9842 • 4pm-2am • mostly women • dancing/DJ • live shows • food served • wheelchair access • woman-owned

### NIGHTCLUBS

**Hotties Bar & Grill** 1083 W 37th St 757/533-5151
• 5pm-1am from 11:30am Sun for drag brunch • lesbians/gay men • dancing/DJ • food served

**The Wave** 4107 Colley Ave (at 41st St) 757/440–5911 • 10pm-2am, clsd Sun, Mon & Wed • lesbians/ gay men • dancing/DJ • live shows • wheelchair access

### RESTAURANTS

**Charlie's Cafe** 1800 Granby St (at 18th) 757/625–0824 • 7am-2pm • some veggie • beer/ wine

**Tortilla West** 508 Oropax St 757/440–3777 • dinner only, Sun brunch, open till 1am • Mexican • plenty veggie/ vegan

### EROTICA

**Leather & Lace** 745 Battlefield Blvd N #104, Chesapeake 757/436–2525 • 11am-8pm, noon-6pm

## Richmond

### ACCOMMODATIONS

**Omni Richmond Hotel** 100 S 12th St (at Cary St) 804/344–7000, 800/843–6664 • gay-friendly • pool • views of city & James River • WiFi • wheelchair access

### BARS

**Babes of Carytown** 3166 W Cary St (at Auburn) 804/355–9330 • 11am-2am, from noon Sat, from 9am Sun • lesbians/ gay men • dancing/DJ • country/ western • karaoke • drag shows • live music • food served • wheelchair access • women-owned

**Barcode** 6 E Grace St (btwn 1st & Foushee Sts) 804/648–2040 • 4pm-2am, from 3pm wknds • mostly gay men • neighborhood bar • karaoke • food served • WiFi • wheelchair access

**Godfrey's** 308 E Grace St (btwn 3rd & 4th) 804/648–3957 • 10pm-close, clsd Mon-Tue, brunch Sun • lesbians/ gay men • dancing/DJ • karaoke • drag shows

### NIGHTCLUBS

**Club Colours** 536 N Harrison St (at Broad) 804/353–9776 • 9pm-3am Sat • lesbians/ gay men • dancing/DJ • multiracial • food served • live shows • wheelchair access

### RESTAURANTS

**Galaxy Diner** 3109 W Cary St 804/213–0510 • 11am-midnight, till 2am wknds • some veggie • full bar

**The Village** 1001 W Grace 804/353–8204 • 8am-2am • American • plenty veggie

## ENTERTAINMENT & RECREATION

**Richmond Triangle Players** 1300 Altamont Ave (at W Marshall St) **804/346–8113** • LGBT-themed plays, films & cabaret

**Venture Richmond** **804/788–6466** • tour the James River • lots of shops, restaurants, etc

## Roanoke

### BARS

**Backstreet Cafe** 356 Salem Ave (off Jefferson) **540/345–1542** • 7pm-2am, clsd Sun-Mon • lesbians/ gay men • neighborhood bar • food served

**Cuba Pete's** 120 Church Ave SW (at First St SW, inside Macado's) **540/342–7231** • 11am-2am • gay-friendly • more gay wknds • also Macado's restaurant • karaoke • wheelchair access

### RESTAURANTS

**Metro Restaurant & Nighclub** 14 Campbell Ave SE • 11:30am-midnight, till 2:30am Fri-Sat • dancing/DJ

## Shenandoah Valley

### ACCOMMODATIONS

**Frog Hollow B&B** 492 Greenhouse Rd (at Rte 11), Lexington **540/463–5444** • gay/ straight • full brkfst • hot tub • also cottage • gay-owned

**The Olde Staunton Inn** 260 N Lewis St, Staunton **540/886–0193, 866/653–3786** • gay/ straight • hot tub • WiFi • nonsmoking

**Piney Hill B&B** 1048 Piney Hill Rd (at Mill Creek Crossroads), Luray **540/778–5261, 800/644–5261** • gay/ straight • country B&B • full brkfst • gay-owned

## Virginia Beach

### ACCOMMODATIONS

**Capes Ocean Resort Hotel** 2001 Atlantic Ave (at 20th St) **757/428–5421, 877/956–5421** • gay-friendly • oceanfront rooms • private balconies • pool • nonsmoking • WiFi • kids ok • wheelchair access

**Ocean Beach Club** 3401 Atlantic Ave (at 34th St) **800/245–1003** • gay-friendly • also cafe & tiki bar • wheelchair access

### BARS

**Klub Ambush** 475 S Lynnhaven Rd (at Lynnhaven Pkwy) **757/498–4301** • 5pm-2am • lesbians/ gay men • neighborhood bar • dancing/DJ • food served • shows • karaoke • gay-owned

**Rainbow Cactus** 3472 Holland Rd (at Diana Lee) **757/368–0441** • 7pm-2am, clsd Mon-Tue • mostly gay men • dancing/DJ • country/ western • drag shows • food served • wheelchair access

### EROTICA

**Nancy's Nook** 1301 Oceana Blvd **757/428–1498** • 24hrs

## Washington

### ACCOMMODATIONS

**Gay Street Inn** 160 Gay St **540/316–9220** • gay-friendly • nonsmoking • WiFi • gay-owned

# WASHINGTON

## Bainbridge Island

### BOOKSTORES

**Eagle Harbor Book Co** 157 Winslow Wy E **206/842–5332** • 9am-7pm, till 9pm Th, till 6pm Sat, 10am-6pm Sun

## Bellevue

see also Seattle

## Bellingham

### BARS

**Rumors** 1119 Railroad Ave (at Chestnut) **360/671–1846** • 4pm-2am • lesbians/ gay men • dancing/DJ • multiracial • wheelchair access

### CAFES

**Tony's Coffee House** 1101 Harris Ave (at 11th), Fairhaven **360/738–4710** • 7am-6pm • plenty veggie • patio • wheelchair access

### RESTAURANTS

**KC's Bar & Grille** 108 W Main St (Washington Ave), Everson **360/966–8838** • 11am-10pm • gay-owned • wheelchair access

**Skylark's Hidden Cafe** 1308 11th St (at McKenzie) **360/715–3642** • 7am-midnight • great soups • full bar • outdoor seating • live jazz wknds

## BOOKSTORES

**Village Books** 1200 11th St (at Harris) **360/671–2626** • 10am-7:30pm, till 7pm Sun • new & used

## EROTICA

**Great Northern Bookstore** 1308 Railroad Ave (at Holly) **360/733–1650**

# Bender Creek

## ACCOMMODATIONS

**Triangle Recreation Camp** PO Box 1226, Granite Falls 98252 • lesbians/gay men • members-only camping on 80-acre nature conservancy • www.camptrc.org

# Bremerton

## INFO LINES & SERVICES

**AA Gay/Lesbian** 700 Callahan Dr (at St Paul's Episcopal) **360/475–0775, 800/562–7455** • 7:30pm Tue

# Everett

## INFO LINES & SERVICES

**AA Gay/Lesbian** 2624 Rockefeller **425/252–2525** • 7pm Sun

# Glacier

## ACCOMMODATIONS

**Mt Baker B&B & Cabins** 9434 Cornell Creek Rd **360/599–2299** • gay/straight • modern chalet • hot tub • kids ok • some shared baths • nonsmoking • WiFi

# Kent

## EROTICA

**The Voyeur** 604 Central Ave S **253/850–8428** • videos • toys • clothing

# La Conner

## ACCOMMODATIONS

**The Wild Iris** 121 Maple Ave **360/466–1400, 800/477–1400** • gay-friendly • inn • nonsmoking • full brkfst • kids ok • WiFi • wheelchair access • gay-owned

# Long Beach Peninsula

## ACCOMMODATIONS

**The Historic Sou'wester Lodge, Cabins & RV Park** Beach Access Rd (38th Pl), Seaview **360/642–2542** • gay-friendly • inexpensive suites • cabins w/ kitchens • vintage trailers • RV hookups • pets ok in cabins & trailers • nonsmoking

**Shakti Cove Cottages** **360/665–4000** • lesbians/gay men • cabins on the peninsula • pets ok • nonsmoking • lesbian-owned

# Mt Vernon

## RESTAURANTS

**Deli Next Door** 202 S 1st St (at Memorial Hwy) **360/336–3886** • 8am-9pm, 9pm-8pm Sun • healthy American • plenty veggie • WiFi • wheelchair access

# Olympia

## INFO LINES & SERVICES

**Free at Last AA** **360/352–7344** • call for info

## ACCOMMODATIONS

**Swantown Inn B&B** 1431 11th Ave SE (at Central St) **360/753–9123, 877/753–9123** • gay-friendly • nonsmoking • full brkfst • WiFi

## BARS

**Hannah's** 123 5th Ave SW (at Columbia) **360/357–9890** • 11am-2am, till midnight Sun-Mon • gay/straight • neighborhood/dive bar • food served

## NIGHTCLUBS

**Jakes on 4th** 311 E 4th **360/956–3247** • noon-2am • lesbians/gay men • dancing/DJ • karaoke

## CAFES

**Darby's Cafe** 211 SE 5th Ave (at Washington) **360/357–6229** • 7am-2pm, 8am-2pm wknds, clsd Mon-Tue • gay/straight • gay-owned

## RESTAURANTS

**Saigon Rendez-Vous** 117 5th Ave SW (btwn Columbia & Capitol Wy) **360/352–1989** • lunch & dinner • Vietnamese • plenty veggie

**Urban Onion** 116 Legion Wy SE (at Capitol) **360/943–9242** • 11am-9pm, 9am-2am wknds • plenty veggie • lounge • wheelchair access

## RETAIL SHOPS

**Dumpster Values** 302 4th (at Franklin) 360/705–3772 • 11am-8pm, noon-6pm Sun • new & used clothing • zines • records • toys • queer women-owned

# Packwood

## ACCOMMODATIONS

**Packwood Lodge** 13807 US Hwy 12 360/496-5333 • gay/straight • small boutique lodge 7 miles from the entrance to Mt Rainier National Park • WiFi • pets/kids ok • gay-owned

# Pasco

## NIGHTCLUBS

**Out & About Restaurant & Lounge** 327 W Lewis 509/543-3796 • 6pm-2am, clsd Mon-Tue • lesbians/gay men • dancing/DJ wknds • karaoke • drag shows • cabaret • 18+ Fri • also restaurant • wheelchair access

# San Juan Islands

## ACCOMMODATIONS

**Inn on Orcas Island** 360/376–5227, 888/886–1661 • gay-friendly • luxury • full brkfst • nonsmoking • wheelchair access • gay-owned

**Lopez Farm Cottages & Tent Camping** 555 Fisherman Bay Rd, Lopez Island 360/468-3555, 800/440-3556 • gay/straight • on 30-acre farm • hot tub • nonsmoking

## ENTERTAINMENT & RECREATION

**Western Prince Whale & Wildlife Tours** 2 Spring St (at Front), Friday Harbor 360/378-5315, 800/757-6722 • whale-watching & wildlife tours April-Oct

# Seattle

## INFO LINES & SERVICES

**Seattle Area Support Groups and Community Center** 114 17th Ave E (at E Thomas) 206/322-2437 • recovery meetings for the GLBTQ community and their family and friends• wheelchair access

## ACCOMMODATIONS

**The Ace Hotel** 2423 1st Ave (at Wall St) 206/448-4721 • gay/straight • kids/pets ok • nonsmoking • WiFi • restaurant & bar

**Alexis Hotel** 1007 1st Ave (at Madison) 206/624-4844, 866/356-8894 • gay-friendly • luxury hotel w/ Aveda spa • kids/pets ok • WiFi • wheelchair access

**Artist's Studio Loft B&B** 16529 91st Ave SW, Vashon Island 206/463-2583 • gay-friendly • on 5 acres • garden • hot tub • nonsmoking

**Bacon Mansion** 959 Broadway E (at E Prospect) 206/329-1864, 800/240-1864 • gay/straight • Edwardian-style Tudor • nonsmoking • WiFi • wheelchair access

**Bed & Breakfast on Broadway** 722 Broadway Ave E (at Aloha) 206/329-8933 • gay/straight • nonsmoking • WiFi

**Gaslight Inn** 1727 15th Ave (at E Howell St) 206/325-3654 • popular • gay/straight • B&B in Arts & Crafts home • pool • WiFi • nonsmoking • gay-owned

**Hotel 1000** 1000 First Ave 206/957-1000, 877/315-1088 • gay-friendly • WiFi • wheelchair access

**Hotel Monaco** 1101 4th Ave (at Spring St) 206/621-1770, 800/715-6513 • gay-friendly • kids/pets ok • WiFi • wheelchair access • also Sazerac Cajun restaurant

**Inn at the Market** 86 Pine St 206/443-3600, 800/446-4484 • gay/friendly • in Pike Place Market

**MarQueen Hotel** 600 Queen Anne Ave N (btwn Roy & Mercer) 206/282-7407, 888/445-3076 • gay/straight • in Theater District • kitchenettes

**Seahurst Garden Studio** 13713 16th Ave SW (at Ambaum Ave), Burien 206/551-7721 • women only • nonsmoking • WiFi • wheelchair access • lesbian-owned

**Sleeping Bulldog Bed & Breakfast** 816 19th Ave S (at S Dearborn St) 206/325-0202 • gay/straight • nonsmoking • WiFi • gay-owned

**The Sorrento Hotel** 900 Madison St 206/622-6400, 800/426-1265 • gay-friendly • restaurant • WiFi

## BARS

**The Baltic Room** 1207 Pine St (at Melrose) 206/625-4444 • 9pm-2am, LGBT night Th • gay/straight • live music

**The Bottleneck Lounge** 2328 Madison St (at John St) 206/323-1098 • 4pm-2am • gay/straight • bar snacks • lesbian-owned

**CC Attle's** 1701 E Olive Way 206/323-4017 • noon-2am • popular • mostly gay men • neighborhood bar • videos • also restaurant • wheelchair access

**Cha Cha Lounge & Bimbo's Cantina** 1013 E Pike St (at 11th Ave) 206/322-0703 • 4pm-2am • gay-friendly • hipster lounge • big burritos • gay-owned

**Changes In Wallingford** 2103 N 45th St (at Meridian) 206/545-8363 • noon-2am • mostly gay men • neighborhood bar • food served • karaoke • videos • wheelchair access

**The Crescent Lounge** 1413 E Olive Wy (at Bellevue) • noon-2am • gay/ straight • neighborhood bar • karaoke nightly • wheelchair access

**The Cuff** 1533 13th Ave (at Pine) 206/323-1525 • 2pm-2am, after-hours wknds, T-dance Sun • popular • mostly gay men • dancing/DJ • country/ western Fri • WiFi • patio • wheelchair access

**Double Header** 407 2nd Ave S Extension (at Washington) 206/464-9918 • 10am-11pm, till 1am Fri-Sat • gay/ straight • neighborhood bar

**Hot Flash Seattle** 1509 Broadway (at Neighbours) 206/252-9333 • T-dance 5pm-9pm 1st & 3rd Sat only • "for seasoned lesbians 36+ (& the women who love us!)" • cover charge

**Hula Hula** 106 1st Ave N (at Denny) 206/284-5003 • 4pm-close • gay-friendly • tiki bar • karaoke

**OutWest** 5401 California Ave SW 206/937-1540 • 4pm-midnight, til 2am Th-Sat • lebians /gay men • neighborhood bar • live Jazz • karaoke

**Poco Wine Room** 1408 E Pine St (at 14th Ave) 206/322-9463 • 4pm-2am • gay/ straight • neighborhood bistropub

**R Place** 619 E Pine St (at Boylston Ave) 206/322-8828 • 4pm-2am, from 2pm wknds • mostly gay men • neighborhood bar • dancing/DJ • food served • karaoke • videos • WiFi • wheelchair access

**Rendezvous** 2322 2nd Ave (at Battery) 206/441-5823 • 4pm-2am • gay/ straight • live bands • cabaret • theater • also restaurant

**The Seattle Eagle** 314 E Pike St (at Bellevue) 206/621-7591 • 2pm-2am • mostly gay men • leather • rock 'n' roll • theme nights • patio • wheelchair access

**Temple Billiards** 126 S Jackson 206/682-3242 • 11am-2am, from 3pm wknds • gay-friendly • more women Wed • food served

**Wildrose Bar & Restaurant** 1021 E Pike St (at 11th) 206/324-9210 • 3pm-2am, 5pm-midnight Mon • mostly women • neighborhood bar • dancing/DJ • karaoke • live shows • food served • wheelchair access

## NIGHTCLUBS

**The Can Can** 93 Pike St #307 (in the Pike Place Market) 206/652-0832 • 6pm-2am • gay/ straight • food served • cabaret

**Contour** 807 1st Ave (at Columbia) 206/447-7704 • 3pm-2am, till 6am Fri-Sat • gay-friendly • fire performances • dancing/DJ • also bar & restaurant

**Dimitriou's Jazz Alley** 2033 6th Ave (at Lenora) 206/441-9729 • gay-friendly • call for events & reservations • live music • nonsmoking • cover charge • also restaurant

**Girl4Girl Productions** • mostly women • dancing/DJ • live shows • go-go dancers • check girl4girlseattle.com for info

**Neighbours Dance Club** 1509 Broadway (btwn Pike & Pine) 206/324-5358 • 9pm-2am, till 3am Th, till 4am Fri-Sat • popular • lesbians/ gay men • dancing/DJ • 2 flrs • also 18+ room Th-Sat • young crowd • wheelchair access

**Purr** 1518 11th Ave (at Pike St) 206/325-3112 • 4pm-2am, from noon wknds • mostly gay men • karaoke * Mexican-inspired food

**Re-bar** 1114 Howell (at Boren Ave) 206/233-9873 • 10pm-2am, clsd Mon • popular • gay/ straight • more women Sat • dancing/DJ Wed-Sun • cabaret/ theater

**Showbox** 1426 1st Ave (at Pike) 206/628-3151 • gay-friendly • live music venue

## CAFES

**The Allegro** 4214 University Wy NE (at NE 42nd St) 206/633-3030 • 7am-10:30pm • WiFi

**Cafe Besalu** 5909 24th Ave NW 206/789-1463 • 7am-3pm, clsd Mon-Tue • great pastries

**Espresso Vivace** 532 Broadway Ave 206/860-5869 • 6am-11pm • popular • WiFi

**Fuel Coffee** 610 19th Ave E 206/329-4700 • 6am-9pm • WiFi

**Kaladi Brothers Coffee** 511 E Pike St (at Summit) 206/388-1700 • 6am-9pm, from 8am wknds • WiFi

**Louisa's** 2379 Eastlake Ave E 206/325-0081 • 7am-9pm, till 10pm Fri-Sat, 8am-3pm Sun

## RESTAURANTS

**Al Boccalino** 1 Yesler Wy (at Alaskan) **206/622-7688** • lunch Tue-Fri, dinner nightly • classy southern Italian

**Bamboo Garden** 364 Roy St (at Mercer St) **206/282-6616** • 11am-10pm • Chinese vegetarian & kosher

**Cafe Flora** 2901 E Madison St **206/325-9100** • lunch, dinner, wknd brunch • vegetarian • beer/ wine • wheelchair accessible

**Canlis** 2576 Aurora Ave N **206/283-3313** • dinner only • fancy seafood

**Dahlia Lounge** 2001 4th Ave (at Virginia) **206/682-4142** • lunch Mon-Fri, dinner nightly, wknd brunch • some veggie • full bar

**Dick's Drive In** 115 Broadway E (at Denny) **206/323-1300** • 10:30am-2am • excellent fries & shakes

**Flying Fish** 300 Westlake Ave N **206/728-8595** • lunch Mon-Fri, dinner nightly, bar till 2am • lesbian chef

**Fresh Bistro** 4725 42nd Ave SW (btwn Alaska St & Edmunds) **206/935-3733** • dinner Mon-Sat, lunch Wed-Fri, wknd brunch

**Glo's** 1621 E Olive Wy (at Summit Ave E) **206/324-2577** • 7am-3pm, midnight -4pm wknds • brkfst only • popular

**Grim's Provisions & Spirits** 1512 11th Ave **206/324-7467** • 3pm-2am, from 10am wkknds, Capitol Hill's most unique three level Restaurant

**Julia's** 300 Broadway E (at Thomas) **206/860-1818** • 8am-11pm, till midnight Fri-Sat • full bar • drag shows Sat

**Kabul** 2301 N 45th St **206/545-9000** • 5pm-9:30pm, till 10pm Fri-Sat • Afghan • some veggie

**Lola** 2000 4th Ave (at Virginia) **206/441-1430** • 6am-midnight, till 2am wknds • popular brunch

**Mama's Mexican Kitchen** 2234 2nd Ave (in Belltown) **206/728-6262** • lunch & dinner • cheap & funky

**Paseo** 4225 Fremont Ave N (at N 43rd St) **206/545-7440** • 11am-9pm, clsd Sun-Mon • Cuban

**Queen City Grill** 2201 1st Ave (at Blanchard) **206/443-0975** • dinner only • popular • fresh seafood • some veggie • full bar • wheelchair access

**Restaurant Zoe** 2137 2nd Ave (at Blanchard) **206/256-2060** • dinner only

**Saint John's Bar & Eatery** 719 E Pike St (at Harvard Ave) **206/245-1390** • 2pm-2am, from 10am wknds

**Snappy Dragon** 8917 Roosevelt Wy NE **206/528-5575** • 11am-9:30pm, 4pm-9pm Sun • Chinese

**Spinasse** 1531 14th Ave E **206/251-7673** • clsd Tue, traditional cuisine of the Piedmont region of Northern Italy

**Sunlight Cafe** 6403 Roosevelt Wy NE (at 64th) **206/522-9060** • 8am-9pm • vegetarian • beer/ wine • wheelchair access

**Szmania's** 3321 W McGraw St (in Magnolia Bluff) **206/284-7305** • dinner nightly • full bar

**Tamarind Tree** 1036 S Jackson St **206/860-1404** • 10am-10pm, till midnight Fri-Sat • Vietnamese

**Teapot Vegetarian House** 345 15th Ave E **206/325-1010** • 11am-10pm • vegan

**Thaiger Room** **206/632-9299** • 11am-10pm, from noon wknds • Thai

**Wild Ginger Asian Restaurant & Triple Bar** 1401 3rd Ave (at Union) **206/623-4450** • lunch Mon-Sat, dinner nightly • popular • bar till 1am

**Wild Mountain** 1408 NW 85th St **206/297-9453** • 8:30am-9pm, clsd Tue • woman-owned

## ENTERTAINMENT & RECREATION

**Alki Beach Park** 1702 Alki Ave SW, West Seattle • popular on warm days

**Garage** 1130 Broadway **206/322-2296** • 3pm-2am • popular • way-cool pool hall • food served • full bar • ladies 1/2 price Sun • also bowling alley • 21+

**Northwest Lesbian & Gay History Museum Project** • exhibits & publication

**Rat City Roller Girls** **206/599-9613** • Seattle's female roller derby league • visit www.ratcityrollergirls.com for events

**Richard Hugo House** 1634 11th Ave **206/322-7030** • noon-6pm, till 5pm Sat, clsd Sun • houses the Zine Archive & Publishing Project • open later for events • also cafe & cabaret

**The Vera Project** corner of Warren Ave N & Republican St (in Seattle Center) **206/956-8372** • queer-friendly • all-ages music arts center

## BOOKSTORES

**Elliott Bay Book Company** 1521 10th Ave **206/624-6600, 800/962-5311** • 10am-10pm, till 11pm Fri-Sat, till 9pm Sun

**Left Bank Books** 92 Pike St (at 1st Ave) 206/622-0195 • 10am-7pm, 11am-6pm Sun • worker-owned collective

### RETAIL SHOPS

**Broadway Market** 401 Broadway E (at Harrison & Republican) • popular mall full of funky, hip stores

**Lifelong Thrift** 1002 E Seneca 206/328-8979 • all sales from donated items fund Lifelong AIDS

**Metropolis** 7321 Greenwood Ave N 206/782-7002 • 10am-6pm, 11am-4pm Sun, clsd Mon cards & gifts

**Two Big Blondes** 2501 S Jackson St (at 25th Ave) 206/762-8620 • 11am-6pm, clsd Sun-Mon • gay/ straight • transgender-friendly • consignment women's clothing for plus sizes • lesbian-owned

### PUBLICATIONS

**The Seattle Lesbian** 206/714-2277 • LGBT online magazine

**SGN (Seattle Gay News)** 206/324-4297 • weekly LGBT newspaper

**The Stranger** 206/323-7101 • queer-positive alternative weekly

### GYMS & HEALTH CLUBS

**Hothouse Spa & Sauna** 1019 E Pike St (at 11th, 2 blocks E of Broadway) 206/568-3240 • noon-midnight, clsd Tue • women only • baths • hot tub • massage

### EROTICA

**Babeland** 707 E Pike (btwn Harvard & Boylston) 206/328-2914 • 11am-10pm, noon-7pm Sun • wheelchair access • lesbian-owned

**Castle Megastore** 206 Broadway Ave E 206/204-0126

## Sequim

### ACCOMMODATIONS

**Sunset Marine Resort** 40 Buzzard Ridge Rd 360/591-4303 • gay-friendly • waterfront cabins • nonsmoking • kids ok • lesbian-owned

## Spokane

### INFO LINES & SERVICES

**AA Gay/ Lesbian** 1700 W 7th Ave #100 509/624-1442 • call for meeting times

### ACCOMMODATIONS

**The Davenport** 10 S Post St 509/455-8888, 800/899-1482 • gay-friendly • pool • WiFi

### RESTAURANTS

**Mizuna** 214 N Howard 509/747-2004 • lunch Mon-Fri, dinner nightly • seasonal menu • plenty veggie • full bar

### BOOKSTORES

**Auntie's Bookstore** 402 W Main Ave (at Washington) 509/838-0206 • 9am-9pm, 11am-6pm Sun-Mon • wheelchair access

## Suquamish

### INFO LINES & SERVICES

**Kitsap Lesbian/ Gay AA** 18732 Division Ave NE (at Congregational Church of Christ) 360/475-0775, 800/562-7455 • 7pm Sun

## Tacoma

### INFO LINES & SERVICES

**AA Gay/ Lesbian** 759 S 45th St (at MCC) 253/474-8897 • 7:30pm Fri

**Rainbow Center** 741 St Helens Ave 253/383-2318 • 1pm-5pm Mon-Fri, till 4pm Sat • community & resource center

**Tacoma Lesbian Concern** 253/777-3357 • social events • resource list • newsletter

### ACCOMMODATIONS

**Chinaberry Hill** 302 Tacoma Ave N 253/272-1282 • gay-friendly • 1889 Victorian inn • also cottage • full brkfst • fireplaces • kids ok • nonsmoking • WiFi

**Hotel Murano** 1320 Broadway Plaza (at S 15th) 253/238-8000, 866/986-8083 • gay-friendly • restaurants & bars • WiFi • wheelchair access

### BARS

**The Mix** 635 St Helens Ave 253/383-4327 • 2pm-2am • lesbians/gay men, ladies night Tue • karaoke

### NIGHTCLUBS

**Club Silverstone** 739 1/2 St Helens Ave (at 9th) 253/404-0273 • 11am-2am • lesbians/ gay men • neighborhood bar • dancing/DJ • karaoke

### CAFES

**Shakabrah Java Cafe** 253/572-2787 • 7am-4pm, from 8am Sun • wheelchair access

### EROTICA

**Castle Megastore** 6015 Tacoma Mall Blvd 253/471-0391

## Vancouver

see also Portland, Oregon

## Whidbey Island

### ACCOMMODATIONS

**Whidwood Inn** 360/720–6228 • gay/ straight • near historic Coupeville • nonsmoking • hot tub • gay-owned

## Winthrop

### ACCOMMODATIONS

**Chewuch Inn** 223 White Ave **509/996–3107, 800/747–3107** • gay-friendly • inn & cabins • E of N Cascades Mtns • hot tub • kids ok • nonsmoking • WiFi • wheelchair access

## WEST VIRGINIA

## Statewide

### PUBLICATIONS

**Out** 724/733–0828 • Pittsburgh's only LGBTQ newspaper since 1973! news, local events, classifieds & more for Western & Central PA, OH & WV

## Charleston

### BARS

**Broadway** 210 Leon Sullivan Wy (at Lee) **304/343–2162** • 12:30pm-3am • mostly gay men • dancing/DJ • live shows

### NIGHTCLUBS

**Atmosphere Ultra Lounge** 706 Lee St **304/343–3737** • 5pm-2am, clsd Mon • lesbians/ gay men • dancing/DJ • drag shows

### ENTERTAINMENT & RECREATION

**Living AIDS Memorial Garden** corner of Washington St E (at Sidney Ave) **304/346–0246**

### BOOKSTORES

**Taylor Books** 226 Capitol St **304/342–1461** • 7:30am-8pm, till 10pm Fri, 9am-10pm Sat, till 3pm Sun • WiFi • also cafe, art gallery & boutique

## Harpers Ferry

### ACCOMMODATIONS

**Laurel Lodge** 844 Ridge St **304/535–2886** • gay-friendly • bungalow overlooking Potomac River gorge • full brkfst • nonsmoking • WiFi • gay-owned

**Laurel Lodge** 844 Ridge St **304/535–2886** • gay-friendly • bungalow overlooking Potomac River gorge • full brkfst • nonsmoking • WiFi • gay-owned

## Huntington

### ACCOMMODATIONS

**Pullman Plaza Hotel** 1001 3rd Ave (at 10th St) **304/525–1001, 866/613–3611** • gay-friendly • full brkfst • pool • nonsmoking • WiFi • wheelchair access

### BARS

**Club Deception** 1037 7th Ave (at 11th St) **304/522–3146** • 5pm-2am • mostly gay men • dancing/DJ • live shows • karaoke • private club • wheelchair access

**The Stonewall** 820 7th Ave (enter in alley) **304/523–2444** • 8pm-3am, clsd Mon-Tue • popular • lesbians/ gay men • dancing/DJ • karaoke • live shows • wheelchair access • gay-owned

### RESTAURANTS

**Sharkey's** 410 10th St **304/523–3200** • 4pm-2:30am, clsd Sun • full bar • karaoke

## Lost River

### ACCOMMODATIONS

**Guest House at Lost River** 288 Settlers Valley Wy (at Mill Gap Rd) **304/897–5707** • lesbians/ gay men • full brkfst • also fine-dining restaurant • full bar • pool • hot tub • gym • nonsmoking • WiFi • gay-owned

### RESTAURANTS

**Lost River Grill & Motel** St Rd 259 **304/897–6482** • 11:45am-9pm, 8am-10pm Sat, 4pm-9pm Mon • full bar • also motel & cabins

**Lost River Trading Post** 295 E. Main St, Wardensville **304/874–3300** • 12pm-7pm Fri, 10am-6pm Sat-Sun • antiques and cafe

## Martinsburg

### EROTICA

**Variety Books & Video** 255 N Queen St (at Race) **304/263–4334** • 24hrs

## Morgantown

### NIGHTCLUBS

**Vice Versa** 335 High St (enter rear) **304/292–2010** • 8pm-3am Th-Sun • lesbians/ gay men • dancing/DJ • karaoke • live shows • private club • 18+ • wheelchair access

## Wheeling

### EROTICA

**Market St News** 1437 Market St (at 14th St) **304/232–2414** • 24hrs, till midnight Sun-Mon

## WISCONSIN

### Algoma

RETAIL SHOPS

**The Flying Pig** N6975 Hwy 42 (at Tenth) 920/487–9902 • 10am-5pm May-Oct, call for hrs off season • art gallery & coffee bar • lesbian-owned

### Appleton

BARS

**Rascals Bar & Grill** 702 E Wisconsin Ave (at Lawe) 920/954–9262 • 5pm-2am, from noon Sun • lesbians/ gay men, ladies night Wed • fish-fry Fri • patio

EROTICA

**Eldorado's** 2545 S Memorial Dr (at Hwys 47 & 441) 920/830–0042

### Eau Claire

INFO LINES & SERVICES

**LGBT Community Center of the Chippewa Valley** 1305 Woodland Ave 715/552–5428 • drop-in 7pm-10pm Fri, call for other hours • library & variety of events

NIGHTCLUBS

**Scooters** 411 Galloway (at Farwell) 715/835–9959 • 3pm-2am • lesbians/ gay men • dancing/DJ • karaoke • drag shows • wheelchair access

### Green Bay

INFO LINES & SERVICES

**Gay AA** 920/432–2600 • call for times & locations

BARS

**Napalese Lounge** 1351 Cedar St 920/432–9646 • 11am-close • mostly gay men • neighborhood bar • DJ Fri-Sat • food served • drag shows • wheelchair access

**Roundabout** 1264 Main St 920/544–9544 • 2pm-2am • lesbians/ gay men

NIGHTCLUBS

**Club XS** 1106 Main St • 7pm-2am • lesbians/ gay men • dancing/DJ

**The Shelter** 730 N Quincy St (at 54302) 920/432–2662 • lesbians/ gay men • dancing/DJ • country/ western • transgender-friendly • food served • karaoke • drag shows • gay-owned

EROTICA

**Lion's Den Adult Superstore** 836 S Broadway (at 5th) 920/433–9640

### Kenosha

**see also Racine**

BARS

**Club Icon** 6305 120th Ave (on E Frontage road of I-94) 262/857–3240 • 7pm-2am, from 3pm Sun, clsd Mon • lesbians/ gay men • dancing/DJ • drag shows

### La Crosse

ACCOMMODATIONS

**Rainbow Ridge Farms B&B** N 5732 Hauser Rd (at County S), Onalaska 608/783–8181, 888/347–2594 • gay-friendly • working hobby farm on 35 acres • WiFi • nonsmoking

BARS

**Chances R** 417 Jay St (at 4th) 608/782–5105 • 3pm-close • lesbians/ gay men • neighborhood bar

**My Place** 3201 South Ave (at East Ave) 608/788–9073 • 3pm-close, from noon wknds • lesbians/ gay men • friendly neighborhood bar • games • gay-owned

**Players** 300 S 4th St (at Jay St) 608/784–4200 • 5pm-2am, from 3pm Fri-Sun, till 2:30am Fri-Sat • popular • lesbians/ gay men • dancing/DJ • transgender-friendly • wheelchair access • gay-owned

EROTICA

**Pleasures** 405 S 3rd 608/784–6350 • DVDs • toys • magazines • lingerie

### Madison

INFO LINES & SERVICES

**OutReach, Inc** 600 Williamson St #P-1 608/255–8582 • 10am-7pm, noon-4pm Sat, clsd Sun

BARS

**Five Nightclub** 5 Applegate Ct (btwn Fish Hatchery Rd & W Beltline Hwy) 608/277–9700, 877/648–9700 • 4pm-2am, from 2pm Sun • popular • lesbians/ gay men • dancing/DJ • karaoke • live shows

**Green Bush** 914 Regent St (at Park) 608/257–2874 • 4pm-midnight, clsd Sun • gay-friendly • also Sicilian restaurant

**Shamrock Bar & Grill** 117 W Main St (at Fairchild) **608/259-8480** • 11am-2am • lesbians/ gay men • popular

**Woof's** 114 King St (on Capitol Sq) **608/204-6222** • 4pm-2am, from noon Sun • lesbians/ gay men • neighborhood bar • leather/ levi • dancing/DJ • food served

### NIGHTCLUBS

**Cardinal** 418 E Wilson St (at S Franklin) **608/257-2473** • 7pm-2am, from 4pm Fri • gay/ straight • dancing/DJ • live music

**Plan B** 924 Williamson St **608/257-5262** • 4pm-2am, from 9pm Sun, clsd Mon • lesbians/ gay men • dancing/DJ • karaoke • 1st & 3rd Fri women's night • Th 18+

**Sotto** 303 N Henry St • 9pm-2am, clsd Sun-Wed • lesbians/ gay men • dancing/DJ, best sound system in the city

### CAFES

**Java Cat** 3918 Monona Dr (at Cottage Grove Rd) **608/223-5553** • 6am-8pm, 7am-8pm Sat-Sun • light food served • WiFi

### RESTAURANTS

**Fromagination** 12 S Carroll (on Capital Sq) **608/255-2430** • 9:30am-6pm, 9am-5pm Sat, clsd Sun

**La Hacienda** 515 S Park St **608/255-8227** • 9am-3am • popular • Mexican • post–Club 5 spot

**Monty's Blue Plate Diner** 2089 Atwood Ave (at Winnebago) **608/244-8505** • 7am-9pm, till 10pm wknds • some veggie • beer/ wine • wheelchair access

### BOOKSTORES

**A Room of One's Own Feminist Books & Gifts** 315 W Gorham St **608/257-7888** • 10am-8pm, till 8pm Sat, noon-5pm Sun • wheelchair access

### PUBLICATIONS

**Our Lives** • LGBT publication • www.ourlivesmadison.com

### EROTICA

**A Woman's Touch** 600 Williamson (at Gateway Mall) **608/250-1928, 888/621-8880** • 11am-6pm, till 8pm Tue-Th, till 7pm Fri-Sat, noon-5pm Sun • wheelchair access

**Red Letter News** 2528 E Washington (btwn North & Milwaukee) **608/241-9958**

## Milwaukee

### INFO LINES & SERVICES

**AA Galano Club** 315 W Court #201 (in LGBT Community Center) **414/276-6936**

**Milwaukee LGBT Community Center** 1110 N Market St, 2nd Fl **414/271-2656** • 10am-10pm, from 6pm Sat, till 5pm Mon, clsd Sun

### ACCOMMODATIONS

**Ambassador Hotel** 2308 W Wisconsin Ave (at N 24th) **414/345-5000, 888/322-3326** • gay/ straight • nonsmoking • WiFi • wheelchair access

**The Brumder Mansion** 3046 W Wisconsin Ave (at N 31st) **414/342-9767, 866/793-3676** • gay-friendly • full brkfst • nonsmoking • WiFi

**Hotel of the Arts/ Days Inn** 1840 N 6th St (at Reservoir Ave) **414/265-5629** • gay-friendly • nonsmoking • WiFi

**The Iron Horse Hotel** 500 W Florida St (at S 5th St) **888/543-4766** • gay-friendly hotel geared toward motorcycle enthusiasts

**The Milwaukee Hilton** 509 W Wisconsin Ave (at 5th St) **414/271-7250, 800/445-8667** • gay-friendly • also restaurant & pub • pool • WiFi • wheelchair access

### BARS

**Art Bar** 722 E Burleigh St (at Fratney) **414/372-7880** • 3pm-2am, from 10am wknds • live entertainment • WiFi • gay-owned

**D.I.X.** 739 S 1st St (at National) **414/231-9085** • 4pm-2am, from noon Sun • mostly gay men • videos

**Fluid** 819 S 2nd St (at W National) **414/643-5843** • 5pm-close, from 3pm Fri, from 2pm wknds • mostly gay men • neighborhood bar

**Hamburger Mary's Milwaukee** 2130 Kinnickinnic **414/988-9324** • 11am-10pm, 10am-midnight wknds • food served • drag shows • karaoke

**Hybrid Lounge** 707 E Brady (at Van Buren) **414/810-1809** • 4pm-close, from 10am Sat-Sun • mostly gay men

**The Nomad** 1401 E Brady St (at Warren) **414/224-8111** • 2pm-2am, from noon wknds • gay-friendly • soccer pub

**Taylor's** 795 N Jefferson St (at Wells) **414/271-2855** • 4pm-close • gay/ straight • neighborhood bar • patio • wheelchair access • gay-owned

**Two** 718 E Burleigh St (at Fratney) / • 7pm-close Wed-Sat • gay/ straight

**Walker's Pint** 818 S 2nd St (at National Ave) 414/643-7468 • 4:30pm-2am, from noon Sun • mostly women • neighborhood bar • dancing/DJ • live shows • karaoke • patio • WiFi • lesbian-owned

**Woody's** 1579 S 2nd St (at Lapham St) 414/672-0806 • 4pm-close, from 2pm wknds • mostly men • neighborhood sports bar • WiFi

## NIGHTCLUBS

**La Cage/ ETC/Montage Lounge** 801 S 2nd St (at National) 414/383-8330 • 6pm-close, from 10pm Fri-Sat • mostly gay men • dancing/DJ • live shows • videos • wheelchair access

## CAFES

**Alterra Coffee Roasters** 2211 N Prospect Ave (at North) 414/273-3753 • 7am-6pm

**Bella Caffe** 189 N Milwaukee St 414/273-5620 • 6am-9pm, till 11pm Fri-Sat, 8am-6pm Sun

**Fuel Cafe** 818 E Center St 414/374-3835 • 7am-10pm, from 8am wknds• WiFi • wheelchair access

## RESTAURANTS

**Beans & Barley** 1901 E North Ave (at Oakland Ave) 414/278-7878 • 8am-9pm • vegetarian cafe & deli

**Coquette Cafe** 316 N Milwaukee St (btwn Buffalo & St Paul) 414/291-2655 • 11am-10pm, till 11pm Fri, 5pm-11pm Sat, 11am-5pm Sun • bistro fare

**Crisp Pizza Bar & Lounge** 1323 E Brady St 414/727-4217 • 4pm-2am, from 11:30am wknds • also full bar

**Harvey's** 1340 W Towne Sq Rd, Mequon 262/241-9589 • dinner nightly • cont'l

**Honeypie Cafe** 2643 S Kinnickinnic Ave (at Potter) 414/489-7437 • 10am-10pm, from 9am wknds, till 9pm Sun • homemade midwestern classics

**The Knick** 1030 E Juneau Ave (at Waverly) 414/272-0011 • 11am-midnight, from 9am wknds • popular • some veggie • full bar • wheelchair access

**La Perla** 734 S 5th St (at National) 414/645-9888 • 11am-10pm, till 11:30pm Fri-Sat • Mexican • also bar

**Lulu** 2261 & 2265 S Howell Ave 414/294-5858 • 11am-2am • also bar till late • live music wknds

**Meritage** 5921 W Vliet St 414/479-0620 • 5pm-10pm, till 11pm Fri-Sat, till 9pm Mon, clsd Sun • American

**Range Line Inn** 2635 W Mequon Rd, Mequon 262/242-0530 • 4:30pm-10pm, clsd Sun-Mon • reservations recommended

**Sanford Restaurant** 1547 N Jackson St 414/276-9608 • dinner only, clsd Sun • Milwaukee fine dining Euro-style

## ENTERTAINMENT & RECREATION

**Boerner Botanical Gardens** 9400 Boerner Dr (in Whitnall Park), Hales Corners 414/525-5600, 414/525-5601 • 8am-dusk • 40-acre garden & arboretum, garden clsd in winter

**Harley-Davidson Museum** 400 Canal St (at N 6th St) 877/287-2789

**Mitchell Park Domes** 524 S Layton Blvd (27th St, at Pierce) 414/257-5611 • 9am-5pm, till 4pm wknd • botanical gardens

**Off the Wall Theatre** 127 E Wells St 414/327-3552 • alternative theatre group

## BOOKSTORES

**OutWords Books, Gifts & Coffee** 2710 N Murray Ave (at Park Pl) 414/963-9089 • 11am-7pm, till 8pm Fri-Sat, noon-6pm Sun • pride items • wheelchair access

**Peoples' Books Co-op** 804 E Center 414/962-0575 • 10am-6pm, noon-4pm Sun

**Woodland Pattern** 720 E Locust St 414/263-5001 • 11am-8pm, noon-5pm wknds, clsd Mon

## EROTICA

**Booked Solid** 7035 W Greenfield Ave (at 70th), West Allis 414/774-7210

# Neenah

## BARS

**ReMixx** 8386 State Road 76 920/725-6483 • 4pm-11pm, till 2:30am Fri-Sat, from 11am Sun, clsd Mon-Tue • lesbians/gay men • neighborhod bar • dancing/DJ • lesbian-owned

# Norwalk

## ACCOMMODATIONS

**Daughters of the Earth** 18134 Index Ave 608/269-5301 • women only • women's land • camping • retreat space • lesbian-owned

## Oshkosh

### BARS

**Deb's Spare Time** 1303 Harrison St (btwn Main & New York) **920/235–6577** • 11am-2am, from 9am wknds • lesbians/ gay men• neighborhood bar • food served • live shows • 18+ • gay-owned

## Racine

### INFO LINES & SERVICES

**LGBT Center of SE Wisconsin** 1456 Junction Ave **262/664-4100** • noon-6pm, 10:30pm-1pm Sat, clsd Sun

### BARS

**Brass Monkey** 1436 Junction Ave • 2pm-2am • gay/straight • neighbor hood bar

## Sheboygan

### BARS

**The Blue Lite** 1029 N 8th St (off Rte 143) **920/457-1636** • 7pm-close, from 3pm Sun • lesbians/ gay men • neighborhood bar • dancing/DJ Fri-Sat

## Sturgeon Bay

### ACCOMMODATIONS

**The Chanticleer Guest House** 4072 Cherry Rd **920/746-0334, 866/682-0384** • popular • gay-friendly • on 70 acres • pool • WiFi • nonsmoking • wheelchair access • gay-owned

## Superior

### BARS

**The Flame** 1612 Tower Ave **715/395-0101** • 3pm-2:30am • lesbians/ gay men • dancing/DJ • live entertainment • karaoke • drag shows • WiFi

**The Main Club** 1217 Tower Ave (at 12th) **715/392-1756** • 3pm-2am • mostly gay men • dancing/DJ • live shows • WiFi • wheelchair access

## Wascott

### ACCOMMODATIONS

**Wilderness Way** 715/466-2635 • lesbians/ gay men • cabins • camping/RV • swimming • kids ok • nonsmoking • wheelchair access • lesbian-owned

## Wausau

### NIGHTCLUBS

**Oz** 320 Washington **715/842–3225** • 7pm-close • mostly gay men • dancing/DJ • karaoke • drag shows • videos

## Wisconsin Dells

### ACCOMMODATIONS

**Rainbow Valley Resort** 4124 River Rd **608/253–1818, 866/553-1818** • lesbians/ gay men • cabins & rooms on 24 acres • pool • WiFi • restaurant & bar

### BARS

**Captain Dix** 4124 River Rd (at Rainbow Valley Resort) **608/253-1818** • 6pm-close, from 11am wknds • lesbians/ gay men • karaoke • also accommodations

# WYOMING

## Cheyenne

see also Fort Collins, Colorado

### INFO LINES & SERVICES

**Wyoming Equality/ United Gays & Lesbians of Wyoming** 307/778-7645 • 10am-2pm Mon-Fri • info • referrals • newsletter • social activities • also youth services

## Etna

### RETAIL SHOPS

**Blue Fox Studio & Gallery** 107452 N US Hwy 89 307/883-3310 • open 7 days • hours vary • pottery, jewelry & mask studio • local travel info • gay-owned

## Evanston

### EROTICA

**Romantix Adult Superstore** 1939 Harrison Dr 307/789-0800 • 7am-2am

## Laramie

### ACCOMMODATIONS

**Cowgirl Horse Hotel** 32 Black Elk Trail **307/745-8794 OR 399-2502** • specializing in women travelers & their horses • men welcome

### BOOKSTORES

**The Second Story** 105 Ivinson Ave **307/745-4423** • 10am-6pm, clsd Sun • independent

## ALBERTA

## Calgary

### INFO LINES & SERVICES

**Front Runners AA** 1227 Kensington Close NW (at Hillhurst United Church) **403/777–1212** • 8:30pm Wed & Sat

### ACCOMMODATIONS

**Calgary Westways Guest House** 216 25th Ave SW **403/229–1758, 866/846–7038** • gay/ straight • full brkfst • hot tub • nonsmoking • pets ok • WiFi • gay-owned

### BARS

**The Back Lot** 209 10th Ave SW (at 1st St SW) **403/265–5211** • 2pm-2am • mostly gay men • martini lounge • patio • wheelchair access

**Ming** 520 17th Ave SW **403/229–1986** • 4pm-2am • gay-friendly • martini lounge • food served

### NIGHTCLUBS

**Backwards Night Club** 628 8th Ave **403/922–4043** • gay/straight • dancing/DJ • massive multi-floor venue in the heart of the downtown

**GirlsGroove** • women's dance parties • check local listings for upcoming events • www.girlsgroove.ca

**Lolita's** 1413 9th Ave SE **403/265–5739** • cabaret/ performance club • also restaurant

**Twisted Element** 1006 11th Ave SW **403/802–0230** • 9pm-close • mostly men • dancing/DJ • karaoke • drag shows • strippers • WiFi

### CAFES

**Caffe Beano** 1613 9th St SW (at 17th Ave) **403/229–1232** • 6am-midnight, from 7am wknds • some veggie • wheelchair access

### RESTAURANTS

**Halo** 13226 Macleod Trail SE **403/271–4111** • lunch & dinner • steak, seafood & wine bar

**Thai Sa-On** 351 10th Ave SW (at 4th) **403/264–3526** • lunch & dinner, clsd Sun

### BOOKSTORES

**Daily Globe News Shop** 1004 17th Ave SW (at 10th St) **403/244–2060** • 9am-10pm • periodicals

### PUBLICATIONS

**Gay Calgary & Edmonton Magazine** **888/543–6960** • monthly LGBT publication

## Edmonton

### INFO LINES & SERVICES

**AA Gay/ Lesbian** 11355 Jasper Ave (at church) **780/424–5900** • 7:30pm Mon • also 8pm Fri at 10804 119th St

**Pride Centre of Edmonton** 10608 105 Ave **780/488–3234** • noon-9pm, 2pm-6:30pm Sat, clsd Sun-Mon

**Womonspace** 9540 111 Ave (Pride Centre of Edmonton) **780/482–1794** • social & recreational society • dances & other events • monthly newsletter

### ACCOMMODATIONS

**Labyrinth Lake Lodge** **780/878–3301** • gay/ straight • lodge on private lake • hot tubs • kids/ pets ok • nonsmoking • WiFi

**Northern Lights B&B** **780/483–1572** • lesbians/ gay men • full brkfst • pool • nonsmoking • gay-owned

### BARS

**Woody's Pub & Cafe** 11723 A Jasper (above Buddy's) **780/488–6557** • 3pm-midnight, from noon-3am wknds • lesbians/ gay men • neighborhood bar • food served • karaoke

### NIGHTCLUBS

**Evolution** 10220 103 St NW **780/424–0077** • 6pm-2am, 8pm-3am Sat, 4pm-midnight Sun • mostly gay men • dancing/DJ 8 drag shows • karaoke

### PUBLICATIONS

**Gay Calgary & Edmonton Magazine** Calgary **888/543–6960** • monthly LGBT publication

## Westerose

### ACCOMMODATIONS

**Pine Trails Getaway** RR1 **780/586–0002** • gay campground • pets ok

## BRITISH COLUMBIA

## Birken

### ACCOMMODATIONS

**Birken Lakeside Resort** 9179 Portage Rd **604/452–3255** • gay-friendly • cabins • campsites • hot tub • swimming • pets ok • lesbian-owned

## Chilliwack

### Restaurants

**Bravo Restaurant & Lounge** 46224 Yale Rd (at Nowell St) **604/792–7721** • 5pm-close, clsd Sun-Tue • martinis • wheelchair access • gay-owned

## Gulf Islands

### Info Lines & Services

**Gays & Lesbians of Salt Spring Island (GLOSSI)** PO Box 644,, Salt Spring Island V8K 2W2 **250/537–7773** • social events • info line

### Accommodations

**Bellhouse Inn** 29 Farmhouse Rd, Galiano Island **250/539–5667, 800/970–7464** • gay/ straight • historic waterfront inn • full brkfst • nonsmoking • WiFi

**Birdsong B&B** 153 Rourke Rd, Salt Spring Island **250/537–4608** • gay/ straight • ocean & harbor views • WiFi

**Hummingbird Lodge B&B** 1597 Starbuck Ln (at Whalebone Dr), Gabriola **250/247–9300, 877/551–9383** • gay-friendly • nonsmoking

## Okanagan County

### Info Lines & Services

**Okanagan Rainbow Coalition** 1476 Water St, Kelowna **250/860–8555** • 24-hr recorded info • support groups • social events • dances

### Accommodations

**Creek View B&B** 1520 Pasadena Rd, Kelowna **250/862–3653** • gay/ straight • swimming • lesbian-owned • nonsmoking • WiFi

**Eagles Nest B&B** 15620 Commonage Rd (at Carrs Landing Rd), Kelowna **250/766–9350, 866/766–9350** • mostly men • overlooking Lake Okanagan • full brkfst • hot tub • nonsmoking • WiFi • gay-owned

### Cafes

**Bean Scene** 274 Bernard Ave, Kelowna **250/763–1814** • 6am-11pm, from 7:30am wknds • patio • wheelchair access

### Restaurants

**Greek House** 3159 Woodsdale Rd, Kelowna **250/766–0090** • 4pm-9pm • cont'l

## Prince George

### Info Lines & Services

**GALA North** **250/562–7124** • 24-hr recorded info • social group • call for drop-in hours & location

### Erotica

**Doctor Love** 1412 Patricia Blvd **250/614–1411**

## Tofino

### Accommodations

**Beachwood** 1368 Chesterman Beach Rd **250/725–4250** • gay-friendly • private apt • steps to the beach • nonsmoking • gay-owned

**BriMar B&B** 1375 Thornberg Crescent **250/725–3410, 800/714–9373** • gay/ straight • on the beach • full brkfst • teens ok

**Eagle Nook Wilderness Resort & Spa** Ucluelet **800/760–2777** • gay-friendly • private log cabins • gourmet meals • health spa

## Vancouver

### Info Lines & Services

**AA Gay/ Lesbian** **604/434–3933**

**The Greater Vancouver Pride Line** **604/684–6869 x290, 800/566–1170** • 7pm-10pm • info & support

**QMUNITY: BC's Resource Centre** 1170 Bute St (btwn Davie & Pendrell Sts) **604/684–5207, 800/566–1170** • also Out on the Shelves LGBT lending library

### Accommodations

**Barclay House B&B** 1351 Barclay St (at Jervis) **604/605–1351, 800/971–1351** • gay/ straight • full brkfst • nonsmoking • WiFi • gay-owned

**Granville B&B** 5050 Granville St (at 34th Ave) **604/739–9002, 866/739–9002** • gay-friendly • nonsmoking • WiFi

**L' Hermitage Hotel** 788 Richards St (at Robson) **778/327–4100** • gay/ straight • pool • nonsmoking • WiFi • wheelchair access

**The Listel Hotel** 1300 Robson Street (at Jervis) **604/684–8461, 800/663–5491** • gay-friendly • boutique hotel • restaurant & bar • swimming • hot tub • gym • nonsmoking • WiFi

**The Loden** 1177 Melville St **604/669–5060, 877/225 6336** • gay/straight • unique luxury boutique hotel • pets ok

**Moda Hotel** 900 Seymour St (at Smithe) **604/683-4251, 877/683-5522** • gay/ straight • restaurant • kids ok • WiFi • also 3 bars

**Nelson House B&B** 977 Broughton St (btwn Nelson & Barclay) **604/684-9793, 866/684-9793** • lesbians/ gay men • full brkfst • jacuzzi in suite • sundeck • WiFi • lesbian- & gay-owned

**"O Canada" House B&B** 1114 Barclay St (at Thurlow) **604/688-0555, 877/688-1114** • gay/ straight • restored 1897 Victorian home • full brkfst • WiFi • gay-owned

**Opus Hotel** 322 Davie St (at Hamilton, Yaletown) **604/642-6787, 866/642-6787** • gay-friendly • hip luxury boutique hotel • also bar & restaurant wheelchair access

**The Sutton Place Hotel** 845 Burrard St (at Smithe) **604/682-5511, 866/378-8866** • gay-friendly • luxurious boutique hotel • nonsmoking • WiFi • pool

**The West End Guest House** 1362 Haro St (at Broughton) **604/681-2889, 888/546-3327** • gay/ straight • full brkfst • nonsmoking • gay-owned

## BARS

**1181** 1181 Davie St (at Bute) **604/687-3991** • 6pm-3am • mostly gay men • upscale cocktail lounge

**The Fountainhead Pub** 1025 Davie St (at Burrard) **604/687-2222** • 11am-midnight, till 2am Fri-Sat • wknd brunch • lesbians/ gay men • neighborhood bar • transgender-friendly • patio

**Guilt and Company** 1 Alexander St (downstairs) **604/288-1704** • 7pm-1am • gay/straight • live shows 8 infused drinks and homemade beef jerky

## NIGHTCLUBS

**816 Granville/ The World** 816 Granville St • midnight-6am Fri-Sun • mostly gay men • dancing/DJ

**Club 23 West** 23 W Cordova (at Carrall) **604/839-5780** • 10pm-4am Fri-Sat • gay/ straight • dancing/DJ

**Crema** **604/875-9907** • women's dance party • www.cremaproductions.com

**Flygirl Productions** **604/839-9819** • women's parties • check www.flygirlproductions.com for details

**Hershe Bar** **604/839-9819** • long wknds only • mega lesbian dance party • check local listings for info

**The Junction** 1138 Davie St **604/669-2013** • 3pm-3am • mostly gay men • food served • dancing/DJ • patio

**The Odyssey** 688 W Hastings St **604/408-8802** • 10pm-3am, from 9pm Th-Sat, clsd Mon-Tue • lesbians/gay men • dancing/DJ

## CAFES

**Coming Home** 753 6th St (at 8th Ave), New Westminster **604/544-5018** • 9am--3pm, clsd Mon • gay-owned

**Delaney's** 1105 Denman St **604/662-3344** • 6am-9pm, from 6:30am wknds • coffee shop

**JJ Bean** 2206 Commercial Dr **604/254-3723** • 6am-10pm

**Rhizome Cafe** 317 E Broadway **604/872-3166** • 11am-10pm, till midnight Fri-Sat, till 3pm Sun, clsd Mon • plenty veggie/vegan • local artists • workshops

**Small Victory** 1088 Homer St **604/899-8892** • 7am-6pm, from 8am wknds • great coffee and bakery

**Sweet Revenge** 4160 Main St (at 26th) **604/879-7933** • 7pm-midnight, till 1am Fri-Sat • patisserie • gay-owned

## RESTAURANTS

**Bin 941 Tapas Parlor** 941 Davie St **604/683-1246** • 5pm-1am, till 2am Fri-Sun • cozy and intimate

**Brioche** 401 W Cordova (at Homer, in Gastown) **604/682-4037** • 7am-8:30pm, 8am-7:30pm wknds • Italian restaurant & bakery

**Cafe Deux Soleils** 2096 Commercial Dr **604/254-1195** • 8am-midnight, till 5pm Sun • lesbians/ gay men • vegetarian • live shows

**Cascade Room** 2616 Main St (at 10th) **604/709-8650** • 5pm-1am, from noon-2am wknds

**Chill Winston** 3 Alexander St **604/288-9575** • 11am-1am • in Gastown

**The Dish** 1068 Davie St **604/689-0208** • 7am-10pm, 9am-9pm Sun • veggie fast food • gay-owned

**Elbow Room Cafe** 560 Davie St (at Seymour) **604/685-3628** • 8am-4pm • great brkfst

**Foundation Lounge** 2301 Main St **604/708-0881** • noon-1am, till 2am wknds • vegetarian

**Hamburger Mary's** 1202 Davie St (at Bute) **604/687-1293** • 8am-3am, till 4am Fri-Sat, till 2am Sun • some veggie • full bar

**Havana** 1212 Commercial Dr **604/253–9119**
• 11am-11pm, from 10am wknds • popular •
Cuban fusion • full bar • patio • also gallery &
theater

**Lickerish** 903 Davie St (at Hornby)
**604/696–0725** • 5:30pm-midnight, till 1am Th-
Sun • global cuisine • cocktail lounge

**Lift Bar & Grill** 333 Menchions Mews
**604/689–5438** • 11:30am-midnight

**Lolita's** 1326 Davie St (at Jervis)
**604/696–9996** • 4:30pm till late, wknd brunch
• innovative Mexican • tiny space but worth
the wait

**Maenam** 1938 W 4th Ave **604/730–5579** •
lunch Tue-Sat, dinner 5pm-midnight • Thai

**Martini's Whole Wheat Pizza** 151 W
Broadway (btwn Cambie & Main)
**604/873–0021** • 11am-2am, from 2pm Sat, till
1am Sun • great pizza • full bar

**Miura Waffle Milk Bar** 829 Davie St
**604/687–2909** • 9am-7pm, from 10am Sat,
clsd Sun

**Naam** 2724 W 4th St (at MacDonald)
**604/738–7151** • 24hrs • vegetarian • live
music • wheelchair access

**Score** 1262 Davie St (at Jervis St)
**604/632–1646** • 11am-late • lesbians/gay
men • sports bar

**Seasons in the Park** Cambie St & W 33rd
Ave **604/874–8008** • from 11:30am, 10:30am
Sun

**Tanpopo Sushi** 1122 Denman (at Pendrell)
**604/681–7777** • lunch & dinner • excellent,
affordable sushi

## ENTERTAINMENT & RECREATION

**Capilano Suspension Bridge** 3735
Capilano Rd, N Vancouver **604/985–7474**

**Cruisey T** leaves from N foot of Denman St
(at Harbor Cruises) **604/551–2628** • Sun
(seasonal) • 4-hour party cruise around
Vancouver Harbour • lesbians/gay men •
dancing/DJ • live shows • food served

**Girl Gig Productions** **604/516–9696** •
women's performance promoters • popular
"Chicks With Picks" series •
www.girlgigproductions.com for info

**Rockwood Adventures** 6578 Acorn Rd,
Sechelt **604/741–0802, 888/236–6606** • rain
forest walks & city tours for all levels w/ free
hotel pickup

**Sunset Beach** Beach Ave, right in the West
End (near Burrard St Bridge) • home of
Vancouver AIDS memorial

**Vancouver Nature Adventures** 1251
Cardero St #2005 **604/684–4922,
800/528–3531** • orca-watching safari • guided
kayaking day trip & beach BBQ • no
experience required • free hotel pickup

**Wreck Beach** below UBC

## BOOKSTORES

**Little Sister's** 1238 Davie St (btwn Bute &
Jervis) **604/669–1753, 800/567–1662 (IN
CANADA ONLY)** • 10am-11pm • popular • LGBT
• wheelchair access

**People's Co-op Bookstore** 1391
Commercial Dr (btwn Kitchener & Charles)
**604/253–6442, 888/511–5556** • LGBT section

## RETAIL SHOPS

**Cupcakes** 1116 Denman St (at Pendrell)
**604/974–1300** • 10am-9pm, till 10pm Fri-Sat •
women-owned cupcake shop • also at 2887 W
Broadway

**Mintage** 1714 Commercial Dr **604/646–8243**
• vintage & future fashions • woman-owned

**Next Body Piercing** 1068 Granville St (at
Nelson) **604/684–6398** • noon-6pm, 11am-
7pm Fri-Sat • also tattooing

## PUBLICATIONS

**Xtra!** **604/684–9696** • LGBT newspaper

## GYMS & HEALTH CLUBS

**Fitness World** 1214 Howe St (at Davie)
**604/681–3232** • day passes

**Spartacus Gym** 1522 Commercial Dr
**604/254–6267**

## EROTICA

**The Love Nest** 119 East 1st St, North
Vancouver **604/987–1175** • 10am-6pm, till
8pm Th-Fri, noon-5pm Sun

**Love's Touch** 1069 Davie St **604/681–7024**

**Womyn's Ware** 896 Commercial Dr (at
Venables) **604/254–2543** • 11am-6pm, till
7pm Th-Fri, till 5:30pm Sun • toys • fetishwear
• lesbian-owned

# Victoria

## ACCOMMODATIONS

**Albion Manor B&B** 224 Superior St
**250/389–0012, 877/389–0012** • gay/straight •
full brkfst • nonsmoking • WiFi • wheelchair
access • gay-owned

**Dashwood Manor Seaside B&B Inn** 1 Cook St (at Dallas Rd) **250/385-5517, 800/667-5517** • gay/straight • heritage designated 1912 British Arts and Crafts Tudor Revival home with great views of the ocean • WiFi • gay-owned

**Inn at Laurel Point** 680 Montreal St (at Quebec St) **250/386-8721, 800/663-7667** • gay-friendly • restaurant • pool • WiFi • nonsmoking • kids/ pets OK • wheelchair access

**Oak Bay Guest House** 1052 Newport Ave **250/598-3812** • gay-friendly • 1912 Tudor-style house • full brkfst • near beaches • kids 10+ ok • nonsmoking

## Bars

**Paparazzi** 642 Johnson St (enter on Broad St) **250/388-0505** • 1pm-2am, till midnight Sun • lesbians/ gay men • dancing/DJ • karaoke • drag shows • videos • wheelchair access

## Nightclubs

**Hush** 1325 Government St (in basement) **250/385-0566** • 9pm-2am, clsd Sun-Tue • gay/ straight • dancing/DJ

## Restaurants

**Green Cuisine** 560 Johnson St #5 (in Market Square) **250/385-1809** • 10am-8pm • vegan • also juice bar & bakery

**Rosie's Diner** 253 Cook St **250/384-6090** • 8am-9pm • '50s & '60s music & videos • wheelchair access • gay-owned

**Santiago's Cafe** 660 Oswego St **250/388-7376** • 11am-9pm • tapas bar • patio • gay-owned

## Entertainment & Recreation

**Butchart Gardens** 800 Benvenuto Ave, Brentwood Bay **250/652-5256, 866/652-4422**

## Bookstores

**Bolen Books** 1644 Hillside Ave #111 (in shopping center) **250/595-4232** • 8:30am-10pm • LGBT section

## Retail Shops

**Oceanside Gifts** 812 Wharf St, Ste 102 (across from Empress Hotel on the lower causeway) **250/380-1777** • 10am-10pm • gifts from across Canada • wheelchair access

# Whistler

## Accommodations

**Best Western Listel Whistler Hotel** 4121 Village Green (at Whistler Way) **604/932-1133, 800/663-5472** • gay-friendly • pool • hot tub • nonsmoking • WiFi • wheelchair access

**Coast Blackcomb Suites at Whistler** 4899 Painted Cliff Rd **604/905-3400, 800/716-6199** • gay-friendly • full bar & restaurant • hot tub • pool • nonsmoking • wheelchair access

**Four Seasons Resort Whistler** 4591 Blackcomb Wy **604/935-3400, 800/268-6282** • gay-friendly • luxury resort & spa • pool • nonsmoking • wheelchair access

**Westin Whistler** 4090 Whistler Wy **604/905-5000, 800/937-8461** • gay-friendly • full-service resort • full bar & restaurant • spa • hot tub • pool • nonsmoking • WiFi • wheelchair access

## Restaurants

**Araxi** 4222 Village Square **604/932-4540** • lunch & dinner • local ingredients • also seafood bar & lounge

**The Bearfoot Bistro** 4121 Village Green **604/932-3433** • 6pm-midnight • excellent wine cellar • reservations recommended

**La Rua** 4557 Blackcomb Blvd **604/932-5011** • 6pm-close, clsd Tue

**Quattro** 4319 Main St **604/905-4844** • dinner nightly • Italian

**Sachi Sushi** 106-4359 Main St **604/935-5649** • lunch & dinner

**Southside Diner** 2102 Lake Placid Rd (off Hwy 99) **604/966-0668** • 7am-midnight • hosts occasional Gay Social

**Trattoria di Umberto** 4417 Sundial Pl **604/932-5858** • lunch & dinner • reservations recommended

## Entertainment & Recreation

➤**Whistler Pride and Ski Festival** • www.gaywhistler.com • last week of January

**Ziptrek Ecotours** PO Box 734 V0N 1B0 **604/935-0001, 866/935-0001** • ziplines crisscross the Fitzsimmons Creek btwn Whistler & Blackcomb

## MANITOBA

### Winnipeg

#### INFO LINES & SERVICES

**Rainbow Resource Centre** 170 Scott St (at Wardlaw) **204/474-0212** • call for hrs, clsd wknds • also info line • many social/ support groups

#### BARS

**Club 200** 190 Garry St (at St Mary Ave) **204/943-6045** • 4pm-2am, 6pm-midnight Sun • lesbians/ gay men • dancing/DJ • karaoke • drag shows • go-go dancers • wheelchair access

**Fame** 279 Garry St **204/414-9433** • 9pm-2am Fri-Sun only • lesbians/ gay men • dancing/DJ • drag shows • transgender-friendly

#### RESTAURANTS

**Buccacino's Cucina Italiana** 155 Osborne St **204/452-8251** • 11am-10pm, till 11pm Fri-Sat, from 10am Sun • live music • full bar • patio

#### BOOKSTORES

**McNally Robinson** 1120 Grant Ave #4000 (in the mall) **204/475-0483, 800/561-1833** • 9am-10pm, till 11pm Fri-Sat, noon-6pm Sun • wheelchair access

#### PUBLICATIONS

**Outwords** **204/942-4599** • LGBT newspaper

## NEW BRUNSWICK

### Fredericton

#### NIGHTCLUBS

**boom!** 474 Queen St **506/463-2666** • 8pm-2am, 4pm-7pm Sun, clsd Mon-Wed • lesbians/ gay men • dancing/DJ

#### RESTAURANTS

**Molly's Cafe** 554 Queen St **506/457-9305** • 9am-10pm, noon-midnight Fri-Sun • full bar • garden patio • some veggie

#### EROTICA

**Pleasures N' Treasures** 558 Queen St **506/458-2048** • 11am-10pm, till 11pm Th-Sat

### Moncton

#### ACCOMMODATIONS

**Auberge Au Bois Dormant Inn** 67 rue John (at Birch) **506/855-6767** • gay-friendly • affordable luxury inn • full brkfst • nonsmoking • WiFi • gay-owned

#### NIGHTCLUBS

**Triangles** 234 St George St (at Archibald) **506/857-8779** • 8pm-2am • lesbians/ gay men • neighborhood bar • dancing/DJ • karaoke Th

#### RESTAURANTS

**Calactus Cafe** 125 Church St (at St George) **506/388-4833** • 11am-10pm • vegetarian

### St John

#### ACCOMMODATIONS

**Mahogany Manor** 220 Germain St **506/636-8000, 800/796-7755** • gay/ straight • full brkfst • nonsmoking • kids ok • wheelchair access • gay-owned

#### NIGHTCLUBS

**Happinez Wine Bar** 42 Princess St **506/634-7340** • 4pm-midnight, till 2am Fri-Sat • gay-friendly

#### RESTAURANTS

**East Coast Bistro** 60 Prince William St **506/642-2822** • lunch & dinner

## NOVA SCOTIA

### Annapolis

#### ACCOMMODATIONS

**By the Dock of the Bay Cottages** 28 Haddock Alley (at Lower Road ), Margaretsville **416/588-1500, 800/407-2856** • gay-friendly • lesbian-owned

### Annapolis Royal

#### ACCOMMODATIONS

**Bailey House B&B** 150 St George St (at Drury Ln) **902/532-1285, 877/532-1285** • gay/ straight • circa 1770 historic waterfront home • full brkfst • nonsmoking • WiFi

**King George Inn** **902/532-5286, 888/799-5464** • lesbians/ gay men • full brkfst • jacuzzi • nonsmoking • WiFi • gay-owned

## Antigonish

### INFO LINES & SERVICES

**Antigonish Women's Resource Centre** 219 Main St, Ste 204 (Kirk Place) **902/863-6221** • 9am-4:30pm Mon-Fri • info • support services & programs

## Digby

### ACCOMMODATIONS

**Harbourview Inn** 25 Harbourview Rd (at Hwy 1), Smith's Cove **902/245-5686, 877/449-0705** • gay-friendly • century-old country inn • full brkfst • pool • kids/pets ok • nonsmoking • WiFi • wheelchair access • gay-owned

## Halifax

### BARS

**The Company House** 2202 Gottingen St **902/404-3050** • 4pm-midnight, from 3pm Th-Fri, till 2am Sat, clsd Sun-Mon • gay/straight • dancing/DJ • live music

**Menz & Mollyz Bar** 2182 Gottingen St, Level 2 (btw Cunard & Agricola) **902/446-6969** • 4pm-2:30am • lesbians/ gay men • neighborhood bar • dancing/DJ • drag shows • karaoke • piano bar

**Reflections Cabaret** 5184 Sackville St (at Barrington) **902/422-2957** • 10pm-4am, clsd Tue-Wed • lesbians/ gay men • dancing/DJ • live shows • cabaret • drag shows • wheelchair access

### CAFES

**Coburg Coffee House** 6085 Coburg Rd **902/429-2326** • 7am-9pm • WiFi

**The Daily Grind** 5686 Spring Garden Rd (near South Park) **902/429-6397** • 8am-6pm, noon-5pm Sun • also newsstand

**The Second Cup** 5425 Spring Garden Rd **902/429-0883** • 7am-11pm, till midnight Th-Sat • WiFi

**Uncommon Grounds** 1030 S Park St **902/404-3124** • 7am-10pm • WiFi

### RESTAURANTS

**Bistro Le Coq** 1584 Argyle St **902/407-4564** • noon-10pm, till midnight Fri-Sat, • Parisian charm and cuisine

**Brooklyn Warehouse** 2795 Windsor St **902/446-8181** • lunch & dinner, clsd Sun

**Chives Canadian Bistro** 1537 Barrington St **902/420-9626** • 5pm-9:30pm

**Heartwood** 6250 Quinpool Rd **902/425-2808** • 11am-9pm, 10am-3pm Sun • vegetarian

### ENTERTAINMENT & RECREATION

**The Khyber** 1588 Barrington St **902/422-9668** • visual & performing arts center

### BOOKSTORES

**Atlantic News** 5560 Morris St (at Queen) **902/429-5468** • 8am-9pm, from 9am Sun

**Trident Booksellers & Cafe** 1256 Hollis St (at Morris St) **902/423-7100** • 8am-5:30pm,10am-5pm Sun • used • popular cafe • WiFi

### RETAIL SHOPS

**Venus Envy** 1598 Barrington St **902/422-0004, 877/370-9288** • 10am-6pm, till 7pm Th-Fri, noon-5pm Sun • "a store for women & the people who love them" • books • sex toys • alternative health products

### PUBLICATIONS

**Wayves** PO Box 34090 Scotia Square B3J 3S1 **902/889-2229** • monthly magazine "for the rainbow community of Atlantic Canada"

### EROTICA

**Night Magic Fashions** 5268 Sackville St **902/420-9309** • clsd Sun

## Tangier

### ACCOMMODATIONS

**Spry Bay Campground & Cabins** 19867 Highway #7 **902/772-2554, 866/229-8014** • gay/ straight • also restaurant & convenience store • lesbian-owned

# ONTARIO

## Grand Valley

### ACCOMMODATIONS

**Rainbow Ridge Resort** Country Rd 109 (at Hwy 25 S) **519/928-3262** • lesbians/ gay men • trailers & tents • located on 72 acres on Grand River • pool • restaurant • dance hall • day visitors welcome • seasonal • pets ok • gay-owned

## Hamilton

### ACCOMMODATIONS

**BurrBrookHaven** 336 8th Concession Rd E (Centre Rd), Carlisle **905/689-7550** • women only • country home, single or groups 8-10 • lesbian-owned

**Cedars Campground** 1039 5th Concession W Rd, Millgrove **905/659–3655, 905/659–7342** • lesbians/ gay men • private campground,seasonal • pool • also bar • dancing/DJ • restaurant wknds • gay-owned

## BARS

**The Embassy Club** 54 King St E (at Houston) **905/522–1100** • noon-3am, nightclub from 10pm wknds • lesbians/ gay men • dancing/DJ • transgender-friendly • karaoke • drag shows • videos

## EROTICA

**Stag Shop** 58 Centennial Pkwy N **905/573–4242** • also 980 Upper James St, 905/385-3300

## Kitchener

### EROTICA

**Stag Shop** 10 Manitou Dr 519/895–1228

## London

### ACCOMMODATIONS

**Hilton Hotel** 300 King St **800/210–9336** • gay-friendly • pool • WiFi • wheelchair access

### NIGHTCLUBS

**Club Lavish** 238 Dundas St **519/667–1222** • 9pm-2am, clsd Sun-Wed • gay/ straight • dancing/DJ • karaoke

### RESTAURANTS

**Blackfriars Bistro** 46 Blackfriars (2 blocks S of Oxford) **519/667–4930** • lunch & dinner, Sun brunch • popular • plenty veggie • full bar

### EROTICA

**Stag Shop** 1548 Dundas St E **519/453–7676** • also 371 Wellington Rd S, 519/668-3334

## Niagara Falls

### ACCOMMODATIONS

**Absolute Elegance B&B** 6023 Culp St (at Main & Ferry) **905/353–8522, 877/353–8522** • gay/ straight • full brkfst • nonsmoking • gay-owned

**Angels Hideaway** 4360 Simcoe St (at River Rd) **905/354–1119** • gay-friendly • full brkfst • nonsmoking

**Britaly B&B** 57 The Promenade (at Charlotte & John), Niagara-on-the-Lake **905/468–8778** • gay-friendly • full brkfst • gay-owned

## Oshawa

### NIGHTCLUBS

**Club 717** 717 Wilson Rd S #7 **905/434–4297** • 7pm-midnight, 9pm-2am Fri-Sat, clsd Mon-Wed • lesbians/ gay men • dancing • drag shows

### EROTICA

**Forbidden Pleasures** 1268 Simcoe St N **905/728-0834**

## Ottawa

### INFO LINES & SERVICES

**Pink Triangle Services** 251 Bank St #301 **613/563–4818** • many groups & services • library • call for times

### ACCOMMODATIONS

**Ambiance B&B** 330 Nepean St **613/563–0421, 888/366–8772** • gay/ straight • full brkfst • some shared baths • kids ok • nonsmoking • WiFi • lesbian-owned

**Brookstreet** 525 Legget Dr **613/271–1800, 888/826–2220** • gay-friendly • pool • golf • also restaurant

**Lord Elgin Hotel** 100 Elgin St **613/235–3333, 800/267–4298** • gay-friendly • pool • also restaurant & bar

**Rideau Inn** 177 Frank St **613/688–2753, 877/580–5015** • gay-friendly • some shared baths • nonsmoking • gay-owned

### BARS

**Centretown Pub** 340 Somerset St W (at Bank) **613/594–0233** • 2pm-2am • lesbians/ gay men • dancing/DJ • leather bar upstairs • Silhouette Lounge piano bar Fri-Sat

**The Lookout** 41 York, 2nd flr (in Byward Market) **613/789–1624** • 2pm-2am, till 9pm Sun • lesbians/ gay men • more women Fri • food served • wheelchair access • lesbian-owned

**Swizzles** 246 Queen St **613/232–4200** • 11am-2am, from 7pm wknds, noon-10pm Tue, clsd Mon • lesbians/ gay men • karaoke • WiFi

### NIGHTCLUBS

**Lotus Lounge** 129 Bank St **613/216–9661** • 10pm-2am Fri, till 7am Sat

**Mercury Lounge** 56 Byward Market Sq (side door upstairs) **613/789–5324** • 8pm-3am, clsd Sun-Tue • popular Wed Hump night party • gay/ straight • dancing/DJ • WiFi

**Zaphod Beeblebrox** 27 York **613/562–1010** • 4pm-2am • gay/ straight • neighborhood bar • dancing/DJ • live music

## CAFES

**Bridgehead Coffee** 366 Bank St (at Gilmour) 613/569–5600 • 7am-9pm • WiFi • gay-owned

**Raw Sugar Cafe** 692 Somerset W 613/216–2850 • vegan & gluten-free options • aslo occasional Femme Tea parties • live music

## RESTAURANTS

**Ahora Mexican Cuisine** 307 Dalhousie St (below Sweet Art ) 613/562–2081 • noon-10pm • gay-owned

**The Buzz** 374 Bank St 613/565–9595 • dinner nightly, Sun brunch • also bar

**Johnny Farina** 216 Elgin St 613/565–5155 • Italian • wheelchair access

**Kinki** 41 York St 613/789–7559 • lunch & dinner • Asian fusion • full bar • DJ • live entertainment • patio

**La Dolce Vita** 180 Preston Street 613/233–6239 • lunch & dinner, except Mon-Wed dinner only • gluten-free menu available

**Shanghai Restaurant** 651 Somerset St W (at Bronson Ave) 613/233–4001 • lunch Tue-Fri, dinner nightly, clsd Mon • also bar • DJ • karaoke

## BOOKSTORES

**Mags & Fags** 254 Elgin St (btwn Somerset & Cooper) 613/233–9651 • till 10pm • gay magazines

## RETAIL SHOPS

**Venus Envy** 226 Bank St 613/789–4646 • 11am-6pm, till 8pm Fri, noon-5pm Sun • award-winning sex shop & bookstore

## PUBLICATIONS

**Capital Xtra!** 416/925–6665 • LGBT newspaper

## EROTICA

**Wicked Wanda's** 382 Bank St 613/820–6032

**Wilde's** 368 Bank St #D (at Gilmour) 613/234–5512 • 11am-7:30pm, till 9pm Fri, noon-5pm Sun • pride items • wheelchair access

# Stratford

## RESTAURANTS

**Down the Street** 30 Ontario St 519/273–5886 • 11am-midnight, clsd Mon • popular • bar till 1am

**Rundles** 9 Cobourg St 519/271–6442 • dinner Tue-Sun, lunch wknds • wheelchair access • gay-owned

# Toronto

## INFO LINES & SERVICES

**519 Church St Community Centre** 519 Church St (on Cawthra Park) 416/392–6874 • 9am-10pm, till 5pm wknds • LGBT info center & cafe • wheelchair access

**AA Gay/ Lesbian** 416/487–5591

**Canadian Lesbian/ Gay Archives** 34 Isabella 416/777–2755 • 7:30pm-10pm Tue-Th & by appt

## ACCOMMODATIONS

**213 Carlton—Toronto Townhouse B&B** 416/323–8898, 877/500–0466 • gay/ straight • some shared baths • nonsmoking • WiFi • gay-owned

**Bonnevue Manor B&B** 33 Beaty Ave (at Queen St & Roncesvalles) 416/536–1455 • gay/ straight • full brkfst • kids ok • nonsmoking • WiFi

**Drake Hotel** 1150 Queen St W (at Beaconsfield) 416/531–5042, 866/372–5386 • gay-friendly • boutique hotel • popular Corner Cafe for brkfst, also roof bar •nonsmoking

**Dundonald House** 35 Dundonald St (at Church) 416/961–9888, 800/260–7227 • mostly gay men • full brkfst • hot tub • sauna • gym • bicycles • nonsmoking • gay-owned

**The Gladstone Hotel** 1214 Queen St W (at Gladstone Ave) 416/531–4635 • gay/ straight • artistic • nonsmoking • WiFi • also Melody bar & cafe

**Hazelton Hotel** 118 Yorkville Ave (at Avenue Rd) 416/963–6300, 866/473–6301 • gay-friendly • luxury property • nonsmoking

**Hotel Le Germain** 30 Mercer St (at Peter St) 416/345–9500, 866/345–9501 • gay-friendly • kids/ pets ok • also restaurant & bar • wheelchair access

## BARS

**Beaver Cafe** 1192 Queen St W (at Northcote Ave) 416/537–2768 • 11am-2am • lesbians/ gay men • DJs • food served • patio • gay-owned

**Bistro 422** 422 College St (at Bathurst St) 416/963–9416 • 5pm-2am • gay/straight • food served

**Boutique Bar** 506 Church St (at Maitland) 647/705–0006 • 2:30pm-2am • lesbians/ gay men • patio

**The Cameron House** 408 Queen St W (at Cameron St) 416/703–0811 • 4pm-close • gay/ straight • live music • also theater

**The Churchmouse & Firkin** 475 Church St (at Maitland) 416/927–1735 • 11am-2am • lesbians/ gay men • English pub • neighborhood bar • leather brunch 3rd Sun

**Dakota Tavern** 249 Ossington Ave (at Dundas) 416/850–4579 • 6pm-2am • gay-friendly • live country music • bluegrass brunch Sun

**The Flying Beaver Pubaret** 488 Parliament St 647/347–6567 • 4pm-close, from 11am Sun, clsd Mon-Tue • gay/straight • live shows • cute patio

**The Hair of the Dog** 425 Church St (at Wood) 416/964–2708 • 11am-2am • gay/ straight • neighborhood pub & restaurant • patio

**Hair of the Dog Pub** 425 Church St 416/964–2708 • 11am-2am, till midnight Sun-Wed • gay/straight • live shows • great patio

**The House on Parliament Pub** 456 Parliament St (at Carlton) 416/925–4074 • 11:30am-2am • gay/ straight • neighborhood bar • food served • rooftop patio

**Melody Bar** 1214 Queen St W (at Gladstone Hotel) 416/531–4635 • 5pm-1am, 6pm-2am Fri-Sat, clsd Sun-Wed • gay/ straight • live music

**O'Grady's** 518 Church St (at Maitland) 416/323–2822 • 11am-2am, till 3am Fri-Sat • gay/ straight • casual dining • huge patio • also lounge upstairs

**Pegasus** 489-B Church St (at Wellesley, upstairs) 416/927–8832 • 11am-2am • lesbians/ gay men • neighborhood bar

**The Raq** 739 Queen St W, 2nd flr (at Palmerston) 416/504–9120 • 5pm-1am, from 4pm Th-Sun, clsd Mon• gay/ straight • DJs • upscale pool hall

**Smiling Buddha** 961 College St (at Dovercourt) 416/516–2531 • 7:30pm-2am • gay/ straight • cabaret • younger crowd

**Sneaky Dee's** 431 College St (at Bathurst) 416/603–3090 • 11am-3am, from 9am Sun • gay-friendly • live bands • kitchen open late • Tex/Mex

**WAYLA (What Are You Looking At )Lounge** 996 Queen St E 406/901–5570 • 5pm-2am • gay/straight • karaoke

**Woody's/ Sailor** 465-467 Church (at Maitland) 416/972–0887 • 1pm-2am • popular • mostly gay men • neighborhood bar • live shows • drag shows • 18+ • wheelchair access

## NIGHTCLUBS

**The Annex Wreck Room** 794 Bathurst St (at Bloor) 416/536–0346 • 10pm-close • gay/ straight • dancing/DJ • bands

**Cherry Bomb** 152a Augusta St (at The Round) 416/923–5300 (CLUB#) • 9pm 3rd Sat • inclusive party for queer women & all of our friends • transgender-friendly • dancing/DJ

**Crews and Tangos** 508 Church St 647/349-7469 • 6pm-2am, from 3pm Th-Sun • mostly gay men • drag shows

**El Convento Rico** 750 College St (at Crawford) 416/588–7800 • 9pm-4am, clsd Mon-Th • gay/ straight • dancing/DJ • Latin/ salsa music • mostly Latino • transgender-friendly • drag shows

**Fly Toronto** 8 Gloucester St (2 streets N of Yonge & Wellesley) 416/925–6222 • Sat only • popular • circuit boys and straight girls • dancing/DJ • cover charge

**Guvernment** 132 Queens Quay E (at Lower Jarvis) 416/869–0045 • gay-friendly • dancing/DJ • visiting big-name DJs

**Lee's Palace/ Dance Cave** 529 Bloor St (at Albany) 416/532–1598 • gay/ straight • live bands • dance cave Mon, Th-Sat

**The Mod Club** 722 College (at Crawford) 416/588–4663 • 10pm Fri-Sat • gay/ straight • dancing/DJ

**Swagger Productions** • parties & events for women of color • weaponoftherevolution.com for details

**Tattoo Rock Parlour** 567 Queen St W (at Denison) 416/703–5488 • 10am-3am Fri-Sun • gay/ straight • dancing/DJ • live shows

**Wrongbar** 1279 Queen St W (at Brock) 415/516–8677 • gay/ straight • dancing/DJ • Big Primpin 1st Fri • check listing for other queer events

## CAFES

**Alternative Grounds** 333 Roncesvalles Ave 416/534–5543 • 7am-7pm

**Fuel Plus** 471Church St 647/352–8807 • 7:30am-10pm, 8:30am-11pm Sat • gay-owned

**JetFuel** 519 Parliament St 416/968–9982 • 7am-8pm • WiFi

**Timothy's** 500 Church St (at Alexander) 416/925–8550 • 7am-midnight, till 3:30am wknds • WiFi

## RESTAURANTS

**AFT Kitchen & Bar** 686 Queen St E 647/346-1541 • 11am-2am • BBQ • nice patio

**Black Hoof** 938 Dundas St W **416/551-8854**
• 6pm-midnight, clsd Tue-Wed • charcuterie &
cheese • not for vegetarians!

**Byzantium** 499 Church St (S of Wellesley)
**416/922-3859** • 5pm-11pm • patio • gay-
owned

**Cafe 668** 885 Dundas St W **416/703-0668** •
lunch & dinner • vegetarian

**Cafe Diplomatico** 594 College (at Clinton,
in Little Italy) **416/534-4637** • 8am-2am, clsd
Mon • Italian

**Corner Cafe** 1150 Queen St W (at Drake
Hotel) **416/531-5042** • 8am-6pm, till 9pm
Wed-Th,till 11pm Fri-Sat • popular brkfst spot

**Easy Restaurant** 1645 Queen St W
**416/537-4893** • 9am-5pm

**Flo's Diner** 70 Yorkville Ave (near Bay St)
**416/961-4333** • 7:30am-4pm Mon till 9pm
Tu-Fri, from 8am -9pm wknds• gay-owned

**Joy Bistro** 884 Queen St E **416/465-8855** •
noon-1am

**Kalendar** 546 College St **416/923-4138** •
10:30am-1am, patio

**La Hacienda** 640 Queen St W (near
Bathurst) **416/703-3377** • noon-1am, from
11am wknds

**Lee Restaurant** 603 King S W **416/504-7867**
• lunch & dinner, Asian fusion, also Madeline's
next door

**Mitzi's Cafe** 100 Sorauren Ave (at Pearson)
**416/588-1234** • 7:30am-4pm, popular wknd
brunch from 9am • gay-owned

**Nota Bene** 180 Queen St W **416/977-6400** •
lunch Mon-Fri, dinner nightly, clsd Sun •
Mediterranean

**Smith** 553 Church St (at Dundonald)
**416/926-2501** • dinner & drinks

**Supermarket** 268 Augusta St (at College)
**416/840-0501** • call for hours • Thai • also
bar w/ DJs

**Urban Herbivore** 64 Oxford St (at Augusta)
**416/927-1231** • 9am-7pm • vegetarian/vegan

**Wine Bar** 9 Church St **416/504-9463** • noon-
11pm • tapas-style dishes

## ENTERTAINMENT & RECREATION

**AIDS Memorial** in Cawthra Square Park

**The Bata Shoe Museum** 327 Bloor St W
**416/979-7799** • 10,000 shoes from over 4,500
years—including the platforms of Elton John &
the pumps of Marilyn Monroe

**Buddies in Bad Times Theatre** 12
Alexander St (at Yonge) **416/975-8555** •
LGBT theater; also Tallulah's cabaret

**Hanlan's Pt Beach** Toronto Islands • nude
beach • 10 minutes from downtown

### BOOKSTORES

**Glad Day Bookshop** 598-A Yonge St (at
Wellesley) **416/961-4161** • 10am-7pm, till
9pm Th-Sat, noon-6pm Sun • LGBT books,
mags & videos

### RETAIL SHOPS

**Out on the Street** 551 Church St
**416/967-2759, 800/263-5747** • 10am-8pm, till
9pm Th-Sat, 11am-7pm Sun • LGBT

**Secrets From Your Sister** 560 Bloor St W
**416/538-1234, 888/868-8007** • 11am-7pm •
"beautiful lingerie in realistic sizes for the
modern woman" • wheelchair access

**Take a Walk on the Wild Side** 161 Gerrard
St E (at Jarvis) **416/921-6112, 800/260-0102** •
"hotel, boutique & club for crossdressers,
transvestites, transexuals & other persons of
gender"

### PUBLICATIONS

**Xtra!** **416/925-6665, 800/268-9872** • LGBT
newspaper

### SEX CLUBS

**Pleasure Palace Toronto** 231 Mutual St (at
Oasis Aqualounge) • occasional women- &
trans-only sex club • check out
www.pussypalacetoronto.com for events

### EROTICA

**Come As You Are** 701 Queen St W (at
Bathurst) **416/504-7934** • 11am-7pm, till
9pm Th-Fri, noon-5pm Sun • co-op-owned
sex store

**Good For Her** 175 Harbord St (near
Bathurst) **416/588-0900, 877/588-0900** •
11am-7pm • women & trans-only hours:
noon-5pm Sun • women's sexuality products •
wheelchair access

**North Bound Leather** 586 Yonge (W of
Wellesley St) **416/972-1037** • toys & clothing
• wheelchair access

**Seduction** 577 Yonge St **416/966-6969**

# Waterloo

## ACCOMMODATIONS

**Colonial Creekside** 485 Bridge St W (at
Lexington) **519/886-2726** • gay/ straight•
pool • WiFi • • gay-owned

## RESTAURANTS

**Ethel's Lounge** 114 King St N (at Spring)
**519/725-2361** • 11:30am-2am • full bar •
patio

EROTICA

**Stag Shop** 7 King St N **519/886–4500**

## Windsor

BARS

**Phog** 157 University Ave W (at Church St) **519/253–1605** • 5pm-2am, from 8pm Sun-Mon • gay-friendly • food served • art & events

**Vermouth** 333 Ouellette **519/977–6102** • 5pm-2am, from 6pm Sat, clsd Sun-Mon • gay-friendly • popular martini lounge

NIGHTCLUBS

**The Loop** 156 Chatham St W (at Ferry St) **519/253–3474** • 10pm-2am, clsd Mon & Wed • gay-friendly • dancing/DJ • live shows • theme nights • young crowd

CAFES

**The Coffee Exchange** 266 Ouellette **519/971–7424** • 7am-11pm, 8am-midnight wknds • WiFi

EROTICA

**Stag Shop** 2950 Dougall Ave **519/967–8798**

## PRINCE EDWARD ISLAND

## Charlottetown

ACCOMMODATIONS

**Evening Primrose** 114 Lord's Pond Rd, Albany **902/437–3134** • gay-friendly • full brkfst • nonsmoking • kids/pets ok • cottage wheelchair access • seasonal • WiFi • lesbian-owned

**The Great George** 58 Great George **902/892–0606, 800/361–1118** • gay-friendly • kids ok • nonsmoking • WiFi • wheelchair access • gay-owned

**The Hotel on Pownal** 146 Pownal St **902/892–1217, 800/268–6261** • gay-friendly • WiFi

**Rodd Charlottetown Hotel** 75 Kent St (at Pownall) **902/894–7371, 800/565–7633** • gay-friendly • pool • kids/pets ok • WiFi • also restaurant & lounge

**Shipwright Inn Heritage B&B** 51 Fitzroy St **902/368–1905, 888/306–9966** • gay-friendly • full brkfst • nonsmoking

BARS

**Baba's Lounge** 81 University Ave **902/892–7377** • 11am-11pm, till midnight Fri-Sat from 5pm Sun • gay-friendly • live bands • also Cedars Lebanese restaurant

ENTERTAINMENT & RECREATION

**Blooming Point** Blooming Point • nude beach

BOOKSTORES

**Book Mark** 172 Queen St (in mall) **902/566–4888** • 9am-8pm, till 9pm Th-Fri, till 5:30pm Sat, clsd Sun

## Hermanville

ACCOMMODATIONS

**Johnson Shore Inn** 9984 Rte 16 **902/687–1340, 877/510–9669** • gay/straight • full brkfst • kids 10+ ok • wheelchair access • lesbian-owned

ENTERTAINMENT & RECREATION

**Prince Edward Distillery** 9984 Route 16 **907/687–2586, 877/510–9669** • Artisan-crafted spirits including Potato Vodka, Wild Blueberry Vodka, and Prince Edward Gin • lesbian-owned

## North Rustico

ACCOMMODATIONS

**Around The Sea** 130 Lantern Hill Dr **866/557–8383** • gay/straight • the world's first rotating house with luxury condo rental suites • WiFi

## York

ACCOMMODATIONS

**Little York B&B** 775 Rte 25 **902/569–0271, 800/953–6755** • gay-friendly • full brkfst • WiFi • gay-owned

## PROVINCE OF QUÉBEC

## Laurentides (Laurentian Mtns)

ACCOMMODATIONS

**Havre du Parc Auberge** 2788 Rte 125 N, St-Donat **819/424–7686** • gay/straight • quiet lakeside inn for nature lovers • full brkfst • gay-owned

**Le Septentrion B&B** 901 chemin St-Adolphe, Morin-Heights/ St-Sauveur **450/226–2665** • lesbians/gay men • full brkfst • pool • hot tub • sauna • nonsmoking • gay-owned

## Magog

### ACCOMMODATIONS

**Au Gîte du Cerf Argenté B&B** 2984 chemin Georgeville Rd (off Hwy 10) **819/847-4264** • gay/ straight • renovated century-old farmhouse • 4 beaches nearby • kids ok • nonsmoking • gay-owned

**Auberge aux Deux Pères** 680 chemin des Peres **819/769-3115, 514/616-3114** • gay-friendly • pool • WiFi • gay-owned

## Montréal

Note: M°=Metro station

### INFO LINES & SERVICES

**AA Gay/ Lesbian** 514/376-9230

**Gay Line/ Gai Ecoute** 514/866-5090 (ENGLISH) • 7pm-11pm

**Gay/ Lesbian Community Centre of Montréal** 2075 rue Plessis #110 (at Ontario) **514/528-8424** • 10am-5:30pm, 1pm-8pm Wed & Fri, clsd wknds • library

**The Village Tourism Information Center/ Gay Chamber of Commerce** 1307 rue Ste-Catherine Est **514/522-1885, 888/595-8110** • 10am-6pm, clsd wknds

### ACCOMMODATIONS

**Alexandre Logan** 1631 rue Alexandre DeSeve (at Logan) **514/598-0555, 866/895-0555** • gay-friendly • WiFi

**Alexandrie Hostel** 1750 Amherst (at Robin) **514/525-9420** • gay-friendly • also bistro • kids/ pets ok • nonsmoking • WiFi • gay-owned

**Auberge le Pomerol** 819 boul de Maisonneuve E (at St-Christophe) **800/361-6896** • gay-friendly • also restaurant • nonsmoking • WiFi

**B&B Le Cartier** 1219 rue Cartier (at Ste-Catherine Est) **514/917-1829, 877/524-0495** • gay/ straight • private studio • WiFi • gay-owned

**B&B Le Terra Nostra** 277 rue Beatty (at Lasalle) **514/762-1223, 866/550-5235** • gay-friendly • full brkfst • nonsmoking • WiFi • woman-owned

**Les Bons Matins** 1401 Argyle Ave **514/931-9167, 800/588-5280** • lesbians/ gay men • apt rental • nonsmoking • WiFi

**Le Chasseur B&B** 1567 rue St-André (at Maisonneuve) **514/521-2238, 800/451-2238** • gay/ straight • Victorian row house • summer terrace • gay-owned

**Hôtel Dorion** 1477 rue Dorion (at Maisonneuve) **514/523-2427, 877/523-5908** • gay/ straight • in the Gay Village • WiFi

**Hotel du Fort** 1390 rue du Fort (at Ste-Catherine) **514/938-8333, 800/565-6333** • gay/ straight • wheelchair access

**Hôtel Gouverneur Montréal Place Dupuis** 1415 rue St-Hubert (at Maisonneuve) **888/910-1111** • gay-friendly • pool • also restaurant & bar • WiFi

**Hotel Lord Berri** 1199 rue Berri (at Ste-Catherine) **514/845-9236, 888/363-0363** • gay-friendly • also Italian resto-bar • WiFi • wheelchair access

**Jade Blue B&B** 1225 de Bullion St (at Ste-Catherine) **514/878-9843, 800/878-5048** • gay/ straight • theme rooms • full brkfst • nonsmoking • WiFi

**L Hotel Montreal** 262 rue St-Jacques W (at St Nicolas) **514/985-0019, 877/553-0019** • gay-friendly • also bar & lounge • WiFi

**Loews Hotel Vogue** 1425 rue de la Montagne (near Ste-Catherine) **514/285-5555, 800/465-6654** • gay-friendly • kids/ pets ok • wheelchair access

**La Loggia Art & Breakfast** 1637 rue Amherst (at Maisonneuve) **514/524-2493, 866/520-2493** • gay/ straight • nonsmoking • in Gay Village • WiFi • gay-owned

**Turquoise B&B** 1576 rue Alexandre DeSève (at Maisonneuve) **514/523-9943, 877/707-1576** • mostly gay men • shared baths • gay-owned

### BARS

**Bar Le Cocktail** 1669 Ste-Catherine Est (at Champlain) **514/597-0814** • 11am-3am • lesbians/ gay men • neighborhood bar • karaoke

**Bar Rocky** 1673 rue Ste-Catherine Est (at Papineau) **514/521-7865** • 8am-close • mostly gay men • drag shows • older crowd

**Cabaret Mado** 1115 rue Ste-Catherine Est (at Amherst, below Le Campus) **514/525-7566** • 11am-3am • popular • lesbians/ gay men • theme nights • dancing/DJ • karaoke • cabaret • drag shows • owned by the fabulous Mado! • wheelchair access

**Club Bolo** 2093 rue de la Visitation (at Association Sportive) **514/849-4777** • 9:30pm-12:30am Fri, special events Sat, T-dance from 3:30pm Sun • lesbians/ gay men • dancing/DJ • country/ western • also lessons • cover charge

**Club Date Piano Bar** 1218 rue Ste-Catherine Est (at Beaudry) 514/521–1242 • 8am-3am • lesbians/ gay men • neighborhood bar • karaoke nightly • piano

**Foufounes Electriques** 87 Ste-Catherine Est (at St-Laurent) 514/844–5539 • 4pm-3am • gay-friendly • dancing/DJ • live bands • patio

**Fun Spot** 1151 rue Ontario Est (at Wolfe) 514/522–0416 • 11am-3am • lesbians/ gay men • neighborhood bar • dancing/DJ • transgender-friendly • food served • drag shows • karaoke • WiFi

**La Relaxe** 1309 rue Ste-Catherine Est, 2nd flr (at Visitation) 514/523–0578 • noon-3am • mostly gay men • neighborhood bar • open to the street • as the name implies, a good place to relax & people-watch

**St-Sulpice** 1680 rue St-Denis (at Ontario) 514/844–9458 • 11am-3am, till midnight Sun • gay/ straight • karaoke • WiFi • large terrace

### NIGHTCLUBS

**Apollon** 1450 rue Ste-Catherine Est • 10pm-3am clsd Mon-Wed • mostly gay men • dancing/DJ

**Circus After Hours** 915 rue Ste-Catherine Est 514/844–3626 • 2am-8am Th & Sun, 1am-10pm Fri-Sat • gay/ straight • dancing/DJ

**Cirque du Boudoir** 514/789–9068 • quarterly • gay/ straight • opulent theme parties • dancing/DJ • performance

**Complexe Sky** 1474 rue Ste-Catherine Est 514/529–6969, 514/529–8989 • noon-3am • lesbians/ gay men • rooftop pool & spa • cabaret & dance club Fri-Sat

**Red Lite (After Hours)** 1755 rue de Lierre, Laval 514/660–7335 • Fri-Sun only 2am-10am • popular • gay-friendly

**Stéréo** 858 rue Ste-Catherine Est (at St-Andre) 514/658–2646 • after-hours Fri-Sun only • gay/ straight • cover • popular

**Unity II** 1171 rue Ste-Catherine Est (at Montcalm) 514/523–2777 • 9pm-close Fri-Sat only • lesbians/ gay men • dancing/DJ • great rooftop terrace • live shows

### CAFES

**Cafe Santropol** 3990 St-Urbain (at Duluth) 514/842–3110 • 11:30am-10pm, from 9am during summer • unique sandwiches • wheelchair access

**Cafe Titanic** 445 St-Pierre (in Old Montréal) 514/849–0894 • 8am-4:30pm, clsd wknds • popular • salad & soup • WiFi

**Kilo** 6744 rue Hutchison 514/270–3024, 877/270–3024 • 9am-5pm, clsd wknds • cakes, coffee & light meals

### RESTAURANTS

**L' Anecdote** 801 rue Rachel Est (at St-Hubert) 514/526–7967 • 7:30am-10pm, from 9am wknds • gay-owned

**Après le Jour** 901 rue Rachel Est (at St-Andre) 514/527–4141 • 5pm-9pm, clsd Mon • Italian/ French • seafood • BYOB • wheelchair access

**Au Pain Perdu** 4489 rue de la Roche 514/527–2900 • 7am-3pm • charming brunch spot in renovated garage

**Bangkok** 1616 rue Ste-Catherine Ouest 514/935–2178 • 9am-9pm • wheelchair access

**Beauty's** 93 Mont-Royal Ouest 514/849–8883 • 7am-3pm, 8am-4pm wknds• diner/ Jewish deli • worth the wait

**La Binerie** 367 Mt-Royal 514/285–9078 • 6am-8pm, 8am-3pm wknds

**Le Cagibi** 5490 boul St-Laurent 514/509–1199 • 9am-1am, from 10:30am wknds, 6pm-midnight Mon • vegetarian • also live music & events

**La Colombe** 554 Duluth Est 514/849–8844 • 5:30pm-midnight, clsd Sun-Mon • BYOB • French

**L' Exception** 1200 rue St-Hubert (at Réné-Lévèsque) 514/282–1282 • 11am-8pm, fill 10pm Sat • terrace

**L' Express** 3927 rue St-Denis (at Duluth) 514/845–5333 • 8am-2am, from 10am Sat-Sun • full bar • great pâté • reservations recommended • wheelchair access

**Fantasie** 1355 rue Ste-Catherine Est 514/523–3466 • dinner only • sushi • gay-owned

**La Strega** 1477 rue Ste-Catherine Est 514/523–6000 • 11am-midnight, from 5pm wknds • inexpensive Italian • some veggie • wheelchair access

**Le Nouveau Palais** 281 rue Bernard W 514/273–1180 • open till 3am wknds, clsd Mon, old school diner

**Le Planète** 1451 rue Ste-Catherine Est (at Plessis) 514/528–6953 • 5pm-10:30pm, brunch only Sun • global cuisine • beer/ wine

**Resto du Village** 1310 rue Wolfe 514/524–5404 • 24hrs • "cuisine canadienne" • WiFi • gay-owned

**Saloon Cafe** 1333 rue Ste-Catherine Est (at Panêt) 514/522-1333 • dinner nightly, lunch wknds only • plenty veggie • big dishes & even bigger drinks

**Schwartz's Deli** 3895 boul St-Laurent 514/842-4813 • 8am-12:30am, till 1:30am Fri, till 2:30am Sat

**Thai Grill** 5101 boul St-Laurent (at Laurier) 514/270-5566 • lunch Mon-Fri, dinner nightly • one of Montréal's best Thai eateries

## ENTERTAINMENT & RECREATION

**Ça Roule** 27 rue de la Commune Est 514/866-0633, 877/866-0633 • join the beautiful people skating & biking up & down Ste-Catherine

**Prince Arthur Est** at boul St-Laurent, not far from Sherbrooke Métro station • closed-off street w/ many outdoor restaurants & cafés • touristy but oh-so-European

## RETAIL SHOPS

**Chez Priape** 1311 Ste-Catherine Est (at Visitation) 514 /521-8451, 800/461-6969 • 10am-8pm, till 9pm Wed, till 10pm Th-Sat, noon-8pm Sun • leather, BDSM, menswear & toys

**Cuir Mont-Royal** 826-A Mont Royal Est (at St-Hubert) 514/527-0238, 888/333-8283 • leather • fetish

**Screaming Eagle** 1424 boul St-Laurent 514/849-2843 • leather shop

## PUBLICATIONS

**2B** 514/521-3873 • English-language LGBT publication covering Québec

**Fugues** 514/848-1854, 888/848-1854 • glossy LGBT bar/ entertainment guide

## EROTICA

**Il Bolero** 6846 St-Hubert (btwn St-Zotique & Bélanger) 514/270-6065 • fetish & clubwear emporium • ask about monthly fetish party

# Quebec City

## RESTAURANTS

**Vertige** 540 Ave Duluth E 514/842-4443 • 5:30pm-10pm, till 11pm Fri-Sat, clsd Sun-Mon

## ACCOMMODATIONS

**ALT Hotel Québec** 1200 av Germain des Prés (at Laurier Blvd), Sainte-Foy 418/658-1224, 800/463-5253 • gay-friendly • non-smoking • WiFi • kids ok • restaurant • wheelchair access • women-owned

**Auberge Place D'Armes** 24 rue Ste-Anne (at St-Louis) 418/694-9485, 866/333-9485 • gay-friendly • nonsmoking • WiFi • restaurant

**Le Château du Faubourg** 429A rue St-Jean (at Claire Fontaine) 418/524-2902 • gay-friendly • B&B in château • nonsmoking • also beauty salon • gay-owned

**Gite TerreCiel** 113 rue Sainte Anne, Baie-Saint-Paul 418/435-0149 • gay/ straight • WiFi • gay-owned

**Hotel Le Clos Saint-Louis** 69 St-Louis (at St-Ursule) 418/694-1311, 800/461-1311 • gay/ straight • boutique hotel located in historic district • nonsmoking • WiFi

**Hôtel Le Germain Dominion 1912** 126 rue St-Pierre (at Marché Finlay) 418/692-2224, 888/833-5253 • gay-friendly • boutique hotel in city's 1st skyscraper • pets ok • wheelchair access

**Hôtel-Motel Le Voyageur** 2250 boul Ste-Anne (at Estimauville) 418/661-7701, 800/463-5568 • gay/ straight • pool • kids/ pets ok • restaurant & bar • WiFi

**Le Moulin de St-Laurent Chalets** 754 chemin Royal, St Laurent, Ile d' Orleans 418/829-3888, 888/629-3888 • gay/ straight • cottages • pool • kids/ pets ok • also restaurant • nonsmoking

## BARS

**Bar Le Drague** 815 rue St-Augustin (at St-Jean) 418/649-7212 • 10am-3am • popular • mostly gay men • neighborhood bar • dancing/DJ Th-Sun • food served • karaoke • cabaret • drag shows • terrace • wheelchair access

**Bar St Matthew's** 889 côte Ste-Geneviève (at St-Gabriel) 418/524-5000 • 11am-3am • lesbians/ gay men • neighborhood bar • patio

## RESTAURANTS

**Le Hobbit** 700 rue St-Jean (at Ste-Geneviève) 418/647-2677 • 9am-10pm • some veggie

**La Piazzetta** 707 rue St-Jean 418/529-7489 • 11am-10:30pm

**Le Poisson d'Avril** 115 quai St-André (at St-Thomas) 418/692-1010, 877/692-1010 • 5pm-close • name is French for "April Fools"

## ENTERTAINMENT & RECREATION

**Fairmont Le Château Frontenac** 1 rue des Carrières 418/692-3861, 800/257-7544 • this hotel disguised as a castle remains the symbol of Québec, come & enjoy the view from outside

**Ice Hotel /Hôtel de Glace** 75, Montée de l'Auberge, Pavillon Ukiuk, Sainte-Catherine-de-la-Jacques-Cartier **418/875-4522, 877/505-0423** • sometimes getting put on ice isn't a bad thing—check this gay-friendly hotel out before it melts away, 9 km E of Québec City in Montmorency Falls Park (Jan-March only)

### PUBLICATIONS

**2B** 514/521-3873 • English-language LGBT publication covering Québec

### EROTICA

**Importation André Dubois** 46 côte de la Montagne (at Frontenac Castle) **418/692-0264** • transgender-friendly • wheelchair access

## St-Georges-de-Beauce

### BARS

**Le Planet** 8450 Blvd Lacroix **418/228-1322** • 2pm-3am, till 10pm Sun, clsd Mon-Tue • gay/ straight • neighborhood bar

# SASKATCHEWAN

## Ravenscrag

### ACCOMMODATIONS

**Spring Valley Guest Ranch** 306/295-4124 • gay/ straight • 1913 character home • also cabin • full brkfst • kids/ pets ok • nonsmoking • also restaurant • gay-owned

## Regina

### NIGHTCLUBS

**The OUTside** 2070 Broad St (at Victoria, at Gay Center) **306/569-1995** • 7pm-3am • lesbians/gay men • dancing/DJ

**Q Nightclub & Lounge** 2070 Broad St (at Victoria) **306/569-1995** • 5pm-2am • lesbians/gay men • dancing/DJ • owned by Gay & Lesbian Community of Regina

### RESTAURANTS

**Abstractions Cafe** 2161 Rose St **306/352-5374** • 9am-6pm, from 11am Sat, clsd Sun • live music

**The Creek in Cathedral Bistro** 3414 13th Ave **306/352-4448** • lunch & dinner, clsd Sun

## Saskatoon

### INFO LINES & SERVICES

**Avenue Community Centre** 201-320 21st St W **306/665-1224, 800/358-1833** • 10am-5pm, till 9pm Wed-Fri,4:30pm-9:30pm Sat • many social/ support groups • queer gift store

**Circle of Choice Gay/ Lesbian AA** 505 10th St E (at Grace Westminster United Church) **306/665-6727** • 8pm Wed

### NIGHTCLUBS

**Diva's** 220 3rd Ave S #110 (alley entrance) **306/665-0100** • 8pm-2am, till 5am Sat, clsd Mon-Tue • lesbians/ gay men • dancing/DJ • drag shows • karaoke • WiFi • private club (guests welcome)

**Pink Lounge & Nightclub** 302 Pacific Ave **306/665-6863** • 7am-2am, till 3am Fri-Sat, clsd Sun-Tue • lesbians/ gay men • dancing/DJ

### RESTAURANTS

**2nd Ave Grill** 10-123 2nd Ave S **306/244-9899** • 11am-10pm, till 11pm Fri-Sat

**The Berry Barn** 830 Valley Rd **306/978-9797** • open daily • seasonal • home-style eatery w/ views of river

**The Ivy Dining & Lounge** 24th St E & Ontario Ave **306/384-4444** • lunch & dinner Mon-Fri, dinner only Sat-Sun

**Prairie Ink** 3130 8th St E **306/955-3579** • 9am-10pm, till 11pm Fri-Sat, till 6pm Sun • also bookstore

### ENTERTAINMENT & RECREATION

**AKA Gallery** 424 20th St W **306/652-0044** • noon-6pm, till 4pm Sat, clsd Sun-Mon • contemporary art & performance

### BOOKSTORES

**Turning the Tide** 525 11th St E **306/955-3070** • noon-8pm, till 10pm Th-Sat • Saskatoon's alternative bookstore

## BAHAMAS

### Nassau

#### NIGHTCLUBS

**Club Waterloo** E Bay St (1/2 mile E of Paradise Island Bridge) **242/393-7324** • 4pm-close • gay-friendly • more women Th • indoor/ outdoor complex w/ 5 bars • dancing/DJ • live music • restaurant • swimming

## BARBADOS

### Bridgetown

#### RESTAURANTS

**The Waterfront Cafe** The Careenage **246/427-0093** • 10am-midnight, clsd Sun • also bar • live music • outdoor seating

## BRITISH VIRGIN ISLANDS

### Tortola

#### ACCOMMODATIONS

**Fort Recovery Villa Beach Resort** West End, Road Town, Tortola **284/541-0955, 855/349-3355** • gay-friendly • private beachfront villas • pool • kids ok • wheelchair access • women-owned

## DOMINICAN REPUBLIC

### Puerto Plata

#### ACCOMMODATIONS

**Tropix Hotel** **809/571-2291** • gay-friendly • full brkfst • garden setting near center of town & beach • pool • kids/ pets ok • lesbian & gay-owned

### Santiago

#### BARS

**Monaco Bar** 40 Av 27 de Febrero, Santo Domingo **809/226-1589** • lesbians/ gay men • dancing/DJ

### Santo Domingo

#### ACCOMMODATIONS

**Caribe Colonial Hotel** Isabel Catolica 159 **809/688-7799** • gay-friendly • boutique hotel • WiFi

**Foreigners Club Hotel** 102 Calle Canela (at Estrelleta) **809/689-3017** • lesbians/ gay men • in Zona Colonial • nonsmoking • WiFi • wheelchair access • gay-owned

**Hotel Aida** Calle El Conde 464 **809/685-7692** • gay-friendly

#### BARS

**Colonial Bar & Disco** 109 Mella Ave (nr Calle Arzobispo Nouel) **809/205-1970** • open Th-Sun • mostly gay men • karaoke

**Esedeku** **809/869-6322** • 8pm-close, from 5pm Sun, clsd Mon • lesbians/ gay men • food served

**Fogoo Discotec** 67 Calle Arzobispo Nouel (btw Espaillat & Santome) **809/205-1970** • mostly gay men • dancing/DJ • drag shows

#### NIGHTCLUBS

**Pure Disco Club** 365 George Washington Ave (at Hotel Meliá) **809/221-6666** • gay/ straight • open till 6am, no shorts or flip flops

**Sunev Bar & Lounge** 203 Calle 19 de Marzo (nr Calle El Conde) **809/221-5167** • 9pm-midnight, till 2am Fri-Sat from 6am Sun, clsd Mon-Tue • mostly gay men • dancing/DJ

#### RESTAURANTS

**El Conuco** 152 Casimiro de Moya (behind Jaragua Hotel) **809/686-0129** • touristy local landmark

**Green Light Cuisine** 20 Heriberto Pieter, Naco **809/732-7719** • sandwiches & salads, fresh & light

**Mamajuana** 451 Avenida Roberto Pastoriza **809/547-1019** • Nuevo Latino

**Onno's Bar** 157 Calle Hostos (at El Conde) **809/689-1183** • DJ on the wknds

#### ENTERTAINMENT & RECREATION

**Parque Duarte** Calle Duarte (at Calle Padre Billini) • Th-Sun nights, this park is the gathering place for young gay Dominicans

## DUTCH & FRENCH WEST INDIES

### Aruba

#### BARS

**Jimmy's Place** Windstraat 32, Oranjestad **297/582-2550** • 5pm-1am, till 3am Fri-Sat, clsd Sun-Mon • gay/straight • neighborhood bar • dancing/DJ • food served

**The Paddock** LG Smith Blvd #13, Oranjestad **297/583-2334, 297/583-2606** • 10am-2am • gay/ straight • neighborhood bar • food served

## RESTAURANTS

**Cafe the Plaza** Seaport Marketplace, Oranjestad **297/583–8826** • 8am-1am, patio

# Barbados

## ACCOMMODATIONS

**Gemini House B&B** 70 Plover Court, Inch Marlow, Christ Church **246/428–7221** • gay-friendly • WiFi

**Inchcape Seaside Villas** **246/428–7006** • private villa rentals • WiFi

## ENTERTAINMENT & RECREATION

**Baxter's Road** Bridgetown • many cafés & bars

# Curacao

## INFO LINES & SERVICES

**Pink House** Charlottestraat 6, Willemstad **5999/462–6616** • LGBT community center, health & rights organization • events

## ACCOMMODATIONS

**The Avila Beach Hotel** 130 Penstraat, Willemstad **800/747–8162** • gay-friendly

**Floris Suite Hotel** Piscadera Bay **5999/462–6111, 800/411–0170** • mostly gay men • pool • WiFi • wheelchair access • gay-owned

**Kura Hulanda** Langestraat 8, Willemstad **888/264–3106 , 5999/434–7700** • gay-friendly • also Jacob's Bar

**Papagayo Beach Resort** Willemstad **800/652–2962 (FROM US), 5999/747–4333** • gay-friendly

## BARS

**Grand Cafe De Heeren** Zuikertuintjeweg 1 **5999/736–0491** • 9am-1am, till 2:30am Th-Fri, clsd Sun • gay/ straight • live shows • also restaurant

**Mundo Bizarro** Nieuwestraat 12 (in the Pietermaai quarter) **5999/461-6767** • gay-friendly • weird & wonderful eatery & café • live shows

**Rainbow Lounge** at Floris Suite Hotel, Piscadera Bay **5999/462–6111** • 5pm-midnight • lesbians/ gay men

## NIGHTCLUBS

**Bermuda Disco** Scharlooweg 72-76 (at the Waaigat, behind the movies), Willemstad **5999/461–4685** • 10pm-4am, popular Fri-Sat • gay-friendly • ladies night Th (mostly straight) • dancing/DJ

**Cabana Beach** at Seaquarium Beach **599/946–5158** • open Wed-Sat • gay-friendly • dancing/DJ • also restaurant

**Tu Tu Tango** Plasa Mundo Merced, Punda **5999/465–4633** • 11pm-4am • more gay Fri • also restaurant

## RESTAURANTS

**Mambo Beach** Bapor Kibra, Seaquarium Beach **5999/461–8999** • 9am-midnight, till 4am Sat • full bar • more gay Sat

**O Mundo** Zuikertuintje Shopping Mall, Willemstad • lunch & dinner • also gay party 2nd Sat

## ENTERTAINMENT & RECREATION

**Cas Abao Beach** • gay-friendly • popular local beach

**Dolphin Academy** Curaçao Sea Aquarium, Bapor Kibra z/n (east of Willemstad, at Sea Aquarium Park) **5999/465–8900, 5999/465–8300** • swim w/ dolphins!

**Jan Thiel Beach** • good people-watching

**Museum Kura Hulanda** Klipstraat 9, Willemstad **5999/434–7765** • African history & culture • Antillean art

**South Caribbean Pride** **5999/462–6111, 800/411–0170** • April/May

# Saba

## ACCOMMODATIONS

**Juliana's Hotel** Dutch West Indies, Windwardside **599/416–2269, 866/783–3319** • gay/ straight • pool • hot tub • full brkfst • ocean & garden views • also Saban-style cottages & restaurant • kids ok • WiFi

**Shearwater Resort** Cliff Side (Booby Hill) **589/416–2498** • gay-friendly • full brkfst • pool • nonsmoking • WiFi • also restaurant • gay-owned

## RESTAURANTS

**Rainforest Restaurant** Windwardside (Dutch WI) **599/416–3888** • brkfst, lunch & dinner • full bar

**Restaurant Eden** The Road (Windwardside), Windwardside **599/416-2539** • 5:30pm-9:30pm, clsd Tue

# St Barthelemy

## ACCOMMODATIONS

**Hotel le Village St-Jean** St-Jean Hill **590–590/27–61–39, 800/651–8366** • gay-friendly • hotel & cottages • pool

**Hotel Normandie** Quartier Lorient **590–590/27-61-66** • gay-friendly • WiFi

**Hotel St-Barth Isle De France** Plage des Flamands 508/528–7727, 800/421–3396 • gay-friendly • ultraluxe hotel

### NIGHTCLUBS

**Le Sélect** Gustavia 590–590/27–86–87 • gay-friendly • more gay after 11pm

### RESTAURANTS

**Le Grain de Sel** Grand Saline Beach 590/524–605 • lunch & dinner • clsd Mon • relaxing setting • ideal before & after sunbathing

### ENTERTAINMENT & RECREATION

**Anse Gouverneur St-Jean Beach** • nudity

**Anse Grande Saline Beach** • nudity • gay section on the left side of Saline

**Orient Beach** • gay beach

## St Maarten

### ACCOMMODATIONS

**Blue Ocean Villas** 352/505–2805 • private villa rentals

**Holland House** 43 Front St, Philipsburg 599/542–2572 • gay-friendly • on the beach • restaurant • bar

### RESTAURANTS

**Cheri's Cafe** Rhine Rd #45 (Maho Reef) 599/54–53–361 • 11am-1:30am, clsd Tue • full bar • dancing • live music • touristy • wheelchair access

## St Martin

### BARS

**Tantra** Rhine Road, Maho Bay, Marigot (at the Marina Royale) 599/545–2861 • 11pm-close Wed, Fri-Sat • gay/ straight

### NIGHTCLUBS

**Eros** Rue Victor Maurasse, Marigot 590/690–881–930 • Sat night • mostly gay men • danicing/DJ • spectacular view from top of the club

### RESTAURANTS

**L' Escapade** 94 Blvd de Grand Case 590–590/87–75–04 • French • some veggie • reservations recommended

**Le Pressoir** 30 Blvd de Grand Case 590–590/87–76–62 • dinner nightly, clsd Sun • French

### ENTERTAINMENT & RECREATION

**Orient Beach** on the northeast side of the island • gay-friendly nude beach

# JAMAICA

## Montego Bay

### ACCOMMODATIONS

**Half Moon** 877/956–625, 866/648–6951 • gay-friendly • upscale resort

## Negril

### ACCOMMODATIONS

**Seagrape Villas** The Cliffs, West End Rd 831/625–1255 (US#) • gay/ straight • 3 seafront villas • excellent sunsets

## Ocho Rios

### ACCOMMODATIONS

**Golden Clouds Villa** North Coast Rd, Oracabessa 941/922–9191, 888/625–6007 • gay-friendly • private estate • full brkfst • fully staffed • jacuzzi • pool • kids ok • wheelchair access • gay-owned

## Port Antonio

### ACCOMMODATIONS

**Hotel Mocking Bird Hill** 876/993–7267, 876/993–7134 • gay-friendly • eco-friendly inn • fresh local food served • pool • massage • kids ok • wheelchair access • lesbian-owned

## Westmoreland

### ACCOMMODATIONS

**Moun Tambrin Retreat** set in the mtns 28 miles from Montego Bay 876/437–4353 • gay/ straight • art deco estate • food served • pool

# MARTINIQUE

## Les Trois Ilets

### ACCOMMODATIONS

**Le Carbet B&B** 18 rue des Alamandas (in Anse Mitan district) 590/596–66–0331 • mostly men • full brkfst • jacuzzi • nude sunbathing • gay-owned

## PUERTO RICO

Please Note: For those with rusty or no Spanish, "carretera" means "highway" and "calle" means "street."

## Baja Sucia

### ENTERTAINMENT & RECREATION

**Playa Sucia/ La Playuela** S of Cabo Rojo Nat'l Wildlife Refuge, Guanica • beautiful, secluded beach

## Bayamon

### BARS

**Start Night Club** 31 Ongay St (behind Clendo lab) 787/536-3579 • open Th-Sat • lesbians/ gay men • drag shows

## Boqueron

### BARS

**El Schamar Bar** at corner of Muñoz Rivera & Jose de Diego 787/851-0542 • 11am-midnight • gay/ straight • drag shows • also hotel

**Sunset Sunrise** 65 Calle Barbosa 787/255-1478 • 10am-close • gay/ straight • older crowd

### RESTAURANTS

**The Fish Net & Roberto's Villa Playera** Calle de Diego 787/254-3163 • best seafood in town

## Ceiba

### ACCOMMODATIONS

**Ceiba Country Inn** Carretera 977 787/885-0471, 888/560-2816 • gay-friendly • dramatic ocean views • also bar • 15 minutes to Vieques/Culebra ferry • WiFi • gay-owned

## Guanica

### ENTERTAINMENT & RECREATION

**Gilligan's Island** take Rd 333 to Copamarina Resort, then take ferry to island 787/821-5706 (FERRY INFO) • beautiful beach located in a biosphere on Southern coast of PR

## Rincon

### ACCOMMODATIONS

**Horned Dorset Primavera Hotel** Apartado 1132 787/823-4030
• gay/ straight • swimming pool • kids 12+ ok

**Lemontree Oceanfront Cottages** Carr 429, km 4.1 (at Carr 115) 787/823-6452, 888/418-8733 • gay/ straight • kids ok • nonsmoking • WiFi • wheelchair access

## San Juan

### INFO LINES & SERVICES

**Centro Communitario LGBTT/ LGBT Community Center** 37 Calle Mayaguez 787/294-9850 • 1pm-9pm, clsd wknds • psychosocial services, support groups, activities

### ACCOMMODATIONS

**Acacia Seaside Inn** 8 Taft St (at McLeary) 787/727-0668, 787/727-0626 • gay-friendly • hotel • kids ok • pool • WiFi

**Casa del Caribe Guest House** Calle Caribe 57, Condado (at Magdalena) 787/722-7139, 877/722-7139 • gay-friendly • B&B in heart of Condado • kids ok • nonsmoking • WiFi

**La Concha** 1077 Ashford Ave, Condado 787/721-7500 • gay/ straight • retro urban showcase & architectural landmark • restaurants & bar

**Coqui del Mar Guesthouse** 2218 Calle General del Valle (at General Patton, Ocean Park) 787/220-4204 • gay-friendly • studios & apts • gay-owned

**El Escondido** PR957 Km 3.3 Bo. Palma Sola, Canovanas 787/989-0403 • gay/straight • pool • a secluded paradise surrounded by 10 acres of lush tropical vegetation, 30 minutes from San Juan

**Hotel El Convento** Calle Cristo 100, Old San Juan (btwn Caleta de las Monjas & Calle Sol) 787/723-9020, 800/468-2779 • gay-friendly • 17th-c former Carmelite convent • pool • WiFi

**Miramar Hotel** 606 Ave Ponce de Leon (at Miramar) 787/977-1000 • gay-friendly • WiFi • also restaurant & bar

**Numero Uno on the Beach** Calle Santa Ana 1, Ocean Park (near Calle Italia) 787/726-5010, 866/726-5010 • gay/ straight • pool • also Pamela's, full bar & grill • kids ok • wheelchair access

**The San Juan Water & Beach Club Hotel** 2 Tartak St (Isla Verde), Carolina 787/728-3666, 888/265-6699 • gay-friendly • boutique hotel on the beach • restaurant & lounge • kids ok • rooftop pool • nonsmoking • WiFi • wheelchair access

## BARS

**Atlantic Beach Bar & Hotel** 1 Calle Vendig, Condado 787/721-6900 • 10am-2am • gay/ straight • great beach location

**Batucada** 15 Ave Carlos Chardon, Hato Rey 787/993-1291 • gay-friendly • neighborhood sports bar & grill • karaoke

**Esechys** 478 Calle Jose Canals (near Calle Rodrigo de Triana, Placita Roosevelt), Hato Rey 787/607-3939 • open Tue-Sun • mostly women • live music Fri

**Oasis** Av Condado 6 (in Condado, next to the San Juan Marriot) 787/721-7145 • 1pm-close • mostly gay men • near beach

**Tia Maria's** 326 Ave Jose de Diego, Parada 22 (at Ponce de León), Santurce 787/724-4011 • 11am-midnight, till 2am Fri-Sat • lesbians/ gay men • neighborhood bar • also liquor shop

## NIGHTCLUBS

**Circo Bar** Calle Condado 650, Parada 18, Santurce 787/725-9676 • 9pm-5am • mostly men • dancing/DJ • karaoke • beware of the neighborhood

## CAFES

**Cafe Berlin** Calle San Francisco 407, Plaza Colón, Old San Juan (btwn Calles Norzagary & O'Donnel) 787/722-5205 • 11am-11pm • popular • espresso bar • plenty veggie

**Kasalta Bakery** 1966 McLeary Ave (at Teniente Matta) 787/727-7340 • 6am-10pm • bakery & deli

## RESTAURANTS

**Aguaviva** 364 Calle La Fortaleza, Old San Juan (at Calle O'Donnell) 787/722-0665 • dinner nightly • fresh seafood & ceviche • wheelchair access

**Ajili Mojili** 1052 Ashford Ave, Condado (at Aguadilla) 787/725-9195 • local specialties • live music • great ambiance

**Al Dente** 309 Calle Recinto S, Old San Juan 787/723-7303 • lunch & dinner, clsd Sun • Italian • also wine bar

**Bebo's Cafe** 1600 Calle Loiza (at Del Parque) 787/268-5087 • cheap & delicious • cafeteria-style Puerto Rican favorites

**Cafe Puerto Rico** 208 O'Donnell, Old San Juan 787/724-2281 • noon-11pm • great mofongo • outdoor seating

**La Casita Blanca** 351 Calle Tapia (off Ave Eduardo Conde, near Laguna Los Corozas) 787/726-5501 • 11am-4pm, till 6pm Th, till 9pm Fri-Sat • amazing local cuisine • best reached by car • no English spoken • beware of neighborhood

**Colombo** 1024 Ashford Ave (at Aguadilla St) 787/725-1212 • 8am-3am • American • also bar • WiFi

**Dragonfly** 364 S Fortaleza St, Old San Juan (across from Parrot Club) 787/977-3886 • opens 5:30pm daily • full bar • Latin/ Asian fusion

**Fleria** 1754 Calle Loiza, Santurce 787/268-0010 • lunch & dinner, clsd Sun-Mon • Greek • some veggie

**El Jibarito** Calle Sol 280 787/725-8375 • Puerto Rican/ criolla • also bar

**Oceano Restaurant & Lounge** 2 Calle Vendig, Condado 787/724-6400 • great beach location • Sun gay party

**The Parrot Club** Calle Fortaleza 363, Old San Juan (btwn Plaza Colón & Callejón de la Capilla) 787/725-7370 • lunch & dinner • chic Nuevo Latino bistro & bar • live music

**Perla** 1077 Ashford Ave, at La Concha Resort, Condado 787/721-7500 • enjoy an upscale dining experience inside a gigantic conch shell • swank!

**Vidy's Cafe** Ave Universidad 104 (Rio Piedras) 787/767-3062 • 10am-1am • plenty veggie • karaoke

## ENTERTAINMENT & RECREATION

**Atlantic Beach** in front of Atlantic Beach Hotel • very gay-friendly beach

**Nuyorican Cafe** San Francisco 312 (by El Callejon) 787/977-1276, 787/366-5074 • live music & arts venue

**Ocean Park Beach** E of Condado • gay/ straight beach • adult-oriented (less kids)

**La Placita/ Plaza del Mercado** Santurce • open-air market by day, street-party by night • lots of bars & restaurants

## ACCOMMODATIONS

**Temptation** 608 Calle Bolivar (Santruce) 787/309-8888 • 10pm-3am, from 5pm Fri • mostly gay men • dancing/DJ • food served

## Vieques Island

### ACCOMMODATIONS

**Bravo!** North Shore Rd (at Lighthouse) **787/741–1128** • gay/ straight • pool • gay-owned

**Casa de Amistad** 27 Benitez Castano **787/741–3758** • gay/ straight • guesthouse in heart of Isabel Segunda • WiFi • gay-owned

**Inn on the Blue Horizon** **787/741–3318** • gay-friendly • country inn & cottages • pool • beach access • restaurant • nonsmoking • WiFi

## TRINIDAD & TOBAGO

### Tobago

### ACCOMMODATIONS

**Grafton Beach Resort** **868/639–0191, 888/790–5264** • gay-friendly • pool • food served

**Kariwak Village Hotel & Holistic Haven** Store Bay Local Rd, Crown Point **868/639–8442, 868/639–8545** • gay-friendly • holistic hotel • kids ok • pool • restaurant • wheelchair access

## VIRGIN ISLANDS

### St Croix

### ACCOMMODATIONS

**King Christian Hotel** 59 Kings Wharf, Christiansted **340/773–6330, 800/524–2012** • gay-friendly • pool • also restaurant

**Sand Castle on the Beach** 127 Smithfield, Frederiksted **340/772–1205, 800/524–2018** • lesbian, gay & straight-friendly • hotel • solar heated pool • WiFi • also restaurant & bar • lesbian & gay-owned

### St John

### ACCOMMODATIONS

**Gallows Point Suite Resort** Cruz Bay **340/776–6434, 800/323–7229** • gay-friendly • beachfront resort • pool • kitchens • also restaurant • full bar • wheelchair access

**Hillcrest Guest House** **340/776–6774, 340/998–8388** • gay-friendly • WiFi • nonsmoking • kids ok

**St John Inn** **800/666–7688, 340/693–8688** • gay-friendly • kids ok • pool • nonsmoking

### RESTAURANTS

**Asolare** Rte 20, Cruz Bay **340/779–4747** • 5:30pm-9:30pm • Asian/ French fusion • hip & elegant

### ENTERTAINMENT & RECREATION

**Salomon Bay** • 20-minute hike on Salomon Beach Trail

### St Thomas

### ACCOMMODATIONS

**Hotel 1829** Government Hill **340/776–1829, 800/524–2002** • gay-friendly • pool • also full bar & restaurant

**Pavilions & Pools Hotel** 6400 Estate Smith Bay **340/775–6110, 800/524–2001** • gay-friendly • 1-bdrm villas each w/ own private swimming pool

### RESTAURANTS

**Mafolie Hotel & Restaurant** 7091 Estate Mafolie **340/774–2790** • great place for lunch with a view

**Oceana Restaurant & Wine Bar** Historic Pointe at Villa Olga **340/774–4262** • on the water's edge • owned by renowned chef Patricia LaCorte

**Virgilio's** 18 Dronningens Gade **340/776–4920** • clsd Sun, great Italian, full bar

### ENTERTAINMENT & RECREATION

**Beach at Emerald Beach Resort** up hill (near airport runway) • walking distance from cruise ship dock

**Morning Star Beach** • popular gay beach

## MEXICO

**Please Note: Mexican cities are often divided into districts or "Colonias," which we abbreviate as "Col." Please use these when giving addresses for directions.**

### Acapulco

### ACCOMMODATIONS

**Casa Condesa** Bella Vista 125 **52–744/484–1616, 800/816–4817 (US & CANADA)** • mostly gay men • full brkfst • near beach • pool

**Hotel Boca Chica** Punta Caletilla (Fraccionamiento las Playas) **800/337–4685** • gay-friendly • pool • also restaurant

**Hotel Encanto** Jacques Cousteau 51 (Fraccionamiento Brisas Marques) **52-744/446-7101** • gay-friendly • pool • WiFi • also restaurant

**Las Brisas** Carretera Escenica 5255 **52-744/469-6900, 866/221-2961 (US#)** • popular • gay-friendly • luxury resort • private pools • kids ok • wheelchair access

## NIGHTCLUBS

**Baby 'O 52-744/484-7474** • 10:30pm-5am, till midnight Sun • gay/ straight

**Cabaré-Tito Beach** Privada de Piedra Picuda 17 PA (nr Torres Gemelas) **52-744/1-24-89-29** • 6pm-3am, from 4pm Th-Sat • lesbians/ gay men • dancing/DJ

**Relax** Calle Lomas de Mar 4 (Zona Dorada) **52-744/482-0421** • 10pm-late, clsd Mon-Wed • popular • lesbians/ gay men • dancing/DJ • drag & strip shows wknds • videos • young crowd

## RESTAURANTS

**100% Natural** Av Costera Miguel Alemán 200 (near Acapulco Plaza) **52-744/485-3982** • 24hrs • fast (healthy) food • plenty veggie

**Becco al Mare 52-744/446-7402** • lunch & dinner • Italian • nice views

**Beto's Restaurant** Av Costera Miguel Alemán 99 (at Condesa Beach) **52-744/484-0473** • 11am-midnight • lesbians/ gay men • full bar • seafood • palapas

**El Cabrito** Av Costera Miguel Alemán 1480 (near Convention Center) **52-744/484-7711** • 2pm-midnight, till 11pm Sun • local favorite • try the roasted goat

**Carlos & Charlie's** Blvd de las Naciones #1813 (in La Isla Shopping Village) **52-744/462-2104** • lunch & dinner • entertainment

**Kookaburra** 3 Fracc (at Marina Las Brisas) **52-744/446-6039** • lunch & dinner • int'l • expensive

**La Cabaña de Caleta** Playa Caleta Lado Oriente s/n (Fracc. las Playas) **52-744/469-8553, 52-744/469-7919** • 9am-9pm • seafood • right on Playa Caleta • great magaritas

**La Tortuga** Calle Lomas del Mar 5 **52-744/484-6985** • noon-midnight, clsd Mon • full bar • good Mexican • seafood • patio • gay-owned

**Shu** Blvd de las Naciones 1813 (Centro Comercial La Isla ) **52-744/462-2001** • Japanese

**Su Casa Angel & Shelly** Av Anahuac 110 **52-744/484-1261, 52-744/484-4350** • seafood • tasty margaritas • great views

**Suntory de Acapulco** Costera Miguel Alemán 36 **52-744/484-8088** • 2pm-midnight • Japanese • gardens

**El Zorrito's** Av Costera Miguel Alemán (at Anton de Alaminos) **52-744/485-3735** • traditional Mexican • several locations along Costera • some all night

# Aguascalientes

## NIGHTCLUBS

**Mandiles** Av Lopez Mateos Poniente 730 W (btwn Agucate & Chabacano) **52-449/153-281** • 10pm-3am Fri-Sat only • lesbians/ gay men • dancing/DJ

# Cabo San Lucas

## ACCOMMODATIONS

**Cabo Villas Beach Resort** Callejon del Pescador s/n (Col. El Medano) **52-624/143-9199, 866/962-2268** • gay-friendly • resort on Medano Beach • pool

**Solmar Suites** Av Solmar 1 **800/344-3349, 310/459-9861 (US#)** • gay-friendly • oceanfront suites at southernmost tip • 2 pools • hot tub

## NIGHTCLUBS

**Las Varitas** Calle Vallentin Gomez Farias (at Camino Viejo a San Jose) **52-624/143-9999** • 9pm-3am, clsd Mon • gay-friendly • dancing/DJ • live shows • rock 'n' roll bar • Ladies Night Fri

## RESTAURANTS

**Mi Casa** Av Cabo San Lucas (at Lazarus Cardenas) **52-624/143-1933** • clsd Sun • lunch & dinner • great chicken mole • reservations recommended

# Cancun

**see also Cozumel & Playa del Carmen**

## ENTERTAINMENT & RECREATION

**Gaytoursmexico by MMT** Av Sunyaxchen 24 **52-998/845-7654** • we specialize in 100% gay excursions on the Yucatan Peninsula

## ACCOMMODATIONS

**Rancho Sak Ol** Puerto Morelos **52-998/871-0181** • gay-friendly • beachfront palapa-style B&B • 30 minutes from Cancún

## Bars

**Picante Bar** Av Tulúm 20, Centro (E of Av Uxmal, next to Plaza Galerías) • 9pm-5am • popular • mostly gay men • dancing/DJ • young crowd • drag shows & strippers Wed-Sat

## Nightclubs

**Karamba** Av Tulúm 9 (Azucenas 2nd flr, SM 22) 52-998/884-0032 • 10:30pm-close, clsd Mon • popular • lesbians/gay men • dancing/DJ • karaoke • drag shows • go-go boys Fri

**Sexy's Club** Av Tulum Plaza Safa Planta Alta 52-998/280-3943 • 10pm-8am, clsd Mon-Tue • mostly gay men • dancing/DJ • cover charge

## Restaurants

**100% Natural** Sunyaxchen 62 52-998/884-0102 • healthy fast food

**Perico's** Av Yaxhilan 61 52-998/884-3152 • noon-1am • traditional Mexican served up w/ huge theatrical flare

## Entertainment & Recreation

**Chichén Itza** • the must-see Mayan ruin 125 miles from Cancún

**Playa Delfines** in the Hotel Zone (next to Hilton's beach) • gay beach

# Chihuahua

## Accommodations

**Hacienda Huiyochi** Copper Canyon 51-1/625-121-8101 • first & only hotel in Copper Canyon that caters to the LGBT community • full brkfst • kids/pets ok

# Ciudad Juárez

see also El Paso, Texas, USA

## Bars

**Club La Escondida** Calle Ignacio de la Peña 366 W • gay/straight • neighborhood bar

## Nightclubs

**G-Life Club** 16 de septiembre 119 (at Constitucion) 52-656/304-4513 • 4pm-9pm Th-Fri and 9am-3pm Sat only • mostly gay men • dancing/DJ

# Copala

## Accommodations

**La Caracola** Antelmo Ventura 68 (2 1/2 hrs from Acapulco) 52-741/101-3047 • gay/straight • pool • WiFi • women-run

# Cordoba

## Bars

**Salon Bar El Metro** Av 7 no. 117–C (btwn Calles 1 & 3) • lesbians/gay men • dancing

# Cozumel

see also Cancún & Playa del Carmen

## Accommodations

**Flamingo Hotel** Calle 6 Norte #81 (at Ave 5) 954/351-9236, 800/806-1601 • gay-friendly • WI • pets ok

# Cuernavaca

## Accommodations

**Casa del Angel** Calle Clavel 18, Col. Satelite (at Begonia) 52-777/512-6775 • gay/straight • contemporary guesthouse on hill overlooking Cuernavaca • hot tub • nonsmoking • full brkfst • gay-owned

**Las Mañanitas** Ricardo Linares 107 52-777/312-8982 & 314-1466, 888/413-9199 (US ONLY) • gay-friendly • gardens • pool • restaurant • peacocks!

**La Nuestra** Calle Mesalina 18 (at Calle Neptuno) 52-777/315-2272, 404/806-9694 • gay/straight • B&B • full brkfst • pool • kids ok • WiFi • lesbian-owned

## Bars

**Barecito** Comonfort 17 (at Morrow) 52-777/314-1425 • 5pm-1am • lesbians/gay men • food served • lesbian-owned

## Nightclubs

**Oxygen** Av Vincente Guerrero 1303 (near Sam's Club) 52-777/317-2714 • 10pm-close, Fri-Sat only • mostly gay men • dancing/DJ • food served • live shows • drag shows • videos • 18+ • young crowd

## Restaurants

**La India Bonita** Dwight Morrow 15 (btwn Morelos & Matamoros) 52-777/312-5021 • 9am-9pm, till 5pm Sun-Mon

**La Maga** Calle Morrow #9 Altos 52-777/310-0432 • clsd Sun, popular lunch buffet • plenty veggie • live music

**Marco Polo** Calle Hidalgo 30 (in front of cathedral, 2nd flr) 52-777/312-3484, 52-777/318-4032 • 1pm-close • Italian (pasta & pizza) • overlooking cathedral

## Entertainment & Recreation

**Diego Rivera Murals** Plaza de Museo (in Cuauhnáhuac Regional Museum)

## Ensenada

### NIGHTCLUBS

**Sublime** Plaza Blanca , 3rd Fl
52-646/128-8798 • 9pm-close • mostly gay
men • dancing/DJ

### RESTAURANTS

**Casamar** Blvd Costero 987 52-646/174-0417
• 8am-10:30pm • popular • seafood • also bar
• Ensenada landmark for 30 years

## Guadalajara

### ACCOMMODATIONS

**Casa Alebrijes Hotel** Libertad 1016, Zona
Centro 52-33/3614-5232 • mostly gay men •
boutique hotel in historic center • two blocks
from gay nightlife area • WiFi • gay-owned

**Casa de las Flores B&B** Santos Degollado
175, Tlaquepaque 52-33/3659-3186,
888/582-4896 • gay-friendly • 15 minutes
from Guadalajara • great brkfsts & margaritas

**Casa Venezuela** Calle Venezuela 459 (at
Col. Americana) 52-33/3826-6590 • gay/
straight • B&B in 100-year-old colonial house •
full brkft • nonsmoking • WiFi • gay-owned

**Hostel Lit** Degollado 413 52-33/1200-5505 •
gay-friendly • WiFi

**Hotel San Francisco** Degollado 267
52-33/3613-3256 • gay-friendly • hotel w/ Old
World charm • close to gay bars • also
restaurant

**Old Guadalajara B&B** Belén 236 (Centro
Histórico) 52-33/3613-9958 • gay/ straight •
nonsmoking • gay-owned

**Orchid House B&B** Juan de Ojeda 75 (at
Ave La Paz) 52-33/3335-19 21 • gay/ straight
• gay-owned

**La Perla B&B** Prado 128, Col. Americana
(Vallarta y Lopez Cotilla) 317/534-2661 • gay/
straight • full brkft • nonsmoking • WiFi •
gay-owned

**La Villa del Ensueño** Florida St 305,
Tlaquepaque 52-33/3635-8792 • gay/ straight
• full brkft

### BARS

**Caudillos Bar** Calle Prisciliano Sánchez 305,
Centro (at Ocampo) 52-33/3613-5445 •
5pm-3am • popular • mostly gay men •
dancing from 9pm • friendly bar • also
restaurant

**Club YeYe** Prisciliano Sánchez 395 (Zona
Centro) 52-33/1337-5253 • 5pm-3am •
lesbians/ gay men • chic video lounge • food
served

**Dona Diabla** Colon 530 • 7pm-3am Wed-
Sun • gay/ straight • shows

**Equilibrio Restaurant & Bar** Ocampo 293
(at Miguel Blanco)

**Maskaras** Calle Maestranza 238 (at
Prisciliano Sánchez) 52-33/3614-8103 •
noon-3am • lesbians/ gay men •
neighborhood bar • colorful atmosphere • live
music • food served

**La Minerva** 8 de Julio #73 52-33/3613-5167
• mostly gay men • karaoke • strippers •
theme nights

### NIGHTCLUBS

**7 Sins** Pedro Moreno 532 (at Donato Guerra,
Zona Centro) 52-33/3658-0713 • mostly gay
men • dancing/DJ

**Black Cherry Grand** Popocatepetl 40 (at
Adolfo Lopez Mateos Sur) 52-33/3647-9024
• 10pm-5am Sat only • mostly gay men •
dancing/DJ

**El Botanero** Calle Javier Mina 1348 (at Calle
54, Sector Libertad) 52-33/3643-0545 • 6pm-
3am, till 1am Sun, clsd Mon-Tue • mostly gay
men • dancing/DJ • food served • karaoke •
drag shows • T-dance Sun • cover charge

**Circus** Galeana 277 (at Prisciliano Sánchez,
Centro Histórico) 52-33/3613-0299 • 9pm-
5am • popular • lesbians/ gay men • dancing
• live shows

**Mónica's** Av Álvaro Obregón 1713 (btwn
Calles 68 & 70, Sector Libertad; no sign, look
for canopy under a big palm tree)
52-33/3643-9544 • 9pm-5am, clsd Mon-Tue •
popular after midnight • mostly gay men •
dancing/DJ • drag & strip shows wknds •
young crowd • cover charge • take a taxi to &
from

**Om Club** Ocampo 270 52-33/3121-9547 •
9am-4pm Th-Sat, 5pm-10pm Sun • mostly gay
men • dancing/DJ

### CAFES

**Dolce Veele** Enrique González Martínez 177
52-33/1523-9593 • 4pm-1am • lesbians/ gay
men • WiFi

**Queer Nation** López Cotilla 611 • 5pm-
midnight, clsd Sun • souvenirs

**Vida Caffe** Av Hidalgo 907 52-33/1181-1834
• 4:30pm-close • lesbians/ gay men

### RESTAURANTS

**Sanborns** Av 16 de Septiembre 127
52-33/3613-6264 • many locations • WiFi

## PUBLICATIONS

**GAYGDL** • online magazine at www.gaygdl.com

**Urbana Revista** • gay lifestyle magazine w/ bars & clubs for Guadalajara & Puerto Vallarta

## Isla Mujeres

### ACCOMMODATIONS

**Casa Sirena** Av Miguel Hidalgo, Centro (at Bravo y Allende) • gay-friendly • Isla Mujeres is a short, 20-minute ferry ride from Cancun • gay-owned

## La Paz

### ACCOMMODATIONS

**La Casa Mexicana Inn** Calle Nicolas Bravo 106 (btwn Madero & Mutualismo) 52-612/125-2748 • open Nov-June • gay/ straight • Spanish/ Moorish retreat • 1 block from La Paz Bay • nonsmoking • WiFi • wheelchair access • woman-owned

**Hotel Mediterrane** Allende 36 (at Malecón) 52-612/125-1195 • gay/ straight • WiFi • nonsmoking • bar & restaurant • sun terrace • gay-owned

### BARS

**Cafe La Pazta** Allende 36 (at Hotel Mediterrane) 52-612/125-1195 • 7am-11pm • gay/ straight • neighborhood bar • also restaurant • young crowd • gay-owned

### NIGHTCLUBS

**Las Varitas** Calle Independencia 111 (at Malecón) 52-612/123-1590 • 9pm-3am, clsd Mon • gay-friendly • dancing/DJ • live shows • rock 'n' roll bar • Ladies Night Fri

## León

### NIGHTCLUBS

**La Madame** Blvd A López Mateos 1709 Oriente (in front of Torre Banamex) 52-477/763-3086 • 10pm-3am, clsd Mon-Wed • mostly gay men • dancing/DJ • drag shows • go-go boys

**Nation** 52-477/716-3695 • gay/ straight • dancing/DJ

## Manzanillo

### ACCOMMODATIONS

**Las Hadas** Av Vista Hermosa s/n (Fracc. Península de Santiago) 52-314/331-0101, 888/559-4329 • gay-friendly • great resort & location

**Red Tree Melaque Inn** Primaveras 32 (30 miles N of Manzanillo), Melaque-Villa Obregon 52-315/355-8917, 480/389-5786 **(US)** • gay-friendly • bungalows • near ocean • pool • kids/ pets ok • nonsmoking • gay-owned

## Mazatlán

### ACCOMMODATIONS

**El Cid Resort** 866/306-6113, 52-669/913-3333 • gay-friendly

**Old Mazatlan Condos** 52-669/981-4361, 866/385-2045 • gay-friendly • swimming • WiFi • gay-owned

**The Pueblo Bonito Emerald Bay** Ave Ernesto Coppel Compaña 201 52-669/989-0525, 800/990-8250 • gay-friendly • resort on 20 acres • jacuzzi • pool • restaurant • piano bar • gym

**Ramada Mazatlán** Av Playa Gaviotas 100 (Zona Dorada) 52-669/983-5333, 800/528-8760 (US#) • gay-friendly • resort • swimming • beach • health club • also popular Joe's Oyster Bar

### BARS

**Pepe Toro** Av de las Garzas 18 (1 block W of Av Camarón Sábalo, Zona Dorada) 52-669/914-4176 • 9:30pm-4am, clsd Mon-Th • popular • mostly gay men • dancing/DJ • drag & strip shows

**Vitrolas Bar** Heriberto Frías 1608 (in Centro Historico) 52-669/985-2221 • 3pm-1am, clsd Mon • lesbians/ gay men • lunch menu • karaoke • drag shows & strippers Sun

### RESTAURANTS

**Cafe Playa Sur** 520/366-8487 • 7am-9pm, clsd Mon • WiFi • gay-owned

**Panamá Restaurant & Pastelería** at Avs de las Garzas & Camarón Sábalo (Zona Dorada) 52-669/913-6977

**Roca Mar** Av del Mar (at Calle Isla de Lobos, Zona Costera) 52-669/981-6008 • till 2am • popular • seafood • full bar • lesbian-owned

## Mérida

### ACCOMMODATIONS

**Angeles de Mérida** Calle 74-A, #494-A (at Calle 57 & Calle 59) 52-999/923-8163 • gay-friendly • B&B in 18th-c home on quietest streets of Mérida • full brkfst • nonsmoking • pool • spa services available

**Los Arcos B&B** Calle 66 52-999/928-0214 • gay-friendly • pool • gay-owned

**Casa Ana B&B** Calle 52 #469 (btwn 51 & 53) 52-999/924-0005 • gay-friendly • pool • nonsmoking • women-owned

**La Casa Lorenzo** Calle 41 #516 A (btwn 62 & 64) 52-999/139-0423 , 866/515-4105 • gay-friendly • pool • nonsmoking • WiFi • gay-owned

**Casa San Juan B&B** 545-A Calle 62 (btwn Calle 69 & Calle 71) 52-999/986-2937, 866/979-6753 • gay/ straight • nonsmoking • kids ok • wheelchair access • gay-owned

**Casa Santiago B&B** Calle 63 #562 (btwn Calles 70 & 72) 52-999/928-9375 • gay/ straight • colonial restored house • pool • nonsmoking • WiFi • wheelchair access • gay-owned

**Gran Hotel** Calle 60 #496 (nr Parque Cepeda Peraza) 52-999/924-7730 & 923-6963 • gay-friendly • historic turn-of-the-century hotel • pets ok • also restaurant

**Las Arecas Guesthouse** Calle 59 #541 (btwn Calle 66 & Calle 68) 52-999/928-3626 • gay-friendly • guesthouse • garden • gay-owned

**Posada Santiago Guesthouse** Calle 57 No 552 (between Calle 66 & 68, Centro Historico) 52-999/924-4258 • gay/ straight • pool • nonsmoking • WiFi • wheelchair access • gay-owned

### Bars

**El Establo** Calle 60 #482 (btwn Calle 56 & 58) 52-999/924-2289 • gay-friendly • dancing/DJ • food served • popular w/ tourists & locals

### Nightclubs

**Pride Disco** Campeche A (200 meters del Puente de Ulman), Anillo Periferico 52-999/946-4401 • mostly gay men • dancing/DJ • strippers • south of town, all taxi drivers know where it is located

### Restaurants

**Cafe La Habana** Calle 59 #511-A (at Calle 62) 52-999/928-6502 • 24hrs • also bar & café

**Cafeteria Pop** Calle 57 (btwn Calle 60 & 62) 52-999/928-6163 • brkfst, lunch & "light dinner" • beer & wine

**La Bella Época** Calle 60 #447 (upstairs in the Hotel del Parque) 52-99/928-1928 • 4pm-1am • Yucatécan cuisine • try to get one of the balcony tables

## Mexico City

Note: M°=Metro station

Note: Mexico City is divided into "Zonas" (ie, Zona Rosa) & "Colonias" (abbreviated here as "Col."). Remember to use these when giving addresses to taxi drivers.

### Info Lines & Services

**Cálamo (LGBT AA)** Av de Chapultepec 465, desd 202 (Col. Juárez) 52-55/5574-1210 • 8pm Mon-Fri, 7pm Sat, 6pm Sun

**Centro Cultural de la Diversidad Sexual** Colima 267 (Col. Roma Norte) 52-55/5514-2565, 52-55/1450-9511 • Mexico City's LGBT center • also cafe

**Jovenes La Villa AA** Calle 521 #248 (nr Ave 510) 52-55/2603-7696

### Accommodations

**Las Alcobas** Presidente Masaryk 390A 52-55/3300-3900 • gay/straight • masterfully designed boutique hotel • two restaurants on site • great location

**Best Western Majestic Hotel** Ave Madero 73, Col. Centro 52-55/5521-8600 • gay-friendly • on the Zócalo Plaza • rooftop restaurant • wheelchair access

**Condesa Haus** Cuernavaca 142 (at Campeche) 52-55/5256-2494, 310/622 4825 (US) • gay-friendly • WiFi • full brkfst • gay-owned

**Downtown México** 30 Isabel la Catolica 52-55/5130-6830 • gay-friendly • magnificent 17th century building, rooftop bar & pool

**Hostal Central Historico Regina** 5 de Febrero #53 (Col. Centro) 52-55/5709-4192 • gay-friendly • also cafe • WiFi

**Hotel Casa Blanca** Lafragua 7 (Col. Tabacalera) 52-55/5096-4500, 800/905-2905 • gay-friendly• pool • restaurant & bar

**Hotel Gillow** Isabel la Católica 17 (Col. Centro) 52-55/5518-1440, 52-55/5510-2636 • gay-friendly • also restaurant & bar

**Hotel Principado** Londres 42 (Col Juarez) 52-55/5533-2944 • gay-friendly

**El Patio 77** Icazbalceta 77 (Col. San Rafael) 52-55/5455-0332, 52-55/5592-8452 • gay-friendly • eco-friendly B&B • WiFi

**The Red Tree House** Culiacan 6 (at Avenida Amsterdam) 52-55/5584-3829 • gay-friendly • stylish B&B • gay-owned

**W Mexico City** Campos Eliseos 252 52-55/9138-1800 • gay-friendly • in trendy Polanco • 2 restaurants & bar • WiFi

## Bars

**42 Bar** Amberes 4 (Zona Rosa) 52-55/5208-0352

**Bar Lili** Calle 65 #7 (Col. Puebla) 52-55/4551-0414 • lesbians/ gay men • neighborhood bar

**Black Out** Amberes 11 (Zona Rosa) 52-55/5511-9247 • gay/ straight • upscale lounge • also restaurant

**La Gayta/ Pussy Bar** Amberes 18 (Zona Rosa) 52-551/055-5873 • lesbians/ gay men • neighborhood bar • young crowd

**Lipstick** Amberes 1 (at Paseo de la Reforma, Zona Rosa) 52-55/5514-4920 • clsd Sun-Wed • gay/ straight • more lesbian Th • lounge • videos • live shows

**El Marrakech Salón** Republica de Cuba 18 (Col. Centro) • lesbians/ gay men • neighborhood bar

**Oasis** República de Cuba 2 (Centro Historico) 52-55/5511-9740 • 3pm-1am, till 3am Fri-Sat • mostly gay men • drag shows • cover charge

**Papi Fun Bar** Amberes 18 (Zona Rosa) 52-55/5208-3755 • lesbians/ gay men • neighborhood bar • young crowd

**Pride Restbar** Alfonso Reyes 281 (Col. Condessa) 52-55/5516-2368

**Tom's Leather Bar** Av Insurgentes 357 (Col. Condesa) 55-84/5564-0728 • 9pm-4am, clsd Mon

**Viena Bar** República de Cuba 3 (Centro Historico) 52-55/5512-0929 • 11am-11pm, clsd Mon-Tue • mostly gay men • beer & tequila only

## Nightclubs

**Butterflies** Calle Izazaga 9 (at Av Lazaro Cárdenas S, Centro Historico) 52-55/5761-1861 • 9pm-3am, till 4:30am Fri-Sat, clsd Mon • popular • lesbians/ gay men • dancing/DJ • 2 flrs • lavish drag shows Fri-Sat • cover charge

**Cabaré-Tito Neón** Calle Londres 161, Local 20-A, Plaza del Angel (Zona Rosa) 52-55/5514-9455 • 6pm-close • mostly gay men • dancing/DJ • go-go dancers

**Club 24** Santa María La Ribera # 24 Del Cuauhtémoc 52-55/2198-2580 • 9am-4am Fri-Sat only • mostly gay men • dancing/DJ

**Envy** Av Las Palmas 500 (Sierra Gamon) • gay/ straight • dancing/DJ

**Hibrido** Calle Londres 161, Plaza del Angel, 2nd flr (Zona Rosa) 52-55/5511-1197 • Th-Sun • lesbians/ gay men • dancing/DJ • strippers

**Liverpool 100** Liverpool 100 (Col. Juarez) 52-55/5208-4507 • 9pm-close Wed, Fri-Sat only • mostly gay men • dancing/DJ

**Living** Bucareli 144 (Col. Juarez) 55-55/5512-7281 • 10pm-close Fri-Sat only • popular • mostly men • popular • theme nights

## Cafes

**B Gay B Proud** Amberes 12-B (Zona Rosa) • food served

## Restaurants

**12:30** Amberes 13 (Zona Rosa) 52-55/5514-5971 • popular before-clubbing hangout

**La Antigua Cortesana** Chiapas 173-A (Col. Roma) 52-55/5584-4678 • 1pm-11pm, till midnight Fri-Sat, till 7pm Sun • popular Mexican cuisine • also bar

**Cafe 22** Montes de Oca 22 (Col. Condesa) 52-55/5212-1533 • 6pm-2am • Mexican & Italian • also shows

**El Cardenal** Calle de Palma 23 52-55/5521-8815 • incredible pastries

**Casa Merlos** Victoriano Zepeda 80 (at Obsevatoria) 52-55/5277-4360 • traditional poblano food • definitely try the molé

**Cote Sud** Orizaba 87 (Col. Roma) 52-55/5219-2981 • 8am-11pm, till midnight Fri, 10am-6pm Sun • French/ tapas

**Fonda San Ángel** Plaza San Jacinto 3, Col. San Ángel (across from Bazar San Ángel) 52-55/5550-1641 & 1942 • popular after 7pm Fri-Sat • classic Mexican dishes

**Ligaya** Nuevo Leon 68 (in Condesa) 52-55/5286-6268 • nouvelle Mexican • dinner nightly • outdoor seating

**La Nueva Opera** Ave Cinco de Mayo 10 (Centro Historico) 52-55/5512-8959 • 1pm-midnight, clsd Sun • legendary cantina since Pancho Villa fired a bullet into the ceiling

**Sanborns** Madera 4 (in Casa de los Azulejos) 52-55/5518-6676 • brkfst, lunch & dinner • superstore

**Xel-Ha** 52-55/5553-5968 • traditional cuisine of the Yucatan

## Entertainment & Recreation

**El Hábito** Madrid 13 (Coyacán District) 52-55/5659-1139 • avant-garde theater & bar

**Museo de Arte Carrillo Gil** Av Revolución 1608 (Col San Angel) 52-55/5550-6260, 52-55/5550-3983 • 10am-6pm, clsd Mon • contemporary art

**Museo de Frida Kahlo** Calle Londres 247 (Coyacán ) 52-55/5554-5999 • 10am-5:45pm, clsd Mon • original paintings, furniture, letters & Frida's dresses • also garden & café

**Museo Templo Mayor** Calle Seminario 8 (at República de Guatemala, enter on plaza, near Cathedral) 52-55/4040-5600 • 9am-5pm, clsd Mon • artifacts from the central Aztec temple at Tenochtitlán

### BOOKSTORES

**El Armario Abierto** Agustín Melgar 25 (Col. Condesa) 52-55/5286-0895 • Mexico's only bookstore specializing in sexuality • some LGBT titles

**Voces en Tinta** Niza 23A (A Entre Reforma y Hamburgo) 52-55/5533-7116 • 10am-9pm • lesbian bookstore & cafe

### RETAIL SHOPS

**Rainbowland** Estrasburgo 31 (Zona Rosa) 52-55/5525-9066

### PUBLICATIONS

**LeS VOZ Magazine** • "The magazine of Mexico's lesbian feminist culture, by & for women"

**Ser Gay** 52-55/1450-9511 • quarterly magazine • covers all Mexico nightlife

## Monterrey

### ACCOMMODATIONS

**Holiday Inn Monterrey Centro** Av Padre Mier 194 N (at Garibaldi, Centro) 52-81/8228-6000 • gay-friendly • near Zona Rosa • pool • also restaurant

### BARS

**Akbal** Abasolo 870B, 2nd flr, Casa del Maíz 52-81/1257-2986 • 9pm-2am, clsd Mon • gay/ straight • more gay Sun

**Casa de Lola** 52-81/8343-6210 • Th-Sat only • mostly gay men • dancing/DJ • karaoke

### NIGHTCLUBS

**Baby Shower** Ocampo 433 Puente (btwn Rayon & Aldama Centro) 52-81/8881-5632 • 9pm-close, clsd Mon-Tue • lesbians/ gay men • dancing/DJ • strippers • videos

**Bizù Disco** 1355 Miguel Hidalgo y Costilla 52-81/8994-4676

**Parking** Allende 120 Ote (btwn Juarez & Guerrero) 52-81/8343-2624 • 10pm-close Wed-Sat • mostly gay men • dancing/DJ

**Vongole & Between Bar** 2121 Eugenio Garza Sada Ave 52-81/8358-7035

## Morelia

### ACCOMMODATIONS

**Casa Camelinas B&B** Jacarandas 172 (Col. Nueva Jacarandas) 52-433/324-5194, 707/942-5083 (US#) • gay-friendly • mostly women • 3 1/2 hours from Mexico City • nonsmoking • also Spanish classes

**Hotel de la Soledad** Ignacio Zaragoza 90 52-443/312-1888 • gay-friendly • in charming old hotel in converted convent • also restaurant & bar

### NIGHTCLUBS

**Con la Rojas** Calle Aldama 343 (Centro) 52-443/312-1578 • 10pm-2:30am, clsd Sun-Tue • mostly gay men • dancing/DJ • cover charge

**Mamá no lo sabe** Aldama 116 (at García Obeso) 52-44/3189-9447 • 10pm-3am • mostly gay men • karaoke

### RESTAURANTS

**Fonda Las Mercedes** Calle Leon Guzmán 47 52-443/312-6113 & 313-3222 • popular • inside beautiful colonial home

## Oaxaca

### ACCOMMODATIONS

**Casa Adobe B&B** Independencia 801 (at Matamoros), Tlalixtac de Cabrera 52-951/517-7268 • gay/ straight • 15 minutes from center of Oaxaca • WiFi • gay-owned

**Casa Colonial** Calle Miguel Negrete 105 (Division Poniente) 52-951/516-5280 • gay-friendly • WiFi • kids/pets ok • wheelchair access

**La Casa de Don Pablo Hostel** Melchor Ocampo 412, Centro (at Rayon St) 52-951/516-8384 • gay/ straight • nonsmoking

**Casa Machaya Oaxaca B&B** Sierra Nevada 164, Col. Loma Linda 52/951-1328203 • gay-friendly • kids ok • private level w/ patio & valley views

**Casa Sol Zipolite** 6 Arco Iris, Col. Arroyo Tres 52-95/8100-0462 • mostly gay men • pool • WiFi • gay-owned • 300 meters from famous Playa Zipolite

**Posada Arigalan** 52-958/111-5801, 956/280-2165 (US) • gay/ straight • perched above the Pacific Ocean • women-run

### NIGHTCLUBS

**Club Privado 502 (aka El Número)** Calle Porfirio Díaz 502 (Centro, ring to enter) • 10pm-close, clsd Sun-Tue • gay/ straight • dancing/DJ • cover charge

**Elefante** 20 de Noviembre 52–951/164-8637

**Gavana Dance Club** Calzada Porfirio Diaz #216 (Col. Reforma) • 9pm-close Th-Sat • gay/straight

### CAFES

**B Proud** Morelos 1107-A • open 9am & 4pm Sun • WiFi

### RESTAURANTS

**El Asador Vasco** Portal de Flores 10-A (Centro) 52–951/514-4755 • popular • great views • authentic Oaxacan cuisine (can you say ¡mole!)

**Casa Crespo** Allende 107 52–951/516-0918 • lunch & dinner, also cooking classes

## Playa del Carmen

**see also Cancún & Cozumel**

### ACCOMMODATIONS

**Acanto Boutique Hotel** 16th St N (btwn 5th Ave & the beach) 631/882-1986 • gay-friendly • pool • nonsmoking • full brkfst based on package

**Aventura Mexicana Hotel** Av 10 (at Calle 24) 52–984/873-1876, 800/455-3417 • gay-friendly • pool • also restaurant & bar

**Hotel Copa Cabana** 5ta Av Norte 52–984/873-0218 • gay-friendly • WiFi • wheelchair access

**Luna Blue Hotel & Bar** Calle 26 (at 5th Av) 415/839-8541

**Reina Roja Hotel** 22 Street (btwn 5th & 10th Ave) 52–984/877-3800 • gay/ straight • pool • WiFi • pets ok

### NIGHTCLUBS

**Playa 69** Av 5 (btwn Calle 4 & Calle 6, ground flr) • 9pm-4am wknds • mostly gay men • dancing/DJ • gay-owned

**Playa Palms** 1st Avenue Bis (btwn 12 & 14th N St) 52–984/803-3908, 888/676-4431 • gay/straight • directly in front of a pristine, white sandy beach in downtown Playa del Carmen • pool

### RESTAURANTS

**100% Natural** Av 5 (btwn 10th & 12th) 52–984/73-2242 • vegetarian

## Puebla

### BARS

**La Cigarra** Ave 5 Poniente 538 (at Calle 7, Centro) 52–222/246-6356 • 6pm-3am • mostly gay men • beer bar • videos

**Franco's Bule Bar** 5 Oriente 402 (Los Sapos) 52–222/232-3409 • 10pm-3am, till 6am Th-Sat, clsd Mon-Tue • mostly gay men • live shows • drag shows • strippers

**Mono** Avenia Juarez 2505 (Colonia La Paz) • gay/straight • small bar in front, dance club in back • food served

### NIGHTCLUBS

**Cabaré-Tito VIP** Av Juarez 2309 Local B (Colonia La Paz), Mexico City • 9pm-close wknds only • lesbians/ gay men • theme nights • dancing/DJ • go-go dancers • drag shows

**Garotos** 22 Orient E 602 (close to Blvd 5 de Mayo, Xenenetla) 52–222/242-4232 • 9pm-3am Fri-Sat only • gay-friendly • dancing/DJ • cover charge

## Puerto Vallarta

### INFO LINES & SERVICES

**Community Center GLBT SETAC** 427 Constitucion (at Manuel M Diéguez) 52–322/224-1974 • AA meetings, movie nights, HIV testing & Spanish classes

### ACCOMMODATIONS

**Blue Chairs Beach Resort** 52–322/222-5040, 888/302-3662 • lesbians/ gay men • pool & beach • WiFi • wheelchair access

**Boana Torre Malibu Condo Hotel** Calle Amapas 325 52–322/222-0999, 52–322/222-6695 • gay/ straight • food served • pool • poolside bar • gay-owned

**Casa Andrea** Calle Francisca Rodriguez 174 52–322/222-1213 • gay/ straight • WiFi

**Casa Cúpula** Callejon de la Igualdad 129, Col. Amapas 52–322/223-2484, 866/352-2511 • lesbians/ gay men • swimming • nonsmoking • WiFi • wheelchair access • gay-owned

**Casa de las Flores** Calle Santa Barbara #359 503 /314-444(US), 52–3222/120-5242 • condos overlooking Los Muertos Beach • gay-owned

**Casa Fantasía** Pinot Suarez 203, Col. Emiliano Zapata (near the Rio Cuale) **52-322/223-2444** • gay/ straight • B&B made up of 3 traditional haciendas • full brkfst • terrace • pool • nonsmoking • wheelchair access • gay-owned

**Los Cuatro Vientos** Matamoros 520 **52-322/222-0161** • gay-friendly • El Nido rooftop bar & restaurant • annual Women's Getaway • pool • WiFi

**Hotel Emperador** Amapas 114 **52-322/222-1767 , 800/523-1158** • gay/ straight • located right on "Los muertos" beach • WiFi

**Hotel Mercurio** **52-322/222-4793, 866/388-2689** • popular • lesbians/ gay men • 1 1/2 blocks from beach • pool • WiFi • gay-owned

**Hotel Torre De Oro** Pulpito 138 (at Olas Altas) **52-322/222-4488** • mostly gay men • near beach • in center of romantic gay quarter • pool • hot tub • full brkfst • also restaurant & lounge

**Villa Safari Condo** Francisca Rodriguez 203 **269/469-0468 (US #)** • gay/ straight • condos • nonsmoking • gay-owned

## BARS

**Los Amigos Bar** Calle Venustiano Carranza 237 (upstairs, next to Paco's Ranch) **52-322/222-7802** • 6pm-4am • lesbians/ gay men • Mexican cantina • patio

**Apaches** Olas Altas 439 (at Rodriguez) **52-322/222-4004** • 5pm-2am, till 1am Sun-Mon • gay/ straight • classy martini bar • tapas • great outdoor seating area • lesbian-owned

**Frida** 301-A Insurgentes (at Venustiano Carranza) **52-322/222-3668** • 1pm-2am, from 7pm Mon-Tue • gay/ straight • Mexican cantina • bears • more gay later in evening • food served • gay-owned

**Garbo** Pulpito 142 (at Olas Altas) **52-322/223-5753** • 6pm-2am • gay/ straight • upscale martini lounge • live music • gay-owned • 18+

**La Noche** Lázaro Cárdenas 257 (Zona Romantica) **52-322/222-3364** • 7pm-2am • lesbians/ gay men

**The Palm/ Viva** Olas Altas 508 (at Rodolfo Gomez) **52-322/223-4818** • 4pm-4am • mostly gay men • dancing/DJ • cabaret

**Reinas** Lazaro Cardenas 361 **52-322/125-9532** • 5pm-2am • mostly gay men • neighborhood bar

**Sama** Olas Altas 510 (at Rodolfo Gomez) **52-322/223-3182** • 4:30pm-2am • lesbians/ gay men • small martini bar w/ sidewalk seating

## NIGHTCLUBS

**CC Slaughter's** Lazaro Cardenas 254 Emiliano (Zapata) **52-322/222-3412** • 6pm-6am • bar and disco

**Club Mañana** Venustiano Carranza #290 (at Col Emiliano Zapata) • 10pm-6am, clsd Sun-Tue • mostly gay men • dancing/DJ

**No Borders** 221 Libertad **52-322/136-8775** • 1pm-2am • lesbians/ gay men • neighborhood bar • rooftop patio

**Paco's Ranch** 237 Ignacio Vallarta **52-322/222-1899** • 10pm-6am • popular • lesbians/ gay men • dancing/DJ • also rooftop terrace • drag shows • cover charge • gay-owned

## CAFES

**A Page in the Sun** 179 Plaza Lázaro Cárdenas (in Zona Romantica) **52-322/222-3608** • 7am-11pm coffee shop & English bookstore

**Cafe San Angel** Olas Altas 449 (at Francisco Rodreguez) **52-322/223-1273** • 7am-1am • sidewalk cafe

**The Coffee Cup** Puesta del Sol L-14 (Marina Vallarta) **52-322/221-2517** • 7am-10pm, clsd Sun in summer • gay-owned

**Uncommon Grounds Buddha Lounge** Lazaro Cardenas 625 **52-322/223-3834** • 5pm-close, clsd Mon-Tue • also aromatherapy & gifts

**Xocodiva** Rodolfo Gomez 118 **52-322/113-0352** • artisinal chocolate • women-owned

## RESTAURANTS

**El Arrayan** Allende #344 (at El Centro) **52-322/222-7195** • 6pm-11pm, clsd Tue • lesbian-owned

**The Blue Shrimp** Olas Altas 366 (Zona Romantica) **52-322/222-4246** • 11am-midnight

**El Brujo** Venustiano Carranza 510 (at Naranjo) **52-322/223-3026** • 1pm-9:30pm, clsd Mon • Mexican/ seafood • worth the wait

**Cafe Bohemio** Rodolfo Gómez 127 (at Olas Altas) **44-322/134-2436** • 5pm-2am, clsd Sun • lesbians/ gay men • open-air cafe • late-evening happy hour • gay-owned

**Cafe de Olla** Calle Basilio Badillo 168 **52-322/223-1626** • 10am-11pm, clsd Tue • popular • Mexican • wait list an hour

**Cafe des Artistes** Calle Guadalupe Sánchez 740 (at Leona Vicario) **52–322/222–3228** • 6pm-11:30pm • popular • upscale French w/a Mexican twist • reservations required

**Chez Elena** Matamoros 520, Centro (at Los Quatro Vientos Hotel) **52–322/222–0161** • 6pm-11pm • seasonal • garden restaurant • also rooftop bar • woman-owned

**Daiquiri Dick's** Olas Altas 314 (on Playa Los Muertos) **310/697–3799** • 8:30am-1:30pm & 5:30pm-11pm, clsd Tue & clsd Sept

**El Dorado** Pulpito 102, Playa de los Muertos **52–322/222–4124** • beach club & restaurant • evening shows

**Le Bistro Jazz Cafe** Isla Rio Cuale 16–A (on the island, at the East Bridge) **52–322/222–0283** • 9am-midnight, clsd Sun • gay-owned

**Lido Beach Club** Malecon 1 Esq Abedul Col Emiliano Zapata **813/855–0190** • 10am-6pm

**Memo's Casa de los Hotcakes** Calle Basilio Badillo 289 **52–322/222–6272** • 8am-2pm • popular • long lines for cheap & good brkfst • indoor patio

**Mezzogiorno Ristorante Italiano** Avenida del Pacifico 33 (North Beach Bucerias Nayarit) **52–329/298–0350** • 6pm-11pm (clsd Mon off-season)

**El Mole de Jovita** 220B Basillo Badillo • 3pm-10pm, clsd Sun, authentic mole

**La Palapa** Pulpito 103, Col Emiliano Zapata **52–322/222–5225** • brkfst, lunch & dinner, beachside dining

**La Piazzetta** Rodolfo Gomez #143 (at Olas Atlas, Romantic Zone) **52–322/222–0650** • 4pm-11pm • Italian

**Planeta Vegetariano** Iturbide 270 (Centro) **52–322/222–3073** • 8am-10pm, clsd Sun • buffet-style

**Red Cabbage** Calle Rivera del Rio 204-A (at Basilio Badillo) **52–322/223–0411** • 5pm-11pm • on Rio Cuale w/ great kitschy decor • lesbian-owned

**The Swedes/ Crows Nest Bar** Púlpito 154 (at Olas Altas) **52–322/223–2353** • 4pm-2am • lesbians/ gay men • Swedish/ European • bar upstairs • gay-owned

**Trio** Guerrero 264 (Centro) **52–322/222–2196** • 6pm-midnight, clsd Sun • patio • live music • reservations advised

## ENTERTAINMENT & RECREATION

**Boana Tours** Calle Amapas 325 (at Casa Boana Torre Malibu) **52–322/222–0099, 52–322/222–6695** • horseback tours daily

**Diana's Cruise the Bay Tour** meet at Los Muertos pier • 9:30am-5pm Th • lesbians/ gay men • cruise on 33-ft trimaran • food served • open bar

**Ladies Outdoor Club Adventures** **52–322/223–9538** • walking tours and day trips • lesbian-owned

**Ocean Friendly** Paseo del Marlin 510-103, Col. Aralias **52–322/225–3774, 044–322/294–0385 (CELL)** • whale-watching tours • Dec 15-March 31

**Playa Los Muertos/ Playa del Sol** S of Rio Cuale • popular • the gay beach • now spans "Blue Chairs" & "Green Chairs"

## PUBLICATIONS

**Gay PV** **52–322/113–0224** • great gay magazine for PV

**Urbana Revista** **52–333/844–6471** • gay lifestyle magazine

## GYMS & HEALTH CLUBS

**Acqua Day Spa & Gym** Calle Constitución 450 (F Rodriguez) **52–322/223–5270** • 7am-9pm, till 5pm Sat, clsd Sun • spa services • also small gym

## EROTICA

**The Closet** Lazaro Cardenas 230 **52–322/223–3030** • noon-9pm

# Querétaro

## NIGHTCLUBS

**Con la Rojas** Ave Constituyentes Pte 42A (Centro) **52–442/212–4795** • 10pm-2:30am, clsd Sun-Wed • mostly gay men • dancing/DJ • cover charge

# San Jose del Cabo

## ACCOMMODATIONS

**El Encanto Inn** **210/858–6649, 52–614/142–0388** • gay-friendly • spa & restaurant • swimming

**One & Only Palmilla** Apartado Postal 52, 23400 **52–624/146–7000, 866/829–2977 (US#)** • gay-friendly • upscale resort w/ golf course • swimming

RESTAURANTS

**Voila Bistro & Catering** 1705 Comonfort (Plaza Paulina) **52–624/130–7569** • noon-10pm, from 4pm Sun • popular • Mexican w/ French twist • full bar • patio

## San Miguel de Allende

ACCOMMODATIONS

**Casa de Sierra Nevada** Calle Hospicio 35 (Centro) **52–415/152–7040, 800/701–1561 (US#)** • gay-friendly • horseback riding • also spa • swimming • patios

**Casa Schuck Boutique B&B** Garita 3, Centro **52–415/152–6618, 937/684–4092** • gay-friendly • boutique hotel • full brkfst • pool • WiFi

**Dos Casas** Calle Quebrada 101 (Guanajuato) **52–415/154–4073** • gay-friendly • full brkfst

**Las Terrazas San Miguel** Santo Domingo 3 **52–415/152–5028, 707/534–1833 (US#)** • gay/ straight • 4 rental homes • nonsmoking • WiFi • gay-owned

RESTAURANTS

**La Azotea** Umaran 6 **52–415/152–4977** • delicious tapas & drinks

**Mezzanine Bistro** Cuna de Allende 11 (at Hotel Vista Hermosa ) **52–415/152–2799** • lunch & dinner, clsd Sun • gay-owned

## Tijuana

BARS

**Luna Sol Lounge** Av Pacifico 640, Playas de Tijuana **52–664/609–4977** • 2pm-midnight • gay/ straight • beach bar • gay-owned

NIGHTCLUBS

**Club Fusion** Calle Larroque 213 **52–664/345–8817** • 8pm-3am Fri-Sun • mostly gay men • dancing/DJ • karaoke • drag shows

**Extasis** Larroque 213 (in Plaza Viva Tijuana, next to the border) **52–664/682–8339** • 8pm-late, clsd Mon-Wed • popular • mostly gay men • women's night Th • dancing/DJ • strippers • cover charge

**Mike's Disco** Av Revolución 1220 (at Calle 6A) **52–664/685–3534** • 8pm-5am, till 3am Th, clsd Wed • lesbians/ gay men • dancing/DJ • drag shows • videos

**Sin Tabu** Av Sanchez Taboada 10291-7 **52–664/681–8138** • gay/ straight

**Terraza 9** Calle 5a (at Av Revolución) **52–664/685–3534** • 5pm-2am, till 5am Fri-Sat, clsd Mon • gay-friendly • dancing/DJ

CAFES

**D'Luna Cafe** Calle 8 #8380 **52–664/321–9735**

## Todos Santos

ACCOMMODATIONS

**The Todos Santos Inn** Calle Legaspi #33 (Topete) **52–612/145–0040** • gay/ straight • in historic district • pool • nonsmoking • also bar • gay-owned

## Tulúm

ACCOMMODATIONS

**Adonis Tulum Riviera Maya Gay Resort & Spa** Carretera Tulum Boca Paila Km 3.8 **800/233–5162, 52–984/871–1000** • mostly gay men • pool

**Casa de las Olas** 10.6km Tulum Beach Rd **52–984/807–3909** • gay-friendly • WiFi • sustainabile beach villa, very secluded that has 5 beautiful ocean front suites

**EcoTulum Resorts & Spa** Carretera Tulum Ruinas Km 5 **54–115/5918–6400, 877/301–4666** • gay-friendly • WiFi

**Om Tulum** Caraterra Ruinas Punta -Allen Km 9.5 **521–98/4114–0538** • gay-friendly • WiFi

**Posada Luna del Sur** Calle Luna Sur 5 **52–984/871–2984** • gay-friendly

## Veracruz

ACCOMMODATIONS

**Hotel Villa del Mar** Blvd Miguel Ávila Camacho 2431 (across street from Playa del Mar beach) **52–229/989–6500** • gay-friendly • hotel w/ separate motel & bungalows • near aquarium

ENTERTAINMENT & RECREATION

**San Juan de Ulua Fortress** • 9am-4:30pm, clsd Mon • impressive early colonial-era floating fortress

**Veracruz Aquarium** Blvd Avila Camacho (at Xicolencat) **52–229/932–7984** • 10am-7pm • one of the largest & best in the world • don't miss it!

## Zacatecas

ACCOMMODATIONS

**Quinta Real Zacatecas** Av Ignacio Rayón 434 (Col. Centro) **52–492/1105–1010, 866/621–9288** • gay-friendly • 5-star hotel built into grandstand of bullfighting ring

## Zihuatanejo

ACCOMMODATIONS

**Hotel Las Palmas** Calle de Aeropuerto (at lot 5) **52-755/557-0634, 888/527-7256** • gay-friendly • full brkfst • pool

NIGHTCLUBS

**Mydori Disco Bar** Calle La Laja s/n (Col. Centro) **52-755/104-5670** • 8pm-4am • lesbians/ gay men • dancing/DJ • drag shows

**Tequila Town** Cuauhtemoc 3 (Col Centro) **52-755/553-8587** • 8pm-4am • gay-friendly • more gay after 11pm • karaoke • videos

# COSTA RICA

## Alajuela

BARS

**Rick's Bar & Restaurant** 500 mts Este Casino Fiesta, carretera Heredia, en Río Segundo de Alajuela **506-2/441-3213** • 6pm-close, from 4pm Sun • lesbians/ gay men

## Chirripó Nat'l Park

ACCOMMODATIONS

**Monte Azul** Contiguo al puente de Chucuyo, Chimirol **506/2742-5222** • gay/ straight • boutique resort, nature preserve & artist colony, less than 2 hrs from Manuel Antonio • restaurant on-site • gay-owned

## Dominical

ACCOMMODATIONS

**Paradise Costa Rica** Escaleras (at San Martin Sur) **800/708-4552** • gay/ straight • vacation villas • lap size pools • nonsmoking • gay-owned

## Guanacaste

ACCOMMODATIONS

**Villa Decary** Nuevo Arenal, 5717 Tilaran **506-2/694-4330, 800/556-0505 (FROM US & CANADA)** • gay-friendly • former coffee farm overlooking Lake Arenal • gay-owned

## Malpais

ACCOMMODATIONS

**Kelea Surf Spa** 949/492-7263 • women-only • surf spa

## Manuel Antonio, Quepos

INFO LINES & SERVICES

**Gay Manuel Antonio** Puntarenas **403/389-8941** • travel information source for gay travellers

ACCOMMODATIONS

**Casa de Frutas** **506-8/825-3257 (CELL), 800/936-9622** • gay/ straight • luxury villa in Tulemar Gardens

**Casitas Eclipse** KM 5 Manuel Antonio Rd **506-2/777-0408** • gay/ straight • detached casitas

**Costa Verde** **506-2/777-0584, 866/854-7958 (FROM US & CANADA)** • gay/ straight • bungalows, studios & apts • pool • gay-owned

**Gaia Hotel & Reserve** km 2.7 Carretera Quepos a Manuel Antonio **506-2/777-9797, 800/226-2515** • gay-friendly • boutique hotel • surrounded by wildlife refuge • full brkfst • pool • WiFi • gay-owned

**Hotel Parador** **506-2/777-1414, 877/506-1414** • gay-friendly • large luxury resort • swimming • also gourmet restaurant • WiFi

**Hotel Villa Roca** **506-2/777-1349** • mostly gay men • great ocean views • near beaches • pool • nonsmoking • gay-owned

**La Mansion Inn** **506-2/777-3489, 800/360-2071** • gay/ straight • luxury hotel • pool • also restaurant • bar • ocean views • gay-owned

**La Posada** **506-2/777-1446** • gay-friendly • 4 bungalows & 2 guest rooms • pool • full brkfst • gay-owned

**Si Como No** **506-2/777-0777, 888/742-6667** • gay-friendly • 25-acre wildlife refuge • also spa • pool • wheelchair access

BARS

**Karma Lounge** under Victoria's Restaurant (50 meters past Super Joseph ) **506/2777 7230** • 6pm-midnight, clsd Mon • mostly men • outside seating

RESTAURANTS

**El Barba Roja** Carretera al Parque Nacional **506-2/777-0331** • 7am-10pm, from 4pm Mon • American • popular • great sunset location

**El Gran Escape & Fish Head Bar** Quepos Centro **506-2/777-0395** • brkfst, lunch, dinner, clsd Tue • seafood • full bar

**Restaurante Gato Negro** KM 5 Manuel Antonio Rd (at Casitas Eclipse) 506-2/777-0408 • 4pm-close • popular • great view • full bar

**Rico Tico** in Hotel Si Como No • brkfst, lunch & dinner • Tex/ Mex • includes use of pool bar • popular • live shows • also Claro Que Sí (seafood restaurant)

## Osa Peninsula

### ACCOMMODATIONS

**Blue Osa Yoga Sanctuary & Spa** 506/8704-7006 • gay/ straight • all meals included • kids/ ok • nonsmoking • WiFi • gay-owned

## Pavones

### ACCOMMODATIONS

**Casa Siempre Domingo B & B** 506/2776-2185 • gay/ straight • pool • WiFi • lesbian-owned

## Playa Sámara

### ACCOMMODATIONS

**Casitas LazDívaz B&B** 506/2656-0295 • gay-friendly • full brkfst • beachfront • wheelchair access • lesbian diva-owned

## Puerto Viejo

### ACCOMMODATIONS

**Banana Azul** 200 meters N of Perla Negra Hotel 506-2/750-2035, 506-2/351-4582 (CELL) • mostly men • full brkfst • nonsmoking • WiFi • gay-owned

### RESTAURANTS

**Koki Beach Restaurant Bar & Lounge** Main St (town center across from water ) 506/8305-0747 • 5pm-11pm, clsd Mon • Latin fusion cuisine • WiFi

## Puntarenas

### ACCOMMODATIONS

**Villa Caletas** Garabito 506/2630-3000 • gay/ straight • restaurant on site • pool • a luxury boutique hotel, 1 hour from San Jose airport

## San Jose

### ACCOMMODATIONS

**Hotel El Mirador** Bello Horizonte, Escazú 506/2289-3981 • mostly men • swimming • conveniently located in Escazú, a suburb of San José

### BARS

**Zona Rosa** 250m norte del Correo Central • lesbians/ gay men • dancing/DJ • karaoke

### ENTERTAINMENT & RECREATION

**Gay Tours Costa Rica** 309-2200 Coronado 506-2/305-8044 • LGBT daily events & excursions

### ACCOMMODATIONS

**Colours Oasis Resort** El Triangulo Noroeste, Blvd Rohrmoser (200 meters before end of blvd) 506-2/296-1880, 866/517-4390 (US & CANADA) • lesbians/ gay men • pool • also bar & restaurant • WiFi • gay-owned

**Hotel Kekoldi** Av 9 (btwn Calles 5 & 7, Barrio Amón) 506-2/248-0804 • gay/ straight • in art deco bldg in downtown • secluded garden • WiFi • gay-owned

**Secret Garden B&B** 506-2/290-3890 • gay/ straight • in historic Rohrmoser district • WiFi • gay-owned

### BARS

**Bar Al Despiste** in front of Mudanzas Mundiales (W of Universal Zapote) 506-2/234-5956 • 6pm-2am, 5pm-10pm Sun, clsd Mon • gay/ straight • theme nights • karaoke

**Casa Vieja** 400 metros al este de la capilla religiosa de Montserrat, Alajuela 506/2440-8525 • 6pm-2am, noon-midnight Sun • lesbians/ gay men • food served

### NIGHTCLUBS

**La Avispa** 834 Calle 1 (pink house btwn Avs 8 & 10) 506-2/223-5343 • 8pm-2am, popular T-dance from 5pm Sun, clsd Mon-Wed • lesbians/ gay men • women's night 2nd & 4th Fri • dancing/DJ

**Azotea** Uruca, de Capris 300 Norte (Plaza Rohrmoser ) 506-2/220-2506 • gay/ straight • dancing/DJ

**El Bochinche** Calle 11 (btwn Avs 10 & 12, Paseo de los Etudiantes), San Pedro 506-2/221-0500 • 7pm-2am, till 5pm Fri-Sat, clsd Sun-Tue • also full restaurant • Mexican • dancing/DJ after 10pm • videos

**Club Energy** Paseo Colon (near 30th, by Pizza Hut) 506/2223-7594 • from 7:30pm Th-Sun • lesbians/ gay men • dancing/DJ • also restaurant

**Puchos** Calle 11 & Av 8 (knock to enter) 506-2/256-1147, 506-2/222-7967 • 8pm-2:30am, clsd Sun • mostly gay men • strippers

## Restaurants

**Ankara** San José de la Montaña (Heredia, San Antonio de Belén, S of church) **50/8326 6646** • clsd Mon-Tue • live music

**Cafe Mundo** Av 9 & Calle 15 (200 meters E of parking lot for INS, Barrio Amón) **506–2/222–6190** • 11am-11pm, 5pm-midnight Sat, clsd Sun • Italian • garden seating • also cafe/ bar • gay-owned

**La Cocina de Leña** in El Pueblo complex **506–2/255–1360** • 11am-11pm • 5 minutes from downtown • reservations recommended

**Machu Picchu** Calle 32 (btwn Aves 1 & 3) **506–2/283–3679** • Peruvian

**Mirador Ram Luna** from center of Aserrí, go 4 kilometers on the road toward Tabarca, Aserrí **506–2/230–3060** • dinner nightly, lunch & dinner wknds, clsd Mon • hillside restaurant w/ amazing views

**Olio** Escalante, Bario California (N of Baselman's, San Pedro/ Los Yoses) **506–2/281–0541** • lunch & dinner, clsd Sun • Spanish • also full bar

**Vishnu Vegetarian Restaurant** Av 1 (btwn Calles 3 & 1) **506–2/256–6063** • 8am-9:30pm

## Entertainment & Recreation

**Mercado Central/ Central Market** Central Avenida (btwn Calles 6 & 8) • bustling market selling food, clothing, souvenirs & more

# San Ramon

## Accommodations

**Angel Valley Farm B&B** 200m N & 300m E of Iglesia de Los Angeles (at Autopista to Arenal Volcano) **506–2/456–4084, 910/805-0149 (US#)** • gay/ straight • full brkfst • kids over 5 & small pets ok • nonsmoking • WiFi • wheelchair access

# Santa Clara

## Accommodations

**Tree Houses Hotel Costa Rica** **506–2/475–6507** • gay/ straight • private treehouses in canopy of trees on wildlife refuge • full brkfst • nonsmoking • lesbian-owned • kids/ pets ok

# Tamarindo

## Accommodations

**Los Altos de Eros** **506/8837–9174, 800/931-1944**

**Cala Luna Hotel & Villas** Playa Langosta (at Playa Tamarindo) **506–2/653–0214, 800/503–5202** • gay-friendly • pools • kids ok

**Hotel Sueño del Mar** Playa Langosta **506–2/653–0284** • gay-friendly • private hacienda on the beach • full brkfst • pool • nonsmoking • WiFi

# ARGENTINA

# Buenos Aires

## Info Lines & Services

**La Casa del Encuentro/ Lesbian Feminist Cultural Center** Rivadavia 3917 **54–1/4982-2550**

**Comunidad Homosexual Argentina** Tomas Liberti 1080 **54–11/4361–6382**

**La Fulana** Callao 339, 5th fl **54–1/6548–9542**

**Pink Point** Avenida de Mayo 1370, 10th flr (at Palacio Barolo) **54–1/4382–8227** • LGBT tourist info

## Accommodations

**1555 Malabia House** Malabia 1555, Palermo Viejo (at Honduras) **54–11/4833–2410** • gay-friendly • pets ok • WiFi

**Be Hotel Buenos Aires** Venezuela 649 (SanTelmo area) **54–11/4136–9393** • gay-friendly • WiFi • restaurant & bar on site • pool

**The Cocker** Av Juan de Garay 458 (at Defensa) **54–1/4362–8451** • WiFi • full brkfst • pets ok • gay-owned

**Faena Hotel & Universe** 445 Martha Salotti St **54–11/4010–9000** • gay/ straight • luxury hotel • WiFi • live shows at The Universe

**Home Hotel** Honduras 5860 **54–11/4778–1008** • gay-friendly boutique hotel • pool • loft apts available • WiFi

**Hotel Intercontinental Buenos Aires** Moreno 809 **888/424-6835 (US#), 54–11/4340–7100** • gay-friendly • WiFi • gym • bar • restaurants

**Hotel Vitrum** 5641 Gorriti **54–1/4776–5030** • gay-friendly • stylish boutique hotel

**Palermo Viejo B&B** Niceto Vega 4629 (at Av Scalabrini Ortiz) **54–11/4773–6012** • gay/ straight • nonsmoking • WiFi • near shopping & gay nightlife • gay-owned

**Rooney's Boutique Hotel** Sarmiento 1775, Piso 3 **54–11/5252–5060** • gay/friendly • exceptional location & free tango classes • WiFi

**Solar Soler B&B** Soler 5676 (at Bonpland) **54-11/4776-3065** • gay-friendly • kids ok • nonsmoking

**Telmho Hotel Boutique** 1086 Defensa St (at Humberto Primo) **54-11/4116-5467** • gay-friendly • WiFi

## BARS

**Bach Bar** Antonio Cabrera 4390 **54-11/5184-0137** • 11pm-close, clsd Mon • lesbians/ gay men • live shows Th-Fri • karaoke • videos

**Bar Jolie** Scalabrini Ortiz 1398 • 9pm-5am Wed only • mostly women • dancing/DJ

**Cero Consecuencia** Cabrera 3769 • 10pm-close, clsd Mon-Tue • lesbians/ gay men

**Flux Bar** Marcelo T de Alvear 980 (at 9 de Julio) **54-11/5252-0258** • 7pm-close, from 8pm wknds, clsd Sun • lesbians/ gay men • dancing/DJ • art • English, Portuguese, & Russian spoken

**Inside** Bartolomé Mitre 1571 **54-11/4372-5439** • 6pm-close • mostly men • also restaurant • live shows • older crowd

**KM Zero** Av Santa Fe 2516 **54-11/4822-7530** • 7pm-close, clsd Sun • also restaurant • lesbians/ gay men • dancing/DJ • drag shows • strippers • videos

**Mundo Bizarro** 1222 Serrano **54-11/4773-1967** • gay-friendly • 1950s American-style cocktail lounge • food served

**Sitges** Córdoba 4119 **54-11/4861-3763** • 10:30pm-4am, till 6am Fri-Sat, clsd Mon-Tue • lesbians/ gay men • women go earlier

## NIGHTCLUBS

**Ambar La Fox** Av Federico Lacroze 3455 (at Alvarez Thomas, at El Teatro) • Sat only • lesbians/ gay men • dancing/ DJ • young, alternative mixed crowd

**Amerika** Gascón 1040 (at Cordoba) **54-11/4865-4416** • open late • mostly gay men • dancing/DJ • cruisy

**Angel's** Viamonte 2168 • midnight-7am Th-Sat • lesbians/gay men • dancing/DJ

**Bahrein** Lavalle 345 • 6pm-7am Wed & Fri, from 10pm Sat, from midnight Tue • gay/ straight • dancing/DJ • also restaurant

**Club 69** Niceto Vega 5510 (btwn Humboldt & Fitzroy, Palermo) **54-1/4779-9396** • 11:30pm Th only • gay/ straight • dancing/DJ • drag shows • performance • over-the-top theme parties

**Club Namunkura** Niceto Vega 5699 (Palermo, at Club M) • 1st Fri only • lesbians/ gay men • dancing/DJ • transgender-friendly

**Cocoliche** Rivadavia 878 • gay/ straight • dancing/DJ

**Fiesta Dorothy** Alsina 940 (near Plaza de Mayo, at Palacio Alsina) **54-11/4334-0097** • huge dance bi-monthly dance party • lesbians/ gay men

**Fiesta Eyeliner** Sarmiento 1272 (at Salon Real) • monthly queer/ alternative dance party • check www.fiestaeyeliner.tk for dates

**Fiesta Oliver** Cordoba 543 (at Sub Club) • 1am Fri only (Fri night) • lesbians/ gay men • dancing/DJ

**Fiesta Plop** Av Federico Lacroze 3455 (at Alvarez Thomas, at El Teatro) • Fri only • lesbians/ gay men • dancing/ DJ • young, alternative mixed crowd

**Glam** Cabrera 3046 **54-11/4963-2521** • midnight-close wknds • mostly gay men • popular • dancing/DJ

**Human** Av Costanera Norte Rafael Obligado (at Av Sarmiento, at Mandalay Complex) • midnight Fri only • mostly gay men • huge dance party

**Juana** 775 Av 44 **54-1/557-6807** • from 11:30pm Fri-Sat only • lesbians/ gay men • dancing/DJ

**Pacha** Av Costanera y Pampa **54-11/4788-4280** • popular dance club • gay-friendly

**Rheo** Marcelino Freyre S/N, Arco 17 (at Crobar) **54-1/3430-2711** • midnight Sat only • mostly gay men • dancing/DJ

**Sub Club** Cordoba 543 • Fri-Sat only • lesbians/ gay men • dancing/DJ

**Unna Fiesta at Glam Disco** • Fri only • mostly women • dancing/DJ • check www.facebook.com/groups/124260580331

## CAFES

**Gout Cafe** Juncal 2124 **54-11/4825-8330** • sandwiches, pastries • gay-owned

**Pride Cafe** Balcarce 869 (in San Telmo) **54-11/4300-6435** • 10am-10pm • live show Th night

## RESTAURANTS

**Arevalito** Arevalo 1478 54–11/4776–4252 • 9am-midnight • vegetarian

**Bio** Humbolt 2192 (Palermo Viejo) 54–11/4774–3880 • lunch & dinner • vegetarian • organic market

**La Cabana** Alicia Moreau de Justo 380 54–11/4314–3710 • brkfst, lunch & dinner • upscale steak house

**Casa Cruz** 1658 Uriarte 54–11/4833–1112 • 8:30pm-3am, later Fri-Sat • upscale, trendy restaurant • also bar

**Cumana** Rodriguez Pena 1149 (at Arenales) 54–11/4813–9207 • popular • warm, cozy and rustic and the restaurant has a variety of Argentinian favorites as well as Italian options

**El Palacio de la Papa Frita** Lavalle 735 (at Maipu) 54–11/4393–5849 • popular • hearty traditional meals • also Av Corrientes 1612, 11/4374-8063

**Filo** San Martin 975 54–11/4311–0312, 54-11/4311–1871 • 8pm-close • Italian • trendy • also art gallery

**Il Materello** Martin Rodriguez 517 (in la Boca nr socccer stadium) 54–11/4307–0529 • very good Italian and everyone loves the lasagna, beware of neighborhood after 4pm

**Mark's Deli & Coffeehouse** El Salvador 4107 (in Palermo) 54–11/4832–6244 • 11am-8pm, till 9pm Sun, clsd Mon

**Naturaleza Sabia** Balcarce 958 (at Carlos Calvo) 54–11/4300–6454 • clsd Mon • vegetarian

**Rave** Gorriti 5092 54–11/4833–7832 • lunch Tue-Sun & dinner nightly

**Sucre** Sucre 676 54–11/4782–9082 • upscale contemporary

**Verde Llama** Jorge Newberry 3623 54–11/4554–7467 • 11am-6pm, till midnight Th-Sat • organic vegetarian cafe

## ENTERTAINMENT & RECREATION

**Casa Brandon** Luis Maria Drago 236 (at Lavalleja) 54–11/4858–0610 • LGBT events, dance parties, poetry readings, art & more • also bar/ restaurant

**La Marshall** Maipu 444 54–11/4912–9043 • 8:30pm Wed • exclusively gay tango lessons

**Museo Evita Peron** Lafinur 2988 (in Palermo) 54–11/4807–9433 • 2pm-7:30pm, clsd Mon

**Out & About Pub Crawl** 54–911/3036–1361 • lesbians/ gay men • make new friends on a tour of the local gay bars

## BOOKSTORES

**Otras Letras** Soler 4796, Palermo 54–1/2060–2942 • 2pm-8pm, from 3pm Sat, clsd Sun • LGBT books & culture

## PUBLICATIONS

**Actitud**

**G-Maps Buenos Aires** Franklin 1463, Florida Oeste 54–11/4730–0729 • free pocket-size gay map of Buenos Aires

**The Ronda** • gay pocket guide w/ local listings • www.theronda.com.ar

# BRAZIL

## Rio de Janeiro

Note: M°=Metro station

## INFO LINES & SERVICES

**Grupo Arco-Iris Rio de Janeiro** Rua do Senado 230 55–21/2222–7286 • 1pm-7pm, till 11pm Sat, clsd Sun • LGBT community center

**Rainbow Kiosk/ Quiosque** Atlantic Av (in front of Copacabana Palace Hotel) 55–21/2275–1641 • popular • 24hrs • lesbians/ gay men • tourist info • drag shows

## ACCOMMODATIONS

**Casa Cool Beans** Rua Laurinda Santos Lobo 136 55–21/2262–0552 • gay/ straight • pool • WiFi • gay-owned

**Casa Dois Gatos** Rua Rosalina Terra 6, Cabo Frio 561/282–0023, 55–22/2645–5806 • mostly gay men • free transportation from Rio airport • pool • WiFi • gay-owned

**Ipanema Plaza** Rua Farme Amoedo (at Rua Prudente de Morais) 55–21/3687–2000 • gay/ straight • near gay beach • rooftop pool • also restaurant

**MyRioCondo.com** 3150 Avenida Atlantica, Apt 901 (Copacabana) 215/847–2397 (US#) • gay/ straight • WiFi • kids ok • gay-owned

**Pousada Internacional** Rua Orlando Carpinelli, Paraty 55–24/3371–7802, 55–24/3371–7806 • gay-friendly • B&B in preserved historic town surrounded by semi-tropical forests • nonsmoking • WiFi • wheelchair access

**Rio Penthouse** 55–21/2541–3882 • gay-friendly • beachfront apts & penthouse suites

## BARS

**Melt** Rua Rita Ludolf 47 55–21/2249–9309 • gay-friendly • lounge • also restaurant • live music

**TV Bar** Av Nossa Senhora de Copacabana 1417 **55–21/2267–1663** • 10pm-5am, 9pm-3am Sun, clsd Mon-Wed • television-themed bar • mostly men • theme nights

## NIGHTCLUBS

**Boite 1140** 1140 Rua Capitao Menezes **55–21/7830–8867** • 11pm-5am Th-Sun • lesbians/ gay men • dancing/DJ • drag shows

**Casa da Matriz** Rua Henrique de Novaes 107 **54–11/2226–9691, 54–11/2266–1014** • 11pm-close, clsd Tue • gay/ straight • dancing/DJ • 18+

**Cine Ideal** Rua da Carioca 64 **55–21/2252–3460** • gay/ straight • dancing/DJ • huge club w/ visting big-name DJs

**Fosfobox** Rua Siqueira Campos 143 **55–21/2548–7498** • open Th-Sun • gay/ straight • underground techno

**Galeria Cafe** Rua Teixeira de Melo 31 (Ipanema) **55–21/2523–8250** • 10:30pm-close, clsd Sun-Tue • gay/ straight • dancing/DJ • also gallery

**Papa G** 42 Almerinda Freitas **55–21/2450–1253** • lesbians/ gay men • dancing/DJ • drag shows • theme nights

**Up Turn** 2000 Av das Americas **55–21/3387–7957** • lesbians/ gay men • dancing/DJ • food served • outdoor seating

**The Week** 154 Rua Sacadura Cabral **55–21/2253–1020** • gay-friendly • dance club

## CAFES

**Cafeína** Rua Farme de Amoedo 43 (Ipanema) **55–21/2521–2194** • 8am-11:30pm

**Copa Cafe** Av Atlantica 3056 **55–21/2235–2947**

**Expresso Carioca** Rua Farme de Amoedo 76 **55–21/2267–8604**

## RESTAURANTS

**Bar d'Hotel** Av Delfim Moreira 696 (2nd flr, inside Marina All Suites Hotel, Leblon) **55–21/2172–1112** • food served all day, bar till late • Mediterranean • see & be seen

**Boox** Rua Br Torre 368 (in Ipanema) **55–21/2522–3730** • upscale restaurant & nightclub

**Cafe del Mar** Av Atlantica 1910 **55–21/7857–8681** • gay-friendly • upscale lounge

**Caroline Cafe** 10 Rua JJ Seabra **55–21/2540–0705** • steak & burgers • full bar

**Gringo Cafe** Rua Barao da Torre 240 **55–21/3813–3972** • American classics

**Maxim's** Av Atlantica 1850 **55–21/2255–7444**

**Pizzaria Guanabara** 1228 Ave Ataulfo de Paiva, Leblon **55–21/2294–0797**

**To Nem Ai** Rua Farme de Amoedo 57 **55–21/2247–8403** • lesbians/ gay men • popular bar w/ outdoor seating

**Via Sete** **55–21/2512–8100** • noon-midnight • plenty veggie

**Zero Zero** Av Padre Leonel Franca 240 (inside planetarium) **55–21/2540–8041** • gay/ straight • more gay Sun • dancing/DJ • upscale restaurant & nightclub

## ENTERTAINMENT & RECREATION

**Copacabana Beach** at Rua Rodolfo Dantas • gay across from Copacabana Palace Hotel

**Farme de Amoedo/ Farme Gay Beach** across from Rua Farme de Amoedo • see & be seen at this popular gay beach

**Ipanema Beach** • gay E of Rua Farme Amoedo

## PUBLICATIONS

**Rio For Partiers** **55–21/2523–9857** • great guide book

# CHILE

## Santiago

Note: M°=Metro station

### ACCOMMODATIONS

**The Aubrey Hotel** Constitución 299-317, Bellavista **56–2/940–2800** • gay-friendly • hip boutique hotel

**Casa Moro** Corte Suprema 177 (at Padre Gomez Vidaurre) **56–2/2696–9499** • lesbians/ gay men • full brkfst • gay-owned

**Lastarria Hotel** Coronel Santiago Bueras 188 **56–2/840–3700** • gay-friendly • luxury boutique hotel

**Le Reve Hotel** Orrego Luco 023, Providencia **56–2/757–6000, 56–2/757–6011** • gay-friendly • luxury boutique hotel

### BARS

**Bar 105** Bombero Nuñez 105 **56–2/403–2990** • 9pm-late Th-Sat • lesbians/ gay men

**Bar de Willy** Av 11 de Septiembre 2214 (Común Providencia) **56–2/381–1806** • 10pm-4am, till 5am wknds • lesbians/ gay men • live shows

**El Closet** Santa Filomena 138 (at Bombero Nuñez) • lesbians/ gay men • karaoke

**Farinelli** Bombero Nuñez 68 (Recoleta) **56–2/732–8966** • 5pm-2am • food served • live shows • drag shows • strippers

**Pub Friend's** Bombero Nuñez 365 (at Dominica, barrio Bellavista) **56-2/777-3979** • 9:30pm-4am, till 5am Fri-Sat • lesbians/ gay men • drag shows

**Vox Populi** Ernesto Pinto Lagarrigue 364 (Bellavista) **56-2/671-1267** • 9:30pm-3am, clsd Sun-Mon • mostly gay men • also restaurant • garden patio

## NIGHTCLUBS

**Blondie** Alameda 2879, loc 104 **56-2/681-7793** • gay/ straight • alternative • dancing/DJ • theme nights

**Bunker** Bombero Nuñez 159 (Bellavista) **56-2/738-2301, 56-2/738-2314** • 11pm-close Fri-Sat • lesbians/ gay men • dancing/DJ • food served • live shows

**Club Ignorancia** Ernesto Pinto Lagarrigue 282 **56-2/8216-3857**

**Club Principe** Pio Nono 398 **56-2/777-6381** • mostly gay men • dancing/DJ • drag shows • strippers

**Nueva Cero** Euclides 1204 par 2 Gran Avenida • mostly gay men • dancing/DJ • drag shows

## CAFES

**Tavelli** Andrés de Fuenzalida 34 (Providencia) **56-2/231-5830** • 8:30am-10pm, from 9:30am Sat • popular

## RESTAURANTS

**Ali Baba** 102 Santa Filomena (Barrio Bellavista, Recoleta) **56-2/732-7036** • Middle Eastern

**Capricho Español** Purisima 65 (barrio Bellavista) **56-2/777-7674** • dinner only • lesbians/ gay men • Spanish • full bar

**La Pizza Nostra** Av Providencia 1975 & Pedro de Valdivia **56-2/231-8941** • Italian

**Santo Remedio** 152 Roman Diaz, Providencia **56-2/235-0984** • 6:30pm-close, from 10:30pm wknds • global cuisine • full bar • live DJs

**El Toro** Loreto 33 **56-2/737-5937** • noon-midnight

## EROTICA

**Japi Jane** Luis Thayer Ojeda 059, Oficina 11 **56-2/234-4917** • 11am-8pm, till 4pm Sat, clsd Sun • women-owned

# AUSTRIA

## Vienna

### INFO LINES & SERVICES

**Hosi Zentrum** Heumuhlgasse 14 **43-1/216-6604** • LGBT political organization • many groups & events • cafe • news magazine

**Rosa Lila Villa** Linke Wienzeile 102 (near Hofmühlgasse, U4-Pilgramgasse) **43-1/586-8150 (WOMEN)** • LGBT center • staffed 5pm-8pm Mon, Wed, Fri • info • gay city maps • also meeting place for various groups • also cafe-bar

### ACCOMMODATIONS

**Altstadt** Kirchengasse 41 **43-1/522-6666** • gay-friendly • located centrally in ancient artist quarter Spittelberg • WiFi

**Arcotel Wimberger** Neubaugürtel 34–36 (at Goldschlagstr) **43-1/521-650** • gay-friendly • restaurant & bar on premises • also fitness club

**Art Hotel** Brandmayergasse 7-9 **43-1/544-5108** • gay-friendly • modern, art-filled hotel

**Boutique Hotel Stadthalle** Hackengasse 20 **43-1/982-4272** • gay/ straight • eco-friendly boutique hotel

**Designapartment Vienna** Glockengasse 25/ 9 **43-650/592-8941** • gay-friendly • full kitchen • terrace • WiFi • gay-owned

**Gay At Home** **43-1/586-1200** • lesbians/ gay men • rental apts around Vienna • gay-owned

**Le Méridien Wien** Opernring 13-15 **43-1/588-900, 800/543-4300** • gay-friendly • pool • sauna • hot tub • also restaurant & bar

**Pension Wild** Lange Gasse 10 (off Lerchenfelder Str) **43-1/406-5174** • mostly gay men • rooms & apts • also restaurant • gay sauna & bar in basement • gay-owned

**Das Tyrol** Mariahilfer Str 15 **43-1/587-5415** • gay-friendly • small luxury hotel

### BARS

**Cafe Cheri** Franzensg 2 **43-650/208-1471** • 10pm-4am • mostly gay men • also cafe

**Cafe Savoy** Linke Wienzeile 36 (at Köstlergasse) **43-1/581-1557** • noon-2am, from 9am Sat-Sun • popular • lesbians/ gay men • upscale cafe-bar

**Felixx** Gumpendorferstr 5 **43-1/920-4714** • 6pm-2am • lesbians/ gay men • food • WiFi

**Frauencafé** Lange Gasse 11 **43-1/406-3754** • 7pm-midnight, till 2am Fri-Sat (sometimes clsd Sun-Mon) • mostly women • transgender-friendly • cafe-bar

**Frauenzentrum Bar** Währingerstr 59 (enter on Prechtlgasse) **43-1/408_5057** • check www.frauenlesbenzentrum-wien.at for events • women • dancing/DJ

**Labris Bar** Biberstrasse 12 **43-1/945-6921** • 6pm-2am, till 4am wknds • mostly women

**Mango Bar** Laimgrubengasse 3 (U4-Kettenbrückengasse) **43-1/920-4714** • 9pm-4am • popular • mostly gay men • gay-owned

**Marea Alta** Gumpendorferstr 28 **43-699/1159-7131** • 7pm-2am, till 4am Fri-Sat, clsd Sun • mostly women • young crowd

**Merandy Lounge** Mollardgasse 17 • 7pm-2am Th, 8pm-6am Fri-Sat • lesbians/ gay men • dancing/DJ

**Peter's Operncafé Hartauer** Riemergasse 9 (at Singer) **43-1/512-8981** • 6pm-2am, clsd Sun-Mon • gay/ straight • food served • terrace

**Red Carpet** Magdalenenstr 2 **43-1/676-782-2966** • lesbians/ gay men • dancing/DJ • younger crowd • theme nights

**Schik** Schikanedergasse 5 • 7pm-2am, till 4am Fri-Sat, clsd Sun • lesbians/ gay men • WiFi

**Studio 67** Gumpendorferstr 67 **43-1/966-7182** • 10am-4am Th-Sat • gay/ straight • dancing/DJ • also upscale lounge

**Village Bar** Stiegengasse 8 (near Naschmarkt) **43-1/676-3848977** • 8pm-3am • mostly men • young crowd

**Wiener Freiheit** Schönbrunner Str 25 (U4-Kettenbrückengasse) **43-1/931-9111** • 8pm-midnight, till 4am Fri-Sat, clsd Sun-Mon • lesbians/ gay men • transgender-friendly • 3 flrs • disco 10pm-4am Fri-Sat • also cafe

## NIGHTCLUBS

**BallCanCan** Schwarzenberg Platz 10 (at Ost Klub) • lesbians/ gay men • dancing/DJ • monthly queer Balkan club

**g.spot** Neubaugasse 2 (at Camera Club) **43-1/523-3063** • 9pm 1st Fri • mostly women • dancing/DJ • monthly parties • check www.gspot.at for dates

**Heaven Gay Night** **43-1/402-1022** • check www.heaven.at for events • mostly men • dancing/DJ • transgender-friendly • strippers • young crowd

**Las Chicas** Lederergasse 11 (at Gerard) • check for dates • women only • dancing/DJ

**Meat Market** • queer electro dance party • check local listings

**Queer Beat** Landstr Hauptstr 38 (at the Viper Room) • 2nd & 4th Sat only • mostly gay men • dancing/DJ

**Up!** Mariahilfer Str 3 (at Lutz Club) • 2nd Fri only • mostly gay men • uplifing house music

**Why Not?** Tiefer Graben 22 (at Wipplinger, U-Schottentor) **43-1/925-3024** • 10pm-close Fri-Sat & before public holidays • mostly gay men • dancing/DJ • live shows • videos • WiFi

## CAFES

**Bakul** Margaretenstr 58 • 9am-2am • also guesthouse

**Cafe Berg** Berggasse 8 (at Wasagasse, U2-Schottentor) **43-1/319-5720** • 10am-1am • popular • lesbians/ gay men • cafe-bar

**Cafe Central** Herrengasse 14 (at Strauchgasse) **43-1/533-3763** • 7:30am-10pm, from 10am Sun & public holidays • "world's most famous coffeehouse"

**Cafe Standard** Margaretenstr 63 **43-1/581-0586** • 8am-midnight, from 11am wknds

**Cafe Stein** Währinger Str 6-8 (near U-Schottentor) **43-1/319-7241** • 7am-1am, from 9am Sun • gay-friendly • cafe-bar • WIFi • terrace

**Das Möbel** Burggasse 10 (Spittelberg) **43-1/524-9497** • 10am-1am • trendy • also art gallery • WiFi

**Point of Sale** Schleifmuhlgasse 12 **43-1/941-6397** • 7am-1am • cafe & deli • also vegan items • WiFi • also bar

**SMart Cafe** Kostlergasse 9 **43-1/585-7165** • 6pm-2am, till 4am Fri-Sat, clsd Sun-Mon • gay/ straight • S/M & fetish cafe

## RESTAURANTS

**Andino** Münzwardeingasse 2 (U4-Pilgramgasse) **43-1/587-6125** • 11am-2am, from 10am Sat, 11am-midnight Sun • Latin American • live music • full bar

**Aux Gazelles** Rahlgasse 5 **43-1/585-6645** • French/ Moroccan restaurant 6pm-midnight • Arabian-style lounge, cafe & deli 11am-2am • also Turkish steam baths noon-10pm

**Bin Im Leo** Servitengasse 14 **43–1/391–7763** • 4pm-midnight, from noon wknds • beer/ wine • plenty veggie

**Cafe-Restaurant Willendorf** Linke Wienzeile 102 (near Hofmuhlgasse, U4-Pilgramgasse) **43–1/587–1789** • 6pm-2am, food served till midnight • plenty veggie • full bar • terrace

**Halle** Museumsquartier 1 **43–1/523–7001** • 10am-2am • modern bistro • artsy crowd

**Kantine** Porzellangasse 19 **43–1/319–5918** • 6pm-2am • Thai

**Motto** Schönbrunner Str 30 (enter on Rüdigergasse) **43–1/587–0672** • 6pm-2am, till 4am Fri-Sat • popular • trendy • also nightclub • patio • reservations recommended

**Santo Spirito** Kumpfgasse 7 **43–1/512–9998** • 6pm-11pm, bar till 2am • classical music

**Schon Schön** Lindengasse 53 (Ecke Andreagasse) • lunch & dinner • fashionable restaurant • also bar • also clothing & hair salon

**Sly & Arny** Lothringerstrasse 22 **43–1/405–0458** • lunch Mon-Fri, dinner nightly, bar till late

**Stöger** Ramperstorffergasse 63 **43–1/544–7596** • 11am-midnight, clsd Sun, from 5pm Mon • Viennese

**Zum Roten Elefanten** Gumpendorferstrasse 3 **43–1/966–8008** • lunch & dinner, open late Fri-Sat, clsd Sun (lunch only in summer)

### ENTERTAINMENT & RECREATION

**Haus der Musik/ House of Music** Seilerstätte 30 **43–1/516–4810** • 10am-10pm • interactive museum of sound • also cafe

**Kunsthistorisches Museum** Maria Theresien-Platz (enter Heldenplatz) **43–1/525–240** • 10am-6pm, till 9pm Th, clsd Mon • not to be missed • works from Ancient Egypt to the Renaissance to Klimt

### BOOKSTORES

**Löwenherz** Berggasse 8 (next to Cafe Berg, enter on Wasagasse, U2-Schottentor) **43–1/317–2982** • 10am-7pm, till 8pm Fri, till 6pm Sat, clsd Sun • LGBT • large selection of English titles

### PUBLICATIONS

**Xtra** • gay magazine

### EROTICA

**Sexworld XXL Store** Mariahilfer Str 49 **43–1/587–6656** • upscale sex shop

**Tiberius** Lindengasse 2 (at Stiftgasse, U3-Neubaugasse) **43–1/522–0474** • clsd Sun • wheelchair access • designer fetish-wear

# CZECH REPUBLIC

## PRAGUE (PRAHA)

Note: M°=Metro station

> Prague is divided into 10 city districts: Praha—1, Praha—2, etc.

## Praha—Overview

### ACCOMMODATIONS

**Apartments in Prague 420/775–588–508, 303/800–0858** • gay/ straight • WiFi • kids/ pets ok

### ENTERTAINMENT & RECREATION

**Letna Park & Beer Garden** • great view of the city

## Praha—1

### ACCOMMODATIONS

**Buddha Bar Hotel** Jakubská 649/8 **420 /221–776–300** • gay/ straight • WiFi • small sexy hotel • pets ok

**Hotel Leonardo** Karolíny Svetle 27 **420 /239–009–239** • gay/ straight • restaurant • WiFi • great location

**Hotel Metropol** Narodni 33 (at Na Perstyne) **420/246–022–100** • gay/ straight • design hotel • all-glass facade

**The ICON Boutique Hotel** V Jame 6 (at Vodickova) **420/221–634–100** • gay/ straight • restaurant & bar • WiFi • wheelchair access

**The Palace Road Hotel Prague** Nerudova 7 (at Malostranske Namesti) **420/257–531–941** • gay/ straight • located in city center • WiFi

### BARS

**Café Bar Flirt** Martinská 5/419 **420/224–248–592** • cafe open 10am-2am, bar open 10pm-2am Fri-Sat • mostly gay men • dancing/DJ Fri-Sat • karaoke

**Friends Bar** Bartolomejská 11 **420/226–211–920** • 7pm-6am • popular • mostly men • dancing/DJ • neighborhood bar • DJ Wed-Sat • videos • WiFi

**K.U. Bar** Rytírská 13 (at Perlová, near Oldtown Square) **420/724–695–910** • 7pm-4am • gay/ straight • upscale & trendy • dancing/DJ • live shows

**Kafirna U Ceského Pána** Kozí 13, Stare Mesto **420/222-328-283** • 1pm-11pm, mostly gay men • small bar popular w/ locals

**Loca Cafe Bar** Smetanovo náb e í 24 **420/212-240-967** • 5pm-2am, till 3am Wed-Th, 4am Fri-Sat • lesbians/gay men, more women Wed • dancing/DJ • food served

## NIGHTCLUBS

**Stage** Stepanska 23 (at Reznicka) **420/252-548-683** • mostly gay men • cafe/restaurant from 4pm • nightclub opens 9pm • karaoke Tue

## CAFES

**Cafe Cafe** Rytirská 10 (at Perlová, near Oldtown Square) **420/224-210-597** • 10am-11pm • popular • WiFi

**Cafe Erra** Konviktská 11 **420/273-136-112** • 10am-midnight • salads, sandwiches & entrées

**Cafe Louvre** Národni 22 (Mº Narodni Trida) **420/224-930-949** • 9am-11:30pm • the favorite hangout of Albert Einstein & Franz Kafka

**Cafe Muzeum** Mezibranska 19 **420/774-454-304** • 10am-11pm, from 1pm wknds

**Q Cafe** Opatovická 166/12 **420/776-856-361** • noon-midnight

## RESTAURANTS

**Campanulla Cafe Restaurant** Velkoprevorske namesti 4 **420/257-217-736** • set in the beautiful garden of The Grand Priory of Bohemia Palace

**Farrango** Dusni 15 **420/224-815-996** • 4pm-midnight, clsd Sun • Thai

**Maitrea** Tynska 6/1064 (nr Old Town Square) **420/221-711-631** • noon-11:30pm • vegetarian

**Noi** Ujezd 19 **420/257-311-411** • 11am-1am • Thai

**Petrinské Terasy** Seminarská Zahrada 393, Malá Strana **420/257-320-688** • noon-11pm • in a former monastery • great view • gay-owned

**Restaurant Dlouhá** Dlouhá 23 (basement) **420/222-329-853** • 11am-11pm

**Staromestska Restaurace** Staromestske namesti 19 **420/224-213-015** • 11am-midnight • local Czech specialties

## ENTERTAINMENT & RECREATION

**NoD Gallery/ Roxy** Dlouhá 33 • experimental theater, dance & performance • also cafe & live music venue

**Sex Machines Museum** Melantrichova 18 **420/227-186-260** • 10am-11pm

## BOOKSTORES

**Globe** Patrossova 6 **420/224-934-203** • English-language bookstore • also cafe

## EROTICA

**Erotic City** Zitna 43 **420/737-221-264**

# Praha—2

## ACCOMMODATIONS

**Balbin Penzion** Balbinova 26 (near Wenceslas Square) **420/222-250-660** • gay/straight • located in city center • full brkfst • WiFi

**Prague Saints** Polska 32 (office location) (at Trebizkeho, at Saints Bar) **420/775-152-041, 420/775-152-042** • lesbians/ gay men • apts in gay Vinohrady district • gay-owned

## BARS

**Club Strelec** Anglicka 2 **420/224-941-446** • 5pm-2am, till midnight Sun • mostly gay men • bear bar on Wed & Sat

**Fan Fan Club** Dittrichova 5 (at Trojanova) **420/776-360-698** • 5pm-2am • mostly gay men • karaoke

**JampaDampa** V Tunich 10 (at Zitna) **420/603-260-678** • 6pm-2am, till 4am Wed, 6pm-6am Fri-Sat, clsd Sun-Mon • popular • mostly women • dancing/DJ • karaoke

**Klub 21** Rimska 21 **420/222-364-720** • 7pm-close, clsd Sun • lesbians/ gay men • cellar bar/ gallery • food • young crowd • mostly Czechs

**Saints** Polska 32 (at Trebizkeho) **420/222-250-326** • 7pm-2am, till 4am wknds • lesbians/ gay men

## NIGHTCLUBS

**Club Saigon** Trebizskeho 9a **420/776-205-880** • 7pm-1am, clsd Sun-Mon • gay/straight • WiFi

**Freedom Night** Trojická 10 (at PM Club) • monthly women's party • check www.djhenriette.cz for details

**Lollypop** Belehradska 120, Vinohrady (at Radost FX) **420/224-254-776, 420/603-193-711** • mostly gay men • huge, bi-monthly party • dancing/DJ

**On** Vinohradska 40 (at Blanicka) **420/222-520-630, 420/776-360-698 (CELL)** • noon-5am • lesbians/ gay men • dancing/DJ • video • 3 levels • darkroom

**Termax** 40 Vinohradska **420/222–710–462** • 10pm-6am Fri-Sat only • popular • mostly gay men • dancing/DJ

**Termix** Trebizskeho 4 (at Vinohradska) **420/222–710–462** • 10pm-5am, clsd Sun-Tue • popular • lesbians/ gay men • dancing/DJ • karaoke

### RESTAURANTS

**Celebrity Cafe** Vinohradska 40 (in Vinohrady) **420/222–511–343** • 8am-2am, noon-3am Sat, noon-midnight Sun • also bar

**Céleste Restaurant & Bar** Rasalnovo nabrezi 1981/80 (at Dancing House) **420/2219–84160** • lunch & dinner, clsd Sun • French dining with great views of the river

**Radost FX** Belehradska 120, Vinohrady **420/224–254–776, 420/603–193–711** • fabulous wknd brunch • vegetarian cafe • also straight nightclub w/ popular bi-monthly gay party Lollypop

## Praha—3

### BARS

**Piano Bar** Milesovská 10 (at Ondrickova) **420/775–727–496** • 5pm-close • lesbians/ gay men • mostly Czech older crowd • food served

**Sapfo** Slezská 74 **420/720–297–420** • 5pm-3am clsd Sun-Mon • mostly women

### CAFES

**Blaze** Husitska 43 **420/777–102–028** • 5pm-close • live music, art & more

### RESTAURANTS

**Restaurant Mozaika** Nitranská 13 **420/224–253–011** • contemporary take on international cuisine • non-smoking

### ENTERTAINMENT & RECREATION

**TV Tower** Mahlerovy sady 1 **420/724–251–286** • get a bird's-eye view of the city from the top of this tower

## Praha—4

### GYMS & HEALTH CLUBS

**Plavecky Stadion Podoli** Podolská 74 **420/241–433–952** • 6am-9:45 pm • gay/ straight • public baths • restaurants • women's sauna Th-Fri & Sun

## Praha—5

### ACCOMMODATIONS

**Andel's Hotel** Stroupeznickeho 21 (at Pizenska) **420/296–889–688** • gay-friendly • restaurant & bar

## Praha—7

### NIGHTCLUBS

**OMG/ Oh My Gay Party** U Pruhonu 3 (at Mecca) • 3rd Sat only • mostly gay men • dancing/DJ

### CAFES

**Duhova Cajovna** Milada Horáková 73 (at Ovenecka) **420/775–269–699** • 3pm-midnight • "Rainbow Tearoom" • food served • WiFi

## Praha—10

### ACCOMMODATIONS

**Ron's Rainbow Guest House** Bulharska 4 (at Finská) **420/271–725–664, 420/731–165–022 (CELL)** • gay/ straight • quiet & friendly • near city center • gay-owned

# DENMARK

## Copenhagen

### INFO LINES & SERVICES

**Kafe Knud** Skindergade 21 **45/3332–5861** • 4pm-10pm Tue & Th only • HIV resource center • cafe open Tue & Th only

**Sabaah** Onkel Dannys Plads 1 • community center for LGBT ethnic minorities • events • meetings

**Wonderful Copenhagen Convention & Visitors Bureau** Vesterbrogade 4A **45/7022-2442 (TOURIST INFO)**

### ACCOMMODATIONS

**Carlton Guldsmeden** Vesterbrogade 66 **45/3322-1500** • gay-friendly

**Copenhagen Admiral Hotel** Toldbodgade 24-28 **45/3374-1414** • gay-friendly • great views • WiFi

**First Hotel Kong Frederik** Vester Voldgade 25 **45/3312-5902**

**First Hotel Skt. Petri** Krystalgade 22 **45/3345-9100** • hotel embodying the ultra-coolest of Scandinavian design • great bar • WiFi • wheelchair access

**First Hotel Twentyseven** Løngangstræde 27 **45/7027-5627**

**Hotel Kong Arthur** Norre Sogade 11 **45/3311-1212**

**Hotel Windsor** Frederiksborggade 30, 1360 **45/3311-0830** • mostly gay men • near gay scene • shared baths • gay-owned

**Radisson Blu Royal Hotel** Hammerichsgade 1 **45/3342-6000**

**The Square** Rådhuspladsen 14
45/3338–1200

## BARS

**Amigo Bar** Schønbergsgade 4, Frederiksberg
45 5/3321–4915 • 10pm-6am • lesbians/ gay
men • neighborhood bar • karaoke

**Cafe Intime** Allegade 25, Frederiksberg
45/3834–1958 • 6pm-2am • gay-friendly •
cafe-bar • piano bar

**Can-Can** Mikkel Bryggers Gade 11
45/3311–5010 • 2pm-2am, till 5am Fri-Sat •
mostly gay men • friendly neighborhood bar

**Centralhjørnet** Kattesundet 18
45/3311–8549 • noon-2am • mostly gay men
• WiFi

**Cosy Bar** Studiestræde 24 (in Latin Quarter)
45/3312–7427 • 10pm-6am, till 8am Fri-Sat •
popular • mostly gay men

**Heaven** Rådhuspladsen 75 45/3333–0806 •
10am-2am, till 5am wknds • lesbians/ gay men
• food served

**Lesbisk Kaffe** Enghavevej 56 • 10am-10pm,
till 1am wknds • mostly women • cafe & bar •
food served • performances • WiFi

**Masken** Studiestræde 33 45/3391–0937 •
2pm-3am, till 5am Fri-Sat • popular • lesbians/
gay men • cafe-bar • WiFi

**Never Mind** Nørre Voldgade 2 45/3311–8886
• 10pm-6am • mostly gay men

**Oscar Bar Cafe** Rådhuspladsen 77
45/3312–0999 • noon-2am • mostly men •
lesbians welcome • food served • great happy
hour • WiFi

**Vela** Viktoriagade 2-4 45/3331–3419 • 8pm-
midnight Wed, till 2am Th, till 5am Fri-Sat • clsd
Sun-Tue • only mostly lesbian bar in town, go
there for the beers and strawberry shots •
neighborhood bar

## NIGHTCLUBS

**Christopher Club** Knabrostræde 3 •
midnight-5am Fri-Sat only • lesbians/ gay men
• dancing/DJ

## CAFES

**Jernbanecafeen** • 7am-2am • WiFi • patio

## RESTAURANTS

**Jailhouse Restaurant & Bar** Studiestraede
12 45/3315–2255 • 3pm-2am, till 5am Fri-Sat
• popular • mostly gay men • bears

**Laekkerier** Borgergade 17F • 8:30am-5pm,
till 10pm Th, from 10am wknds • organic take-
out

**Luna's Diner** Vesterbrogade 42
45/3322–4757 • 10am-midnight, till 1am Fri-
Sat

**Tight** Hyskenstraede 10 45/3311–0900 •
5pm-10pm, from noon wknds • Canadian,
French & Australian

## ENTERTAINMENT & RECREATION

**Amager Strandpark** • beach 5 km from
city center

**Bellevue Beach** • mostly gay beach • left
end is nude

**Kifak** Staldgade 8 • venue for LGBT special
events

**Warehouse 9** Bygning 66 (enter from
parking lot in front of Oksenhallen, in the
meatpacking district) 45/3322–2847 • queer
art, music, performance & more

## PUBLICATIONS

**Out & About** 45/4093–1977

## EROTICA

**Lust** Mikkel Bryggersgade 3A 45/3333–0110 •
erotica for women

# ENGLAND

## LONDON

London is divided into 6 regions:
   London—Overview
   London—Central
   London—West
   London—North
   London—East
   London—South

## London—Overview

### BARS

**Glass Bar** • women's parties around
London • check www.theglassbar.org.uk for
events

### NIGHTCLUBS

**Exilio** 44–(0)79/5698–3230 • 9:30pm-2:30am
twice a month on Sat, call for location •
lesbians/ gay men • dancing/DJ • Latino/a

**Torture Garden** 44–020/7700–1441 • the
worlds largest fetish/ body art club • check
www.torturegarden.com for events

### ENTERTAINMENT & RECREATION

**The Women's Library, London
Metropolitan University** Old Castle St
44–020/7320–2222 • clsd Sun • also cafe •
museum • cultural center • call for events •
nonsmoking

## PUBLICATIONS

**Diva** 44-020/7424-7400 • glorious glossy magazine for lesbians & bisexual women

**g3** 44-020/7724-9898 • free monthly lesbian glossy

# London—Central

London—Central includes Soho, Covent Garden, Bloomsbury, Mayfair, Westminster, Pimlico & Belgravia

## ACCOMMODATIONS

**Dover Hotel** 42/44 Belgrave Rd 44-020/7821-9085 • gay-friendly • WiFi

**Fitz B&B** 15 Colville Place (btwn Charlotte & Whitfield ) 44-(0)78/3437-2866 • lesbians/ gay men • 18th-c townhouse • nonsmoking • WiFi • gay-owned

**George Hotel** 58–60 Cartwright Gardens (N of Russell Square) 44-020/7387-8777 • gay-friendly • full brkfst • some shared baths • kids ok

**Hazlitt's** 6 Frith St (Soho Sq) 44-020/7434-1771 • gay-friendly • WiFi

**Lincoln House** 33 Gloucester Pl, Marble Arch (at Baker St) 44-020/7486-7630 • gay/ straight • B&B • full brkfst • WiFi • wheelchair access

**Marble Arch Inn** 49-50 Upper Berkeley St 44-020/7723-7888 • gay-friendly

**Z Hotel** 17 Moor St 44-020/3551-3700 • gay/ straight • WiFi • great Soho location

## BARS

**The Admiral Duncan** 54 Old Compton St (Soho) 44-020/7437-5300 • pub hours • popular • lesbians/ gay men • neighborhood bar • transgender-friendly

**Bar Soho** 23-25 Old Compton St (at Frith St) 44-020/7439-0439 • noon-1am, till 3am Fri-Sat, from 2pm Sun

**Circa** 62 Frith St 44-020/7734-6826 • 4pm-1am • mostly gay men • dancing/DJ

**Compton's of Soho** 51-53 Old Compton St (at Dean St) 44-020/7479-7961 • noon-midnight, till 10:30pm Sun • mostly gay men • food served Sun • wheelchair access

**Dog & Duck** 18 Bateman St (at Frith St) 44-020/7494-0697 • 10am-11:30pm • gay/ straight • neighborhood bar • food served

**Duke of Wellington** 77 Wardour (Soho) 44-020/7439-1274 • pub hours • gay/ straight • snacks

**The Edge** 11 Soho Square (at Oxford St) 44-020/7439-1313 • 3pm-1am, till 3am Fri-Sat, till 11:30pm Sun • popular • dancing/DJ • live music • good food • outdoor seating • wheelchair access

**Freedom Bar** 66 Wardour St (off Old Compton St) 44-020/7734-0071 • 4pm-3am, from 2pm Fri-Sat, 2pm-11:30pm Sun • lesbians/ gay men • dancing/DJ • food served • young crowd

**Friendly Society** 79 Wardour St (the basement at Old Compton, enter Tisbury Ct) 44-020/7434-3805 • 4pm-11pm, till 10:30pm Sun • lesbians/ gay men • young crowd

**G-A-Y Bar** 30 Old Compton St (at Frith) 44-020/7494-2756 • noon-midnight • lesbians/ gay men • basement women's bar

**Green Carnation** 4-5 Greek St (Soho Sq) 44-020/8123-4267 • 4pm-2am • inspired by the time & life of Oscar Wilde

**Ku Bar/ Ku Klub** 30 Lisle St (Leicester Sq) 44-020/7437-4303 • noon-3am, till 10:30pm Sun • lesbians/ gay men • karaoke • young crowd • WiFi • also Soho bar at 25 Frith St

**Madam JoJo's** 8-10 Brewer St (at Rupert) 44-020/7734-3040 • mostly gay men • live shows • Tranny Shack Wed

**The New Bloomsbury Set** 76 Marchmont St (at Tavistock Pl) 44-020/7383-3084 • 4pm-11pm, 2pm-10:30pm Sun • gay/ straight

Note: "Pub hours" usually means 11am-11pm Mon-Sat and noon-3pm & 7pm-10:30pm Sun

**The Retro Bar** 2 George Ct (at Strand) 44-020/7321-2811 • pub hours • lesbians/ gay men • neighborhood bar • dancing/DJ • karaoke

**Ruby Tuesday** 30 Lisle St (at Ku Bar, Leicester Sq) 44-020/7437-4303 • 2nd Tue only • mostly women • dancing/DJ • entertainment

**Rupert Street** 50 Rupert St (off Brewer) 44-020/7292-7141 • pub hours • popular • lesbians/ gay men • upscale "fashiony-types" • food served • wheelchair access

**She Soho** 23A Old Compton St 44-020/7437-4303 • 4pm-11:30pm, till midnight Fri-Sat, till 10:30pm Sun • mostly women

**Star at Night** 22 Great Chapel St (at Hollen St) 44-020/7494-2488 • 6pm-11:30pm, clsd Sun-Mon • lesbians/ gay men • dancing/DJ • relaxed cafe/ bar • live shows

**The Village Soho** 81 Wardour St (at Old Compton) 44-020/7478-0530 • 4pm-1am, till 11:30pm Sun • popular • mostly gay men • 18+ • young crowd • wheelchair access

**The Yard** 57 Rupert St (off Brewer) 44-020/7437-2652, 871/426-2243 • pub hours • popular • mostly gay men • 2 levels • young crowd • food served • wheelchair access

## NIGHTCLUBS

**Code** 5 Greek St (at Green Carnation, Soho) 44-079/5652-9649 • last Fri only • mostly women • dancing

**G-A-Y Club** Under the Arches, Villers St (at Heaven) 44-020/7734-6963 • 11pm-3am • popular • mostly gay men • dancing/DJ • live shows • young crowd • Camp Attack Fri • cover charge

**Heaven** 9 The Arches (off Villers St) 44-020/7930-2020 • the mother of all London gay clubs • call for hours/ events • mostly gay men • dancing/DJ

**KU Bar Frith St** 25 Frith St (at Old Compton St, Soho) 44-020/7287-7986 • noon-11pm, till midnight wknds • mostly men • dancing/DJ

**The Shadow Lounge** 5-7 Brewer St (Soho) 44-020/7317-9270 • 10pm-3am, clsd Sun • mostly gay men • dancing/DJ • private club

## CAFES

**Balans Cafe** 34 Old Compton St 44-020/7439-3309 • 24hrs • popular • lesbians/ gay men • all-day brkfst • terrace

**Caffe Nero** 43 Frith St 44-020/7434-3887 • 7am-2am, till 4am Sat

**Flat White** 17 Berwick St 44-020/7734-0370 • 8am-7pm, 9am-6pm wknds • Australian-style cafe

**LJ Coffee House** 3 Winnett St (at Rupert) 44-020/7434-1174 • 7:30am-7pm, 10am-8pm Sat, from 1pm Sun • cozy cafe • street views

**Milk Bar** 3 Bateman St 44-020/7287-4796 • 8am-7pm, till 5pm wknds • wheelchair access

## RESTAURANTS

**Cha Cha Moon** 15-21 Ganton St 44-020/7297-9800 • noon-11pm, till 10pm Sun • inexpensive Chinese

**Food for Thought** 31 Neal St, downstairs (Covent Garden) 44-020/7836-0239 • noon-8:30pm, till 5:30pm Sun • vegetarian • inexpensive hole-in-the-wall • BYOB

**The Gay Hussar** 2 Greek St (on Soho Square) 44-020/7437-0973 • lunch & dinner, clsd Sun • Hungarian • wheelchair access

**Mildred's** 45 Lexington 44-020/7494-1634 • noon-11pm, clsd Sun • popular • vegetarian • plenty vegan

**Randall & Aubin** 16 Brewer St (at Walkers Court) 44-020/7287-4447 • noon-11pm • casual French • good people-watching

**Wagamama Noodle Bar** 10-A Lexington St 44-020/7292-0990 • noon-11pm • Japanese • nonsmoking • chain w/ locations throughout city

## BOOKSTORES

**Gay's the Word** 66 Marchmont St (near Russell Sq Underground) 44-020/7278-7654 • 10am-6:30pm, 2pm-6pm Sun

## RETAIL SHOPS

**Prowler Soho** 5–7 Brewer St (behind Village Soho bar) 44-020/7734-4031 • 11am-10pm, noon-8pm Sun • popular • large gay department store

# London—West

London—West includes Earl's Court, Kensington, Chelsea & Bayswater

## ACCOMMODATIONS

**Cardiff Hotel** 5, 7, 9 Norfolk Sq (Hyde Park) 44-020/7723-9068 • gay-friendly • B&B hotel in 3 Victorian townhouses • some shared baths • WiFi

**Millennium Bailey's Hotel** 140 Gloucester Rd (at Old Brompton Rd, Kensington) 44-020/7373-6000 • located in the heart of Kensington • also restaurant & bar

**Myhotel Chelsea** 35 Ixworth Place (at Elystan St, Chelsea) 44-020/7225-7500, 44-020/7637-2000 • gay-friendly • stylish boutique hotel in Chelsea

**Parkwood Hotel** 4 Stanhope Pl (Marble Arch) 44-020/7402-2241 • gay-friendly • full brkfst • nonsmoking

## BARS

**Richmond Arms** 20 The Square (at Princes, Richmond) 44-020/8940-2118 • pub hours • lesbians/ gay men • dancing/DJ • professional crowd • karaoke • drag shows • cabaret

**West Five (W5)** 6 Popes Ln (South Ealing) 44-020/8579-3266 • 7pm-close, clsd Mon-Tue • lesbians/ gay men • cabaret • lounge • piano bar • garden

## RESTAURANTS

**The Churchill Arms** 119 Kensington Church St 44-020/7727-4242 • inexpensive, fantastic Thai • also pub

**The Gate** 51 Queen Caroline St, Hammersmith • lunch & dinner, clsd Sun, vegetarian

**Star of India** 154 Old Brompton Rd 44-020/737-2901 • lunch & dinner • upscale

## ENTERTAINMENT & RECREATION

**Walking Tour of Gay SOHO** 56 Old Compton St (at Admiral Duncan Pub) 44-020/7437-6063 • 2pm Sun • world-famous historical walking tour covering over 600 years of gay history in London's "square mile of sin"

# London—North

**London—North includes Paddington, Regents Park, Camden, St Pancras & Islington**

## ACCOMMODATIONS

**Ambassadors Bloomsbury** 12 Upper Woburn Pl (at Euston Rd, Bloomsbury) 44-020/7693-5400 • gay-friendly • near Kings Cross St Pancras & Euston Stations • Italian restaurant on-site • nonsmoking

**Ossian Guesthouse** 20 Ossian Rd (at Mt Pleasant Villas, Crouch Hill) 44-020/8340-4331 • gay-friendly • Victorian house on quiet street in quiet suburb

**The Royal Park Hotel** 3 Westbourne Terr (Hyde Park) 44-020/7479-6600 • gay-friendly • intimate luxury hotel • sauna & gym • WiFi

## BARS

**Duke of Wellington** 119 Balls Pond Rd 44-020/7275-7640 • 3pm-midnight, till 1am Fri-Sat • gay/ straight • popular w/ lesbians • food served

**G-A-Y Late** 5 Goslett Yard (Camden Town) • 11pm-3am • mostly gay men

**The George Music Bar** 114 Twickenham Rd (Isleworth) 44-020/8560-1456 • 5pm-close, from noon wknds • transgender-friendly • cabaret • gay-owned

**King William IV (KW)** 77 Hampstead High St (Hampstead) 44-020/7435-5747 • pub hours • lesbians/ gay men • food served • beer garden

## NIGHTCLUBS

**Club Kali** 1 Dartmouth Park Hill (at The Dome) 44-020/7272-8153 (DOME #) • 10pm-3am 3rd Fri • popular • lesbians/ gay men • dancing/DJ • mostly Asian • transgender-friendly • South Asian music • cover charge

**Dream Bags Jaquar Shoes** 32-36 Kingsland Rd 44-020/7729-5830 • noon-1am • jam-packed club in a former shoe shop • also art exhibts

**East Bloc** 217 City Rd (at Shepherdess Walk, Old Street) 44-020/7253-0367 • 10pm-4am, till 6am Fri-Sat, clsd Mon-Wed • mostly men • electro dance club in funky basement space

**Egg** 200 York Way (Kings Cross) 44-020/7871-1111 • 10pm-6am Sat, until late afternoon Sun • gay/ straight • dancing/DJ

**Habibi London** 99-100 Turnmills (Farringdon) • 10:30pm last Fri only • lesbians/ gay men • Middle Eastern

## RESTAURANTS

**Manna** 4 Erskine Rd (at Ainger Rd, Camden) 44-020/7722-8028 • lunch Tue-Sun, dinner nightly • vegetarian • reservations recommended

**Providores and Tapa Room** 109 Marylebone High St (at New Cavendish St) 44-020/7935-6175 • lunch & dinner • Asian fusion

## ENTERTAINMENT & RECREATION

**Rosemary Branch Theatre** 2 Shepperton Rd 44-020/7704-2730 (BAR), 44-020/7704-6665 (THEATRE) • gay/ straight • also restaurant & bar • many gay-themed plays

# London—East

**London—East includes City, Tower, Clerkenwell & Shoreditch**

## ACCOMMODATIONS

**Andaz Liverpool Street** 40 Liverpool St (near Bishopsgate, at Liverpool Street Station) 44-020/7961-1234 • restaurants, bars, gym

**The Hoxton** 81 Great Eastern St 44-020/7550-1000 • gay-friendly • also restaurant • nonsmoking • WiFi

## BARS

**Bar Music Hall** 134 Curtain Rd (Shoreditch) 44-020/7729-7216 • 11am-midnight, till 3am Fri-Sat • gay-friendly • great wknd brunch • dancing/DJ • live shows

**Bethnal Green Working Men's Club** 42-44 Pollard Row (at Squirries St, Bethnal Green) 44-020/7739-7170 • lesbians/ gay men • performance art • cabaret • drag shows • transgender-friendly

**Dalston Superstore** 117 Kingsland High St (at Sandringham Rd) 44-020/7254 2273 • noon-2am • gay/ straight • neighborhood bar • food served • WiFi

**The Macbeth** 70 Hoxton St (at Crondall St, Old St) 44-020/ 7749-0600 • 8pm-1am • gay/ straight • live shows • terrace

**The Old Ship** 17 Barnes St (Stepney) 44-020/7790-4082 • from 4pm Mon, from 7pm Wed-Sat, from 6pm Sun, clsd Tue • lesbians/ gay men • neighborhood bar • cabaret • wheelchair access

## NIGHTCLUBS

**Kaos at Stunners** 566 Cable St (at Butcher Row, Cable St Studios, Limehouse) • monthy parties • check www.kaoslondon.com • transgender • dancing/DJ • private club

**Pelucas y Tacones** 6 Shoreditch High St (at Concrete/ Pizza East) • 9pm-2am 2nd Sat only • queer disco party

**Pout** 2-3 Old Change Court (at Yager Bar) • 8pm 2ndSat only • mostly women • dancing/DJ

**Unskinny Bop** 42-44 Pollard Row (Bethnal Green Club) • 9pm 3rd Satonly • mostly women • dancing/DJ • live music

**Urban Desi** 18-20 Houndsditch (at Dukes) • 11pm-5am 2nd Sat • lesbians/ gay men • dancing/DJ • mostly South Asian

**Way Out Club** 14 New London St (at Gilt Bar, corner of Crutched Friers and Seething Ln) 44-(0)20/7264-1910 • 9pm-4am Sat only • transsexuals & their friends • dancing/DJ • live shows • private club • cover charge

## CAFES

**Pogo Cafe** 76 Clarence Rd 44-020/8533-1214 • 12:30pm-9pm, from 11am Sun • vegan • volunteer-run • queer social space

## RESTAURANTS

**Bistrotheque** 23-27 Waderson St 44-020/8983-7900 • expensive & glamorous • also cabaret shows after dinner

**Bonds Restaurant & Bar** 5 Threadneedle St 44-020/7657-8090 • lunch & dinner Mon-Fri, just bar service & snacks wknds, space formerly a bank lobby

**Cafe Spice Namaste** 16 Prescott St 44-020/7488-9242 • lunch Mon-Fri, dinner nightly, clsd Sun • Indian

**Canteen** 2 Crispin Pl (Spitalfields) 44-(0)84/5686-1122 • place to be for brkfst

**Hoxton Square Bar & Kitchen** 2-4 Hoxton Square 44-020/9613-1171 • great dark spot for brkfst • live music

**Les Trois Garçons** 1 Club Row (at Bethnal, Shoreditch) 44-020/7613-1924 • 6pm-midnight, clsd Sun • eclectic decor • reservations recommended

**Lounge Lover** 44-020/7012-1234 • fancy cuisine in a posh lounge • reservations required • wheelchair access

**Royal Oak** 73 Columbia Rd (at Hackney Rd, Old St) 44-020/7729-2220 • 4pm-11pm, from noon Fri-Sun • popular Sun for the Columbia Rd Flower market

**Saf** 63-97 Barkers Building, High Street (in Kensington, at Wholefoods Market) 44-020/7368-4555 • lunch & dinner, also bar till midnight • upscale vegan/ raw food

## EROTICA

**Expectations** 75 Great Eastern St (Shoreditch) 44-020/7739-0292 • 11am-7pm, till 8pm Sat, noon-5pm Sun • leather/ rubber store • also mail order

**Sh! Women's Erotic Emporium** 57 Hoxton Sq (off Old St, Shoreditch) 44-020/7613-5458 • noon-8pm • men very welcome when accompanied by a woman

# London—South

London—South includes Southwark, Lambeth, Kennington, Vauxhall, Battersea, Lewisham & Greenwich

## ACCOMMODATIONS

**Griffin House** 22 Stockwell Green 44-020/7096-3332 • lesbians/ gay men • 2 rental apts near Vauxhall Gay Village & West End • WiFi • gay-owned

## BARS

**BackCOUNTER** 7-11 S Lambeth Rd (Vauxhall) 44-020/3693-9600 • 5pm-late, clsd Mon-Tue • gay/straight • neighborhood bar • DJ/dancing • food served • WiFi • wheelchair access

**Bar Wotever** 372 Kennington Ln (at Royal Vauxhall Tavern) • 6pm-midnight Tue • dancing/DJ • genderqueers & their admirers

**Battersea Barge** Riverside Walk Nine Elms Ln (Vauxhall) 44-020/7498-0004 • call for events • gay-friendly • cabaret • comedy • food served • gay-owned

**The Cambria** 40 Kemerton Rd (Denmark Hill) 44-020/7737-3676 • upmarket eclectic pub • gay/straight • food served • beautiful back garden

**George & Dragon** 2 Blackheath Hill (Greenwich) **44-020/8691-3764** • 6pm-2am, till 4am Fri-Sat • mostly gay men • live shows • cabaret

**Kazbar** 50 Clapham High St (Clapham) **44-020/7622-0070** • 5pm-midnight, till 1am Fri-Sat, from 1pm Sun • lesbians/ gay men

**The Little Apple** 98 Kennington Ln **44-020/7735-2039** • noon-midnight, till 3am Sat • lesbians/ gay men • dancing/DJ • transgender-friendly • food served • terrace • wheelchair access

**Prince of Greenwich** 72 Royal Hill (Greenwich) • 4pm-11pm, from noon Fri-Sat • mostly gay men • neighborhood bar • food served • drag shows

**The Star & Garter** 227 High St (Bromley) **44-020/8466-7733** • pub hours • lesbians/ gay men • karaoke • WiFi • wheelchair access

**The Two Brewers** 114 Clapham High St (Clapham) **44-020/7819-9539** • 4pm-2am, till 4am Fri-Sat, from 2pm Sun • lesbians/ gay men • dancing/DJ • karaoke • cabaret

### NIGHTCLUBS

**Black Sheep Bar** 68 High St (at S Norwood Hill, Croydon) **44-020/8680-2233** • gay/ straight • theme nights • alternative club

**Bootylicious** 1 Nine Elms (at Club Colosseum) • 11pm 3rd Sat • popular black gay club

**Fire** 47B S Lambeth Rd (Vauxhall) **44-020/3242-0040** • after-hours, Sat mornings & Sun afternoons • gay/ straight • dancing/DJ • cover charge

**Hard On** 66 Albert Embankment (at Union, in Vauxhall) **44-020/7533 402 985** • 3rd Sat only • mLesbians/gay men • fetish party • large play area with equipment • private club

**Horse Meat Disco** 349 Kennington Ln (at the Eagle) **44-020/7793-0903** • 8pm Sun only • lesbians/ gay men • dancing/DJ • popular queer dance party

**Royal Vauxhall Tavern** 372 Kennington Ln (Vauxhall) **44-020/7820-1222** • 8pm-late, 9pm-3am Fri-Sat, 2pm-midnight Sun • mostly gay men • popular wknds • more women Sat for Duckie • dancing/DJ • transgender-friendly • food served • wheelchair access

### RESTAURANTS

**COUNTER Vauxhall Arches** 7-11 S Lambeth Rd (Vauxhall) **44-020/3693-9600** • 7am-midnight, bar and brasserie in the centre of Vauxhal

### ENTERTAINMENT & RECREATION

**Oval Theatre Cafe Bar** 52-54 Kennington Oval **44-020/7582-0080** • 6pm-11pm Tue-Sat (cafe) • inquire about current theatre & art

# FRANCE

# PARIS

Note: M°=Métro station

Paris is divided by arrondissements (city districts); 01=1st arrondissement, 02=2nd arrondissement, etc

## Paris—Overview

Note: When phoning Paris from the US, dial the country code + the city code + the local phone number

### INFO LINES & SERVICES

**Centre Gai et Lesbien** 63 rue Beaubourg **33-1/4357-2147** • drop-in evenings • call for other events/ groups

**Gay AA** 7 rue Auguste Vacquerie (at St George's Anglican) **33-1/4634-5965** • 7:30pm Tue, see calendar for other times

### ACCOMMODATIONS

**Gay Accommodation Paris** 271, rue du Faubourg Saint Antoine **33-1/4348-1382** • studios for rent in central Paris • gay-owned

### NIGHTCLUBS

**Womexx** • mostly women • dancing/DJ • lesbian parties in cool spaces • www.womexx.fr

### PUBLICATIONS

**Têtu** **33-1/5680-2080** • stylish & intelligent LGBT monthly (en français)

## Paris—01

### ACCOMMODATIONS

**Hotel Louvre Richelieu** 51 rue de Richelieu (M° Palais-Royal) **33-1/4297-4620** • gay/ straight • nonsmoking • WiFi

**Hotel Louvre Saint-Honoré** 141 rue Saint-Honoré (at rue du Louvre) **33-1/4296-2323** • gay/ straight • full brkfst • kids ok • WiFi • wheelchair access

### BARS

**Le Banana Cafe** 13-15 rue de la Ferronnerie (near rue St-Denis, M° Châtelet) **33-1/4233-3531** • 6pm-dawn • lesbians/ gay men • dancing/DJ • tropical decor • theme nights • piano bar • live shows • young crowd • wheelchair access • terrace

**Bar du Kent'z** 2-4 rue Vauvilliers (M°
Chatelet-Les Halles) **33–1/4221–0116** •
mostly gay men • 1920s style cocktail lounge

**Le Tropic Cafe** 66 rue des Lombards (M°
Châtelet) **33–1/4013–9262** • 4pm-5am •
lesbians/ gay men • dancing/DJ Fri-Sat •
transgender-friendly • kitschy, fun bar • tapas
served • terrace • wheelchair access

**Le Velvet** 43 rue Saint Honore
**33–1/4221–1360** • clsd Sun-Mon •
lesbians/gay men

### RESTAURANTS

**L' Amazonial** 3 rue Ste-Opportune (at rue
Ferronnerie, M° Châtelet) **33–1/4233–5313** •
lunch & dinner, brunch wknds • • Brazilian/
int'l • cabaret • drag shows • heated terrace •
wheelchair access • gay-owned

**Au Diable des Lombards** 64 rue des
Lombards (at rue St-Denis, M° Châtelet)
**33–1/4233–8184** • 8am-1am • American • full
bar • terrace

**Marc Mitonne** 60 rue de l'Arbre-Sec (M° Les
Halles) **33–1/4261–5316** • 6pm-2am, clsd
Sun-Mon • live shows • cabaret

**La Poule au Pot** 9 rue Vauvilliers (M° Les
Halles) **33–1/4236–3296** • 7pm-5am, clsd
Mon • clsd Aug • bistro • traditional French

### ENTERTAINMENT & RECREATION

**Forum des Halles** 101 Porte Berger (M°
Châtelet-Les Halles) **33–1/4476–9656** •
underground sports/ entertainment complex
w/ museums, theater, shops, clubs, cafes &
more

### GYMS & HEALTH CLUBS

**Club Med Gym** 147 rue St–Honoré (M°
Louvre) **33–1/4020–0303** • gay/ straight • day
passes available • many locations throughout
the city

## Paris—02

### BARS

**La Champmeslé** 4 rue Chabanais (at rue
des Petits Champs, M° Pyramides)
**33–1/4296–8520** • 4pm-3am, till 7am Fri-Sat,
clsd Sun • popular • mostly women • theme
nights • older crowd • WiFi • wheelchair
access • a lesbian landmark, in business for
over 20 years

### NIGHTCLUBS

**Rex Club** 5 blvd Poissonière (M° Bonne
Nouvelle) **33–1/4236–1096** • gay-friendly •
call for events • clsd August • cover

### CAFES

**Stuart Friendly** 16 rue Marie Stuart
**33–1/4233–2400** • noon-11pm, till midnight
Fri-Sat, till 5:30pm Sun • "straight-friendly" cafe
• food served

### RESTAURANTS

**Le Lezard Cafe** 32 rue Etienne Marcel
**33–1/4233–2273** • full bar • terrace year
round

**Le Loup Blanc** 42 rue Tiquetonne (M°
Etienne-Marcel) **33–1/4013–0835** • 7:30pm-
midnight, till 1am Sat, also brunch 11am-
4:30pm Sun • popular • lesbians/ gay men

## Paris—03

### ACCOMMODATIONS

**Absolu Living** 236 rue St Martin
**33–1/4454–9700** • lesbians/ gay men • fully
furnished apts in central Paris • short & long-
term stays • gay-owned

**Adorable Apartment in Paris** (M°
Rambuteau) **415/287–0306 (US#)** • gay-
friendly • in heart of Marais • nonsmoking •
lesbian & gay-owned

**Hôtel du Vieux Saule** 6 rue de Picardie
**33–1/4272–0114** • gay-friendly

**Hotel Jules & Jim** 11 rues Gravilliers
**33–1/4454–1313** • gay/ straight • gay-owned

### BARS

**Le CUD Club** 12 rue des Haudriettes
**33–1/4277–4412** • 11pm-6am, till 7am wknds
• mostly men • dancing/DJ • young crowd

**Le Duplex** 25 rue Michel-Le-Comte (at rue
Beaubourg, M° Rambuteau) **33–1/4272–8086**
• 8pm-2am, till 4am Fri-Sat • lesbians/ gay
men • neighborhood bar • bohemian types •
live shows • WiFi

**La Mutinerie** 176–178 rue St-Martin (near
rue Réaumur, M° Rambuteau)
**33–1/4272–7059** • 4pm-2am • mostly women
• neighborhood bar • young crowd

**Le Tango/ La Boite à Frissons** 13 rue au
Maire (M° Arts-et-Metiers) **33–1/4272–1778** •
10:30pm-5am, clsd Mon • lesbians/ gay men •
food served

### EROTICA

**Rex** 42 rue de Poitou (at rue Charlot, M° St-
Sébastien-Froissard) **33–1/4277–5857** • 1pm-
8pm, clsd Sun • new, custom & secondhand
leather & S/M accessories

## Paris—04

### ACCOMMODATIONS

**Historic Rentals** 800/537-5408 (US#) • gay-friendly • 1-bdrm apt • full kitchen • nonsmoking • WiFi

**Hôtel Beaubourg** 11 rue Simon le Franc (btwn rue Beaubourg & rue du Temple, M° Hôtel-de-Ville) **33-1/4274-3424** • gay/straight • next to Centre Pompidou • WiFi

**Hôtel de la Bretonnerie** 22 rue Ste-Croix-de-la-Bretonnerie (M° Hôtel-de-Ville) **33-1/4887-7763** • gay-friendly • 17th-c hotel w/ Louis XIII decor

**Hôtel du Vieux Marais** 8 rue du Plâtre (M° Hôtel-de-Ville) **33-1/4278-4722** • gay-friendly • centrally located • WiFi

**Paris At Home** 33-06/1991-5828 • lesbians/ gay men • B&B & apts • gay-owned

### BARS

**3W Kafe** 8 rue des Ecouffes (M° St Paul) **33-1/4887-3926** • 5pm-2am, till 4am Fri-Sat • popular • mostly women • dancing/DJ • live shows • young crowd

**Au Mange Disque** 15 rue de la Reynie (at Boule de Sebastopol) **33-1/4804-7817** • 11am-2am, from 5pm Sun-Mon • mostly gay men • theme nights • colorful, modern decor

**Le Carrefour** 8 rue des Archives (at rue de la Verrerie) **33-1/4029-9005** • 6am-2am • mostly gay men • neighborhood bar • good location & terrace

**Cox** 15 rue des Archives (at rue Ste-Croix-de-la-Bretonnerie, M° Hôtel-de-Ville) **33-1/4272-0800** • 5:30pm-2am, from 4:30pm Fri-Sun • mostly gay men • dancing/DJ • huge terrace

**Dandy's Cafe** 9 rue Nicolas Flamel **33-1/4271-4582** • 2pm-2am • mostly gay men

**L' Enchanteur** 15 rue Michel Lecomte (M° Rambuteau) **33-1/4804-0238** • 6pm-6am, clsd Mon • lesbians/ gay men • karaoke

**Les Filles de Paris** 57 rue Quincampoix **33-1/4271-7220** • 10pm-5am Wed-Sat, also restaurant from 7pm, clsd Sun-Mon • gay/straight • dancing/DJ • drag shows, burlesque & cabaret

**Le Freedj** 35 rue Ste-Croix-de-la-Bretonnerie (at rue du Temple, M° Hôtel-de-Ville) **33-1/4029-4440** • 6pm-4am • lesbians/ gay men • bar upstairs, club downstairs

**L' Imprevu Cafe** 9 rue Quincampoix **33-1/4278-2350** • 3pm-2am, from 1pm Sun • mostly gay men • low key neighborhood cafe/ bar • food served

**Les Jacasses** 5 rue des Ecouffes (M° St Paul) **33-1/4271-1551** • 5pm-2am • mostly women • men welcome

**Morgan Bar** 25 rue du Roi de Sicile **33-1/4277-0666** • lesbians/ gay men • dancing/DJ • WiFi

**L' Oiseau Bariolé** 16 rue Saint-Croix-de-la-Bretonnerie (M° Hotel de Ville) **33-1/4272-3712** • lesbians/ gay-men • 5pm-close • quiet

**L' Open Cafe** 17 rue des Archives (at rue Ste-Croix-de-la-Bretonnerie, M° Hôtel-de-Ville) • 11am-2am, till 4am Fri-Sat • popular • lesbians/ gay men • sidewalk cafe-bar

**Le Raidd** 23 rue du Temple (M° Hotel de ville) **33-1/4277-0488** • 5pm-5am • mostly men • dancing/ DJ • go-go boys

**Sly Bar** 22 rue des Lombards **33-1/8253-2781** • mostly gay men • neighborhood bar • dancing/DJ

**Le So What** 30 rue du Roi de Sicile (M° Hôtel-de-Ville) • 9pm-2am, 10pm-4am Fri-Sat, clsd Sun-Tue • lesbians/ gay men • stylish new bar • dancing/DJ • lesbian-owned

**Les Souffleurs** 7 rue de la Verrerie (M° Hôtel-de-Ville) **33-1/6421-8133** • lesbians/ gay men • artsy younger crowd • events in the basement

**Le Troisieme Lieu** 62 rue Quincampoix **33-1/4804-8564** • 6pm-2am, clsd Sun • mostly women • also restaurant & nightclub

**Le Voulez-Vous** 18 rue du Temple (M° Hôtel-de-Ville) **33-1/4459-3857** • 11am-2am • lesbians/ gay men • lounge & restaurant • terrace

**Yono** 37 rue Vieille du Temple **33-1/4274-3165** • 6pm-2am, 4:30pm-11pm Sun, clsd Mon • lesbians/ gay men • dancing/DJ, cozy basement bar • also restaurant

**Ze Baar** 41 rue des Blancs Manteaux (at rue du Temple) **33-1/4271-7508** • 5pm-2am • mostly gay men • neighborhood bar • also restaurant

### CAFES

**Le Kofi du Marais** 54 rue Ste-Croix-de-la-Bretonnerie (M° Hôtel de Ville) **33-1/4887-4871** • 7pm-midnight, clsd Sun • lesbians/ gay men • coffee & light meals

## RESTAURANTS

**4 Pat** 4 rue St Merri **33-1/4277–2545** • noon-2am • dancing/DJ • Italian menu

**Les Agités** 15 rue de la Reynie (at Boule de Sebastopol) **33-1/8389–5309** • 7pm-2am, clsd Sun-Mon

**L' Alimentari** 6 Rue des Ecouffes **33-1/4277–2459** • very good small trattoria

**Le Chant des Voyelles** 4 rue des Lombards (M° Châtelet) **33-1/4277–7707** • 11:30am-3pm & 6:30pm-midnight, open all day in summer • traditional French • terrace

**Etamine Cafe** 13 rue des Ecouffes (at rue des Rosiers, M° Hotel de Ville) **33-1/4478–0962** • noon-midnight, clsd Mon • also bar

**Le Gai Moulin** 10 rue Ste-Merri (at rue du Temple, M° Hôtel-de-Ville) **33-1/4887–0600** • noon-midnight • lesbians/ gay men • French/int'l

**HD Diner** 6-8 Square Ste-Croix de la Bretonnerie **33-1/4277–6934** • 11am-midnight • 50's style diner

**La Pas-Sage-Oblige** 29 rue du Bourg-Tibourg (M° Hôtel-de-Ville) **33-1/4041–9503** • lunch & dinner • vegetarian

**Les Piétons** 8 rue des Lombards (M° Châtelet) **33-1/4887–8287** • noon-2am • Spanish/ tapas • also bar

**Who's** 14 rue Saint Merri (M° Rambuteau) **33-1/4272–7597** • noon-6am

**Woo Bar** 3 rue Pierre au Lard (M° Rambuteau) **33-1/4272–7597** • noon-6am

## BOOKSTORES

**Les Mots à la Bouche** 6 rue Ste-Croix-de-la-Bretonnerie (near rue du Vieille du Temple, M° Hôtel-de-Ville) **33-1/4278–8830** • 11am-11pm, 1pm-9pm Sun • LGBT • English titles

## RETAIL SHOPS

**Abraxas** 9 rue St-Merri **33-1/4804–3355** • tattoos • piercing • large selection of body jewelry

## EROTICA

**Dollhouse** 24 rue du Roi de Sicile (at Ferdinand Duval) **33-9/5074–5974** • women's erotica store

# Paris—05

## RESTAURANTS

**L' AOC** **33-1/4354–2252** • lunch & dinner, clsd Sun

**Le Petit Prince** 12 rue de Lanneau (M° Maubert-Mutualité) **33-1/4354–7726** • 7:30pm-midnight • popular • French

## ENTERTAINMENT & RECREATION

**Open-Air Sculpture Museum** Quai Saint-Bernard • along the Seine btwn the Jardin des Plantes & the Institut du Monde Arabe

# Paris—06

## ACCOMMODATIONS

**The Hotel Luxembourg Parc** 42 rue de Vaugirard **33-1/5310–3650** • gay/ straight • great location

## BARS

**La Venus Noire** 25 rue de l'Hirondelle (M° St-Michel) • 6pm-1am, till 2am Fri-Sat, clsd Sun • mostly women • neighborhood bar • live music

# Paris—08

## ACCOMMODATIONS

**François 1er** 7 rue Magellan **33-1/4723–4404** • gay-friendly • boutique hotel near les Champs-Elysées • also bar

**Hôtel le Lavoisier** 21 rue Lavoisier **33-1/5330–0606, 866/376–7831 (US#)** • gay-friendly • 19th-c townhouse • WiFi

**Prince de Galles** 33 Avenue George V **33-1/5323–7777** • gay-friendly • legendary jewel of the Parisian Art Deco movement near les Champs-Elysées • WiFi

## NIGHTCLUBS

**Escualita** 128 rue de la Boetie (at Club "MadaM") • midnight Sun only • mostly men • transgender-friendly • fab tranny dance party • all are welcome

**Le Queen** 102 av des Champs-Élysées (btwn rue Washington & rue de Berri, M° Georges-V) **33-8/5389–0890** • midnight-dawn, more gay Sun • popular • gay/ straight • dancing/DJ • drag shows • young crowd • selective door • cover charge

# Paris—09

## ACCOMMODATIONS

**The Grand** 2 rue Scribe **33-1/4007–3232, 888/424–6835 (US#)** • gay-friendly • ultraluxe art deco hotel • WiFi

## BARS

**Rosa Bonheur** 1 rue Botzaris **33-1/4200–0045** • gay-friendly • more gay Sun, arrive before 6pm to avoid the line

## NIGHTCLUBS

**Folies Pigalle** 11 place Pigalle (M° Pigalle) **33-1/4878-5525, 33-1/4280-1203 (BBB INFO LINE)** • midnight-dawn • gay/ straight • dancing/DJ • theme nights • transgender-friendly • multiracial • cover charge

**Fox Club** 9 rue Frochot **33-1/4281-0923** • 6pm-2am, 7pm-5am Fri-Sat, clsd Sun-Tue • mostly women • dancing/DJ

**Glass** 7 rue Frochot (in Pigalle) **33-9/8072-9883** • 7pm-2am • gay/straight • dancing/DJ • popular with locals Mon

## Paris—10

### BARS

**L' Okubi** 219 rue St-Maur (M° Goncourt) **33-1/4201-3508** • 6pm-2am, clsd Sun • lesbians/ gay men • dancing/DJ

## Paris—11

### ACCOMMODATIONS

**Le 20 Prieure Hotel** 20 rue du Grand Prieuré **33-1/4700-7414** • gay/ straight • WiFi

**Le General Hotel** 5/7 rue Rampon **33-1/4700-4157** • gay-friendly • WiFi • wheelchair access

**HI Matic** 71 rue de Charonne • gay-friendly • a new urban eco-lodging concept • WiFi • wheelchair access • gay-owned

**Hôtel Beaumarchais** 3 rue Oberkampf (btwn bd Beaumarchais & bd Voltaire, M° Filles-du-Calvaire) **33-1/5336-8686** • gay/ straight • beautiful hotel • WiFi

### BARS

**Le Bataclan** 50 blvd Voltaire (at Bataclan club, M° Saint Ambroise) **33-1/4314-0030** • gay-friendly • live music venue • more gay for the Follivores & Crazyvores • call for events

**Follivores/ Crazyvores** 50 blvd Voltaire (M° Saint Ambroise) **33-1/4314-0030** • lesbians/ gay men • monthly sing-along dance parties • Follivores is 1960s-1990s French pop • Crazyvores is English-speaking • kitsch factor very high!

### NIGHTCLUBS

**Les Disquaires** 6 rue des Taillandiers (M° Bastille) **33-1/4021-9460** • gay/ straight • dance bar • live bands

### CAFES

**Cannible Café** 93 Rue Jean-Pierre Timbaud **33-1/4929-0040** • an old-fashioned Parisian café in Belleville • WiFi

**Le Pause Cafe** 41 rue de Charonne **33-1/4806-8033** • 8am-2am, 9am-8pm Sun • food served

### RESTAURANTS

**Le Tabarin** 3 rue Amelot **33-1/4807-1522** • lunch Sun-Fri, dinner Sun-Sat • lesbians/ gay men • full bar • piano bar

### ENTERTAINMENT & RECREATION

**L' ArtiShow** 3 cite Souzy **33-1/4002-1803** • cabaret • also lunch & dinner served

### BOOKSTORES

**Violette & Co** 102 rue de Charonne (at boulevard Voltaire, M° Charonne) **33-1/4372-1607** • 11am-8pm, 2pm-7pm Sun, clsd Mon • LGBT & feminist • English titles • art shows • lesbian-owned

### EROTICA

**Démonia** 22 ave Jean Aicard (at rue Oberkampf, M° St-Maur) **33-1/4314-8270** • clsd Sun • BDSM shop • lingerie • videos • toys

## Paris—12

### SEX CLUBS

**Atlantide** 13 rue Parrot (M° Gare de Lyon) **33-1/4342-2243** • gay/ straight sauna w/ sexual atmosphere • men, women, transgender-friendly • private cabins • also bar

## Paris—14

### ENTERTAINMENT & RECREATION

**Friday Night Fever** Place Raoul Dautry (btwn Montparnasse office tower & Montparnasse train station) • 10pm-1am Fri (weather-permitting), meet 9:30pm • rollerblade through the city • gay/ straight

### GYMS & HEALTH CLUBS

**Amphibi** 73 rue Hallé (at rue Bézout, M° Alesia) **33-1/4047-5090** • sauna where everyone is welcome: gay, straight, bisexual, transgendered

## Paris—15

### ACCOMMODATIONS

**Platine Hotel** 20 rue Ingénieur Robert Keller **33-1/4571-1515** • gay/ straight • Marilyn Monroe and 1950's theme • WiFi • wheelchair access

## Paris—16

### ACCOMMODATIONS

**Keppler** 10 rue Keppler **33–1/4720–6505** • gay-friendly • near major tourist stops • also bar • kids/ pets ok • WiFi

## Paris—17

### RESTAURANTS

**Sans Gêne** 112 rue Legendre **33–1/4627–6782** • 5pm-2am, Sun brunch, clsd Mon • also bar

## Paris—18

### BARS

**Karambole Cafe** 10 rue Hegesippe Moreau (M° Place de Clichy or La Fourche) **33–1/4293–3068** • 9am-2am, from 6pm Sat, clsd Sun • gay/ straight • artsy cafe by day • DJs by night

**Le Tagada Bar** 40 rue Trois-Frères (M° Abesses) **33–1/4255–9556** • 6pm-2am, clsd Mon • mostly gay men • upscale food

### ENTERTAINMENT & RECREATION

**Michou** 80 rue des Martyrs (at Blvd de Clichy, M° Pigalle) **33–1/4606–1604** • infamous drag cabaret • dinner show

## Paris—19

### CAFES

**Cafe Cherie** 44 Blvd de la Villette (M° Belleville) **33–1/4202–0205** • 8am-2am • gay/ straight • live music & DJs starting at 10pm • WiFi

## Paris—20

### ACCOMMODATIONS

**Mama Shelter** 109 rue de Bagnolet **33–1/4348–4848** • gay/ straight • great location on the Right Bank • kichenettes • also restaurant & cool local bars • WiFi

### ENTERTAINMENT & RECREATION

**Père Lachaise Cemetery** bd de Ménilmontant (M° Père-Lachaise) • perhaps the world's most famous resting place, where lie such notables as Chopin, Gertrude Stein, Oscar Wilde, Sarah Bernhardt, Isadora Duncan, Edith Piaf & Jim Morrison

# GERMANY

# BERLIN

**Berlin is divided into 5 regions:**
**Berlin—Overview**
**Berlin—Kreuzberg**
**Berlin—Prenzlauer Berg–Mitte**
**Berlin—Schöneberg-Tiergarten**
**Berlin—Outer**

## Berlin—Overview

### INFO LINES & SERVICES

**Gay AA for English Speakers** at Mann-O-Meter **49–30/787–5188** • 5pm Tue, also Gay AA 8pm Th

**Lesbenberatung (Lesbian Advice)** Kulmer Str 20a (in Kreuzberg) **49–30/215–2000** • switchboard & center • staffed 10am-5pm, till 7pm Tue & Th

**Mann-O-Meter** Bülowstr 106 (at Nollendorfplatz) **49–30/216–8008** • 5pm-10pm • gay switchboard & center • also cafe • also B&B referral service

**Sonntags Club** Greifenhagener Str 28 (S/U-Schönhauser Allee) **49–30/449–7590** • info line 10am-6pm daily • LGBT info • also cafe-bar • 5pm-midnight • women's night Fri 8pm

**Spinnboden Lesbian Archive & Library** U-Bahn 8, Bernauerstr (in 2nd courtyard, 2nd flr) **49–30/448–5848** • call for hours • also by appt

### NIGHTCLUBS

**MegaDyke Productions** **49–30/179 59 12 738** • popular parties & events for lesbians, including L-Tunes at SchwuZ & annual pride events for lesbians in other locations • see www.megadyke.de for more details

### RESTAURANTS

**Paris Bar** Kantstrasse152 **49–30/313–8052** • bistro & bar

### ENTERTAINMENT & RECREATION

**Fritz Music Tour** **49–30/3087–5633** • visit the haunts of David Bowie, Nina Hagen, Iggy Pop & Rammstein, among other popular musical acts

**The Jewish Museum Berlin** Lindenstr 9-14 **49–30/2599–3300** • 10am-8pm, till 10pm Mon • German-Jewish history & culture

**Schwules (Gay) Museum** U6/U7 Mehringdamm 61 **49–30/6959–9050** • 2pm-6pm, till 7pm Sat, clsd Tue • guided tours 5pm Sat (in German) • exhibits, archives & library

## PUBLICATIONS

**Siegessäule** 49–30/235–5390 • free monthly LGBT city magazine (in German) • awesome maps

# Berlin—Kreuzberg

## ACCOMMODATIONS

**Hotel Transit** Hagelberger Straße 53–54 49–30/789–0470 • gay-friendly • loft-style hotel in 19th-c factory • also bar

**The Mövenpick Hotel** 49–30/230–060 • gay-friendly • convenient location • also space-agey bar

## BARS

**Barbie Bar** Mehringdamm 77 (at Kreuzbergstr) 49–30/6956–8610 • 3pm-close • lesbians/ gay men • lounge • terrace

**Bierhimmel** Oranienstr 183 (U-Kottbusser Tor) 49–30/615–3122 • 9am-3am, from 1pm wknds • gay/ straight • young crowd

**Galander** Grossbeerenstr 54 (nr Mehringdamm) 49–30/2850–9030 • 6pm-2am • gay/ straight • lovely 20's cocktail bar • small snacks served

**Mobel Olfe** Reichenbergerstrasse 177 (at Skalitzer) 49–30/2327–4690 • 8pm-close Tue-Sun • popular • lesbians/ gay men

**Rauschgold** Mehringdamm 62 (U-Mehringdamm) 49–30/7895–2668 • 8pm-close • lesbians/ gay men

**Roses** Oranienstr 187 (at Kottbusser Tor) 49–30/615–6570 • 10pm-close • popular • lesbians/ gay men • transgender-friendly • young crowd

**Sofia** • open 9am, from 11am Sat & 8pm Sun • lesbians/ gay men

## NIGHTCLUBS

**L-tunes** Mehringdamm 61 (at SchwuZ) 49–30/179 59 12 738 • 10pm last Fri only • mostly women, queer friends welcome • dancing/DJ • events

**SchwuZ (SchwulenZentrum)** Mehringdamm 61 (enter through Café Sundstroem) 49–30/629–088 • from 11pm Fri-Sat • mostly gay men • more women last Fri • dancing/DJ • live/ drag shows • young crowd • wheelchair access

**Serene Bar** Schwiebusser Str 2 49–30/6904–1580 • lesbians/ gay men • popular Girls Bar Th • Girls Dance 10pm Sat

**SO 36** Oranienstr 190 (at Kottbusser Tor) 49–30/6140–1306, 49–30/6140–1307 • popular • gay/ straight • dancing/DJ • transgender-friendly • live shows • videos • young crowd • wheelchair access • theme nights include Café Fatal (ballroom dancing) & Gayhane (Turkish night)

## CAFES

**Melitta Sundström** Mehringdamm 61 (at Gneisenaustr, U-Mehringdamm) 49–30/692–4414 • 10am-11pm • lesbians/ gay men • terrace • wheelchair access • also LGBT bookstore

**Sudblock** Admiralstrasse 1-2 • 10am-7pm • lesbians/ gay men • live entertainment

## RESTAURANTS

**Amrit** Oranienstr 202 49–30/612–5550 • noon-1am • Indian

**Jolesch** Muskauer Strasse 1 49–30/612–3581 • Austrian culture in Kreuzberg

**Restaurant Z** Friesenstr 12 49–30/692–2716 • 5pm-1am • Greek/ Mediterranean

## SEX CLUBS

**Be Cunt** Görlitzer Str 71 (at Club Culture Houze) 49–30/6170–9669 • 2nd Tue of the month • trans, dykes, genderfucks, femmes, tomboys & female queers

**Club Culture Houze** Görlitzer Str 71 (off Skalitzer Str) 49–30/6170–9669 • 2nd Tue lesbian night, gay male theme nights Mon, Th & Sun, gay/ straight other nights

## EROTICA

**Altelier Dos Santos** Mehringdamm 119 (U Platz der Luftbrucke) 49–30/5059–9919 • noon-6pm, till 4pm Sat • high quality custom leather & fetish wear • lesbian-owned

**Playstixx** Heimstrasstrasse 6 49–30/6165–9500 • makers & sellers of silicone toys for women & lovers

**Sexclusivitäten** Fürbringer Str 2 49–30/693–6666 • lesbian sex shop • Open Salon sex party noon-8pm Fri • also escort service

# Berlin—Prenzlauer Berg-Mitte

## ACCOMMODATIONS

**Andel's Hotel** Landsberger Allee 106 49–30/453–053 • gay-friendly • WiFi • also restaurant • wheelchair access

**Arte Luise Kunsthotel** Luisenstr 19 (Mitte) 49–30/284–480 • gay-friendly • former palace near River Spree

**Intermezzo Hotel for Women** Gertrud-Kolmar Str 5 (at Brandenburger Tor) **49–30/2248–9096** • women only • wheelchair access

**Schall & Rauch Pension** Gleimstr 23 (at Schönhauser Allee) **49–30/339–723** • lesbians/gay men • also bar & restaurant

## BARS

**Besenkammer Bar** Rathausstr 1 (at Alexanderplatz, under the S-Bahn bridge) **49–30/242–4083** • 24hrs • lesbians/gay men • tiny "beer bar"

**Betty F\*\*\*** Mulackstrasse 13 (at Gormannstrasse) • from 10pm • lesbians/gay men • tiny neighborhood bar

**Marietta** Stargarder Str 13 **49–30/4372–0646** • 10am–2am, till 4am Sat-Sun • lesbians/gay men

**Perle** Sredzkistrasse 64 • 7pm-close, clsd Sun-Mon • lesbians/gay men • innovative lighting & electronica

**Privatleben** Rhinowerstr 12 (at Gleimstra) **49–30/4320–5851** • from 6pm • lesbians/gay men • small friendly bar

**Reingold** Novalisstr 11 (U-Oranienburger Str) **49–30/4985–3450** • from 7pm, clsd Sun-Mon • gay/straight • more gay Th • food served • lesbian-owned cocktail lounge

**Sanatorium 23** Frankfurter Allee 23 **49–30/4202–1193** • from 3pm • gay/straight • trendy cafe/bar • also guesthouse

**Sharon Stonewall** Kleinen Präsidentenstr 3 (at Hackescher Market) **49–30/2408–5502** • 8pm-2am, till 4:30am Fri-Sat, clsd Mon • lesbians/gay men • WiFi

**Zum Schmutzigen Hobby/ Nina's Bar** Revalerstrasse 99 • 6pm-close • lesbians/gay men • dancing/DJ • drag shows • transgender-friendly

## NIGHTCLUBS

**Berghain** Am Wrietzener Bahnhof (off Strasse der Pariser Kommune, near Ostbahnhof station) **49–30/2936–0210** • lesbians/gay men • converted power station is now popular dance club

**Chantals House of Shame** • 11pm Th & Bad Girls club monthly parties

**Girls Town** Karl-Marx-Allee 33 (at Kino International, U-Schillingstr) **49–30/2475–6011** • 2nd Sat every other month • mostly women • dancing/DJ • huge, popular lesbian club

**GMF** Alexanderstrasse 7 (at Week End, U-Alexanderplatz) **49–30/2809–5396** • mostly gay men • Sun only 11pm-close

**Irrenhouse** Am Friedrichshain 33 (at Geburtstagsklub) • 3rd Sat • lesbians/gay men • dancing/DJ • drag shows • transgender-friendly • Nina Queer's monthly drag party

**KitKat Club** Kopenickerstrasse 76 (enter on Bruckenstrasse) **49–30/2173–6841** • 8pm-close Th, 11pm-8am Fri-Sat • gay/straight • also S/M club • cabaret

**Klub International** Karl-Marx-Allee 33 (at Kino International, U-Schillingstr) **49–30/2475–6011** • 11pm-close, 2nd Sat lesbian night • mostly gay men • dancing/DJ • cover charge

**Milkshake** Warschauer Str 34 (at Monstrer Ronson's) • check milkshakegirls.de for events • mostly women • dancing/DJ • transgender-friendly

**Spy Club** Friedrichstr/ Unter den Linden (at Cookies) **49–30/2809–5396** • last Sat only • lesbians/gay men • dancing/DJ

## CAFES

**Anna Blume** Kollwitzstrasse 83 **49–30/4404–8749** • 8am-2am • great brkfst

**Cafe Seidenfaden** Dircksenstr 47 (U-Alexanderplatz) **49–30/283–2783** • 10am-6pm, noon-8pm Sat, clsd Sun • women only • drug- & alcohol-free cafe • info board • nonsmoking

**November** Husemannstr 15 (at Sredzkistr) **49–30/442–8425** • 10am-2am • lesbians/gay men • cafe-bar • terrace • brkfst buffet wknds

**Poor and Literate** Kopenhagenerstr 77 **49–30/4403–9520** • 4pm-9pm Th-Sun • live shows • beer/wine • WiFi • lesbian/queer gathering place, cafe by day, bar by night • lesbian-owned

## RESTAURANTS

**Anda Lucia** Savignyplatz 2 **49–30/5471–0271** • 6pm-10pm • tapas bar

**Cavallino Rosso** Hannoversche Strasse 2 **49–30/2790–8314** • modern and cosy atmosphere

**The Kosher Classroom** Auguststrasse 11-13 **49–30/3300–6070** • traditional Jewish cuisine, vegan meals and specialties from the sea

**Rice Queen** Danziger Str 13 (U-Eberswalder Str) **49–30/4404–5800** • 5pm-11pm, from 2pm wknds • Asian fusion

**Schall & Rauch Wirtshaus** Gleimstr 23 (at Schönhauser Allee) **49–30/443–3970** • 10am-close • lesbians/ gay men

**Thüringer Stuben** Stargarder Str 28 (at Dunckerstr, S/U-Schönhauser Allee) **49–30/4463–3339** • 4pm-1am, from noon Sun • full bar

### BOOKSTORES

**Ana Koluth** Schönhauser Allee 124 **49–30/8733–6980** • 10am-8pm, till 6pm Sat, clsd Sun • lesbian-owned

### EROTICA

**Blackstyle** Seelower Str 5 (S/U-Schönhauser Allee) **49–30/4468–8595** • clsd Sun • latex & rubber wear

# Berlin—Schöneberg-Tiergarten

### ACCOMMODATIONS

**Arco Hotel** Geisbergstr 30 (at Ansbacherstr, U-Wittenbergplatz) **49–30/235–1480** • gay/ straight • centrally located • kids/ pets ok • wheelchair access • gay-owned

**Axel Hotel Berlin** Lietzenburger Str 13/15 **49–30/2100–2893** • mostly gay men • WiFi

**Bananas Berlin** Geisbergstr 41 **49–30/2196–1768** • mostly gay men • WiFi • central location in a quiet area • gay-owned

**Hotel California** Kurfürstendamm 35 (at Knesebeckstr, U-Uhlandstr) **49–30/880–120** • gay-friendly • cafe/ bar • nonsmoking flr • kids ok

**Hotel Hansablick** Flotowstr 6 (at Bachstr, off Str des 17 Juni) **49–30/390–4800** • gay-friendly • full brkfst • kids/ pets ok • WiFi

**Hotel Zu Hause** Kleiststrasse 35 (at Eisenacher Str) **49–(0)30/2362–6522** • gay/ straight • WiFi • gay-owned

### BARS

**Blond** Eisenacher Str 3a (at Fuggerstr, U-Nollendorfplatz) **49–30/6640–3947** • 10am-2am • gay/ straight • food served • WiFi

**Green Door** Winterfeldstr 50 **49–30/152–515** • 6pm-3am, till 4am Fri-Sat * gay/straight • cute decor

**Hafen** Motzstr 19 (at Eisenacher Str, U-Nollendorfplatz) **49–30/211–4118** • 8pm-close • mostly gay men • transgender-friendly • live shows

**HarDie's Kneipe** Ansbacherstr 29 (in Wittenberplatz) **49–30/2363–9841** • noon-midnight, till 2am wknds • mostly gay men • cafe/ pub

**Heile Welt** Motzstrasse 5 **49–30/2191–7507** • 6pm-4am • popular • lesbians/ gay men

**Incognito** Hohenstauffenstr 53 (off Luther Str, U-Viktoria Luise Platz) **49–30/2191–6300** • 6pm-4am • lesbians/ gay men • trangender-friendly

**Kumpelnest 3000** Lützowstr 23 (at Potsdamer Str, U-Kurfürstenstr) **49–30/261–6918** • 5pm-5am, till 8am Fri-Sat • popular wknds • gay-friendly • cocktail bar • dancing/DJ • transgender-friendly • young crowd

**Neues Ufer** Haupstrasse 157 (U-Bahn Kleistpark) **49–30/7895–7900** • 11am-2am, clsd wknds • lesbians/ gay men • older crowd

**Prinz Knecht** Fuggerstr 33 (U-Nollendorfplatz) **49–30/236–27444** • 3pm-2am • popular • mostly gay men

**Pussy-Cat** Kalckreuthstr 7 (U-Nollendorfplatz) **49–30/213–3586** • 6pm-6am • lesbians/ gay men

**Storks** Kleiststrasse 7 **49–30/2362–4700** • 10pm-late, 24hrs wknds • mostly gay men • small bar & bistro

### NIGHTCLUBS

**Propaganda** Nollendorfplatz 5 (at Goya Theater) • 2nd Sat only • mostly gay men • dancing/DJ • drag shows

### CAFES

**Begine** Potsdamer Str 139 (at Bülowstr) **49–30/215–1414** • meeting point for women

**Cafe Berio** Maaßenstr 7 (at Winterfeldtstr, U-Nollendorfplatz) **49–30/216–1946** • 7am-midnight, from 8am wknds • popular • brkfast all day • also bar • seasonal terrace • wheelchair access

**Cafe Savigny** Grolmanstr 53–54 (at Savignyplatz) **49–30/4470–8386** • 9am-midnight • artsy crowd • full bar • terrace

### RESTAURANTS

**Boccacelli 2** Martin-Luther-Str. 134 **49–30/7889–0988** • Italian cuisine

**Café des Artistes** Fuggerstr 35 **49–30/2363–5249** • noon-midnight • great food & nice staff

**Diodata** Goltzstrasse 51 **49–30/2191–7884** • 11am-11pm, 10am-3pm Sun • Viennese

**Gnadenbrot** Martin-Luther-Str 20a **49–30/2196–1786** • 3pm-1am • cheap & good

**Hamburger Mary's** Lietzenburger Str 15 (in theAxel Hotel) **49–30/2100–2895** • brkfst & dinner, full bar • mostly gay men • drag shows • karaoke • wheelchair access • gay-owned

**Les 3 Veuves de Wilmersdorf** Fechnerstrasse 30 **49–30/8600–8251** • excellent burgers

**More** Motzstrasse 28 (at Martin-Lutherstrasse) **49–30/2363–5702** • 9am-midnight • popular

**Ottenthal** Kantstrasse 153 **49–30/313–3162** • cuisine of Austria

**Sissi** Motzstr 34 **49–30/2101–8101** • great Austrian food, terrace & location

**Witty's Organic Food** Wittenbergplatz • organic snack bar • look for the rainbow flags

## ENTERTAINMENT & RECREATION

**Xenon Kino** Kolonnenstr 5-6 **49–30/7800–1530** • gay & lesbian cinema

## BOOKSTORES

**Prinz Eisenherz Buchladen** Motzstrasse 23 **49–30/313–9936** • 10am-8pm, clsd Sun • LGBT books, comics and magazines in German, French & English • also a gallery • gay-owned

# Berlin—Outer

## ACCOMMODATIONS

**Artemisia Women's Hotel** Brandenburgischestr 18 (at Konstanzerstr) **49–30/873–8905, 49–30/869–9320** • the only hotel for women in Berlin • a real bargain • quiet rooms • bar • sundeck w/ view • some shared baths • nonsmoking rooms available

**Charlottenburger Hof** Stuttgarter Platz 14 (at Wilmersdorfer Str) **49–30/329–070** • gay-friendly • centrally located • also cafe & bar open 24hrs

## BARS

**Himmelreich** Simon Dach Str 36 (off Warschauer Str, in Friedrichshain, U-Frankfurter Tor) **49–30/2936–9292** • from 7pm Mon-Fri, 2pm-close wknds • lesbians/ gay men • women's night Tue

**Monster Ronsons** Warschauerstr 34 **49–30/8975–1327** • 7pm-6am • lesbians/ gay men • popular karaoke bar

**Silver Future** Weserstr 206 (Neükölln) **49–30/7563–4987** • 2pm-2am, till 3am Th-Sat

## NIGHTCLUBS

**Die Busche** Warschauer Platz 18 **49–30/296–0800** • 10pm-5am, tilll 7am Fri-Sat, clsd Tue & Th • popular • lesbians/ gay men • dancing/DJ • live shows • terrace • cover charge

**Mermaids** Falckensteinstr 47 (at Comet Club) • 10pm 3rd Sat, May-Oct only • mostly women • dancing/DJ • also between parties on the 2nd Fri at Hafenbar Marianne Mariannenstr 6

## CAFES

**Schrader's** Malplaquetstr 16b (at Utrechter Str, Wedding) **49–30/4508–2663** • also bar • gay-owned

## RESTAURANTS

**Cafe Rix** Karl-Marx-Str 141 (in Neükolln) **49–30/686–9020** • 9am-midnight • Mediterranean • plenty veggie • also bar

**Kurhaus Korsakow** Grunbergerstrasse 81 (in Friedrichshain) **49–30/5473–7786** • 5pm-close, from 9am wknds, clsd Mon

# IRELAND

## Dublin

## INFO LINES & SERVICES

**AA** 105 Capel St (at Outhouse) **353–1/873–4999** • 6pm Tue & 7:45pm Fri

**Dublin Lesbian Line** **353–1/872–9911** • 7pm-9pm Mon & Th .

**Gay Switchboard Dublin** **353–1/872–1055** • 6:30pm-9:30pm, 4pm-6pm wknds

**Outhouse** 105 Capel St **353–1/873–4999** • LGBT community center, cafe, library, meetings

## ACCOMMODATIONS

**The Arlington Hotel Temple Bar** 16 Lord Edward St **353–1/670–8777** • gay/ straight • conveniently located with restaurant & bar

**The Clarence** 6-8 Wellington Quay **353–1/407–0800** • gay-friendly • owned by Bono & The Edge of U2 • kids ok • WiFi • wheelchair access

**The Dylan** Eastmoreland Place **353–1/660–3000** • gay/ straight • restaurant & bar

**Fitzwilliam Hotel** St Stephen's Green **353–1/478–7000** • gay-friendly • bar & restaurant

**Inn On the Liffey** 21 Upper Ormond Quay **353–1/677–0828** • lesbians/ gay men • WiFi • gay-owned

**The Merchant House** 8 Eustace St (Temple Bar Area) **353–1/633–4477** • gay/ straight • WiFi • gay-owned

**Waterloo House** 8-10 Waterloo Rd **353–1/660–1888** • 5-star hotel • gay/ straight • restaurant & bar

## BARS

**Front Lounge** 33 Parliament St
**353–1/670–4112** • noon-11:30pm, till 2am Sat
• popular • lesbians/ gay men • dancing/DJ •
transgender-friendly • karaoke

**The George aka Bridies** 89 S Great George
St **353–1/478–2983** • 2pm-2:30am, till
11:30pm Mon-Tue, till 1am Sun • popular •
lesbians/ gay men • dancing/DJ • drag shows •
karaoke

**Panti Bar** 7-8 Capel St **353–1/874–0710** •
5pm-close • lesbians/ gay men • dancing/DJ •
food • drag shows • wheelchair access

## NIGHTCLUBS

**Mother** Exchange St (at Copper Alley,
Arlington Hotel) • 10:30pm Sat only •
lesbians/ gay men • dancing/DJ

**Nimhneach** • gay/ straight • fetish & BDSM
party • strict dress code • see
www.nimhneach.ie for dates & location

## CAFES

**3Fe** 54 Middle Abbey St (Twisted Pepper
Bldg) **353–1/661–9329** • 10am-7pm, noon-
6pm Sun • run by barista champion

**Irish Film Institute Bar & Restaurant** 6
Eustace St (in Temple Bar) **353–1/679–5744** •
lunch & dinner • next to independent cinema
• light meals • plenty veggie

**Lovinspoon Cafe** 13 N Frederick St
**353–1/804–7604** • 7am-6pm, clsd Sun (except
summers)

## RESTAURANTS

**Brasserie Sixty6** 66 S Great Georges St
**353–1/400–5878** • brkfst, lunch, dinner, wknd
brunch • WiFi

**La Cave** 28 S Anne St **353–1/679–4409** •
12:30pm-close, from 6pm Sun • French

**The Chameleon** 1 Lower Fownes St
**353–1/671–0362** • 5pm-11pm, from 3pm Sun,
clsd Mon • Indonesian

**Cornucopia** 19 Wicklow **353–1/677–7583** •
8:30am-9pm, till 10:30pm Sat, from noon Sun
• affordable vegetarian

**DavyByrnes** 21 Duke St **353–1/677–5217** •
11am-11pm • famous pub frequented by
James Joyce

**L' Ecrivain** 109A Lower Baggot St
**353–1/661–1919** • lunch Mon-Fri, dinner
Mon-Sat, clsd Sun • also piano bar •
reservations recommended

**Eden** 7 South William St **353–1/670–6887** •
lunch & dinner, wknd brunch • patio dining

**F.X. Buckley** 2 Crow St **353–1/671–1248** •
5:30pm-close • steak & seafood

**Fire Restaurant** Mansion House, Dawson
St **353–1/676–7200** • 5:30pm-close, noon-
3pm jazz lunch Sat, clsd Sun

**Odessa** 14 Dame Court **353–1/670–7634** •
lunch & dinner, wknd brunch • local hot spot •
also nightclub w/ drag shows

**Shack** 24 E Essex St **353–1/679–0043** •
lunch & dinner

**Trocadero** 4 Saint Andrew St
**353–1/677–5545** • 5pm-midnight, clsd Sun

**The Winding Stair Restaurant** 40 Lower
Ormond Quay **353–1/872–7320** • lunch &
dinner • Irish • young crowd • also bookshop

## BOOKSTORES

**Chapters Bookstore** Ivy House, Parnell St
**353–1/872–3297** • LGBT section

**The Winding Stair Bookshop** 40 Lower
Ormond Quay **353–1/872–7320** • 10am-6pm,
till 7pm Th-Sat, from noon Sun • also
restaurant

## PUBLICATIONS

**GCN (Gay Community News)** Unit 2
Scarlet Row, Essex St W, Temple Bar, 8
**353–1/675–5025** • monthly LGBT newspaper
• many resources

# ITALY

## Rome

Note: M°=Metro station

## INFO LINES & SERVICES

**Gay Help Line** 800/713–713 • 4pm-8pm,
clsd Sun

## ACCOMMODATIONS

**2nd Floor B&B** via San Giovanni in
Laterano 10 **39–06/9604–9256** • lesbians/gay
men • in the heart of Rome's gaylife • WiFi •
gay-owned

**58 Le Real de Luxe** Via Cavour 58, 4th flr
(near Colosseum) **39–06/482–3566,
0039/347–182–9387 (CELL)** • gay/ straight •
B&B inn • kids ok • nonsmoking • WiFi •
wheelchair access

**Albergo Del Sole al Pantheon** Piazza della
Rotonda 63 **39–06/678–0441** • gay-friendly •
4-star hotel • jacuzzi • kids ok

**Ares Rooms** Via Domenichino 7
**39–06/474–4525, 39–340/278–1248 (CELL)** •
gay-friendly • some shared baths

**B&B In And Out Rome** Via Arco del Monte (at Viale Trastevere) **39–339/784–0653** • gay/ straight • in 18th-c palace • kids/ pets ok • nonsmoking • WiFi • wheelchair access • lesbian-owned

**Best Place** Via Turati 13 **39–329/213–2320** • lesbians/ gay men • reservations required

**Claridge Hotel** Via Liegi 62 **39–06/845–441** • gay-friendly • near Borghese park • gym w/ sauna & Turkish bath

**Daphne Veneto** Via di San Basilio 55 **39–06/8745–0086** • gay-friendly • small, cozy inn in heart of historical Rome • kids ok • nonsmoking • also Daphne Trevi at Via degli Avignonesi 20

**Discover Roma** Via Castelfidardo 50 **39–06/4470–3154** • lesbians/ gay men • woman-owned

**Domus Valeria B&B** Via del Babuino 96, Apt 14 (Spanish Square) **39–339/232–6540** • lesbians/ gay men • shared baths • WiFi • gay-owned

**Franklin** Via Rodi 29 **39–06/3903–0165** • gay-friendly • music-themed hotel w/ CD library

**Gayopen B&B** Via dello Statuto 44, Apt 18 (at Via Merulana, Piazza Vittorio) **39–06/482–0013** • gay/ straight • B&B • full brkfst • kids/ pets ok • lesbian & gay-owned

**Hotel Altavilla** Via Principe Amedeo 9 **39–06/474–1186** • gay-friendly • pets ok • also bar

**Hotel Edera** Via A Poliziano 75 **39–06/7045–3888** • gay-friendly • WiFi

**Hotel Labelle** Via Cavour 310 **39–06/679–4750** • lesbians/ gay men • near the Roman Forum

**Hotel Malu** Via Principe Amedeo 85/a **39–06/9603–1250** • gay-friendly • WiFi • near Termini Station

**Hotel Scott House** Via Gioberti 30 **39–06/446–5379** • gay-friendly

**Hotel Welcome Piram** Via Amendola 7 **39–06/4890–1248** • lesbians/ gay men • hot tubs

**Nicolas Inn** Via Cavour 295 (at Via dei Serpenti) **39–06/9761–8483, 39–338/937–8387** • gay-friendly • near the Colosseum & Roman Forum • nonsmoking • WiFi • native English speaker

**Orsa Maggiore for Women** Via San Francesco di Sales 1/a (at Via della Lungara) **39–06/689–3753** • women only • inside 16th-c former convent • nonsmoking

**Pensione Ottaviano** Via Ottaviano 6 **39–06/3973–8138** • gay-friendly • in quiet area near St Peter's Square • hostel

**The Rainbow B&B** Viale Giulio Cesare 151 **39–06/347–507–0344 (CELL), 39–06/348–3343689** • lesbians/ gay men • WiFi

**Relais Conte di Cavour de Luxe B&B** Via Farini 16 (at Via Cavour) **39–06/482–1638** • gay-friendly • great location • WiFi

**Relais le Clarisse** Via Cardinale Merry del Val 20 (at Viale Trastevere) **39–06/5833–4437** • gay/ straight • nonsmoking • WiFi • on historic site in central Rome • lesbian-owned

**Scalinata di Spagna** Piazza Trinità dei Monti 17 (M° Piazza di Spagna) **39–06/6994–0896, 39–06/679–3006 (BOOKING #)** • gay-friendly • roof garden • kids/ pets ok • nonsmoking • WiFi

**Valadier** Via della Fontanella 15 **39–06/361–1998** • gay-friendly • kids ok • 2 restaurants & piano bar • WiFi

## BARS

**Coming Out** Via San Giovanni in Laterano 8 (near Colosseum) **39–06/700–9871** • 7:30pm-2am • popular • lesbians/ gay men • dancing/DJ • transgender-friendly • food served • live music Th • karaoke • lesbian-owned

**Garbo** Vicolo di Santa Margherita 1a (in Trastevere, Tram 8) **39–06/581–2766, 39–34/9815–1446** • 10pm-3am, clsd Mon • lesbians/ gay men • cocktail bar • food served • gay-owned

**Il Giardino dei Ciliegi** Via dei Fienaroli 4 **39–06/580–3423** • 5pm-2am, from 1pm Sun • lesbians/ gay men • tea salon & bar

## NIGHTCLUBS

**L' Alibi** Via di Monte Testaccio 40–44 (M° Piramide) **39–06/574–3448** • 11:30pm-5am, clsd Mon-Wed • popular • lesbians/ gay men • dancing/DJ • theme nights • live shows • rooftop garden in summer • young crowd

**Amigdala** Via delle Conce 14 (at Rising Love) • Sat only • check site for dates: www.amigdalaqueer.it • lesbians/ gay men • dancing/DJ • electronica & queer culture

**Frutta e Verdura** Via Placido Zurla 68-70 (in Casilina) **39–347/244–6721 (ENGLISH), 39–348/879–7063 (ITALIAN)** • 4:30am-10am Sun & public holiday evenings • lesbians/ gay men • dancing/DJ

**Gorgeous** Via del Commercio 36 (at Alpheus) **39–06/574–7826** • 11pm-5am Sat • lesbians/ gay men • dancing/DJ

**Muccassassina** via di Portonaccio 212 (at Qube) **39-06/541-3985** • 10:30pm-5am Fri only (Sept-June) • popular • lesbians/ gay men • dancing/DJ • live shows • young crowd • cover charge

**Venus Rising** Via Libetta 13 **39-06/574-8277** • last Sun only • special events for women • checkwww.facebook.com/venusrisingroma for upcoming parties

## CAFES

**Oppio Caffè** Via delle Terme di Tito 72 **39-06/474-5262, 39-347/510-8594 (CELL)** • brkfst, lunch & dinner • open 24hrs in Aug • popular • lesbians/ gay men • full bar • live shows • terrace w/ great view

## RESTAURANTS

**Aroma** via Labicana 125 • one of the finest dining experiences in Rome

**Asino Cotto Ristorante** Via dei Vascellari 38 (in Travestere, Tram 8) **39-06/589-8985** • lunch & dinner, clsd Mon • creative gourmet Mediterranean • reservations required • gay-owned

**La Carbonara** Via Panisperna 214 **39-06/482-5176** • lunch & dinner, clsd Sun • classic Roman cuisine since 1906

**Cecilia Metella** Via Appia Antica, 125/127/129 • located in the center of the Appia Antica Park

**Città in Fiore** Via Cavour 269 **39-06/482-4874** • lunch Th-Mon, dinner nightly • lesbians/ gay men • Chinese

**Ditirambo** Piazza della Cancelleria 74-75 (near Campo dei Fiori) **39-06/687-1626**

**La Focaccia** Via della Pace 11 **39-06/6880-3312** • 11am-2am • pizza

**Gelateria San Crispino** Via Panetteria 42 (near Trevi Fountain) **39-06/679-3924** • noon-12:30am, till 1:30am Fri-Sat, clsd Tue • gelato!

**Glass Hostaria** Vicolo Del Cinque 58 • ultra-modern gem

**Il Pagliaccio** Via Dei Banchi Vecchi 129 • cuisine that spans the globe in the fusion of flavors

**La Rosetta** Via della Rosetta 8-9 • fish-only restaurant right in the heart of Rome

**Marco G** Via Garibaldi, 56 • Fresh & Simple

**Mater Matuta** Via Milano 47 (basement) **39-06/4782-5746** • lunch Mon-Fri, dinner nightly • also wine bar

**Osteria del Pegno** Vicolo Montevecchio 8 (Plaza Navona) **39-06/6880-7025** • lunch & dinner, clsd Wed winter • large pizza selection • wheelchair access

**Ristorante da Dino** Via dei Mille 10 (at Piazza Indipendenza) **39-06/491-425** • clsd Wed • family-run Roman food at reasonable prices • near Termini Station

**La Taverna di Edoardo II** Vicolo Margana 14 **39-06/6994-2419** • 7:30pm-midnight, clsd Tue • lesbians/ gay men • full bar • wheelchair access

## ENTERTAINMENT & RECREATION

**Gay Village 39-06/753-8396** • gay summer festival

## RETAIL SHOPS

**Hydra II** Via Urbana 139 **39-06/489-7773** • leather, vinyl, clubwear, western, vintage & more

**Souvenir Rainbow** via San Giovanni in Laterano 26 **39-06/7720-4593** • 9am-9pm • gay gifts

## EROTICA

**Alcova** Piazza Sforza Cesarini 27 (at Corso Vittorio Emanuele II) **39-06/686-4118** • fetish shop

## TRAVEL AGENTS

**Through Eternity Tours Italy** Via Astura 2/B **39-06/700-9336** • walking tours of Rome • get 10% off by using the code "Damron10" • gay-owned

# NETHERLANDS

# AMSTERDAM

Amsterdam is divided into 5 regions:
Amsterdam—Overview
Amsterdam—Centrum
Amsterdam—Jordaan
Amsterdam—Rembrandtplein
Amsterdam—Outer

## Amsterdam—Overview

### INFO LINES & SERVICES

**COC-Amsterdam** Rozenstraat 14 (at Prinsengracht, in the Jordaan) **31-20/626-3087** • info line 10am-5pm, also cafe 8pm-11:30pm Wed-Fri • also sponsors women's parties at clubs around town • www.cocamsterdam.nl for info

**Gay/ Lesbian Switchboard 31-20/623-6565** • noon-10pm, 4pm-8pm wknds • English spoken

**Pink Point** Westermarkt (Raadhuisstraat & Keizersgracht, in the Jordaan by Homomonument) **31–20/428–1070** • 10am-6pm • info on Homomonument & general LGBT info • friendly volunteers • queer souvenirs & gifts

## NIGHTCLUBS

**Fuckin' Pop Queers/ Ultrasexi/ Multisexi** • lesbians/ gay men • monthly queer dance parties at different clubs around the city • check ultrasexi.com for details

**Girlesque** • mostly women (cool gay guys welcome) • huge quarterly dance parties • check www.girlesque.nl for info

## ENTERTAINMENT & RECREATION

**The Anne Frank House** Prinsengracht 263-267 (in the Jordaan) **31–20/556–7105 (RECORDED INFO), 31–20/556–7100** • the final hiding place of Amsterdam's most famous resident

**Boom Chicago** Leidseplein 12 (Leidseplein Theater) **31–20/423–0101 (TICKETS)** • English-language improv comedy • distributes free Boom! guide to Amsterdam

**Gay and Lesbian History Walks 31–20/628–689–775** • mention Damron & you get 10% off

**MacBike** Stationsplein 12 (next to Centraal Station) **31–20/620–0985** • rental bikes & map for self-guided tour of Amsterdam's gay points of interest, also 4 other locations

**The van Gogh Museum** Paulus Potterstr 7 (on the Museumplein) **31–20/570–5200** • under renovations, check www.vangoghmuseum.nl for updates

## PUBLICATIONS

**Gay & Night 31–20/788–1360** • free monthly bilingual entertainment paper w/ club listings

**Gay News Amsterdam 31–20/679–1556** • bilingual paper • extensive listings

# Amsterdam—Centrum

## ACCOMMODATIONS

**Amsterdam B&B Barangay 31–6/2504–5432** • gay/ straight • 1777 town house • near tourist attractions • full brkfst • nonsmoking • WiFi • gay-owned

**Amsterdam Central B&B** Oudebrugsteeg 6-II (at Warmoesstraat) **31–62/445–7593** • lesbians/ gay men • B&B apts in 16th-c guesthouse • WiFi • full brkfst • gay-owned

**Crowne Plaza Amsterdam City Centre** NZ Voorburgwal 5 **31–20/620–0500, 877/227–6963 (US#)** • gay-friendly • pool • restaurant & bar • wheelchair access

**Hotel The Exchange** Damrak 50 **31–20/523–0080** • gay/straight • an independent design hotel in central Amsterdam that playfully weaves together fashion and architecture in unique rooms

**Mauro Mansion** Geldersekade 16 (at OZ Kolk) • gay/ straight • 9-room boutique-style hotel, set in a 16th century canal house

**NH City Centre Hotel** Spuistraat 288–292 **31–20/420–4545** • gay-friendly • kids/ pets ok • WiFi • wheelchair access

**NH Grand Hotel Krasnapolsky** Dam 9 (at Warmoesstraat) **31–20/554–9111** • gay-friendly • full-service hotel • in the city center opposite Royal Palace • WiFi • wheelchair access

**Palace B&B** Spuistraat 224 **31–6/3169–3878** • gay/ straight • 1794 bldg w/ indoor garden • nonsmoking • WiFi • gay-owned

**Park Plaza Victoria Amsterdam** Damrak 1-5 (opposite Centraal Station) **31–20/623–4255** • gay-friendly • 4-star hotel • pool • gym • restaurants & bar • WiFi • wheelchair access

**Winston Hotel** Warmoesstraat 129 **31–20/623–1380** • gay-friendly • hipster hotel • rockers & artists • popular bar • live DJs • gallery • some shared baths

## BARS

**De Barderij** Zeedijk 14 (at OZ Kolk) **31–20/420–5132** • noon-1am, till 3am Fri-Sat • mostly gay men • large neighborhood bar/ brown café • older crowd

**Cafe Mandje** Zeedijk 63 (at Stormsteeg) **31–20/622–5375** • gay/ straight • originally opened in 1927 as Amsterdam's first gay bar by dyke-on-bike Bet van Beeren

**De Engel van Amsterdam** Zeedijk 21 (at OZ Kolk) **31–20/427–6381** • 1pm-1am, till 3am Fri-Sat • mostly gay men • patio

**Getto** Warmoesstraat 51 (at Niezel) **31–20/421–5151** • 4pm-1am, till 2am Fri-Sat, till midnight Sun, clsd Mon • popular • lesbians/ gay men • live DJs • also restaurant till 11pm

**Prik** Spuistraat 109 **31–20/320–0002** • 4pm-1am, till 3am Fri-Sat • lesbians/ gay men • food served • patio

## NIGHTCLUBS

**Club Stereo** Jonge Roelensteeg 4 (at Kalvertstraat) **31–20/770-4037** • 7pm-1am, till 3am Fri-Sat • gay/ straight • dancing/DJ • live shows

## CAFES

**Dampkring** Haarlemmerstraat 44 **31–20/638-0705** • smoking coffeeshop • great fresh OJ

**Gary's Late Night** TT Vasumweg 260 **31–20/637-3643** • noon-3am, till 4am Fri-Sat • popular • fresh muffins & bagels • organic fair-trade coffee

**Puccini Bomboni** Staalstraat 17 **31–20/626-5474** • If you love chocolate, do we have a cafe for you!

## RESTAURANTS

**Cafe de Jaren** Nieuwe Doelenstraat 20-22 **31–20/625-5771** • 10am-1am, till 2am Fri-Sat • some veggie • full bar • terrace

**Cafe Latei** Zeedijk 143 (in Red Light District) **31–20/625-7485** • 8am-6pm, from 9am Sat, from 11am Sun • Indian food • great coffee hangout • WiFi

**Greenwoods** Singel 103 (near Dam Square) **31–20/623-7071** • English-style brkfst & tea snacks

**Hemelse Modder** Oude Waal 11 **31–20/624-3203** • 6pm-10pm • popular • lesbians/ gay men • French/ int'l • also full bar • wheelchair access • gay-owned

**Japans Restaurant An** Weteringschans 76 (at Vijzerstraat) **31–20/624-4672** • lunch & dinner, clsd Sun-Mon • Japanese • patio • cash only

**Krua Thai** Staalstraat 22 **31–20/622-9533** • 5pm-10:30pm • terrace • wheelchair access

**Het Land van Walem** Keizersgracht 449 **31–20/625-3544** • lunch & dinner • int'l • inexpensive • local crowd • canalside terrace • wheelchair access • lesbian-owned

**Maoz** Muntplein 1 **31–20/420-7435** • 11am-1am, till 3am wknds • vegetarian

**'t Sluisje** Torensteeg 1 **31–20/624-0813** • 6pm-close, clsd Mon-Tue • popular steak house • lesbians/ gay men • transgender-friendly • full bar (open later) • drag shows nightly

**Song Kwae** Kloveniersburgwal 14 (near Nieuwmarkt & Chinatown) **31–20/624-2568** • 1pm-10:30pm • Thai • full bar • terrace

## BOOKSTORES

**The American Book Center** Spui 12 **31–20/625-5537** • 10am-8pm, till 9pm Th, 11am-6:30pm Sun • large LGBT section • wheelchair access

**Boekhandel Vrolijk Gay & Lesbian Bookshop** Paleisstraat 135 (at Spuistraat, near Dam Square) **31–20/623-5142** • 11am-6pm, 10am-5pm Sat, from 1pm Sun

## RETAIL SHOPS

**Gays & Gadgets** Spuistraat 44 **31–20/330-1461** • gifts, gadgets, clothing, cards

**Magic Mushroom** Spuistraat 249 **31–20/427-5765** • 11am-7pm, till 8pm Fri-Sat • "smartshop": magic mushrooms & more • also Singel 524

## GYMS & HEALTH CLUBS

**Splash** Looiersgracht 26-30 **31–20/624-8404** • gym & wellness center

## EROTICA

**Absolute Danny** Oudezijds Achterburgwal 78 (in the Red Light District) **31–20/421-0915** • 11am-9pm • upscale erotica • woman-owned

**Black Body** Spuistraat 44 **31–20/626-2553** • clsd Sun • rubber clothing specialists • leather • toys • DVDs • wheelchair access

**Christine Le Duc** Spui 6 **31–20/624-8265**

**DeMask** Zeedijk 64 **31–20/423-3090** • 11am-7pm, clsd Sun • rubber & leather clothing

**Female & Partners** Spuistraat 100 **31–20/620-9152** • 11am-6:30pm, from 1pm Mon,till 9pm Th, 1pm-6pm Sun • fashions & toys for women

# Amsterdam—Jordaan

## ACCOMMODATIONS

**Chic and Basic Amsterdam** Herengracht 13-19 (at Brouwersgr) **31–20/522-2345** • gay-friendly • "the quiet hotel"

**The Dylan** Keizersgracht 384 (at Runstraat) **31–20/530-2010** • gay-friendly • sleep in high style • also restaurant

**Hotel Pulitzer** Prinsengracht 315–331 (at Reestraat) **31–20/523-5235** • gay-friendly • occupies 24 17th-c buildings on 2 of Amsterdam's most picturesque canals

**Hotel Rembrandt Centrum** Herengracht 255 (at Hartenstraat) **31–20/622-1727** • gay/ straight • canalside hotel near Dam Square

**Maes B&B** Herenstraat 26 (at Keizersgr) **31–20/427–5165** • gay/ straight • nonsmoking • WiFi • gay-owned

**Marnixkade Canalview Apartments** **31–6/1012–1296** • lesbians/ gay men • fully furnished apts in 19th-c canal house on a quiet canal in heart of Jordaan • nonsmoking • WiFi • gay-owned

**Sunhead of 1617** Herengracht 152 (at Leliegracht & Raadshuisstraat) **31–20/626–1809** • gay/ straight • full brkfst • kids/ pets ok • nonsmoking • also several canal apts • WiFi • gay-owned

## BARS

**Cafe de Gijs** Lindengracht 249 (at Lijnbaansgr) **31–20/638–0740, 31–6/2537–3674** • 4pm-1am • 1st Wed of month social gathering for transvestites & transsexuals, from 6pm

**Saarein 2** Elandsstraat 119 (at Hazenstraat) **31–20/623–4901** • 4pm-1am, till 2am Fri-Sat, clsd Mon • mostly women • food served • brown cafe

## NIGHTCLUBS

**de Trut** Bilderdijkstraat 165 (at Kinkerstraat) **31–20/612–3524** • 10pm-3am Sun only • lesbians/ gay men • hip underground dance party in legalized squat • alternative • young crowd

## CAFES

**Cafe 't Smalle** Egelantiersgracht 12 **31–20/623–9617** • 10am-1am, till 2am wknds • brown cafe • full bar • outdoor seating

**Lab111** Arie Biemondstraat 111 **31–20/616–9994** • noon-1am, till 3am Fri-Sat, lab turned cafe • lab turned cafe • live music

## RESTAURANTS

**Balthazar's Keuken** Elandsgracht 108 **31–20/420–2114** • open plan kitchen gives the feeling of an intimate dinner

**Bojo** Lange Leidsedwarsstraat 49–51 (near Leidseplein) **31–20/622–7434** • 11am-9pm, from 4:30pm wknds • popular • Indonesian

**De Bolhoed** Prinsengracht 60 (at Tuinstr) **31–20/626–1803** • noon-10pm, from 11am Sat • vegetarian/ vegan

**Burger's Patio** 2e Tuindwarsstr 12 **31–20/623–6854** • 6pm-1am • Italian • plenty veggie

**Foodism** Nassaukade 122 (at Hugo de Grootstraat) **31–20/486–8137** • 5pm-10pm • good Mediterranean food • funky & fun

**Freud** Spaarndammerstraat 424 **31–20/688–5548** • lunch & dinner, clsd Sun-Mon

**Granada** Leidsekruisstraat 13 **31–20/625–1073** • 5pm-close • Spanish • tapas • also bar • live music wknds

**De Vliegende Schotel** Nieuwe Leliestraat 162 **31–20/625–2041** • 4pm-11:30pm • vegetarian/ vegan

## ENTERTAINMENT & RECREATION

**Homomonument** Westermarkt (Raadhuisstraat/Keizersgracht) • moving sculptural tribute to lesbians & gays killed by Nazis

## BOOKSTORES

**Xantippe Unlimited** Prinsengracht 290 **31–20/623–5854** • 1pm-6pm, from 10am Sat, noon-5pm Sun • women's bookstore • lesbian section • English titles • lesbian-owned

## RETAIL SHOPS

**Dare to Wear** Buiten Oranjestraat 15 **31–20/686–8679** • piercing, jewelry & accessories

**House of Tattoos** Haarlemmerdijk 130c **31–20/330–9046** • 11am-6pm, from 1pm Sun • great tattoos, great people

## SEX CLUBS

**Sameplace** Nassaukade 120 **31–20/475–1981** • gay/ straight • men only Mon • transgender-friendly • dancing/DJ • theme nights • darkroom

# Amsterdam—Rembrandtplein

## ACCOMMODATIONS

**Amsterdam House** 's Gravelandseveer 7 (at Kloveniersburgwal) **31–20/626–2577 (OFFICE), 31–20/624–6607 (HOTEL)** • gay-friendly • hotel, apts & houseboats

**Dikker & Thijs Fenice Hotel** Prinsengracht 444 (at Leidsestraat) **31–20/620–1212** • gay-friendly • great location • nonsmoking rooms • bar & restaurant

**Eden Hotel** Amstel 144 **31–20/530–7878** • gay-friendly • 3-star hotel • nonsmoking rooms • brasserie overlooking River Amstel • WiFi • wheelchair access

**Hotel de l'Europe** Nieuwe Doelenstraat 2-8 **31–20/531–1777** • gay-friendly • grand hotel on the River Amstel • fitness center • pool

**Hotel Monopole** Amstel 60 (at Kloveniersburgwal) **31–20/624–6271** • gay-friendly • centrally located • nonsmoking rooms available • kids ok • also Cafe Rouge

**Hotel The Golden Bear** Kerkstraat 37 (at Leidsestraat) **31–20/624–4785** • lesbians/ gay men • great place to stay in central Amsterdam • WiFi • gay-owned

**Hotel Waterfront** Singel 458 (at Koningsplein) **31–20/421–6621** • gay-friendly • rooms & studios • brkfst • located in city's center

**ITC Hotel** Prinsengracht 1051 (at Utrechtsestraat) **31–20/623–0230, 31–20/623–1711** • lesbians/ gay men • 18th-c canal house • great location • also bar & lounge • WiFi • lesbian- & gay-owned

**Seven Bridges** Reguliersgracht 31 (at KeizersGracht) **31–20/623–1329** • gay-friendly • small & so elegant • canalside w/ view of 7 bridges (surprise!) • brkfst brought to you

## BARS

**Cafe Rouge** Amstel 60 (at Kloveniersburgwal) **31–20/420–9881** • 4pm-1am, till 3am wknds • mostly gay men • neighborhood bar

**Chez Rene** Amstel 50 (at Kloveniersburgwal) **31–20/420–3388** • 8pm-3am, till 4am Fri-Sat • lesbians/ gay men • lesbian-owned

**Het Dwarsliggertje Cafe** Reguliersdwarsstraat 105 **31–61/677–8599** • 3pm-1am, till 3am Fri-Sat • mostly gay men • neighborhood bar

**Entre Nous** Halvemaansteeg 14 (at Reguliersbreestr) **31–20/623–1700** • 9pm-3am, till 4am Fri-Sat • lesbians/ gay men • neighborhood bar

**Hot Spot Cafe** Amstel 102 (at Bakkersstr) **31–20/622–8335** • 9pm-3am, from 8pm Fri-Sun • mostly gay men • neighborhood bar

**Ludwig** Reguliersdwarsstraat 37 (at St Jorisstraat) **31–20/625–3661** • 7pm-1am, till 3am Fri-Sat, clsd Mon-Tue • mostly gay men • dancing in the back • terrace

**Mankind** Weteringstraat 60 (at Weteringschans) **31–20/638–4755** • noon-11pm, clsd Sun • mixed crowd • canalside terrace • food served till 8pm • Dutch/ English • WiFi

**Soho** Reguliersdwarsstraat 36 (at St Jorisstraat) **31–20/422–3312** • 6pm-3am, till 4am Fri-Sat, from 4pm Sun • popular • lesbians/ gay men • young crowd • afterwork cocktails and dance club

**Taboo** Reguliersdwarsstraat 45 **31–20/775–3963** • 5pm-3am, from 4pm wknds • lesbians/ gay men • neighborhood bar

**Vivelavie** Amstelstraat 7 (at Rembrandtplein) **31–20/624–0114** • 3pm-3am, till 4am Fri-Sat • mostly women

**Het Wapen van Londen** Amstel 14 (at Vijzelstraat) **31–6/1539–5317** • 4pm-1am, till 2am Fri-Sat • popular cafe-bar • mostly gay men • terrace

## NIGHTCLUBS

**Club Roque** Amstel 178 (at Wagenstraat) • 11pm-5am, clsd Sun-Tue • lesbians/ gay men • dancing/DJ

**Studio 80** Rembrandtplein 17 (at Amstelstraat) **31–20/521–8333** • 11pm-3am Th, 11pm-5am Fri-Sat • gay/ straight • dancing/DJ

## CAFES

**Betty, Too** Reguliersdwarsstraat 29 (at Leidsestraat) • 10am-1am • occasional gay events

**Happy Feelings** Kerkstr 51 **31–20/423–1936** • 11am-midnight, till 1am Fri-Sat • smoking coffeeshop • publisher's choice

**Lunchroom** Reguliersdwarsstr 31 (at Koningsplein) **31–20/622–9958** • 10am-7pm • terrace open in summer • gay-owned

**The Other Side** Reguliersdwarsstr 6 (at Koningsplein) **31–72/625–5141** • 11am-1am • mostly gay men • smoking coffeeshop • gay-owned

## RESTAURANTS

**Garlic Queen** Reguliersdwarsstr 27 **31–20/422–6426** • 6pm-close, clsd Mon-Tue • even the desserts are made w/ garlic!

**Golden Temple** Utrechtsestr 126 **31–20/626–8560** • 5pm-9:30pm • mix of Indian, Mexican & Mediterranean • oldest vegetarian & vegan restaurant in city • nonsmoking

**De Huyschkaemer** Utrechtsestraat 137 **31–20/627–0575** • noon-1am, till 3am wknds

**Red** Keizersgracht 594 **31–20/320–1824** • informal and warm ambiance

**Rose's Cantina** Reguliersdwarsstr 40 (near Rembrandtplein) **31–20/625–9797** • 5pm-11pm • popular • Tex-Mex • full bar

**Saturnino** Reguliersdwarsstr 5 **31–20/639–0102** • noon-midnight • Italian • full bar • gay-owned

## EROTICA

**Mail & Female** Nieuwe Vijzelstraat 2, 1017 HT **31–20/623–3916** • erotic fashions & toys for women

## Amsterdam—Outer

### ACCOMMODATIONS

**Between Art & Kitsch** Ruysdaelkade 75-2 (at Daniel Stalpertstraat) **31-20/679-0485** • gay-friendly • near museums • WiFi

**The Collector B&B** De Lairessestr 46 hs (in museum area) **31-6/1101-0105 (CELL), 31-20/673-6779** • gay-friendly • B&B • full brkfst • WiFi • kids ok • gay-owned

**Conscious Hotel Vondelpark** Overtoom 519 **31-20/820-3333** • gay/straight • WiFi • wheelchair access

**Dumas & Considine B&B** Roeterstraat 18 (at Nieuwe Achtergracht) **31-20/624-0174** • gay-friendly • full brkfst • powered by green energy • kids ok • nonsmoking • WiFi • gay-owned

**Freeland Hotel** Marnixstraat 386 (at Leidsegracht) **31-20/622-7511** • gay-friendly • 2-star hotel • full brkfst • WiFi • gay-owned

**Hemp Hotel** Frederiksplein 15 (at Achtergracht) **31-20/625-4425** • only in Amsterdam: sleep on a hemp mattress, eat a hemp roll (THC-free) for brkfst or drink hemp beer in the Hemp Temple bar

**Hotel Arena** Gravesandestraat 51 (at Mauritskade) **31-20/850-2400** • gay-friendly • huge hotel in former orphanage • popular nightclub in former chapel • WiFi • also restaurant & cafe-bar

**Hotel Kap** Den Texstraat 5 **31-20/624-5908** • gay/straight • bikes available to rent • also self-catering apt • gay-owned

**Hotel Rembrandt** Plantage Middenlaan 17 (at Plantage Parklaan) **31-20/627-2714** • gay-friendly • beautiful brkfst room w/ 17th-c art • near Rembrandtplein • nonsmoking

**Lloyd Hotel** Oostelijke Handelskade 34 **31-20/561-3636, 31-20/561-3604** • gay-friendly • hip hotel for all budgets in cool Eastern Harbor area • WiFi

**NL Hotel** Nassaukade 368 (at B Toussaintstraat) **31-20/689-0030** • gay/straight • WiFi • gay-owned

**Prinsen Hotel** Vondelstraat 36-38 (near Leidseplein) **31-20/616-2323** • gay-friendly • also bar

### NIGHTCLUBS

**Flirtation** Oostelijke Handelskade 4 (at Piet Heinkade, at Club Panama) • bi-monthly women's dance party • check local listings for next event

**Melkweg** Lijnbaansgracht 234 (at Leidseplein) **31-20/531-8181** • gay/straight • popular live-music venue • restaurant • theater • cinema • gallery

### RESTAURANTS

**Het Bosch** Jollenpad 10 **31-20/644-5800** • French cuisine with modern twists

**De Peper** Overtoom 301 **31-20/412-2954** • 7pm-close Sun, Tue & Th-Fri • sliding scale, volunteer-run vegan cafe • also monthly queer & women's parties

**Rijsel** Marcusstraat 52b **31-20/463-2142** • classic meets '60s interior with a modern industrial feel

**De Waaghals** Frans Halsstraat 29 **31-20/679-9609** • 5pm-9:30pm • int'l vegetarian

**White Elephant Thai** Van Woustraat 3 **31-20/679-5556**

# SCOTLAND

## Edinburgh

### INFO LINES & SERVICES

**The Edinburgh LGBT Centre** 58A & 60 Broughton St **44-0131/556-9471**

**The Edinburgh LGBT Centre** 58A & 60 Broughton St **44-0131/556-9471**

**LGBT Centre for Health & Wellbeing** 9 Howe St **44-0131/523-1100**

### ACCOMMODATIONS

**94DR** 94 Dalkeith Rd **44-131/662-9286** • gay/straight • guesthouse central location • full brkfst • WiFi • gay-owned

**Ardmor House** 74 Pilrig St (at Leith Walk) **44-0131/554-4944** • lesbians/gay men • Victorian • kids/pets ok • nonsmoking • wheelchair access • gay-owned

**Averon Guest House** 44 Gilmore Pl **44-0131/229-9932** • gay-friendly • comfortable guesthouse in city center • full brkfst • nonsmoking

**Ayden Guest House** 70 Pilrig St **44-0131/554-2187** • gay/straight • guesthouse in quiet, central location • in-house chef cooks fabulous brkfst • WiFi • lesbian-owned

**Garlands** 48 Pilrig St (off Leith Walk) **44-0131/554-4205** • gay/straight • Georgian town house • full brkfst • nonsmoking • WiFi • gay-owned

**Sheraton Grand Hotel and Spa** 1 Festival Sq 44–131/229–9131 • gay-friendly • newly-renovated • gym & pool

**Tigerlily** 125 George St 44–131/225–5005 • gay-friendly • glamorous bar & restaurant • WiFi

**The Witchery by the Castle** Castlehill (The Royal Mile) 44–0131/225.5613 • gay-friendly • B&B • full brkfst • theatrical suites at the gates of Edinburgh castle • also restaurant

## BARS

**The Auld Hoose** 23-25 St Leonards St 44–0131/668–2934 • noon-1am, from 12:30pm Sun • gay/ straight • neighborhood bar • food served

**Cafe Habana** 22 Greenside Pl 44–0131/558–1270 • 1pm-1am • lesbians/ gay men • theme nights • popular pre-clubbing • WiFi

**Cafe Nom de Plume** 60 Broughton St 44–0131/478–1372 • 11am-11pm, till 1am Fri-Sat • food served

**CC Bloom's** 23 Greenside Pl (at Leith Walk) 44–0131/556–9331 • 6pm-3am, from 7pm Sun • mostly gay men • dancing/DJ • live shows • theme nights

**Elbow** 133-135 E Claremont St 44–0131/556–5662 • 11am-1pm • gay/straight • bar & bistro

**LAGRAD (Lesbian and Gay Real Ale Drinkers )** 2 Montrose Terrace (at the Regent) 44–0131/661–8198 • first Monday of the month

**Newtown Bar** 26-B Dublin St 44–0131/538–7775 • noon-1am, till 2am Fri-Sat • lesbians/ gay men • dancing/DJ • food served • WiFi

**Planet** 6 Baxter's Pl (at Leith Walk) 44–0131/556–5551 • 4pm-1am • lesbians/ gay men • popular • food served

**The Regent** 2 Montrose Terrace 44–0131/661–8198 • noon-1am, from 12:30pm Sun • mostly gay men • food served • WiFi

**The Street** 2 Picardy Pl 44–0131/556–4272 • noon-1am • gay/ straight • dancing/DJ • food served • patio

**Theatre Royal Bar** 25-27 Greenside Pl 44–0131/557–2142 • noon-midnight • gay-friendly • good ale • food served

**Woodland Creatures** 260 - 262 Leith Walk 44–0131/629–5509 • 11am-1pm • gay/straight • cool café bar • live music

## NIGHTCLUBS

**GHQ** 4 Picardy Pl 44–0131/550–1780 • 9pm-3am • lesbians/ gay men • dancing/DJ • theme nights

## CAFES

**Cafe Lucia** 13–29 Nicolson St (next to Edinburgh Festival Theatre) 44–0131/662–1112 • 10am-10pm

**Filmhouse Cafe** 88 Lothian Rd 44–0131/229–5932, 44–0131/228–2688 (CINEMA) • 10am-11:30pm, till 12:30am • beer/ wine • also cinema

## RESTAURANTS

**Blue Moon** 1 Barony St 44–0131/556–2788 • 11am-midnight, from 10am wknds • popular • lesbians/ gay men • famous for macaroni cheese • gay-owned

**Henderson's** 94 Hanover St 44–0131/225.2131 • organic vegetarian • also deli & cafe • beer/ wine

**Tower Restaurant & Terrace** National Museum of Scotland, Chambers St (at George IV Brigde) 44–0131/225–3003 • lunch & dinner • panoramic views of Edinburgh's castle & historic skyline • wheelchair access

**Valvona & Crolla** 19 Elm Row 44–0131/556–6066 • clsd Sun • oldest Italian deli in Scotland

## ENTERTAINMENT & RECREATION

**Black Kilt Tours** 125b Grange Loan 44–786/416–5362 • tailor-made driver/guided tours of Scotland for the LGBT community and friends, gay-owned

## BOOKSTORES

**Bobbie's Bookshop** 220 Morrison St 44–0131/538–7069 • 10am-5pm, clsd Sun

**Word Power Books** 43-45 W Nicolson St 44–0131/662–9112 • 10am-6pm, noon-5pm Sun • independent & radical • events

## RETAIL SHOPS

**Q Store** 5 Barony St 44–0131/477–4756 • 11am-7pm Sat-Wed, till 6pm Sat, 1pm-5pm Sun • pride store

## NATIONAL PUBLICATIONS

**ScotsGay** 44–0131/539–0666 • Scotland's premier magazine for lesbians, gays, bisexuals & friends • published monthly

## EROTICA

**Fem 2 Dom** 25 Easter Rd 44–0131/623–6969 • 10am-9pm, from noon Sun • toys, clothing & videos

# SPAIN

## Barcelona

**Note: M°=Metro station**

### INFO LINES & SERVICES

**Casal Lambda** Verdaguer y Callís 10 (M° Drassanes) 34/93-319-5550 • 5pm-9pm • community center • cafe • archives • library • also publish magazine

**Col-Lectiu Gai de Barcelona (CGB)** 34/934-534-125 • staffed 7pm-9pm Mon-Sat • also publishes Info Gai

**Coordinadora Gai Lesbiana** Vicant d'Hongria 156, E-08014 34/900-601-601 • 7pm-9pm Mon-Fri, 6pm-8pm Sat • nat'l gay group

### ACCOMMODATIONS

**Agua Alegre** c/ Roger de Lluria 47 (M° Catalunya) 34/93-487-8032 • gay/ straight • garden terrace

**Barcelona City Centre** 34/653-900-039 • mostly gay men • in Eixample District • kids/ pets ok • WiFi • gay-owned

**California Hotel** Rauric 14 (at Ferran, M° Liceu) 34/93-317-7766 • gay/ straight

**Casa de Billy Barcelona** Rambla Catalunya 85, Piso 5, Puerta 1 (at Mallorca) 34/93-426-3048 • gay/ straight • shared baths • full brkfst • nonsmoking • WiFi

**Catalonia Diagonal Centro** Balmes 142-146 34/93-415-9090 • gay-friendly • kids ok • food served • WiFi • wheelchair access

**Catalonia Portal de l'Àngel** Avenida Portal de L'Angel 17 34/93-318-4141 • gay-friendly • WiFi • pool

**Éos** Gran Via de los Corts Catalanes 575 (M° Universitat) 34/93-451-8772, 34/617-931-439 • lesbians/ gay men • B&B in gay district • gay-owned

**Fashion House** Bruc 13 Principal 34/63-790-4044 • lesbians/ gay men • shared baths

**GayStay BCN** C / Piquer 15, Pral 3 (at Carrer de Mata) 34/676-145-909 • mostly men • WiFi • gay-owned

**HCC Regente** Rambla de Catalunya 76 34/93-487-5989 • gay-friendly • in 1913 art nouveau bldg • pool • WiFi • wheelchair access

**HCC Taber** Arago 256 34/93-487-3887 • gay-friendly • in art nouveau bldg designed by Doménech i Montaner • WiFi

**Hostal Baires** 34/93-319-7774 • gay-friendly • in Barrio Gótico

**Hostal Que Tal** Mallorca 290 (at Bruch) 34/93-459-2366 • mostly gay men

**Hotel Colon** Avenida Catedral 7 34/93-301-1404 • gay-friendly

**Hotel Axel** Aribau 33 (at Consell de Cent) 34/93-323-9393 • lesbians/ gay men • full brkfst • pool • WiFi • also restaurant • also Skybar • wheelchair access

**Hotel Catalonia Fira** Av. Gran Via N 50 (Plaza Europa) 34/93-236-0000 • gay-friendly • WiFi • new 4-star hotel in the heart of old Barcelona

**Hotel Majestic Barcelona** Paseo de Gracia 68 (in city center) 34/93-488-1717 • gay-friendly • 5-star hotel • rooftop pool • wheelchair access

**Room Mate Emma** Carrer Rosselló 205 34/932-385-606 • gay-friendly • nighclub vibe • WiFi

### BARS

**Aire/ Sala Diana** Valencia 236 (btwn Enriq. Granados & c/ Balmes) 34/93-451-8462 • 11pm-3am, clsd Sun-Wed • seasonal • gay/ straight, more women Sun • dancing/DJ • cafe-bar

**Al Maximo** Assaonadora 25 • clsd Sun-Mon • lesbians/ gay men • neighborhood bar

**El Balcon des Aquiles** Lleo 9 • 7pm-3am • mostly gay men • neighborhood bar • theme nights

**Bar Plata** Consejo de Ciento 233 (at Urgell) • 5pm-3am • mostly gay men

**BimBamBum** Casanova 48 • 11pm-3am, clsd Mon-Tue • mostly gay men • dancing/DJ

**Black Bull** Muntaner 64 34/934-515-104 • 8pm-2:30am • mostly gay men

**El Cangrejo** Villarroel 86 • 10:30pm-3am, clsd Mon-Tue • popular • lesbians/ gay men • dancing/DJ

**La Chapelle** Muntaner 65 • mostly gay men • cafe by day

**Chiringuito GayLorenzo** Ed Dulce Deseo de Lorenzo (Playa de la Mar Bella) • summer gay beach bar

**La Cueva** Calàbria 91 • open 4pm, clsd Mon • lesbians/ gay men • drag shows

**Dacksy** Consell de Cent 247 34/934-519-925 • 5pm-3am • lesbians/ gay men • trendy cocktail lounge • dancing/DJ

**Lust** Casanova 75 (at Consell de Cent) • 9pm-2:30am, clsd Mon, pre-clubbing bar • lesbians/ gay men

**La Madame** Ronda Sant Pere 19-21 (M° Urquinaona) **34/93-426-8444** • from midnight Sun only • gay/ straight • dancing/DJ

**Moeem** Muntaner 11 **34/659-229-033** • 6pm-3am • lesbians/ gay men • cheap drinks

**Museum Cafe & Club** Sepulveda 178 (at Urgell) • 6:30pm-3am • mostly gay men

**People Lounge** Villarroel 71 (M° Urgell) **34/93-451-5986** • 8pm-3am • mostly gay men • food served

**Punto BCN** Muntaner 63-65 (at Y Aragón, Metro, M° Universitat) **34-93/451-9152** • 6pm-2:30am • popular • mostly gay men • upscale cafe-bar • wheelchair access

**La Sue BCN** Villarroel 60 **34/933-236-153** • cozy lesbian bar with local artists can exhibit their art and read their books

**Zelig** **34/93-441-5622** • 7pm-2am, till 3am wknds, clsd Mon • gay/ straight • dancing/DJ • food served

## Nightclubs

**Arena Classic** Diputació 233 (at Balmes, M° Universitat) **34/93-487-8342** • 12:30am-5am Fri-Sat only • popular • mostly gay men • dancing/DJ • Spanish music • live shows • cover charge

**Arena Sala Madre** Balmes 32 (at Diputació, M° Universitat) **34/93-487-8342** • 12:30am-5am, clsd Mon (except in Aug) • popular • mostly gay men • dancing/DJ • food served • live shows • cover charge

**Centrik Weekend Bar** Aribau 30 • 11pm-3am Fri-Sat • mostly gay men

**Les Fatales** • mostly women • dancing/DJ • parties around Barcelona • check lesfatales.org for details

**Metro** Sepúlveda 185 (M° Universitat) **34/93-323-5227** • midnight-5am, from 1am Mon • popular • mostly gay men • dancing/DJ • leather • drag shows • cover charge

**Souvenir Barcelona** Noi del Sucre 75 (Viladecans) • after-hours club 6am-1pm Sat-Sun & holidays

## Cafes

**La Concha del Barrio Chino** Guardia 14 (M° Liceu) **34/93-302-4118** • 4pm-3am • gay/ straight • dancing/DJ • transgender-friendly

## Restaurants

**7 Portes** Passeig d'Isabel II, 14 **34/93-319-3033, 34/93-319-2950** • 1pm-1am • Catalan • upscale • over 150 years old!

**El Berro** Diputació 180 **34/933-236-956** • 7am-3am, from 9am wknds • inexpensive diner-style restaurant • also bar

**Botafumeiro** El Gran de Gràcia 81 **34/93-218-4230, 34/93-217-9642** • 1pm-1am • Galician seafood • full bar • reservations recommended

**Castro** Casanova 85 (M° Urgell) **34/93-323-6784** • 1pm-4pm & 9pm-midnight, clsd Sun • Catalan • full bar • live shows

**dDivine** Balmes 24 (M° Universitat) **34/93-317-2248** • 9:30pm-1am, clsd Sun-Tue • dinner show hosted by "Divine" • lesbians/ gay men • reservations recommended

**Eterna** Consell de Cent 127-129 (at Villarroel) **34/93-424-2526** • 1pm-4pm Mon-Fri, 9:30pm-midnight Th-Sat, clsd Sun • lesbians/ gay men • drag shows

**La Flauta Magica** c/ de Banys Vells 18 (M° Jaume I) **34/93-268-4694** • dinner nightly • vegetarian/ organic • wheelchair access

**Iurantia** Casanova 42 (M° Urgell) **34/93-454-7887** • lunch Mon-Fri, dinner Mon-Sat, clsd Sun • pizzeria • reservations recommended

**Little Italy** Carrer del Rec 30 (near Passeig del Born) **34/93-319-7973** • 1pm-4pm & 9pm-midnight • live jazz

**Madrid-Barcelona** Carrer d'Arago 282 (M° Passeig de Gracia) **34/93-215-7027** • lunch & dinner, clsd Sun • located on old railway line • Catalan

**Marquette** Diputació 172 (M° Universitat) **34/93-162-3905** • 6pm-3am • Italian food •

**Sazzerak** **34/93-451-1138** • full bar

**Tafino** Consejo de Ciento 193 • 1pm-4pm Mon-Fri, 8:30pm-midnight Tue-Sat

**Tu Sabes** **34/615-999-282** • 7pm-midnight Th, 9pm-3am Fri-Sat

**La Veronica** Rambla de Raval 2-4 **34/93-329-3303** • 1pm-1am, clsd Mon • popular pizzeria • terrace

## Entertainment & Recreation

**Chernobyl Beach** take the Metro to Sant Roc • popular gay beach

**Mar Bella** • popular gay beach

**Museu Picasso** Montcada 15-23 **34/93-256-3000** • early Picasso works

**Parc Guell** Mount Tibidado • mosiacs & sculpture by Gaudi

**Sant Sebastiàn** • popular gay beach

## BOOKSTORES

**Antinous** Josep Anselm Clavé 6 (btwn Las Ramblas & Ample, M° Drassenes) 34/93-301-9070 • clsd Sun • LGBT • books • gifts • also cafe • wheelchair access

**Cómplices** Cervantes 2 (at Avinyó, M° Liceu) 34/93-412-7283 • 10:30am-8:30pm, from noon Sat, clsd Sun • LGBT • Spanish & English titles

**Nosotr@s** Casanova 56 (M° Urgell) 34/93-451-5134 • LGBT books • magazines • gifts • videos • DVDs

## EROTICA

**Erotic Museum of Barcelona** Ramblas 96 34/93-318-9865 • 10am-midnight (seasonal hours)

**Harmony Love** 34/93-405-3300

**Kitsch** Muntaner 17-19 (at Gran Vía) 34/93-453-2052 • 10am-10pm, from 5pm Sun

## TRAVEL AGENTS

**Rainbow Barcelona Tours** Via de les Corts Catalanes 581 USA 34-63/318-553 • gay tours of the city and travel services

# Madrid

**Note: M°=Metro station**

## INFO LINES & SERVICES

**COGAM (Colectivo de Lesbianas, Gays, Transexuales, y Bisexuales de Madrid)** Puebla 9 (Bajo) 34/91-522-4517 • LGBT center • groups • library • also cafe-bar

## ACCOMMODATIONS

**Camino de Soto** Puente de la Reine 18, Soto del Real 34-66/744-1351 • gay/ straight • located 40 minutes from Madrid • full brkfst • pool • WiFi • gay-owned

**Chueca Pension** Gravina 4 34/91-523-1473 • mostly gay men • hostel • kids ok • WiFi

**Hostal CasaChueca** Calle San Bartolomé 4 (at San Marcos) 34/91-523-8127 • mostly gay men • WiFi • gay-owned

**Hostal La Fontana** Valverde 6, 1° (M° Gran Vía) 34/91-521-8449, 34/91-523-1561 • lesbians/ gay men • WiFi

**Hostal la Zona** Calle Valverde 7, 1 & 2 (at Gran Vía) 34/91-521-9904 • mostly gay men • full brkfst • all rooms w/ private baths & balconies • WiFi • gay-owned

**Hostal Puerta del Sol** Plaza Puerta del Sol 14, 4° (at Calle de Alcalá, M° Sol) 34/91-522-5126 • gay-friendly • centrally located • WiFi • wheelchair access

**Hotel Catalonia Gaudí** Gran Vía 7-9 (at Alcalá) 34/91-531-2222 • gay-friendly • WiFi • kids ok • wheelchair access

**Hotel Urban Madrid** Carrera de San Jerónimo 34 34/91-787-7770 • gay-friendly • upscale hotel w/ 3 restaurants & rooftop pool • WiFi

**Pensión Madrid House** Barbieri 1 34/651-387 535 • gay/ straight • one block from Chueca Square • WiFi • gay-owned

## BARS

**El 51** Hortaleza 51 (in Chueca) 34/91-521-2564 • 6pm-3am, from 4pm wknds • popular • mostly gay gay men • upscale cocktail lounge

**Enfrente** Infantas 12 (M° Gran Vía) 34/68-779-1462 • 8pm-3am • mostly gay men • leather • DJs Th & Sun

**Fu3l** San Marcos 16 (at Barbieri) • 7pm-3:30am, mostly gay men, bears

**Fulanita de Tal** Calle del Conde de Xiquena 2 (at Prim) • mostly women • stylish & hip • dancing/DJ

**El Gallinero** San Carlos 6 (in Lavapies area) • 7:30pm-midnight, till 2:30am Th-Sat, clsd Mon • mostly women • lesbian-owned

**Gris** • 10pm-3am, from 9pm Th-Sat, clsd Sun-Mon • lesbians/ gay men • reduced drink prices until 11:30pm • music bar

**LL** Pelayo 11 (M° Chueca) 34/91-523-3121 • 5pm-close • popular • mostly gay men • neighborhood bar • dancing • strippers • drag shows • videos

**El Mojito** Olmo 6 (in Lavapies area) 34/91-531-1141 • 9pm-3am, till 3:30am Fri-Sat • lesbians/ gay men • cocktail bar • great music

**Museo Chicote** Calle Gran Via 12 34/915-326-737 • 9pm-3am • gay/ straight • '50s style lounge • food served • live shows

**La Ochenta (80)** Calle de la Sombrerería 8 (in Lavapies area) • 80's music

**Rick's** Calle del Clavel 8 (at Infantas, M° Gran Vía, ring to enter) 34/91-531-9186 • 11pm-6am, open later Fri-Sat, 9pm-2am Sun • popular • mostly gay men • dancing/DJ

**Rimmel** Calle de Luis de Góngora 2 (M° Chueca) • 7pm-3am • mostly gay men • 2 for 1 drinks till 11:30pm

**El Rincón Guay** Embajadores 62 (Lavapiés quarter) 34/914-68-37-00 • 9am-2am • lesbians/ gay men • neighborhood bar/ cafe • WiFi

**Sacha's** Plaza de Chueca 1 (M° Chueca) • 8pm-3am • lesbians/ gay men • dancing/DJ • drag shows • terrace

**Sixta** Calatrava 15 (M° La Latina) 34/913-663-018 • 10pm-2am, 3pm-midnight Sun, clsd Mon-Wed • packed on Sun afternoon • gay/ straight • gay-owned

**Tántalo** Libertad 14 34/915-213-127 • 6pm-2:30am • mostly gay men • WiFi

**Truco** Calle de Gravina 10 (at Plaza de Chueca) 34/91-532-8921 • 8pm-close, clsd Mon-Tue • popular • mostly women • dance bar • great parties • seasonal terrace

**Why Not** San Bartolomé 6 (M° Gran Vía) • 9pm-3am, till 5am Fri-Sat • mostly gay men • dancing/DJ

## Nightclubs

**Boite** Calle Tetuan 27 (Plaza del Carmen) 34/91-522-9620 • gay/ straight • dancing/DJ • check listings for gay club nights

**Club 33** Cabeza 33 (M° Antón Martín) 34/91-369-3302 • midnight-6am, from 6pm Sun, clsd Mon-Wed • popular wknds • women only • men welcome as guests • dancing/DJ • cabaret • cover charge

**Dark Hole** Pelayo 80-82 • 1am -6am Sat, gay goth club

**Escape** Gravina 13 (at Plaza de Chueca) 34/91-532-5206 • 10pm-5am Wed-Sun • mostly women • dancing/DJ • live shows

**Griffin's** Marqués de Valdeiglesias 6 (M° Banco de España) 34/91-522-2079 • 11pm-late • mostly gay men • dancing/DJ • drag shows • entertainment

**Joy Eslava** Arenal 11 (M° Sol) 34/91-366-3733 • 11:30pm-6pm Sat only • popular • fabulous crowd • converted theater

**Long Play** Plaza de Vázquez de Mella 2 • midnight-6am wknds only • lesbians/ gay men • dancing/DJ • young crowd

**Ohm** Plaza de Callao 4 (at Sala Bash, M° Callao) 34/91-531-0132 • midnight-close Fri-Sat • popular • gay/ straight • dancing/DJ • go-go dancers

**Polana** Barbieri 10 (M° Chueca) 34/91-532-3305 • 10pm-5am • trendy • lesbians/ gay men • dancing/DJ

**Tábata** Vergara 12 (next to Teatro Real, M° Opera) 34/91-547-9735 • 11:30pm-late Wed-Sat • lesbians/ gay men • dancing/DJ • young crowd • cover charge

**Week-end** Plaza de Callao 4 (at Ohm Club) 34/91-541-3500 • midnight-6am Sun • popular • lesbians/ gay men • dancing/DJ • alternative • cover charge

## Cafes

**El Apolo** Barco 18 34/915-210-830 • 8am-3pm & 6pm-2am, 10am-2am Sat, from 5pm Sun

**Cafe Acuarela** Gravina 10 (M° Chueca) 34/91-522-2143, 34/91-570-6907 • 3pm-3am, from 11am Sat-Sun • lesbians/ gay men • bohemian cafe-bar • cocktails

**Cafe Figueroa** Augusto Figueroa 17 (at Hortaleza, M° Chueca) 34/91-521-1673 • 4pm-midnight, till 2:30am wknds • lesbians/ gay men • also bar

**Cafe la Troje** Pelayo 26 (at Figueroa, M° Chueca) 34/91-531-0535 • 5pm-2am • lesbians/ gay men • full bar

**D'Mystic** Gravina 5 (M° Pelayo) 34/91-308-2460 • 9:30am-close • gay/ straight • popular • hot food served • hip cafe-bar in Chueca area

**Mama Inés** Hortaleza 22 (M° Chueca) 34/91-523-2333 • 10am-2am • sandwiches • pies

**XXX Cafe** Clavel 2 (M° Gran Vía) 34/91-532-8415 • 1pm-1am • mostly gay men • food served • cabaret wknds

## Restaurants

**Al Natural** Zorrilla 11 (M° Sevilla) 34/91-369-4709 • lunch & dinner, no dinner Sun • vegetarian

**Antigua Taqueria** Calle Cabestreros 7 (in Lavapies area) 34/915-308-270 • 11am-midnight, till 2am Fri-Sat • Tex-Mex • lesbian-owned

**El Armario** San Bartolomé 7 (btwn Figueroa & San Marcos, M° Chueca) 34/91-532-8377 • lunch & dinner • lesbians/ gay men • Mediterranean

**Artemisa** Ventura de la Vega 4 (at Zorrilla) 34/91-429-5092 • lesbians/ gay men • vegetarian • also Tres Cruces 4 location

**Barandales** Menorca, 31 34-91/557-2152 • specialize in castilian food from two castilian provinces

**La Berenjena** Calle Marqués de Toca 7 (in Lavapies area) **34/914-675-297** • 8pm-2am, from 1:30pm wknds, till midnight Sun, clsd Mon • lesbian-owned

**La Berenjena** Calle Marqués de Toca,7 (in Lavapies area) **34/914-675-297** • 8pm-2am, from 1:30pm wknds, till midnight Sun, clsd Mon • lesbian-owned

**Botin** **34/91-366-4217** • one of the oldest restaurants in the world (open since 1725) & an old Hemingway haunt

**Cafetín La Quimera** Sancho Davila, 34 • offers a typical flamenco show

**Colby** **34/91-521-2554** • 9:30am-close, from 11:30am Sun

**Divina La Cocina** Colmenares 13 (at San Marcos, Mº Chueca) **34/91-531-3765** • lunch & dinner • lesbians/ gay men • elegant & trendy

**Ecocentro** Esquilache 2, 4, y 6 (at Pablo Iglesias, Mº Rios Rosas) **34/91-553-5502** • open till midnight • vegetarian • natural foods • also shop • herbalist school

**El Chambao** Manuel Malasana 16 (at Calle de Monteleon) • tapas restaurant • also bar

**La Gastrocroqueteria de Chema** Calle Segovia 17 **34/913-642-263** • dinner nightly from 9pm, lunch wknds from 2pm, romantic space serving traditonal tapas

**Gula Gula** Gran Via 1 (Mº Gran Via) **34/91-522-8764** • lunch & dinner • popular • lesbians/ gay men • buffet/ salad bar • drag shows • reservations required

**La Gamella** Calle Alfonso XII, 4 • Spanish and American cuisine

**La Gloria** Paseo Infanta Isabel, 5 • fine seasonal dishes

**Marsot** Pelayo 6 (Mº Chueca) **34/91-531-0726** • lunch & dinner

**Mercado de la Reina** Calle Gran Vía 12 **34/915-213-198** • 9am-2am, hip and happening with high quality food

**Momo** Calle de la Libertad 8 **34/91-532-7162** • lunch & dinner • nonsmoking • charming staff • gay-owned

**ORIO Madrid** C/ Fuencarral 49 **34-93/342-5411** • great tapas

**Paris Tokyo** Plaza Vázquez de Mella 12 **34/915-216-128** • noon-2am • fine dining with a disco vibe • gay-owned

**El Rincón de Pelayo** Pelayo 19 (Mº Chueca) **34/91-521-8407** • lunch & dinner • lesbians/ gay men

**Sama-Sama** San Bartolomé 23 (Mº Chueca) **34/91-521-5547** • lunch & dinner, clsd Sun • Balinese decor • also Infante 5 location

**Shikku** Lagasca, 5 **34-91/344-1664** • chic Japanese

**Taberna el Olivar** Calle Olivar 54 (in Lavapies area) • 7pm-midnight, from 1pm Fri-Sun, clsd Tues • lesbian-owned

**Taberna La Bola** Calle Bola, 5 **34/9157-6930** • best of the castillan cuisine

**Vegaviana** Pelayo 35 **34/913-080-381** • lunch & dinner, clsd Sun-Mon • vegetarian

**Villa Cazorla** Calle Castillo 14 **34-91/665-7578** • surrounded by Parque del Castillo and Bosque Pinar

## BOOKSTORES

**A Different Life** Pelayo 30 (Mº Chueca) **34/91-532-9652** • 11am-10pm • LGBT • books • magazines • music • videos • sex shop downstairs

**Berkana Bookstore** Hortaleza 64 **34/91-522-5599** • 10:30am-9pm, from noon Sat-Sun • LGBT • ask for free gay map of Madrid • wheelchair access

## PUBLICATIONS

**Shangay Express** **34/91-445-1741** • free bi-weekly gay paper • also publishes Shanguide

## GYMS & HEALTH CLUBS

**Gimnasio V35** Valverde 35 (Mº Gran Via) **34/91-523-9352** • 8:30am-11pm, 10am-10pm Sat, clsd Sun

**Holiday Gym Princesa** Serrano Jover 3 (Mº Argüelles) **34/91-547-4033** • central location • pool

## EROTICA

**Amantis** Pelayo 46 **34/91-702-0510**

**La Jugueteria** Travesia de San Mateo 12 **34-91/308-7269** • 11am-3pm & 5pm-9pm, clsd Sun • very lesbian friendly

**Los Placeres de Lola** Doctor Fourquet, 34 **34/91-468-6178** • noon-10pm, clsd Sun • women & their companions only • toys, leather, books & videos • also cafe

# Sitges

## ACCOMMODATIONS

**Antonio's Guesthouse** Passeig Vilanova 58 **34/93-894-9207** • mostly men • WiFi • also apts • gay-owned

**B My Guest B&B** Ctra Sant Pere de Ribes 34/639–534–979 • women-only penthouse apt • WiFi • lesbian-owned

**Los Globos** Avda Ntra Sra de Montserrat 43 34/93–894–9374 • lesbians/ gay men • kids/ pets ok • also bar • brkfst buffet • WiFi • wheelchair access • gay-owned

**Hotel Antemare** Verge de Montserrat 48-50 34/93–894–7000 • gay-friendly • pool • 1 block from beach

**Hotel Liberty** Isla de Cuba 45 (at Artur Carbonell) 34/93–811–0872 • lesbians/ gay-men • seasonal • nonsmoking • WiFi • wheelchair access • gay-owned

**Hotel Renaixença** Illa de Cuba 13 , 08070 34/93–894–8375 • mostly gay men • some shared baths • hotel bar

**Hotel Romàntic** Sant Isidre 33 34/93–894–8375 • gay/ straight • full brkfst • some shared baths • seasonal • kids/ pets ok • also full bar

**Hotel Santa Maria** Paseo de la Ribera 52 34/93–894–0999 • gay/ straight • clean & modest • great restaurant

**Medium Sitges Park Hotel** Calle Jesus 16 34/938–940–205 • gay/ straight • pool, restaurant, bar & garden • WiFi • wheelchair access

**Parrot's Hotel** Joan Tarrida 16 34/93–894–1350 • lesbians/ gay men • WiFi • also bar & restaurant

**San Sebastian Playa** Port Alegre 53 305/538–9697 (US#), 866/376–7831 (in US) • gay-friendly • pool • also bar/ restaurant • nonsmoking • wheelchair access

**Sitges Royal Rooms** 34/64–998–1148 • mostly gay men • WiFi • gay-owned

### BARS

**Azul** Sant Bonaventura 10 34/93–894–7634 • 9pm-3am • mostly gay men • neighborhood bar

**Dark/ DSB** Bonaire 14 • 5pm-3am • mostly men • sleek lounge

**Mojito & Co** Plaza Industrial 1 • 5pm-3am • mostly men • breezy lounge w/ outdoor seating

**Parrot's Pub** Plaza Industria 2 (at Primero de Mayo) 34/93–894–7881 • 5pm-close, seasonal • popular • lesbians/ gay men • live shows • patio • also restaurant

**Ruby's Terrace** Joan Tarrida Ferratges 14 • from 8pm • mostly gay men • drag shows • terrace

**XXL** Joan Tarrida Ferratges 7 • 11pm-3:30am (wknds only off-season) • popular • mostly gay men • dancing/DJ

### NIGHTCLUBS

**Bourbon's** Sant Bonaventura 13 34/93–894–3347 • 10:30pm-3:30am (Sat only off-season) • popular • mostly gay men • dancing/DJ • videos • young crowd

**Comodín** Tacó 4 34/93–894–1698 • 10pm-3am,,mostly gay men • dancing/DJ • drag shows

**Mediterraneo** Sant Bonaventura 6 34/93–894–3347 • 11pm-3:30am • popular • mostly gay men • dance bar • patio

**Orek's** Bonaire 13 • 10pm-3am (only Fri-Sat in winter) • mostly gay men • dancing/DJ • strippers • darkroom

**Organic** Bonaire 15 34/93–894–2230 • opens 2:30am (wknds only off-season) • mostly gay men • transgender-friendly • dancing/DJ • singles party Th • darkroom • cover charge

**El Piano** Bonaventura 37 34/93–814–6245 • 10pm-3am • lesbians/ gay men • piano bar • cabaret

**Queenz** Bonaire 17 • 10pm-3:30am, seasonal • mostly men • DJs • drag shows • cabaret

**Ricky's** • midnight-6am, clsd Mon • gay/ straight, more gay Fri

**Trailer** Angel Vidal 36 • 1am-6am, seasonal • popular • mostly gay men • dancing/DJ

### CAFES

**Cafe Al Fresco** Carrer Major 33 34/93–811–3307 • 9am-midnight

**Cine Cafe** Jesus 55 34/662–560–050 • 10am-midnight, clsd Tue • mostly gay men • Anglo-American • gay-owned

**Mont Roig Cafe** Marques de Montroig 11-13 34/93–894–8439 • 9am-3am • patio • WiFi • also full bar

### RESTAURANTS

**Air Coco** Paseo Maritim 2 34/93–894–2445 • clsd Mon • popular • patio seating • water views • reservations recommended

**Alma** Tacó 16 34/93–894–6387 • 8pm-close (clsd Tue-Wed off-season) • lesbians/ gay men • French • terrace

**Beach House** Sant Pau 34 34/93–894–9029 • brkfst & dinner , friendly service from the owners themselves • full bar • patio • gay-owned

**El Celler Vell** 34/93-811-1961 • dinner nightly, lunch Fri-Sun, clsd Wed • traditional Catalan

**Ma Maison** Bonaire 28 34/93-894-6054 • lunch & dinner • popular • lesbians/ gay men • French • full bar • terrace

**Mezzanine** Espalter 8 34/93-894-9940 • dinner only • French

**Pic Nic** Paseo de la Ribera 34/93-811-0040 • in front of gay beach • also internet cafe

**Sitthai** Bonaire 29 34/938-111-6 58 • 8pm-midnight, clsd Wed

**So Ca/ Southern California** Sant Gaudenci 9 34/93-894-3046 • 1pm-close • also bar

**El Trull** Mossèn Felix Clará 3 (off Major) 34/93-894-4705 • dinner only, clsd Wed • popular • lesbians/ gay men • French/ int'l

### ENTERTAINMENT & RECREATION

**Gay Beach (Platja de la Bassa Rodona)** • in front of Calipolis Hotel & Picnic cafe

**Gay Beach Party** La Playa De La Bossa Rodona • midnight-6am Tue in season

**Playa De Las Balmins** • turn left then pass a long beach strip & then climb a hill past a cemetery

**Playa del Muerto** • exclusively gay beach 50 minutes walk from the center of Sitges • also beach bar

### RETAIL SHOPS

**Laguna Beach Shop** Sant Josep 25 34/938-947-204 • 10:30am-2pm, 5pm-9pm

# JAPAN

## Tokyo

### ACCOMMODATIONS

**Capitol Tokyu** 10-3 Nagata-cho 2-chome (Chiyoda-ku) 81-3/3581-4511, 800/428-6598 • gay-friendly • near the Diet

**Four Seasons Hotel** 10-8 Sekiguchi 2-chome (Bunkyo-ku) 81-3/3943-2222 • gay-friendly • wheelchair access • pool • surrounded by historic Japanese garden

**HI Tokyo Central Hostel** 18F Central Plaza (1-1 Kagurakashi, Shinjuku-ku) 81-3/3235-1107 • gay-friendly • 11pm curfew

**Hotel Century Southern Tower** 2-2-1 Yoyogi (Shibuya-ku) 81-3/5354-0111 • gay-friendly • near gay district

**Hotel Sunroute Plaza Shinjuku** 2-3-1 Yoyogi (Shibuya-ku) 81-3/3375-3211 • gay-friendly • near gay district

**Keio Plaza Hotel** 2-2-1 Nishi Shinjuku 81-3/3344-0111 • gay-friendly • swimming • restaurants & bars

**Park Hyatt** 3-7-1-2 Nishi Shinjuku 81-3/5322-1234 • gay-friendly • kids ok • restaurant & lounge • luxury hotel featured in Lost in Translation • pool • spa

**Shinjuku Prince Hotel** 30-1 Kabuki-cho 1-chome (Shinjuku-ku) 81-3/3205-1111, 800/542-8686 (US) • gay-friendly • WiFi

**Shinjuku Washington Hotel** 3-2-9 Nishi-Shinjuku (Shinjuku-ku) 81-3/3343-3111 • gay-friendly

**Tokyu Stay** 5-9-8 Nishi Shinjuku 81-3/3370-1090 • gay-friendly • great location

### BARS

**Advocates Cafe** 1-F, Dai-7 Tenka Bldg (Shinjuku 2-18-1) 81-3/3358-3988 • 6pm-4am, till 1am Sun • cafe-bar • lesbians/ gay men • young crowd

**Alamas Cafe** 1/F Garnet Bldg, Shinjuku 2-12-1 81-3/6457-4242 • 6pm-2am, till 5am Fri-Sat, 3pm-midnight Sun • lesbians/ gay men • dancie club at night

**Arty Farty** 2F, #33 Kyutei Bldg (Shinjuku 2-11-7), Shinjuku-ku 81-3/5362-9720 • 6pm-5am, from 7pm Fri, from 5pm wknds, till 3am Sun • mostly gay men • dancing/DJ • young crowd

**Bridge** Shinjuku Ni-chome 13-16 (Sensho Building 6F) • 8pm-5am • lesbians/gaymen

**Campy! Bar** Shinjuku Ni-chome 12-10 (Musashino Building 1F) • 8pm-5am • lesbians/gaymen • drag shows

**DNA** 81-3/3341-4445 • 3pm-5am • gay/ straight • neighborhood bar

**GB** B1, Shinjuku Plaza Bldg (Shinjuku 2-12-3), Shinjuku-ku 81-3/3352-8972 • 8pm-2am, till 3am Fri-Sat • mostly gay men

**Gold Finger** Shinjuku Ni-chome 12-11 • 9pm-5am • lesbians/gaymen • Sat women only • karaoke

**Hug** Shinjuku 2-15-8 81-3/5379-5085 • 9pm-5am, clsd Sun • women only • karaoke • cover charge

**Keivi** 4F Yoshino Bldg, 17-10 Sakuragaoka 81-3/3496-0006 • 6pm-midnight • mostly gay men • neighborhood bar

**Kinsmen** 2F Shinjuku 2-12-16 (near Shinjuku Sanchome Station) 81-3/3354-4949 • 7pm-1am, till 3am Fri-Sat, clsd Mon • lesbians/ gay men

**Kusuo** 3F Sunflower Bldg (Shinjuku 2-17-1) 81–3/3354–5050 • 8pm-4am, till 5am wknds • mostly men • dancing /DJ

**Monsoon** Shimazaki Bldg 6F (2-14-9 Shinjuku) 81–3/3354–0470 • 3pm-6am • mostly gay men • small, inexpensive bar

**Peach** 1F (Shinjuku 2-15-8) 81–3/3351–7034 • 11pm-7am, clsd Sun-Mon • women only • in a brick building next to 'Hug' & across from 'Agit' • look for the peach mark on the door • cover charge

**Tac's Knot** 2F, Rm 202 (Shinjuku 3-11-12) 81–3/3341–9404 • 8pm-2am • lesbians/ gay men • also art exhibitions

**Tamago** 1F Yamahara Heights Bldg (Shinjuku 2-12-15) 81–3/3351–4838 • 9pm-5am • women only • drag king shows

**Town House** Ginza 6 Shinbashi, Bldg 1-11-15 (Minato-ku) 81–3/3289-8558 • 6pm-midnight, from 4pm Sat, clsd Sun • mostly gay men • karaoke

**Usagi** on lock U facing block V, 5th Fl (up the narrow stairs) • mostly gay men • great balcony

**Warai-Tei** 301 Nakae Bldg III, 2F (2-15-13 Shinjuku) 81–3/3226-0830

**Wordup Bar** 2-10-7 2F TOM Bld Shinjuku 81–3/3353–2466 • mostly gay men • dancing/DJ

## NIGHTCLUBS

**Agit** 81–3/3350-8083 • 8pm-6am • lesbians/ gay men • karaoke • lesbian-owned

**Arch** B1F Hayakawa Bldg (Shinjuku 2-14-6) 81–3/3352–6297 • lesbians/ gay men • dancing/DJ • check www.clubarch.net for info on men-only & women-only nights

**Club Zinc** Shinjuku 2-14-6 (across from Shinjuku Park) 81–3/3352–6297 • 8pm-4am • lesbians/ gay men • 1st Th women's party called Bar Monalisa

**Diamond Cutter** B1F Hayakawa Bldg (Shinjuku 2-14-6, at Club Arch) 81–3/3352–6297 (ARCH) • check www.diamondcutter.jp for dates • women only • dancing/DJ • cabaret

**Motel #203** 81–3/6383-4649 • 8pm-5am, till 2am Sun, clsd Tue • popular happy hour 8pm-9pm • women only • dancing/DJ

**Rehab Lounge** 81–3/3355–7833 • 7pm-2am, till 3am Fri-Sat • popular happy hour 7pm-9pm • mostly gay men • dancing/DJ

**Shangri-La** 2-2-10, Shinkiba (at ageHa, Studio Coast) 81–3/5534-2525 • bi-monthly • mostly men • popular • dancing/DJ

**Warehouse** Fukao Bldg B 1-4-5 (exit 7 Azabu Juban station) 81–3/6230 0343 • gay/ straight • large underground club host Red gay nights

## RESTAURANTS

**Angkor Wat** 1-38-13 Yoyogi (Shibuya-ku) 81–3/3370-3019 • lunch & dinner • Cambodian

**Ban Thai** 1-23-14 Kabuki-cho, 3rd flr (Shinjuku) 81–3/3207-0068 • lunch & dinner

**Chin-ya** 1-3-4 Asukusa 81–3/3841-0010 • lunch & dinner • serving shabu-shabu & sukiyaki since 1880

**Edogin** 4-5-1 Tsukiji (Chuo-ku) 81–3/3543-4401 • 11am-9:30pm, till 8pm Sun • popular • sushi

**Gonpachi** 1-13-11 Nishi Azabu, 1F, 2F (Minato-ku) 81–3/5771-0170 • 11:30am-5am • multiple locations

**Kakiden** 3-37-11 Shinjuku, 8th flr 81–3/3352-5121 • lunch & dinner • upscale Japanese

**Kitchen Five** 4-2-15 Nishi-Azabu (Minato-ku) 81–3/3409-8835 • 6pm-9:45pm • Mediterranean • woman chef

**Kozue** 3-7-1-2 Nishi Shinjuku (at the Park Hyatt) 81–3/5323-3460 • lunch and dinner daily, on a clear day you can see Mount Fuji from the hotel's exquisite contemporary Japanese restaurant , dress code

**Las Chicas** Jingumae 5-47-6 (off Shibuya), Shibuya-ku 81–3/3407-6865 • 11:30am-11pm • English spoken

**Maisen** 4-8-5 Jingu-mae (Shibuya-ku) 81–3/3470-0071 • specializes in tonkatsu

**Moti** 3F Roppongi Hama Bldg (6-2-35 Roppongi) 81–3/3479-1939 • noon-10pm • Indian

**New York Grill** 3-7-1-2 Nishi Shinjuku (at Park Hyatt Hotel, 52nd flr) 81–3/5322-1234 • lunch & dinner • reservations recommended

**The Pink Cow** 1-3-18 Shibuya, Shibuya-ku (Villa Modernuna B-1, across from Aoyama Park Tower) 81–3/3406-5597 • 5pm-late, clsd Mon

**Sasa-no-yuki** 2-15-10 Negishi (Taito-ku) 81–3/3873-1145 • 11am-9pm, clsd Mon • serving homemade tofu for 300 years

**Tenmatsu** 1-6-1 Dogen-zaka (Shibuya-ku) 81–3/3462-2815 • tempura

**Teyandei** 2-20-1 Nishi Azabu (Minato-ku) **81–3/3407–8127** • a cozy izakaya in a 2 story house on a quiet discrete street with more residences than businesses, also other locations

**Yuian** 2-6-1 Nishi-Shinjuku 52nd Fl (in the Shinjuku Sumitomo Bldg) **81–3/3342-5671** • 5:30-1030pm, upscale Japanese pub (Izakaya) on the 52nd floor and the window tables have amazing views

### RETAIL SHOPS

**Isetan Men's** 3-14-1 Shinjyuku 1-11-15 **81–3/3352-1111**

### GYMS & HEALTH CLUBS

**Gold's Gym Harajuku** 6-31-17 Jingumae (Shibuya-ku) **81–3/5766-3131** • 24 hrs, except Sun, many gay members

### TRAVEL AGENTS

**Magnet Tours** 2-11-14 Nishishinbash Bldg 2F (Minato-ku) **81–3/3500-4819** • tour operator in Japan to focus specifically on LGBT travelers

# THAILAND

## Bangkok

### INFO LINES & SERVICES

**Gay AA** 12/3 Silom Rd (at the Coffee Society) **66–2/231-8300** • 7pm Th

### ACCOMMODATIONS

**Baan Saladaeng** 69/2 Soi Saladaeng 3, Saladaeng Rd (Silom, Bangrak) **66–2/2636-3038** • gay-friendly • upscale • near gay scene

**Bangkok Rama Place, City Resort & Hotel** 1546 Pattanakarn Rd (in Suan-Luang District) **66–2/722-6602-10** • gay-friendly • full brkfst • pool • kids ok • also restaurant • WiFi • wheelchair access • lesbian-owned

**D&D Inn** 68-70 Khaosan Rd (Phranakorn) **66–2/629-0526** • gay-friendly • central location • pool • "life's little luxuries at a price you can afford"

**Elephantstay** Royal Elephant Kraal & Village (74/1 M3 Tumbol Suanpik), Phra Nakhon Si Ayutthaya **66–81/668-7727, 66–87/116-3307** • gay/ straight • live w/, care for & learn about elephants • near Lopburi River • 1 hour to Bangkok • lesbian-owned

**Furama Silom** 59 Silom Rd **66–2/237-0488** • gay-friendly • pool • sauna • gym • restaurant • bar

**Heaven@4 Hotel** Sukhumvit Soi 4 **66–2/656-9450** • gay/ straight • WiFi • also bar

**Hotel de Moc** 78 Prajatipatai Rd, Pra-Nakorn **66–2/282-2831-3, 66–2/629-2100-5** • gay-friendly • pool • WiFi • wheelchair access

**Lub d** 4 Decho Rd (Silom, Bangrak) **66–2/634-7999** • gay-friendly • hostel w/ some private rooms • WiFi

**Luxx** 6/11 Decho Rd **66–2/635-8800** • gay-friendly • style-conscious, minimalist design hotel • full brkfst • WiFi

**Old Bangkok Inn** 607 Pra Sumen Rd (at Rajdamnern Ave, in Pra Nakhon) **66–2/629-1787** • environmentally-friendly • full brkfst • kids/ pets ok • nonsmoking

**Omyim Lodge** 72-74 Naratiwat Rd Silom **66–2/635-0169** • gay/ straight • full brkfst • nonsmoking • kids ok • WiFi • lesbian & gay-owned

**Pinnacle Hotel** 17 Soi Ngam Duphli, Rama 4 Rd, Sathorn **66–2/287-0111** • gay/ straight • fitness center

**Regency Park Hotel** 12/3 Sukhumvit 22, Soi Sainamthip **66–2/259-7420** • gay-friendly • located in heart of Bangkok • full brkfst • pool

**Sheraton Grande Sukhumvit** 250 Sukhumvit Rd **66–2/649-8888** • gay-friendly • tropical garden • pool WiFi • wheelchair access • also Thai & Italian restaurant

**Tarntawan Place Hotel** 119/ 5-10 Surawong Rd **66–2/238-2620** • centrally located • kids ok • discount for gays • WiFi • wheelchair access

### BARS

**70 Bar's** 231/16 Sarasin (Chitlom) **66–2/253-4433** • lesbians/ gay men • dancing/DJ • retro lounge

**The Balcony Pub & Restaurant** 86–88 Silom Soi 4 (off Silom Rd) **66–2/235-5891** • 5:30pm-close • popular • mostly gay men • karaoke • terrace

**Bed Supperclub** 26 Soi Sukhumvit 11, Sukhumvit Rd, Klongtoey-nua, Wattana **66–2/651-3537** • 7:30pm-close • gay/ straight • dancing/DJ • dinner served in bed

**Club Love Remix** Ramkhamhaeng Soi 89/2 **66–2/378-4345, 66–1/987-4946** • gay/ straight • dancing/DJ • young crowd • also restaurant

**@Diamond** 10/17 Silom Soi 2/1 **66–2/234-0459** • 6pm-2am • mostly men • neighborhood bar • food served

**Expresso** 8/10-11 Silom Rd, Soi 2 (Bang Rak) • mostly gay men • relaxed café-bar

**Golden Dome** 252/5 Ratchadapisek Rd Soi 18 (Huay Khwang) **66-2/692-8202** • lesbians/ gay men • cabaret • shows nightly at 5pm, 7pm & 9pm

**JJ Park** 8/3 Silom Rd, Soi 2 (Bang Rak) **66-2/235-1227** • 10:30pm-2am • gay/ straight • food • live music

**Maxi's Bar & Restaurant** 38/1-2 Soi Pratoochai Suriwong Rd **66-2/2266-4225** • 6pm-2am • mostly gay men

**One Night Only** Silom Soi 4, 74-1 **66-89/499-0303** • 6pm-3am • mostly gay men • small bar on the first floor, also lounge & outside area

**Telephone Pub & Restaurant** 114/ 11 Silom Rd, Soi 4 **66-2/234-3279** • 6pm-1am • lesbians/ gay men • karaoke • WiFi • food served

## NIGHTCLUBS

**DJ Station** 8/6-8 Silom Rd, Soi 2 (Bang Rak) **66-02/266-4029** • 10:30pm-2am • lesbians/ gay men • dancing/DJ

**G-Star** Ratchada Rd, Soi 8 (Din Daeng) **66-2/643-8792** • 7pm-2am • mostly gay men • dancing/DJ

**Happen** 8/14 Silom Soi 2 • 8pm-late, busy after 11pm • mostly gay men • karaoke

**Pharaoh's Music Bar** 104 Silom Soi 4 (above Sphinx) **66-2/234-7249** • 7pm-2am • gay/ straight • food • karaoke

**X Boom** Soi Anuman Ratchathon, Suriwong, Bangkok • opens at 8pm • popular 'after-hours' place • mostly gay men • dancing/DJ • go-go dancers

## CAFES

**Bug & Bee** 18 Silom Rd, Suriyawong (Bang Rak) **66-2/233-8118** • 24hrs

**Coffee Society** 12/3 Silom Rd (Suriyawong, Bang Rak) **66-2/235-9784** • 24hrs • WiFi • also art gallery

**Dick's Cafe Bangkok** 894/7–8 Soi Pratuchai (Duangthawee Plaza, off Surawong Rd) **66-2/637-0078** • 11am-2am • European-style cafe in the heart of the action

**Rocket Coffeebar** Sukhumvit Soi 49 **66-2/662-6638** • nice terrace

## RESTAURANTS

**Cabbages & Condoms** 6 Soi 12 Sukhumvit Rd (at Birds & Bees Resort) **66-2/229-4611** • 11am-10pm • Thai food w/ safe-sex education

**Coyote on Convent** 1/2 Sivadon Bldg Convent (Silom Bangrak) **66-2/631-2325** • 11am-midnight • Mexican • ladies night 6pm-8pm Th & 10pm-midnight Sat

**Crêpes & Co** 59/4 Langsuan Soi 1 (Ploenchit Rd, Lumpini) **66-2/653-3990** • 9am-11pm • lounge • full bar

**Eat Me** Soi Pipat 2 (off Soi Convent) **66-2/238-0931** • 3pm-1am • upscale • also gallery • live music

**Full Moon** 144/2 Silom Soi 10 **66-2/634-0766** • Thai food • gay-owned

**Hemlock** 56 Phra Arthit Rd, Chanasongkram **66-2/282-7507** • 5pm-midnight, clsd Sun • traditional Thai food • more lesbian wknds

**Indigo** 6 Convent Rd (off Silom Rd) **66-2/235-3268** • noon-1am, clsd Sun • patio • full bar • French

**Loy Nava Dinner Cruises** 37 Charoen Nakorn Rd, Klongsan **66-2/437-4932** • traditional Thai cuisine on rice barge on Chao Phraya River • reservations required

**Mali** 43 Sathorn Soi 1 **66-2/679-8693** • 8am-11pm • Thai & int'l • gay-owned

**Mango Tree** 37 Soi Tantawan (off Suriwong Rd) **66-2/236-2820** • popular • reservations recommended • traditional Thai food • live music nightly

**May Kaidee** 111 Tanao Rd, Bang-lam-phu (behind Burger King) **66-9/137-3173** • 9am-11pm • innovative vegetarian • also 33 Samen Rd (Soi 1)

**O...Ho...** 2/8 Soi Sri Bumphen **66-2/286-5292** • 9am-midnight • Thai & Western menu • gay-owned

**Once Upon a Time** 32 Soi Petchaburi 17, Pratunam **66-2/252-8629** • 11am-11pm • Thai

**Sphinx** 100 Silom Soi 4 **66-2/234-7249** • 6pm-1am • popular • Thai & Western • mostly gay men • full bar • karaoke • terrace

**Sweet Basil** 1 Srivieng Rd (Si Lom, Bang Rak) **66-02/234-1889** • 11:30am-9pm • popular • Vietnamese food

**Zup Zip** 674 Soi 101, Lad Prao Rd **66-081/734-2759** • 6pm-2am • popular w/ local lesbians • lesbian-owned

## ENTERTAINMENT & RECREATION

**Calypso Cabaret** 296 Phaya Thai Rd, Pathumwan (at Asia Hotel) **66-2/261-6355** • lesbians/ gay men • cabaret • drag shows nightly at 8:15pm & 9:30pm

**Mambo** 59/28 Sathu-phararam 3 Rd
**66-2/294-7381-2** • cabaret • shows nightly at
7:15pm & 10pm

# AUSTRALIA

## Sydney

### INFO LINES & SERVICES

**The Gender Centre** **61-2/9569-2366** •
9am-4:30pm Mon-Fri, free services for
transgender/ transsexual people & their
partners/ friends/ families

**Lesbian & Gay Counselling Service**
**61-2/8594-9596, 1-800/18-4527 (OUTSIDE
SYDNEY)** • 5:30pm-10:30pm • info & support

### ACCOMMODATIONS

**Best Western Hotel Stellar** 4 Wentworth
Ave (at Oxford St) **61-2/9264-9754** • gay/
straight • kitchenette in each room • WiFi •
cafe & bar

**Brickfield Hill B&B Inn** 403 Riley St (at
Foveaux), Surry Hills **61-2/9211-4886** • gay/
straight • Victorian terrace-house in gay district
• near beaches & downtown • WiFi • gay-
owned

**Chelsea Guest House** 49 Womerah Ave (at
Oswald Ln), Darlinghurst **61-2/9380-5994** •
gay/ straight • Victorian w/ Italianate courtyard
• nonsmoking • gay-owned

**Kirketon Boutique Hotel** 229 Darlinghurst
Rd (at Farrell Ave) **61-2/9332-2011,
800/332-920 (AUSTRALIA ONLY)** • gay-friendly •
also restaurant & bars • kids ok • WiFi

**Medusa** 267 Darlinghurst Rd (at Liverpool),
Darlinghurst **61-2/9331-1000** • gay-friendly •
modern boutique hotel • WiFi

**Nomads Westend** 412 Pitt St (at Goulburn
St) **61-2/9211-4588, 1800/013-186** • gay-
friendly • budget/ backpacker's
accommodations • cafe • wheelchair access

**Pensione Hotel** 631-635 George St (at
Goulburn St) **61-2/9265-8888, 800/885-886** •
gay-friendly • close to the Capital theatre

**Victoria Court Hotel Sydney** 122 Victoria St
(at Orwell, Potts Point) **61-2/9357-3200,
1800/630-505 (IN AUSTRALIA)** • gay-friendly •
historic B&B-inn in elegant Victorian • full
brkfst • WiFi

### BARS

**Bar Cleveland** 433 Cleveland St (at Bourke),
Surry Hills **61-2/9698-1908** • 10am-2am, till
4am Fri-Sat, till midnight Sun • gay/ straight •
cocktail lounge • DJ • young crowd

**The Beauchamp** 265 Oxford St (at S
Dowling), Darlinghurst **61-2/9331-2575** •
noon-2am popular • gay/ straight •
neighborhood bar • food served • pronounced
"Bee-chum" • gay-owned

**Beresford Sundays** 354 Bourke St (at
Albion St), Surry Hills **61-2/9357-1111** • from
noon Sun • lesbians/ gay men • fun in the sun

**The Colombian** 117-123 Oxford St (at Crown
St), Darlinghurst **61-2/9360-2151** • 9am-6am
• lesbians/ gay men • dancing/DJ • theme
nights

**Green Park Hotel** 360 Victoria St (at
Liverpool), Darlinghurst **61-2/9380-5311** •
10am-2am, noon-midnight Sun • more gay
Sun • stylish bar

**The Imperial Hotel** 35 Erskineville Rd,
Newtown **61-2/9519-9899** • lesbians/ gay
men • dancing/DJ • food served • drag shows

**Lava Bar** 2 Oxford St (top flr of Burdekin
Hotel), Darlinghurst **61-2/9331-3066** • 11am-
1am, 4pm-4am Sat • gay/ straight • popular w/
lesbians Fri till 4am • live shows

**The Oxford** 134 Oxford St (at Bourke St,
Taylor Square), Darlinghurst **61-2/8324-5200**
• 10am-close • popular • lesbians/ gay men •
3 bars include the Polo Lounge, Supper Club
& Gilligans

**The Palms On Oxford** 124 Oxford St (at
Bourke St, Taylor Square), Darlinghurst
**61-2/9357-4166** • 8pm-late, clsd Mon-Wed •
dancing/DJ

**The Stonewall** 175 Oxford St (at Bourke),
Darlinghurst **61-2/9360-1963** • noon-6am,
from 9am wknds • popular • mostly gay men •
dancing/DJ • drag shows

**ZanziBar** 323 King St (at Phillips St),
Newtown **62-2/9519-1511** • gay-friendly •
food served

### NIGHTCLUBS

**ARQ** 16 Flinders St (at Taylor Square),
Darlinghurst **61-2/9380-8700** • 9pm-late Th-
Sun, clsd Mon-Wed • popular • mostly gay
men • dancing/DJ • drag shows Th • cover
charge

**Bitch** **61-2/439-430-428** • hot weekly
women's parties • also big events on long
wknds • www.bitchnews.com.au

**Chicks With Picks** 20 Broadway Rd (at
Kensington St, at Clare Hotel), Ultimo • 2nd
Sun only • women's open mic

**Hellfire** 85-91 Oxford St (at Midnight Shift), Darlinghurst • monthly parties check facebook.com/TheSydneyHellfireClub for dates• gay/ straight women-oriented fetish party • dancing/DJ • alternative • leather • burlesque • live shows • cover charge

**Home** Tenancy 101, Cockle Bay Wharf (at Wheat Rd, Darling Harbour) 61-2/9266-0600 • open Fri-Sun • popular • gay-friendly • hosts Homesexual (www.homesexual.com.au)

**Kitty Bar** 35 Erskineville Rd (at The Imperial Hotel), Erskineville 61-2/9380-8700 • last Fri only • popular • mostly women • dancing/DJ • live shows • cover charge

**The Midnight Shift** 85 Oxford St (at Riley), Darlinghurst 61-2/9358-3848 • 2pm-3am, till 12:30 am Mon-Wed, till 6am Fri-Sat • popular • mostly gay men

**Nevermind** 163 Oxford St, Darlinghurst • Fri-Sun only • gay/ straight • theme nights • cutting edge electronic music

**Pussycat Club** 134 Oxford St (at The Oxford Hotel ), Darlinghurst 61-2/9331-3467 • 3rd Sat only • mostly women • trans-friendly • dancing/DJ • cabaret & burlesque shows • all queers welcome

**Queer Central** 199 Enmore Rd (at Sly Fox Hotel), Enmore 61-2/9557-1016 • 9pm Wed only • mostly women • dancing/DJ • live performances

**Slide** 41 Oxford St (at Pelican) 61-2/8915-1899 • 6pm-3am, 5pm-4am Fri, 7pm-4am Sat-Sun, clsd Mon-Tue • lesbians/ gay men • dancing/DJ • also restaurant • live music • cabaret

**Sly Fox** 199 Enmore Rd, Enmore 61-2/9557-1016 • lesbians/ gay men • karaoke

**Velvet Wednesdays** 324 King St (at the Bank Hotel), Newtown • 8pm Wed only • mostly women • dancing/DJ

## Cafes

**Fratelli Fresh Waterloo** 7 Danks St 61-2/9699-3161 • 9am-6pm, 8am-4pm Sat, 10am-4pm Sun • Italian vegetarian

**Victoire** 285 Darling St 61-2/9818-5529 • great bread

**Vinyl Lounge Cafe** 17 Elizabeth Bay Rd, Elizabeth Bay 61-2/9326-9224 • 7am-4pm, from 8am wknds, clsd Mon • lesbians/ gay men • light menu • plenty veggie • cash only

## Restaurants

**10 William Street** 10 William St 61-2/9360-3310 • 5pm-midnight, from noon Fri-Sat, • Italian quirky wine bar

**Bentley Restaurant & Bar** 320 Crown St (Surry Hills) 61-2/9332-2344 • noon-late, clsd Sun- Mon • tapas & small plates • excellent wine

**Bertoni Casalinga** 281 Darling St 61-2/9818-5845 • 6am-6:30pm • Italian

**Bills Surry Hills** 359 Crown St (Surry Hills) 61-2/9360-4762 • 7am-10pm • great ricotta pancakes

**Billy Kwong** 3/355 Crown St (Surry Hills) 61-2/9332-3300 • sustainable local & organic Chinese from 6pm daily • reservations recommended • wheelchair access

**The Boathouse on Blackwattle Bay** 123 Ferry Road (Glebe) 61-2/9518-9011 • lunch & dinner Tue-Sun • gourmet seafood • some veggie • great view • reservations required

**Chu Bay** 312a Bourke St, Darlinghurst 61-2/9331-3386 • 5:30pm-11pm • Vietnamese • some veggie

**Fu Manchu** 249 Victoria St, Darlinghurst 61-2/9360-9424 • lunch & dinner • chic noodle bar • plenty veggie • nonsmoking • cash only

**Iku Wholefood Kitchen** 25a Glebe Point Rd, Glebe 61-2/9692-8720, 800/732-962 • lunch & dinner • creative vegan/ macrobiotic fare • nonsmoking • outdoor seating • cash only

**Kujin** 41b Elizabeth Bay Rd, Elizabeth Bay 61-2/9331-6077 • lunch & dinner, clsd Mon • Japanese

**Queen Victoria Hotel/ Razors Bistro** 167 Enmore Rd, Enmore 61-2/9517-9685 • pub food, good burgers • WiFi

**Sean's Panaroma** 270 Campbell Parade, Bondi Beach 61-2/9365-4924 • open 6pm , from noon Sat-Sun, clsd Mon-Tue

**Thai Kanteen** 541 Military Rd (at Harbour St), Mosman 61-2/9960-3282 • dinner nightly, clsd Sun • modern Thai • gay-owned

**Thai Pothong** 294 King St (Newtown) 61-2/9550-6277 • lunch & dinner • Thai • wheelchair access

## Entertainment & Recreation

**Bondi Beach** Bondi Beach • Sydney's most popular beach • more gay at north end

**Bronte Beach** • check out the pool above the cliffs

**Lady Jane Beach/ Lady Bay Beach**
Watsons Bay • crowded nude beach • mostly
men

**Obelisk Beach** Middle Head Rd (at
Chowder Bay Rd) • mostly men • gay beach •
nudity permitted

**Sydney by Diva** departs from Oxford Hotel
(in Taylor Square), Darlinghurst
61–2/9310-0200 • tour Sydney w/ drag queen
host

**Sydney Gay/ Lesbian Mardi Gras** 94
Oxford St, Darlinghurst 2010 61–2/9383-0900
• the wildest party under the rainbow on this
planet (see www.mardigras.org.au)

**The Women's Library** 8-10 Brown St
61–2/9557-7060 • "books, journals,
ephemera, & art by, for, & about women"

### BOOKSTORES

**The Bookshop Darlinghurst** 207 Oxford St
(near Darlinghurst Rd), Darlinghurst
61–2/9331-1103 • 10am-10pm • Australia's
oldest LGBT bookstore • staff happy to help w/
tourist info

**Gertrude & Alice** 46 Hall St (Bondi Beach)
61–2/9130-5155 • second-hand books • also
coffee shop

### RETAIL SHOPS

**House of Priscilla** 47 Oxford St,
Darlinghurst 61–2/9286-3023 • wigs,
costumes & more

### PUBLICATIONS

**LOTL Magazine** 61–2/9332-2725 •
Lesbians on the Loose • monthly magazine

**SX Weekly** 61–2/9360-8934 • free gay/
lesbian weekly

**Sydney Star Observer** 61–2/8263-0500 •
weekly newspaper w/ club & event listings

### GYMS & HEALTH CLUBS

**City Gym** 107–113 Crown St (at William St),
E Sydney 61–2/9360-6247 • day passes
available

**Gold's Gym Sydney** 58 Kippax St (level 1),
Surry Hills 61–2/9211-2799 • 5:30am-9pm,
8am-6pm Sat, till 5pm Sun

### SEX CLUBS

**Aarows** 17 Bridge St (at Pitt St), Rydalmere
61–2/9638-0553 • 24hrs • lesbians/ gay men •
transgender-friendly • 18+

### EROTICA

**House of Fetish** 288 Crown St, Darlinghurst
61–2/9380-9042 • clsd Mon-Tues

## CRUISES

*Women Only*

**Olivia Travel 800/631–6277** 434 Brannan St, San Francisco, CA 94107 • exclusive cruise, resort & escape vacations for lesbians • *www.olivia.com*

*Gay/Lesbian*

**Aquafest 800/592–9058** 4801 Woodway #400-W, Houston, TX 77056 • LGBT groups mingle w/ mixed clientele on major cruise lines • *www.aquafestcruises.com*

**Gayribbean Cruises 877/560–8318** Dallas, TX • gay & lesbian group cruise organizer • fabulous destinations • annual Halloween cruise from Galveston, TX • *www.gayribbeancruises.com*

**R Family 917/522–0985** 5 Washington Ave, Nyack, NY 10960 • family-friendly vacations designed especially for the LGBT community • *www.rfamilyvacations.com*

**RSVP Vacations 800/328–7787** gay & lesbian cruise vacations • *www.rsvpvacations.com*

## LUXURY TOURS

**DavidTravel 949/427–0199** 310 Dahlia Pl, Ste A, Corona del Mar, CA 92625-2821 • full-service travel agency & tour operator • small luxury group departures & customized travel for individuals & groups • milestone events, including honeymoons! • *www.DavidTravel.com*

## GREAT OUTDOORS ADVENTURES

*Women Only*

**Adventures in Good Company 410/435–1965, 877/439–4042** 5913 Brackenridge Ave, Baltimore, MD 21212 • outdoor & adventure travel for women of all ages & abilities • *www.adventuresingoodcompany.com*

**Call of the Wild Adventure Travel 650/265–1662, 888/378–1978** 20834 Solstice Dr, Bend, OR 97701 • hiking, camping & cultural trips for all levels in Western US & more • longest-running adventure travel company for women • *www.callwild.com*

**Chicks with Picks & Chicks Rock 970/626–4424** PO Box 486, Ridgway, CO 81432 • ice climbing & rock climbing for women • all levels welcome • *www.chickswithpicks.net*

**Herizen™ Life Adventures Int'l Inc SKYPE:/VALMA - HERIZEN** 101-5170 Dunster Rd #176, Nanaimo, BC V9T 6M4, Canada • women-only retreats • sailing, yoga, riding & more in Baja, Mexico, Belize, British Columbia & British Virgin Islands • *www.herizenlifeadventures.com*

**Mariah Wilderness Expeditions 530/626–6049, 800/462–7424** PO Box 1160, Lotus, CA 95651 • unique vacations for women on roads less traveled • multi-sport adventures • unique cultural & eco-explorations • *mariahrafting.com*

**WalkingWomen 0114/241–2774** York, United Kingdom • women's walking vacations for all levels • England, Scotland, Ireland, Wales, Europe, & as far as Nepal & South Africa! • *www.walkingwomen.com*

**Wild Women Expeditions 888/993–1222** PO Box 264, Woody Point, NF A0K 1P0, Canada • Canada's outdoor adventure company for women • kayaking • hiking • cycling • yoga & more • decidedly dykey! • *wildwomenexp.com*

**Winter Moon Summer Sun 218/848–2442** 3388 Petrell, Brimson, MN 55602 • dogsledding trips in winter • kayaking Lake Superior in summer • rustic accommodations w/ meals provided • *www.wintermoonsummersun.com*

**WomanTours 585/424–2124, 800/247–1444** 3495 Winton Place, Bldg E-245, Rochester, NY 14623 • fully supported bicycle tours for women • call for a free catalog • *www.womantours.com*

**Women On A Roll 310/839–2500** 3842 Main Street #B, Culver City, CA 90232 • travel, sporting, cultural & social club for women • wide range of events & trips • largest lesbian organization in Southern California • *www.womenonaroll.com*

**Women's Flyfishing® 907/274–7113** PO Box 243963, Anchorage, AK 99524 • women-only fly-fishing schools & guided trips for women & couples in Alaska, Argentina & Mexico • we provide all gear & equipment • beginners welcome! • *www.womensflyfishing.net*

**Women's Holidays /61 266840178** PO Box 5417, Lismore, NSW 2480, Australia • international escapes & adventures for women • also hosts The Women's Accomodation Network • *www.bushwise.co.nz*

*Mostly Women*

**Venus Charters 305/304–1181** Garrison Bight Marina, Key West, FL 33040 • snorkeling & dolphin-watching • light-tackle fishing • commitment ceremonies • *www.venuscharters.com*

*Gay/Lesbian*

**Alyson Adventures, Inc 305/296–9935, 800/825–9766** 626 Josephine Parker Dr #206, Key West, FL 33040 • award-winning adventure travel & active vacations • hiking, biking & multi-sport activities • *www.hetravel.com*

**Journeyweavers 607/277–1416** 313 Washington St, Ithaca, NY 14850 • group & individual outdoor adventure & birding trips in Costa Rica & beyond • *www.journeyweavers.com*

**Out in Alaska 907/339–0101** 1819 Dimond Dr, Anchorage, AK 99507 • adventure travel throughout Alaska for LGBT travelers • your best bet for a fun & authentic Alaska vacation! • *www.outinalaska.com*

**Undersea Expeditions 858/270–2900, 800/669–0310** 758 Kapahulu Ave #100-1188, Honolulu, HI 96816 • gay & lesbian scuba adventures worldwide • *www.UnderseaX.com*

*Gay/Straight*

**Natural Habitat Adventures 303/449–3711, 800/543–8917** PO Box 3065, Boulder, CO 80307 • up-close encounters w/ the world's most amazing wildlife in its natural habitat • *www.nathab.com*

## SPIRITUAL/HEALTH VACATIONS

*Gay/Lesbian*

**Spirit Journeys 201/483–3111, 800/754–1875** 134 River Rd, New Milford, NJ 97646 • spiritual retreats, workshops & adventure trips throughout the US & abroad • *www.spiritjourneys.com*

## THEMATIC TOURS

*Women Only*

**Canyon Calling Adventures for Women 928/282–0916** 200 Carol Canyon Dr, Sedona, AZ 86336 • worldwide multi-activity adventure trips for moderately fit women, including the premiere trip to New Zealand w/ Kiwi company founder • *www.canyoncalling.com*

**Sights & Soul Travels 240/750–0597, 866/737–9602** 13610 Chrisbar Ct, Germantown, MD 20874 • small group, upscale, women-only trips to 32 destinations in Europe, Africa, South America & Asia • *www.sightsandsoul.com*

*Mostly Women*

**French Escapade 510/483–5713, 888/483–5713** 2389 Blackpool Pl, 94577 San Leandro • discover France, Belgium, Spain & Switzerand in small groups • sightseeing, painting, cooking tours • some women-only trips • lesbian owned/run • *www.frenchescapade.com*

*Gay/Lesbian*

**Planetdwellers 61–2/8667–3336** Shop 47 Elizabeth Bay Rd, Elizabeth Bay, NSW 2011, Australia • LGBT tours of Australia • come to OZ! • *www.planetdwellers.com.au*

**Venture Out 415/626–5678, 888/431–6789** 575 Pierce St #604, San Francisco, CA 94117 • high-end, escorted, small-group tours for gay & lesbian travelers to countries around the world • *www.venture-out.com*

*Gay/Straight*

**Brazil Ecojourneys 55–48/3389–5619** Estrada Rozalia Paulina Ferreira 1132, Armação, 88063-555 Florianopolis, Brazil • lesbian-owned Brazil tour operator • *www.brazilecojourneys.com*

**Wild Rainbow African Safaris 800/423–1945** 308 Jones St, Ukiah, CA 95482 • bespoke African safaris lead by Jody Cole • *www.wildrainbowsafaris.com*

## VARIOUS TOURS

*Gay/Straight*

**Ishpingo Tours 866/456–3325** LGBT tour specialists for Ecuador & the Galapagos • *www.ishpingotours.com*

➤**Thanks Babs, the Day Tripper 702/370–6961** Las Vegas, NV • *www.thanksbabs.com*

**Zoom Vacations 773/772–9666, 866/966–6822** Chicago, IL • takes gay group travel to the next level • experience the best of a destination w/ surprises, insider events & a sense of magic • *www.zoomvacations.com*